Software Requirements Engineering

Second Edition

Software Requirements Engineering

Second Edition

Edited by Richard H. Thayer and Merlin Dorfman
Foreword by Alan M. Davis

Original contributions by:

Sidney C. Bailin	Kevin Forsberg	James D. Palmer
Alan M. Davis	Laura M. Ippolito	John Reilly
Merlin Dorfman	Hal Mooz	Hossein Saiedian
Richard E. Fairley		Richard H. Thayer
Stuart R. Faulk		Dolores R. Wallace

IEEE Computer Society Press
Los Alamitos, California

Washington • Brussels • Tokyo

IEEE Computer Society Order Number BP07738
ISBN 0-8186-7738-4
Library of Congress Number 96-45235

Additional copies may be ordered from:

IEEE Computer Society
Customer Service Center
10662 Los Vaqueros Circle
P.O. Box 3014
Los Alamitos, CA 90720-1314
Tel: + 1-714-821-8380
Fax: + 1-714-821-4641
E-mail: cs.books@computer.org

IEEE Service Center
445 Hoes Lane
P.O. Box 1331
Piscataway, NJ 08855-1331
Tel: + 1-732-981-0060
Fax: + 1-732-981-9667
mis.custserv@computer.org

IEEE Computer Society
Asia/Pacific Office
Watanabe Bldg., 1-4-2
Minami-Aoyama
Minato-ku, Tokyo 107-0062
JAPAN
Tel: + 81-3-3408-3118
Fax: + 81-3-3408-3553
tokyo.ofc@computer.org

Cover art design by Alex Torres

IEEE

COMPUTER
SOCIETY

Contributors of Original Papers

Dr. Sidney C. Bailin, Knowledge Evolution, Inc., 1748 Seaton Street, NW, Washington DC 20009

Dr. Alan M. Davis, University of Colorado at Colorado Springs, Colorado Springs, CO 80933-7150

Dr. Merlin Dorfman, Lockheed Martin Missiles & Space Company, Inc., P.O. Box 3504, Sunnyvale, CA 94088-3504

Mr. Jon K. Digerness, North Coast Graphics, 7418 Kanai Avenue, Citrus Heights, CA 95621 (illustrator)

Dr. Richard E. Fairley, Colorado Technical University, 4435 N. Chestnut Street, Colorado Springs, CO 80907-3896

Dr. Stuart R. Faulk, Department of Computer and Information Science, Deschutes Hall, University of Oregon, Eugene, OR 97403, USA

Dr. Kevin Forsberg, Center for Systems Management, 19046 Pruneridge Avenue, Cupertino, CA 95041

Ms. Laura M. Ippolito, Computer Systems Laboratory, National Institute of Standards and Technology, Gaithersburg, MD 20899-0001

Dr. Hossein Saiedian, Department of Computer Science, University of Nebraska at Omaha, Omaha, NE 68182-0500

Mr. Hal Mooz, Center for Systems Management, 19046 Pruneridge Avenue, Cupertino, CA 95041

Dr. James D. Palmer, 860 Cashew Way, Fremont, CA 94536

Mr. John Reilly, MetaSolv, 14900 Landmark, Suite 530, Dallas, TX 75240

Dr. Richard H. Thayer, Department of Computer Science, California State University at Sacramento, Sacramento, CA 95819

Ms. Dolores R. Wallace, Computer Systems Laboratory, National Institute of Standards and Technology, Gaithersburg, MD 20899-0001

Foreword

Alan M. Davis

Colorado Springs, Colorado

The first edition of *System and Software Requirements Engineering*— the first compilation ever of the "great works of requirements engineering"—was a monumental success. This, the second edition, now retitled *Software Requirements Engineering*, is even more impressive. Richard Thayer and Merlin Dorfman have an uncanny ability to sift through the hundreds of papers written on the subject and cull those that contain nuggets. It is the presence of these golden nuggets that makes the collection so superb.

Thayer and Dorfman bridge the gap between academia and industry. Within these covers you'll find ideas that are ready now for widespread dissemination and use. Whether reprinted or original, the editors have avoided papers of a highly research-oriented nature; instead, they have dwelt on papers that are practical.

In the seven years since the first edition was published, progress in requirements engineering has been painfully slow. Although many projects have started to embrace sound requirements engineering principles, a remarkable number still see requirements as a chore. As a result, we still see projects that skip requirements engineering entirely, or call their design a requirements specification just so it looks like they care about requirements. The progress that has occurred can best be described as "back to basics." Projects that practice "back to basics" do simple things. They maintain lists of their requirements in databases (where annotating, sorting, filtering, and cross-referencing are easy). They prototype systems before baselining requirements. They involve customers and users in the requirements process. They strive to find ways of reducing complexity and computer jargon in their requirements. They avoid approaches that claim to be panaceas.

This book goes a long way toward helping us comprehend all aspects of requirements engineering. Like the first edition, it serves requirements practitioners, student, managers, and scholars well. It contains some gems found nowhere else, and it reprints the best of the practical literature.

Preface to the Second Edition

Richard H. Thayer
Merlin Dorfman

Much has changed in the field of requirements engineering since the first edition of this tutorial was published 6 years ago. Some of the more important changes since 1990 are as follows:

- The increased recognition of the importance of requirements engineering and the risks of doing it incorrectly or insufficiently (the inability to produce complete, correct, and unambiguous software requirements) is still considered the major cause of software failure today

- An increase in the number of conferences and workshops devoted exclusively to requirements engineering, for example, the International Symposium on Requirements Engineering, held in odd-numbered years, and the International Conference on Requirements Engineering, held in even-numbered years

- An increased number of books and journals devoted to requirements engineering, for example, *Requirements Engineering Journal* (Springer-Verlag London, Ltd.), Davis, A.M., *Software Requirements: Analysis and Specification* (Prentice-Hall International, Englewood Cliffs, N.J.)

- The inclusion, in the *Capability Maturity Model for Software* (published in 1993 by the Software Engineering Institute), of requirements engineering as a "Key Process Area" in defining a mature software development process

- The increased development of commercially available tools that support requirements engineering functions

- The emergence of subspecialties of requirements engineering, for example, requirements elicitation, requirements verification, and requirements traceability

- More extensive use of the concept of operations (ConOps) document, which was first invented and described in the literature more than 15 years ago

- More extensive practice of the validation and verification of requirements. As with the ConOps document, this is not a new idea, but is now much more accepted

This tutorial describes the current state of the practice of requirements engineering, primarily for software systems but also for systems that may contain other elements such as hardware and people. Every attempt has been made to select good, current tutorial papers for this tutorial. A paper published in the 1980s or even the 1970s is not by definition "old" or out of date. Some very fine papers, published 10–15 years ago, are still current and are the best available description of the subject under consideration. Papers selected for inclusion in this tutorial were carefully checked against the following criteria, to determine if they:

- Accurately described the state of the practice for the given topic; if a small portion of a paper was perhaps outdated, this was explained in the chapter introduction

- Covered the state of the practice for the given topic thoroughly and evenly

- Defined the basic terms

- Avoided presenting new, unproved concepts, with no reasonable prediction as to their future

- Did not try to sell one tool or concept over all others

- Are easy to read, for example, contained no gratuitous (unnecessary) mathematics

- Are organized in a hierarchical manner (top-level concepts discussed first, second-level concepts discussed next, and so forth)

- Provided a list of additional references

- Were written by an expert in the area (*to assure all of the above*)

Our criteria are, of course, idealized. Even these "rules" were violated if there was a good reason. On the basis of these criteria, we have selected papers in the following six chapters:

Chapter 1:   Introductions, Issues, and Terminology

Where there were good existing papers, either from the first edition of this tutorial or elsewhere, we have used them. A large number of the papers from the first edition are still current and topical. We have also sought out new papers and revisions of papers from the first edition from noted authors in the field.

This tutorial is one of a set of tutorials on "software system engineering" published or to be published by the IEEE Computer Society Press:

- R.H. Thayer (ed.), *Software Engineering Project Management*, IEEE Computer Society Press, Los Alamitos, CA, 1997

- M. Dorfman and R.H. Thayer (eds.), *Software Engineering*, IEEE Computer Society Press, Los Alamitos, CA, 1997

- R.H. Thayer and A.D. McGettrick (eds.), *Software Engineering—A European Perspective*, IEEE Computer Society Press, Los Alamitos, CA, 1993

Duplication of papers across tutorials has been kept to a minimum. In a few cases, particularly important papers are duplicated in order that each tutorial can stand alone.

We would like to acknowledge the support provided by the following people.

- Dr. William (Bill) Sanders, Managing Editor, Computer Society Press

- Ms. Cheryl Smith, Acquisitions Assistant, Computer Society Press

- Ms. Lisa O'Conner, Tutorial Production Editor, Computer Society Press

Merlin Dorfman, PhD
Lockheed Martin Missiles & Space Company
Sunnyvale, California

Richard Thayer, PhD
California State Unviersity, Sacramento
Sacramento, California

Preface

The purpose of this tutorial is to assemble under one cover a comprehensive body of knowledge about systems and software requirements engineering. Emphasis is on software requirements analysis and specifications, system engineering and its interface with software engineering, as well as information on subjects that are affected by system and software requirements, such as verification and validation, management, and configuration management. An additional volume, *Standards, Guidelines, and Examples: System and Software Requirements Engineering,* edited by Merlin Dorfman and Richard H. Thayer and published by the IEEE Computer Society Press, contains material that may be considered as an appendix to this tutorial.

This tutorial contains 44 original papers and reprints on system and software requirements engineering, a glossary of over 1400 system/software engineering terms applicable to requirements engineering, an "Annotated Bibliography" of books and reports with over 50 entries, and a list of "Selected References and Other Readings" with over 300 entries.

This tutorial is intended for:

- *Managers:* The tutorial provides an overview of system and software requirements issues and describes many of the "popular" software requirement methodologies and tools. Included are descriptions of software requirements specifications and methodologies, descriptions of several "new" software process models and their relationships to requirements engineering, discussions on software requirements reviews and verification, and approaches to managing the requirements activities. Several case studies are provided.

- *System and software system engineers:* The tutorial describes the front end of the software lifecycle and the difficulties interfacing with the system specifications. It also presents a basic understanding of system and software system engineering: partitioning, allocation, and flowdown of system requirements to software; software requirements analysis; and specification writing.

- *Software engineers, programmers, analysts, and other computer personnel:* The tutorial contains a general description of procedures and techniques for analyzing and specifying system and software requirements, and for writing a good requirements specifications, as well as descriptions of a number of state-of-the-art methodologies, representation methods, tools, and techniques.

- *Hardware engineers:* The tutorial describes how system specifications are partitioned and allocated to software, the techniques and tools for analyzing and describing software specifications, and how software interfaces with hardware.

- *College-level students and their teachers:* The tutorial offers sufficient background and instructional material to serve as a main or supplementary text for a course in system/software requirements analysis and specifications, in other words, requirements engineering.

This tutorial takes the view that system and software requirements engineering is the technical "center" of any system and/or software development project. Papers were selected that either describe this technical center or describe activities that interact with it (e.g., project management, configuration management, and reviews and walkthroughs). This approach provided a framework for selecting appropriate papers and assembling original material. This tutorial also takes the view that the techniques, tools, and procedures used for system engineering are similar, if not identical, to those used for software engineering.

Both original and reprinted papers are organized into chapters according to their impact on system and software requirements. Chapter 1 starts with a paper that introduces system and software engineering. Other papers in the chapter define and describe software engineering and the effect requirements have on the engineering process. Terminology and issues are also discussed.

Chapter 2 contains papers describing system engineering, operational concepts, methods for deriving software requirements from system requirements, and the application of system engineering principles to software called software system engineering.

Chapter 3 contains papers on "classic" software requirements analysis and the five types of requirements—functional, performance, external interfaces, design constraints, and quality metrics—as well as an approach to representing a software requirements specification by a users' manual. Chapter 3 also includes the most popular standard in software engineering, the IEEE *Guide to Software Requirements Specifications*.

Chapter 4 contains papers on ways to analyze and document software requirements. The papers deal with the classic (non-realtime) and modern (realtime) approaches to structured analysis, data-structured approaches, object-oriented methods, a method based on interface analysis, and formal (mathematically based) approaches to requirements engineering.

Chapter 5 contains papers on automated approaches to software requirements analysis (called requirements tools or computer-aided software engineering (CASE) tools). Classic tools such as SREM (Software Requirements Engineering Methodology) are described as well as innovative, experimental tools such as the knowledge-based system called *Requirement Apprentice*. Requirements analysis and documentation tools for personal computers are also presented, as well as some general purpose tools, such as Fourth Generation Languages (4GLs) and automated traceability tools.

Chapter 6 is concerned with managing the software requirements engineering activity and with testing and verification of system and software requirements. Papers describe a management view of requirements; the verification, validation, walkthrough/inspection, and review of requirements; and the part configuration management plays in the requirements phase.

Chapter 7 begins with three papers that provide different perspectives on the overall strategy of software development. It continues with detailed discussion of two new software development paradigms—reuse and prototyping—and their impact on software requirements.

Chapter 8 is devoted to case studies. Four case studies highlight the application of information hiding, realtime structured analysis, prototyping, and formal specification methods.

All papers, whether original or reprinted, are tutorial in nature and are intended to explain some aspects of system and/or software requirements engineering. Every attempt was made to use the latest information. However, recent papers that present the latest (as yet unproven) technology were, as a rule, excluded. The papers in this tutorial explain the best state-of-the-practice in specifying and documenting system and software requirements.

In order to fill gaps in the published literature, the authors of this tutorial contacted experienced, seasoned authors and practitioners in the areas of system and software engineering and asked them to write or revise papers for the tutorial. Each of these original papers has been independently refereed through the IEEE Computer Society peer review process. The following authors, listed alphabetically, have contributed original or revised papers to this tutorial:

- Dr. Peter P. Chen (Chen & Associates) describes the Entity-Relationship approach to data modeling that he pioneered.

- Mr. Peter Coad (Object International, Inc.) and Mr. Edward Yourdon have written about a new, but rapidly growing, approach, Object-Oriented Analysis, and its advantages over conventional methods.

- Dr. Alan M. Davis (George Mason University), chair of the IEEE working group for a "Guide for Software Requirements Specifications," has written a paper on software requirements analysis and specifications that is based on the IEEE standard.

- Dr. Merlin Dorfman (Lockheed Missiles & Space Company, Inc.) has written an introductory paper on system and software requirements and the application of allocation, partitioning, flowdown, and traceability to system engineering.

- Mr. Richard F. Flynn (Lockheed Missiles & Space Company, Inc.) and Dr. Merlin Dorfman have updated their 1984 paper, "ARTS: An Automated Requirements Traceability System," to reflect recent improvements in ARTS and to relate their experiences in supporting the system.

- Dr. Hassan Gomaa (George Mason University) has written a paper that emphasizes the difference between rapid and evolutionary prototyping.

- Mr. Charles P. Hollocker (Northern Telecom, Inc.), chair of the IEEE working group for a "Standard for Software Reviews and Audits," has prepared a paper on requirements reviews, walkthroughs, and inspections.

- Dr. Norman R. Howes (Institute for Defense Analyses) has rewritten his paper on the procedure for substituting a user manual for a requirements specification.

- Mr. Steven E. Keller and Mr. Laurence G. Kahn (Dynamics Research Corporation) and Mr. Roger B. Panara (Rome Air Development Center) have written a paper on quality metrics for software requirements. This paper incorporates the R&D work done at RADC on Software Quality Attributes. There were no existing papers on software quality metrics as applied to software requirements.

- Mr. Robert J. Lano (Lano Enterprises) has written a paper on the operations concept document. The operations concept document is one of the most valuable tools in system engineering today and is required on most government contracts. There is no other existing public paper on the subject.

- Dr. John H. Manley (University of Pittsburgh) has contributed a paper on a new software development lifecycle strategy. Manley's two-track lifecycle model separates and shows the interrelationships between the management lifecycle and the technical lifecycle. The impact of system and software requirements on this model is highlighted.

- Mr. E. Dale Nelsen (Lockheed Missiles & Space Company, Inc.) has contributed an original paper on requirements allocation and flowdown, entitled "System Engineering and Requirement Allocation." One of the most important issues in system engineering today is how to properly partition, allocate, flowdown, and trace system requirements to software implementation.

- Dr. Arthur Pyster (Software Productivity Consortium) has prepared a paper on a new software development strategy called the *Synthesis Process*. This new process acknowledges and uses iteration, prototyping, and incremental development. It is specifically intended to promote the reuse of software.

- Mr. J. Douglas Sailor (Lockheed Missiles & Space Company, Inc.) has written a paper on system engineering patterned after the Defense Systems Management College textbook, *Systems Engineering Management Guide*. Sailor was the author of the first edition of the text. There were no existing papers that provided a view of system engineering to the necessary breadth and depth.

- Dr. Hasan Sayani (Advanced Systems Technology Corporation) has written a history and current status report on the Problem Statement Language/Problem Statement Analyzer (PSL/PSA).

- Dr. Cyril P. Svoboda (Advanced Systems Technology Corporation) has written on realtime and non-realtime structured analysis, consolidating the research and implementation activities in structured analysis over the past 13 years.

- Dr. Richard H. Thayer (California State University, Sacramento) and Dr. Winston W. Royce (SoftwareFirst) have written a paper on software system engineering that outlines and describes the system engineering approach to developing software.

- Dr. Joseph E. Urban (Arizona State University) has contributed a new paper on formal requirements analysis methods and executable specifications.

- Dr. Raymond T. Yeh (Syscorp International) and Dr. Peter A. Ng (New Jersey Institute of Technology) have contributed a general description of software requirements analysis and specifications from a management perspective. Dr. Yeh also wrote the foreword to the tutorial.

- Dr. Pamela Zave (AT&T Bell Laboratories) has modified her paper on "Assessments," which shows a taxonomy of the various software requirements analysis methods and techniques.

No successful endeavor has ever been carried through by one person alone. This is one of the measures of management, and this tutorial is no exception. The authors would like to thank the people and organizations that supported us in this effort, including:

- Ms. Margaret Brown, Managing Editor, IEEE Computer Society Press, for removing much of the drudgery in writing a book.

- Dr. Garry Kampen and his editors, for their review and comments.

- Ms. Barbara Dietrich of California State University, Sacramento, California, for her part in writing the glossary.

- Mr. Joseph Kramer of the library of California State University at Sacramento, for his research help.

- California State University at Sacramento, Computer Science Graduate Class in *Advanced Software Requirements Analysis* (Fall 1988), for reviewing all the papers in this tutorial and providing their frank opinions.
- Mr. Jon Digerness of Carmichael, California, for providing the illustrations that accompany the introductions to each chapter.

Richard H. Thayer
California State University, Sacramento

Merlin Dorfman
Lockheed Missiles & Space Company, Inc.

Contents

Introduction to Tutorial

Software Requirements Engineering

Software requirements engineering is the science and discipline concerned with establishing and documenting software requirements. It consists of:

- *Software requirements elicitation*—The process through which the customers (buyers and/or users) and the developer (contractor) of a software system discover, review, articulate, and understand the users' needs and the constraints on the software and the development activity.

- *Software requirements analysis*—The process of analyzing the customers' and users' needs to arrive at a definition of software requirements

- *Software requirements specification*—The development of a document that clearly and precisely records each of the requirements of the software system

- *Software requirements verification*—The process of ensuring that the software requirements specification is in compliance with the system requirements, conforms to document standards of the requirements phase, and is an adequate basis for the architectural (preliminary) design phase

- *Software requirements management*—The planning and controlling of the requirements elicitation, specification, analysis, and verification activities

Many of the papers in this tutorial directly support this model of requirements (see Table 1).

In turn, *system requirements engineering* is the science and discipline concerned with analyzing and documenting system requirements. It involves transforming an operational need into a system description, system performance parameters, and a system configuration. This is accomplished through the use of an iterative process of analysis, design, trade-off studies, and prototyping.

Software requirements engineering has a similar definition as the science and discipline concerned with analyzing and documenting software requirements. It involves partitioning system requirements into major subsystems and tasks, then allocating those subsystems or tasks to software. It also transforms allocated system requirements into a description of software requirements and performance parameters through the use of an iterative process of analysis, design, trade-off studies, and prototyping.

A *system* can be considered a collection of hardware, software, data, people, facilities, and procedures organized to accomplish some common objectives. In software engineering, a system is a set of software programs that provide the cohesiveness and control of data that enables the system to solve the problem.

The major difference between system requirements engineering and software requirements engineering is that the origin of system requirements lies in user needs while the origin of software requirements lies in the system requirements and/or specifications. Therefore, the system requirements engineer works with users and customers, eliciting their needs, schedules, and available resources, and must produce documents understandable by them as well as by management, software requirements engineers, and other system requirements engineers.

The software requirements engineer works with the system requirements documents and engineers, translating system documentation into software requirements which must be understandable by management and software designers as well as by software and system requirements engineers. Accurate and timely communication must be ensured all along this chain if the software designers are to begin with a valid set of requirements.

Table 1: Model for Software Requirements Engineering

Requirements Activity	Reference Document
Requirements Elicitation	K. Forsberg and H. Mooz, "System Engineering Overview" R.E. Fairley and R.H. Thayer, "The Concept of Operations: The Bridge from Operational Requirements to Technical Specifications" J.A. Goguen and C. Linde, "Techniques for Requirements Elicitation" J. Rumbaugh, "Getting Started: Using Use Cases to Capture Requirements"
Requirements Analysis	S. Faulk, "Software Requirements: A Tutorial" G. Kotonya and I. Sommerville, "Requirements Engineering with Viewpoints" C.P. Svoboda, "Structured Analysis" J. Reilly, "Entity-Relationship Approach to Data Modeling" S.C. Bailin, "Object-Oriented Requirements Analysis" R. Viennau, "A Review of Formal Methods" H. Saiedian, "Formal Methods in Information Systems Engineering"
Requirements Specification	S. Faulk, "Software Requirements: A Tutorial" A.M. Davis, "A Comparison of Techniques for the Specification of External System Behavior" J. Reilly, "Entity-Relationship Approach to Data Modeling" S.C. Bailin, "Object Oriented Requirements Analysis" IEEE Std 830-1993, *IEEE Recommended Practice for Software Requirements Specifications* IEEE Std 1233-1993, *IEEE Guide for Developing System Requirements Specifications*
Requirements Verification	D.R. Wallace and L.M. Ippolito, "Verifying and Validating Software Requirements Specifications" J.D. Palmer, "Traceability" A. Davis et al., "Identifying and Measuring Quality in a Software Requirements Specification"
Requirements Management	R.T. Yeh and P.A. Ng, "Software Requirements—A Management Perspective"

Chapter 1

Introductions, Issues, and Terminology

1. Introduction to Chapter

It is a well-documented belief that the failure to develop and document good requirements specifications is the major cause of software development failures.[1,2,3] The purpose of Chapter 1 is to identify some of the major issues in software requirements development and to define terms used both in and around system and software engineering.

The problems with writing good, correct, complete, and measurable system and software requirements specifications are a major issue in software development today. Some of the major issues of concern in the requirements area are:

- The inability of engineers to write a correct software requirements specification

- The desire of managers to truncate requirements activity because they believe that the major effort in any software development is programming and testing

- The lack of cooperation by customers when it comes to verifying that the software requirements are correct, and the lack of understanding of the structure and purpose of the software requirements specifications

- The problems associated with identifying which tool and/or methodology to use in developing and representing a software requirements specification

- The lack of knowledge that system requirements are essential to the development of good software requirements, or the unwillingness to act in accordance with that knowledge

- The lack of training of system engineers on how to partition and allocate system functions to software

- The desire of senior management in many large corporations to place personnel with little software knowledge or experience in positions of responsibility over what is essentially a major software project

Terminology causes many problems because of the newness of the computer science and software engineering fields. Many terms do not have universally accepted definitions. System engineers, computer scientists, and software development groups define things in different ways. One of the purposes of this tutorial is to provide a common set of definitions that can be used in the area of system and software requirements engineering.

The four articles in this chapter were selected to introduce the tutorial, provide definitions, and establish the requirements engineering issues and problems. The first article, by the co-editor of the tutorial, Dr. Merlin Dorfman, sets the tone for the entire tutorial and establishes the definition of system and software requirements engineering. The article by Harwell et al. defines software requirements and provides a taxonomy of software requirements definitions. An article by Scharer looks at requirements from both the user's and developer's point of view. The last article, by Siddiqi and Shekaran, Program Co-Chairs of the 1996 International Conference on Requirements Engineering, summarizes the current state of research and practice.

2. Description of Articles

The first article, "Requirements Engineering" by Merlin Dorfman, is an overview of this tutorial. In this article, Dorfman discusses the value of good requirements and specifications, the place of requirements analysis in the life cycle, and the framework for developing system requirements. The article introduces the concepts of architectural design, allocation, flowdown, and traceability. It also explains the application of configuration management, interface definition, and verification and validation to the requirements activity. A brief introduction is given to some of the tools and methods to be discussed in detail later in the tutorial.

The second article in the chapter, "What Is a Requirement?" by Richard Harwell, Erik Aslaksen, Ivy Hooks, Roy Mengot, and Ken Ptack, does an excellent job in defining many of the terms associated with requirements engineering. While there may be some differences of opinion in discussing some of these definitions, for the most part they appear to be those definitions in common use today. The article defines differences between:

- *Derived and primary* (also called *"allocated"*) *requirements*
- *Qualitative and quantitative requirements.* The authors define qualitative requirements as being unmeasurable requirements and quantitative requirements as being measurable requirements. One of the major research areas in software engineering is in determining how to measure qualitative requirements
- *Project and product requirements.* Product requirements would be part of a requirements specification and project requirements would be part of a statement of work (SOW) or management plan
- *Mandatory requirements, guidance* (also called *"desirable requirements"*), *and information* (also called *"notes"*)

The article also attempts to separate requirements from "design;" however, it does recognize that a "design" (sometimes called a *design constraint*) can be a requirement. The article concludes with a discussion about three attributes of a requirements specification: (1) completeness, (2) lack of ambiguity, and (3) scope (also called "measurable"). A discussion in Chapter 3 will indicate that there are a number of other attributes that can also be applied to a specification document.

"Pinpointing Requirements" by Laura Scharer does a very fine job of defining the major issues involved in writing a software requirements specification. She points out that analysts and users harbor grave doubts about each other. The origins of these attitudes are obvious—failure encourages blame. Users are disenchanted, because developers constantly bungle new system developments; and developers are disenchanted because they alone are blamed for the failures.

This article is about software development for an in-house user; in other words, the user belongs to the same parent company as the software development team. Because of this situation, the relationship between the developer and user is much closer than in a contract situation.

Scharer points out the problems that exist between experienced and inexperienced users and between experienced and inexperienced software developers. She goes on to discuss some realistic goals and how to improve the relationship between the developer and the user. For instance, a thorough evaluation is needed as to whether or not the system can be defined. The article also points out 12 different environmental factors that influence the software development process.

The article goes on to define methods for controlling the system, for selecting a user for the project team, and for training the user, and presents a well-defined approach to developing a software system.

The last article, by Jawed Siddiqi and M. Chandra Shekaran, "Requirements Engineering: The Emerging Wisdom," reports on some of the work being done to improve software requirements. The article examines a number of different ways to answer the question, "What constitutes a requirement?" Other issues discussed in the article are as follows:

- Prioritizing requirements
- Coping with incompleteness
- Making requirements methods and tools more accessible

The article concludes with a statement that the authors believe there is a greater need to narrow the gap between research and practice.

References

1. Alford, M.W., and J.T. Lawson, *Software Requirements Engineering Methodology (Development)*, RADC-TR-79-168, U.S. Air Force, Rome Air Development Center, Griffiss AFB, New York, N.Y., 1979.

2. Davis, A.M., *Software Requirements: Analysis and Specification*, Prentice-Hall, Englewood Cliffs, N.J., 1990.

3. Faulk, S.R., "Software Requirements," in *Software Engineering*, M. Dorfman and R.H. Thayer, eds., IEEE Computer Society Press, Los Alamitos, Calif., 1997.

Requirements Engineering

Merlin Dorfman

Lockheed Martin Missiles & Space Company
Sunnyvale CA 94088-3504

Abstract

Requirements engineering is presented and discussed as a part of systems engineering and software systems engineering. The need for good requirements engineering, and the consequences of a lack of it, are most apparent in systems that are all or mostly software. Requirements engineering approaches are closely tied to the life cycle or process model used. A distinction is made between requirements engineering at the system level and at lower levels, such as software elements. The fundamentals of requirements engineering are defined and presented: elicitation; decomposition and abstraction; allocation, flowdown, and traceability; interfaces; validation and verification. Requirements development approaches, tools, and methods, and their capabilities and limitations, are briefly discussed.

I. Introduction

When the "Software Crisis"[1] was discovered and named in the 1960s, much effort was directed at finding the causes of the now-familiar syndrome of problems. The investigations determined that requirements deficiencies are among the most important contributors to the problem: "In nearly every software project which fails to meet performance and cost goals, requirements inadequacies play a major and expensive role in project failure."[2] Development of the requirements specification "in many cases seems trivial, but it is probably the part of the process which leads to more failures than any other."[3]

It was determined that the benefits of good requirements include:

- Agreement among developers, customers, and users on the job to be done and the acceptance criteria for the delivered system
- A sound basis for resource estimation (cost, personnel quantity and skills, equipment, and time)
- Improved system usability, maintainability, and other quality attributes
- The achievement of goals with minimum resources (less rework, fewer omissions and misunderstandings)

It was also observed that the value of good requirements, and the criticality of doing them well, increased dramatically with the size and complexity of the system being developed. Additionally, software-intensive systems seemed to have more inherent complexity, that is, were more difficult to understand, than systems that did not contain a great deal of software; thus these systems were more sensitive to the quality of their requirements.

The products of a good requirements analysis include not only definition, but proper documentation, of the functions, performance, internal and external interfaces, and quality attributes of the system under development, as well as any valid constraints on the system design or the development process.

As the value of good requirements became clear, the focus of investigation shifted to the requirements themselves: how should they be developed? How can developers know when a set of requirements is good? What standards, tools, and methods can help; do they exist, or must they be developed? These investigations are by no means complete: not only are new tools and methods appearing almost daily, but overall approaches to requirements, and how they fit into the system life cycle, are evolving rapidly. As a result, requirements engineering has been well established as a part of systems engineering. Requirements engineers perform requirements analysis and definition on specific projects as well as investigate in the abstract how requirements should be developed.

II. Requirements Engineering and the Development Life Cycle

Many models exist for the system and/or software life cycle, the series of steps that a system goes through from first realization of need through construction, operation, and retirement.[4] (Boehm[5] provides a good overview of many existing models, and presents as well a risk-driven approach that includes many other models as subsets; Davis et al.[6] describe conditions under which various models might be used.) Almost all models include one or more phases with a name like "requirements analysis" or "user needs development." Many models require generation of a document called, or serving the function of, a requirements specification. Even those that do not call for such a document, for example Jackson System Development, have a product such as a diagram or diagrams that incorporate or express the user's needs and the development objectives.[7]

A few of the better-known life cycle models are briefly discussed in the following sections, and the way requirements engineering fits into them is presented.

A. Baseline Management

Among the most extensively used models are Baseline Management and the Waterfall, on which Baseline Management is based.[8] (Baseline Management differs from the Waterfall in that it specifically requires each life cycle phase to generate defined products, which must pass a review and be placed under configuration control before the next phase begins.) In these models, as shown in Figure 1, determination of requirements should be complete, or nearly so, before any implementation begins. Baseline Management provides a high degree of management visibility and control, has been found suitable for developments of very large size in which less complex methods often fail, and is required under many military standards and commercial contracts. This model, however, has been somewhat discredited, because when large complex systems are developed in practice it is usually impossible to develop an accurate set of requirements that will remain stable throughout the months or years of development that follow completion of the requirements. This essential and almost unavoidable difficulty of the Waterfall and Baseline Management models had been noted for many years[9,10] but was brought to the attention of the U.S. defense software community by a Defense Science Board report authored by F. Brooks.[11] Brooks pointed out that the user often did not know what the requirements actually were, and even if they could be determined at some point in time they were almost certain to change. To resolve this problem Brooks recommended an Evolutionary model, as is discussed below. The approach advocated by Brooks provides the following advantages:

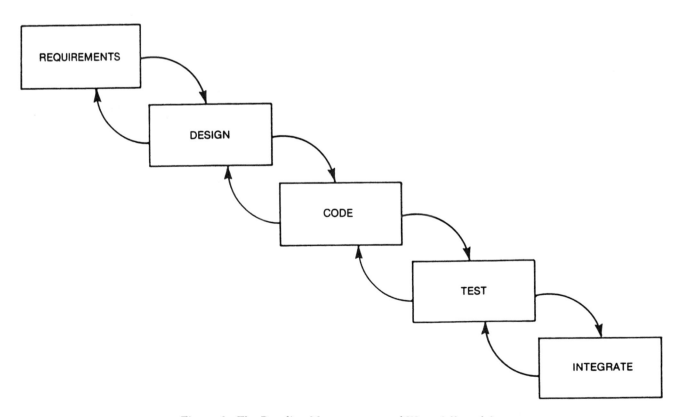

Figure 1. The Baseline Management and Waterfall models.

- The user is given some form of operational system to review (a prototype or early evolution), which provides better definition of the true needs than can be achieved by reading a draft specification. This approach avoids what Brooks identified as the unacceptable risk of building a system to the a priori requirements.

- Delivery of some operational capabilities early in the development process—as opposed to the delivery of everything after many months or years—permits incorporation of new requirements and of capabilities that did not exist or were not feasible at the start of development.

B. Prototyping

The Prototyping life cycle (Figure 2) is one approach to the use of an operational system to help determine requirements.[12] In this model, some system capability is built with minimum formality and control to be run for or by the user, so that requirements can be determined accurately. Several successive prototypes will usually be built. The amount of requirements analysis that precedes prototyping depends on the specifics of the problem. It is normally recommended that the prototype should be used only to help generate a valid set of requirements; after the requirements are available, they should be documented, and development should proceed as in the Baseline Management model. If this recommendation is followed, the prototyping portion of the life cycle may be considered as a tool or method supporting requirements analysis within the Baseline Management model.

Many tools and methods are available to help support prototyping. The term *rapid prototyping* is associated with some of them, to distinguish them from other forms, such as development of high-risk hardware and software components, which is a slow, expensive process. Much of rapid prototyping is concentrated in two application areas: user interfaces and heavily transaction-oriented functions such as database operations. In these areas, a distinction can be made between prototyping tools and approaches that provide only "mockups" (simulate the system's response to user actions) and those that actually perform the operations requested by the user. In the latter category are the so-called Fourth Generation Languages (4GLs),[13,14] which provide methods of generating code for user operations included within the 4GL's capability. Such tools provide the option of retaining the prototype as (part of) the final system; considerations of execution time and efficiency of memory usage are weighed against the time and cost of building a system using the Baseline Management model and requirements determined from the rapid prototyping effort.

C. Incremental Development

The Incremental Development life cycle model calls for a unitary requirements analysis and specification effort, with requirements and capabilities allocated to a series of increments that are distinct but may overlap each other (Figure 3). In its original conception the requirements are assumed to be stable, as in the Baseline Management model, but in practice the requirements for later increments may be changed through technology advancement or experience with the early deliveries; hence this model may in effect be not very different from the Evolutionary Development model described next.

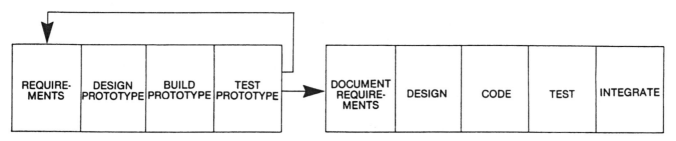

Figure 2. The Prototyping life cycle model.

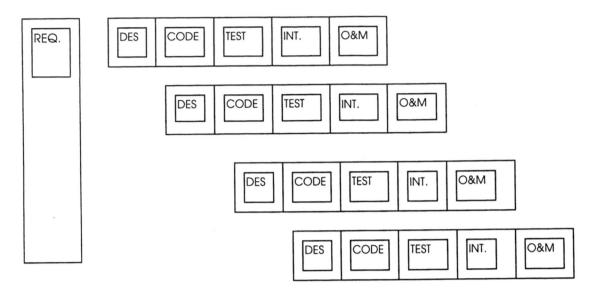

Figure 3. The Incremental Development model.

D. Evolutionary Development

The Evolutionary Development life cycle calls for a series of development efforts, each of which leads to a delivered product to be used in the operational environment over an extended period of time (Figure 4). In contrast with the Prototyping model, in which the purpose of each early product is only to help determine requirements, each delivery or evolution provides some needed operational capability. However, there is feedback from users of the operational systems that may affect requirements for later deliveries.

Each delivery in this model represents a full development cycle, including requirements analysis. The deliveries may overlap, as shown in Figure 4, or one delivery may be completed before the next is begun. The product of each requirements analysis phase is an addition or improvement to the product(s) of the requirements analysis phase of the previous delivery. Similarly, the implementation portions of each delivery may add to, or upgrade, products of earlier deliveries. With this understanding, each delivery may be looked at as a small example of a Baseline Management life cycle, with a development process and time span small enough to minimize the problems discussed above.

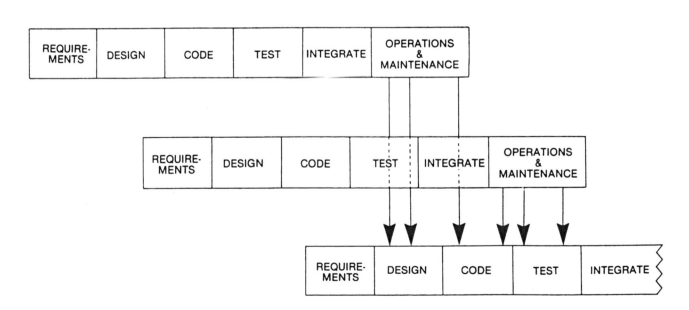

Figure 4. The Evolutionary Development model.

10

E. The Spiral Model

Boehm[5] describes the Spiral model, an innovation that permits combinations of the conventional (Baseline Management), Prototyping, and Incremental models to be used for various portions of a development. It shifts the management emphasis from developmental products to risk, and explicitly calls for evaluations as to whether a project should be terminated. Figure 5 summarizes the Spiral model.

The radial coordinate in Figure 5 represents total costs incurred to date. Each loop of the spiral, from the (−x) axis clockwise through 360 degrees, represents one phase of the development. A phase may be specification oriented, prototyping oriented, an evolutionary development step, or one of a number of other variants; the decision on which form to use (or whether to discontinue the project) is made at each crossing of the (−x) axis by evaluating objectives, constraints, alternatives, and status (particularly risk).

The Spiral model thus makes explicit the idea that the form of a development cannot be precisely determined in advance of the development: the re-evaluation at the completion of each spiral allows for changes in user perceptions, results of prototypes or early versions, technology advances, risk determinations, and financial or other factors to affect the development from that point on.

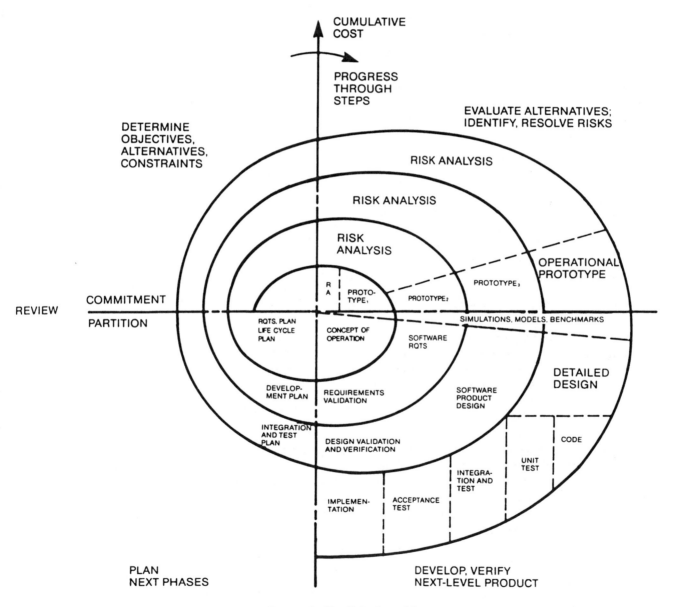

Figure 5. The Spiral model.

11

Boehm has referred to the Spiral model as a "process model generator": given a set of conditions, the Spiral produces a more detailed development model.[15] For example, in the situation where requirements can be determined in advance and risk is low, the Spiral will result in a Baseline Management approach. If requirements are less certain, other models such as the Incremental or Prototyping can be derived from the Spiral. And, as mentioned above, re-evaluation after each spiral allows for changes in what had been (tentatively) concluded earlier in the development.

III. System and Software Requirements

System and software requirements are often treated together because the tools and methods used to derive them, and the techniques of documenting them, are very similar. (It may be remarked that most of the tools and methods originated with software developers and were then found to be appropriate for system use as well.) However, some important differences between system and software requirements should be pointed out.

System requirements describe the behavior of the system as seen from the outside, for example, by the user. Although requirements documents and specifications cannot easily be read by users,[16] the system requirements serve at least as a partial communications vehicle to the more technically inclined users, or to a purchasing organization, as well as to analysts and designers who are concerned with the development of system elements or components.

Requirements for elements below the system level, whether they are for elements that are all hardware, all software, or composite (both hardware and software), are normally of minimal interest to users. These requirements serve to communicate with the developers, who need to know what is expected of the elements for which they are responsible, and who also need information about those elements with which they must interface.

This distinction is important for several reasons. First, like any communications vehicle, a requirements document should be written with its intended audience in mind. The degree to which nontechnical users must read and understand a requirements document is a factor in how it is written. Second, and perhaps most important, the skills and experience of the requirements developers must be considered. All too frequently, systems engineers with limited software knowledge are responsible for software-intensive systems. They not only write system-level requirements, which demands knowledge of what functions and per-

formance a software-intensive system can be expected to meet; they also allocate functions and requirements to hardware and software. Thus the software developers are asked to develop designs to meet requirements that may be highly unrealistic or unfeasible. Software developers seem to be reluctant to get involved in systems engineering; one of the results is that the development of software elements often starts with poor requirements.

The U.S. Air Force Aeronautical Systems Center has recognized the importance of systems engineering to a software development by including in its Software Development Capability Evaluation (SDCE)[17] material about systems engineering capability and its interface with software engineering. The SDCE is an instrument used to help acquisition organizations determine whether bidders who have submitted proposals for a software contract are likely to be able to perform acceptably.

Section IV carries further the distinction between system and software requirements as the approach to generating requirements for all system elements is outlined.

IV. Fundamentals of Requirements Engineering

This section presents the overall framework within which requirements engineering takes place. Information about tools and methods is not presented here; at this point concern is focused on the sequence of events.

Several taxonomies have been proposed for requirements engineering. Prof. Alan Davis has proposed the following[18]:

- Elicitation
- Solution determination
- Specification
- Maintenance

Another is that requirements engineering consists of elicitation, analysis, specification, validation/verification, and management. The comparison with Davis's is straightforward—validation/verification is included in maintenance, and management is implicit in all four of Davis's activities.

A system of any but the smallest size will be decomposed into a hierarchy of elements. Starting with the lowest levels, the elements are integrated into larger-size elements at higher levels, back up to the full system (Figure 6). Several approaches are available for development of the hierarchy, but all produce definitions of elements at all levels of the hierarchy. In the functional approach (implied by the element names used in Figure 6), the elements represent the parts of the system that will meet particular system requirements or carry out particular system capabilities. In a physical decomposition, the elements will represent physical components of the system. In a data-driven approach, the components will contain different parts of the key data needed by the system, and most likely also the operations carried out on that data. In an object-oriented approach, the components will consist of *objects* that include not only physical components of the system but also the data and functions (operations) needed by those physical components.

After the lowest-level elements (*Units* in Figure 6) are defined, they are separately developed and then integrated to form the next larger elements (*Programs* in Figure 6). These elements are then integrated into larger-size elements at the next level, and so on until the entire system has been developed, integrated, and tested. Thus the life cycle models presented earlier can be seen to be oversimplified in that they do not account for the development and integration of the various elements that compose the system. This aspect can be considered to be outside the responsibility of the requirements engineer, but, as discussed below, it affects cost, feasibility, and other factors that bring the realities of implementation to the

development of requirements, in contrast to the strict separation of "what" and "how" often postulated for system development.

The requirements engineer needs to be concerned with all the requirements work that takes place. As described above, this includes requirements for the entire system, for composite (hardware and software) elements at lower levels, and for all-hardware and all-software elements. It should be noted at this point that references to *the* "requirements specification" are meaningless for any but the smallest systems; there will be several or many requirements specifications.

A. System Requirements

Next is described the mechanics of filling out the system hierarchy with requirements.[19,20] It should be pointed out that, although the hierarchy used as an example is functional, the process, and the traceability aspects that accompany it, are valid whether the decomposition is functional, physical, data driven, or object oriented.

Early in the development process, the system-level requirements are generated. A primary tool used in generating the system requirements is the Concept of Operations or ConOps document,[16] a document that is narrative in form and describes the environment and operation of the system to be built. An important part

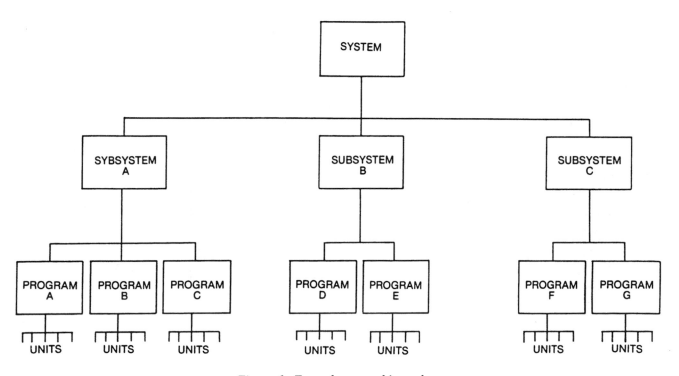

Figure 6. Example system hierarchy.

of the development of both the ConOps and the system requirements is the process of requirements elicitation, which is defined as working with the eventual users of the system under development to determine their needs.[21] Elicitation involves an understanding of psychological and sociological methods as well as system development and the application domain of the system to be built.

While the system requirements are being developed, requirements engineers and others begin to consider what elements should be defined in the hierarchy. By the time the system requirements are complete in draft form, a tentative definition of at least one and possibly two levels should be available. This definition will include names and general functions of the elements. Definition of the system hierarchy is often referred to as *partitioning*.

B. Allocation

The next step is usually called *allocation*. Each system-level requirement is allocated to one or more elements at the next level; that is, it is determined which elements will participate in meeting the requirement. In performing the allocation, it will become apparent that (1) the system requirements need to be changed (additions, deletions, and corrections), and (2) the definitions of the elements are not correct. The allocation process therefore is iterative, leading eventually to

a complete allocation of the system requirements, as shown in Figure 7. The table in Figure 7 shows which element or elements will meet each system requirement; all requirements must be allocated to at least one element at the next level. In this example, we have called the level below system the Subsystem level; in practice, the names are arbitrary, depending on the number of levels in the entire hierarchy and the conventions in use by the systems engineering organization. Figure 7 shows that the system-level requirement denoted as SYS001 is allocated to subsystems A and B, SYS002 is allocated to A and C, and so forth.

C. Flowdown

The next step is referred to as *flowdown*. (The reader should be aware that this nomenclature is not universal.) Flowdown consists of writing requirements for the lower-level elements in response to the allocation. When a system requirement is allocated to a subsystem, the subsystem must have at least one requirement that responds to that allocation. Usually more than one requirement will be written. The lower-level requirement(s) may closely resemble the higher-level one, or may be very different if the system engineers recognize a capability that the lower-level element must have in order to meet the higher-level requirement. In the latter case, the lower-level requirements are often referred to as *derived*.

SYSTEM REQUIREMENTS	SUBSYSTEM A	SUBSYSTEM B	SUBSYSTEM C
SYS 001	X	X	
SYS 002	X		X
SYS 003		X	
SYS 004	X	X	X
SYS 005			X
SYS 006		X	
SYS 007	X	X	

Figure 7. Example of allocation of system requirements.

14

The level of detail increases as we move down in the hierarchy. That is, system-level requirements are general in nature, while requirements at low levels in the hierarchy are very specific. A key part of the systems engineering approach to system development is *decomposition* and *abstraction:* the system is partitioned (decomposed) into finer and finer elements, while the requirements start at a highly abstract (general) level and become more specific for the lower-level elements. Large software-intensive systems are among the most logically complex of human artifacts, and decomposition and abstraction are essential to the successful management of this complexity.

When flowdown is done, errors may be found in the allocation, the hierarchy definition, and the system requirements; thus the flowdown process is also iterative and may cause parts of previous processes to be repeated. Figure 8 shows the results of the first level of the flowdown process: a complete set of requirements for each of the subsystems. System-level requirement SYS001 was allocated to subsystems A and B; subsystem requirements (in this example, SSA001, SSA002, and SSB001) are written in response to the allocation. Similarly SYS002 was allocated to A and C, and subsystem requirements SSA003, SSA004, SSA005, SSC001, and SSC002 are the flowdown of SYS002 to subsystem levels. The result is a complete set of requirements for each of the subsystems. After completion of this level of flowdown, allocation of the subsystem requirements is carried out to the next level, followed by flowdown to that level. Again the processes are iterative and changes may be needed in the higher-level definition, allocation, or flowdown.

The process of partitioning, allocation, and flowdown is then repeated to as low a level as needed for this particular system; for software elements this is often to the module level. Figure 9 emphasizes the iterative nature of this process at each level in the many levels of partitioning, allocation, and flowdown.

SYSTEM REQUIREMENT	SYSTEM A REQUIREMENT	SYSTEM B REQUIREMENT	SYSTEM C REQUIREMENT
SYS 001	SSA 001 SSA 002	SSB 001	—
SYS 002	SSA 003 SSA 004 SSA 005	—	SSC 001 SSC 002
SYS 003	—	SSB 002 SSB 003	—
SYS 004	SSA 006 SSA 007	SSB 004 SSB 005 SSB 006	SSC 003
SYS 005	—	—	SSC 004 SSC 005
SYS 006	—	SSB 007 SSB 008	—
SYS 007	SSA 008 SSA 009	SSB 009	—

Figure 8. Example of flowdown of system requirements.

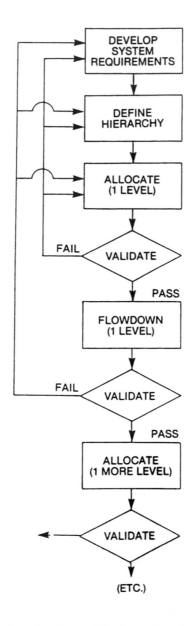

Figure 9. Iteration in partitioning, allocation, and flowdown.

D. Traceability

The number of requirements proliferates rapidly during the allocation and flowdown process. If we assume that there are four levels in the hierarchy, that each element partitions to four at the next level, that each requirement is allocated to two of the four, and that each flowdown results in three requirements per allocated element (all reasonable assumptions), there will be more than 250 requirements in the hierarchy for each system-level requirement. Keeping track of all these requirements is essential, to make sure that all requirements are properly flowed down to all levels, with no requirements lost and no "extras" thrown in.

Reading and understanding the requirements to answer these questions is difficult enough; without a way to keep track of the flowdown path in a hierarchy of thousands of requirements, it becomes impossible. Traceability is the concept that implements the necessary bookkeeping.[19,20] Establishment of traceability as allocation and flowdown are done helps ensure the validity of the process. Then, if changes are needed (such as a system-level requirement due to user input, or a lower-level requirement due to a problem with allocation, flowdown, or feasibility), traceability enables the engineer to locate the related requirements, at higher and lower levels, that must be reviewed to see if they need to be changed.

Figure 10 shows the traceability path corresponding to the allocation and flowdown in Figures 7 and 8. System requirement SYS001 traces downward to SSA001, which in turn traces downward to PGA001, PGA002, and PGB001. SYS001 also traces to SSA002, which further traces to PGA003, PGC001, and PGC002. Upward traceability also exists, for example, PGB001 to SSA001 to SYS001. A similar hierarchy exists through SYS001's allocation and flowdown to subsystem B. Other formats such as trees and indented tables can be used to illustrate traceability, as in Dorfman and Flynn.[19]

Note that, while allocation and flowdown are technical tasks, traceability is not strictly an engineering function: it is a part of requirements management and is really only "bookkeeping." A case can be made that more of the requirements problems observed in system development are due to failures in requirements management than to technical functions. In the Software Engineering Institute's Capability Maturity Model for Software,[22] these nontechnical aspects of requirements management are important enough that they are one of the six "Key Process Areas" that a software development organization must satisfy to move beyond the first, ad hoc or chaotic level of maturity.

E. Interfaces

An additional step is interface definition. Before development of system requirements can begin, the system's external interfaces (the interfaces between the system and the outside world) must be known. As each level of partitioning, allocation, and flowdown takes place, the interfaces of each element to the rest of the system must be specified. This definition has two parts. First, interfaces defined at higher levels are made more specific; that is, the external interfaces to the entire system are identified as to which subsystem(s) actually perform the interface. Second, internal interfaces at that level are defined, that is, the subsystem-to-subsystem interfaces needed to enable each subsystem to meet the requirements allocated to it.

Figure 11 illustrates this concept. In the top diagram, *A* represents an external interface of the system, for example, an output produced by the system. When subsystems 1, 2, 3, and 4 are defined, as shown in the lower diagram, *A* is identified to subsystem 1, that is, the output originates in subsystem *A*, and internal interfaces, such as *B* between 3 and 4, are found to be necessary. This process continues throughout development of the hierarchy.

SYSTEM REQUIREMENT	SUBSYSTEM A REQUIREMENT	PROGRAM A REQUIREMENT	PROGRAM B REQUIREMENT	PROGRAM C REQUIREMENT
SYS 001	SSA 001	PGA 001 PGA 002	PGB 001	—
	SSA 002	PGA 003	—	PGC 001 PGC 002
SYS 002	SSA 003		PGB 002 PGB 003	—
	SSA 004	PGA 004	PCB 004	PGC 003
	SSA 005	PGA 005	PCB 005 PCB 006	PGC 004 PGC 005

Figure 10. The requirements traceability path.

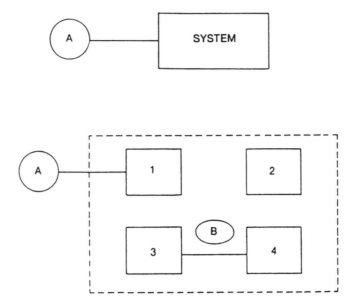

Figure 11. Increasing detail of interface definition.

It is also possible that errors in partitioning, allocation, and flowdown will be discovered when interface definition is taking place, leading to iteration in those earlier steps.

F. The Refined Life Cycle Model

Next, let's examine the implications of the above processes for the life cycle models discussed earlier. It should now be apparent that the single "Requirements Analysis" phase, even if extended to "System Requirements Analysis" and "Software Requirements Analysis," is inadequate. The life cycle model should account for the multiplicity of levels in the hierarchy, and furthermore should recognize that the various subsystems and other elements at any level do not need to be synchronized. That is, if we are willing to accept the risk that flowdown to the last subsystem will surface some errors in partitioning or allocation, we can phase the subsystems, and of course the lower-level elements as well.

Figure 12 is the more realistic, and more complicated, life cycle chart that results from the above considerations. Although it builds on a Baseline Management approach, the nesting and phasing shown will apply to any of the models discussed earlier, or to combinations. The key features of Figure 12 are as follows:

1. For all but the lowest level of the hierarchy, the implementation phase of its life cycle becomes the entire development cycle for the next lower elements. Thus the subsystems

have their development cycle shown as a phase of the system life cycle.

2. Elements at any level may be phased. Thus the subsystems are shown as starting and finishing their development cycles at different times. This approach has at least two advantages:

    *   Staff can be employed more efficiently, since the schedules for each element can be phased to avoid excessive demand for any technical specialty at any time

    *   Integration can be carried out in a logical fashion, by adding one element at a time, rather than by the "big bang" approach of integrating all or many elements at the same time

G. Validation and Verification

A final point in the framework of fundamentals relates to another requirements management task, the review of the requirements.[23] Validation and verification of the partitioning, allocation, flowdown, and interfaces is equally as important as their generation. It has been shown repeatedly that requirements errors not found until later in the development cycle are many times more expensive to fix than if they were found before the requirements phase was completed.[24] The Baseline Management model requires that all the requirements at all levels be fully and properly reviewed before design and implementation begin. The life cycle models

18

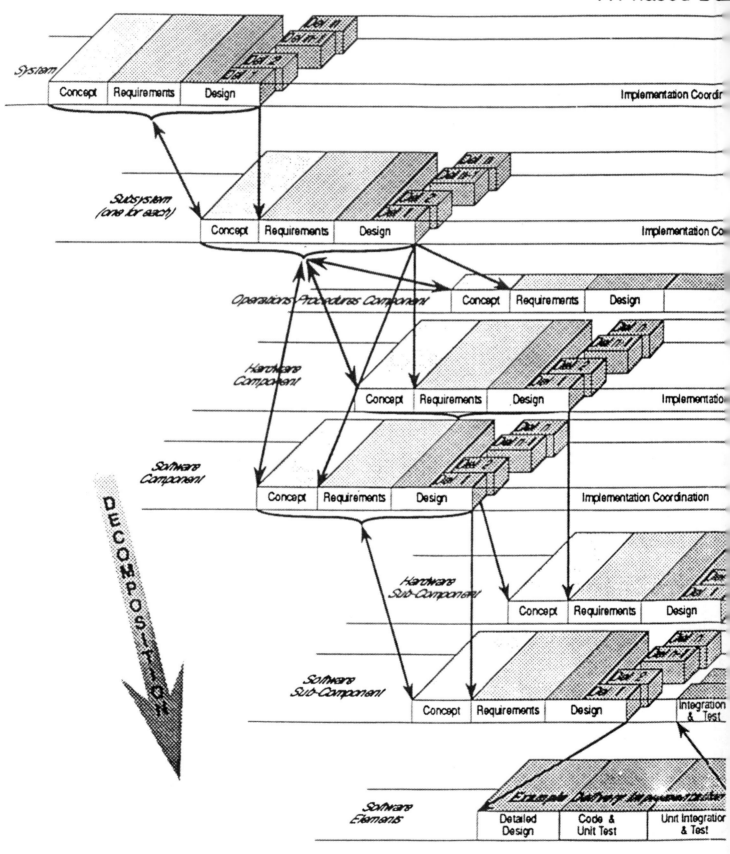

fe-Cycle

ivery Model

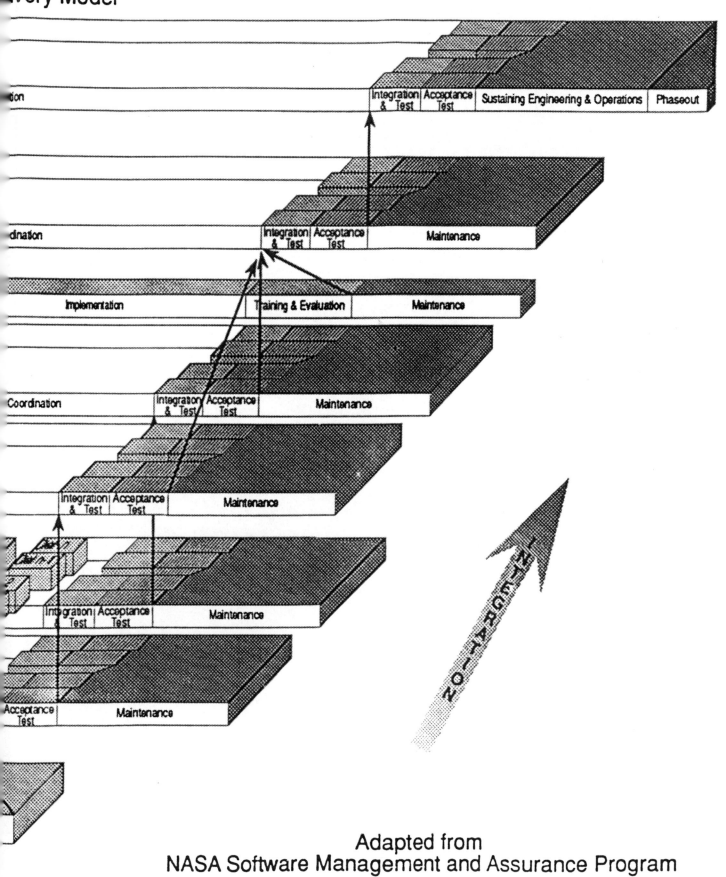

Adapted from
NASA Software Management and Assurance Program

wherein the requirements are not all determined and "frozen" before design begins specify review of requirements as they are considered ready to be the basis for some design and further development.

The attributes of a good requirements specification are addressed by Boehm.[23] Among the most important attributes are the following:

- Clear/unambiguous
- Complete
- Correct
- Understandable
- Consistent (internally and externally)
- Concise
- Feasible

It should be apparent that the evaluation of a requirements specification with respect to these attributes may be highly subjective and qualitative. Davis et al.[25] demonstrate the extreme difficulty of attempting to quantify the degree to which a specification exhibits these qualities. Nevertheless, these attributes are so important that the verification and validation of requirements against these criteria must be carried out, to the degree possible and as quantitatively as possible. Boehm[23] and Davis et al.[25] address approaches to validation and verification of requirements.

V. Requirements Engineering and Architectural Design

In the previous section, an overview is given of the process of partitioning, allocation, and flowdown. The result of this process (a definition of the hierarchy down to some level, generation of the requirements for all elements, and determination of the interfaces between them) is known as the *architectural design* or *top-level design* of the system. Although it is called a design, requirements engineering is involved throughout the process. What, then, is the distinction between requirements analysis and design in this process?

Requirements analysis is often defined as the "what" of a problem: implementation free; containing objectives, not methods. Design, then, is the "how": the implementation that will meet the requirements. The two are supposed to be kept distinct, although of course the feasibility of meeting a requirement always needs to be considered. However, if you look closely at the process of generating the architectural design, you will see that both requirements analysis and design are involved.[26]

The generation of system-level requirements is, to the extent possible, a pure "what," addressing the desired characteristics of the complete system. The next steps, determining the next level of the hierarchy and allocating system requirements to the elements, are in fact a "how": they do not address objectives beyond the system requirements, but they define a subsystem structure that enables the requirements to be met. Flowdown is again a "what," determining what each element should do (functions, performance, and so on).

Development of the architectural design is, then, a process in which the steps of requirements analysis and design alternate, with more detail being brought out at each cycle. The output of requirements analysis is input to the next stage of design, and the output of design is input to the next stage of requirements analysis.[27] If different people perform the two functions, one person's requirement is the next person's design, and one person's design is the next person's requirements.[28]

Pure requirements analysis, like pure design, can only go so far. Both disciplines are needed to achieve the desired result, a system that meets its user's needs. Note that the character of requirements analysis, like that of design, changes as we move down in the hierarchy: requirements analysis for a low-level element is much more detailed, and involves knowledge of previous design decisions. The tools and methods used for "analysis" do in fact support all aspects of architectural design development: partitioning, allocation, and flowdown. They therefore are useful in both the requirements analysis and design stages of the process.

VI. Requirements Engineering Practices

The principles of requirements engineering described above are valid and important, but for practical application additional specifics are needed. These specifics are provided by methods and tools. A *method*, sometimes referred to as a *methodology*, describes a general approach; a *tool*, usually but not always automated, provides a detailed, step-by-step approach to carrying out a method.

A. Methods

Requirements analysis methods may be roughly divided into four categories, as shown in Figure 13. The categorizations should not be regarded as absolute: most methods have some of the characteristics of all the categories, but usually one viewpoint is primary.

Process-oriented methods take the primary viewpoint of the way the system transforms inputs into outputs, with less emphasis on the data itself and control aspects. Classical structured analysis (SA)[29] fits into

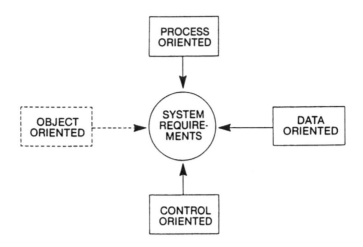

Figure 13. Categories of requirements analysis methods.

this category, as do Structured Analysis and Design Technique (SADT),[30] and formal methods such as VDM[31] and Z.[32]

Data-oriented methods emphasize the system state as a data structure. While SA and SADT have secondary aspects of the data viewpoint, Entity-Relationship modeling[33] and JSD[7] are primarily data oriented.

Control-oriented methods emphasize synchronization, deadlock, exclusion, concurrence, and process activation and deactivation. SADT and the real-time extensions to SA[34,35] are secondarily control oriented. Flowcharting is primarily process oriented.

Finally, object-oriented methods base requirements analysis on classes of objects of the system and their interactions with each other. Bailin[36] surveys the fundamentals of object-oriented analysis and describes the variations among the several different methods in use.

B. Tools

The number of tools that support requirements engineering is growing rapidly, and even the most cursory survey is beyond the scope of this paper. Nevertheless, some discussion of the characteristics of requirements engineering tools, and trends in these characteristics, is in order.

Davis[18] has classified requirements tools as follows:

- Graphical editing
- Traceability
- Behavior modeling
- Databases and word processing—not designed for requirements engineering, but used in requirements applications
- Hybrid (combinations of the above)

Early requirements tools, such as SREM[37] and PSL/PSA,[38] were stand-alone, that is, were not integrated with any other tools, and supported the requirements analysis function by providing automation, either for a specific method or a group of methods. These tools consisted of hundreds of thousands of lines of code and ran on large mainframe computers. PSL/PSA used only very limited graphics in its early versions but later versions had improved graphics capabilities. SREM made heavy and effective use of graphics from the beginning. Both included some form of behavior modeling. In this same time frame, stand-alone traceability tools began to be developed.[19]

By the mid-1980s, integrated software development environments began to become available that, while they were more complex software products than the earlier tools, ran on powerful (usually UNIX-based) workstations that were smaller in size and lower in cost than mainframes. Examples include Software through Pictures,[39] CADRE Teamwork, and similar products. These environments included requirements analysis tools, which generally supported one of the standard graphical analysis methods, and might also include traceability tools that enabled the requirements to be traced through design, implementation, and test. Some of the integrated environments provided a choice of analysis tools, such as tools that supported different methods. As computers continued to become smaller, more powerful, and lower in cost, full software development environments (known as Computer-Aided Software Engineering [CASE] or Software Engineering Environments [SEE]) became available on desktop computers, and economics permitted providing such a computer to each member of the development team and networking them together.

CASE environments seemed full of promise during the late 1980s but somehow that promise has not been translated into pervasive use in the embedded systems and scientific software markets[40]; perhaps there was a perception that the environments supported a Waterfall or Baseline Management model of end-to-end software development better than the Prototyping, Evolutionary, or Incremental models that became increasingly popular. The requirements tools that are part of these integrated environments are, of course, limited to the market penetration of the environments themselves. In the application area of transaction-oriented systems such as financial and database, tools implementing an Entity-Relationship model such as Texas Instruments's Information Engineering Facility have revolutionized the way software is developed, but in the scientific and embedded application areas stand-alone tools, if any, are used. Perhaps the current trend toward object-oriented technologies will revitalize the market for tools and for integrated tool environments.

C. The Role of Tools and Methods

In conclusion, a few words are in order about the role of tools and methods in requirements engineering, and indeed across the full scope of software and systems engineering. Proper use of tools and methods is an important part of process maturity as advocated by the Software Engineering Institute,[22] and process maturity has been shown to lead to improvements in a software development organization's productivity and quality.[41] It has equally been shown that developers cannot adopt or purchase methods and tools and just throw them at the problem. Selection of tools and methods requires study of their applicability and compatibility with the organization's practices. A process must be identified that meets the organization's needs; methods must be selected that support the process, with tool availability one of the factors to be considered; then and only then should tools be purchased. Commitment, training, and the time to make the transition are essential. Tools and methods are not a panacea: if selected and used correctly they can provide great benefits; if regarded as magic solutions or otherwise misused, they will prove an expensive failure.

References

1. Naur, P. and B. Randell, eds., "Software Engineering: Report on a Conference Sponsored by the NATO Science Commission," Garmisch, Germany, 7–11 Oct. 1968. Scientific Affairs Division, NATO, Brussels, Jan. 1969.

2. Alford, M.W. and J.T. Lawson, "Software Requirements Engineering Methodology (Development)," RADC-TR-79-168, U.S. Air Force Rome Air Devel-

opment Center, Griffiss AFB, NY, June 1979 (DDC-AD-A073132).

3. Schwartz, J.I., "Construction of Software, Problems and Practicalities," in *Practical Strategies for Developing Large Software Systems*, E. Horowitz, ed., Addison-Wesley, Reading, Mass., 1975.

4. IEEE Standard 610.12-1990, "IEEE Standard Glossary of Software Engineering Terminology," IEEE, New York, N.Y., 1990.

5. Boehm, B.W., "A Spiral Model of Software Development and Enhancement," *Computer*, Vol. 21, No. 5, May 1988, pp. 61–72.

6. Davis, A.M., E.H. Bersoff, and E.R. Comer, "A Strategy for Comparing Alternative Software Development Life Cycle Models," *IEEE Trans. Software Eng.*, Vol. 14, No. 10, Oct. 1988, pp. 1453–1461.

7. Cameron, J.R., "An Overview of JSD," *IEEE Trans. Software Eng.*, Vol. 12, No. 2, Feb. 1986, pp. 222–240.

8. Royce, W.W., "Managing the Development of Large Software Systems," *Proc. IEEE Wescon*, 1970. Reprinted in *Proc. 9th Int'l Conf. Software Eng.*, IEEE Computer Society Press, Los Alamitos, Calif., 1987, pp. 328–338.

9. McCracken, D.D. and M.A. Jackson, "Life Cycle Concept Considered Harmful," *ACM Software Eng. Notes*, Vol. SE-7, No. 2, 1982, pp. 29–32.

10. Gladden, G.R., "Stop the Life Cycle, I Want to Get Off," *ACM Software Eng. Notes*, Vol. SE-7, No. 2, Apr. 1982, pp. 35–39.

11. Brooks, F.P., Jr., Chairman, *Report of the Defense Science Board Task Force on Military Software*, Office of the Under Secretary of Defense for Acquisition, U.S. Department of Defense, Washington D.C., Sept. 1987.

12. Gomaa, H. and D.B.H. Scott, "Prototyping as a Tool in the Specification of User Requirements," *Proc. 5th Int'l Conf. Software Eng.*, IEEE Computer Society Press, Los Alamitos, Calif., 1981, pp. 333–342.

13. Verner, J. and Graham T., "Third-Generation versus Fourth-Generation Software Development," *IEEE Software*, Vol. 5, No. 4, July 1988, pp. 8–14.

14. Cobb, R.H., "In Praise of 4GLs," *Datamation*, July 15, 1985, pp. 36–46.

15. Boehm, B.W., ed., *Software Risk Management*, IEEE Computer Society Press, Los Alamitos, Calif., 1989, p. 434.

16. Fairley, R.E. and R.H. Thayer, "The Concept of Operations: The Bridge from Operational Requirements to Technical Specifications," in *Software Engineering*, M. Dorfman and R.H. Thayer, eds., IEEE Computer Society Press, Los Alamitos, Calif., 1997.

17. *Acquisition Software Development Capability Evaluation* (2 volumes), AFMC Pamphlet 63–103, Depart-

ment of the Air Force, HQ Air Force Material Command, Wright-Patterson AFB, OH, June 15, 1994.

18. Davis, A.M., private communication, 1996.

19. Dorfman, M. and R.F. Flynn, "ARTS—An Automated Requirements Traceability System," *J. Systems and Software*, Vol. 4, No. 1, 1984, pp. 63–74.

20. Palmer, J.D., "Traceability," in *Software Engineering*, M. Dorfman and R.H. Thayer, eds., IEEE Computer Society Press, Los Alamitos, Calif., 1997, pp. 266–276.

21. Goguen, J.A. and C. Linde, "Techniques for Requirements Elicitation," *Proc. Int'l Symp. Requirements Eng.* IEEE Computer Society Press, Los Alamitos, Calif., 1993.

22. Paulk, M.C. et al., *Capability Maturity Model for Software, Version 1.1*, CMU/SEI-93-TR-24, Software Engineering Institute, Carnegie Mellon University, Pittsburgh, P.A., Feb. 1993. See also Paulk, M.C., et al., *Key Practices of the Capability Maturity Model for Software, Version 1.1*, CMU/SEI-93-TR-25, Carnegie Mellon University, Pittsburgh, P.A., Feb. 1993.

23. Boehm, B.W., "Verifying and Validating Software Requirements and Design Specifications," *IEEE Software*, Vol. 1, No. 1, Jan. 1984, pp. 75–88.

24. Boehm, B.W., *Software Engineering Economics,* Prentice-Hall, Englewood Cliffs, N.J., 1981.

25. Davis, A. et al., "Identifying and Measuring Quality in a Software Requirements Specification," *Proc. 1st Int'l Software Metrics Symp.,* IEEE Computer Society Press, Los Alamitos, Calif., 1993.

26. Swartout, W. and R. Balzer, "On the Inevitable Intertwining of Specification and Design," *Comm. ACM*, Vol. 27, No. 7, July 1982, pp. 438–440.

27. Hatley, D.J., and I.A. Pirbhai, *Strategies for Real-Time System Specification*, Dorset House, New York, N.Y., 1987.

28. Davis, A.M., *Software Requirements: Objects, Functions, and States*, Prentice-Hall, Englewood Cliffs, N.J., 1993.

29. Svoboda, C.P., "Tutorial on Structured Analysis," in *System and Software Requirements Engineering*, R.H. Thayer and M. Dorfman, eds., IEEE Computer Society Press, Los Alamitos, Calif., 1990.

30. Ross, D.T., "Structured Analysis (SA): A Language for Communicating Ideas," *IEEE Trans. Software Eng.*, Vol. 3, No. 1, Jan. 1977, pp. 16–33.

31. Bjoerner, D., "On the Use of Formal Methods in Software Development," *Proc. 9th Int'l Conf. Software Eng.*, IEEE Computer Society Press, Los Alamitos, Calif., 1987, pp. 17–29.

32. Norris, M., "Z (A Formal Specification Method). A Debrief Report," STARTS, National Computing Centre, Ltd., 1986. Reprinted in *System and Software Requirements Engineering*, R.H. Thayer and M. Dorfman, eds., IEEE Computer Society Press, Los Alamitos, Calif., 1990.

33. Reilly, J.R., "Entity-Relationship Approach to Data Modeling," in *Software Requirements Engineering,* 2nd ed., R.H. Thayer and M. Dorfman, eds., IEEE Computer Society Press, Los Alamitos, Calif., 1997.

34. Ward, P.T. and S.J. Mellor, *Structured Development Techniques for Real-Time Systems* (3 vols.), Prentice-Hall, Englewood Cliffs, N.J., 1985.

35. Hatley, D.J., "The Use of Structured Methods in the Development of Large Software-Based Avionics Systems," AIAA Paper 84-2592, *Proc. 6th Digital Avionics Systems Conf.*, AIAA, New York, N.Y., 1984.

36. Bailin, C.A., "Object Oriented Requirements Analysis," in *Encyclopedia of Software Engineering*, John J. Marciniak, ed., John Wiley & Sons, New York, N.Y., 1994.

37. Alford, M.W., "SREM at the Age of Eight: The Distributed Computing Design System," *Computer*, Vol. 18, No. 4, Apr. 1985, 36–46.

38. Sayani, H., "PSL/PSA at the Age of Fifteen: Tools for Real-Time and Non-Real-Time Analysis," in *System and Software Requirements Engineering*, R.H. Thayer and M. Dorfman, eds., IEEE Computer Society Press, Los Alamitos, Calif., 1990, 403–417.

39. Wasserman, A.I. and P.A. Pircher, "A Graphic, Extensible Integrated Environment for Software Development," *ACM SIGPLAN Notices*, Vol. 12, No. 1, Jan. 1987, pp. 131–142.

40. Lewis, T., "The Big Software Chill," *Computer*, Vol. 29, No. 3, Mar. 1996, pp. 12–14.

41. Herbsleb, J. et al., "Benefits of CMM-Based Software Process Improvement: Initial Results," CMU/SEI-94-TR-13, Software Engineering Institute, Carnegie Mellon University, Pittsburgh, P.A., Aug. 1994.

What Is A Requirement?

Richard Harwell
Lockheed Aeronautical Systems Company
86 S. Cobb Drive; Marietta, GA 30063-0685

Erik Aslaksen
University of Technology, Sydney, and
Ewbank Preece Sinclair Knight
PO Box 572, St. Leonards
Sydney, NSW 2065 Australia

Ivy Hooks
Bruce G. Jackson & Assoc., Inc.
17629 El Camino Real, Suite 207
Houston, TX 77058

Roy Mengot
Texas Instruments
PO Box 650311
Dallas, TX 75075

Ken Ptack
PRC, Inc.
Crystal Gateway One, Suite 1211
1235 Jefferson Davis Highway
Arlington, VA 22202

Abstract. Each contract specialist, lawyer, engineer, systems engineer, manager, or anyone else involved in *the transition of vision into product*, has his or her own definition of a requirement. With the rare exception, all are applicable and meaningful – but most are forgotten or ignored in the crunch to produce an effective requirements document under constrained schedule and funding environments. Yet, the need for effective requirements generation is probably the number one priority today in product development needs. Rather than approaching this problem from the theoretical or apriori standpoint, this paper examines the nature of a requirement through a process of identifying key characteristics and relationships from the viewpoint of the requirements manager/analyst and the requirements user (design team). It also discusses the importance of determining that requirements convey a need (as opposed to a directed solution), and ascertaining quality in terms of contextual adequacy.

INTRODUCTION

This is the first of three papers addressing the topic *"What is a requirement?"*. It concentrates on: (1)the use of characteristics and relationships to analyze and integrate requirements sets, (2) identification of the transition from requirement to design, and (3) determining quality in terms of completeness, lack of ambiguity, and scope. The second paper expands on the concept of requirements characteristics to include selected optional characteristics which may be used by requirements analysts for special purpose needs. The last in the series is an in-depth examination of *"Requirement Structure"*, providing a means of assisting the requirements analyst in better understanding the structure of an individual requirement from a linguistic and contextual standpoint.

THE REQUIREMENT ENVIRONMENT

All projects begin with a statement of requirements, whether it be an innovator's simple statement of concept, a formal DoD System Specification, or a Marketing Analysis. However, the "rush" to convert concepts to products – the "real stuff" you can touch and manipulate – often overpowers the requirements development process. This, in turn, hampers the ability to produce the concept as originally envisioned. Prior papers on this subject range from an examination of requirements from a micro-specification viewpoint to academic treatises on the theory of requirement constructs. However, program personnel frequently set aside such treatises as being too difficult to interpret and apply in the day to day efforts of getting the job done.

This paper establishes a means of identifying the clear-cut characteristics of a requirement which can be used by both requirements analysts and design teams. These characteristics can help determine the source, applicability, depth, and other factors needed for assessing and implementing an integrated, and coherent, requirements set. Analysis of assigned characteristics can help a design team identify whether a specific requirement establishes a quantifiable threshold, if it needs further analysis to determine its impact, or if it can be treated as a goal or customer desire.

In a specification environment it is a common practice to identify multiple classes of requirements (i.e., functional requirement, reliability requirement, constraints, etc.) according to a designated specification structure. However, in a requirements management system environment (database), a specification is simply a "slice" of the database according to pre-defined attributes. In this environment, requirements classes are treated as a specified characteristic of a requirement (or as a relationship/attribute to a requirement), rather than as a separate class of requirements. Therefore, this paper is based on the concept that:

If it mandates that something must be accomplished, transformed, produced, or provided, it is a requirement – period.

The qualifiers follow – in the form of characteristics and relationships. This allows a requirement to be the focus, i.e., the key player or authority, for all related information in a requirements management database environment. Yet, this approach preserves the use of familiar identifiers (albeit in a different format) for use in specification-based developments. In the latter case, a *reliability requirement* becomes a requirement having the qualifier *reliability* as one of its relationships (other relationships might include *radar subsystem, WBS 1237, MTBF, etc.*).

REQUIREMENTS CHARACTERISTICS

Although it may be difficult to find the "right" definition of a requirement that provides us with omnipotent insight into requirements generation forevermore, we can consistently identify the "fingerprints" of a requirement. There are nine characteristics in all – three essential characteristics and six optional characteristics, as shown in Tables 1 and 2, respectively. As noted in the tables, each of these characteristics has subsets which may be used as deemed appropriate for each program. (The terms "program" and "project" are synonymous in this paper.) A discussion of the three fundamental characteristics, with examples, follow.

Requirement Type. The *requirement type* identifies the source and contractual applicability of a requirement. There are only two requirements types:

• Primary. Those requirements (whatever their form – contract provision, specification, database, market analysis, etc.) levied on a contractor/producer under force of contract. The identification is unambiguous. If it is: (1) contractually applicable, or has the force of a contract as in a market analysis, and (2) comes from a source external to program personnel, it's a primary requirement. An example would be *"The payload shall be transported into orbit in the payload bay"*.

• Derived. Those requirements (whatever their source – internal, supplier, team member, customer, etc.) that are generated apart from the primary requirements. The identification is unambiguous. If it is not a primary requirement, it is a derived requirement. An example would be *"The payload shall have a diameter of less than 14 feet"*. The specifying of payload diameter is derived from the payload bay size based on the original primary requirement. That derivation may have been accomplished by the Contractor's Program Manager, be the result of a trade analysis, or physical examination of an object. Or it may have been suggested by the customer's Contracting Officer – but not as an amendment to the contract. It doesn't matter, it is still a derived requirement with the primary requirement as it's parent for traceability.

The requirement type enables the product team to assess the difficulties associated with changing a requirement. By definition, if it is a primary requirement, a Contract Change, or perhaps a new market analysis, will be required. But if it is a derived requirement, the decision to change (as long as the change is within the scope of the "parent" primary requirement) rests with program management.

With respect to requirements entered into a database, there may be a need to modify the exact customer statement – particularly when a specification combines several different requirements into a single sentence. The precise splitting of such a requirement, including the creation of transitional phrases, does not constitute a derived requirement because *no assumptions or expansions* of the primary requirement will have been made. However, each split-out segment will be a child of the parent (original) primary requirement.

Requirement Application. The *requirement application* identifies the object of a requirement. There are only two requirements applications:

• Product Parameter. A product parameter is a requirement that applies to the product or service to be developed. The identification is unambiguous. If it directly acts on the product or service, it is a product parameter. Examples of such requirements would include *"The external surfaces of all equipment shall be painted white"*, and *"The operator training program shall result in a pass rate of not less than 95% for qualified candidates"*.

Product parameters have two primary subdivisions:

• *Qualitative.* – This product parameter contains **no measurable requirement.** An example would be *"The mixer shall produce a mixture of homogeneous appearance"*. A qualitative product parameter usually necessitates further analysis to determine suitable quantifiable criteria; i.e., usually necessitates the development of derived requirement(s), with the qualitative product parameter serving as the parent.

• *Quantitative* – This product parameter contains **a measurable requirement.** An example would be *"The mixer shall produce a mixture having a fineness granularity of XYZ within five minutes "*. A quantitative product parameter may have children, but such children would be generated for the purpose of specifying particular approaches to meeting this measurable requirement.

• *Program Parameter.* A program parameter is a requirement that applies to the activities associated with enabling the creation of a product or service, such as conducting tradeoffs or holding design reviews. This also includes contract provisions which define the customer/contractor relationship; e.g., confidentiality, intellectual property rights, warranties, etc. In short, a program parameter defines activities related to the technical and administrative management of product development. The identification is unambiguous. If it does not directly act on the product or service, it is a program parameter. Examples of such requirements would include *"The contractor shall develop a concept of operations"* or *"The contractor shall conduct internal design reviews every two weeks."*

Program Parameters have three primary subdivisions:

• *Task* – Identifies an analysis or other effort to be performed. Examples would include *"Prepare a Systems Engineering Management Plan"* or *"Perform an analysis of the structural loads on the bridge pylons"*.

• *Compliance Evaluation* – Identifies the methodology for measuring compliance with parameter. (There should be a verification program parameter associated with each product parameter.)

• *Regulatory* – Identifies administrative elements such as *"Deliverable data shall be furnished with unlimited rights to the Government"*.

Requirement Compliance Level. The requirement compliance level identifies the depth of compliance mandated for a requirement. There are only three compliance levels:

• **Mandatory.** Whether a primary or derived requirement, it *must be implemented.* Such requirements usually include a *"shall"* statement in their structure. If it is a *primary requirement* and is not achievable, then a contract change or deviation/waiver is necessary. If it is a *derived requirement* and is not achievable, then a briefing must be presented to management (or in rare instances, the customer) for lessening of the requirement. An example might be a directive to use an in-house component, which is not deemed to conform to a primary requirement. If there are no alternatives to the derived requirement in such an instance, it is very likely that a higher ordered (parent) primary requirement may not be achievable and will also need to be changed. •

• **Guidance.** Whether a primary or derived requirement, it is *desirable that it be implemented.* In general, failure to implement does not constitute non-compliance so long as it can be demonstrated that a reasonable degree of implementation was attempted. This is equivalent to specifying a goal or desire on the part of the customer or management. An example would be *"Use Mil-Std-499B as a guide in implementing the systems engineering process."*

• **Information.** This unique characteristic is essential when requirements management systems (requirements databases) are used in lieu of hard copy source documents. By strict interpretation, these "requirements" are not actually requirements, but *are non-binding statements which significantly influence the context, meaning, and understanding of other requirements.* An example might be a reference to the customer's reasoning for specifying a particular approach or requirement.

Priority. This characteristic identifies the relative importance of a requirement in terms of implementation, particularly in establishing criteria for trade studies. In a cost reimburseable environment, a customer may use priorities to mandate that certain elements must be completed before a specified ceiling is reached. The priority characteristic may also be used for establishing the sequence in which specified design or test activities should occur. Unlike the other characteristics, the values of priority will be dependent on program and company needs.

REQUIREMENT ALLOCATION AND/OR RELATIONSHIP ASSIGNMENT

Determining the characteristics of a given requirement enables the product team to understand nature of a requirement. Correspondingly, allocation of a requirement (or assignment of a relationship to a requirement in a database) enables the product team to visualize and understand the interactive and interdependent nature of a balanced requirements set. This insight is achieved by being able to scope and group an otherwise disconnected series of requirements into meaningful structures for analysis and implementation.

After the characteristics are defined, anomalies identified, and decisions made with respect to team handling of the anomalies (until customer or management resolution), the product team is primarily interested in identifying requirements applicable to the team components. As with requirements characteristics, definition of the allocation/relationship assignment process should be approached from the viewpoint of the user. Therefore, the initial effort is usually the assignment of responsibility (i.e., ownership) of each requirement to the respective team. As the program progresses, this assignment may change, but a known baseline for performance responsibility will maintained.

The key in this effort is not the specifics of the allocation (each program has its own needs), nor the process followed (each company has its own version of the systems engineering process). Rather, the key is establishing an agreed upon hierarchy of relationships that will enable the teams to examine large quantities of requirements (potentially hundreds of thousands on some programs) according to program needs. For example, a typical relationship hierarchy might include the following:

• **Product Elements** – Segments, subsystems, interface components, etc.

• **Keywords** – Indices (terms not usually appearing in requirements text such as "affordability", "mission applicability", etc.), work breakdown structure (WBS) elements, technical budgeting, trade study references, etc.

• **Parent/Child Relationships** – Traceability between higher and lower level requirements

• **Assignments to Specifications** – Identification of the various specifications into which the requirement will be incorporated

• **Test Plan/Test Methods Applicability** – Identification of the applicable test plan reference and methods for demonstrating compliance

• **Other Assignments, Observations, and Discriminators.**

Particularly when used in conjunction with a requirements management system, these relationships enable product teams to examine requirements through insights gained by selective groupings. These examinations will help to further identify anomalies for resolution, but more importantly they can help to *integrate* the requirements statements and thus identify before *integrated test and evaluation* the suitability of a given requirements set to accomplish the customer's objective.

REQUIREMENT VERSUS DESIGN IMPLEMENTATION

There are two aspects of this issue of *"Is it a requirement or is it a design implementation?"* The first occurs when the customer mandates a design solution as a requirement. The other occurs when the product team generates derived requirements which actually may be design solutions instead of requirements. Both aspects are discussed below.

Requirements – Needs Versus Implementation.

An RFP was released last summer for the development of a requirements management tool. The first requirement was to "provide a database". The statement is one of implementation and not of need, and it is common to find such statements in requirements documents. Requirements documents should state *what* is needed, not *how* it is to be provided. Yet this is a common mistake made by requirements authors.

Most authors do not intend to state implementation, they simply do not know how to state the requirement correctly. In the case above, the author of the document continued with many valid requirements -

• Provide the capability for traceability between requirements *(Qualitative product parameter)* ,

• Provide the capability to add attributes to requirements *(Qualitative product parameter)*,

• Provide the ability to sort requirements *(Qualitative product parameter)* .

Granted, each of these requirements will result in a database type of system, but a separate requirement for a database was not needed.

There are two major dangers in stating implementation. The one most often cited is that of forcing a design when not intended. If all the needs can be met without a database, then why state the need for a database. If they cannot be met another, or better, way, then a database will be the selected design solution.

The second danger is more subtle and potentially much more detrimental. By stating implementation, the author may be lulled into believing that all requirements have been covered. In fact, very important requirements may be missing. This may result in the contractor/producer conforming with the requirements document, yet not delivering a system or product which accomplishes the customer's real intent. For example, providing a database in the above instance will not be sufficient for someone needing a requirements management tool. It is the capabilities of the requirements management tool that are needed.

At each level of requirements development the problem of needs versus implementation will occur. At the system level the requirements must state *WHAT* is needed. The system designer will determine *HOW* this can be accomplished – and then must define *WHAT* is needed at the subsystem level. The subsystem designer will determine *HOW* the need can be met – and then must define *WHAT* is needed at the component level, and so forth.

Another illustration of how implementation creeps into needs statements is that of a proposed system requirement on a different program which included the expression *"landing in TBD sea state conditions"*. Since there was no vehicle design – the vehicle could have landed in water or on land – it was difficult to justify this requirement as written. On being asked *why* such a requirement was needed, the author indicated the real concern was about crew rescue. If the vehicle were to land in the water, rescue by helicopter could only be accomplished under certain sea conditions. In further discussions, however, it was noted that if the vehicle made a landing on the ground, there would also be a limited amount of time to reasonably leave the crew inside and unattended – an equal crew rescue concern. The requirement, therefore, was changed to reflect the real need *"time to remove the crew from the vehicle"*.

To ensure that a requirement statement represents a need and not an implementation, ask *WHY* the requirement is needed. If this does not lead to a "real" need statement, then the original requirement statement is probably appropriate, citing a need rather than implementation.

When Does the Transition Occur From Requirement to Design Implementation?

The second aspect of the requirements versus implementation concern most often occurs with software development. Many of the systems engineering and software engineering interface difficulties stem from the fact that software developers views the continuum from customer requirement to acceptable code as a requirements process – rather than as a transition from requirement to design to product. Stated in another way, what the systems engineer may view as a *"design solution"* , the software engineer may view as a lower level *"requirement"*. The same concern occurs in hardware development as the requirements process progresses to lower and lower levels. A point is reached when the question must be asked: *Is this a requirement or a design solution?"* There are no absolute answers. But establishing a general guideline such as the following is feasible:

- If there are no viable alternatives which can be implemented, other than the statement in question – it's highly probable the statement is a design solution. In effect, it's mandating a solution as discussed above. As such, it should be removed from whatever requirements document intended and included in a design description document , a drawing, or code.

- However, even if there is a lack of viable alternatives, when implementation as a design solution is not feasible without further customer or systems engineering interface, it should continue to be treated as a requirement (particularly in software development). This is due to the fact that implementation is dependent upon an understanding of the context in which the requirement/solution is to be implemented, and as such, cannot stand alone as a true design solution.

Requirement Quality

Definition Of Requirement Quality.

The quality of an object or process is often defined as the degree to which it meets specification requirements. It is sometimes also defined as fitness for purpose. So what is the specification of a requirement, what is its purpose?

Execution of a requirement may be considered to occur as an interface between two processes: *The definition process, in which an intellectual intent (concept) is transformed into a written statement (specification), and the interpretation process, in which the written statement is transformed into the intellectual input to a process which produces a set of more detailed (derived) requirements or design description.*

The purpose of a requirement is to reproduce in the mind of the reader the intellectual content which was in the mind of the writer. *The quality of a requirement is then the extent to which this takes place.*

Two features of this definition emerge :

- The quality of a requirement is not an absolute characteristic – it is only defined relative to the reader.

- The quality of a requirement is not a measurable trait – it can only be inferred a posteriori.

The first of these features is inherent in the nature of a requirement and would be a feature of any definition of quality. The second feature is a result of the high level of the definition; a much more detailed (and complex) definition could have been introduced which would be measurable. This is not considered to be a particularly practical solution. Instead, the approach will be to define some subordinate traits/factors which are more easily measurable.

Necessary Elements for Requirement Quality.

Completeness. A requirement must be complete in the sense that it provides all the program-specific (i.e. non common domain) information necessary for the user to carry out the next process step. To understand what this means, consider the case where the next step is development of derived (i.e. more detailed) requirements. Such a step consists of analyzing the parent requirements, identifying the options available to satisfy these requirements, choosing the best option, specifying (i.e. giving new, more detailed/derived requirements), and finally verifying that these derived requirements will collectively achieve the intent of the parents. The crucial activity here is choosing the best option; the criterion for making that choice is determined by the given requirements. For example, a requirement for minimum weight will give a different choice than one for minimum cost. Conversely, the absence of a requirement to differentiate among options for a specific parameter implies that parameter is not a criteria for completeness. For example, if the requirement says nothing about the color of the equipment, the author of the requirement does not care and cannot complain if the equipment turns out, say, shocking pink. If the author does care, then the requirement was not complete.

These examples demonstrate that completeness of a requirement is dependent upon the author's intent. Therefore, while it is possible to measure or test for completeness, such measurement is only possible in conjunction with the author.

Lack of Ambiguity. A requirement must be unambiguous in the sense that different users (with similar backgrounds) would give the same interpretation to the requirement. This has two aspects. On the one hand there is the aspect of grammatical ambiguousness, i.e. the poorly constructed sentence. On the other hand there is the aspect of ambiguousness arising from a lack of detail allowing different interpretations.

The first of these can be measured or tested independently of author or user, but the second aspect can be measured only in conjunction with a set of users, since it depends on what assumptions the user makes automatically, i.e. as a result of the user's background knowledge.

Scope. A requirement must be properly scoped in the sense of providing a definite amount of information. Poor requirements in this regard include motherhood statements as "shall use their best efforts", "shall ensure the highest system integrity", "shall be of a high quality", "shall provide a reliable service", etc. Although scope is intrinsic to the requirement; measurement of the depth of scope would need a procedure tailored to the program needs.

CONCLUSION

The accurate translation of a customer's need by the product team is essential. Identifying requirements characteristics, determining that the stated requirement conveys a need (as opposed to a directed solution), and ascertaining contextual adequacy are essential for assessing the accuracy of translation before the product team proceeds. These criteria enable the analysis team to better understand the customer's intent and to better identify where disjoints, ambiguities, and conflicts exist early in the program. The objective is to be able to integrate a collection of requirements (preferably through manipulation in a database using these characteristics and relationships as "grouping" devices) and to establish their achievability prior to design implementation – rather than during test and evaluation. In addition, as we learn the effects certain combinations of characteristics and relationships have on the development process, we can more readily identify potential difficulties and correct them before we are committed to an approach that may be impracticable.

CATEGORY	CHARACTERISTIC
Type	**A. Primary** – Usually a contract requirement, but may be a requirement in a pre-contract document Also may be a requirement established by Marketing or survey teams as in Commercial applications.
	B. Derived – Derived from Primary Requirements or higher level Derived Requirements.
Application	**A. Product Parameter** – The Product Parameter refers to a requirement which applies to the product or service to be developed. It may be adjusted for a specific application or phase. For example, some programs and tools distinguish between a "design" and a "constraint " parameter. Other programs may need to distinguish between "design," "build," and "operate". In any application, subsets may include: 1. **Qualitative** – Not directly measurable • *Functional (What it does/A capability of the product)* • *Process (Leading to a result/product)* 2. **Quantitative** – Directly measurable. • *Performance* • *Design Point (Altitude, endurance, temperature, mix-rate, etc.)* • *Procedural (Specified sequence of events, specified algorithm)* • *Physical (What it is)*
	B. Program Parameter – The Program Parameter refers to a requirement which is not directly involved in the development, production, or operation of the product. But rather pertains to programmatic activity associated with supporting these aforementioned aspects. There must be a "Compliance Evaluation Program Parameter" for each product parameter which specifies how accomplishment of the product parameter can be measured. 1. **Task** *(Perform an analysis, build to a product specification, operate a system, etc.)* 2. **Compliance Evaluation** *(Measure compliance with a product parameter.)* 3. **Regulatory** *(Administrative , corporate policies/practices, etc.)*
Compliance Level	**A. Mandatory** – Typically a "shall" statement – mandates conformance. **B. Guidance (Goal) (Objective)** – Typically a "will" statement – accomplishment is desired/preferred. It is still essential to demonstrate and document why accomplishment is not achievable, if requirement is not met. **C. Information** – Statement supporting or giving insight to a measurable requirement, the absence of which would lead to a misunderstanding of the associated requirement. (A practice necessitated by the use of databases in requirements management systems which will be used by the team in lieu of the source document.)
Priority	The particular values of priority will be program and company dependent

Table 1. – Essential Requirements Characteristics

Good requirements definition can be an important factor in the success of a system development project.

PINPOINTING REQUIREMENTS

by Laura Scharer

One of the most common reasons systems fail is because the definition of system requirements is bad.

Why are we consistently unable to produce a good statement of requirements? Because it is difficult; we have a poor attitude about working with users (and vice versa); our expectations for this phase of systems design is different from the users' expectations; we let the situation control us; and we don't always use the techniques that are most appropriate.

More specifically:

• Sophisticated problem solving is required to produce good statements of requirements. Problems must be translated into corrective goals, which must be translated into solutions, which must in turn be reduced to functional terms. There is no guarantee that the functions will create the desired results.

• The articulation of requirements is unusually difficult. Functions and processes are not easily described.

• System requirements change, and the definition must be able to absorb these changes.

• Tools and techniques for optimizing the definition process are not generally available.

• Heavy user involvement can introduce interpersonal and project management problems.

• User motivation is difficult because reinforcement for their work is traditionally postponed until the implementation stage, by which time they have learned to expect disappointment.

• The definition process can become highly political.

• Definition is mentally taxing.

• Compromises which will eventually disenchant some of the users and analysts are required.

• We have no real yardstick other than the ultimate success or failure of the system; there is no way to judge the quality of our definition.

While we can't expect these difficul-

ties to disappear, we can minimize their impact.

Analysts and users harbor grave doubts about each other (Table I), and the origins of these attitudes are obvious. Failure encourages blame. Users are disenchanted because we consistently bungle new system development; we are disenchanted because we alone are blamed for the failures. Somehow, even when users participate heavily in the definition process, they succeed with the help of unquestioned corporate mores in abdicating responsibility for system results. In other words, users provide the system definition but the systems people are responsible for it.

However, we should not expect users to metamorphose into analysts just because they are sitting on a project team. Remember:

• Assume that the user is trained in his own functional field but not necessarily in systems skills. Give him work assignments involving existing system education and new system definition—work that he can perform better than an analyst just because he is a user.

• The user's primary objective on the project is to protect his own interests. Let him.

• If you have recruited good users for the project team, they are usually good workers who receive recognition in the company and have confidence in their own abilities. In other words, they have delicate egos. It is very easy to insult users' intelligence by appropriate work assignments: we can't give them all the dirty work.

• The systems group, although responsible for project management, has no real organizational authority over users on the project team. The users can't be forced to do anything for the project.

• Users need periodic, if not constant, attention. After we've received all their input, we can't leave them hanging. Provide written status reports on a regular schedule and contact them personally whenever possible.

Another problem is that users and analysts don't even share a common goal for the definition process. Certainly both groups

would agree that the objective of requirements definition is to produce a specification of what the system will do.

ANALYSTS DEFINE SYSTEM

Let's define what the system will do from the analyst's point of view. We are to produce this definition, but we impose some conditions on it. For one thing, the definition must be translatable into a system design. This requires that it be a functional specification, expressed in terms of processes, outputs, inputs, and data structures. We want the definition to be precise, clear and not open to misinterpretation. Quite understandably, we hope that the definition will be complete, because design is optimized when all features are known and can thus be integrated neatly into databases and programs. In the best of situations, the specification is frozen so that design, coding, and testing will never have to be reworked.

Now, two important time constraints surface which affect the definition of the system and the system itself. Because the systems group is responsible for the project, we ask that the definition be produced within the time allotted to this project phase. The specification activity to do this must have a definite beginning and end, and the end of this phase must precede the beginning of the design phase. Additionally, we must insist that the system thus defined can be implemented within project schedules and budget, both of which are usually preset before definition begins and thus before the real size and complexity of the system are known.

Finally, analysts are interested in developing a definition for a good system. We want to specify a system that is not only technically feasible but also elegant. We want integrated functions, clean and simple databases, efficient computer runs, and economical output.

Now, let's start again, this time from the user's point of view.

The users seem to be more satisfied with a qualitative definition which, in many cases, specifies the system in generalities and in terms of benefits to be derived. To reach the level of detail that analysts desire, the users must actually enter what they consider to be problem solving, or design (how) mode: they must arrive at functions that will solve their problems. They can't quite understand us when we distinguish our whats and hows: we're usually thinking a step ahead of them (Table II).

The qualitative nature of the user's definition suggests that it is to be interpreted, to be fleshed out in greater detail, at a later time. But the users, since you are asking them what they want and since they're telling you, expect that all requests will be met in the new system. They are often sincerely puzzled by arguments of technical feasibility or advisability, especially because they usually believe firmly that they need all requested features in order to achieve their stated goals.

Flexibility is a key consideration for the users. The system specification must be changeable with their needs, as must be the system after it is developed. This emphasis on flexibility also suggests that the users do not consider system definition to be a front-end activity with a definite ending point; it becomes, in essence, an ongoing process.

Finally, users are simply interested in defining a system that will work. They are not as interested in the project budget as they are in the impact of the system on their individual budgets. They want the system to perform specified functions without flaw, to be operationally efficient for their people, and to achieve the subjective goals.

USERS DEFINE SYSTEMS

Users who try to define a system with the analysts' goals in mind can find themselves in a predicament, particularly when one of the following is true:
• The system in question is just not definable by traditional means.
• The system can be defined but the user doesn't really know what he wants.
• The user knows what he wants but can't articulate it.

To defend themselves—to produce a system specification that will satisfy the analysts despite the above conditions—users have developed strategies which by now are classic.

The Kitchen Sink. This strategy, employed by users who throw everything into their system definition, has as its outstanding characteristics exaggeration and a protective overstatement of needs. An overabundance of reports, exception processing, and politically motivated system features are also symptomatic. The Kitchen Sink also provides a marvelous cover-up for the user who doesn't know what he wants but who can bury

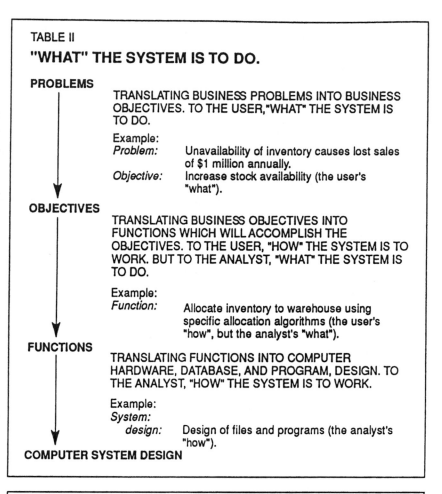

TABLE II

"WHAT" THE SYSTEM IS TO DO.

PROBLEMS

TRANSLATING BUSINESS PROBLEMS INTO BUSINESS OBJECTIVES. TO THE USER, "WHAT" THE SYSTEM IS TO DO.

Example:
Problem: Unavailability of inventory causes lost sales of $1 million annually.
Objective: Increase stock availability (the user's "what").

OBJECTIVES

TRANSLATING BUSINESS OBJECTIVES INTO FUNCTIONS WHICH WILL ACCOMPLISH THE OBJECTIVES. TO THE USER, "HOW" THE SYSTEM IS TO WORK. BUT TO THE ANALYST, "WHAT" THE SYSTEM IS TO DO.

Example:
Function: Allocate inventory to warehouse using specific allocation algorithms (the user's "how", but the analyst's "what").

FUNCTIONS

TRANSLATING FUNCTIONS INTO COMPUTER HARDWARE, DATABASE, AND PROGRAM, DESIGN. TO THE ANALYST, "HOW" THE SYSTEM IS TO WORK.

Example:
System:
design: Design of files and programs (the analyst's "how").

COMPUTER SYSTEM DESIGN

TABLE III

THE OBJECTIVE OF REQUIREMENTS DEFINITION

Objective: To define what the system will do.

ANALYSTS	USERS
Functional definition	Qualitative definition
Precise	Interpretation to be expected
Complete	All requests to be met
Frozen	Flexible definition
Definition produced within alloted time	Definition an ongoing process
Resulting system implemented within project schedule and budget	Favorable impact of system on departmental budgets
Good system	System will work

that fact in the sheer volume of his requests.

Smoking: Known also by its full name, "Smoke Gets in Your Eyes," this strategy is practiced by the user who sets up a smokescreen by requesting 10 system features, knowing that he really wants only one of them. The nine extra requests give him bargaining power. The Smoker is usually a rather experienced user who is consciously manipulating the definition process (as contrasted to the Kitchen Sink user, who is usually naive in believing that he really needs

everything he asks for). In both cases, the full set of system requirements submitted by the users must be reduced to one that is necessary, sufficient, manageable, and achievable Surprisingly, despite his premeditation, the Smoker is easier to work with because he has a realistic idea of what he really wants.

The Same Thing. Sometimes a euphemism for the embarrassing words, "I don't know," sometimes a sign of laziness, the Same Thing is manifest by the statement: "Just give me the same thing I'm getting

Users provide the system definition, but the systems people are responsible for it.

now." The statement may be qualified in many ways, such as, ". . . but more accurately," or ". . . more timely," or ". . . but computerize it." The user who employs the Same Thing is often quite satisfied he has told the analysts everything they need to know to proceed. The only thing the analysts really know, however, is that the user probably isn't aware of what his current system does, and that he doesn't want to take the time for an introspective review of his own functions and problems. Here, the systems group has little chance of succeeding because only the user can fully discover his own needs and problems.

Each time we witness one of these syndromes, we are reminded that despite our prodding and despite users' (usually) good intentions, they just don't seem to produce the kind of system specification we envision. It would be easy to play the blame game here and conclude that users are not capable of system definition, but it would be more productive to reexamine our goals for the definition process and to ask if our objective is possible to achieve.

A concept known as definability can help us answer that question.

CAN WE DEFINE IT?

Definability is the ability of a system to be defined; it is not a repeat of the "feasibility" question (can a computerized solution to this problem be developed at all?). Rather, it assesses the relative ease or difficulty of defining this system in this environment, and is assigned a loose value on a scale from "low" to "high." By assessing definability, you have an opportunity to establish more realistic goals for the definition process and to select definition techniques that are most appropriate to your situation.

Definability is affected by characteristics of the system itself. For example:

Type of system. Transaction processors and reporting systems—with very traditional accounting systems at one extreme —are functionally specific, finite, and quite tangible, and hence highly definable. At the other extreme, management support systems, decision support systems, simulators, and other systems that may be lumped together as "management information systems" are by nature less definable, because their purpose is to support a dynamic and changing management environment.

Size of system. Size is measured in several ways, including:
- number of functions performed
- number of departments affected
- number of individuals contributing to the definition
- number of subsystems
- number of system interfaces

<table>
<tr><td colspan="2">TABLE I</td></tr>
<tr><td colspan="2">THE USER - ANALYST RELATIONSHIP</td></tr>
<tr><td>HOW WE SEE USERS</td><td>HOW USERS SEE US</td></tr>
<tr><td>They. . .</td><td>We. . .</td></tr>
<tr><td>Don't really know what they want.</td><td>Don't understand "the business."</td></tr>
<tr><td>Can't articulate what they want.</td><td>Handle company politics awkwardly.</td></tr>
<tr><td>Have too many "needs" which are politically motivated.</td><td>Try to tell them how to do their jobs.</td></tr>
<tr><td>Want everything right now.</td><td>Can't translate a system definition into a successful system.</td></tr>
<tr><td>Can't prioritize needs.</td><td>Say no all the time.</td></tr>
<tr><td>Want "me first," not company first.</td><td>Place too much emphasis on technicalities.</td></tr>
<tr><td>Refuse responsibility for the system.</td><td>Are always over budget.</td></tr>
<tr><td>Are unable to provide a definition for a system that will work.</td><td>Are always late.</td></tr>
<tr><td>Are not committed to system development projects.</td><td>Ask users for time and effort even to the detriment of their primary duties.</td></tr>
<tr><td>Are unwilling to compromise.</td><td>Set unrealistic standards for requirements definition.</td></tr>
<tr><td>Can't remain on schedule.</td><td>Are unable to respond quickly to legitimately changing needs.</td></tr>
</table>

As size increases, definability decreases and the possibility for error and omission is greater. There is also a hesitancy to attack each element of a very large system with the thoroughness that is possible with smaller systems.

Complexity of system. Complexity decreases the definability of a system. It is determined by:
- number of variables
- degree of interdependence of the variables
- number of databases accessed and updated
- difficulty of logic
- degree of flexibility
- need for specialized knowledge (e.g., mathematical, statistical, forecasting)

Similarity to existing systems. Definability is enhanced when experience data for similar systems is available.

Environmental factors can also have an overriding influence on the definition process. These include:

1. *Users' understanding of their own needs.* Definability is positively affected by users who know what they want, or who at least can work with analysts to discover what they want.

2. *Consensus among users.* Definability is increased when each user department

makes an effort to gain a consensus opinion before going to the systems group with requests.

3. *Systems' understanding of user needs.* Analysts who know the business application favorably impact definability.

4. *Ability to communicate ideas.* Definability often suffers because users and analysts cannot communicate with each other. Development of system models, or use of a structured documentation format which uses an unambiguous language, can help.

5. *Accessibility to all affected users.* "Representative" user participation is usually mandatory because of the size of the user community affected by a new system. But definability is enhanced by direct user contact, so analysts should make an effort to talk to as many users as possible.

6. *Systems development experience.* Definability increases when analysts and users have experience in new systems development. Experienced participants have more realistic expectations as well as the knowledge and skills that contribute to successful definition.

7. *Personalities.* Good users improve definability. A good user is willing to make decisions, sticks by his decisions, cooper-

Definability is enhanced when experience data for similar systems is available.

ates, and thinks positively and aggressively.

8. *Availability of human resources*. Project staffing that places appropriate emphasis on front-end definition by including users and analysts with specification skills is important. More often, however, there are a disproportionate number of programmers on the project team.

9. *Project length*. The longer project minimizes definability because it gives the users more time to change their mind and the environment more time to change around the system.

10. *Schedule*. Definability decreases when inadequate time is allowed for the definition process.

11. *Budget*. Monies allocated to a project translate into available man hours; time for consulting, training, and software aids; and proportion of time assigned to front-end work.

12. *Corporate stress*. Corporate pressure, project visibility, reasonableness of expectations for system results, and the time and budget allowed for a system all influence definability. Unreasonable stress leads to fear, frustration, defeatism, and mistakes, but some degree of stress and attention, some feeling of high-level support and of accountability for results, can enhance the quality of the definition process.

CONTROL THE SYSTEM

Our goal should be to control the system before it controls us. Reduction of the system is accomplished by examining each proposed feature to determine whether it is valid and necessary.

1. Before definition begins, develop a precise scope document which clearly demarcates project boundaries. Obtain written acceptance of project scope from the users, then utilize the scope document to weed out requests that do not belong with this system.

2. Break the system into smaller pieces to be attacked separately. This may increase interface considerations, but it will also increase the possibility for understanding completely each part of the system.

3. Separate transaction-oriented portions of the system from management support sections so they can be considered as distinct entities.

4. Require users to justify each requested feature, in terms of either decisions, supported, benefits derived, or money saved.

5. Ask the users to assign a relative priority to each of their requests. This is helpful because it takes the pressure of saying no off the systems group and it provides a framework for partitioning the system into smaller pieces.

6. Find a similar system in another or-

ganization and learn as much as you can from their experiences.

7. Reduce the number of variables and of databases affected by the system.

8. Eliminate flexibility that users cannot realistically control. Determine whether flexibility is needed to support changing conditions of normal operations or if it is requested only to handle rare exceptions.

9. Reject a system feature if your equipment or your personnel do not possess the required technical capabilities for implementing it (the technical veto).

10. Reject a system feature if it will consume computer time, disk storage, printer time, or other machine resources out of proportion to its potential benefits (the operations veto).

11. Reject a system feature (or features, taken together) if they cannot be implemented with available manpower within imposed time constraints (the manpower veto)

In other words, if you recognize that the system is getting out of hand, speak up. Go formally on record with your recommendations for reduction. Submit amendments to the official project documents describing scope, feasibility, and cost justification, and require user approval of these changes. Because the system may be altered significantly by reduction, the corporate view of the system and the time and money allocated to it may also change, hopefully so that expectations are more realistic than in earlier project phases.

We also have an opportunity to control the external factors. Our goals in controlling the environment should be to surround ourselves with good users, to strengthen the base of knowledge upon which the users and the analysts are building, and to place realistic constraints on the project.

Users heavily influence the atmosphere of a project, so they should be chosen for the project team very carefully. Be sure that every area impacted by the system is represented. Balance the team so that users are equally represented, not only in numbers, but also in rank, authority, and seniority. Select users who can and will truly function as representatives. As representatives, a user must:

● provide regular status reports to his constituents

● give everyone a chance to contribute to the definition and to review formal definition documents

● present consensus opinions to the systems group

● favorably influence his constituents toward the project

● relate well to persons above and below him in his area

● have authority to commit his area in matters such as policy, budget, and interdepartmental procedures

● be accountable for his performance as a representative

Select users who have a thorough knowledge of their functional areas and of corporate policies, procedures, and organizational nuances which could affect definition. Look for users who enjoy being busy, are positively motivated to work on the project, and are organized, flexible, realistic, decisive, responsible, and able to express themselves.

TRAINING THE USERS

You undoubtedly are reading this list with a growing smile on your face because such users don't exist. We can strengthen the background knowledge of project participants by conducting a thorough existing system review with heavy user participation; providing books, seminars, or coursework in this particular business application; and providing formal training in the requirements definition technique which will be used in the project.

All these considerations—from getting good users assigned to the project to training them well—require time, money, and corporate commitment, which lead us to our final opportunity for controlling the environment. We must do two things for ourselves. First, we must take the time to make realistic project estimates for time, manpower, and money. Then, we must be honest when communicating these constraints to corporate management. In this way we can establish a realistic schedule which gives us time to do things right; work with a budget that is adequate for staffing the project and educating participants; gain some credibility with management by sticking to budget and schedule; reduce undue stress.

When confronted by an undefinable system, the users are faced with the impossible task of deciding what they want without knowing if what they want will work. They must perform some very difficult activities, such as reducing problem solutions to functional terms, visualizing system components and their interaction and effect on everyday operations, and discriminating between alternative approaches.

Unfortunately, the only sure way to determine if a system will work is to try it. Often users find themselves in the frustrating position of defining and building a system, only to realize that the system they really need will have to come next time.

Our goal should be to control the system before it controls us.

We must realize that in many cases the users need to try a system before they can define it. Prototyping addresses this problem. With prototyping, construction of a quick and dirty system begins after the bare minimum of a specification has been prepared. This quick and dirty system has one purpose, and that is to show the users what they are asking for, giving them some working knowledge of the results that can be achieved by the system they have defined. There is no attempt to create a good system from the technical or operational point of view, but rather to build a working, scaled model of the critical and most difficult portions of the system. After definition is complete, the prototype will be discarded and replaced by the operating version of the system.

Prototyping is relatively untried, so we don't have a great deal of experience data available. Examination of the concept reveals several potential benefits:
• The prototype system provides a concrete frame of reference for the users and analysts. Most important, the users can see how their definition has been interpreted by the systems group. The understanding of the analysts is evident by what they do rather than by what they say.
• The time lag between system definition and system demonstration is minimized. System demonstration and implementation are different, but they have traditionally occurred at the same time. This time lag has been very expensive to development projects, since changes are not discovered until considerable time and effort have already been invested in design and coding.
• Definitional changes can be incorporated into the model rather rapidly. encouraging active user participation and enthusiastic feedback.
• Prototyping is more attuned to the normal style and work habits of the users—usually managers—who sit on the project team. Emphasis is placed on active, hands-on evaluation of a working system rather than passive study and review of written documents.
• The technique provides at least some programmers—the ones working on the prototype—with closer user contact and longer project involvement, resulting in greater understanding of the permanent system.
• Experience data gained during prototyping can favorably influence the design of the permanent system.

There are, of course, potential drawbacks. Prototyping may be overkill for very simple systems and yet too involved for the whole of an extremely large system. Prototyping is unproven, quite different, and potentially expensive, so management support for the technique can be lacking. In addi-

tion, prototyping is not an academically pleasing technique. Distinctly bounded project phases are absent, and the prototype itself replaces the formal documentation which traditionally evolves during the definition stage. Finally, prototyping is so new that the high-level programming tools and the personnel skills required to perform prototyping are not generally available.

WELL-DEFINED APPROACH

Systems that promise to be difficult to define require an orderly, methodical approach to needs analysis and requirements definition. In these instances, functional definition will occur in a more traditional mode, as a bounded, front-end project phase, with development of an official written specification for the system.

In selecting a definition technique for these cases, we will want one which is repeatable (based on general concepts which can be applied to many situations), productive (efficient use of analyst and user time), and which, of course, produces a high-quality system definition.

We have several formal methodologies available. The characteristics which these techniques have in common are:
1. strict separation of functional specification (what the system is to do) from system design (how the system is to work)
2. development of a definition that is, however, easily translated into a physical system design
3. orderly decomposition of system requirements from the highest to the lowest level
4. representation of system requirements as a logical model expressed in graphic terms, using a minimum of textual explanation
5. active participation of the user groups, with emphasis on the user's role as a review agent
6. strict attention to system boundaries
7. separation of activities analysis from data analysis
8. documentation technique that is relatively easy to change and that records the evolution of the system definition
9. procedure for using the methodology is well defined and training materials are available

Traditional definition, despite its drawbacks, still has its place for one very simple reason: it is familiar, so users feel comfortable with it.

Characteristics of traditional definition are:

1. Textual description is the predominant definition tool, resulting in a specification document that is lengthy, ambiguous, and boring.
2. Top-down decomposition is not a requirement, and as a result, functions are described to inconsistent levels of detail.
3. Requirements are presented in list form rather than modeled; dynamic system flows and relationships are lost in the static, piece-by-piece specification.
4. Data analysis is deemphasized, if performed at all.

Traditional definition is also relatively inexpensive, if we consider its cost alone and not the costs incurred during design and coding to make up for inadequate specifications. Also, there is little or no learning curve involved with traditional definition in most organizations.

So, because it is comfortable, and perhaps not always by choice, it appears that we will be performing requirements definition using traditional techniques for some time to come. Rather than resigning ourselves to failure, we can borrow some of the important principles of prototyping and the well-defined methods to improve the results of definition activity. And rather than perpetuating the traditional methodologies without improvement, we can subtly begin to change common practice so that we accomplish a transition toward more structured techniques without unduly alienating the users or our managers.

We can begin by placing renewed emphasis on illustration of the functional specifications. Illustration may be in the form of charts or graphs, but should also include visitations to other companies with similar systems, walk-throughs of the proposed system with the users, and simulations of everyday procedures using newly defined functions and reports. And after coding begins, we can provide sample output to users as it becomes available, rather than waiting for official system implementation. Results of incremental testing can thus be used almost as a prototype, providing a concrete point of reference and eliciting comments from users much earlier than under normal circumstances.

We should also encourage use of a systematic approach to definition. We can use top-down decomposition to assure that all functions have been discovered and explored. We can also make a conscious effort to perform data analysis in addition to function analysis, thus providing at least external data needs to the design team.

The initiative for improving requirements definition must be ours, but it is an effort which is sure to be repaid with increased success. ✱

Unfortunately, the only sure way to determine if a system will work is to try it.

REQUIREMENTS ENGINEERING:
THE EMERGING WISDOM

JAWED SIDDIQI, *Sheffield Hallam University,* and M. CHANDRA SHEKARAN, *Microsoft*

Developments in requirements engineering, as in system development, have come in waves. The next wave of requirements techniques and tools will account for the problem and development context, accommodate incompleteness, and recognize the evolutionary nature of requirements engineering.

The field traditionally known as system analysis was first applied to information systems, and so had an organizational and application orientation. The field of requirements engineering seeks to incorporate an engineering orientation into systems analysis.

The most widely known, and perhaps the most significant, products of this engineering orientation are the various development methods and their associated automation support tools. Unfortunately, many of these prescriptive methods pay little or no attention to how context influences decomposition and evolution. Practitioners, who are used to focusing on context, find these methods to be inadequate. So the gap between practice and research is still very wide.

The conventional wisdom about requirements engineering is rapidly evolving, however, and the latest research is taking context into account.

Developments in requirements engineering are following trends in system development: In the first wave of system development, the focus was on writing code. Small and large system development alike were viewed as a single activity, not an organized process with several stages. The next wave saw the introduction of the development life cycle, of which requirements analysis was the first phase. Next came the adoption of evolutionary development models and the acknowledgment, at least from practitioners, that implementation may often proceed from incomplete requirements. The evolution of

Reprinted from *IEEE Software*, Vol. 13, No. 2, Mar. 1996, pp. 15–19.

requirements engineering has benefited from both the information-systems and software-engineering paradigms. Today a variety of approaches judiciously mix techniques borrowed from both strands. Definitive claims about the superiority of one paradigm over the other are not only premature but of little practical use. Such debates distract us from addressing important fundamental questions that include:

♦ What activities should be included in requirements engineering?

♦ What constitutes a requirement?

♦ What issues of practice need further attention?

REQUIREMENTS-ENGINEERING ACTIVITIES

Most software-engineering professionals believe that the requirements phase has its own life cycle. The phases of it have been given different labels. In the '80s Herb Krasner identified five phases: need identification and problem analysis; requirements determination; requirements specification;

requirements fulfillment; and requirements change management.[1] More recently, Matthias Jarke and Klaus Pohl proposed a three-phase cycle: elicitation, expression, and validation.[2]

However the phases may be sliced, it has long been realized that requirements evolve through a series of iterations. The Inquiry Cycle Model proposed by Colin Potts and colleagues takes this view.[3] It integrates three phases — documentation, discussion, and evolution — and has stakeholders use scenarios to identify and validate requirements. The validation is accomplished by stakeholders challenging proposed requirements with the intent of obtaining a clearer understanding of the justifications for the requirements' existence. On the basis of this validation, stakeholders can freeze or change a requirement in the final phase.

The software-engineering community had focused its efforts on the problem-analysis phase, which is what many decomposition methods address. In general terms, these methods are designed to help the analyst define the

range of all possible solutions. More specifically, according to Alan Davis, the problem-analysis phase encompasses learning about the problem, understanding the needs of the potential users, discovering who the user really is, and understanding all the constraints on the solution.[4] The outcome — the requirements-specification document — is assumed to be a complete description of the product's external behavior.

Lately, the software-engineering community has extended this decomposition paradigm to propose that systems can be built using a standard repertoire of components. Jarke and Pohl have suggested, for example, that one-shot requirements-engineering projects may be replaced by a "requirements-engineering practice," which puts together standard components in innovative fashions rather than continuing the practice of reinventing the components themselves.[2]

As we've said, the biggest drawback of the reductionist view of partitioning things into smaller parts is that context will influence the decomposition.

Indeed, for Jarke and Pohl the juxtaposition of vision and context is at the heart of managing requirements. They define requirements engineering as a process of establishing visions in context and proceed to define context in a broader view than is typical for an information-systems perspective. Jarke and Pohl partition context into three worlds: subject, usage, and system. The subject represents a part of the outside world in which the system — represented by some structured description — exists to serve some individual or organizational purpose or usage.

WHAT CONSTITUTES A REQUIREMENT?

The oldest and perhaps most widely shared piece of conventional wisdom is that requirements constitute a complete statement of what the system will do without referring to how it will do it. The resiliency of this view is indeed surprising since researchers have long argued against this simple distinction.[5]

Clearly, requirements and design are interdependent, as practitioners surely realize. Perhaps the continuing prevalence of the "what vs. how" distinction is due to the well-meaning desire on the part of requirements engineers to avoid overconstraining implementers. Other reasons for the persistence of this debate are explored elsewhere.[6]

Another common distinction is the separation of functional (or behavioral) and nonfunctional requirements. Again, practitioners have found that, for many applications, this distinction is not clear. Some requirements that may appear to be nonfunctional at first become, in due course, functional. In the past, most researchers have focused on functional requirements. The article by Barry Boehm and Hoh In in this issue reflects the more recent trend to direct attention to nonfunctional requirements issues. For some time now, the software community has realized the need to broaden its view of requirements to consider the context

within which the system will function. Alex Borgida, Sol Greenspan, and John Mylopoulos' work on the use of conceptual modeling as a basis for requirements engineering was a major signpost in directing researchers to this perspective.[7] The article by Hans Nissen and his colleagues in this issue reports on recent experiences in applying conceptual-modeling techniques.

More recently, Michael Jackson has advanced another way to look at context.[8] Jackson faults current software-development methods for focusing on the characteristics and structure of the solution rather than the problem. Software, according to Jackson, is the description of some desired machine,

The oldest, most widely held piece of conventional wisdom is that requirements are complete.

and its development involves the construction of that machine. Requirements are about purposes, and the purpose of a machine is found outside the machine itself, in the problem context. He has, therefore, argued for a shift towards a problem-oriented approach that seeks to distinguish different characteristics and structures in the application domain. Adopting this problem-oriented approach means that the requirements for a system can simply be viewed as relationships among phenomena in the domain and a specification is a restricted kind of requirement; it is restricted because it must be expressed in terms of domain phenomena that are shared with the machine to be constructed.

This characterization of requirements and specification is indeed very general. However, Jackson animates it into a method by devising a general

problem frame, analogous to those proposed by the mathematician, George Polya. In Polya's terms, software development is a three-part problem: the domain, the requirements, and the machine. Jackson argues that for any method to be powerful it must exploit the specific features of the problem and because problem features vary widely, we need a repertoire of methods each suitable for a certain class of problems. This view puts the knowledge of both the domain expert and the analyst at the heart of requirements engineering.

Joseph Goguen shares Jackson's broad view of requirements.[9] But, while Jackson's distinctive contribution is primarily concerned with how requirements are represented, Goguen's novel contribution centers on how requirements should be produced. Goguen argues that requirements are information, and all information is *situated* and it is the situations that determine the meaning of requirements. Taking context (or situations) into account means paying attention to both social and technical factors. Focusing on technical factors alone fails to uncover elements like tacit knowledge, which cannot be articulated. Therefore, an effective strategy for requirements engineering has to attempt to reconcile both the technical, context insensitive, and the social, contextually situated factors.

For Goguen, requirements are not things "out there" flying about like butterflies. Nor is the job of the analyst to find some suitable net to capture them. Requirements emerge from the social interactions between the system users and the analyst. This goes beyond taking multiple viewpoints of the different stakeholders and attempting to reconcile them because it does not attempt, *a priori*, to construct some abstract representation of the system. Current methods of eliciting tacit information, such as questionnaires, interviews, introspection, and focus groups are inadequate, as Goguen points out.

Instead, he advocates "ethnomethodology." In this approach, the analyst gathers information in naturally occurring situations where the participants are engaged in ordinary, everyday activities. Furthermore, the analyst does not impose so-called "objective," preconceived categories to explain what is occurring. Instead, the analyst uses the categories the participants themselves implicitly use to communicate.

Trends in the last decade have made the requirements-as-contract model irrelevant to most developers today.

REALITY CHECK

Descending from the lofty considerations of the fundamental nature of requirements, here we recommend some practical issues that require greater attention. A careful examination of these issues actually reveals a considerable level of compatibility with the perspective shifts urged by Jackson and Goguen.

Most requirements-engineering work to date has been driven by organizations concerned with the procurement of large, one-of-a kind systems. In this context, requirements engineering is often used as a contractual exercise in which the customer and the developer organizations work to reach agreement on a precise, unambiguous statement of what the developer would build.

Trends in the last decade — system downsizing, shorter product cycles, the increasing emphasis on building reusable components and software architectural families, and the use of off-the-shelf or outsourced software — have significantly reduced the percentage of systems that fit this profile. The requirements-as-contract model is irrelevant to

most software developers today.

Other issues are more important:

◆ *Supporting market-driven inventors.* The bulk of the software developed today is based on market-driven criteria. The requirements of market-driven software are typically not elicited from a customer but rather are created by observing problems in specific domains and inventing solutions. Here requirements engineering is often done after a basic solution has been outlined and involves product planning and market analysis. The paramount considerations are issues such as available market window, product sizing, feature sets, toolkit versus vertical application, and product fit with the development organization's overall product strategy. Classical requirements engineering offers very little support for these problems. Only recently have researchers begun to acknowledge their existence.[10]

◆ *Prioritizing requirements.* Competitive forces have reduced time to market, causing development organizations to speed development by deliberately limiting the scope of each release. This forces developers to distinguish between desirable and necessary (and indeed, between levels of needed) features of an envisioned system. Further, modifying certain noncritical requirements may enable an envisioned system to be realized using one or more off-the-shelf components. Yet there has been little progress to date on mechanisms for prioritizing requirements and making choices on which of those among a set of optional requirements will be satisfied by a given system release.

◆ *Coping with incompleteness.* One impetus for the switch in the '80s to the evolutionary development model was the recognition that it was virtually impossible to make all the correct requirements and implementation decisions the first time around. Yet most requirements research agendas continue to emphasize the importance of ensuring completeness (in the sense

of having no missing parts) in requirements specifications. However, incompleteness in requirements specifications is a simple reality for many practitioners. Some may even claim that completeness in real-world requirements specifications is a utopian state about as achievable as getting it right the first time! Goguen echoes this view in his criticism of current methods for their prescriptiveness and their insistence on the existence of a complete specification.[9] The real challenge is how to decide what kinds and levels of incompleteness the developer can live with. To this end we need techniques and tools to help determine appropriate stopping conditions in the pursuit of complete requirements specifications — enabling such clarification to be postponed to a later development stage (or a later "spiral" in the system's evolution).

◆ *Integrating design artifacts.* Developers need faster ways to conveniently express the problem to be solved and the known constraints on the solution. Often, getting to this fast outweighs the risk of overconstraining design. As Shekaran and others have observed elsewhere, requirements engineering becomes more of a design and integration exercise in this context.[11] We need "wide-spectrum" requirements techniques that can capture and manipulate design-level artifacts, such as off-the-shelf components. To date, there have been very few concrete results in providing support for the task of evaluating alternative strategies for satisfying requirements (a "design-like" task). However, the burgeoning interest and activity in requirements tracing may offer some solutions in the near future. In this issue, Pinheiro and Goguen offer an early look at tool support that can be provided for tracing requirements.

◆ *Making requirements methods and tools more accessible.* Today, many practitioners use general tools like word processors, hypertext links, and spreadsheets for many requirements engineering tasks. Given the wide variety of contexts in which requirements are determined and systems are built, researchers may be well-advised to focus on specific requirements subproblems (for example, tracking and managing software priorities) and consider building automation support in the form of add-ons to existing general-purpose tools. Less accessible to practitioners are methods that prescribe a major overhaul of an organization's requirements process and the use of large, monolithic tools.

W e believe the key mission for the requirements-engineering community is to continually narrow the ever-growing gap between research and practice. To that end, we close with some apt advice from the poet Stevie Smith, cited by Peter Checkland:[12]

It is very nice to have feet on the ground if you are a feet-on-the-ground person. I have nothing against feet-on-the-ground people. And its very nice to have feet off the ground if you are a feet-off-the-ground person. I have nothing against feet-off-the-ground people. They are all aspects of truth or motes in the coloured rays that come from coloured glass and stains the white rays of eternity. ◆

REFERENCES

1. H. Krasner, "Requirements Dynamics in Large Software Projects, A Perspective on New Directions in the Software Engineering Process," *Proc. IFIP*, Elsevier, New York, pp. 211-216.

2. M. Jarke and K. Pohl, "Requirements Engineering in 2001: (Virtually) Managing a Changing Reality," *Software Engineering*, Nov. 1994, pp. 257-266.

3. C. Potts, K. Takahashi, and A. Anton, "Inquiry-Based Requirements Analysis," *IEEE Software*, Mar. 1994, pp. 21-32.

4. A Davis, *Software Requirements, Analysis and Specification*, Prentice-Hall, Englewood Cliffs, N.J., 1990.

5. W. Swartout and R. Balzer, "On the Inevitable Intertwining of Specification and Design," *Comm ACM*, July 1982, pp. 438-440.

6. J. Siddiqi, "Challenging Universal Truths in Requirements Engineering," *IEEE Software*, Mar. 1994. pp. 18-19.

7. A. Borgida, S. Greenspan, and J. Mylopoulos, "Knowledge Representation as the Basis for Requirements Specifications," *Computer*, Apr. 1985, pp. 82-91.

8. M. Jackson, *Software Requirements and Specifications*, Addison-Wesley, Reading, Mass., 1995.

9. J. Goguen, "Formality and Informality in Requirements Engineering," *Proc. IEEE Int'l Conf. Requirements Eng.*, IEEE CS Press, Los Alamitos, Calif., 1996.

10. C. Potts, "Invented Requirements and Imagined Customers: Requirements Engineering for Off-the-Shelf Software," *Proc. Int'l Symp. Requirements Engineering*, IEEE Press, New York, 1995, pp. 128-130.

11. M.C. Shekaran and J.F. Tremlett, "Reasoning about Integration Issues During Requirements Definition: A Knowledge-Based Approach," *Proc. Int'l Conf. Systems Integration*, IEEE CS Press, Los Alamitos, Calif.. 1992, pp. 229-239.

12. P. Checkland, *Systems Thinking, Systems Practice*, John Wiley, Chichester, UK, 1990.

Chapter 2

System and Software System Engineering

1. Introduction to Chapter

System and software system engineering are the first steps in the development of any software-intensive system. *System engineering* is the application of scientific and engineering efforts to[1]:

1. Transform an operational need into a description of system performance parameters and a system configuration through the use of

an iterative process of definition, synthesis, analysis, design, test, and evaluation

2. Integrate related technical parameters and ensure compatibility of all related functional and program interfaces in a manner that optimizes the total system definition and design

3. Integrate reliability, maintainability, safety, survivability, human factors, and other such factors into the total engineering effort to meet cost, schedule, and technical performance objectives

Software system engineering is also a technical and management process. The technical process is the analytical effort necessary to transform an operational need into a software design of the proper size and configuration, and its documentation in requirements and design specifications. The management process involves assessing the risk and cost, integrating the engineering specialties and design groups, maintaining configuration control, and continuously auditing the effort to ensure that cost, schedule, and technical performance objectives are satisfied to meet the original operational need.[2]

The purpose of this chapter is to introduce the concept of system engineering and to present another view of the major system engineering tools: partitioning, allocation, flowdown, and traceability. It starts with an article on system engineering by Forsberg and Mooz and then takes a look at the interfacing document, called a "concept of operations document," between the customer and the developer. The chapter then discusses how a concept of operations (ConOps) document can bridge the gap between user needs and expectations and the technical software requirements specifications (SRS).

The tutorial concludes with an article titled "Software System Engineering: An Engineering Process" by Dr. Richard Thayer, co-editor of this tutorial, on how to apply system engineering principles to software.

2. Description of Articles

The first article, "System Engineering Overview," by Kevin Forsberg and Hal Mooz of the Center for Systems Management, was written especially for this revision and hence emphasizes the relationship between system engineering and software engineering. Forsberg and Mooz begin with examples of good and bad system engineering and then move to a discussion of the current environment for system engineering. A typical system engineering organization within a project is presented, along with the impact of the typical organization on the need for teamwork.

The authors next discuss the activities in the system development life cycle, using the "Vee chart" as the primary representation, and show how the common life-cycle models (such as the Waterfall, incremental development, and evolutionary development models) and a research and development project are represented.

Finally, the process of system engineering is discussed, with its major activities of project initiation, system analysis and design (the most intensive period of system engineering activity), and system integration and verification.

The second article, "The Concept of Operations: The Bridge from Operational Requirements to Technical Specifications," was written by Richard E. Fairley and Richard H. Thayer. This article presents the relatively new concept of developing a "needs" document that will bridge the gap between the customer and the more formal software requirements specifications. The article describes the role of the *concept of operations* (ConOps) document in the specification and development of a software-intensive system. It also describes the process of developing a ConOps, its uses and benefits, who should develop it, and when it should be developed. A detailed outline of the ConOps document is provided as an appendix to the article.

The last article, by Thayer, applies the concept of systems engineering to software and is entitled "Software System Engineering: An Engineering Process." This article also describes the application of system engineering principles, activities, tasks, and procedures to the development of a software system. This application, called *software system engineering*, is the overall integrating concept that encompasses the managerial and technical activity that controls the cost, schedule, and technical achievement of the developing software system. The article argues that "software engineering" should have been called "software system engineering" because the modern techniques, tools, and activities for what we call "software engineering" were derived from modern-day system engineering. This article recognizes the difference between software systems engineering and software engineering just as system engineering is recognized as being different from hardware engineering (all types).

This article partitions systems engineering (and eventually software system engineering) into five activities:

- *Problem definition (requirements analysis)*—Determines needs and constraints through analyzing the requirements and interfacing with the customer
- *Solution analysis (design)*—Determines a set of possible ways to satisfy the requirements; studies and analyzes the possible solutions; and selects the optimum one
- *Process planning*—Determines the cost of the product, the delivery schedule, and methods of controlling the project and product
- *Process control*—Establishes process, reviews progress and intermediate products, and takes corrective action when necessary
- *Product evaluation (verification, validation, and testing)*—Tests, demonstrates, and analyzes the final product and documentation

The article looks at the most important software system engineering tools and techniques. Each technique is examined and its application to software system engineering is discussed. Finally, the software development process is partitioned into five general phases and each phase is partitioned into a number of software system engineering processes. The activities and tasks associated with each process are described.

References

1. MIL-STD-499A, "Engineering Management" (USAF), U.S. Department of Defense, May 1, 1974.

2. Adapted from Sailor, J.D., "System Engineering Overview," in *System and Software Engineering Requirements,* Thayer, R.H., and M. Dorfman, eds., IEEE Computer Society Press, Los Alamitos, Calif., 1989.

System Engineering Overview[*]

Kevin Forsberg and Harold Mooz
© 1996 Center for Systems Management
19046 Pruneridge Avenue
Cupertino, CA 95014

Abstract

System engineering is both a thought process for approaching a design and a specific technical discipline. As such, the process exists at every level in the project hierarchy. Whether the system is a large "design-from-scratch" project, or a project to expand on existing capability, or a nondevelopment project based on existing designs, the concept of system engineering is equally applicable. The system architect, who is responsible for determining the overall technical approach to meet the customer's need, is the instigator and orchestrator of the techniques discussed herein.

Detailed system engineering tools appropriate to the software environment are presented in other articles in this book. In fact, many of the tools used in system engineering have their origin in software engineering (functional flow diagrams, data flow diagrams, documentation of the concept of operations, and so on.). Emphasis on object-oriented requirements development and design has made it even more clear in practice that the system engineering management approach for software and hardware is identical. However, the application of these tools must be understood in the framework of overall system evolution and the system engineering process. The purpose of this article is to provide that framework.

1. Introduction

1.1. Background

System engineering is a term widely used in industry. However, there is no universal understanding of system engineering as a discipline. We once asked the senior manager at a major computer manufacturing company in Silicon Valley (California) if he had system engineers on his staff. He responded, "Of course. If your system breaks down, we send a system engineer to your facility with a bag of parts to repair it."

Our objective in this article is to describe system engineering as a process within a project environment and to outline the techniques and associated tools of this vital function.

System engineering is as much a philosophy as it is an engineering discipline. System engineering is a way of thinking and doing. Poor system management is *the* major factor contributing to troubled projects. System engineering is a major technical management discipline within the system management environment with the focus of "doing the right things right." System engineering provides the technical heart of any project. A number of authors, notably Blanchard,[1] have

expressed this philosophy, either directly or indirectly, in their articles and text books. Our philosophy, as expressed in our book,[2] is that system engineering is an integral part of project management, and must first be understood from that perspective. Other authors, for instance Boardman,[3] have emphasized the mathematical approaches, such as queuing theory and linear programming, which are valuable tools in generating data that the system engineer may find useful—and in some cases, essential—as decision aids. However, without the context of the entire process, the results from detailed tools cannot be properly applied.

Effective system engineering requires good judgment even more than technical skills. Knowledgeable people have raved about the success of the Lockheed Skunk Works,[4] which in 1945 produced America's first operational jet fighter (the P-80), and in 1962 produced the world's fastest airplane (the SR-71, which held the world speed record for 30 years), with a project cycle time less than half of what others required. The reason for success is not that they were isolated from bureaucratic controls (although they were), or that they produced effective products with minimal documentation (which they did), or that they had supercomputers (which they did not). Rather their

---

success is based primarily on the fact that the leader of the Skunk Works, Kelly Johnson, was a perceptive and intuitive system engineer.

The system engineer must have a broad perspective: understanding all stakeholders, evaluating and orchestrating multidisciplines, and developing the context within which the project solution will ultimately be expected to operate. This implies that there needs to be a systematic exploration of the user's or stakeholders' needs, the context of implementation, and evaluation of areas of high risk and opportunity early in the project study phase. The more system engineering is applied early in a project, the more likely it is that the project will evolve in a controlled and efficient fashion.

Examples of proficient system engineering often go unreported. The Olympic games, and all that goes to support them, provide highly visible examples of success (and failure) in the commercial environment. The metrics are smooth operations, satisfied participants and attendees, and positive financial return to the sponsoring community. The Lillehammer, Norway winter Olympics in 1994 were very successful, as were the 1984 Los Angeles, California summer Olympics. Both ran smoothly and returned substantial profit to the cities involved. In contrast, at the Atlanta, Georgia

Olympics (1996), IBM suffered a number of high-profile glitches on their $40 million Olympic information integration effort, with the result that the 12 news wire services that had contracted with the Atlanta Olympics committee had trouble obtaining complete, accurate competition results, and some problems were still unresolved even after the closing ceremonies. As Caldwell reported,[5] "IBM carried off a nearly flawless performance on most technical fronts. But, as Luis Estrada (the IBM program manager) concedes, the process broke down *because user requirements were not understood* [italics added]." Good system engineering—even though it was not called by that name—made the difference between meeting goals or not.

Commercial companies seldom measure both the costs and benefits of a meaningful study period before initiating project development, so comparative data are difficult to obtain for projects started with and without good system engineering. NASA, however, has collected and shared information with the public about their projects. Figure 1, based on NASA data, illustrates the benefit of a study phase as measured by the overrun incurred during system development. This chart shows that a thorough study can often prevent the time lost and the funds wasted on requirements-driven rework.

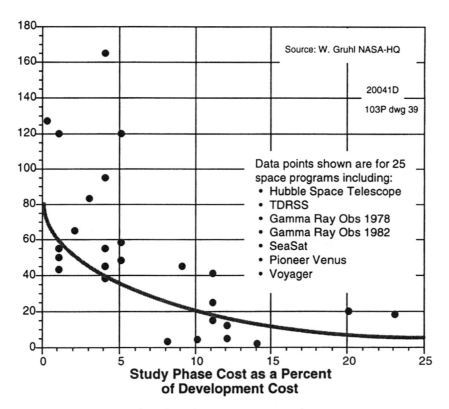

Figure 1. Benefits of management commitment.

If there is little or no study done before initiating project development, project overruns can increase by factors of two or more. An example is provided by the GOES (Geostationary Operational Environment Satellite) satellite project initiated in 1985. This project was critical to replacing weather satellites then in use, which were expected to become inoperative by the end of the 1980s. The satellites provided critical data for commercial weather stations throughout the United States. At the time of project initiation the plan was for first launch in 4 years (1989) and a total budget of $500 million. Since the GOES satellite was a replacement for existing weather satellites, the project manager and customer decided that the study period could be skipped to save time, even though they should have known better. The first satellite was 5 years late and the costs soared to over three times the original estimate. More than that, the specifications established are so stringent that the last satellite in the series will still require a deviation to the specification in year 2005. The huge cost overrun and substantial schedule impact were not expected by the project team. The critical decision to skip the study period was made without understanding the resulting system risk, and, as noted in the article, "Blundersat,"[6] the project was almost canceled by an angry Congress.

Other major projects have suffered similar fates. The Treasury Department announced in 1996 that its decade-long, multibillion-dollar effort to modernize the Internal Revenue Service's computers is "badly off the track" and must be rethought from top to bottom. Congressional subcommittee chairman Jim Lightfoot criticized the IRS performance. The IRS's fundamental problem is not technology, but "a lack of effective management," said Lightfoot. "This is not rocket science." Effective system engineering is clearly missing. In the future, said the deputy director of Treasury, each step in the project will have a clear "system architecture document."

The need for effective system engineering is not limited to large commercial or government projects. The authors were personally associated with a small ($160,000) project to put an existing relational data management system, written in Ada, onto a customer-specified computer system, and perform searches of a three million-entry database within a "reasonable" amount of time. Since Ada code is almost entirely machine independent, this project was viewed as low risk, and we violated our own principles by not insisting on a thorough system engineering evaluation (a study period) before signing the contract. We relearned several painful lessons. First, "almost" is a deadly word. Second, even though the computer manufacturer had an Ada compiler on a similar model, "similar" is also a deadly word. Third, "reasonable time" is untestable,

and was ultimately a fatal flaw. We did not get paid for our year-long effort.

The system engineering challenge is to ensure development of the optimum solution that meets all technical requirements and provides the proper balance of system performance, life cycle costs, and development schedule. In addition, the system engineer must balance considerations of project risk and product quality with the other three drivers. To accomplish this, system engineering must be an interdisciplinary approach that evolves and verifies a set of system product and process solutions that are integrated, balanced, and satisfy customer needs. System engineering encompasses all of the efforts related to the development process, including science, engineering, integration, producibility, and affordability. System engineering includes the end-to-end process and must consider *in the initial development* the requirements of operations and maintenance, including the user training, required equipment and documentation, procedures, data, product phase-out, and, if appropriate, disposal.

In the mid-1980s the Software Engineering Institute (SEI) developed their Capability Maturity Model (CMM), which has become an industry standard for assessing the maturity and appropriate use of *software* development processes within a corporation. This has been valuable for focusing management attention on the need for a managed software development process. No such counterpart to the CMM exists for system engineering (although several initiatives at the SEI and the International Council Of System Engineering [INCOSE] are underway, and several beta versions are in use). Yet, just as for successful software development, successful implementation of system engineering depends on a managed process. The system engineer must be the advocate to ensure that this process is followed and is effective.

The system engineer is the leader of the concurrent engineering team. System engineering responsibility begins with identification of user requirements and includes in-process validation that user needs are being addressed as the project evolves. That responsibility includes ultimate validation that stakeholder needs have been satisfied in the operations and maintenance phase, and ends at the point of system retirement (decommissioning or disposal). The system engineer must be the advocate for the optimum system life cycle cost, even though in many projects the project initiation is driven by minimum acquisition cost or lowest initial production cost, with little regard for the total environment. A pilot friend of ours once said that "the three most useless things in the world are: runway behind you, altitude above you, and money in the out-years." It is hard to sell a project approach that increases initial acquisition costs in order to save money in operations a decade later. This is part of the system engineer's challenge.

The system engineer has responsibilities that include:

- Technical interface with the customer
- Requirements definition, management, analysis, and flowdown
- Verification planning and audit
- Validation planning and audit
- Interface management
- Risk and opportunity analysis and management
- Change management and configuration control

1.2. System Engineering, Software System Engineering, Mechanical System Engineering...

As a thought process and a disciplined approach to problem solving, the concept of system engineering and the tools described herein are applied at all levels of a project from the highest level system down to the lowest level components. In some project organizations, there is a function formally called system engineering. Within an integrated product team supporting one segment or portion of the project, there may be a similar system engineering function but it is often called by the discipline name, such as software system engineering or electromechanical system engineering. At lower levels where there are multiple designs being evolved for different components, there may be a design integration function that is system engineering at a lower level of decomposition. In each instance the philosophy of approach and process should be the same, although the definition of "the system" changes with project decomposition. For the context of this tutorial, software system engineering is a subset of overall project system engineering. If the sole purpose of the project is to produce a software product, then system engineering and software system engineering are synonymous. The methods and tools discussed apply in either case.

1.3. Current Environment

After consulting with more than 100 commercial as well as government-focused corporations during the past 15 years, it is clear to us that system engineering is not well understood, and often is not recognized as a necessary discipline. Even in organizations dealing with customers who demand sophisticated system engineering support, the approach is varied and inconsistent.

Compounding this problem is downsizing within major corporations, which has resulted in retirement or release of experienced project managers and system engineers. Technically competent but inexperienced engineers are being assigned to manage projects and to conduct system engineering. The loss of the knowledge base with the departing experienced personnel has resulted in a situation where there is little retention of lessons learned.

This has led to a number of significant issues:

1. *User requirements are often not well identified and documented.* The user requirements are unclear, and in fact confusion exists in who the users are. In a commercial environment, the marketing organization is often the "surrogate" user, attempting to distill user requirements from a variety of different potential buyers. The development team is often working at cross purposes with marketing, because they feel that as developers they "know the product better and can provide what the user 'really needs.'" Often all stakeholders are not considered in developing user requirements. This problem is not limited to large projects, as Norman effectively illustrates in his book, *The Design of Everyday Things.*[7]

2. *Insufficient system studies and analyses are performed during the study period.* This results in a lack of understanding of how to sequence the project throughout the project cycle phases and how to establish a development strategy (grand design, incremental development, evolutionary development, technology introduction). There is inadequate project review and approval to ensure selection of an optimum system concept. The tendency is to rush to a point design, and there is insufficient involvement of the developer in the operational requirements and system concept studies.

3. *The development team is directed to respond to incomplete project specifications containing TBDs (to be determined) that the buyer will not commit to resolving by a specified date.* This causes inaccurate costing and scheduling for the project. When the user or customer resolves the TBDs, there is usually a project cost and schedule adjustment required. The system engineer is responsible for ensuring timely TBD resolution.

4. *The system concept and operational environment are not well understood.* Past opera-

tional experience is often not adequately considered in the studies defining the project. The flowdown of user operational requirements to the development system specifications is imprecise. The initial system development does not consider incremental development or upgrade strategy as a deliberate part of the process. System obsolescence as a result of rapidly changing technology is not adequately addressed. In particular, defining those parts of the system that require easy change-out to accommodate new technology is sometimes ineffectively addressed.

5. *The problem context of implementation is not adequately defined.* The user is "too busy" to work with the development team to create a User Concept of Operations document. The developers do not understand the user's environment. Only a subset of users is identified, and a deficient project solution is created. For instance, the developers create a software system in a nonstandard language, and the user has no trained people to maintain the system.

6. *The schedule and budget estimates for the project evolution are not realistic.* The buyer underestimates the time to do the project. The unrealistic schedule results in budget underestimates. This results in a project destined for schedule slips and cost overruns from the outset. The project may be driven by artificial schedule constraints such as the need to make a new product announcement at an annual convention. The artificial constraints force unreasonable development shortcuts to support these commitments. The eagerness to see a project initiated causes the project team to commit to an unaltered set of requirements even if the budget has been cut.

7. *There is often insufficient preparation for system operation.* System life cycle provisioning is not considered or is poorly implemented during the project evolution. Operations and maintenance procedures are not considered during the study period and are ignored during the development period, resulting in the fielding of a defective solution and inadequate training of system operators. In one major project all deliverable software documentation was eliminated to save development cost, even though the customer was expected to maintain for decades the 1.5 million line-of-code system consisting of six different computer languages.

8. *Rapidly changing technology creates pressure to shorten the project cycle time.* This results in some cases in inappropriate shortcuts of the system engineering and project management process. It may also result in premature commitment to unproved technology.

9. *The pressure to shorten project cycle times creates pressure to accept point designs.* This creates pressure to minimize or eliminate risk and opportunity management studies during the study period. Often past experience on cost and schedule is not rationally applied to future work. To meet an aggressive release date, one major microchip manufacturer chose to reduce the planned schedule for product development, first by making early selection of a point design, and second by deleting all rework from the project plan, even though experience had shown that two and sometimes three iterations during certain phases of the activity had always been required. The company was embarrassed when they missed announced release dates that had been committed to by aggressive and optimistic management.

Proper implementation of the system engineering process—and the commitment by executive management, project management, and the project team to follow the process—will avoid the negative consequences of the above issues.

1.4. Common Vocabulary

Effective system engineering on a project will help to establish a common vocabulary, a common discipline, and a common philosophy of approach. In order to achieve the common discipline and philosophy of approach, all members of the team need to have a common understanding of the terms used on the project. For instance the term *prototype* has a very clear definition in Webster's dictionary and a very precise meaning in a hardware project environment, where prototype is a "fully compliant, fully operational" version against which all future systems will be replicated. In a software environment the word *prototype* has a less precise meaning and can apply to a user requirements feasibility model or an algorithm demonstration model, but rarely, if ever, refers to a fully compliant software system that is then to be replicated. Other terms, such as the definition of levels in a system hierarchy, are also significantly different in hardware and software environments, and yet both are part of the same project. The establishment of a common vocabulary is essential to communication, and the lack of a solid vocabulary leads to confusion and miscommunication. Part of the system engineering role is to ensure that this common understanding is created and to promulgate it throughout the project team.

1.5. Summary

System engineering is the discipline that forces high value decisions early to bound and reduce risk and enhance opportunities on the project. System engineering is also the discipline responsible for ensuring an orderly process is followed throughout the project cycle. System engineering is the technical conscience of the project.

2. System Engineering: A Team Responsibility

2.1. Teamwork

System engineering encompasses many disciplines and requires a broad perspective. While the system engineer can orchestrate the process, he or she usually does not have the breadth of knowledge in all required disciplines to implement them without specialty team involvement. Consequently teamwork is essential in managing the technical development process. There are four key aspects of teamwork, as discussed by Chiroini and Forsberg.[8] A team is a group of two or more people working together with:

- A common goal
- Acknowledged interdependency
  - Competency
  - Respect
  - Trust
- Acceptance of a common code of conduct
- A shared reward

From the perspective of system engineering, all four of the above are important, but the system engineering process will develop the acknowledged interdependency and help focus the team on the common goal. The team members consist of the project manager, the system engineer and staff, designers, integrators, testers, trainers, operators, customers, users, quality assurance, configuration management, logistics, and other system effectiveness organizations. It is not the responsibility of the system engineer to be expert in all of these areas. It *is* the responsibility of the system engineer to know when and how to involve the appropriate disciplines.

2.2. Concurrent Engineering

Concurrent engineering integrates the design of a product and its development, manufacturing, coding, and other support processes starting in the study period and continuing throughout the development project, considering all elements of the product life cycle from conception through disposal. Its goal is to encourage involvement of all appropriate stakeholders and the use of lessons learned to influence the problem solution. Concurrent engineering is a concept that has been practiced and articulated for several decades, but has come into vogue once again as a solution to certain current difficulties in projects.

One effective implementation of the concurrent engineering concept is the use of integrated product teams (IPTs), where each responsible team is focused on the development of a single component within the overall system. Issues such as reliability, maintainability, supportability, producibility, inspectability, and human factors are all considered early in the development process to thereby produce a more effective high-quality design. It creates an environment to improve the efficiency and results of talented people working interactively.

The system engineer is responsible for establishing the requirements for each of the integrated product teams and for managing the interfaces between the teams. One of the reasons that projects relying on integrated product teams sometimes fail is that the system engineering role in providing interface requirements and integration between teams has not been acknowledged and accepted by the IPT members and their management. This is, in fact, the primary weakness of the IPT approach in practice. Again, the requirements development process must be consistent with concurrent engineering. System engineering itself should be conducted in a concurrent engineering environment.

2.3. Typical System Engineering Organization

The system engineer on a small project is usually the project manager. On a larger project, the system engineer is one of the key technical personnel on the project, working as a partner with the chief project engineer (who is responsible for the evolution of the design) and the chief system architect, a common position in software development projects. Figure 2 shows a typical system engineering organization on a project with fifty people and highlights the areas that need to be addressed by the system engineer or system engineering team on an effort of any size. Figure 3 illustrates the relationship of system engineering to other organizations. System engineering is focused on the development of project requirements and the flow-

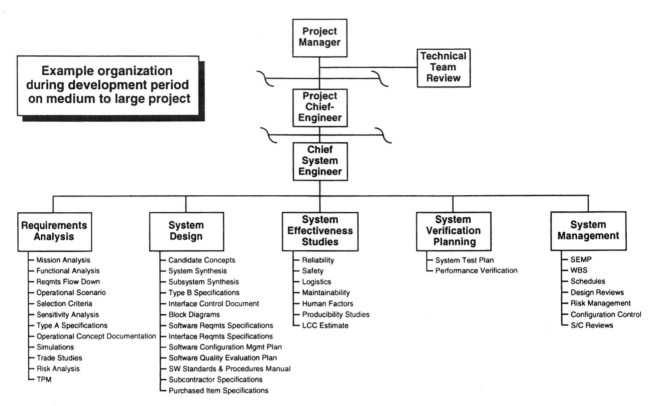

Figure 2. Typical project system engineering organization during the development period.

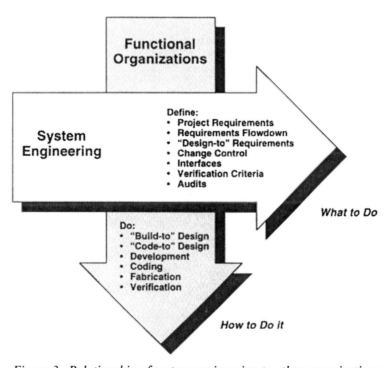

Figure 3. Relationship of system engineering to other organizations.

down of these requirements to the "design-to" documentation. The system engineer defines what is to be done. The functional organizations or integrated product teams determine how to do it. The project manager negotiates when work must be done, who will do it, and how much it will cost. Figure 4 emphasizes the importance of the system engineer in orchestrating the evolution of the project, starting from initial concept through delivery of the functioning system and its performance in the operational environment. The vision of the system engineer as the orchestrator of the activities is important because he or she must draw on many skills to perform the detailed work required.

In a research environment the project manager or principal research investigator may self-generate requirements for the project.[9] In the more usual case the project requirements are defined by external means and the project team is formulated to produce a product that satisfies those needs. The most effective organization is one in which the project office consists of a "quadrad": the project manager, the chief systems engineer, project business manager, and the project engineer (Figure 5). The chief system engineer is responsible for managing the requirements (what is to be

done). The project engineer or software chief architect is responsible for orchestrating the evolution of the implementation (how to do it). The integrated product teams should be end item oriented so that every major component of the system has a responsible individual team leader.

The integrated product (or process) team concept is a very effective way of organizing. Each integrated product team has a project engineer as the leader, and the team consists of all necessary disciplines to get the job done (hardware, software, manufacturing, reliability, and so on). The one deficiency in this structure is that functional disciplines, such as software engineering, are dispersed across a number of product teams. There needs to be a mechanism to ensure consistency of process, such as the software development methodology, across all teams. This is addressed at the project manager's level by having a representative of the software design organization assigned (part- or full-time, as required) to the project manager's staff, as shown in the dashed box in Figure 5. This person, who may also have a dual role as a member or leader of an IPT, oversees all software activities on all IPTs, with a focus on process. The system engineer must work with the process-oriented experts from each of the technical

Figure 4. The chief system engineer (whose job is sometimes performed by the deputy project manager for engineering)

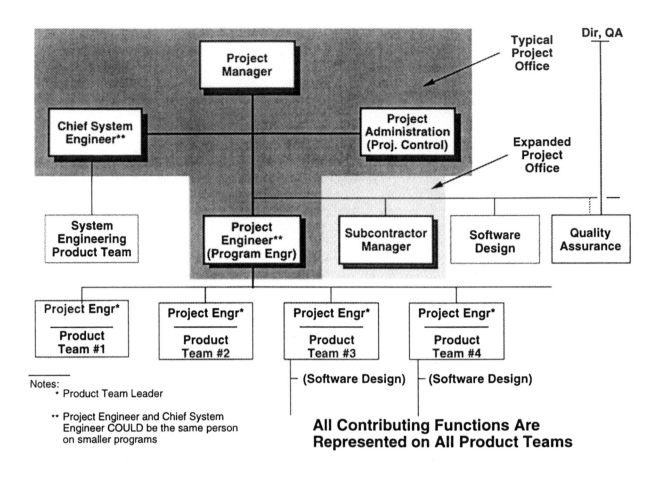

Figure 5. Typical industry project team organization.

disciplines to ensure that requirements are being met and that the appropriate engineering processes are followed, particularly in instances where process control is essential to ensure a quality product.

In a project using integrated product teams, the system engineer performs the critical task of managing the interfaces between all the IPTs on the project, and ensuring that the various IPT products integrate into a validated functioning system solution. The project manager must vest the necessary authority in the system engineer to make this happen, and the IPT leaders must agree to cooperate with the system engineer.

Another vital role of the system engineer is to assist the project manager and marketing in keeping the project sold. Especially in a commercial environment, marketing is the connecting link between customer or user and system engineering. System engineering is the essential role that ensures that the marketing organization does not oversell capabilities and commit to something that cannot be achieved. System engineering and marketing must maintain a proper balance. Marketing must strive to avoid overcommitting; system engineering must strive to be responsive to cus-

tomer needs rather than reacting negatively to changing system requirements and constraints.

3. System Development Life Cycle

3.1. The Project Cycle

Every project has a cycle, which consists of technical, business, and budget aspects. The system engineer is responsible for managing the technical aspects of the project cycle.[10] There are many different ways of describing the details of the project cycle but they all have common characteristics, as shown in Figure 6. The government project cycles have a formal study period, as illustrated by pre-Phase A through Phase B in the NASA environment or the User Requirements Definition Phase through a Source Selection Phase in a typical nonmilitary government agency. In a commercial environment the study period starts with a Product Requirements Definition Phase and concludes with a Product Proposal Phase.

Regardless of the details of the cycle, the system engineer is responsible for managing the complete life

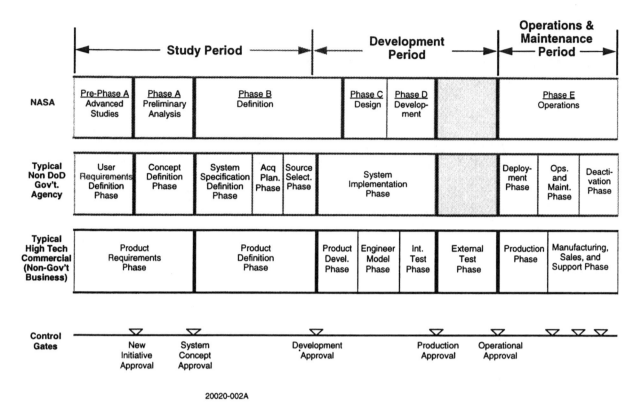

	Study Period					Development Period			Operations & Maintenance Period		
NASA	Pre-Phase A Advanced Studies	Phase A Preliminary Analysis	Phase B Definition			Phase C Design	Phase D Development		Phase E Operations		
Typical Non DoD Gov't. Agency	User Requirements Definition Phase	Concept Definition Phase	System Specification Definition Phase	Acq Plan. Phase	Source Select. Phase	System Implementation Phase			Deployment Phase	Ops. and Maint. Phase	Deactivation Phase
Typical High Tech Commercial (Non-Gov't Business)	Product Requirements Phase		Product Definition Phase			Product Devel. Phase	Engineer Model Phase	Int. Test Phase	External Test Phase	Production Phase	Manufacturing, Sales, and Support Phase
Control Gates	New Initiative Approval	System Concept Approval		Development Approval			Production Approval	Operational Approval			

20020-002A

Figure 6. Commercial and government project cycles.

cycle, starting in the earliest phase, with focus on requirements definition, system concept, architecture, and decomposition. In the midportion of the project life cycle system engineering focuses on interface management, design audit, and requirements management. During the concluding phases of the development cycle, system engineering focuses on integration, requirements verification and validation, operations support, and deactivation planning. It is important to recognize that planning for operational and deactivation issues starts early in the study period, since the system must be designed with operational needs and deactivation considerations as requirements.

3.2. Technical Aspects of the Project Cycle ("Vee" Chart)

3.2.1. Decomposition and Definition. Envision a project cycle that contains all of the project activities, products resulting from those activities, and control gates at which the maturity and completeness of those products are reviewed and accepted (see Reference 2, pp. 75–77). Further envision that this project cycle contains only the technical portion of the total project cycle; it is pinned to the wall on the left side at the

initial statement of user requirements, and is also pinned to the wall on the right side where the product satisfying the user requirements is ready for delivery. If we now envision that this cycle chart is made of an elastic material, we can pull downward on the cycle chart in the middle, where the fabrication and coding occur. The project cycle becomes a Vee representing increasing levels of decomposition (Figure 7).

In this Vee, the left leg represents the decomposition and definition of the project. The decomposition is the hierarchical functional and physical partitioning of any system into hardware assemblies, software components, and operator activities that can then be scheduled, budgeted, and assigned to a responsible manager. If the system contains only commercial off-the-shelf (COTS) products or reusable software components, from an object-oriented library, for instance, there may be only a few levels in the hierarchy, with many parallel elements at a given level. In such a case the focus is not on creating a new design, but rather on integrating the system elements to achieve the overall system performance. Interface software may be created through icon-driven screen builders. However, experience has proven that the principles of system and software engineering still must be followed, and the following discussion still applies.

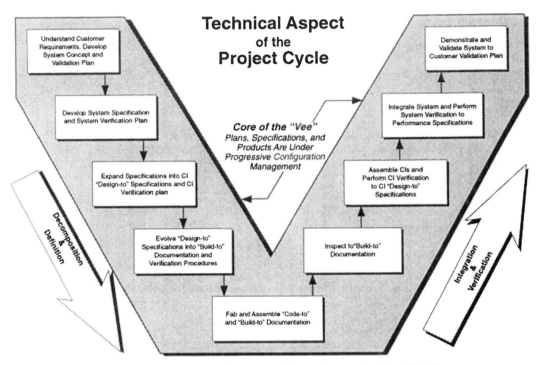

Technical Aspect of the Project Cycle

Figure 7. The technical aspect of the project cycle (the "Vee").

The definition process during decomposition creates documented "design-to specifications," "build-to," and "code-to" documentation that defines the functional and physical content of the entity and the associated interfaces.

The right leg of the Vee represents the integration and verification of the system, starting at the lowest level and building to the completed solution. Integration is the successive combining and testing of system hardware assemblies, software components, and operator tasks to progressively demonstrate the performance and compatibility of subelements, elements, and segments of the system. Verification is the timely, methodical process of determining that the system, during its evolution and ultimately as developed, meets all specified requirements. Verification assures that the system is being built right. Validation, which is also part of this process, assures that the right system is being built, that is, it meets user needs.

3.2.2. Core of the Vee. Figure 7 shows a depiction of the core of the Vee for a five-level hierarchy. The Vee chart is very similar to the waterfall depiction first documented by Royce in 1970.[11] The waterfall representation has been widely used for many years, and is still current (see Blanchard,[1] p. 123). The waterfall is often identified (incorrectly) as a software-only life cycle; it applies equally well to any system.

In the Vee representation the left leg follows the same pattern as in the waterfall. When the lowest level of detail in fabrication or coding is reached, the water-

fall methodology depicts a continually descending set of blocks through integration and verification. In the Vee, however, the blocks ascend to the right to represent increasingly complete portions of the overall system, with the last block being the validated system ready for operations in the user environment.

There are many variants of the Vee model that allow for incremental and evolutionary development. These are discussed in subsequent sections. It is important, however, to understand the concept for a simple example that is sometimes called the grand design, in which requirements are defined at the outset and then addressed in a sequential fashion.

3.2.3. Detailed Vee Chart. The critical aspects of decomposition and definition are illustrated in Figure 8. A fundamental concept in the Vee chart is that time and baseline maturity move from left to right. As baseline decisions are made, increasing portions of the Vee are included in the approved baseline. This starts with the user requirements statement, which is placed under configuration management and formal change control once agreement has been reached with the user.

In any project, baseline decisions can and should be challenged. The consequences of changes to baseline decisions can have profound impact on project performance, however. This is dramatically illustrated in the failure of Apollo 13, and reaffirms the adage, "no change is a small change." The liquid oxygen tank that exploded in flight had been originally designed for 28 volts (for the internal heating elements), since the spacecraft had a 28-volt on-board electrical system. About 1 year after the design work began, the customer changed the requirement to 65 volts for the tank systems, since the ground test equipment could produce that voltage in preflight checkout. The design team caught almost all of the affected elements in the tanks, and made the appropriate changes. The "almost" missed one thermocouple, which, through a number of minor ground handling problems, overheated and subsequently caused the flight failure (see Lovell and Kluger,[12] pp. 370–380). The waterfall model depicts the challenging of baseline decisions as upward-diagonal arrows.[11] This implies an easy revisiting of all decisions, even the earliest user requirements. In the Vee model these upward iterations are also shown, but they are vertical (Figure 8), since one cannot go back in time. This depiction has been effective in communicating to the project team, executive management, and the customer the potential consequences of late iterations of baseline agreements.

As one moves down the left leg of the Vee, details are developed to define the next lower level in the system hierarchy and this is shown in Figure 8 as "the baseline being considered." The off-core studies are the iterative evaluations of alternative approaches to find an optimum solution for the baseline at the next level of decomposition; of equal importance is the emphasis on the risk and opportunity identification at each step (see Forsberg and Mooz[13,14]). The off-core

studies have as their focus the early identification of risk issues to ensure that an antigravity machine is not being requested. There are examples of major systems that were undertaken because the higher level requirements looked entirely plausible, but when the details were developed, they were found to be impossible to meet. As noted earlier, such a system was the GOES satellite in which the specification established in 1985 was so stringent that it still will not be met in the year 2005, when the last satellite in the series is to be launched.

The off-core studies should focus on critical issues as illustrated in Figure 9. These studies start at the very beginning of the project. In the earliest phase the purpose is to bound the user requirements to ensure that an achievable project is being defined. The studies may involve top-level analytical efforts or may drive to the lowest level of the hierarchy, creating software functional requirements prototypes or hardware mockups or perhaps even software and hardware detailed operational components to prove that specific requirements can be achieved within time or performance constraints. Note the use of the of the phrase *software functional requirements prototyping* to provide a more definitive meaning of the purpose of a software prototype at this stage of the project. These off-core studies are under engineering direction, as opposed to project control, and their results influence, but are not necessarily part of, the system baseline.

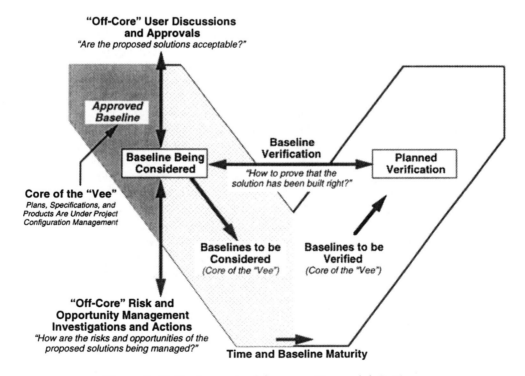

Figure 8. Critical aspects of decomposition and definition.

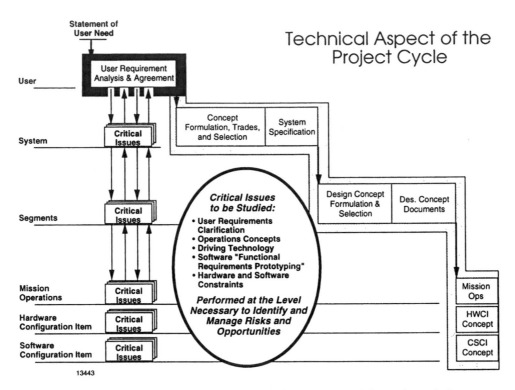

Figure 9. Critical issues to be studied at the start of the study period.

An equally important consideration is the identification of opportunities in the off-core studies, wherein minor changes to the system might yield a cheaper or more effective system, or might allow for a more comprehensive system to be developed for minimal cost impact. As the risk and opportunities evolve, and as the concepts for the system mature, there must be upward iteration with the user to ensure that the user requirements have been appropriately addressed, and that the user is supportive of the evolving solution. Also, the system engineer should periodically ask the user, "Is meeting this user requirement really worth the cost to you?" This is part of the validation process to ensure that the system will not only meet specification but will be considered high value by the user. Another aspect of the upward iteration is that the user must be made aware of the system expectations so there are no unpleasant surprises on completion of the delivered system.

As the requirements are defined for the baseline being considered, the planned verification must be simultaneously considered (Figure 8). This has the benefit of ensuring that requirements are verifiable and that valid needs, such as "user friendly" or "rapid response," are put in quantifiable terms.

Figure 10 illustrates the iterative process at a later stage of development where the user requirements, the system concept, and system specification have been appropriately studied. The project baseline has been approved to the point shown in the cross-hatched area. The development of the design concepts for each of the segments, the next level in the hierarchy shown in Figure 10, has both upward iteration with the system specification or user requirement updates and downward iteration to identify risks and opportunities. Iterations focus on the critical issues shown in Figure 10, now including issues such as affordability assessment, environmental impact, and system failure modes analyses. These early studies are critical because they surface design approaches that, when implemented, may yield a defective system if hazards have not been thought through completely. An example is the radiation couch produced by a Canadian firm in the late 1980s. Patients receiving radiation therapy for cancer were strapped to the couch and treated with either high-energy, short-duration beams or with low-energy, long-duration beams. The treatment dose is set manually, and the machine is then controlled by software. The software design did not consider the hazard of an operator choosing the high-energy beam and a long duration time cycle. Consequently there was no provision for emergency shut-down. Seven people died a few months after treatment as a direct result of this defect.

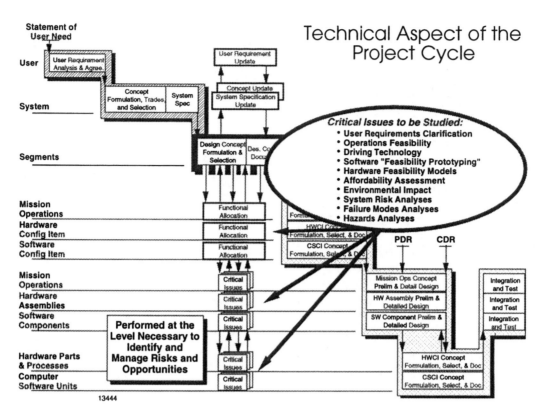

Figure 10. Critical issues to be studied at the start of the development period.

Many people resist the idea of a defined project cycle with an evolving baseline, claiming it constrains creativity. On the contrary, it should enhance creativity. Figure 11 emphasizes that there are upward arrows to indicate iteration with the maturing baseline, but there are no horizontal arrows from one phase to the next because it is only necessary that at each step the design is proven to be achievable and that the key risks and opportunities have been identified and acted on. Thus the solution at *step b* in the process shown in Figure 11 could be quite different from the solution considered at *step a*, and both could be very different from the final solution chosen at *step d*. The creative process is to continuously improve the off-core approaches, which are under local engineering control, until the final solution is identified at *step d*. The solution developed at step d will become part of the baseline at the control gate for that level of detail, and then will be managed under formal configuration management.

In the previous charts we focused on the concept of an evolving baseline under progressive configuration control. The project baseline contains all technical, cost, schedule, and deliverable requirements that are sufficiently mature to be managed by configuration management and formal change control. The system engineer is responsible for managing the technical baseline. The technical baseline is first established by placing the user requirements under change control. Note that "change control" does not mean "change prevention."

Off-core studies used to identify risks and opportunities are usually under local engineering control and are not part of the baseline. Without the formality of a controlled baseline, the project team is faced with designing to a set of free-floating system requirements. There is an adage that says, "Meeting requirements and walking on water are equally easy—if both are frozen." The mistake is in allowing the user requirements to float, while freezing the results of detailed studies early in the project cycle (the off-core activities). As an example, in the early 1990s a consortium of major corporations launched a commercial venture to provide nation-wide cellular telephone coverage, using a fleet of satellites. The consortium had not yet settled on the system concept, but decided to initiate the detailed software development anyway because "time was of the essence to stay ahead of the competition." After 6 years, and a lot of money spent on software, the system was not yet in operation.

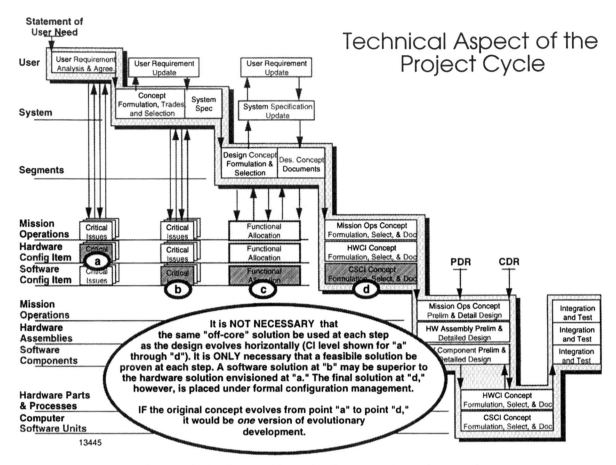

Figure 11. Evolution of lower-level concepts from phase to phase.

Once the detailed assemblies are built, coded, or procured, the integration of the system begins. The critical aspects of the integration and verification process are illustrated in Figure 12. Here downward off-core iterations are focused on problem investigation and resolution. Upward iterations are focused on resolution of problems that require a waiver or deviation if the system cannot meet the anticipated requirements.

3.2.4. Other Representations. The Vee depiction of the technical aspects of the project cycle is one view of this process. Another model commonly used in the software environment is the *spiral model*, developed by Boehm[15] and shown in Figure 13. The power of the spiral model is that it highlights the progressive need for risk analysis and prototyping (although it would be more illuminating to understand the different objectives of each of these prototypes). Figure 13 has numbers added to relate the spiral model to the Vee. Figure 14 shows that the spiral model can be overlaid on the Vee model when a horizontal, instead of spiral, time base is used. Both models represent the same approach. It is the authors' experience

that the Vee depiction provides a more accurate understanding of the process.

3.2.5. Summary of the Vee. The core of the Vee (Figure 7) represents the decisions that are placed under progressive configuration management. The Vee:

- Displays the relationship of verification planning to requirements development

- Reflects the concept of decomposition

- Illustrates system-level versus detail-level decomposition and integration activities

- Emphasizes baseline definition and configuration management

- Emphasizes ongoing risk and opportunity management (off-core activities)

- Illustrates impact of time and maturity

- Provides a basis for understanding the implication of incremental and evolutionary development approaches

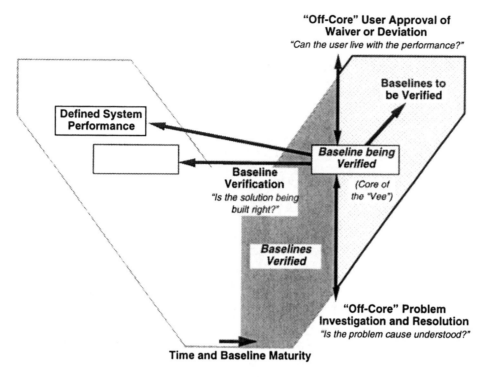

Figure 12. Critical aspects of integration and verification.

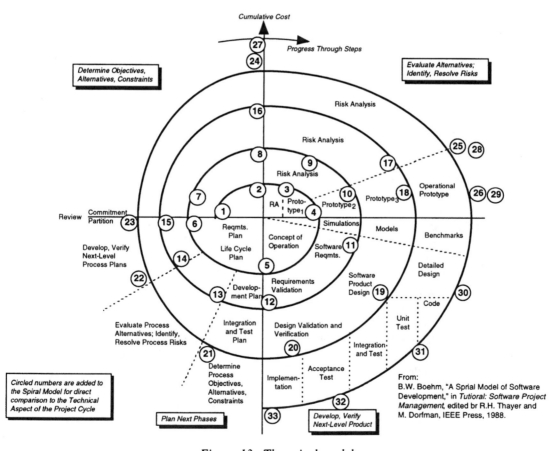

Figure 13. The spiral model.

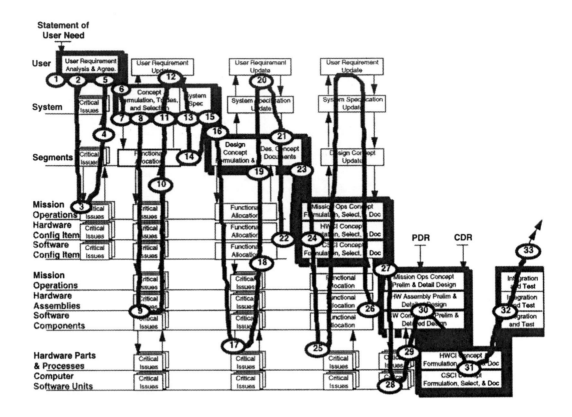

Figure 14. The spiral model overlaid on the "Vee."

3.3. Incremental and Evolutionary Development

3.3.1. Incremental Development—Single Delivery.
As explained in Forsberg and Mooz,[16] the Vee can be used to describe other development approaches. Key to successful implementation of both of the incremental development approaches (Figures 15 and 16) is that the system is considered as a whole from development of the user requirements statement through the preliminary design review (PDR). At or after PDR, incremental development options can be considered.

For incremental development with a single delivery, all increments must be completed before a functional system can be fielded. This concept is used when all requirements can be specified a priori and incremental development is desired for cost effectiveness, for security reasons, to make better use of scarce resources, or to initiate the development of long lead, critical technology. The graphical depiction of incremental development with a single delivery is shown in Figure 15.

An example that is easy to visualize is the development of the space shuttle. In the late 1960s many studies were performed to determine the optimum configuration for the space shuttle. Since all components were to be reusable, the driving technical issue was the development of a large, reusable rocket engine. Although the engines on the Saturn were more than adequate to boost the shuttle to orbit, they were one-time-use only. Thus in 1970 the space shuttle engine contract was awarded. Two years later, increment two was awarded for the space shuttle orbiter itself. In the intervening 2 years additional studies showed that a better design for the orbiter could be achieved with five engines rather than three. This was no longer a possibility, however, since the large engines under development were designed for three engines, not five, on the orbiter itself. As a consequence the orbiter design was constrained. Incremental development entails some project risk, and tradeoffs must be made before the project is initiated, since the early increments may constrain the freedom of choice during later increments.

3.3.2. Incremental Development–Incremental Delivery.
This approach is used when all requirements can be specified a priori, but when incremental development is desired to provide early but limited functionality. It provides preplanned incremental increases in performance and may be used in environments to accommodate budget limitations or to shorten the delivery span for an otherwise long development cycle. This concept is illustrated in Figure 16.

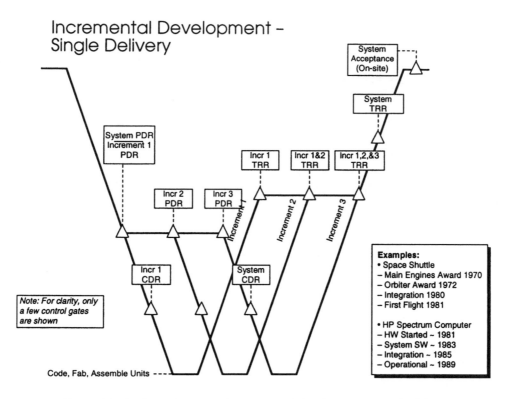

Figure 15. Technical aspect of incremental development—single delivery.

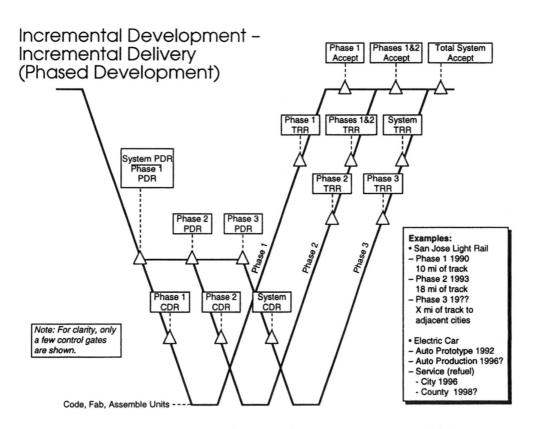

Figure 16. Technical aspects of incremental development—incremental delivery.

The first increment(s) in an incremental development–incremental delivery approach are developed and delivered to allow assembly into an operational system with limited functionality. Later increments add increased functionality. An example would be a computer system that is upgraded with later versions of software, improved hardware technology, and increased capacity.

Another example would be the implementation of a light rail system, which has been common in American cities in the 1990s. In San Jose, California, the first phase provided for the purchase of the light rail cars, the maintenance facilities, and 10 miles of track. The promise to the voters was that freeway traffic would be diminished because people would ride the light rail cars. The voters were disappointed because traffic did not diminish, but were encouraged to wait until the second increment, which would add additional track. Phase two was implemented about 3 years later and had a total of about 18 miles of track, which also did not reach the residential community and thus did not reach its objective of reducing freeway traffic. The voters were very reluctant to approve the third increment, which is still pending. This highlights a major concern of the incremental delivery process, since the

functionality provided in the first increment must be sufficiently attractive to encourage the users to wait for and potentially to fund subsequent increments. If important capabilities are not available until the final increment, there may never be a final increment.

3.3.3 Evolutionary Development. A third strategy is called *evolutionary development* (Figure 17). This is appropriate when the project requirements cannot be specified a priori and the development process itself is expected to uncover unforeseen needs and system applications. It is also applicable to a research and development environment.[9] In this model new or enhanced functionality is added to the functioning system at each iteration to satisfy newly discovered needs. An example would be the evolution of word-processing systems in the 1970s. The early vision might have been simply to enhance the capabilities of a typewriter by allowing spell check and spell correction of the last word typed, as opposed to a whole document.

In the evolutionary development model it is not necessary that the first iteration produce a functioning system, but the more iterations that are required before a useful product is produced, the less likely it is that funding will be available for the final version.

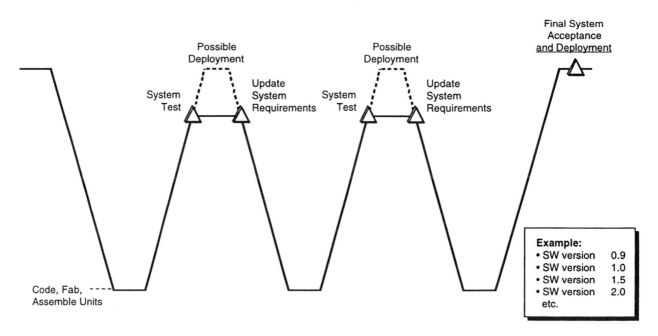

Figure 17. Technical aspects of an evolutionary design.

3.4. Technology Insertion Management

A new product developed in research laboratories may be the starting point for a new project.[9] The new capability may provide a new and unexpected opportunity for solving existing problems or may create the opportunity to do something never before contemplated (such as the Post-it, developed as a result of research into adhesives). The new technology may trigger the identification of user requirements and this is then the start of the detailed assessment through the Vee process. The project manager and system engineer must manage the maturing of that new technology as the project evolves to ensure that it is available in time to incorporate into the system.

4. System Engineering Process

4.1. Project Initiation

4.1.1. Requirements-Driven Process. System engineering is a requirements-driven process. If there are no requirements, there is no project. It is the system engineer who, working with others (marketing, customers, users, developers, competitors), initiates the exploration into ideas that will ultimately define a user need, and from that, a project (Figure 18). The origin of the requirements (the *stimulus* in Figure 18) can be self-generated,[9] but more typically the require-

ments are in response to a recognized need on the part of a user, or a new opportunity to apply existing or new technology, or some new challenge previously not considered. All of these are sources of stimuli leading to an idea for a new business opportunity, a new set of user requirements, and a new project.

4.1.2. Users, Customers, Stakeholders, and Providers. In defining the user requirements for a project, it is important to understand that there are many stakeholders, not just the users, who have an interest in, and an influence on, a project. Some stakeholders may be regulatory agencies, other stakeholders may be executive management. In this discussion it is useful to offer the following definitions:

- Stakeholder—Any group, individual, or organization that is affected by, or can affect, the project

- User—Any stakeholder who will work with the system in some capacity, and so must understand it from that perspective

- Customer(s)—The person(s) with the money to pay for the project or its end product. The customer is not necessarily a user

- Provider (Seller)—The intermediate parties in the project chain who respond to the customers

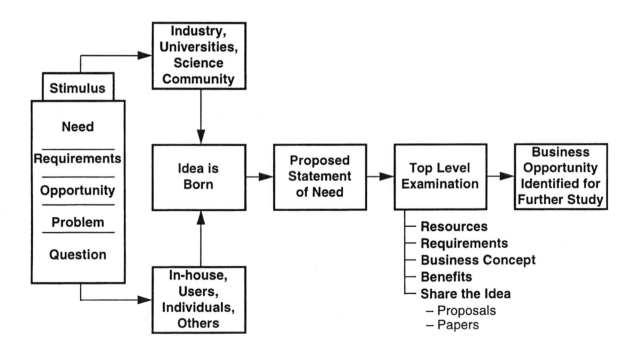

Figure 18. Project genesis.

In a commercial environment there often will be thousands, if not tens of thousands, of users of a specific product, and they all are stakeholders in the development process. When there is a large user community, the project team can deal only with representatives of that community, sometimes called *surrogate users*. Marketing serves as a surrogate user, filtering the multitude of user requirements into a viable set to which the project team can then respond.

In some instances a separate organization is established to represent the needs of a large group of users. This is not an easy task, and it sometimes meets with mixed success. Consumer advocate organizations are one example. Another example is the Space Telescope Science Institute, which was established specifically to coordinate the user requirements from thousands of independent principal investigators worldwide for the Hubble Space Telescope design and operations. In this instance, the process was not done well, and the initial relationship between the Space Telescope Science Institute (the users), NASA (the customer), and the industry contractors (the providers) was often acrimonious and unnecessarily destructive, as described by Chaisson in his book, *The Hubble Wars: Astrophysics Meets Astropolitics in the Two-Billion-Dollar Struggle over the Hubble Space Telescope.*[17] It has finally become an effective relationship during the operational period.

Another useful perspective is that members of the project team are all stakeholders in the project. They are simultaneously providers to those who have defined their work tasks, and customers for those who are supporting them in the creation of their end product. An important concept is that the entity at each level of decomposition is someone's system, with customers and providers, and should be managed as such.

4.2. System Analysis and Design Process

4.2.1. Overview. A clear statement of user need initiates the first round through the system analysis and design process shown in Figure 19. The output from the process is a set of agreed-to requirements (with buyer approval) for the next level in the hierarchy. This process is situational and is repeated over and over at descending levels in the hierarchy. Figure 20 illustrates the situational nature of the process as applied to the sequential project cycle.

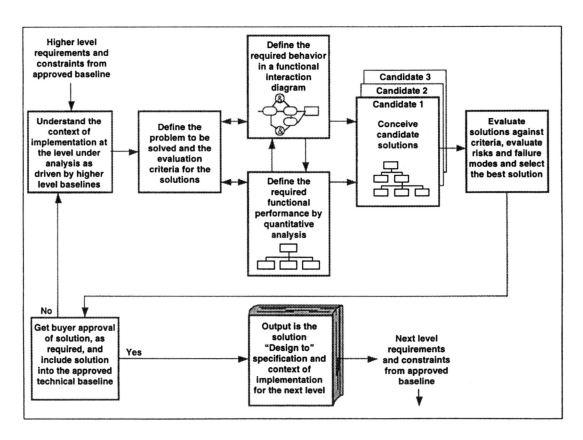

Figure 19. System analysis and design process.

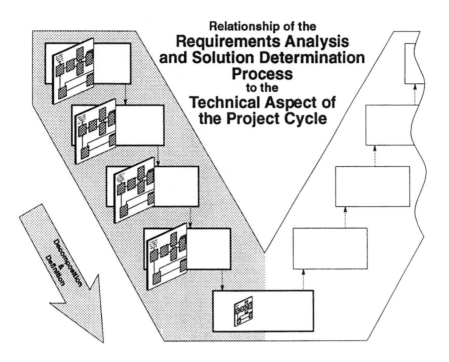

Figure 20. Relationship of the requirements analysis and solution determination process to the technical aspects of the project cycle.

At every decomposition level the following questions must be answered:

- What is the problem to be solved and in what context?
- What must the solution do (functionality)?
- How well must the solution do it (performance)?
- Within what constraints? Within what interfaces?
- What level of risk is acceptable (as a system design philosophy)?
- How will the best option be selected from candidate solutions?
- How will it be proven that the solution meets the requirements (verification and validation planning)?
- What documentation is required?

Note that it is not necessary to carry all segments or configuration items to the same level of detail in the system decomposition. Imagine that you are responsible for developing and testing a collision-avoidance system for use on corporate jets. The proj-ect requires purchase of an airplane and the installation of commercial off-the-shelf (COTS) hardware and your proprietary software on the plane. The $10 million airplane is one segment, and no further break-down is required. The $1 million detection system is another segment. Within that segment the COTS hardware needs to be defined only at the configuration item level to identify functionality, performance, and interface requirements—and to verify compliance. The proprietary software may have to be defined down to the component level to ensure proper requirements definition and development management. If a design approach emphasizing reuse (such as object-oriented design) is used, and if an adequate development library of software objects exists, it may be satisfactory to stop at the configuration item level for software definition as well. The system engineer must tailor the level of decomposition based on risk.

4.2.2. What Is the Problem to Be Solved and in What Context? A primary responsibility of the system engineer is to ensure clear customer communications about what is wanted and what is to be provided. Figure 21 illustrates the difficulty, because written words do not convey unambiguously what is desired and expected. Lack of clarity at the beginning can lead to major difficulty as the project evolves.

Figure 21. Example of confused customer communications.

For example, several years ago the chief financial officer (CFO) at a major corporation complained to the director of management information systems (MIS) that it took days to get the financial reports each time he requested them. The CFO demanded that they provide him with real-time response at the terminal on his desk. After an intense 6 months, linking corporate offices throughout the United States into a real-time system, the director of MIS announced to the CFO that the system was ready for his evaluation. The CFO was ecstatic with the instant response; he said he thought a real-time system would take at least 30 minutes to provide the needed data. The MIS director said, "If I had known that you were willing to wait 30 minutes for the reports, we could have completed your system in 2 months for $10 million, instead of the $100 million this one cost us."

There are many tools available to help define and understand the implications of the user needs. One such tool that has been widely discussed, and for which books have been written, is quality function deployment, and its popular implementation: the House of Quality.[18,19] The purpose of these tools is to clarify "What do you mean by that?" One should also use other techniques such as documentation review, interviews, focus groups, surveys, comment cards, and direct observation to provide a "check and balance" through use of multiple approaches.

Thoroughness and care are required to clarify and identify all requirements properly, and it takes time and training to do it right. In 1992 a major shipping company, with ship, truck, and rail components, decided to "modernize the computers and software for their US-based ground system." They chose to use the Quality Function Deployment approach[19] to identify the system requirements, rather than simply improving the mechanization of their current way of doing business. They expected to devote several months to the requirements definition; they were surprised that the eighteen-person team, from twelve locations, had to meet twice a month in person for 18 months to complete the House of Quality. The team leader said that all participants, including executive management, felt the process was extremely valuable, and well worth the time invested. The final set of user requirements was significantly different from what was initially envisioned.

Once the stakeholder requirements have been defined, it is important to determine their relative importance. An order-of-magnitude reasonableness test or investment of resources required to achieve a stakeholder's objective, combined with a comparison with current capability, can provide insight in establishing priorities. Often a user who has no direct responsibility for cost and schedule on the project can define requirements that are very expensive to meet and that may provide only marginal utility.

An illustration of improper priorities is documented in the history of the NeXT computer development.[20] Steve Jobs spent a substantial amount of time and money in his startup operation trying to produce a "perfect" black case for the NeXT computer. A "perfect" black case is very difficult to make because black finish highlights any imperfections. As a matter of priority, was this a proper focus for a computer manufacturer, who was at that time slowly going out of business? How many users really cared about having a black computer case on their desk? Was the black case really a system requirement?

Finally, it is essential to provide the context within which the requirements are to be met. At a system level, the context is provided by the Concept of Operations document,[21] which is written from the user's point of view. At lower levels of the project hierarchy the context within which the lower level requirements are to be met is defined by system engineering in the entity specification, usually in a descriptive introduction.

The Concept of Operations document should address the following issues: what, where, when, who, why, and how. To develop that understanding, it is necessary to envision and understand the user's environment. Even in the design of simple products, Norman[7] (pp. 151–158) notes that designers often think they understand (but really do not) user needs better than the users, and their customers (buyers) often do not have user satisfaction as a goal either. Again, remember there are many levels of users in a system and all appropriate stakeholders should be considered at this point. Also, we often say what a system will do; it is often useful to define what a system will *not* do, because it highlights implied requirements and minimizes misunderstandings at a later date.

Once the system requirements—and constraints—have been defined, it is useful to develop a behavior model to illustrate and define the full scope of the user requirements and the user environment. The behavior model should include all of the operational considerations, including reliability, maintainability, availability, human factors, decommissioning, security issues if any, and any other operational aspects. The customer should then be asked to validate the behavior or requirements understanding model. This is the stage where you must think the entire system through and define all of the system requirements and constraints. As they found in Apollo 13, late changes (to accommodate ground handling as opposed to flight conditions) can lead to disaster.

4.2.3. What Must the Solution Do (Functionality)? A number of tools exist for determining the functional requirements of the system. Perhaps the simplest is the functional flow block diagram (FFBD), which has been used for 40 years or more. The diagram by itself is incomplete since it does not enforce any logic constraints, and interfaces between the functions need to be defined with the aid of another tool (the N^2 diagram). Variants such as data flow diagrams or command flow diagrams are also widely used. One of the most powerful representations is the behavior diagram, which is a complete and self-consistent logic diagram. The use of the behavior diagram has been automated in the CASE tool, RDD-100, where RDD stands for Requirements Driven Development, and where CASE stands for Computer-Aided System (not Software) Engineering. The RDD pro-

gram can display the data in functional flow block diagrams, N^2 diagrams, and other common formats if the user wishes to do so.

The primary error that the authors have seen in practice is that system engineers sometimes focus on the functions that the organization is to perform (design an airplane), rather than the functions that the system is to perform (carry 150 people coast to coast). The objective of functional analysis is to develop a system (or lower-level component) specification. While functional analysis could be used to develop an organizational chart, do not mix that task with system analysis.

4.2.4. How Well Must the Solution Do It (Performance)? All systems have performance requirements. We were once told by a knowledgeable expert that functionality could be specified for software, but performance could not be. That is no longer a valid statement, if it ever was. It is possible, however, that seemingly reasonable system performance requirements cannot be met when the system components are defined and it is found that their performance is inconsistent with the system requirement (recall the GOES example). This is why the off-core studies early in the project cycle are so critical to project success, and to the setting of reasonable expectations (Figure 11).

Performance analysis is closely tied to functional analysis; when you know what is to be done, you must now determine how fast or how often or how well it must be done. The performance analysis starts with a system-level requirement (for example, the data search must be completed within 3 seconds maximum, or the fully loaded plane must fly 550 knots nonstop coast to coast). These top-level requirements must be flowed down either by derivation (analysis), or by allocation (judgment based on experience). One can compute the component response necessary to support the system-level 3-second requirement. The weight necessary to perform a given function on a new airplane cannot be easily calculated a priori, and past experience is used to make an initial allocation, which must be then verified as the design matures.

Inability to meet the performance requirements may force a re-examination of the user requirements and priorities (an upward iteration in Figure 8 or 10). For example, in 1964 the contract was awarded for development of the C-5A. One of the driving user requirements was that this new cargo plane must provide front-line battlefield support. This meant that the plane—which was three times bigger than any airplane in existence at that time—must land in a plowed field, and go over a 6-inch curb at full landing speed (try that in your car sometime). The past experience was that the landing gear was 5 percent of the dry structural weight. In precontract studies the designers assumed that landing gear would be 10 percent of the dry structural weight. As the lower-level designs were developed, it was found that the landing gear weight was 20 percent of dry structural weight, with severe impact on payload. The resolution was to change user requirements; the front-line support requirement was dropped, and the C-5A can land only on improved runways.

4.2.5. Within What Constraints? Within What Interfaces? Design constraints must be identified and documented, or the user may be presented with a system that has serious operational limitations. In one major software development the buyer "forgot" to provide constraints on the language used. As a consequence each supplier used a different language, and, since documentation was not specified, there are no manuals, except for high-level user guides, for system maintenance. This is on a 1.5-million line of code development that has an expected operational life of 25 years. The customer now expects to have to recode all the software for support and maintenance reasons.

Design constraints can be obvious things such as maximum power consumption, maximum weight, maximum memory, material compatibility, mean time between repair, mean time to repair, and so on. It can include upward and downward compatibility, provisions for future growth, or requirements for portability.

Interfaces must be defined for interaction with external systems, as well as between components internal to the system. For systems making extensive use of nondevelopment items, interface identification and management is the most important system engineering function. This is the single biggest cause of project failures in COTS projects. Anyone who has tried to use a "standard computer interface" to project computer-generated images at a remote conference facility can attest that this is a nontrivial exercise. At one conference the authors were presented with a box of twelve connection cables, none of which worked; one fit, but the strands of smoke emanating from our computer were not encouraging.

4.2.6. What Level of Risk Is Acceptable (as a System Design Philosophy)? Risk and opportunity management are an ongoing part of every project. However, that is not what is meant here. The issue is what constitutes project success; are you after an aggressive exploration of new technology, or are you after a safe, totally reliable system based on well-proven technology?[14]

Consider the development and implanting of a mechanical heart valve. Twenty-five years ago a mechanical valve was being considered for the first time. A 50 percent success rate would have been considered good; the alternative to the patient was certain death. Today the mechanical valve must have 100 percent reliability, and the operation to implant it must have a 95 percent or better success rate. Anything less will land you in court. Would you be willing to introduce new valve design that can be injected in place, instead of requiring a major operation, but with an 80 percent chance of success?

In 1996 public television broadcast a program on the early days of America's first reconnaissance satellite system (the Corona program). The first twelve launches in the early 1960s were failures, yet at the time—and even today—the program was considered very successful. Would your management support you if you had twelve successive $100 million dollar failures in a row? Are you, your management, and your customer risk averse in decisions to introduce new approaches in your project? Figure 22 identifies a number of risk decisions that are driven by the project's risk philosophy. All of these decisions have direct cost, schedule, and quality impact.

4.2.7. How Will the Best Option Be Selected from Candidate Solutions? After the requirements to be met have been defined, then alternative solutions must be considered. There must be an orderly process for comparing these alternatives. The fundamental process is shown in Figure 23.

There are several well-established decision analysis tools available that use this fundamental process. The Kepner–Tregoe Associates (KTA) approach[22] has been successfully used for more than 30 years, and it is still valid today. It is basically a weighted matrix for scoring alternatives. Some people dislike weighted scoring because it seems too mechanical. Such opinions miss the point. This is a judgmental process, and the numbers are an effective aid in helping you handle many variables in a consistent way.

An alternative approach is to use the analytical hierarchy process.[23] This approach appeals to engineers because the relative weights between alternatives are found by computing the eigenvalues and eigenvectors of a weighting matrix. Since there are PC-based computer programs available to do the mechanics of the process, it is easily available to everyone. However, just as for the KTA approach, the results are judgmental, and the numbers are only an aid in combining many factors in a simple-to-handle approach.

Regardless of what technique you adopt, as a system engineer you should be able to use these tools routinely and effectively.

4.2.8. How Will It Be Proven That the Solution Meets the Requirements (Verification and Validation Planning)? As requirements are developed, approaches must be developed to verify that they have been met (Figure 8). This forces the early development of the Verification and Validation plan. It also forces the requirements to be written so that they can be verified.

Issue	High Risk	Low Risk
Certification	None	Full pedigree
Commercial Applications	Maximum	Selected use
Cost	Mandatory limit	Desirable target
Design for growth	None	Planned
Expendable margins	None	High
Inspection	None	100%
New Technology	High use	No
Part De-rating	None	Substantial
Qualification	None	Full with high margins
Redundancy	None	Full
Reliability	Low	High
Schedule	Mandatory limit	Desirable target
Sparing	None	Full
Verification	None	100%

103 9607

Figure 22. Risk decisions that are driven by risk philosophy.

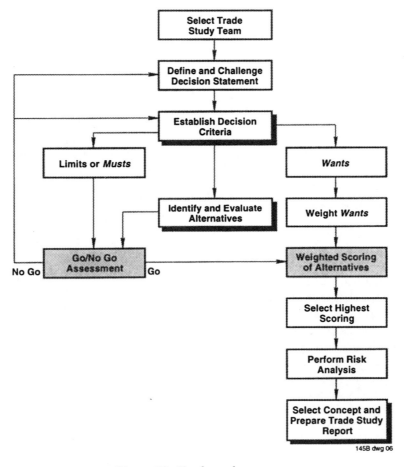

Figure 23. Trade study process.

In the example cited in Section 1.1, the software program failed the user requirement to perform a data search in a "reasonable" amount of time. Attention to the verification plan at the start of the project—before the contract was signed—would have avoided this unverifiable requirement, which became a disastrous pitfall at the end of the project.

4.2.9. What Documentation Is Required?

There is a saying, "A short pencil is better than a long memory." The amount and type of documentation must be tailored to the project needs. One measure is to ask what the risk is if a mistake is made on the project because decisions are not documented. If someone offers to bring in lunches for you and your officemates, and you order a vegetarian salad, would you care if they brought you an anchovy pizza instead? If so, you had better ask that next time they document your order in writing.

As the system definition matures, the technical baseline also matures by addition of the system requirements document, the concept definition document, the system specifications, the "design-to" specifications, the "build-to" and "code-to" documentation and ultimately the "as built," "as tested," "as accepted," and "as operated" documents. The level of documentation and detail required under configuration management depends on the criticality of the project, the number of people involved, the number of subcontractors, the number of personnel at remote sites, and so on. The documentation method must be tailored to each project to ensure baseline decisions are appropriately communicated to all who must take action on the basis of those decisions.

The studies of off-core critical issues (Figures 8 to 12) should be documented by the person performing the work. Such engineering studies are kept under informal engineering control, but should be part of the project data set.

4.3. System Integration and Verification Process

In a perfect world the integration and verification process runs smoothly from detailed level to completed system. If the system analysis and design process was not properly followed, if there were changes to system-level requirements, if interface management was not rigorously followed, if the system partitioning was poorly selected so that the interfaces are complex, if ..., the system integration and verification process becomes the most challenging part of the project. This is especially true when time and project funding run out. The process in this phase is simple; the implementation is usually not. In commenting on IBM's performance at the 1996 Atlanta Olympics,[5] one cus-

tomer said, "Their stats collection and commentator systems are wonderfully designed. It was the deployment and integration that killed them."

The system integration and verification process is illustrated in Figure 24. Components of the system are integrated and are subjected to verification (tests, analysis, inspection, or demonstration) to ensure readiness for integration with the next assembly. If no deficiencies are detected, then integration proceeds to the next level. If deficiencies are detected, either they are corrected or uncorrectible deficiencies are accepted through a waiver or deviation process. If a component is modified to correct a deficiency or if some deficiency is accepted through a waiver, a regression test is necessary to ensure that these changes from what was planned do not affect the performance of other parts of the system. Figure 24 is a situational process that is repeated multiple times through the hierarchy as the system is assembled.

5. Conclusion

System engineering is an end-to-end process that is critical to project success. The process has been clearly defined. It is up to executive management and project management to insist on implementation of that process and empower the project team to do so. It is up to the system engineer to enforce the process discipline.

System engineering requires good judgment, "uncommon" sense, and team-building skills to succeed. Computerized tools and mathematical knowledge are useful—and in some cases essential—for decision support, but they are not the essence of the discipline.

References

1. Blanchard, B.S., *System Engineering Management,* John Wiley & Sons, New York, N.Y., 1991.

2. Forsberg, K. and H. Mooz, with Howard Cotterman, *Visualizing Project Management*, John Wiley & Sons, New York, N.Y., 1996.

3. Boardman, J., *Systems Engineering, An Introduction*, Prentice-Hall, Englewood Cliffs, N.J., 1990.

4. Rich, B. and L. Janos, *Skunk Works*, Little, Brown & Company, New York, N.Y., 1994.

5. Caldwell, B., "No Management Medals; IBM's Olympic Woes Not a Technology Issue," *Information Week*, Aug. 19, 1996, p. 80.

6. Kuznik, F., "Blundersat," *Air and Space Smithsonian*, Dec. 1993/Jan. 1994, pp. 41–47.

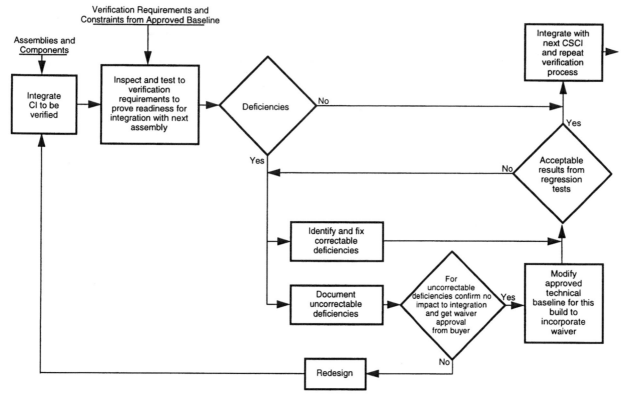

Figure 24. System integration and verification process.

7. Norman, D.A., *The Design of Everyday Things*, Currency Book by Doubleday, New York, N.Y., 1989.

8. Chiroini, J. and K. Forsberg, "The Work Element in Teamwork," *Proc. IPMA 1996 World Congress on Project Management*, 1996.

9. Forsberg, Kevin, "'If I Could Do That, Then I Could...,' System Engineering in a Research and Development Environment—As Illustrated by the Evolution of the Space Shuttle Tiles," *Proc. Int'l Council for System Eng. (INCOSE) Symp.*, (also included in the supplement: Best Presentations of the Fifth Annual International Symposium), 1995.

10. Forsberg, K. and H. Mooz, "The Relationship of System Engineering to the Project Cycle," *Proc. Nat'l Council for System Eng. (NCOSE) Conf.*, 1991, pp. 57–65.

11. Royce, W.W., "Managing the Development of Large Software Systems," *Proc. IEEE WESCON*, 1970, pp. 1–9. Reprinted in *Tutorial: Software Engineering Project Management*, R.H. Thayer, ed., IEEE Computer Society Press, Los Alamitos, Calif., 1988.

12. Lovell, J. and J. Kluger, *Apollo 13*, Simon & Schuster (Pocket Books Division), New York, N.Y., 1994.

13. Forsberg, K. and H. Mooz, "Relating Risk and Opportunity Management to the Project Cycle," *Proc. Int'l Council for System Eng. (INCOSE) Conf.*, 1995.

14. Forsberg, K. and H. Mooz, "Risk and Opportunity Management," *Proc. Int'l Council for System Eng. (INCOSE) Conf.*, 1995.

15. Boehm, B.W., "A Spiral Model of Software Development," in *Tutorial: Software Engineering Project Management*, R.H. Thayer and M. Dorfman, eds., IEEE Computer Society Press, Los Alamitos, Calif., 1988, pp. 128–142.

16. Forsberg, K. and H. Mooz, "Application of the 'Vee' to Incremental and Evolutionary Development," *Proc. Int'l Council for System Eng. (INCOSE) Conf.*, 1995.

17. Chaisson, E.J., *The Hubble Wars: Astrophysics Meets Astropolitics in the Two-Billion-Dollar Struggle over the Hubble Space Telescope*, Harper Collins, New York, N.Y., 1994.

18. Hauser, J.R. and D. Clausing, "The House of Quality," *Harvard Business Review*, May–June 1988, pp. 63–73.

19. Guinta, L. and N. Praizler, *The QFD Book: The Team Approach to Solving Problems and Satisfying Customers through Quality Function Deployment*, AMACOM Books (a division of American Management Association), New York, N.Y., 1993.

20. Stross, R.E., *Steve Jobs & The NeXT Big Thing*, Macmillan, New York, N.Y., 1993, pp. 117–143.

21. Fairley, R., R. Thayer, and P. Bjorke, "The Concept of Operations: The Bridge from Operational Requirements to Technical Specifications," *Proc. 1st Int'l Conf. Requirements Eng.*, IEEE Computer Society Press, Los Alamitos, Calif., 1994, pp. 40–47.

22. Kepner, C. and B. Tregoe, *The New Rational Manager,* Princeton Research Press, Princeton, N.J., 1981.

23. Saaty, T., "Priority Setting in Complex Problems," *IEEE Trans. Eng. Management,* Aug. 1983, pp. 140–155.

The Concept of Operations:
The Bridge from Operational Requirements to Technical Specifications*

Richard E. Fairley
Colorado Technical University

Richard H. Thayer
California State University, Sacramento

Abstract

This paper describes the role of a Concept of Operations (ConOps) document in specification and development of a software-intensive system. It also describes the process of developing a ConOps, its uses and benefits, who should develop it, and when it should be developed. The ConOps described in this paper is compared to other forms of operational concept documents. A detailed outline for ConOps documents is provided in an appendix to the paper.

Introduction

The goal of software engineering is to develop and modify software-intensive systems that satisfy user needs, on schedule and within budget. Accurate communication of operational requirements from those who need a software-intensive system to those who will build the system is thus the most important step in the system development process. Traditionally, this information has been communicated as follows: The developer analyzes users' needs and buyer's requirements and prepares a requirements specification that defines the developers' understanding of those needs and requirements.[1] The users and buyer review the requirements specification and attempt to verify that the developer has correctly understood their needs and requirements. A draft users' manual is sometimes written by the developer to assist users and buyer in determining whether the proposed system will operate in a manner consistent with their needs and expectations. A prototype of the user interface may be constructed to demonstrate the developers' understanding of the desired user interface.

This traditional way of specifying software requirements introduces several problems: First, the buyer may not adequately convey the needs of the user community to the developer, perhaps because the buyer does not understand those needs. Second, the developer may not be expert in the application domain, which inhibits communication. Third, the users and buyer often find it difficult to understand the requirements produced by the developer. Fourth, the developer's requirements specification typically specifies system attributes such as functions, performance factors, design constraints, system interfaces, and quality attributes, but typically contains little or no information concerning operational characteristics of the specified system [ANSI/IEEE Std 830-1984]. This leaves the users and buyer uncertain as to whether the requirements specification describes a system that will provide the needed operational capabilities.

A draft version of the users' manual can provide some assurance that the developer understands user/buyer needs and expectations, but a draft version of the manual may not be written. If it is written, considerable time and effort have usually been spent by the time it is available for review. Major changes can require significant rework. Furthermore, it is difficult to demonstrate that the correspondences among technical specifications, users' manual, and (undocumented) operational requirements are complete and consistent.

A prototype of the user interface can be helpful, but there is a danger that demonstration of an acceptable user interface will be taken as assurance that the developer understands all of the users' operational needs. In summary, the traditional approach does not facilitate communication among users, buyer, and developer; nor does it emphasize the importance of specifying the operational requirements for the envisioned system.

---

* A version of this paper will appear in *Annals of Software Engineering*.

1 Users are those who will interact with the new or modified system in the performance of their daily work activities; users include operators and maintainers. The buyer is a representative of the user community (or communities) who provides the interface between users and developer: the developer is the organization that will build (or modify) and deliver the system.

Concept analysis helps users clarify their operational needs, thereby easing the problems of communication among users, buyer, and developer. Development of a Concept of Operation document (ConOps) to record the results of concept analysis provides a bridge from user needs into the system development process. Ideally, concept analysis and development of the ConOps document are the first steps in the development process; however, (as discussed below) developing a ConOps at later stages of the system lifecycle is also cost-effective.

Subsequent sections of this paper describe the evolution of the ConOps technique, the concept analysis process, the Concept of Operations document, roles to be played by a ConOps, some guidelines on when and how to develop a ConOps, development scenarios and a process for developing the ConOps, the recommended format for a ConOps, and some issues concerning maintenance of a ConOps throughout the development process and the operational life of a software system.

History of the ConOps Approach

One of the earliest reports on formalizing the description of operational concepts for a software system is contained in a 1980 TRW report by R.J. Lano: "A Structured Approach for Operational Concept Formulation" [TRW SS-80-02]. The importance of a well-defined operational concept (for example, definition of system goals, missions, functions, components) to the success of system development is emphasized in the report. The report presented tools, techniques, and procedures for more effectively accomplishing the system engineering tasks of concept formulation, requirements analysis and definition, architecture definition, and system design.

In 1985, the Joint Logistics Commanders' Joint Regulation "Management of Computer Resources in Defense Systems" was issued. This Joint Regulation included DoD-STD-2167, which contained a Data Item Description (DID) entitled "Operational Concept Document" (OCD) [Dl-ECRS-8x25, DoD-Std-2167, 1985]. The purpose of this DID was to describe the mission of the system, its operational and support environments, and the functions and characteristics of the computer system within an overall system. The OCD DID was folded into the System/Segment Design Document [Dl-CMAN-80534, DoD-Std-2167A, 1988] in the revised version of DoD-STD-2167 [DoD-Std-2167A].

Operational concepts were moved into Section 3 of the System/Segment Design Document (SSDD), which tended to place emphasis on overall system concepts rather than software concepts. Because the OCD was no longer a stand-alone document in 2167A, many users of 2167A did sufficiently emphasize operational concepts. For software-only projects, use of the SSDD was often waived. In these cases, there was no other place within the 2167A DIDs to record operational concepts for a software-intensive system. As a result, several other government agencies, including NASA and the Federal Aviation Administration, produced their own versions of the original 2167 DID for documenting operational concepts within the 2167A framework.

Another DoD standard, DoD-Std-7935A for development of information systems, required that the functional description of the proposed information system be contained in Section 2 of that document. The Functional Description in 7935A provided little guidance on how to develop a ConOps document; furthermore, it was very specific to the information systems domain, emphasized functionality only, and allowed little flexibility for new methods and techniques of software system development.

In recognition of the importance of well-defined operational concepts to successful development of a software system, Mil-Std 498 for Software Development and Documentation, which has replaced 2167A and 7935A, includes a Data Item Description for an Operational Concept Document (OCD). The authors of this paper played a leading role in developing the draft version of the Operational Concept Document (OCD) for the Harmonization Working Group that prepared Mil-Std-498. The OCD in Mil-Std 498 is similar to the ConOps outline contained in Appendix A of this paper. IEEE Standard 1498, the commercial counterpart of Mil-Std-498 (which currently exists in draft form) incorporates an OCD similar to the one in Appendix A.

The American Institute of Aeronautics and Astronautics (AIAA) published a document titled "Operational Concept Document (OCD) Preparation Guidelines" [AIAA OCD 1992]. The AIAA OCD compares favorably with the ConOps presented in this paper; however, in the opinion of this paper's authors, the tone and language used in the AIAA OCD is biased to the developer's view of user needs rather than the users' operational view. The AIAA OCD is also biased toward embedded, real-time systems.

A major goal for the ConOps presented here is to provide a means for users of information processing systems, who are knowledgeable in their application domain but not expert in software engineering, to describe their needs and wants from their point of view; in other words, the recommended Guide is more user-oriented than existing standards and guidelines, which tend to be systems-oriented and developer-oriented.

Another difference between existing standards and the ConOps recommended in this paper is that this paper emphasizes the importance of describing both the current system's and the proposed system's characteristics, even though that may result in some redundancy in the document. The advantages of redundancy are considered to outweigh the problems.

The Concept Analysis Process

Concept analysis is the process of analyzing a problem domain and an operational environment for the purpose of specifying the characteristics of a proposed system from the users' perspective. The traditional system development process emphasizes functionality with little concern for how that functionality will be used. Concept analysis emphasizes an integrated view of a system and its operational characteristics, rather than focusing on individual functions or pieces of a system. A major goal of concept analysis is to avoid development of a system in which each individual function meets its specifications, but the system as a whole fails to meet the users' needs.

Concept analysis should be the first step taken in the overall system development process. It identifies the various classes of users and modes of operation,[2] and provides users with a mechanism for defining their needs and desires. Concept analysis is also useful to surface different users' (and user groups') needs and viewpoints, and to allow the buyer (or multiple buyers) to state their requirements for the proposed system. This process is essential to the success of the subsequent system development effort. Users have an opportunity to express their needs and desires, but they are also required to state which of those needs are essential, which are desirable, and which are optional. In addition, they must prioritize the desired and optional needs. Prioritized user needs provide the basis for establishing an incremental development process and for making trade-offs among operational needs, schedule, and budget.

Concept analysis helps to clarify and resolve vague and conflicting needs, wants, and opinions by reconciling divergent views. In the case where several user groups (or buyer groups) have conflicting needs, viewpoints, or expectations, concept analysis can aid in building consensus. In some cases, it may be determined that no single system can satisfy all of the divergent needs and desires of multiple user groups and buyer agencies. It is better to make that determination earlier rather than later.

Concept analysis is an iterative process that should involve various people. The analysis group should include representatives from the user, buyer, and developer organizations, plus any other appropriate parties such as training and operational support. In cases where a development organization has not been selected at the time of concept analysis, the developer role may be filled by in-house development experts or consultants.

The results of concept analysis are recorded in the ConOps document, which serves as a framework to guide the analysis process and provides the foundation document for all subsequent system development activities (analysis, design, implementation, and validation). The ConOps document should say everything about the system that the users and buyer need to communicate to those who will develop the system.

The ConOps document should be repeatedly reviewed and revised until all involved parties agree on the resulting document. This iterative process helps bring to the surface many viewpoints, needs, wants, and scenarios that might otherwise be overlooked.

The Concept of Operations (ConOps) Document

The ConOps document describes the results of the conceptual analysis process. The document should contain all of the information needed to describe the users' needs, goals, expectations, operational environment, processes, and characteristics for the system under consideration. Essential elements of a ConOps include:

- A description of the current system or situation
- A description of the needs that motivate development of a new system or modification of an existing system
- Modes of operation for the proposed system
- User classes and user characteristics
- Operational features of the proposed system
- Priorities among proposed operational features
- Operational scenarios for each operational mode and class of user
- Limitations of the proposed approach
- Impact analysis for the proposed system

A detailed outline for a ConOps document containing these elements is provided in Appendix A to this paper.

---

2 Diagnostic mode, maintenance mode, degraded mode, emergency mode, and backup mode must be included, as appropriate, in the set of operational modes for a system environment, processes, and characteristics for the system under consideration.

A ConOps document should, in contrast to a requirements specifications, be written in narrative prose, using the language and terminology of the users' application domain. It should be organized to tell a story, and should make use of visual forms (diagrams, illustrations, graphs, and so forth) whenever possible. Although desirable, it is not necessary that the needs and wants expressed in a ConOps be quantified; that is, users can state their desire for "fast response" or "reliable operation." These desires are quantified during the process of mapping the ConOps to the requirements specification and during the flowdown of requirements to the system architecture. During system development, the impact of trade-offs among quantified system attributes (such as response time and reliability) must be explored within the limits of available time, money, and the state of technology.

A ConOps document should be tailored for the application domain, operational environment, and intended audience. This means that the terminology, level of abstraction, detail, technical content, and presentation format should adhere to the objectives for that particular ConOps document. The following points are worth making in this regard:

1. A ConOps document must be written in the users' language. This does not necessarily imply that it cannot use technical language, but rather that it should be written in the users' technical language if the users are experts in a technical domain. If the ConOps document is written by the buyer or developer the authors must avoid use of terminology associated with their own discipline.

2. The level of detail contained in a ConOps should be appropriate to the situation. For example, there may be instances wherein a high-level description of the current system or situation is sufficient. In other instances, a detailed description of the current system or situation may be necessary. For example, there may be no current system: A detailed statement of the situation that motivates new system development with extensively specified operational scenarios for the envisioned system may be required. Or, the new system may be a replacement for an existing system to upgrade technology while adding new capabilities. In this case, a brief description of the existing system would be appropriate, with more detail on the new capabilities to be provided. The level of detail also depends on whether the ConOps document is for a system as a whole, or whether there will be separate ConOps documents for each system segment (for example, checkout, launch, on-orbit, and ground support elements for a spacecraft system) with an umbrella ConOps that describes operational aspects of the entire system.

3. The presentation format used in a ConOps document will vary, depending on the application of the document. In some user communities, textual documents are the tradition, while in others, storyboards are used. Examples of this difference can be seen by comparing the styles of communication in the information processing and command-and-control domains, for instance. The presentation format should be adjusted to accommodate the intended audience of the ConOps, although the use of visual forms is recommended for all audiences.

4. The comprehensive outline of a ConOps document, as presented in Appendix A, may not apply to every system or situation. If a particular paragraph of the outline does not apply to the situation under consideration, it should be marked "Not Applicable (N/A);" however, for each paragraph marked N/A, a brief justification stating why that paragraph is not applicable should be provided in place of the paragraph. "Not Applicable" should be used only when the authors of a ConOps are confident that the paragraph does not apply to the situation, and not simply because the authors don't have the required information. For example, if the authors do not know whether alternatives and trade-offs were considered (paragraph 8.3 of the ConOps outline), they should determine that fact. In the interim period, the paragraph can be marked "TBD." If they determine no alternatives or trade-offs were considered, the paragraph can be marked "not applicable." In this case, a brief justification stating why alternatives and trade-offs were not considered should be included.

To summarize, the ConOps format presented in Appendix A should be tailored to produce an efficient and cost-effective mechanism for documenting user needs and for maintaining traceability to those needs throughout the development process.

Roles for ConOps Documents

The ConOps document can fill one of several roles, or some combination thereof:

1. To communicate users' and buyer's needs/requirements to the system developers. The ConOps author might be a buyer, presenting users' views to a developer; or a user presenting the users' view to a buyer and/or a developer. In this case, the ConOps is used by the developer as the basis for subsequent development activities.

2. To communicate a developer's understanding to users and/or buyer. The developer might produce a ConOps document as an aid in communicating the technical requirements to users and buyer, or to explain a possible solution strategy to the users and/or buyer. In this case, the ConOps is reviewed by the users and buyer to determine whether the proposed approach meets their needs and expectations.

3. To communicate a buyer's understanding of user needs to a developer. In this case, the buyer would develop the ConOps, obtain user concurrence, and use the ConOps to present user needs and operational requirements to the developer.

4. To document divergent needs and differing viewpoints of various user groups and/or buyers. In this case, each user group and/or buyer might develop (or commission development of) a ConOps to document their particular needs and viewpoints. This would be done as a prelude to obtaining a consensus view (see Role 5), or to determine that no single system can satisfy all of the various users' needs and buyers' requirements.

5. To document consensus on the system's characteristics among multiple users, user groups, or multiple buyers. In this case, the ConOps provides a mechanism for documenting the consensus view obtained from divergent needs, visions, and viewpoints among different users, user groups, and buyers before further development work proceeds.

6. To provide a means of communication between system engineers and software developers. In this case, the ConOps would describe user needs and operational requirements for the overall system (hardware, software, and people) and provide a context for the role of software within the total system.

7. To provide common understanding among multiple system/software developers. In cases where multiple system development and/or software development organizations are involved, the ConOps can provide a common understanding of how the software fits into the overall system, and how each software developer's part fits into the software portion of the system. In this case, there may be multiple ConOps documents, related in a hierarchical manner that mirrors the system partitioning.

Variations on, and combinations of, these roles might be found under differing circumstances. For example, the ConOps process might play Roles 4 and 5 to obtain and document consensus among user groups and buyers prior to developer selection; the consensus ConOps document would then fill Role 1 by providing the basis for subsequent development activities by the developer.

Additional roles for the ConOps include:

8. Providing a mechanism to document a system's characteristics and the users' operational needs in a manner that can be verified by the users without requiring them to have any technical knowledge beyond what is required to perform their job functions.

9. Providing a place for users to state their desires, visions, and expectations without requiring them to provide quantified, testable specifications. For example, the users could express their need for a "highly reliable" system, and their reasons for that need, without having to produce a testable reliability requirement.

10. Providing a mechanism for users and buyer(s) to express their thoughts and concerns on possible solution strategies. In some cases, there may be design constraints that dictate particular approaches. In other cases, there may be a variety of acceptable solution strategies. The ConOps allows users and buyer(s) to record design constraints, the rationale for those constraints, and to indicate the range of acceptable solution strategies.

When Should the ConOps be Developed?

Development of a ConOps document should be the first step in the overall development process, so that it can serve as a basis for subsequent development activities.

The ConOps might be developed

1. Before the decision is made to develop a system. In this case, the ConOps document would be used to support the decision process.

2. Before the request for proposals (RFP) or in-house project authorization is issued. The ConOps would be included in the RFP package or project authorization.

3. As the first task after award of contract, so that the developer can better understand the users' needs and expectations before subsequent system development activities are started.

In cases (1) and (2), development of the ConOps document will be initiated by the users or the buyer (although the document author might be a developer; possibly the developer who will later develop the system). In case (3), development of the ConOps can be initiated by, and/or developed by, the user, buyer, or developer.

Concept analysis and preparation of a ConOps document can also be quite useful even if initiated at a later stage of the system life cycle. If, during system development, so many diverging opinions, needs, visions, and viewpoints surface that the development process cannot continue successfully, a ConOps document can provide a common vision of the system. The ConOps document for the Hubble Space Telescope System is a good example of this situation [Hubble 1983]. It was written after several attempts to develop a requirements specification; however, potential users of the space telescope could not agree on the operational requirements. The ConOps document provided the vehicle for obtaining a consensus, which in turn provided a basis for generating detailed operational requirements.

The developer who is building a system might want to develop a ConOps document, even as the requirements specifications are being generated. The developer might want the ConOps as a high-level overview and introduction to the system to serve as a guideline for the development team. Developers concerned about understanding user needs might develop a ConOps document as an aid to successfully developing a system that meets the users' needs and expectations.

A ConOps document might be developed during the operational phase of the system life cycle to support users, operators, and maintainers of the system. It might happen that potential system users do not want to use it because they do not understand the system's operational capabilities, or because they do not understand how the system would fit into their working environment. To solve these problems, the buyer or the developer might develop a ConOps document to "sell" the system to potential users.

A ConOps is also helpful to new users, operators, and maintainers who need to understand the operational characteristics of a system. The ConOps can also be used to explain the system's operational characteristics to prospective buyers who were not involved in initial system development.

If the involved parties deem it to be useful, a ConOps document can be developed at any time during the system life cycle; however, some major benefits of the document and the process of developing it are lost if it is developed after the requirements specification is baselined.

Scenarios for Developing the ConOps

Ideally, concept analysis and development of the ConOps document should be done by the users. However, depending on the purpose and timing of development, the ConOps might be developed by the users, the buyer, or the developer. Regardless of who develops the ConOps, it must reflect the views of, and be approved by, the user community.

A high degree of user involvement in concept analysis and review of the ConOps document is crucial to a successful outcome, even if concept analysis and development of the ConOps document are done by the buyer or the developer. In these cases, the buyer or developer must engage the users in the process to ensure a correct and comprehensive understanding of the current system or situation and the users' needs, visions, and expectations for the new system. One way to ensure the necessary interactions is to establish an interdisciplinary team consisting of representatives from all user groups, from the buyer(s), and from the developer(s). However, the focus must never be allowed to shift from the users' operational perspective to the buyer's or developer's perspective.

One benefit of having the users write the ConOps document is that it ensures the focus will stay on user-related issues. However, the users may not know how to develop a ConOps document or be able to realistically envision what a new system can accomplish, that is they may not know the capabilities of existing technology. To reduce the impact of these problems, qualified personnel can be brought in to assist the users in developing the ConOps document.

One benefit of having the developers write the ConOps document is that they will, in most cases, have comprehensive knowledge of available technologies, and thus may be able to propose alternative (and better) ways of solving the users' problems. Another benefit of a developer-produced ConOps is that the ConOps analysis process will provide the developer with a good understanding of the users' problems, needs, and expectations, which facilitates subsequent development activities.

An advantage of a buyer-developed ConOps is that the buyer may have a good understanding of the user community, the developer organization, the political realities of the situation, and the budgetary constraints that may exist. This knowledge can be invaluable in producing a ConOps for a system that will satisfy user needs and that can be delivered within political and budgetary constraints.

Regardless of who takes primary responsibility for producing the ConOps document, it is important that all parties (users, buyers, developers) be involved in the analysis process and that everyone contribute their particular viewpoint to development of the ConOps.

A Development Process for the ConOps

The approach described below is intended as a guideline. If the approach conflicts with what seems to be most appropriate in a specific situation, the guideline should be modified to fit that situation. For instance, there may be no current system; or the new system may be a modification of a current system; or the new system may be a total replacement for an outdated (manual or automated) system. Topics emphasized in the ConOps may be different in each situation.

1. Determine the objectives, roles, and team members for the ConOps process. This will normally be determined by the situation that motivates development of the ConOps document.

2. Tailor the recommended ConOps document format and obtain agreement on an outline for the ConOps document. This is important so that everyone understands the agreed-upon format and content areas of the document.

3. Describe the overall objectives and shortcomings of the current system. Also, determine and document the overall objectives for the new or modified system. If there is no current system, describe the situation that motivates development of a new system.

4. If there is an existing system, describe the that system's scope and boundaries, and identify any external systems and the interfaces to them. Also, establish and describe in general terms the scope and boundaries for the new or modified system, and identify the major external systems and interfaces to it.

5. Describe operational policies and constraints that apply to the current system or situation and any changes to those policies and constraints for the new system.

6. Describe the features of the current system or situation. This includes the system's operational characteristics, operational environment and processes, modes of operation, user classes, and the operational support and maintenance environments.

7. State the operational policies and constraints that will apply to the new or modified system.

8. Determine the operational characteristics of the proposed system, that is, describe the characteristics the proposed system must possess to meet the users' needs and expectations.

9. Document operational scenarios for the new or modified system. Scenarios are specified by recording, in a step-by-step manner, the sequences of actions and interactions between a user and the system. The following approach can be used to develop and document operational scenarios:

   - Develop a set of scenarios that, to the extent possible, covers all modes of operation, all classes of users, and all specific operations and processes of the proposed system.

   - Walk through each scenario with the appropriate users and record information concerning normal operating states and unusual conditions that are relevant to the operation of the proposed system.

   - During the walk-throughs, establish new scenarios to cover abnormal operations such as exception handling, stress load handling, and handling of incomplete and incorrect data.

   - Establish new scenarios whenever a branch in the thread of operation is encountered. Typically, walking through the "normal" scenarios will uncover additional scenarios. Different users may also have different views of some scenarios. If these variations are significant, include them as separate scenarios.

- Repeatedly develop scenarios until all operations, and all significant variations of those operations, are covered.
- For each operational scenario, develop an associated test scenario to be used in validating the operational aspects of the delivered system in the user environment. Establish traceability between operational scenarios and test scenarios.

10. After the scenarios have been developed, validate the description of the proposed system and the operational scenarios by walking through all of the scenarios with representatives from all user groups and all classes of users for all operational modes.

11. Obtain consensus on priorities among the operational scenarios and features of the proposed system. Group the scenarios and operational features into essential, desirable, and optional categories; prioritize scenarios and features within the desirable and optional categories. Also, describe scenarios and features considered but not included in the proposed system.

12. Analyze and describe the operational and organizational impacts the proposed system will have on users, buyer(s), developers, and the support/maintenance agencies. Also, include significant impacts on these groups during system development.

13. Describe the benefits, limitations, advantages, and disadvantages of the proposed system, compared to the present system or situation.

Recommended Format of a ConOps Document

The recommended format of a ConOps document accommodates the objective of describing a proposed system from the users' point of view, in user terminology. The following format is recommended. Appendix A contains a detailed version of this outline.

1. Introduction to the ConOps document and to the system described in the document.
2. List of all documents referenced in the ConOps document.
3. Description of the current system or situation, including scope and objectives of the current system, operational policies and constraints, modes of operation, classes of users, and the support environment for the current system. If there is no existing system, describe the reasons that motivate development of a new system.
4. Nature of proposed changes and/or new features, including the justification for those changes and/or features.
5. Operational concepts for the proposed system, including scope and objectives for the proposed system, operational policies and constraints, modes of operation, classes of users, and the support environment for the proposed system.
6. Operational scenarios describing how the proposed system is to perform in its environment, relating system capabilities and functions to modes of operation, classes of users, and interactions with external systems.
7. Operational and organizational impacts on the users, buyers, developers, and the support and maintenance agencies, during system development and after system installation.
8. Alternative and trade-offs considered but not included in the new or modified system; analysis of benefits, limitations, advantages, and disadvantages of the new or modified system.
9. Notes, acronyms and abbreviations, appendices, and glossary of terms

This organization of a ConOps document provides a logical flow of information beginning with a description of the current system, transitioning through considerations of needed changes and the rationale for such changes, and leading to a description of the new or modified system. This will guide the reader through the description of the systems (both the current system or situation and the proposed system) in a simple and intuitive way.

Maintaining the ConOps

A ConOps should be a living document that is updated and maintained throughout the entire life cycle (development process and operational life) of the software product. During system development, the ConOps document must be updated to keep users informed of the operational impacts of changes in requirements, the system design, operational policies, the operational environment, and other users' needs. During the operational life of the software product, the

ConOps must be updated to reflect the evolutionary changes to the system.

It is important to maintain the ConOps document under configuration control, and to ensure that user and buyer representatives are members of the change control board for the ConOps. Placing the ConOps under configuration control will protect the document from uncontrolled changes, and through the formal process of updating and notification, help to keep all parties informed of changes. A major benefit of this approach is that users and buyers are involved in reviewing and approving the changes. This minimizes the surprise factor that can occur when a delivered system is not the same as the system users thought they agreed to at the requirements review.

The ConOps document should also be updated and maintained under configuration control throughout the operational life of the associated system. During the operational life of the system, a ConOps can aid the support, maintenance, and enhancement activities for the system in much the same way that it helped during development. Specifically, it can be used to communicate new operational needs and impacts that result in modifications, upgrades, and enhancements. Furthermore, the ConOps provides a communication tool to familiarize new personnel with the system and the application domain.

Traceability should be established and maintained among the ConOps document, the system/software requirements specifications, and the acceptance/regression test scenarios. It is important for the developer (or maintainer) to be able to demonstrate to the users, buyer, and themselves that every essential user need stated in the ConOps document, and the desirable and optional features implemented, can be traced to and from the system specifications and to and from the delivered capabilities in the final product.

Summary and Conclusions

This paper has described the evolution of the ConOps approach, the conceptual analysis process, the Concept of Operations document, roles to be played by a ConOps, some guidelines on when to develop a ConOps, development scenarios and a development process for developing the ConOps, the recommended format for a ConOps, and some issues concerning the maintenance of a ConOps throughout the development process and operational life of a software system.

As software engineers, we become so involved in the technology of software development and modification that we sometimes forget our fundamental charter: to develop and modify software-intensive systems that satisfy user needs, on time and within budget. Performing conceptual analysis and develop-

ing and maintaining a Concept of Operations document provides the bridge from users' operational requirements to technical specifications. All subsequent work products (requirements specs, design documents, source code, test plans, users' manual, training aids, and maintenance guide, for example) should flow from the ConOps. Maintaining the ConOps and the traceability of work products to the ConOps will not guarantee success; however, it can increase the probability that we will develop systems that satisfy users' needs for efficient and effective tools that help them accomplish their work activities.

Acknowledgments

The authors would like to acknowledge the support of the following individuals in preparing the ConOps Guide: Per Bjorke, Dr. Merlin Dorfman, Dr. Lisa Friendly, and Jane Radatz.

References

[AIAA OCD, 1992] AIAA Recommended Technical Practice, Operational Concept Document (OCD), Preparation Guidelines, Software Systems Technical Committee, American Institute of Aeronautics and Astronautics (AIAA), Mar. 1, 1992.

[ANSI/IEEE Std 830-1984] ANSI/IEEE Standard 830-1984: IEEE Guide for Software Requirements Specifications, The Institute of Electrical and Electronic Engineers, Inc., approved by the American National Standards Institute July 20, 1984.

[Dl-CMAN-80534, DoD-Std-2167A, 1988] System/Segment Design Document (SSDD), Dl-CMAN-80534, U.S. Department of Defense, Feb. 29, 1988.

[DI-ECRS-8x25, DoD-Std-2167, 1985] Operational Concept Document (OCD), Dl-[ECRS-8x25] U.S. Department of Defense, June 4, 1985.

[DoD-Std-2167A, 1988] Military Standard: Defense System Software, Development, DoD-Std-2167A, U.S. Department of Defense, Feb. 29, 1988.

[DoD-Std-7935A, 1988] Functional Description (FD), DoD Automated Information Systems (AIS) Documentation Standards, DoD-Std-7935A, U.S. Department of Defense, Oct. 31, 1988, pp. 19–37.

[Hubble, 1983] Science Operations Concept, Part 1 (Final), Space Telescope Science Institute, Prepared for NASA Goddard Space Flight Center, Greenbelt, MD, May 1983.

[Lano, 1988] Lano, R.J., "A Structured Approach For Operational Concept Formulation (OCF)," TRW-SS-80-02, TRW Systems Engineering and Integration Division, Redondo Beach, Calif., Jan. 1980. Also in *Tutorial: Software Engineering Project Management*, edited by R. Thayer, Computer Society Press, Los Alamitos, Calif., 1988.

Appendix A

Outline for a Concept of Operations Document

Software System Engineering:
An Engineering Process

Richard H. Thayer
California State University, Sacramento
Sacramento, CA 95819

Abstract

This article describes the application of system engineering principles to the development of a software system. This application, called software system engineering, is the concept that combines the management and technical activities that control cost, schedule, and technical achievement of the developing software system. This article recognizes the difference between software system engineering and software engineering, just as system engineering is recognized as being different from hardware engineering (all types).

In this article, the software development process is partitioned into five general activities: problem definition, solution analysis, process planning, process control, and product evaluation. Tools that support these activities are described and are related to system engineering functions.

Key Words—code and component testing, problem definition, process control, process planning, product evaluation, software design, software integration, software requirements generation, software system engineering, software system testing, solution analysis, system definition, system engineering

1. Introduction

This article describes the application of system engineering principles to the development of a computer software system. The activities, tasks, and procedures that make up the principles are known as *software system engineering*. The purpose of this article is to separate proper system engineering processes from software component engineering processes so that the principles and procedures of system engineering can be applied to software development.

Software system engineering (SwSE) is the technical management of a software development. It is the concept that combines the management and technical activities that control the cost, schedule, and technical achievement of the software system. SwSE applies the procedures, practices, technologies, and know-how of system engineering along with the technical process of software engineering, and ensures that the highest quality software product is produced within cost and schedule constraints. *Know-how* means the skill, background, and wisdom to apply knowledge effectively in practice.

This article recognizes the difference between SwSE and software engineering, just as system engineering is recognized as being different from hardware engineering (all types). SwSE supports the premise that the quality of a software product depends on the quality of the process used to create it. *The products of both system engineering and SwSE are documents.* This is in contrast to hardware (component) engineering, in which the products are the devices or components being produced, and software engineering, in which the products are computer programs (software) and the documentation necessary to use, operate, and maintain them.

Software system engineering is not a job description; it is a process. Software system engineering can be done by many organizations and people: system engineers, managers, software engineers, programmers, and, not to be ignored, customers and users. Many practitioners consider SwSE to be a special case of system engineering. Others consider SwSE to be the dominant discipline for computer-based systems.

System engineering and SwSE are often overlooked in a software development project. Systems that are all software and/or run on commercial, off-the-shelf computers are often considered just software projects, not system projects, and no effort is expended to develop a system engineering approach. Ignoring the systems aspects of the project often results in software that will not run on the hardware selected, will not integrate with hardware and other software systems, and frequently contributes to the so-called "software crisis."[1,2]

1.1. The Role of Software in Systems

The dominant technology in many technical systems is software. *Software often provides the cohesiveness and control of data that enable the system to solve problems.* Software also provides the flexibility to work around hardware or other problems, particularly those discovered late in the development cycle.

Figure 1[3] illustrates the concept that it is software that ties system elements together. For this reason, software is frequently a more complex part of any system and is often the technical challenge. In this example, software is what makes a combination of radar, people, radios, airplanes, communications, and other equipment work together to provide an air traffic control system. It is also noted that "management information systems (MIS)" are software systems that tie organizational entities together.

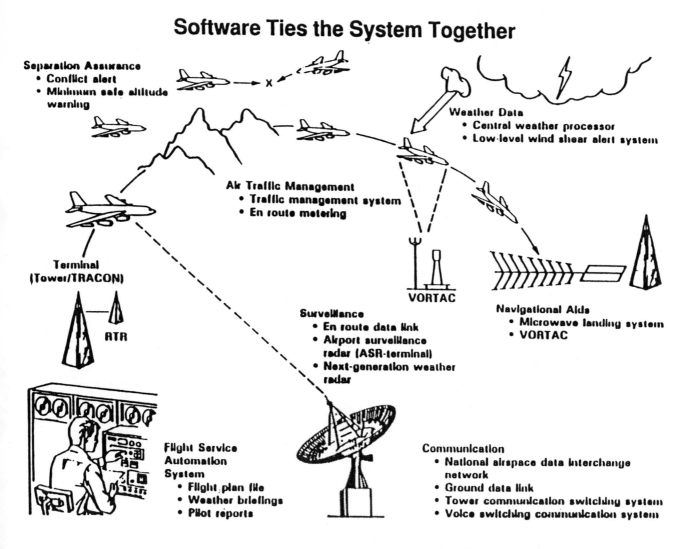

Figure 1. Software ties the system together. (Credit: Logicon, Incorporated.)

1.2. Scope of Software System Engineering

Software system engineering is a necessary activity regardless of the type of software that is being developed. Software system engineering can be applied to commercial, scientific, or military software projects, both in real-time and batch systems. The ability to apply SwSE is not restricted by the size or complexity of the software product. Software system engineering covers the total life cycle.

Software system engineering is applicable in system development under a number of different hardware/software configurations:

1. Systems in which software is not a technical challenge: Software engineering and production costs are small in comparison with hardware engineering and hardware production costs

2. Systems in which software is the technical challenge and dominant technical feature of the system (sometimes called "software-intensive systems"): The cost of software engineering and production is minor in comparison with hardware production costs

3. Systems in which software is the technical challenge and dominant cost of the system (often called "software systems")

Software system engineering is most valuable under configurations 2 and 3 above. Under configuration 1, SwSE plays a very minor role (once it has been determined that software is not dominant). In configuration 2, system engineering and SwSE should work together with full recognition that many crucial decisions fall under SwSE. *Unfortunately, the dominant cost of hardware components focuses management's attention on hardware rather than software.* This often results in:

- Selection of hardware too early in the development cycle (when the software requirements are analyzed, the selected hardware turns out to be inappropriate).
- Poor cost and schedule estimates for software
- Inappropriate hardware–software allocation
- Software development started late in the development cycle
- Software cost and schedule overruns
- Software problems being ignored until they become a crisis

Equally important (from a software engineering viewpoint) is configuration 3, where SwSE is the system engineering discipline.

1.3. Why Is Software System Engineering Necessary?

More and more new systems are being developed today, and many of these new systems are highly dependent on properly operating software systems. *Thus software is larger and more complex now than at any time in history.* This trend is caused by:

- The availability of cheap computer hardware, which motivates system requirements
- More and more system solutions being provided by software rather than hardware
- Increased software complexity caused by increased system complexity
- Customers who want more reliable and usable software systems
- Customers who want the capability and flexibility of software (which can only be applied if built into the software system)

As a result, software development costs are growing and software takes much longer to build. These extremely large and complex systems require technical system management and the oversight of system engineering. Without this system engineering approach the following problems often result:

- Complex software systems become unmanageable
- Costs are overrun and schedules are missed
- Unacceptable risks are sometimes taken
- Unacceptable system engineering procedures (or none at all) are used
- Erroneous decisions are made early in the life cycle that prove very costly in the end
- Subsystems and components that are developed independently do not integrate properly
- Parts and components never get built or requirements are not met
- The delivered system fails to work properly
- Parts of the system must be reworked after delivery (called maintenance)

Software system engineering is necessary in order to build the "new order" of computer-dependent systems now being sought by government and industry.

1.4. Definitions

A *system* is a collection of elements related in a way that allows the accomplishment of some common objective. The key words are *related* and *a common objective*. Unrelated terms and elements without a common objective would not be a system but parts of other systems. This concept is illustrated in Figure 2.

A *man-made system* is a collection of hardware, software, people, facilities, procedures, and other factors organized to accomplish a common objective. A *software system* is, therefore, a man-made system that consists of a collection of programs and documents that together allow the accomplishment of a set of requirements with software.

System engineering (SE) is the application of scientific and engineering efforts to (1) transform an operational need into a system description and performance parameters through the use of an iterative process of definition, analysis, synthesis, design, test, and evaluation; (2) integrate related technical parameters and ensure compatibility of all related functional and program interfaces in a manner that optimizes the total system definition and design; and (3) integrate reliability, maintainability, safety, survivability, human factors, and other such considerations into the total engineering effort to meet cost, schedule, and technical performance objectives.[4]

Software system engineering is related to SE and is likewise both a technical and management process. The *technical process* of SwSE is the analytical effort necessary to transform an operational need into a description of a software system; a software design of the proper size, configuration, and quality; its documentation in requirements and design specifications; the procedures necessary to verify, test, and accept the finished product; and the documentation necessary to use, operate, and maintain the system.

Software engineering is:

- The practical application of computer science, management, and other sciences to the analysis, design, construction, and maintenance of software and its associated documentation

- An engineering science that applies the concepts of analysis, design, coding, testing, documentation, and management to the successful completion of large, custom-built computer programs under constraints of time and budget

- The systematic application of methods, tools, and techniques to achieve a stated requirement or objective for an effective and efficient software system

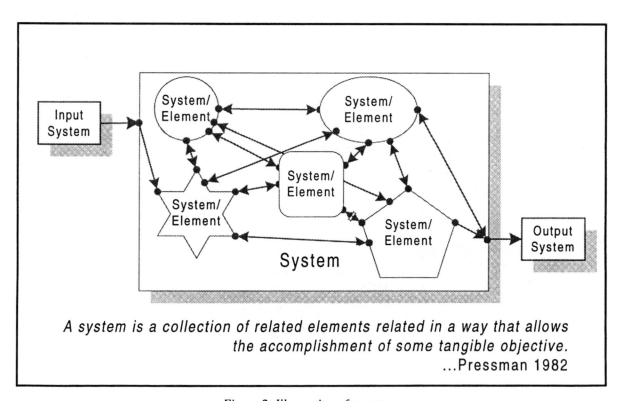

A system is a collection of related elements related in a way that allows the accomplishment of some tangible objective.
...Pressman 1982

Figure 2. Illustration of a system.

Figure 3 illustrates the relationships between system engineering, software system engineering, and software engineering. Initial analysis and design and final system integration and testing are done by the traditional SE. During the initial stages of developing the software, SwSE is responsible for software requirements analysis and architectural design. Software system engineering is also responsible for the final testing of the software system. Finally, the component design for the system is called *software engineering*.

The *management process* involves assessing the risks and costs of the software system, establishing a master schedule, integrating the various engineering specialties and design groups, maintaining configuration control, and continuously auditing the effort to ensure that cost and schedule are met and technical requirements objectives are satisfied.[5]

Figure 4 illustrates the relationships between project management, software system engineering, and software engineering. Project management has overall management responsibility for the project and authority to commit resources. Software system engineering has the responsibility for determining the technical approach, making technical decisions, interfacing with the technical customer, and approving and accepting the final software product. Software engineering is responsible for developing the software design, coding the design, and developing software configuration items (subsystems).

1.5. Role of Software System Engineering

Software system engineering is responsible for the overall technical management of the system and the verification of the final system products. It is responsible for the activities and tasks listed in Table 1. This is not meant to be an all-inclusive list but to give some knowledge of the types of tasks and responsibilities of SwSE.

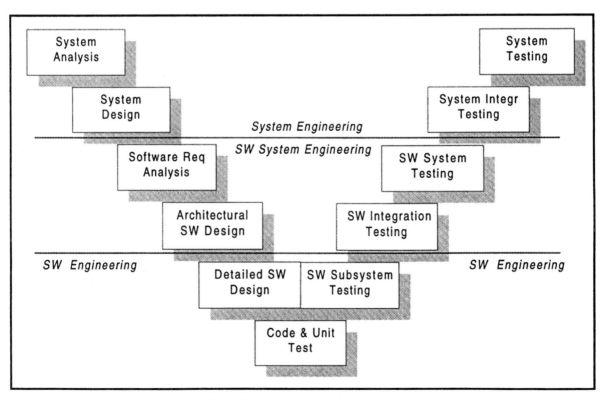

Figure 3. Engineering relationships.

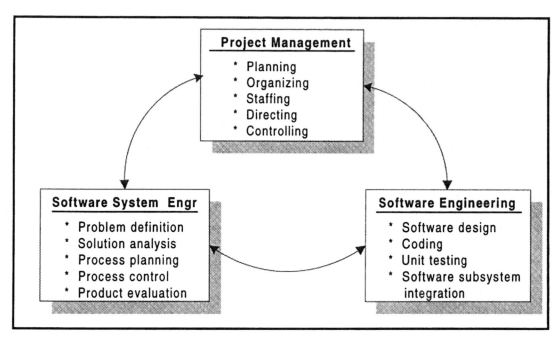

Figure 4. Management relationships.

Table 1. Activities and Tasks of Software System Engineering

Interface technically with the customer	Manage interface control working group
Determine project effort and schedule	Develop verification and validation procedures and plans
Determine technical risk	
Define and document requirements	Develop testing plans, procedures, and cases
Perform requirements functional analysis and flowdown	Establish standards, practices, and methodologies
Determine system data throughput and storage	Conduct external and internal reviews
Perform trade-off studies and time-line analysis	Verify and audit technical products
Develop prototypes	Manage software system configuration and change
Design and document top-level system architecture	Identify technology needs
Define and document technical interfaces	Manage subcontractor technical direction

1.6. Overview of Article

As discussed in Section 1.3, SwSE can be used in a number of different circumstances and hardware/software configurations. The principal viewpoint of this article is the application of SE to hardware/software systems in which software is the technical challenge (configuration 2). Many of the SwSE procedures can be applied to configuration 1, and most of them can be applied to configuration 3.

This article provides guidance for project managers, software engineers, analysts, or students in the procedures and documentation necessary to accomplish the SwSE process in software development. It separates the required activities from the optional activities requirements, environment, and/or circumstances surrounding the project.

This article uses a simplified life-cycle development process (model), called a *waterfall chart*,[6] as the framework to discuss the activities and tasks of SwSE. (These concepts are equally applicable to System Engineering.) These activities and tasks are identified as a series of individual processes in each phase of the software development. The characteristic activities and tasks for each process are analyzed and defined.

Section 2 discusses the functions and activities of SE and SwSE. Section 3 lists and describes the various tools and techniques of SE and SwSE. Section 4 describes the SwSE approach as a step-by-step process.

2. Software Systems Engineering

2.1. System Engineering

System engineering is the practical application of scientific, engineering, and management skills to transform a user's need into a description of a system configuration that best satisfies that need in an effective and efficient way. The product of SE is documents, not operational hardware and software.

According to H.C. Alberts, a professor at the Defense System Management College (Fort Belvoir, Virginia) who teaches SE, the term *system engineering* was first proposed in 1956 by H. Hitch, Chairman of the Aeronautical Engineering Department at Pennsylvania State University.[7] Hitch was trying to develop an engineering discipline that could concentrate on the development of large systems that used many diverse engineering disciplines. These system development efforts were typically for long-term systems.

2.2. Software System Engineering

The practical application of SE is to transform a user's need into a description of a software system configuration that best satisfies that need in an effective and efficient way. The term *software system engineering* is credited to Dr. Winston W. Royce, an early leader in software engineering, in the early 1980s.[8]

2.3. Functions of System and Software Engineering

System engineering involves (note that the term in parentheses is the typical name given to this function in SwSE):

- *Problem definition (requirements analysis)*—Determines needs and constraints through analyzing the requirements and interfacing with the customer
- *Solution analysis (design)*—Determines the set of possible ways of satisfying the requirements and constraints; studies and analyzes the possible solutions; and selects the optimum one
- *Process planning*—Determines the cost of the product, the delivery schedule, and methods of controlling the project and product
- *Process control*—Establishes process, reviews progress and intermediate products, and takes corrective action when necessary
- *Product evaluation (verification, validation, and testing)*—Tests, demonstrates, and analyzes the final product and documentation

System engineering (SE) is the overall technical management of a system development project.

2.4. Problem Definition (Requirements Analysis)

Determines needs and constraints through analyzing the requirements and interfacing with the customer. Specifically, SE must:

- Identify "what" the system must do (without assuming "how" it will be accomplished)
- Prepare a concept of operations (ConOps) document if not already done
- Develop specifications (system and software)
- Define documentation requirements
- Define requirements baseline

Some of the tools that are useful in supporting this effort are as follows (see Section 3 for a complete description):

- *Concept of operations (ConOps) document*—Describes the overall systems characteristics from an operational (user's) viewpoint
- *Specifications*—Documentation of requirements and constraints that satisfy the mission "needs"
- *Baseline*—A formal description of a system product that has been accepted and agreed on by all parties concerned with the system product
- *Work breakdown structures (WBS)*—A tool for representing relationships
- *Functional flow block diagrams (FFBD)*—A tool for "roughing out" the major functions and their interfaces
- *Data flow diagrams*—A tool for representing dependencies
- *N-squared (N^2) charts*—An aid to establishing and representing system and subsystem interfaces
- *Timeline analysis*—Depicts the concurrence, overlap, and sequential relationship of time-critical functions and related tasks
- *Prototyping models*—Demonstrates potential requirements (and design) to the user
- *Test compliance matrix*—A representation method for displaying which methods will be used to verify ("test") each software requirement

2.5. Solution Analysis (Design)

Solution analysis determines the set of possible ways of satisfying the requirements and constraints; studies and analyzes the possible solutions; and selects the optimum one. Specifically, SE must:

- Answer the "how" question (conceptual design)
- Postulate possible technical approaches
- Determine all technology selection factors and risks
- Conduct trade-offs of alternative approaches to the "how" question
- Select the best combination of system elements to determine a solution that will meet users' objectives and support requirements
- Determine if additional analysis, synthesis, or trade-off studies are required to make selections
- Develop system specifications
- Identify the physical interfaces
- Assure traceability of requirements

Some of the tools that are useful in supporting this effort are as follows (see Section 3 for a complete description):

- *Work breakdown structures (WBS)*—A tool for representing the components of a system or the activities of a process (or both)
- *Internal specifications*—Internal technical documents
- *Interface control*—Method for controlling the system and software interfaces
- *Trade studies*—A formal decision analysis method

2.6. Process Planning

Process planning is used to determine the amount of effort to develop, deliver, and control the project and product. Specifically, SE must:

- Plan the engineering workload
- Determine project effort and schedule
- Determine technical and managerial risks
- Establish planning and control methods
- Select standards and practices for development
- Update plans when necessary

Some of the tools that are useful in supporting this effort are as follows (see Section 3 for a complete description):

- *System life-cycle model*—A representation of the steps and activities necessary to develop a software system
- *Work breakdown structures (WBS)*—A tool for representing relationships
- *Cost-estimation models*—a predictive cost-estimation tool based on statistical science (rather than intuition)
- *Computer-aided project management tools*—Automated tools in support of project management activities
- *Risk assessment*—Identifying areas of potential risk with the associated probability of occurrence and seriousness

2.7. Process Control

Process control establishes process, reviews progress and intermediate products, and takes corrective action when necessary. Specifically, SE must:

- Establish standards and procedures for development
- Measure progress and intermediate product quality
- Evaluate the development process
- Develop the integration and system test plans
- Conduct in-process design reviews
- Take corrective action if process fails to meet plan or standard

Some of the tools that are useful in supporting this effort are as follows (see Section 3 for a complete description):

- *Baseline management*—Partitions the project into manageable phases: requirements, design, implementation, and test
- *Configuration management*—Controlling the documents
- *Quality assurance*—A set of procedures and methods for verifying the products and processes of a systems development
- *Verification and validation*—A rigorous methodology for evaluating the correctness and quality of the software

- *Technical performance measurements (TPM)*—Measuring essential performance parameters
- *Interface control working groups (ICWG)*—Controlling the interfaces
- *Requirements tracing tool*—A mechanism for tracking requirements to finished product
- *Design reviews/audits*—A periodic check on progress

2.8. Product Evaluation (Verification, Validation, and Testing)

Product evaluation tests, demonstrates, and analyzes the final product and documentation. Specifically, SE must:

- Evaluate the final product
- Verify that the product requirements have been met
- Provide project historical data

Some of the tools that are useful in supporting this effort are as follows (see Section 3 for a complete description):

- Test compliance matrix—A representation method for displaying which methods will be used to verify ("test") each software requirement
- *Verification and validation*—An SwSE process that implements a rigorous methodology for evaluating the correctness and quality of the software throughout the life cycle
- *Testing*—The controlled exercise of the program code in order to expose errors
- *Verification*—A group term that includes those methods and procedures that are used to "prove" that the system performs as required

3. Software System Engineering Process

This section of the article describes the SwSE approach as a step-by-step process. Five major steps are listed:

- System definition phase
- Software requirements engineering phase
- Software design
- Code and component testing phase
- Integration and system testing phase

In several instances the major process is divided into two subprocesses, for example, the system definition phase is partitioned into the system analysis and the system design subphases. Each phase and subphase is composed of:

- Inputs
- Processes
- Outputs
- Control gates

Some of the steps are run together. If two similar activities are performed at the same time, or by the same organizational entity, or they have a common input or output, they will be discussed as the same step.

3.1. System Definition Phase

The purpose of the SE phase is to determine a functional and performance description of the final system (that is, determine the requirements) and to separate those requirements that can best be solved by software from those that should be solved by hardware or manual procedures.

The system definition phase is initiated when it is recognized that a problem exists, which can best be solved by building and operating a software-driven system. It is terminated when the system requirements are known, a decision has been made as to top-level (preliminary) architecture of the system, the system requirements baseline is determined, and the various planning activities are completed.

The following sections describe each of the processes in the system definition phase.

3.1.1. System Analysis and Specifications

3.1.1.1. Inputs

(1) *System needs and requirements*—A statement, either oral or written, that establishes the needs and/or requirements for the system

(2) *External environment*—The circumstances, objects, and conditions that surround the system to be built; they include political, market, cultural, organizational, and physical influences as well as standards and policies that govern what the system must do or how it will do it

(3) *Standards and policies*—Corporate instruction on methods and approaches to

provide general guidance on the system and software development

(4) *Statement of work (SOW)*—A description of all the work required to complete a project

3.1.1.2. Process

(1) Determine the system needs and/or requirements. Develop requirements specifications.

The first step in any system activity is to investigate, determine, and document the system requirements in a system requirements specification (SysRS) and/or a software requirements specification (SRS).

A *system requirement* is (1) a system capability needed by a user to solve a problem or achieve an objective, and/or (2) a system capability that must be met or possessed by a system or system component to satisfy a contract, standard, specification, or other formally imposed document.[9]

Regardless of the mix of hardware, software, or manual procedures, the resulting document is usually called a *system requirements specification*.

A system requirements specification (SRS) is frequently the initial document prepared in a technical development—software or nonsoftware—that sets forth the requirements for a system or portion of a system (sometimes called a *system segment*). It is a written document that describes in detail what is needed to satisfy the customers' and users' needs. Typically included are functional requirements and external interfaces, as well as performance requirements (sometimes called *mission requirements*), design constraints, and quality attributes of the finished system. System requirements specifications are sometimes referred to simply as *system specifications*.

One of the most important sources of system requirements is the concept of operations (ConOps) document. In SE/SwSE, the ConOps document is normally produced as the first step in the system definition phase of a given program. The ConOps document should be (but is not always) prepared by the customer or buyer.

(2) Generate and document management and technical plans and strategies. Perform risk management.

Concurrently with the development of the system requirements, management plans are generated and documented. The system management plan provides management and control of the project from the beginning through product delivery and sign-off. As part of the planning effort, perform risk assessment and develop a risk management plan for the project.

The *system engineering management plan* (SEMP) is a management document written by the system developer that identifies the technical plans, organizational configuration, functions and responsibilities, management techniques, analysis, simulations, technical performance measurement parameters, and schedules that will be initiated, tracked, or employed on the program. The SEMP is supported by a number of specialty plans such as the activities in specific critical areas (example: software project management plan), and, together with these plans, serves as a top-level technical management master plan.[10]

(3) Develop verification, validation, and preliminary test plan for the system. Generate a test compliance matrix.

The verification and validation (V&V) plan defines the V&V activities and tasks at each software life-cycle phase, identifies the development products necessary to verify the ongoing process, and establishes criteria for starting and stopping each V&V activity. In addition, V&V planning includes selecting the most cost-effective V&V tools and techniques for each phase and developing an organization and staff to accomplish the plan.

Included in the V&V plan, or developed separately, is the preliminary test plan, which is derived from the requirements specifications. The test (verify) compliance matrix will demonstrate that all requirements can be verified. Requirements that cannot be verified will be eliminated or changed to a form that can be verified.

(4) Establish a configuration management system and software quality assurance plan.

A configuration management (CM) system applicable to the project is developed and documented. Individuals responsible for CM are identified.

Standards and procedures applicable to the customer, project, and development organization are developed or adopted from another source. A software quality assurance (SQA) system is selected. An SQA plan is written, and individuals responsible for SQA are identified

(5) Verify the system requirements. Perform peer reviews on the software products.

Using the V&V plan developed earlier, the system requirements are verified against the customers requirements and needs. The ConOps document, if available, should be used to represent the customer's needs and requirements. Perform peer reviews (inspections and walkthroughs) on the software products. Pay particular attention to those products (software requirements, risk management plan) that are the most critical.

(6) Review the products of the phase and obtain joint concurrence among developers, customers, and users.

The system requirements specifications and other products of the system requirements phase are reviewed by an appropriate review team composed of the developers, customers, and potential users of the system. This is a major milestone review called the system requirements review (SRR). If the SRR and other phase products are found to be acceptable the developers are permitted to proceed to the system design phase.

(7) Produce the system requirements baseline and place under configuration management.

At the completion of an acceptable SRR, the system requirements specifications are baselined as the functional baseline and placed under CM.

3.1.1.3. Outputs

(1) *System requirements specifications*—Describes the system specifications

(2) *Interface requirements specifications*—Describes the system interface requirements, if not part of the system requirements specifications

(3) *Test compliance matrix*—Used during the requirements phase to determine if the requirements are testable and during the testing phase to define what test to use on which requirements

(4) *System engineering management plan*—Used throughout the project to monitor and control the project

(5) *Risk management plan*—To identify the high-risk tasks in order to avoid or prevent risks with the highest probability of occurrence

(6) *Configuration management plans*—A plan for controlling changes to the system baseline

(7) *System requirements baseline*—The baseline that describes the system requirements

3.1.1.4. Control Gates

(1) *System requirements review*—An acceptable SRR will permit the project to proceed to the system design phase

3.1.2. System Design

3.1.2.1. Inputs

(1) *System requirements specifications*—A description of the to-be-delivered system

(2) *Interface requirements specifications*—A description of the necessary interfaces to the external world

(3) *System engineering management plan*—A plan as to how the system will be developed and delivered

3.1.2.2. Process

(1) Determine how best to implement the requirements. Perform trade studies and time-line analysis.

Conduct engineering studies on the most effective and efficient design for the system. Use trade studies (also called trade-off analysis) to define the best design trading off cost, schedule, performance, and risk. Use time-line analysis to ensure that the performance of the system meets timing requirements.

(2) Develop top-level system design and interface requirements. Allocate system requirements to top-level components.

Use results of engineering studies to design the optimum system. Partition the requirements into major system components (called *configuration items*). These configuration items can be all hardware, all software, or a mixture. Allocate all requirements to one or more of these configuration items. Derive new requirements where necessary to achieve system requirements.

(3) Develop preliminary software system requirements and interface specifications.

Describe software configuration items in a preliminary software requirements specification. Identify the interfaces between the software system and external entities and between configuration items. Use the N^2 charts as an interface design and representation tool.

(4) Verify the system design.

Using the V&V plan developed earlier, verify the system against the system requirements.

(5) Review the products of the phase and obtain joint concurrence among developers, customers, and users.

The system design specifications and other products of the system design phase are reviewed by an appropriate review team composed of the developers, customers, and potential users of the system. This is a major milestone review called the system design review (SDR). If the system design and other phase products are found to be acceptable the developers are permitted to proceed on to the software requirements phase.

(6) Update the system requirements baseline; produce the system design baseline; and place under configuration management.

At the completion of an acceptable SRR, the system design specifications are baselined in the allocated baseline and placed under CM. Any changes in the system requirements specifications are noted and forwarded to the appropriate configuration control authority.

3.1.2.3. Output

(1) *System design description*—Describes the system design

(2) *System interface design description*—Describes the system interface design, if not part of the system design specifications

(3) *Preliminary software requirements specifications*—Describes the software requirements

(4) *Preliminary software interface requirements*—Describes the software interfaces, if not part of the software requirements specifications

(5) *System design baseline (allocated baseline)*—The baseline that describes the top-level system design

3.1.2.4. Control Gates

(1) *System design review (SDR)*—An acceptable SDR will permit the project to proceed to the software requirements phase

3.2. Software Requirements Generation Phase

The purpose of the software requirements generation phase is to define the software requirements and interface specifications in sufficient detail to allow the software designer to design the software system accurately.

The software requirements generation phase is initiated when customer and user requirements have been properly identified, a top-level system design is complete, software subsystems are identified, and all customer/user requirements have been properly allocated (assigned) to one or more of these subsystems. The phase ends when the software requirements are known and documented for each software subsystem, the preliminary user manual is written, the verification, validation, and test documents are developed, and a software requirements baseline is identified and accepted by the developers, customers, and users.

The following sections describe each of the processes in the software requirements generation phase.

3.2.1. Inputs

(1) *System design description*—Describes the system design

(2) *System interface design description*—Describes the system interface design if not part of the system design specifications

(3) *Preliminary software requirements specifications*—Describes the software requirements

(4) *Preliminary software interface requirements*—Describes the software interfaces, if not part of the software requirements specifications

(5) *System engineering management plan*—A plan as to how the system will be developed and delivered

3.2.2. Process

(1) Establish a software requirements specification for each software subsystem.

Flowdown the system requirements to the software configuration items (CIs) that had previously been identified by the system design process. Software requirements can be identified as belonging to one or several different categories[11]:

- *Functional requirements*—A requirement specifying functions that a system or system component must be capable of performing

- *Performance requirements*—A requirement specifying performance characteristics that a system or system component must possess, such as speed, accuracy, frequency

- *External interface requirements*—A requirement specifying hardware, software, or database elements that a system or system component must interface, or setting forth constraints on formats, timing, or other factors caused by such an interface

- *Design constraints*—A requirement affecting or constraining the design of a software system or software system component, for example, language requirements, physical hardware requirements, software development standards, and software quality assurance standards

- *Quality attributes*—A requirement specifying the degree to which software possesses attributes that affects quality; such as correctness, reliability, maintainability, portability

(2) Develop external software interfaces. Establish an interface control working group (ICWG).

Identify and document the external interfaces between software CIs and other outside entities (either hardware or other software systems) and internal interfaces between software CIs. Establish an ICWG (or equivalent organization) to maintain the interfaces. All changes to any interface must be approved by the ICWG.

(3) Trace requirements between top-level requirements and software requirements.

Using the requirements tracing system, trace and document the forward and backward trace between a system design (the source) and the software requirements (the results). Document the results in a requirements tracing report and present it in the software specifications review.

(4) Write a software project management plan.

Concurrently with the development of the software requirements, a software management plan is generated and documented. The software management plan provides the management and control of the project from the project beginning through product delivery and sign-off.

The *software project management plan* (sometimes called the *software development plan* or *software engineering project plan*) is the controlling document for managing a software project.[12] A software project management plan (SPMP) defines the technical and managerial functions, activities, and tasks necessary to satisfy the requirements of a software project, as defined in the project agreement. All other management plans (configuration management plan, software quality assurance plan, and so on) are considered to be part of the software project management plan.

Perform risk assessment and develop a risk management plan for the software project.

(5) Write a preliminary software user manual.

The *user manual* (UM) is a document prepared by the developer and used to provide the customer and/or user personnel with the necessary instructions on how to use and operate the software system. The manual contents and format are specifically designed to meet the needs of the intended users.

The preliminary user manual is developed early in the software development process for the following reasons:

- It provides a description of the software system in the user's own terms. (This is applicable only to software systems that are not transparent to the user. In other words, the user is aware that the software system is performing its functions.)

- It provides a means of verifying the software requirements. The user manual is prepared from the software requirements specifications because the requirements specifications describe the finished system. If the software requirements specifications contain errors of omission, incompleteness, or incorrectness, these errors will likely be discovered by the users during their review of the user manual.[13]

- It provides guidance to designers on how to make a system usable and assists in writing test documents.

(6) Develop test documentation for the system and acceptance testing.

The software V&V test plan and procedures started during the system definition phase are completed during the software requirements generation phase. Plans and procedures are added on how to verify many of the nonfunctional requirements, such as performance, external interfaces, design constraints, and quality attributes.

Preliminary V&V test documents like those described below are developed for each software subsystem and identified by a separate software requirement specification:

- *Test plan*—A document describing the scope, approach, resources, and schedule of intended testing activities. It identifies test items, the features to be tested, the testing tasks, who will do each task, and any risks requiring contingency planning. It also determines what, when, and how the software will be tested and defines the pass/fail criteria

- *Test design specification*—A document specifying the details of the test approach for a software feature or combination of software features and identifies the associated tests. It shows in detail what items will to be tested

- *Test procedure specification*—A document specifying a sequence of actions for the execution of a test. It is a step-by-step description of the process of testing

- *Test case specification*—A document specifying inputs, predicted results, and a set of execution conditions for a test item. It defines the input and output data used in the test[14]

This form of testing that is based only on the software requirements specifications is called *black-box testing* (also called *functional testing*). Black-box testing is a software test strategy that derives its test specifications and case data from the external specifications and requirements of the system. This is in contrast to *white-box testing,* in which the internals of the code are specifically exercised. Methods for black-box testing include nominal testing (expected values), random testing, and testing at boundary values (both inside and outside the boundaries). It verifies the end results at the system level but does not check on how the system is implemented. It also does not assume that all statements in the program are executed. A good test document should include both black-box and white-box testing.

The preliminary test documents are developed early in the software development process to accomplish several things:

- They provide a means of verifying the software requirements. The test documents are prepared from the requirements specifications because the requirements specifications describe the finished system. In the event the software requirements specification contains errors of omission, incompleteness, or incorrectness, this will likely be discovered by the test developers early in the life cycle. No requirement is complete until its testability has been demonstrated in a test planning document.

- The engineering exercise that goes into developing a test suite is similar to the exercise that goes into engineering the software system (see Table 2). When the system testers are independent of the software developers, a fresh examination of the software requirements can frequently uncover overlooked requirements, ambiguous statements, and other errors.

(7) Verify the software requirements and interface documents.

In this phase, the software requirement specifications are verified against the system requirements and the architectural design. The verification function looks for bad software requirements—incorrect, incomplete, ambiguous, or untestable—and noncompliance with the system functional and nonfunctional requirements.

Some of the tools and procedures used by V&V in this phase include requirements traceability analysis, requirements evaluation, requirements interface analysis, and test planning.[15] Some additional tools are control flow analysis, data flow analysis, algorithm analysis, simulation analysis, in-process audits, and requirements walkthroughs.

Development documents	Testing documents
Project management plan	Test plan
Requirements specifications	Test design specifications
Design specifications	Test procedure specifications
Coding	Testing
Applications data	Test case specifications

(8) Review the products of the phase and obtain joint concurrence among developers, customers, and users.

A *software specification review* (SSR) is a milestone review conducted to finalize software requirements so that the software developer can initiate top-level software design. The SSR is conducted when software requirements have been sufficiently defined to evaluate the developer's responsiveness to and interpretation of the system/segment-level technical requirements. A successful SSR will be predicated on the customer's and/or developer's determination that the software requirements specification and interface specifications form a satisfactory basis for proceeding into top-level design phase.[16]

(9) Produce the software requirements baseline and place under configuration control.

The *software requirements baseline* is the initial software configuration identification established at the end of the software requirements generation phase. This baseline is established by an approved software requirements and interface specification and placed under formal configuration control by joint agreement between the developer and the customer. Department of Defense developers would call this the *software allocated baseline*.

3.2.3. Outputs

(1) *Software requirements and interface specifications*—Describes the software system and interface specifications

(2) *Preliminary user manual*—Describes the actions the software user must take to effectively use the system

(3) *Preliminary test documents*—Defines the test plans, test specifications, test process, and test cases for the system and acceptance tests

(4) *Software project management plan*—Used throughout the project to monitor and control the project

(5) *Software requirements baselines*—The baseline that describes the software requirements

3.2.4. Control Gates

(1) *Software specifications review (SSR)*—An acceptable SSR will permit the project to proceed to the software design phase

3.3. Software Design Phase

The purpose of the software design phase is to design the software system in sufficient detail so that the subsystem can be correctly programmed (coded) and tested.

The software design phase is initiated when software requirements have been properly identified and documented and the draft user manual and draft test documents have been developed. This phase ends when the software design documentation is judged to be complete and correct by a formal review, the preliminary operator and maintenance manuals are written, and a product baseline is established.

The following sections describe each of the processes in the software design phase.

3.3.1. Architectural Design

3.3.1.1. Inputs

(1) *Software requirements specifications*—Describes the system specifications

(2) *Software interface requirements specifications*—Describes the system interface requirements, if not part of the system requirements specifications

(3) *Software requirements baselines*—Describes the software requirements baseline

3.3.1.2. Process

(1) Allocate system requirements to top-level software components (configuration items). Complete the final system trade studies. Produce a software architectural design description.

Software design is the process of designing a system by identifying its major components, decomposing them into their low-level components, and iterating until the desired level of detail is achieved. *Architectural design* (sometimes called *top-level design* or *preliminary design*) typically includes definition and structuring of computer program components and data, definition of the interfaces, and preparation of timing and sizing estimates.

The product of architectural design is the architectural design description (or specification). Architectural design description includes such information as the

- Overall processing architecture
- Functions allocated to lowest level (but not described in detail)

- Data flow, database, and associated processors
- Control of processing
- System utilities and operating system interfaces
- External and internal interfaces
- Allocated storage and throughput

The design represents a logical satisfaction of the requirements by a specific approach.

(2) Trace requirements from architectural design to software requirements.

Using the requirements tracing system trace and document the forward and backward trace between the software requirements (the source) and the software design (the results). Document the results in a requirements tracing report and present it in the preliminary design review.

(3) Initiate a unit development folder (UDF or software development folder [SDF]).

Initiate a UDF for each "unit" of the software system. The lowest level of the design can be defined as units for the purpose of the UDF. Each UDF will have the allocated software requirements including any assigned design constraints, metrics, and data. Cost and schedule information for the unit is also provided. A WBS is an excellent tool for analyzing the system and determining the lowest level design.

(4) Develop test documentation for integration testing.

The test documents are reviewed and updated where necessary. Test procedures and test case descriptions should be added to test any new capabilities added to the system.

The test procedures developed in the preliminary test documents were concerned primarily with black-box testing. Not all system attributes can be tested completely in that manner. Another method that tests the internal workings of a system is called *white-box testing* (also called *structural testing*), which can be developed after the design is complete.

White-box testing is a software test methodology at the module level in which test procedures and test cases are derived from the internal structure of the program. It may execute all the statements or branches in the program to check on how the system is implemented. Some methods of white-box testing are statement coverage, branch coverage, and path coverage.

Other items that must be updated or developed are the test compliance matrix, which must be updated to account for the "as-designed" configuration, and additional computer systems and hardware needed for checkout.

(5) Verify the software design and interface documents.

In this phase, the software design specifications are verified against the software requirements and the top-level system design. The verification function looks for incomplete or incorrect design, inefficient and unmaintainable design, poor user interfaces, and poor documentation.

The minimum V&V tasks are design traceability analysis, design evaluation, interface analysis, and updating the V&V test plan and test design specifications for component testing, integration testing, system testing, and acceptance testing.[17] The V&V activity then reports the discrepancies found between these levels of life-cycle documents and other major problems.

(6) Review the products of the phase and obtain joint concurrence among developers, customers, and users.

The architectural design description and other products of the software design phase are reviewed by an appropriate review team composed of the developers, customers, and potential users of the system. This is a major milestone review called the preliminary design review (PDR). If the architectural design and other phase products are found to be acceptable the developers are permitted to proceed on to the system design phase.

Special note: The term *architectural design* has gradually replaced the early term *preliminary design* as being more appropriate for the activities involved. The acronym for the "appropriate review" (architectural design review, ADR) did not catch on, so we still use the term *preliminary design review* (PDR) for the architectural design phase review.

(7) Produce the software architectural design baseline and place under configuration control.

The *architectural design baseline* is the top-level product baseline. This baseline is established by an approved software architectural design and interface specification and placed under formal configuration control by joint agreement between the developer and the customer. Many projects do not formally establish this baseline.

3.3.1.3. Outputs

(1) *Software architectural description*—Describes the architectural design

(2) *Software interface design description*—Describes the external interface design

(3) *Unit development folder (UDF)*—A set of unit development folders for each "unit" of design

(4) *Test documentation*—An update of the system and acceptance test documents

3.3.1.4. Control Gates

(1) *Architectural (preliminary) design review (PDR)*—An acceptable PDR will permit the project to proceed to the software design phase

3.3.2. Detailed Design

3.3.2.1. Inputs

(1) *Software architectural description*—Describes the architectural design

(2) *Software interface design description*—Describes the external interface design

(3) *Unit development folder (UDF)*—A set of unit development folders for each "unit" of design

3.3.2.2. Process

(1) Design the detailed-level software system. Maintain the interfaces and traceability.

Detailed design (sometimes called *low-level design*) is the process of refining and expanding the software top-level designs. This allows for more detailed descriptions of the processing logic, data structures, and data definitions, to the extent that the design is complete enough to be implemented (coded).

The product of the detailed design is the detailed design specifications, which describe the exact detailed configuration of a computer program. Each entity (sometimes called module) identified by the architectural design will contain the following information[18]:

- *Identification*—The name of the entity. Two entities shall not have the same name

- *Type*—A description of the kind of entity; for example, subprogram, module, procedure, process, or data store

- *Purpose*—A description of why the entity exists; describes the specific functional and performance requirements for which the entity exists

- *Function*—A statement of what the entity does; for example, a functional attribute shall state the transformation applied by the entity to inputs to produce the desired outputs

- *Subordinates*—The identification of all entities that compose this entity; used to identify parent/child structural relationships

- *Dependencies*—A description of the relationships of this entity with other entities; describes the other entities and conditions under which they either use or are used by the subject entity

- *Interface*—A description of how other entities interact with this entity; describes the methods of interaction and the rules governing those interactions

- *Resources*—A description of the elements used by the entity that are external to the design; identifies and describes all the resources external to the design that are needed to perform its function, for example, physical devices, software services, and processing resources

- *Processing*—A description of the rules used by the entity to achieve its function. A refinement of the functional attribute. Describes the algorithm to perform a specific task and contingencies when necessary

- *Data*—A description of the data elements internal to the entity; describes the method of representing initial values, use, format, and acceptable values

The design can be represented by a continuation of the methodologies started in the top-level design (data flow diagrams, flowcharts, structure charts, PDL, Warnier–Orr charts, and many of the modern CASE tools). Another popular detailed design tool is pseudocode to describe the individual software modules.

(2) Write preliminary operator manual and software maintenance manual.

The preliminary operator and maintenance manuals are preliminary versions of two of the three deliverable documents used to support a software system.

An *operator manual* is a document used by the operators of a system (in contrast to the users) to enable them to support the users and operate the system. On many systems, particularly modern desk-top computers, the operator and the user are the same, and, as a result, the operator and user manuals are combined.

The *maintenance manual* is the legacy the software developers leave to aid future software engineers in maintaining the system. A maintenance manual (sometimes called a *software maintenance document*) is a software engineering project deliverable document that is used to describe the software system to software engineers and programmers who are responsible for maintaining the software in the operation and maintenance phase of the life cycle.

Software maintenance is the performance of those activities required to keep a software system operational and responsive after it is accepted and placed into production.[19] Maintenance includes the modification of the software after delivery to correct faults, improve performance or other quality attributes, or adapt the product to a changed environment.

(3) Update the software verification, validation, and test documents.

The V&V plans and test documents are reviewed and updated where necessary. Test procedures and test case descriptions should be added to test any new capabilities added to the system.

(4) Verify the software design documents.

In this phase, the software detail design specifications are verified against the architectural design software requirements. The verification function looks for incomplete or incorrect design, inefficient and unmaintainable design, poor user interfaces, and poor documentation.

The minimum V&V tasks are design traceability analysis, design evaluation, and interface analysis. The V&V activity then reports the discrepancies found between these levels of life-cycle documents and other major problems.

(5) Review the products of the phase and obtain joint concurrence among developers, customers, and users.

The software design products are reviewed jointly by the developers, customers, and users. The purpose of these reviews is to obtain concurrence on the top-level and detailed design.

The detailed design description and other products of the software design phase are reviewed by an appropriate review team composed of the developers, customers, and potential users of the system. This is a major milestone review called the critical design review (CDR). If the design and other phase products are found to be acceptable the developers are permitted to proceed on to the coding and unit testing phase.

(6) Update the software requirements baselines; produce the build-to software product baseline; and place under development controls.

The software requirements baseline is the initial configuration of the software architecture. The *product baseline* is the final delivered configuration of the system. To distinguish between the product baseline that exists before the product is built, and the product baseline after the product is built, the former is called the "build-to" baseline and the latter is referred to as the "as-built" baseline. The build-to baseline is not placed under formal configuration control, but under development control—a local control maintained by SwSE and administered by the program support librarian.

3.3.2.3. Outputs

(1) *Software detailed design description*—A description of the software detailed design

(2) *Software interface design description*—A description of the internal software interfaces

(3) *Preliminary operator manual*—A draft of the operators manual

(4) *Preliminary maintenance manual*—A draft of the maintenance manual

(5) *Build-to software baseline*—A final product baseline that is to be coded and tested

3.3.2.4. Control Gates

(1) *Detailed (critical) design review (CDR)*—An acceptable CDR will permit the project to proceed to the code and unit testing phase

3.4. Code and Component (Unit) Testing Phase

The purpose of the code and component (frequently called *unit*) testing phase is to code and test the individual software components.

The code and component testing phase is initiated when the software design has been properly identified and documented and the verification procedures have been updated. The phase ends when the design has been transformed into software, the component testing is complete, the product baseline is updated, and the product is ready for final testing and review.

The following sections describe each of the processes in the code and component testing phase.

3.4.1. Inputs

(1) *Software detailed design description*—A description of the detailed design

(2) *Software interface design description*—A description of the internal software interfaces

3.4.2. Process

(1) Implement (code) the software design.

The detailed design is turned into machine-readable code. Programming is performed in accordance with the standards and procedures contained in the software project management plan. Progress and quality are monitored by code walkthroughs.

(2) Test and debug the individual components of the system.

The basic component of a software system is a module or unit. The testing of a unit is normally done by the developer (programmer) of the unit. Unit testing is the process of ensuring that the unit executes as intended. It usually involves testing all statements and branch possibilities (white-box testing). Some of the errors found could be missing design features, design features added but not required, programs that do not handle the proper input data, and unfriendly and difficult user interfaces. Formal testing (sometimes with informal test procedures) is called *unit testing*. Informal unit testing by the programmer is called *debugging*.

Component testing would involve testing larger programs of the system, but would not typically involve integration testing.

(3) Complete the validation and test documentation and prepare for formal testing.

The VV&T documentation is updated to account for the changes in the system made during the implementation phase. V&V and testing procedures are maintained under configuration control, as are software products. The programming support librarian keeps the approved completed copy of the plans, procedures,

test data and test results that have been developed by the project.

(4) Verify the code and other products. Conduct code walkthroughs.

In this phase, the software code is verified against the software top-level and detailed design. The verification function looks for incomplete or incorrect code, inefficient and unmaintainable implementation, poor user interfaces, and poor documentation.

The minimum verification tasks are source code traceability analysis, source code evaluation, software code interface analysis, source code documentation evaluation, continue test case development, and continue test procedure specifications.[20] The verification activity then reports the discrepancies found between these levels of life-cycle documents and other major problems or noncompliances to SwSE.

A *code walkthrough* (sometimes called *inspection* or *peer review*) is a software engineering quality assurance procedure in which a designer or programmer leads one or more members of the development team through a segment of design or code that he or she has written, while other members ask questions and make comments about technique, style, possible errors, violation of development standards, and other problems.

(5) Conduct the test readiness review and obtain concurrence among developers, customers, and users.

A *test readiness review* (TRR) is a milestone review to determine if the software test procedures are complete and to ensure that the software developer is prepared for formal software system testing. The results of any informal testing will also be reviewed. The TRR will be attended by developer, customer, and user representatives. With their concurrence, the developers can proceed to performing integration and testing of the system.

(6) Update the requirements and product (as-built) baseline.

The requirements and product baselines are updated to account for the changes in the system during the implementation phase. The resulting baseline is called the "as-built" product baseline as distinguished from the "build-to" product baseline. The as-built product baseline is placed under formal configuration control.

3.4.3. Outputs

(1) *Tested software at the component (unit)*

level—The completed software system ready for integration testing

(2) *Unit test report*—The results of the unit testing

(3) *"As-built" software baseline*—A final product baseline that has been coded and tested

3.4.4. Control Gates

(1) *Test readiness review (TRR)*—An acceptable TRR will permit the project to proceed to the integration and testing phase

3.5. Integration and System Testing Phase

The purpose of the integration and testing phase is to integrate the components, programs, subsystems, and other interfacing entities into a tested, finished system. This may or may not include acceptance testing. It does not include installation and checkout.

The software system integration and system testing phase is initiated when the code has been developed, software components have been independently verified, and the software is ready for integration and testing. This phase ends when the software system components are integrated into a software system, verified against the software requirements, integrated and verified with the total hardware/software system, the final products are audited, and a software product baseline is identified and accepted by the customers, users, and developers.

The following sections describe each of the processes in the integration and system testing phase.

3.5.1. Software Integration and Testing

3.5.1.1. Inputs

(1) *Tested software*—Software that has been unit tested and is determined to be ready for integration and system testing

3.5.1.2. Process

(1) Integrate the software units and components into larger components and perform integration testing.

Software integration testing involves integrating the components of the software system and testing the integrated system to determine if the system works as required. Integration testing can be either incremental or nonincremental. Incremental testing involves testing a small part of the system and then incrementing the configuration of the system-under-test by adding one component at a time and testing after each increment. Nonincremental testing involves assembling all the components of the system and testing them all at once. Hardware engineers call this the "smoke test," that is, "let's test it all at once and see where the smoke rises." Since software failures don't smoke, it is often difficult to tell where a system has failed when all the components are being tested at one time. Incremental testing has proven to be a more successful approach.

There are two separate strategies to incremental testing: top-down testing and bottom-up testing (see Figure 5). *Top-down testing* is the process of integrating the system-under-test, progressively, from top to bottom, using simulations of low-level components (called *stubs*) during testing to complete the system. This is in contrast to *bottom-up testing*, which is the process of incrementing the system-under-test, progressively, from bottom to top, using software drivers to simulate top-level components during testing.

Each of these strategies has a number of different advantages and disadvantages. Some of these advantages and disadvantages are listed in Table 3.

At first glance, bottom-up testing appears to have the most advantages and least disadvantages. However, advantage 3 under top-down testing and disadvantage 2 under bottom-up testing provide significant management advantages through increased customer satisfaction and visibility of progress, so that top-down testing is often the preferred method.

(2) Conduct software validation and testing in conformance with formal software verification, validation, and testing documents.

In this process, the completed software system is verified against the design and validated against the system and software requirements. Tests are conducted in conformance with formal test documents and the test compliance matrix. As described earlier, *verification* is the process of determining whether or not the products of a given phase of the software development cycle fulfill the requirements established during the previous phase. *Validation* is the process of ensuring that what is built corresponds to what was actually required; it is concerned with the completeness, consistency, and correctness of the requirements.

During the software system testing phase, the software system is verified against the build-to baseline to determine if the final program properly implements the design. At roughly the same time, the software system is tested and validated against the original system and software requirements specification to see if the product was built correctly.

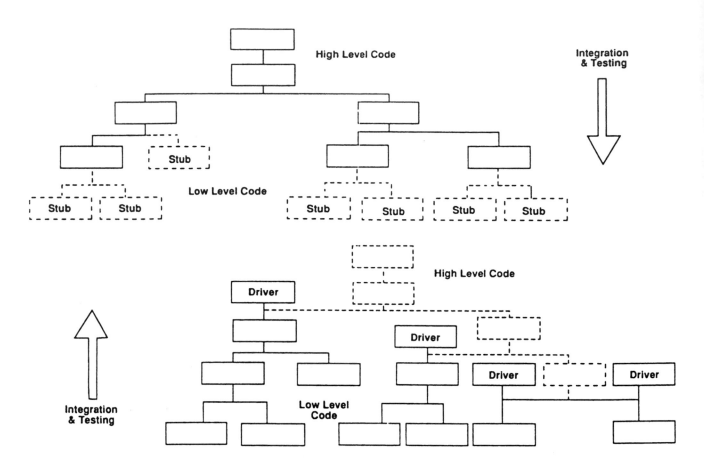

Figure 5. Top-down testing versus bottom-up testing.

Table 3. Comparison of Top-Down versus Bottom-Up Testing[21]

Top-down testing	
Advantages	**Disadvantages**
1. More productive if major flaws occur toward the top of the program.	1. Stub modules must be produced.
2. Representation of test cases is easier.	2. Stub modules are often complicated.
3. Earlier skeletal programs allow demonstration (and improve morale)	3. The representation of test cases in stubs can be difficult.
	4. Observation of test output is more difficult.
Bottom-up testing	
1. More productive if major flaws occur toward the bottom of the program.	1. Driver modules must be produced.
2. Test conditions are easier to create.	2. The program as an entity does not exist until the last module is added.
3. Observation of test results is easier.	

(3) Integrate the software system with the hardware components and conduct system validation in conformance with formal system verification, validation, and test documents.

In this process, the software system is integrated with the hardware components and system integration testing is conducted. This phase does not include acceptance testing unless requested and contracted for. System testing validates the entire software system against system and performance requirements, using a simulated environment and real contrived data. Contrived data are better than "real" data for system testing. This provides "stress" data that might not be received from real sources except in the most unusual circumstances.

When required, qualification or acceptance testing can be conducted by the customer, or by the developer for the customer, to demonstrate that the software meets its specified requirements. Acceptance testing validates the software against acceptance criteria in the users' environment with the final hardware–software configuration.

(4) Complete the user manual, operator manual, and maintenance manual.

The user manual, operator manual, and maintenance manual are also the products of the software development process. The users carry out the system functions; the operators are responsible for facility operation, recovery, periodic backup, and so forth.

The user manual, described earlier, communicates with the users of the system and tells them how to use the software system. The user manual would also include positional handbooks. The operator manual provides instructions on how to operate the system. Operator and user manuals are frequently combined, particularly when intended for use with personal computers.

The user manual is initiated during the software requirements generation phase, primarily as a check on the software requirements specifications. The operator and maintenance manuals are initiated during the software design phase. These manuals are reviewed, audited for accuracy, corrected where necessary, and delivered to the customer along with the finished software.

(5) Review the products of the phase and obtain joint concurrence among developers, customers, and users.

The formal qualification review (FQR) is the test, inspection, or analytical process by which hard-ware/software products at the end-item level are verified to have met contractual performance requirements.

(6) Update the software product ("as-tested") baseline and place under configuration control.

During the software system testing phase, the requirements baselines and product baselines are updated to account for the changes in the system during the implementation and integration phases. The final product baseline is called the "as-tested" product baseline and placed under formal configuration control. This is the baseline that is carried forward to the operation and maintenance phase of the life cycle.

(7) Conduct final audits and reviews and "sell off" the product.

The *functional configuration audit* (FCA) is a formal examination of functional characteristics from test data for a hardware/software system prior to acceptance to verify that the item has achieved the performance specified in its requirements baselines. The *physical configuration audit* (PCA) is a formal examination of the configuration of a hardware/software system against its technical documentation in order to establish the product or operational baseline.

Functional and physical configuration audits are performed on all items of software and hardware. The functional configuration audit is conducted on the software at the completion of formal software testing. The physical configuration audit may be conducted at the completion of the formal software testing or after system integration and testing.

On concurrence of the customer, the final system is turned over to the customer for future installation and operation.

3.5.1.3. Outputs

(1) *Completed and validated system*—The final product for delivery to the customer

(2) *Completed and validated documentation*— The final product for delivery to the customer

3.5.1.4. Control Gates

(1) *Final audits and reviews*—An acceptable final audit and review will permit the project to be delivered to the customer

4. Summary and Conclusions

Conducting software engineering without conducting SE puts a project in jeopardy of being incomplete or the components not working together, and exceeding its cost and scheduled budget.

System engineering and SwSE are primarily disciplines used in the front end of the system life cycle for technical planning and at the very late part of the life cycle to verify that the plans have been met. A review of the emphasis in this article will show that much of the work of planning and SE is done during the top-level requirements analysis and top-level design phases. The other major activity of SwSE is the final validation and testing of the completed system.

System engineering principles, activities, tasks, and procedures can be applied to software development. This article has summarized, in broad steps, what is necessary to implement SwSE on either a hardware-software system (that is primarily software) or on an almost totally software system. Software system engineering is not cheap, but it is cost effective.

References

1. Gibbs, W.W., "Software's Chronic Crisis," *Scientific American*, Sept. 1994, pp. 86–95.

2. Royce, W.W., "Current Problems," in *Aerospace Software Engineering: A Collection of Concepts*, C. Anderson and M. Dorfman, eds., American Institute of Aeronautics, Inc., Washington, D.C., 1991.

3. Fujii, R., Speaker, "IEEE Seminar in Software Verification and Validation," Logicon, Inc.—Two-day public seminar presented by the IEEE Standards Board, July 1989.

4. Department of Defense, MIL-STD-499A, *Engineering Management (USAF)*, May 1, 1974.

5. Sailor, J.D., "System Engineering Overview," in *Tutorial: System and Software Engineering Requirements*, edited by R.H. Thayer and M. Dorfman, IEEE Computer Society Press, Los Alamitos, Calif., 1989.

6. Royce, W.W., "Managing the Development of Large Software Systems," *Proc. IEEE WESCON*, 1970, pp. 1–9. Reprinted in *Tutorial: Software Engineering Project Management*, edited by R.H. Thayer, IEEE Computer Society Press, Los Alamitos, Calif., 1988.

7. Alberts, H.C., "System Engineer—Managing the Gestalt," in *System Engineering Management Course Syllabus*, The Defense System Management College, Fort Belvoir, V.A. 1988.

8. Royce, W.W., "Software Systems Engineering," a seminar presented during the Management of Software Acquisition course, Defense Systems Management College, Fort Belvoir, V.A., 1981–1988.

9. Adapted from *IEEE Standard Glossary of Software Engineering Terminology*, ANSI/IEEE Std 729-1983, IEEE, Inc., New York, 1983.

10. *System Engineering Management Guide*, 2nd Ed., Technical Management Department, Defense Systems Management College, Fort Belvoir, V.A., 1986.

11. ANSI/IEEE Std 830-1984, *IEEE Guide for Software Requirements Specifications*, IEEE, Inc., New York, N.Y., 1984.

12. Fairley, R.E., "A Guide for Preparing Software Project Management Plans," in *Tutorial: Software Engineering Project Management*, edited by R.H. Thayer, IEEE Computer Society Press, Los Alamitos, Calif., 1988.

13. Howes, N.R., "On Using the Users' Manual as the Requirements Specification II," in *Tutorial: System and Software Engineering Requirements*, edited by R.H. Thayer and M. Dorfman, IEEE Computer Society Press, Los Alamitos, Calif., 1989.

14. ANSI/IEEE STD-829-1983, *IEEE Standard for Software Test Documents*, IEEE, Inc., New York, N.Y., 1983.

15. ANSI/IEEE STD-1012-1986, *Standard for Software Verification and Validation Plans*, IEEE, Inc., New York, N.Y., 1986.

16. MIL-STD 1521B (USAF), *Technical Reviews and Audits for Systems, Equipment, and Computer Programs* (proposed revision), Joint Policy Coordination Group on Computer Resource Management, U.S. Government Printing Office, Washington, D.C., 1985.

17. ANSI/IEEE STD-1012-1986, *Standard for Software Verification and Validation Plans*, IEEE, Inc., New York, N.Y., 1986.

18. ANSI/IEEE STD 1016-1987, *IEEE Recommended Practices for Software Design Description*. IEEE, Inc., New York, N.Y., 1987.

19. Martin, R.J. and W.M. Osborne, *Guidance on Software Maintenance*, National Bureau of Standards Reports on Computer Science and Technology, NBS Special Publication 500-106, U.S. Government Printing Office, Washington, D.C., Dec. 1983.

20. ANSI/IEEE STD-1012-1986, *Standard for Software Verification and Validation Plans*, IEEE, Inc., New York, N.Y., 1986.

21. Myers, G.J., *The Art of Software Testing*, John Wiley & Sons, New York, N.Y., 1979.

IEEE Std 1362-1998

(Incorporates
IEEE Std 1362a-1998)

IEEE Guide for Information Technology— System Definition—Concept of Operations (ConOps) Document

Sponsor
Software Engineering Standards Committee
of the
IEEE Computer Society

Approved 19 March 1998
IEEE-SA Standards Board

Abstract: The format and contents of a concept of operations (ConOps) document are described. A ConOps is a user-oriented document that describes system characteristics for a proposed system from the users' viewpoint. The ConOps document is used to communicate overall quantitative and qualitative system characteristics to the user, buyer, developer, and other organizational elements (for example, training, facilities, staffing, and maintenance). It is used to describe the user organization(s), mission(s), and organizational objectives from an integrated systems point of view.
Keywords: buyer, characteristics, concept of operation, concepts of operations document, ConOps, developer, operational requirements, scenario, software-intensive system, software system, system, user, user requirements, viewpoint

The Institute of Electrical and Electronics Engineers, Inc.
345 East 47th Street, New York, NY 10017-2394, USA

IEEE Standards documents are developed within the IEEE Societies and the Standards Coordinating Committees of the IEEE Standards Board. Members of the committees serve voluntarily and without compensation. They are not necessarily members of the Institute. The standards developed within IEEE represent a consensus of the broad expertise on the subject within the Institute as well as those activities outside of IEEE that have expressed an interest in participating in the development of the standard.

Use of an IEEE Standard is wholly voluntary. The existence of an IEEE Standard does not imply that there are no other ways to produce, test, measure, purchase, market, or provide other goods and services related to the scope of the IEEE Standard. Furthermore, the viewpoint expressed at the time a standard is approved and issued is subject to change brought about through developments in the state of the art and comments received from users of the standard. Every IEEE Standard is subjected to review at least every five years for revision or reaffirmation. When a document is more than five years old and has not been reaffirmed, it is reasonable to conclude that its contents, although still of some value, do not wholly reflect the present state of the art. Users are cautioned to check to determine that they have the latest edition of any IEEE Standard.

Comments for revision of IEEE Standards are welcome from any interested party, regardless of membership affiliation with IEEE. Suggestions for changes in documents should be in the form of a proposed change of text, together with appropriate supporting comments.

Interpretations: Occasionally questions may arise regarding the meaning of portions of standards as they relate to specific applications. When the need for interpretations is brought to the attention of IEEE, the Institute will initiate action to prepare appropriate responses. Since IEEE Standards represent a consensus of all concerned interests, it is important to ensure that any interpretation has also received the concurrence of a balance of interests. For this reason, IEEE and the members of its societies and Standards Coordinating Committees are not able to provide an instant response to interpretation requests except in those cases where the matter has previously received formal consideration.Comments on standards and requests for interpretations should be addressed to:

> Secretary, IEEE Standards Board
> 445 Hoes LaneP.O. Box 1331
> Piscataway, NJ 08855-1331
> USA

Note: Attention is called to the possibility that implementation of this standard may require use of subject matter covered by patent rights. By publication of this standard, no position is taken with respect to the existence or validity of any patent rights in connection therewith. The IEEE shall not be responsible for identifying patents for which a license may be required by an IEEE standard or for conducting inquiries into the legal validity or scope of those patents that are brought to its attention.

Authorization to photocopy portions of any individual standard for internal or personal use is granted by the Institute of Electrical and Electronics Engineers, Inc., provided that the appropriate fee is paid to Copyright Clearance Center. To arrange for payment of licensing fee, please contact Copyright Clearance Center, Customer Service, 222 Rosewood Drive, Danvers, MA 01923 USA; (508) 750-8400. Permission to photocopy portions of any individual standard for educational classroom use can also be obtained through the Copyright Clearance Center.

Introduction

[This introduction is not a part of IEEE Std 1362-1998, IEEE Guide for Information Technology — System Definition — Concept of Operations (ConOps) Document.]

Purpose

This guide presents format and contents of a concept of operations (ConOps) document to be used when developing or modifying a software-intensive system. A software-intensive system is a system for which software is a major technical challenge and is perhaps the major factor that affects system schedule, cost, and risk. In the most general case, a software-intensive system is comprised of hardware, software, people, and manual procedures. To make this guide more readable, the term "system" will be used to mean a software-intensive system that includes elements to be developed or modified, in addition to software. The term "software system" will be used to mean a software-intensive system in which software is the only component to be developed or modified.

This guide does not specify the exact techniques to be used in developing the ConOps document, but it does provide approaches that might be used. Each organization that uses this guide should develop a set of practices and procedures to provide detailed guidance for preparing and updating ConOps documents. These detailed practices and procedures should take into account the environmental, organizational, and political factors that influence application of the guide.

The heart of the ConOps described in this guide is contained in Clauses 3 through 5.

— Clause 3 describes the existing system (manual or automated) that the user wants to replace;
— Clause 4 provides justification for a new or modified system and any restrictions on that system; and
— Clause 5 describes the proposed system.

The outlines for Clause 3 and Clause 5 are almost identical. This is not to say that the contents of the finished ConOps document will be identical. On the contrary, the contents should be very different. The outlines are the same to remind developers of the items that should be included and the actions to be taken.

Not all software projects are concerned with development of source code for a new software product. Some software projects consist of a feasibility study and definition of product requirements. Other projects terminate upon completion of product design or are only concerned with modifications to existing software products. Applicability of this guide is not limited to projects that develop operational versions of new products, nor is it limited by project size or scope. Small projects may require less formality than large projects, but all components of this guide should be addressed by every software project.

The ConOps approach provides an analysis activity and a document that bridges the gap between the user's needs and visions and the developer's technical specifications. In addition, the ConOps document provides the following:

— A means of describing a user's operational needs without becoming bogged down in detailed technical issues that shall be addressed during the systems analysis activity.

— A mechanism for documenting a system's characteristics and the user's operational needs in a manner that can be verified by the user without requiring any technical knowledge beyond that required to perform normal job functions.

— A place for users to state their desires, visions, and expectations without requiring the provision of quantified, testable specifications. For example, the users could express their need for a "highly reliable" system, and their reasons for that need, without having to produce a testable reliability requirement. [In this case, the user's need for "high reliability" might be stated in quantitative terms by the buyer prior to issuing a request for proposal (RFP), or it might be quantified by the developer during requirements analysis. In any case, it is the job of the buyer and/or the developer to quantify users' needs.]

— A mechanism for users and buyer(s) to express thoughts and concerns on possible solution strategies. In some cases, design constraints dictate particular approaches. In other cases, there may be a variety of acceptable solution strategies. The ConOps document allows users and buyer(s) to record design constraints, the rationale for those constraints, and to indicate the range of acceptable solution strategies.

Intended uses

This guide is intended for use in a variety of situations by a variety of users including the following:

— Acquirers using ISO/IEC 12207:1995, Information technology—Software life cycle processes, will find the current guide suitable for satisfying the requirements of 5.1.1.1:

"The acquirer begins the acquisition process by describing a concept or a need to acquire, develop, or enhance a system, software product or software service."

— Users who formerly applied MIL-STD-498, Software Development and Documentation, and related standards will find that the ConOps document described in this guide is very similar to the operational concept description (OCD) included in MIL-STD-498.

— Users of EIA/IEEE J-STD-016-1995, EIA/IEEE Interim Trial-Use Standard for Information Technology Software Life Cycle Processes Software Development Acquirer—Supplier Agreement will find that the ConOps document described in this guide is substantively identical to the OCD included in EIA/IEEE J-STD-016-1995.

— Other users will find this guide useful in facilitating communication among the various stakeholders in a project.

Software as part of a larger system

Software projects are sometimes parts of larger projects. In these cases, the software ConOps document may be a separate document or it may be merged into the system level ConOps document.

Overview

This guide contains four clauses. Clause 1 defines the scope of this guide. Clause 2 provides references to other IEEE standards that should be followed when applying this guide. Clause 3 provides definitions of terms that are used throughout the guide. Clause 4 contains an overview and a detailed specification of the ConOps document, including required components that should be included, and optional components that may be included in project plans based on this guide.

Responsible organization

Ideally, the ConOps document should be written by representatives of the user community. In practice, other individuals or organizations may write the ConOps (e.g., the buyer, a third party consultant, and/or the software developer). In these cases, it is essential that user representatives be involved in reviewing, revising, and approving the ConOps document. The primary goal for a ConOps document is to capture user needs, and to express those needs in the user's terminology.

Audience

This guide is intended for users and buyers of software systems, software developers, and other personnel who prepare and update operational requirements for software-intensive systems and monitor adherence to those requirements.

Evolution of plans

Developing the initial version of the ConOps document should be one of the first activities completed on a software project. As the project evolves, the nature of the work to be done and details of the work will be better understood. The ConOps document should be updated periodically to reflect the evolving situation. Thus, each version of the document should be placed under configuration control.

Terminology

This guide follows the 1996 edition of the IEEE Standards Style Manual. The terms *should, may, might,* and *suggest* are used to indicate actions that should be used to develop a good ConOps document but that are not mandatory. However, the authors of a ConOps document should consider using all aspects of this guide to insure a complete and effective document.

The ConOps document is sometimes called an operational concept document (OCD).

History

Use of a ConOps document was first documented in Lano, R. J., "A Structured Approach for Operational Concept Formulation," TRW SS-80-02, TRW Defense and Space Systems Group, Redondo Beach, CA, 1980. In 1992 the Software Systems Technical Committee of the American Institute of Aeronautics and Astronautics (AIAA), developed a standard for an OCD.

This ConOps guide originated in October 1993, as a Master of Science thesis at California State University, Sacramento, and was supported by the U.S. Office of Research and Development. It was accepted as MIL-STD-498, Data Item Description (DID), by the DoD-Std-2167A Harmonizing Working Group with few changes. MIL-STD-498-1995 became IEEE Std 1498-1995, which was redesignated J-STD-016-1995.

The IEEE Standards Board approved the project authorization request (PAR) for development of this guide in June 1993. The first draft was submitted to the Software Engineering Standards Committee (SESC) on 8 August 1995; it was returned on 1 November 1995 with a request that the guide be harmonized with certain other specified software engineering standards. The second draft was submitted to the SESC on 28 February 1996. This draft was balloted on 21 August 1996.

Participants

This guide was written by the IEEE Guide for a Concept of Operations Document Working Group, which is part of the IEEE Computer Society. The following three individuals are the authors of this guide:

Richard H. Thayer
Richard E. Fairley
Per Bjorke

Other individuals who supported the development of this guide are:

Jed Bartlett	Merlin Dorfman	Randy Paul
Boris I. Cogan	Rajko Milovanovic	Jane Radatz

The following persons were on the balloting committee:

Mikhail Auguston	Peter A. Berggren	Alan L. Bridges
Robert E. Barry	H. Ronald Berlack	Kathleen L. Briggs
Mordechai Ben-Menachem	Audrey C. Brewer	Thomas G. Callaghan

Stuart Ross Campbell
Leslie Chambers
Keith Chan
John P. Chihorek
S. V. Chiyyarath
Antonio M. Cicu
Theo Clarke
Darrell Cooksey
W. W. Geoff Cozens
Gregory T. Daich
Hillary Davidson
Neil Davis
Bostjan K. Derganc
Michael P. DeWalt
Dave Dikel
Charles Droz
John W. Fendrich
Julian Forster
Eva Freund
Juan Garbajosa-Sopena
Julio Gonzalez-Sanz
L. M. Gunther
John Harauz
Rob Harker
William Hefley
Manfred Hein
Mark Heinrich
Mark Henley

Umesh P. Hiriyannaiah
Fabrizio Imelio
George Jackelen
Vladan V. Javonovic
Frank V. Jorgensen
William S. Junk
George X. Kambic
David W. Kane
Judith S. Kerner
Robert J. Kierzyk
Motti Y. Klein
Dwayne L. Knirk
Shaye Koenig
Thomas M. Kurihara
J. Dennis Lawrence
Michael Lines
Dieter Look
David Maibor
Philip P. Mak
Tomoo Matsubara
Scott D. Matthews
Patrick McCray
Bret Michael
Alan Miller
Millard Allen Mobley
James W. Moore
Kartik C. Mujamdar

Mike Ottewill
Donald J. Pfeiffer
John G. Phippen
Peter T. Poon
Margaretha W. Price
Kenneth R. Ptack
Andrew P. Sage
Stephen R. Schach
Norman F. Schneidewind
Gregory D. Schumacher
Robert W. Shillato
Richard S. Sky
Alfred R. Sorkowitz
Donald W. Sova
Fred J. Strauss
Michael Surratt
Douglas H. Thiele
Booker Thomas
Patricia Trellue
Richard D. Tucker
Theodore J. Urbanowicz
Glenn D. Venables
Camille S. White-Partain
Charles D. Wilson
Paul R. Work
Weider D. Yu
Janusz Zalewski
Peter F. Zoll

The following individuals were part of the Life Cycle Data Harmonization working group for IEEE Std 1362a-1998:

Leonard L. Tripp, *Chair*

Edward Byrne
Paul R. Croll
Perry DeWeese
Robin Fralick
Marilyn Ginsberg-Finner
John Harauz
Mark Henley

Dennis Lawrence
David Maibor
Ray Milovanovic
James Moore
Timothy Niesen
Dennis Rilling

Terry Rout
Richard Schmidt
Norman F. Schneidewind
David Schultz
Basil Sherlund
Peter Voldner
Ronald Wade

The following persons were on the balloting committee for IEEE Std 1362a-1998:

Eduardo W. Bergamini
H. Ronald Berlack
Richard E. Biehl
Juris Borzovs
David W. Burnett
Michael Caldwell
Antonio M. Cicu
Francois Coallier
Virgil Lee Cooper
W. W. Geoff Cozens
Paul R. Croll

Geoffrey Darnton
Taz Daughtrey
Bostjan K. Derganc
Perry R. DeWeese
Leo Egan
Jonathan H. Fairclough
Richard E. Fairley
John W. Fendrich
Jay Forster
Kirby Fortenberry
Eva Freund

Roger U. Fujii
Marilyn Ginsberg-Finner
Julio Gonzalez-Sanz
Lewis Gray
L. M. Gunther
David A. Gustafson
John Harauz
Rob Harker
William Hefley
Debra Herrmann
Umesh P. Hiriyannaiah

112

David Johnson
Frank V. Jorgensen
William S. Junk
Ron S. Kenett
Judith S. Kerner
Robert J. Kierzyk
Thomas M. Kurihara
John B. Lane
J. Dennis Lawrence
Mary Leatherman
William M. Lively
Stan Magee
David Maibor
Robert A. Martin
Patrick D. McCray
James W. Moore
Pavol Navrat

Donald J. Ostrom
Lalit M. Patnaik
Mark Paulk
John G. Phippen
Alex Polack
Peter T. Poon
Kenneth R. Ptack
Larry K. Reed
Ann E. Reedy
Donald J. Reifer
Annette D. Reilly
Andrew P. Sage
Helmut Sandmayr
Stephen R. Schach
Norman F. Schneidewind
David J. Schultz
Robert W. Shillato
David M. Siefert

Lynn J. Simms
Carl A. Singer
Fred J. Strauss
Toru Takeshita
Richard H. Thayer
Douglas H. Thiele
Booker Thomas
Patricia Trellue
Glenn D. Venables
John W. Walz
Camille S. White-Partain
Scott A. Whitmire
P. A. Wolfgang
Paul R. Work
Janusz Zalewski
Geraldine Zimmerman
Peter F. Zoll

When the IEEE-SA Standards Board approved this standard on 19 March 1998, it had the following membership:

Richard J. Holleman, *Chair*
Donald N. Heirman, *Vice Chair*
Judith Gorman, *Secretary*

Satish K. Aggarwal
Clyde R. Camp
James T. Carlo
Gary R. Engmann
Harold E. Epstein
Jay Forster*
Thomas F. Garrity
Ruben D. Garzon

James H. Gurney
Jim D. Isaak
Lowell G. Johnson
Robert Kennelly
E. G. "Al" Kiener
Joseph L. Koepfinger*
Stephen R. Lambert
Jim Logothetis
Donald C. Loughry

L. Bruce McClung
Louis-François Pau
Ronald C. Petersen
Gerald H. Peterson
John B. Posey
Gary S. Robinson
Hans E. Weinrich
Donald W. Zipse

*Member Emeritus

Kim Breitfelder
IEEE Standards Project Editor

Contents

IEEE Guide for Information Technology— System Definition—Concept of Operations (ConOps) Document

1. Scope

This guide prescribes the format and contents of the concept of operations (ConOps) document. A ConOps is a user-oriented document that describes system characteristics of the to-be-delivered system from the user's viewpoint. The ConOps document is used to communicate overall quantitative and qualitative system characteristics to the user, buyer, developer, and other organizational elements (e.g., training, facilities, staffing, and maintenance). It describes the user organization(s), mission(s), and organizational objectives from an integrated systems point of view.

This guide may be applied to all types of software-intensive systems: software-only or software/hardware/people systems. The concepts embodied in this guide could also be used for hardware-only systems, but this mode of use is not addressed herein. The size, scope, complexity, or criticality of the software product does not restrict use of this guide. This guide is applicable to systems that will be implemented in all forms of product media, including firmware, embedded systems code, programmable logic arrays, and software-in-silicon. This guide can be applied to any and all segments of a system life cycle.

This guide identifies the minimal set of elements that should appear in all ConOps documents. However, users of this guide may incorporate other elements by appending additional clauses or subclauses to their ConOps documents. In any case, the numbering scheme of the required clauses and subclauses should adhere to the format specified in this guide. Various clauses and subclauses of a ConOps document may be included by direct incorporation or by reference to other supporting documents.

2. References

This guide shall be used in conjunction with the following publications. In particular, the standards on requirements and plans should be consulted in preparing the ConOps. When the following standards are superseded by an approved revision, the revision shall apply.

IEEE Std 610.12-1990, IEEE Standard Glossary of Software Engineering Terminology.[1]

---

[1]IEEE publications are available from the Institute of Electrical and Electronics Engineers, 445 Hoes Ln., P.O. Box 1331, Piscataway, NJ 08855-1331, USA.

IEEE Std 828-1998, IEEE Standard for Software Configuration Management Plans.

IEEE Std 830-1998, IEEE Recommended Practice for Software Requirements Specifications.

IEEE Std 1058-1998, IEEE Standard for Software Project Management Plans.

IEEE Std 1058.1-1987 (Reaff 1993), IEEE Standard for Software Project Management Plans.

IEEE Std 1061-1992, IEEE Standard for Software Quality Metrics Methodology.

IEEE 1062, 1998 Edition, IEEE Recommended Practice for Software Acquisition.

IEEE Std 1074-1997, IEEE Standard for Developing Software Life Cycle Processes.

IEEE 1233, 1998 Edition, IEEE Guide for Developing System Requirements Specifications.

IEEE/EIA 12207.0-1996, IEEE/EIA Standard—Industry Implementation of ISO/IEC 12207:1995, for Information Technology— Software life cycle processes.

IEEE/EIA 12207.1-1997, IEEE/EIA Guide for Information Technology— Software life cycle processes—Life cycle data.

3. Definitions

The definitions listed here establish meanings within the context of this guide. Definitions of other terms that may be appropriate within the context of this guide can be found in IEEE Std 610.12-1990.

3.1 analysis: The process of studying a system by partitioning the system into parts (functions, components, or objects) and determining how the parts relate to each other.

3.2 buyer: (A) An individual or organization responsible for acquiring a product or service (for example, a software system) for use by themselves or other users. *See also:* **customer. (B)** The person or organization that accepts the system and pays for the project.

3.3 concept analysis: The derivation of a system concept through the application of analysis. *See also:* **analysis.**

3.4 concept of operations (ConOps) document: A user-oriented document that describes a system's operational characteristics from the end user's viewpoint. *Synonym:* **operational concept description (OCD).**

3.5 constraint: An externally imposed limitation on system requirements, design, or implementation or on the process used to develop or modify a system.

3.6 contract: In project management, a legally binding document agreed upon by the customer and the hardware or software developer or supplier; includes the technical, organizational, cost, and/or scheduling requirements of a project.

3.7 customer: (A) An individual or organization who specifies the requirements for and formally accepts delivery of a new or modified hardware or software product and its documentation; the customer may or may not be the ultimate user of the system. There are potentially many levels of customers, each with a different level of requirements to satisfy. The customer may be internal or external to the development organization for the project. *See also:* **user. (B)** An individual or organization who acts for the ultimate user of a new or modified hardware or software product to acquire the product and its documentation. *See also:* **buyer.**

3.8 developer: An organization that develops software products; "develops" may include new development, modification, reuse, reengineering, maintenance, or any other activity that results in software products, and includes the testing, quality assurance, configuration management, and other activities applied to these products. *Synonym:* **supplier.**

3.9 environment: The circumstances, objects, and conditions that surround a system to be built; includes technical, political, commercial, cultural, organizational, and physical influences as well as standards and policies that govern what a system must do or how it will do it.

3.10 functionality: The capabilities of the various computational, user interface, input, output, data management, and other features provided by a product.

3.11 mode: A set of related features or functional capabilities of a product, (e.g., on-line, off-line, and maintenance modes).

3.12 N^2 diagram: A system engineering or software engineering tool for tabulating, defining, analyzing, and describing functional interfaces and interactions among system components. The N^2 diagram is a matrix structure that graphically displays the bidirectional interrelationships between functions and components in a given system or structure.

3.13 operational concept description (OCD): *See:* **concept of operations (ConOps) document.**

3.14 priority: A rank order of status, activities, or tasks. Priority is particularly important when resources are limited.

3.15 problem domain: A set of similar problems that occur in an environment and lend themselves to common solutions.

3.16 request for proposal (RFP): A request for services, research, or a product prepared by a customer and delivered to prospective developers with the expectation that prospective developers will respond with their proposed cost, schedule, and development approach.

3.17 scenario: (A) A step-by-step description of a series of events that may occur concurrently or sequentially. **(B)** An account or synopsis of a projected course of events or actions.

3.18 software-intensive system: A system for which software is a major technical challenge and is perhaps the major factor that affects system schedule, cost, and risk. In the most general case, a software-intensive system is comprised of hardware, software, people, and manual procedures.

3.19 software life cycle: The system or product cycle initiated by a user need or a perceived customer need and terminated by discontinued use of the product. The software life cycle typically includes a concept phase, requirements phase, design phase, implementation phase, test phase, installation and checkout phase, operation and maintenance phase, and, sometimes, retirement phase. These phases may overlap in time or may occur iteratively.

3.20 software system: A software-intensive system for which software is the only component to be developed or modified. *See also:* **software-intensive system.**

3.21 solution domain: The environment in which a solution or set of solutions resides. *See also:* **problem domain.**

3.22 supplier: *See:* **developer.**

3.23 system: (A) A collection of interacting components organized to accomplish a specific function or set of functions within a specific environment. **(B)** A group of people, objects, and procedures constituted to achieve defined objectives of some operational role by performing specified functions. A complete system includes all of the associated equipment, facilities, material, computer programs, firmware, technical documentation, services, and personnel required for operations and support to the degree necessary for self-sufficient use in its intended environment.

3.24 traceability: The identification and documentation of derivation paths (upward) and allocation or flowdown paths (downward) of work products in the work product hierarchy. Important kinds of traceability include: to or from external sources to or from system requirements; to or from system requirements to or from lowest level requirements; to or from requirements to or from design; to or from design to or from implementation; to or from implementation to test; and to or from requirements to test.

3.25 user: (A) An individual or organization who uses a software-intensive system in their daily work activities or recreational pursuits. **(B)** The person (or persons) who operates or interacts directly with a software-intensive system.

3.26 user need: A user requirement for a system that a user believes would solve a problem experienced by the user.

4. Elements of a ConOps document

This clause describes each of the essential elements of a ConOps document. These elements should be ordered in the sequence of clauses and subclauses shown in Table 1. Each version of a ConOps document based on this guide should contain a title and a revision notice that uniquely identifies the document. Revision information may include the project name, version number of the document, date of release, approval signatures, a list of subclauses that have been changed in the current version of the document, and a list of version numbers and dates of release of all previous versions of the document. The approved ConOps document should be placed under configuration control.

As indicated in Table 1, the preface of a ConOps document provides information that the writer wants the reader to know prior to reading the document. The preface should include the purpose of the document, the scope of activities that resulted in its development, who wrote the document and why, the intended audience for the document, and the expected evolution of the document.

A table of contents, a list of figures, and a list of tables should be included in every ConOps document, as indicated in Figure 1.

```
Title page
Revision chart
Preface
Table of contents
List of figures
List of tables
1. Scope
        1.1 Identification
        1.2 Document overview
        1.3 System overview
2. Referenced documents
3. Current system or situation
        3.1 Background, objectives, and scope
        3.2 Operational policies and constraints
        3.3 Description of the current system or situation
        3.4 Modes of operation for the current system or situation
        3.5 User classes and other involved personnel
        3.6 Support environment
4. Justification for and nature of changes
        4.1 Justication of changes
        4.2 Description of desired changes
        4.3 Priorities among changes
        4.4 Changes considered but not included
5. Concepts for the proposed system
        5.1 Background, objectives, and scope
        5.2 Operational policies and constraints
        5.3 Description of the proposed system
        5.4 Modes of operation
        5.5 User classes and other involved personnel
        5.6 Support environment
6. Operational scenarios
7. Summary of impacts
        7.1 Operational impacts
        7.2 Organizational impacts
        7.3 Impacts during development
8. Analysis of the proposed system
        8.1 Summary of improvements
        8.2 Disadvantages and limitations
        8.3 Alternatives and trade-offs considered
9. Notes
Appendices
Glossary
```

Figure 1—ConOps document outline

4.1 Scope (Clause 1 of the ConOps document)

Clause 1 provides an overview of the ConOps document and the system to which it applies.

4.1.1 Indentification (1.1 of the ConOps document)

This subclause contains the identifying number, title, and abbreviation (if applicable) of the system or subsystem to which this ConOps applies. If related ConOps documents for an overall system have been developed in a hierarchical or network manner, the position of this document relative to other ConOps documents should be described.

4.1.2 Document overview (1.2 of the ConOps document)

This subclause summarizes and expands on the purposes of motivations for the ConOps document. The intended audience for the document should also be mentioned. In addition, this subclause describes any security or privacy considerations associated with use of the ConOps. This subclause also outlines the remaining parts of this guide.

The purposes of a ConOps document will, in most cases, be:

— To communicate the user's needs for and expectations of the proposed system to the buyer and/or developer; or

— To communicate the buyer's or developer's understanding of the users' need and how the system shall operate to fulfill those needs.

However, a ConOps document might also serve other purposes, such as building consensus among several user groups, among several buyer organizations, and/or among several developers.

The audience of a ConOps document can be a variety of people.

— Users might read it to determine whether their needs and desires have been correctly specified by their representative or to verify the developer's understanding of their needs.

— Buyers might read it to acquire knowledge of the user's needs and/or developer's understanding of those needs.

— Developers will typically use the ConOps document as a basis for system development activities, and to familiarize new team members with the problem domain and the system to which the ConOps applies.

4.1.3 System overview (1.3 of the ConOps document)

This subclause briefly states the purpose of the proposed system or subsystem to which the ConOps applies. It describes the general nature of the system, and identifies the project sponsors, user agencies, development organizations, support agencies, certifiers or certifying bodies, and the operating centers or sites that will run the system. It also identifies other documents relevant to the present or proposed system.

A graphical overview of the system is strongly recommended. This can be in the form of a context diagram, a top-level object diagram, or some other type of diagram that depicts the system and its environment.

Documents that might be cited include, but are not limited to: the project authorization, relevant technical documentation, significant correspondence, documents concerning related projects, risk analysis reports, and feasibility studies.

4.2 Referenced documents (Clause 2 of the ConOps document)

This clause lists the document number, title, revision, and date of all documents referenced in the ConOps document. This clause should also identify the source for all documents not available through normal channels.

4.3 Current system or situation (Clause 3 of the ConOps document)

Clause 3 describes the system or situation (either automated or manual) as it currently exists. If there is no current system on which to base changes, this subclause describes the situation that motivates development of the proposed system. In this case, the following subclauses will be tailored as appropriate to describe the motivating situation.

This clause also provides readers with an introduction to the problem domain. This enables readers to better understand the reasons for the desired changes and improvements.

4.3.1 Background, objectives, and scope (3.1 of the ConOps document)

This subclause provides an overview of the current system or situation, including as applicable, background, mission, objectives, and scope. In addition to providing the background for the current system, this subclause should provide a brief summary of the motivation for the current system. Examples of motivations for a system might include automation of certain tasks or countering of certain threat situations. The goals for the current system should also be defined, together with the strategies, solutions, tactics, methods, and techniques used to accomplish them. The modes of operation, classes of users, and interfaces to the operational environment define the scope of the proposed system, which are summarized in this clause and defined in greater detail in subsequent clauses.

4.3.2 Operational policies and constraints (3.2 of the ConOps document)

This subclause describes any operational policies and constraints that apply to the current system or situation. Operational policies are predetermined management decisions regarding the operations of the current system, normally in the form of general statements or understandings that guide decision making activities. Policies limit decision-making freedom but do allow for some discretion. Operational constraints are limitations placed on the operations of the current system. Examples of operational constraints include the following:

— A constraint on the hours of operation of the system, perhaps limited by access to secure terminals
— A constraint on the number of personnel available to operate the system
— A constraint on the computer hardware (for example, must operate on computer X)
— A constraint on the operational facilities, such as office space

4.3.3 Description of the current system or situation (3.3 of the ConOps document)

This subclause will contain the major portion of the description of the current system. It provides a description of the current system or situation, including the following, as appropriate:

a) The operational environment and its characteristics;

b) Major system components and the interconnection among those components;

c) Interfaces to external systems or procedures;

d) Capabilities, functions, and features of the current system;

e) Charts and accompanying descriptions depicting inputs, outputs, data flows, control flows, and manual and automated processes sufficient to understand the current system or situation from the user's point of view;

f) Cost of system operations;

g) Operational risk factors;

h) Performance characteristics, such as speed, throughput, volume, frequency;

i) Quality attributes, such as: availability, correctness, efficiency, expandability, flexibility, interoperability, maintain-ability, portability, reliability, reusability, supportability, survivability, and usability; and

j) Provisions for safety, security, privacy, integrity, and continuity of operations in emergencies.

Since the purpose of this clause is to describe the current system and how it operates, it is appropriate to use any tools and/or techniques that serve this purpose. It is important that the description of the system be simple enough and clear enough that all intended readers of the document can fully understand it. It is also important to keep in mind that the ConOps document shall be written using the users' terminology. In most cases, this means avoidance of terminology specific to computers (i.e., "computer jargon").

Graphical tools should be used wherever possible, especially since ConOps documents should be understandable by several different types of readers. Useful graphical tools include, but are not limited to, work breakdown structures (WBS), N^2 charts, sequence or activity charts, functional flow block diagrams, structure charts, allocation charts, data flow diagrams (DFD), object diagrams, context diagrams, storyboards, and entity-relationship diagrams.

The description of the operational environment should identify, as applicable, the facilities, equipment, computing hardware, software, personnel, and operational procedures used to operate the existing system. This description should be as detailed as necessary to give the readers an understanding of the numbers, versions, capacity, etc., of the operational equipment being used. For example, if the current system contains a database, the capacity of the storage unit(s) should be specified, provided the information exerts an influence on the users' operational capabilities. Likewise, if the system uses communication links, the capacities of those links should be specified if they exert influence on factors such as user capabilities, response time, or throughput.

Those aspects of safety, security, and privacy that exert influence on the operation or operational environment of the current system should be described.

The author(s) of a ConOps document should organize the information in this subclause as appropriate to the system or situation, as long as a clear description of the existing system is achieved. If parts of the descriptions are voluminous, they can be included in an appendix or incorporated by reference. An example of material that might be included in an appendix would be a data dictionary. An example of material to be included by reference might be a detailed manual of operational policies and procedures for the current system.

4.3.4 Modes of operation for the current system or situation (3.4 in the ConOps document)

This subclause describes the various modes of operation for the current system or situation (e.g., operational, degraded, maintenance, training, emergency, alternate-site, peacetime, wartime, ground-based, flight, active, and idle modes). All of the modes that apply to all classes of users should be included. Important modes to include are degraded, backup, and emergency modes, if such exist. This is especially true if these modes involve different geographical sites and equipment that have significant impacts on the operational aspects of the system.

This subclause can be further divided into lower-level subclauses, one for each mode described. System processes, procedures, and capabilities or functions should be related to each mode, as appropriate, perhaps using a cross-reference matrix.

4.3.5 User classes and other involved personnel (3.5 of the ConOps document)

A user class is distinguished by the ways in which users interact with the system. Factors that distinguish a user class include common responsibilities, skill levels, work activities, and modes of interaction with the system. Different user classes may have distinct operational scenarios for their interactions with the system. In this context, a user is anyone who interacts with the existing system, including operational users, data entry personnel, system operators, operational support personnel, software maintainers, and trainers.

This subclause can be organized further, as follows, if it is helpful in communicating the content.

4.3.5.1 Organizational structure (3.5.1 of the ConOps document)

This subclause describes the existing organizational structures of the various user groups and user classes that are involved with the current system. Organizational charts are useful graphic tools for this purpose.

4.3.5.2 Profiles of user classes (3.5.2 of the ConOps document)

This subclause provides a profile of each user class for the current system. If some users play several roles, each role should be identified as a separate user class.

Each user class for the current system, including operators and maintainers, should be described in a separate subclause. Each of these should provide a description of the user class, including responsibilities, education, background, skill level, activities, and modes of interaction with the current system.

4.3.5.3 Interactions among user classes (3.5.3 of the ConOps document)

This subclause describes interactions among the various user classes involved with the current system. In particular, interactions among user groups, operators, and maintainers should be described. Interactions that occur among the users of the system, and between users and non-users, both within the organization and across organizational boundaries, if they are relevant to the operation of the existing system, should be described. Informal as well as formal interactions should be included.

4.3.5.4 Other involved personnel (3.5.4 of the ConOps document)

This subclause describes other personnel who will not directly interact with the system, but who have an influence on, and are influenced by, the present system. Examples include executive managers, policy makers, and the user's clients. Although these individuals do not have hands-on interaction with the system, they may significantly influence, and be influenced by, the new or modified system.

4.3.6 Support environment (3.6 of the ConOps document)

This subclause describes the support concepts and support environment for the current system, including the support agency or agencies; facilities; equipment; support software; repair or replacement criteria; maintenance levels and cycles; and storage, distribution, and supply methods.

4.4 Justification for and nature of changes (Clause 4 of the ConOps document)

Clause 4 of the ConOps document describes the shortcomings of the current system or situation that motivate development of a new system or modification of an existing system. This clause provides a transition from Clause 3 of the ConOps, which describes the current system or situation, to Clause 5 of the ConOps, which describes the proposed system. If there is no current system on which to base changes, this subclause should so indicate and provide justification for the features of the new system.

4.4.1 Justification for changes (4.1 of the ConOps document)

This subclause should:

a) Briefly summarize new or modified aspects of the user needs, missions, objectives, environments, interfaces, personnel, or other factors that require a new or modified system;

b) Summarize the deficiencies or limitations of the current system or situation that make it unable to respond to new or changed factors; and

c) Provide justification for a new or modified system.

    1) If the proposed system is to meet a new opportunity, describe the reasons why a new system should be developed to meet this opportunity.

    2) If the proposed system improves a current operation, describe the rationale behind the decision to modify the existing system (e.g., to reduce life cycle costs or improve personnel efficiency).

    3) If the proposed system implements a new functional capability, explain why this function is necessary.

4.4.2 Description of desired changes (4.2 of the ConOps document)

This subclause summarizes new or modified capabilities, functions, processes, interfaces, and other changes needed to respond to the factors identified in 4.1. Changes should be based on the current system described in Clause 3 of the ConOps document. If there is no existing system on which to base changes, this subclause should summarize the capabilities to be provided by a new system. This description should include the following, as appropriate:

a) *Capability changes.* Description of the functions and features to be added, deleted, and modified in order for the new or modified system to meet its objectives and requirements.

b) *System processing changes.* Description of the changes in the process or processes of transforming data that will result in new output with the same data, the same output with new data, or both.

c) *Interface changes.* Description of changes in the system that will cause changes in the interfaces and changes in the interfaces that will cause changes in the system.

d) *Personnel changes.* Description of changes in personnel caused by new requirements, changes in user classes, or both.

e) *Environment changes.* Description of changes in the operational environment that will cause changes in the system functions, processes, interfaces, or personnel and/or changes that should be made in the environment because of changes in the system functions, processes, interfaces, or personnel.

f) *Operational changes.* Description of changes to the user's operational policies, procedures, methods, or daily work routines caused by the above changes.

g) *Support changes.* Description of changes in the support requirements caused by changes in the system functions, processes, interfaces, or personnel and/or changes in the system functions, processes, interfaces, or personnel caused by changes in the support environment.

h) *Other changes.* Description of other changes that will impact the users, but that do not fit under any of the above categories.

4.4.3 Priorities among changes (4.3 of the ConOps document)

This subclause identifies priorities among the desired changes and new features. Each change should be classified as essential, desirable, or optional. Desirable and optional changes should be prioritized within their classes. If there is no existing system on which to base changes, this subclause should classify and prioritize the features of the proposed system.

a) *Essential features.* Features that shall be provided by the new or modified system. The impacts that would result if the features were not implemented should be explained for each essential feature.

b) *Desirable features.* Features that should be provided by the new or modified system. Desirable features should be prioritized. Reasons why the features are desirable should be explained for each desirable feature.

c) *Optional features.* Features that might be provided by the new or modified system. Optional features should be prioritized. Reasons why the features are optional should be explained for each optional feature.

Classifying the desired changes and new features into essential, desirable, and optional categories is important to guide the decision making process during development of the proposed system. This information is also helpful in cases of budget or schedule cuts or overruns, since it permits determination of which features must be finished, and which ones can be delayed or omitted.

4.4.4 Changes considered but not included (4.4 of the ConOps document)

This subclause identifies changes and new features considered but not included in 4.2 of the ConOps document, and the rationale for not including them. By describing changes and features considered but not included in the proposed system, the authors document the results of their analysis activities. This information can be useful to other personnel involved with system development, whether it be users, buyers, or developers should they want to know if a certain change or feature was considered, and if so, why it was not included. In software especially, there are few, if any, outward signs of what has been changed, improved or is still unsafe or unsecure (e.g., in certain scenarios or workarounds).

4.4.5 Assumptions and constraints (4.5 of the ConOps document)

This subclause describes any assumptions or constraints applicable to the changes and new features identified in this clause. This should include all assumptions and constraints that will affect users during development and operation of the new or modified system. An assumption is a condition that is taken to be true. An example of an assumption is that the system workload will double over the next two years, thus a new system with higher performance is required. A constraint is an externally imposed limitation placed on the new or modified system or the processes used to develop or modify the system. Examples of constraints include external interface requirements, and limits on schedule and budget.

4.5 Concepts for the proposed system (Clause 5 of the ConOps document)

This clause describes the proposed system that results from the desired changes specified in Clause 4 of the ConOps document. This clause describes the proposed system in a high-level manner, indicating the operational features that are to be provided without specifying design details. Methods of description to be used and the level of detail in the description will depend on the situation. The level of detail should be sufficient to fully explain how the proposed system is envisioned to operate in fulfilling users' needs and buyer's requirements.

In some cases, it may be necessary to provide some level of design detail in the ConOps. The ConOps should not contain design specifications, but it may contain some examples of typical design strategies, for the purpose of clarifying operational details of the proposed system. In the event that actual design constraints need to be included in the description of the proposed system, they shall be explicitly identified as required to avoid possible misunderstandings.

NOTE — If some of the features of the proposed system are the same as the features of the original system, then the comment "no change" should appear after the subclause number and name.

4.5.1 Background, objectives, and scope (5.1 of the ConOps document)

This subclause provides an overview of the new or modified system, including, as applicable, background, mission, objectives, and scope. In addition to providing the background for the proposed system, this subclause should provide a brief summary of the motivation for the system. Examples of motivations for a system might include automation of certain tasks or taking advantage of new opportunities. The goals for the new or modified system should also be defined, together with the strategies, solutions, tactics, methods, and techniques proposed to achieve those goals. The modes of operation, classes of users, and interfaces to the operational environment define the scope of the proposed system, which are summarized in this subclause and defined in greater detail in subsequent subclauses.

4.5.2 Operational policies and constraints (5.2 of the ConOps document)

This subclause describes operational policies and constraints that apply to the proposed system. Operational policies are predetermined management decisions regarding the operation of the new or modified system, normally in the form of general statements or understandings that guide decision-making activities. Policies limit decision-making freedom, but do allow for some discretion. Operational constraints are limitations placed on the operations of the proposed system. Examples of operational constraints include the following:

— A constraint on the hours of operations of the system, perhaps limited by access to secure terminals;
— A limiting constraint on the number of personnel available to operate the system;
— A limiting constraint on the computer hardware (e.g., must operate on computer X); and
— A limiting constraint on the operational facilities, such as office space.

4.5.3 Description of the proposed system (5.3 of the ConOps document)

This subclause will contain the major portion of the description of the proposed system. It provides a description of the proposed system, including the following, as appropriate:

a) The operational environment and its characteristics;

b) Major system components and the interconnections among these components;

c) Interfaces to external systems or procedures;

d) Capabilities or functions of the proposed system;

e) Charts and accompanying descriptions depicting inputs, outputs, data flow, and manual and automated processes sufficient to understand the proposed system or situation from the user's point of view;

f) Cost of systems operations;

g) Operational risk factors;

h) Performance characteristics, such as speed, throughput, volume, frequency;

i) Quality attributes, such as: reliability, availability, correctness, efficiency, expandability, flexibility, interoperability, maintainability, portability, reusability, supportability, survivability, and usability; and

j) Provisions for safety, security, privacy, integrity, and continuity of operations in emergencies.

Since the purpose of this subclause is to describe the proposed system and how it should operate, it is appropriate to use any tools and/or techniques that serve that purpose. It is important that the description of the system be simple enough and clear enough that all intended readers of the document can fully understand it. It is important to keep in mind that the ConOps shall be written in the user's language. In most cases, this means avoidance of terminology specific to computers—in other words, "computer jargon."

Graphics and pictorial tools should be used wherever possible, especially since ConOps documents should be understandable be several different types of readers. Useful graphical tools include, but are not limited to, WBS, N^2 charts, sequence or activity charts, functional flow block diagrams, structure charts, allocation charts, DFDs, object diagrams, storyboards, and entity relationship diagrams.

The description of the operational environment should identify, as applicable, the facilities, equipment, computing hardware, software, personnel, and operational procedures needed to operate the proposed system. This description should be as detailed as necessary to give the readers an understanding of the numbers, versions, capacity, etc., of the operational equipment to be used. For example, if the proposed system contains a database, the capacity of the storage units should be specified, provided that information influences the users' operational capabilities. Likewise, if the system uses communication links, then the capacities of those links should be specified if they exert influence on user capabilities or response time.

Those aspects of safety, security, and privacy that exert influence on the operation or operational environment of the proposed system should be described.

The author(s) of a ConOps document should organize the information in this subclause as appropriate to the system or situation, as long as a clear description of the proposed system is achieved. If parts of the description are voluminous, they can be included in an appendix or incorporated by reference. An example of material that might be included in an appendix would be a data dictionary. An example of material to be included by reference might be a detailed manual of operation policies and procedures for the proposed system.

4.5.4 Modes of operation (5.4 of the ConOps document)

This subclause describes the various modes of operation for the proposes system (for example, regular, degraded, maintenance, training, emergency, alternate-site, peacetime, wartime, ground-based, flight, active, and idle modes). Include all of the modes that apply to all user classes. Important modes to include are degraded, backup, and emergency modes, if such exist. This is especially true if these modes involve different geographical sites and equipment that have significant impacts on the system.

This subclause can be further divided into lower-level subclauses, one for each mode described. System processes, procedures, and capabilities or functions should be related to each mode.

4.5.5 User classes and other involved personnel (5.5 of the ConOps document)

A user class is distinguished by the ways in which the users interact with the system. Factors that distinguish a user class include responsibilities, skill level, work activities, and mode of interaction with the system. Different user classes may have distinct operational scenarios for their interactions with the system. In this context, a user is anyone who will interact with the proposed system, including operational users, data entry personnel, system operators, operational support personnel, software maintainers, and trainers.

This subclause can be further divided into lower-level subclauses if it is helpful in communicating the content.

4.5.5.1 Organizational structure (5.5.1 of the ConOps document)

This subclause describes the organizational structures of the various user groups and user classes that will be involved with the proposed system. Organizational charts are useful graphic tools for this purpose.

4.5.5.2 Profiles of user classes (5.5.2 of the ConOps document)

This subclause provides a profile of each user class for the proposed system. If some users play several roles, each role should be identified as a separate user class.

Each user class for the proposed system, including operators and maintainers, should be described in a separate subclause. Each subclause should provide a description of the user class, including responsibilities, education, background, skill level, activities, and envisioned modes of interaction with the proposed system.

4.5.5.3 Interactions among user classes (5.5.3 of the ConOps document)

This subclause describes interactions among the various user classes that may be involved with the proposed system. In particular, interaction among user groups, operators, and maintainers should be described. Interactions that will occur among the users of the proposed system, and between users and non-users, both within the organization and across interfacing organizations, if they are relevant to the operation of the proposed system, should be described. Informal as well as formal interactions should be included.

4.5.5.4 Other involved personnel (5.5.4 of the ConOps document)

This subclause describes other personnel who will not directly interact with the system, but who have an influence on, and are influenced by, the present system. Examples include executive managers, policy makers, and the user's clients. Although these individuals do not have hands-on interaction with the system, they may significantly influence and be influenced by, the new or modified system.

4.5.6 Support environment (5.6 of the ConOps document)

This subclause describes the support concepts and support environment for the proposed system, including the support agency or agencies; facilities; equipment; support software; repair or replacement criteria; maintenance levels and cycles; and storage, distribution, and supply methods.

4.6 Operational scenarios (Clause 6 of the ConOps document)

A scenario is a step-by-step description of how the proposed system should operate and interact with its users and its external interfaces under a given set of circumstances. Scenarios should be described in a manner that will allow readers to walk through them and gain an understanding of how all the various parts of the proposed system function and interact. The scenarios tie together all parts of the system, the users, and other entities by describing how they interact. Scenarios may also be used to describe what the system should not do.

Scenarios should be organized into clauses and subclauses, each describing an operational sequence that illustrates the roles of the system, its interactions with users, and interactions with other systems. Operational scenarios should be described for all operational modes and all classes of users identified for the proposed system. Each scenario should include events, actions, stimuli, information, and interactions as appropriate to provide a comprehensive understanding of the operational aspects of the proposed system. Prototypes, storyboards, and other media, such as video or hypermedia presentations, may be used to provide part of this information.

In most cases, it will be necessary to develop several variations of each scenario, including one for normal operation, one for stress load handling, one for exception handling, one for degraded mode operation, etc.

Scenarios play several important roles. The first is to bind together all of the individual parts of a system into a comprehensible whole. Scenarios help the readers of a ConOps document understand how all the pieces interact to provide operational capabilities. The second role of scenarios is to provide readers with operational details for the proposed system; this enables them to understand the users' roles, how the system should operate, and the various operational features to be provided.

Scenarios can also support the development of simulation models that help in the definition and allocation of derived requirements, identification, and preparation of prototypes to address key issues.

In addition, scenarios can serve as the basis for the first draft of the users' manual, and as the basis for developing acceptance test plans. The scenarios are also useful for the buyer and the developer to verify that the system design will satisfy the users' needs and expectations.

Scenarios can be presented in several different ways. One approach is to specify scenarios for each major processing function of the proposed system. Using this approach, this clause would contain one subclause for each process. Each subclause would then contain several more lower-level subclauses, one for each scenario supported by that process. An alternative approach is to develop thread-based scenarios, where each scenario follows one type of transaction type through the proposed system. In this case, each subclause would contain one scenario for each interaction type, plus scenarios for degraded, stress loaded, and back-up modes of operation. Other alternatives include following the information flow through the system for each user capability, following the control flows, or focusing on the objects and events in the system.

Scenarios are an important component of a ConOps, and should therefore receive substantial emphasis. The number of scenarios and level of detail specified will be proportional to the perceived risk and the criticality of the project.

4.7 Summary of impacts (Clause 7 of the ConOps document)

This clause describes the operational impacts of the proposed system on the users, the developers, and the support and maintenance organizations. It also describes the temporary impacts on users, buyers, developers, and the support and maintenance organizations during the period of time when the new system is being developed, installed, or trained on.

This information is provided in order to allow all affected organizations to prepare for the changes that will be brought about by the new system and to allow for planning of the impacts on the buyer agency or agencies, user groups, and the support maintenance organizations during the development of, and transition to the new system.

4.7.1 Operational impacts (7.1 of the ConOps document)

This subclause should be further divided into lower-level subclauses to describe the anticipated operational impacts on the user, development, and support or maintenance agency or agencies during operation of the proposed system. These impacts may include the following:

— Interfaces with primary or alternate computer operating centers;
— Changes in procedure;
— Use of new data sources;
— Changes in quantity, type, and timing of data to be input into the system;
— Changes in data retention requirements;
— New modes of operation based on emergency, disaster, or accident conditions;
— New methods for providing input data if the required data are not readily available;
— Changes in operational budget; and
— Changes in operational risks.

4.7.2 Organizational impacts (7.2 of the ConOps document)

This subclause should be further divided into lower-level subclauses to describe the anticipated operational impacts on the user, development, and support or maintenance agency or agencies during operation of the proposed system. These impacts may include the following:

— Modification of responsibilities; responsibilities;
— Addition or elimination of job positions; positions;
— Training or retraining users; users;
— Changes in numbers, skill levels, position identifiers, or locations of personnel; personnel; and
— Numbers and skill levels of personnel needed for contingency operation at one or more alternate sites following an emergency, disaster, or accident.

4.7.3 Impacts during development (7.3 of the ConOps document)

This subclause should be further divided into lower-level subclauses that describe the anticipated impacts on the user, development, and support or maintenance agency or agencies during the development project for the proposed system. These impacts may include the following:

— Involvement in studies, meetings, and discussions prior to award of the contract;
— User and support involvement in reviews and demonstrations, evaluation of initial operating capabilities and evolving versions of the system, development or modification of databases, and required training;
— Parallel operation of the new and existing systems; and
— Operational impacts during system testing of the proposed system.

4.8 Analysis of the proposed system (Clause 8 of the ConOps document)

This clause provides an analysis of the benefits, limitations, advantages, disadvantages, and alternatives and trade-offs considered for the proposed system.

4.8.1 Summary of improvements (8.1 of the ConOps document)

This subclause provides a qualitative (and to the extent possible, quantitative) summary of the benefits to be provided by the proposed system. This summary should include the below items, as applicable. In each case, the benefits should be related to deficiencies identified in 4.1 of the ConOps.

— *New capabilities.* Additional new features or functionality.
— *Enhanced capabilities.* Upgrades to existing capabilities.
— *Deleted capabilities.* Unused, obsolete, confusing, or dangerous capabilities removed.
— *Improved performance.* Better response time, reduced storage requirements, improved quality, etc.

4.8.2 Disadvantages and limitations (8.2 of the ConOps document)

This subclause provides a qualitative (and to the extent possible, quantitative) summary of the disadvantages and/or limitations of the proposed system. Disadvantages might include the need to retrain personnel, rearrange work spaces, or change to a new style of user interface; limitations might include features desired by users but not included, degradation of existing capabilities to gain new capabilities, or greater-than-desired response time for certain complex operations.

4.8.3 Alternatives and trade-offs considered (8.3 of the ConOps document)

This subclause should describe major alternatives considered, the trade-offs among them, and rationale for the decisions reached. In the context of a ConOps document, alternatives are operational alternatives and not design alternatives, except to the extent that designs alternatives may be limited by the operational capabilities desired in the new system. This information can be useful to determine, now and at later times, whether a given approach was analyzed and evaluated, or why a particular approach or solution was rejected. This information would probably be lost if not recorded.

4.9 Notes (Clause 9 on the ConOps document)

This clause should contain any additional information that will aid understanding of a particular ConOps document. This clause should include an alphabetical listing of all acronyms and abbreviations, along with their meanings as used in this document, and a list of any terms and definitions needed to understand the document.

4.10 Appendices (Appendices of the ConOps document)

To facilitate ease of use and maintenance of the ConOps document, some information may be placed in appendices to the document. Charts and classified data are typical examples. Each appendix should be referenced in the main body of the document where that information would normally have been provided. Appendices may be bound as separate documents for easier handling.

4.11 Glossary (Glossary of the ConOps document)

The inclusion of a clear and concise definition of terms used in the ConOps document (but that may be unfamiliar to readers of the ConOps document) is very important. A glossary should be maintained and updated during the processes of concept analysis and development of the ConOps document. To avoid unnecessary work due to misinterpretations, all definitions should be reviewed and agreed upon by all involved parties.

Annex A

IEEE/EIA 12207.1-1997 Compliance Statement

(Informative)

A.1 Overview

The Software Engineering Standards Committee (SESC) of the IEEE Computer Society has endorsed the policy of adopting international standards. In 1995, the international standard, ISO/IEC 12207, Information technology—Software life cycle processes, was completed. That standard establishes a common framework for software life cycle processes, with well-defined terminology, that can be referenced by the software industry.

In 1995 SESC evaluated ISO/IEC 12207 and decided that the standard should be adopted and serve as the basis for life cycle processes within the IEEE Software Engineering Collection. The IEEE adaptation of ISO/IEC 12207 is IEEE/EIA 12207.0-1996. It contains ISO/IEC 12207 and the following additions: improved compliance approach, life cycle process objectives, life cycle data objectives, and errata.

The implementation of ISO/IEC 12207 within the IEEE also includes the following:

— IEEE/EIA 12207.1-1997, IEEE/EIA Guide for Information Technology—Software life cycle processes—Life cycle data;

— IEEE/EIA 12207.2-1997, IEEE/EIA Guide for Information Technology—Software life cycle processes—Implementation considerations; and

— Additions to 11 existing SESC standards (i.e., IEEE Stds 730, 828, 829, 830, 1012, 1016, 1058, 1062, 1219, 1233, and 1362) to define the correlation between the data produced by existing SESC standards and the data produced by the application of IEEE/EIA 12207.1-1997.

NOTE — Although IEEE/EIA 12207.1-1997 is a guide, it also contains provisions for application as a standard with specific compliance requirements. This annex treats IEEE/EIA 12207.1-1997 as a standard.

In order to achieve compliance with both this standard and IEEE/EIA 12207.1-1997, it is essential that the user review and satisfy the data requirements for both standards.

When this standard is directly referenced, the precedence for conformance is based upon this standard alone. When this standard is referenced with the IEEE/EIA 12207.x standard series, the precedence for conformance is based upon the directly referenced IEEE/EIA 12207.x standard, unless there is a statement that this standard has precedence.

A.1.1 Scope and purpose

Both this standard and IEEE/EIA 12207.1-1997 place requirements on a ConOps document. The purpose of this annex is to explain the relationship between the two sets of requirements so that users producing documents intended to comply with both standards may do so.

A.2 Correlation

This clause explains the relationship between this standard and IEEE/EIA 12207.0-1996 in the following areas: terminology, process, and life cycle data.

A.2.1 Terminology correlation

Both this standard and IEEE/EIA 12207.0-1996 have similar semantics for the key terms of change, constraints, environment, modes of operation, policy, and system.

A.2.2 Process correlation

This standard places no requirements on process.

A.2.3 Life cycle data correlation and concept of operations documents

The information required in a ConOps document by this standard and the information required in a ConOps document by IEEE/EIA 12207.1-1997 are similar. It is reasonable to expect that a single document could comply with both standards. Both documents use a process-oriented context to describe the content of a ConOps document.

A.2.4 Life cycle data correlation between other data in IEEE/EIA 12207.1-1997 and this standard

This sublause correlates the life cycle data other than a ConOps document between IEEE/EIA 12207.1-1997 and this standard. It provides information to users of both standards.

Table A-1—Life cycle data correlation between other data in IEEE/EIA 12207.1-1997 and IEEE Std 1362-1998

Information item	IEEE/EIA 12207.0-1996 subclause	Kind	IEEE/EIA 12207.1-1997 subclause	IEEE Std 1362-1998 subclause
System architecture and requirements allocation description	5.3.3.1, 5.3.3.2	Description	6.25	4.5.3

A.3 Document compliance

This clause provides details bearing on a claim that a ConOps document complying with this standard would also achieve "document compliance" with the ConOps document described in IEEE/EIA 12207.1-1997. The requirements for document compliance are summarized in a single row of Table 1 of IEEE/EIA 12207.1-1997. That row is reproduced in Table A.2.

Table A-2—Summary of requirements for a ConOps document excerpted from Table 1 of IEEE/EIA Std 12207.1-1997.

Information item(s)	IEEE/EIA 12207.0-1996 subclause	Kind	IEEE/EIA 12207.1-1997 subclause	References
ConOps	5.1.1.1	Description	6.3	IEEE Std 1362-1998 EIA/IEEE J-STD-016, F.2.1 Also see the following for guidance on the use of notations: ISO 5806: 1984 ISO 5807: 1985 ISO 8631: 1989 ISO 8790: 1987 ISO 11411: 1995

The requirements for document compliance are discussed in the following subclauses:

— A.3.1 discusses compliance with the information requirements noted in column 2 of Table A.2 as prescribed by Clause 5.1.1.1 of IEEE/EIA 12207.0-1996.

— A.3.2 discusses compliance with the generic content guideline (the "kind" of document) noted in column 3 of Table A.2 as a "description." The generic content guidelines for a "description" appear in 5.1 of IEEE/EIA 12207.1-1997.

— A.3.3 discusses compliance with the specific requirements for a ConOps document noted in column 4 of Table A.2 as prescribed by 6.3 of IEEE/EIA 12207.1-1997.

— A.3.4 discusses compliance with the life cycle data objectives of Annex H of IEEE/EIA 12207.0-1996 as described in 4.2 of IEEE/EIA 12207.1-1997.

A.3.1 Compliance with information requirements of IEEE/EIA 12207.0-1996

The information requirements for a ConOps document are those prescribed by 5.1.1.1 of IEEE/EIA 12207.0-1996. In this case, those requirements are substantially identical with those considered in A.3.3 of this standard.

A.3.2 Compliance with generic content guidelines of IEEE/EIA 12207.1-1997

The generic content guidelines for a "description" in IEEE/EIA 12207.1-1997 are prescribed by 5.1 of IEEE/EIA 12207.1-1997. A complying description shall achieve the purpose stated in 5.1.1 and include the information listed in 5.1.2 of IEEE/EIA 12207.1-1997.

The purpose of a description is:

IEEE/EIA 12207.1-1997, subclause 5.1.1: Purpose: Describe a planned or actual function, design, performance, or process.

A ConOps document complying with this standard would achieve the stated purpose.

Any description complying with IEEE/EIA 12207.1-1997 shall satisfy the generic content requirements provided in 5.1.2 of that standard. Table A.3 of this standard lists the generic content items and, where appropriate, references the subclause of this standard that requires the same information. The third column lists information that shall be added in order to comply with the generic content requirements.

Table A-3—Coverage of generic description requirements by ConOps document listed in IEEE Std 1362-1998

IEEE/EIA 12207.1-1997 generic content	Corresponding subclauses of IEEE Std 1362-1998	Additions to requirements of IEEE Std 1362-1998
a) Date of issue and status	—	Date of issue and status should be provided in the Revision Chart or as an additional clause after the Glossary, Configuration management.
b) Scope	4.1 Scope (Clause 1 of the ConOps document)	—
c) Issuing organization	—	Issuing organization should be identified and referenced in the Revision Chart or as an additional clause after the Glossary, Configuration management.
d) References	4.2 Referenced documents (Clause 2 of the ConOps document)	—
e) Context	4.3 Current system or situation (Clause 3 of the ConOps document)	—
f) Notation for description	—	The definition of, or appropriate references to a definition of, the notation used for the system overview graphics should be included in 1.3 of the ConOps document if the system graphics are included.
g) Body	4.4 Justification for and nature of changes (Clause 4 of the ConOps document) 4.5 Concepts for the proposed system (Clause 5 of the ConOps document) 4.6 Operational scenarios (Clause 6 of the ConOps document) 4.7 Summary of impacts (Clause 7 of the ConOps document)	—
h) Summary	4.8 Analysis of the proposed system (Clause 8 of the ConOps document)	—
i) Glossary	4.11 Glossary (Glossary of the ConOps document)	—
j) Change history	—	Change history for the ConOps document should be provided or referenced in an additional clause after the Glossary, Configuration management.

A.3.3 Compliance with specific content requirements of IEEE/EIA 12207.1-1997

The specific content requirements for a ConOps document in IEEE/EIA 12207.1-1997 are prescribed by 6.3 of IEEE/EIA 12207.1-1997. A complying ConOps document shall achieve the purpose stated in 6.3.1 and include the information listed in 6.3.3 of IEEE/EIA 12207.1-1997.

The purpose of the ConOps document is:

IEEE/EIA 12207.1-1997, subclause 6.3.1: Purpose: Describe, in users' terminology, how the system should operate to meet the users' needs for the system.

A ConOps document complying with IEEE/EIA 12207.1-1997 shall satisfy the specific content requirements provided in 6.3.3 of that standard. Table A.4 of this standard lists the specific content items and, where appropriate, references the subclause of this standard that requires the same information. The third column lists information that shall be added in order to comply with the specific content requirements.

Table A-4—Coverage of specific ConOps document requirements by requirements by ConOps document listed in IEEE Std 1362-1998

IEEE/EIA Std 12207.1-1997 specific content	Corresponding subclauses of IEEE Std 1362-1998	Additions to requirements of IEEE Std 1362-1998
a) Generic description information	4.1 Scope (Clause 1 of the ConOps document)	See Table A.2
b) Description of current situation or system	4.3 Current system or situation (Clause 3 of the ConOps document)	—
c) Justification for and nature of changes	4.4 Justification for and nature of changes (Clause 4 of the ConOps document)	—
d) Concepts of the proposed system	4.5 Concepts for the proposed system (Clause 5 of the ConOps document)	—
e) Operational scenarios	4.6 Operational scenarios (Clause 6 of the ConOps document)	—
f) Summary of impacts	4.7 Summary of impacts (Clause 7 of the ConOps document)	—
g) Analysis of the proposed system	4.8 Analysis of the proposed system (Clause 8 of the ConOps document)	—
h) Priorities, assumptions, constraints, advantages, limitations, alternatives, and trade-offs considered	4.8.1 Summary of improvements 4.8.2 Disadvantages and limitations 4.8.3 Alternatives and tradeoffs considered	—

A.3.4 Compliance with life cycle data characteristics

In addition to the content requirements, life cycle data shall be managed in accordance with the objectives provided in Annex H of IEEE/EIA 12207.0-1996.

NOTE — The information items covered by this standard include plans and provisions for creating software life cycle data related to the basic types "requirements data" and "user data" in H.4 of IEEE/EIA 12207.0-1996. Requirements data provides for the following: expected functionality, operational context, performance constraints and expectations, basis for qualification testing, and key decision rationale. User data provides the following: software overview, system access information, commands and responses, error messages, operational environment, and key decision rationale.

A.4 Conclusion

The analysis suggests that any ConOps document complying with this standard and the additions shown in Table A.3 and Table A.4 will comply with the requirements of a ConOps document in IEEE/EIA 12207.1-1997. In addition, to comply with IEEE/EIA 12207.1-1997, any document shall support the life cycle data objectives of Annex H of IEEE/EIA 12207.0-1996.

Chapter 3

Software Requirements Analysis and Specifications

1. Introduction to Chapter

Software requirements can be defined in several different ways[1]:

- A software capability needed by a user to solve a problem or achieve an objective

- A software capability that must be met or possessed by a system or system component to satisfy a contract, standard, specification, or other formally imposed document

- A short description sometimes used in place of the term "software requirements specification"

Software requirements analysis is the process of studying user needs to arrive at a definition of software requirements. A *software requirements specification* is the document that clearly and precisely describes each of the essential requirements (functions, performance, design constraints, and quality attributes) of the software and the external interfaces. Each requirement should be defined in such a way that its achievement is capable of being objectively verified by a prescribed method; for example, test, demonstration, analysis, and inspection.[2]

Chapter 3 contains articles on "classic" software requirements. Chapter 3 also contains the most popular standard in software engineering: the *IEEE Recommended Practice for Software Requirements Specifications.* Published along with this standard is the *IEEE Guide for Developing System Requirements Specifications.*

This chapter looks at software requirements from the basic premise that the requirement analysis determines what the customer needs, and the specification document, produced as a result of the analysis, documents those needs. This view is held regardless of the tools and methodology that might be used to arrive at the needs and specifications.

2. Description of Articles

"Techniques for Requirements Elicitation," by Joseph A. Goguen and Charlotte Linde, is one of the best articles from the *Proceedings of the International Symposium on Requirements Engineering* in 1993. It is also one of the few recent articles on requirements elicitation. Requirements elicitation is a recent addition to requirements engineering.

This article surveys and evaluates several elicitation techniques for computer-based systems, paying particular attention to dealing with social issues. The techniques surveyed include introspection, interviews, questionnaires, focus groups, discussion groups, and protocol and discourse analysis. Although these techniques are relatively untried in requirements engineering, the authors believe there is promise in the approach, particularly for the last three techniques listed. Two of the techniques discussed under focus groups are the popular JAD and RAD (joint application development and rapid application development, respectively).

The article discusses the social interaction between individuals and the requirements analyst's ability to extract the correct requirements from a group of users.

"Getting Started: Using Use Cases to Capture Requirements," by James Rumbaugh, reports on a requirements elicitation method called "use cases." The article starts by discussing *user-centered analysis* as the best method of determining software requirements. *User-centered analysis* is a process of capturing requirements from the users' point of view. Rumbaugh reports that many people consider user-centered analysis to be the *best* way to solve the *right* problem.

Use cases are a user-centered analysis technique. *Use cases* identify scenarios between system components and one or more external entities that stimulate the system. Use cases are written as natural language text descriptions. Each scenario describes a task from the user's point of view. Details of how the system works internally are irrelevant to a use case.

The next article in this chapter, by Stuart Faulk of the University of Oregon, is an excellent overview of software requirements engineering. This original article also appears in the IEEE tutorial *Software Engineering.* The article argues that software requirements engineering is a subset of software engineering.

Faulk shows that "requirements problems are persistent, pervasive, and costly," and describes the difficulties that arise in the development and documentation of software requirements. He shows how a disciplined approach can help solve requirements problems. He summarizes current and emerging methods for software requirements engineering and concludes with the observation that, while it may be impossible to do a perfect job of software requirements, a systematic approach can contribute to successful software development.

The fourth article in this chapter is "Requirements Engineering with Viewpoints," by Gerald Kotonya and Ian Sommerville. It is reprinted from the January 1996 issue of the *Software Engineering Journal,* a joint publication of the U.K. Institution of Electrical Engineers and the British Computer Society.

After reviewing some of the causes of poor requirements specifications and the characteristics of a good requirements engineering approach, the authors describe the use of viewpoints. Viewpoints represent the interests of different parties in the development and use of the system. The parties may be direct users or may have an indirect stake in how others develop and use the system, such as the viewpoint of security and systems planning in the development of an automated teller system.

Kotonya and Sommerville next describe viewpoint-oriented requirements definition (VORD), a process for requirements engineering. The process has three steps:

1. Identification and structuring of viewpoints
2. Documentation of the identified viewpoints
3. Specification of the viewpoint requirements

An example of the application of VORD is given, and viewpoint analysis is discussed in more detail. A VORD tool set is described. Finally, some limitations of the method are presented, such as VORD is limited to a service-oriented view of a system and lacks direct support for control and concurrency.

As the title says, the article by Alan Davis et al., "Identifying and Measuring Quality in a Software Requirements Specification," is concerned with how to produce a quality software requirements specification. A software requirements specification is a document that describes all of the external observable behavior and characteristics expected of a software system. A quality software requirements specification is one that contributes to the successful creation of the software system.

This article looks at the concept of quality in a software requirements specification and defines attributes that contribute to that quality. The article identifies twenty-four metrics that could be used to measure quality in a software requirements specification. The article then treats each metric separately and provides:

- A description of the metric
- An example of the application of the metric

- A subjective quality metric for the attribute
- A short discussion on methods by which the attribute could be improved

In summary, the article defines twenty-four qualities that the software requirements specification should exhibit. It provides an impressive list of references and in eighteen cases a quantitative metric for the quality attributes.

The next-to-last article is a copy of IEEE Standard 830-1993, *IEEE Recommended Practice for Software Requirements Specifications*. This recommended practice is an outstanding thesis on what should be contained in a software requirements specification. A recommended practice, in the IEEE standards hierarchy, not only contains those items that are mandatory in a software requirements specifications but also includes suggested procedures.

This recommended practice, which was written by the Working Group for Software Requirements Specifications, Software Engineering Standards Subcommittee of the Technical Committee on Software Engineering of the IEEE Computer Society, was chaired by Edward R. Byrne. The purpose of this recommended practice was to provide mandatory contents for a software requirements specification and to describe a "good" software requirements specification. The recommended practice also describes several alternative approaches to specifying software requirements. This recommended practice contains criteria that may be used in evaluating a software requirements specification.

The purpose of the document is to:

- Help software customers accurately describe what they want to attain
- Help software suppliers understand exactly what the customer wants
- Help individuals in companies:

  —Develop a standard outline for their organization's requirements specifications

—Develop additional local support items such as a software requirements specification quality checklist, or a writer's handbook

The final article in this chapter and the second standard included in the tutorial is the *IEEE Guide for Developing System Requirements Specifications*, IEEE standard P1233-1993. This guide was developed by a working group from the IEEE Computer Society Software Engineering Standards Committee, chaired by Louis E. Miller, and as of this writing is still in draft form. The purpose of this guide is to provide a procedure for capturing system requirements. This guide serves analysts by providing a clear definition for identifying well-formed system requirements and ways of organizing them. This guide should be used to help the analyst capture requirements at the beginning of the system requirements phase. It can also be used to clarify what constitutes a good requirement and provide an understanding of where to look to identify different requirement sources.

This guide is viewed as a means of developing a document that can be used to communicate system requirements from a customer to a technical group that will develop the system, that is, it acts as a bridge between the customer and the developer. In Chapter 2 the concept of operations (ConOps) document was viewed as fulfilling the same role. Therefore, the ConOps document can be viewed as a predecessor document to the system requirements specification and both of them as predecessor documents to the software requirements specification.

References

1. Adapted from *IEEE Standard Glossary of Software Engineering Terminology,* ANSI/IEEE Std 729-1983, IEEE, New York, N.Y., 1983.

2. ANSI/IEEE Std 830-1984, *IEEE Standard for Software Requirements Specifications,* IEEE, NY, 1984. Reprinted in *System and Software Engineering Requirements,* Thayer, R.H., and M. Dorfman, eds., IEEE Computer Society Press, Los Alamitos, Calif., 1990.

Techniques for Requirements Elicitation*

Joseph A. Goguen
Centre for Requirements and Foundations
Oxford University Computing Lab

Charlotte Linde
Institute for Research on Learning
Palo Alto, California

Abstract

This paper surveys and evaluates techniques for eliciting requirements of computer-based systems, paying particular attention to how they deal with social issues. The methods surveyed include introspection, interviews, questionnaires, and protocol, conversation, interaction, and discourse analyses. Although they are relatively untried in Requirements Engineering, we believe there is much promise in the last three techniques, which grew out of ethnomethodology and sociolinguistics. In particular, they can elicit tacit knowledge by observing actual interactions in the workplace, and can also be applied to the system development process itself.

1   Introduction

A basic question in Requirements Engineering is how to find out what users really need. Research has shown that many large projects fail because of inadequate requirements [5]; moreover, this inadequacy is often related to social, political and cultural factors. This paper describes and assesses techniques for requirements elicitation. We first review some traditional techniques, including introspection, questionnaires, interviews, focus groups, and protocol analysis. Then we discuss some techniques from discourse analysis, which we take to include conversation and interaction analyses, as well as the analysis of discourse structure. Finally, we compare the various approaches. There is a fairly large bibliography.

Developing a large system[1] is a complex and difficult process. In the early days of computing, there was no particular organisation to this process: programmers just sat down and tried to write code that would be useful. Today, few doubt that a task that can consume hundreds of person-years should be carefully planned and managed. Therefore the system "life cycle" has been broken into a number of so called "phases," of which Requirements Engineering is the earliest phase[2] that lies largely within Computing Science. The requirements phase is typically preceeded by business planning, and is formally initiated by the client.

It is more accurate to view the division of the life cycle into phases as a management technique, than as a model of how the system development process actually proceeds; i.e., the life cycle phases are a useful scheme for classifying the activities that occur in system development, but it is far from true that these activities occur in strict linear order. Suchman [43] explains that naturally occurring plans are typically used as after-the-fact explanations to lend coherence to past events. Indeed, requirements are constantly reconsidered in both design and coding, and often activities that can be classified as Requirements Engineering are done by programmers and managers relatively near system delivery, or even after system delivery. Moreover, much of this work remains undocumented. (See [8] for an ethnographic study that supports these assertions.)

Once a need is expressed and an initial plan developed, the requirements team tries to identify what properties the system should have to meet that need. Note that setting up a requirements team involves choosing representatives of the client; their background knowledge and experience can play a very strong rôle in the development process. Relevant properties may include not just high-level functional requirements, but also response time, cost, security, portability, reliability, and modifiability. In addition, there may be requirements for the development process, such as certain quality control procedures, reporting schemes, tools, or limits on cost or time. Some of these are not easily quantified; the imprecision may even be desirable, to accommodate the trade-offs that inevitably arise.

The next phase after requirements is "design," where engineers try to fix the main components of the system, their requirements, and interactions. This resembles how an architect designs a house, once requirements have been agreed with a client. A more detailed design phase may follow. (Of course, an actual execution of this idealised plan will generally interleave the various activities.)

The analogy with architecture should make it clear that eliciting requirements can be far from easy: clients may change their minds once they see the possibilities more clearly, and discoveries made during later phases may also force retrofitting requirements. The requirements of real systems are rarely static. There are very good reasons why clients often do not, or cannot, know exactly what they need; they may want to see models, explore alternatives, and envision new possibilities. Often these possibilities are closely intertwined with social, political, legal, financial, and/or psychological factors. For example, certain ways of using a database

---

*The research reported in this paper has been supported by a contract with British Telecom.

[1] There is little difference between the development cycles of software and hardware systems, and most real systems involve both aspects.

[2] There is no widely accepted terminology for phases, nor even any widely accepted division into phases.

Reprinted from *Proc. Int'l Symp. Requirements Engineering,* 1993, pp. 152–164.

may be illegal; others may be politically undesirable; some may be incompatible with the corporate organisation of the user (e.g., they may cross administrative boundaries); others may be too slow unless very expensive equipment is used. In the extreme, a project may be doomed, because no system can be built that satisfies its requirements or because the agreed requirements do not reflect the real needs.

A major goal of Requirements Engineering is to avoid such problems. This will often involve putting significant effort into requirements elicitation. Unfortunately, Requirements Engineering is an immature discipline, perhaps not entirely unfairly characterised as a battlefield occupied by competing commercial methods[3], firing competing claims at each other, and leaving the consumers weary and confused.

1.1 Why Social Science?

The problems of requirements elicitation cannot be solved in a purely technological way, because social context is much more crucial than in the programming, specification and design phases. Some Computing Scientists might think that requirements elicitation is where science stops and chaos begins. This raises the fundamental questions of whether there *is* any order in the social world, and if so, how it can be studied. If there is order in the social world, then a precise understanding of how it is constructed and maintained should help with methodology for requirements elicitation. If not, then requirements elicitation must remain a mysterious process, fraught with frequent unexplained failures, and occasional unexplained successes.

The premise of this paper, as of social science generally, is that the social world *is* ordered. We also make two further assertions: social order may not be immediately obvious, or immediately describable, by common sense; and social order cannot be assumed to have an *a priori* structure. Therefore, social order can only be determined by immersion in the actual unfolding of social phenomena, rather than (for example) by collecting statistics about the occurrence of certain pre-given categories. Detailed arguments for these assertions are given later.

The majority of computer-based systems are developed without any systematic help from the social sciences (sociology, psychology, linguistics, anthropology, etc.). This means that the needs of the user, both as individual and as organisation, are not addressed systematically; in general, they are only incompletely known to the development team, and there are often some serious misconceptions. Among the systems that have been developed with some help from the social sciences, most have used only classical experimental psychology (e.g., ergonomics for keyboard layout, or the psychology of perception for display colours). Many efforts have tried to model the cognitive process of individual users, but this approach has not been very successful with the larger social, political, and cultural factors that so often cause failure.

[3] What we call "methods" are often called "methodologies" by practitioners. But in an academic context, the word "methodology" should properly be used for the study and comparison of methods, and that is how we use it in this paper.

Very few system development efforts have tried to use any social science methods beyond (for example) elementary guidelines for the conduct of interviews. Among these, very few indeed have tried to use techniques based on what we regard as the most promising areas, namely ethnomethodology and sociolinguistics (see [17, 28] for related discussion).

It seems worth emphasising that many requirements methods available in the marketplace, even though they may refer to certain social, organisation, or linguistic issues, do not do so in a systematic manner, and in fact, do not have any proper scientific basis at all. Of course, this is not to deny that there may be a great deal of practical experience behind the recommendations and notations of some of the better methods, or that they may be useful in many practical situations.

This paper begins to explore a scientific basis for requirements elicitation, by considering the basic issue of how to acquire the necessary information. Introspection is undoubtedly the most common current source of information; but experience shows that it can be very misleading. Interviews and questionnaires are also widely used, and sometimes protocol analysis is used. Any of these can be useful. But this paper argues that conversation, interaction, and discourse analyses are more detailed and precise, and hence likely to be more accurate.

Acknowledgements

The first author wishes to thank Kathleen Goguen for many valuable comments on this paper, and the members of the Centre for Requirements and Foundations at Oxford for their friendly enthusiasm. Both authors wish to thank Dr. Susan Leigh Star for her very helpful comments on a draft of the paper.

2 Introspection

Introspection is the first and most obvious method for trying to understand what properties a system should have in order to succeed. It amounts to imagining what kind of system I would want if I were doing this job, using this equipment, etc. This method can be very useful, but it has the problem that the introspection of an expert in a different field, such as Requirements Engineering, is unlikely to reflect the experience of actual users. Experts tend to work from what they remember or imagine of themselves; for user interface design, this experience can be very far from the questions, assumptions and fears of actual users. In viewing tapes of novice users learning a new interface, interface designers and cognitive scientists were consistently shocked by what they saw as incompetent and inconsistent behaviour [25]. For example, experts might be surprised that, when a word processer does something a user finds surprising, such as centering a headline further to the right than expected, the user does not attempt to understand why; in fact, users seem to believe that computers just are sometimes puzzling or irritating, and that it is not necessary or valuable to explain why. Cognitive scientists may be surprised at this, because their model suggests that a user who finds that a model is incorrect should correct the model. Designers may be upset because they feel that the subjects are not using their designs correctly.

Similarly, requirements engineers cannot introspect what work settings look like, or the conditions under which a new technology will be learned. For example, many subjects must learn to use new technology in conditions that require multiple and ongoing splitting of attention. However, requirements rarely take account of this.

Finally, we note that the phrase "naive user" can confuse the issue. So called naive users are often experts in their own speciality, about which the requirements engineers are naive. Although this is obvious, the point is that the phrase focuses attention on the users' relation to the new technology, and may suggest that the users' task is to learn the technology properly and fully, instead of just doing their own job better using the new technology.

We conclude not that introspection is an inadmissible method, as claimed by many current psychologists, but rather that introspection without careful consideration of its limits can be (and often is) highly inaccurate (an interesting discussion of introspection can be found in [47]). Hence, we suggest that if there is room for doubt, introspection should be checked by some of the more empirical methods described below.

3 Interviews

Interviews are used in an extraordinary variety of domains, and are often quite successful; see [30] for a good survey. This section discusses questionnaires, open ended interviews, and focus groups, showing that the interview process involves some (usually unstated) assumptions about the interaction between interviewer and subject. We argue that some of these assumptions are quite problematic, and raise doubts about using these methods for some applications.

3.1 Questionnaire Interviews

Questionnaire interviews are very widely used, and have the benefit of appearing scientific, because they use statistical analysis. The following is from a discussion by Suchman and Jordan ([46] p. 232):

1. There is an unresolved tension between the survey interview as an interactional event and as a neutral measurement instrument. On the one hand, the interview is commonly acknowledged to be fundamentally an interaction. On the other hand, in the interest of turning the interview into an instrument, many of the interactional resources of ordinary conversation are disallowed.

2. The success of the interview as an instrument turns on the premise that (a) relevant questions can be decided in advance of the interaction and (b) questions can be phrased in such a way that, as long as they are read without variation, they will be heard in the intended way and will stimulate a valid response.

3. The premises of 2. fail insofar as (a) topics that come from outside the conversation run the risk of irrelevance, and (b) as an ordinary language procedure, the survey interview is inherently available for multiple interpretations of the meaning of both questions and answers.

4. Compared with ordinary conversation, the survey interview suppresses those interactional resources that routinely mediate uncertainties of relevance and interpretation.

Suchman and Jordan [46] argue that validity is not assured by having the same words repeated to subjects in each interview, because these words will mean different things to different people in different contexts. In normal interaction, these issues of interpretation are negotiated between participants; but in a survey interview, the method and training given to interviewers specifically forbids such negotiation. The following example should make this point more vivid [46][4]:

I: Generally speaking, do you usually think of yourself as a Republican, Democrat, Independent, or what?

R: As a person.

I: As a Republican::

R: No.

I: Democrat::

R: No.

I: Independent or what.

R: Uhm:: I think of myself as a (pause) Christian.

I: Okay. (writing) But politically, would you have any particular:: (inaudible)

R: I am one of Jehovah's Witnesses so, you know, when it comes to::

I: I see.

R: So I'm, I am acclimated toward government, but it is that of Jehovah God's kingdom.

I: Yes.

Here, the interviewer presupposes a system of political categories, and asks the respondent to choose one for self identity. But the respondent does not share this system, and thus cannot choose. This mismatch could be the beginning of an interesting exploration of the respondent's religious and political categories, and in an ordinary conversational situation, probably would be. But because this is forbidden for survey interviewers, this fascinating informant probably ends up as a bleached "Don't Know" or "Other." The point is a general one: categories and concepts that are transparent to one community can be entirely opaque to members of another community, and the fact that this opacity exists may not be noticed in the course of discussions unless specific attention is paid to the possibility.

Here is another example (cited in [30]) of an answer that must be classified as "other":

I: Are you a virgin?

R: Not yet.

---

[4]In this transcription system, colons after a sound indicate that it is lengthened, and the number of colons indicates the degree of lengthening.

3.2 Open ended Interviews

The open ended interview is much used in anthropology and psychology, and avoids many problems of the questionnaire method. In it, the interviewer poses a question, and then allows subjects to answer as they wish. The interviewer may probe for more detail, but does not set the terms of the interview. This sounds much more benign than the survey interview, but the issues of whether the question asked can be answered at all, and whether the answer is part of the normal discourse repertoire of the speaker, still remain.

Let us first consider questions that cannot be answered at all. For example, in linguistics and education research, subjects are sometimes asked how they tie their shoelaces. This produces some marvelous examples of linguistic incompetence. But there is no reason why subjects *should* be competent at this task, because people do not tell each other how to tie bowknots — rather, it is taught by showing. (But a sailor or a ship model maker may give a much more competent performance, because these experts have vocabulary for knots and the parts of knots.)

Let us generalise. People know how to do many things that they cannot describe. It is a commonplace in ethnography that people's descriptions of how they weave a basket or choose a chief or write a program bear a complex and opaque relation to how they can be seen to do these things when they are observed. This problem is so familiar that it has a nickname in social science: the *say-do problem*; also, philosophers speak of *tacit knowledge*. The moral is this: Don't ask people to describe activities that they do not normally describe, or if you do, then don't believe the answers.

Now let us consider interview questions that people can and do answer in what seems a useful way, and ask how this compares with their practice; we must consider not only the practice that they describe, but also their discourse practice. For this, we must compare the discourse produced when the topic is elicited with that produced in a related but non-elicited situation; that is, we ask whether the interview data is the same, is wholly different, or bears some partial but regular similarity to the non-elicited speech. One approach is to observe spontaneous speech. For example, in studying apartment layout descriptions, we can observe whether they occur in spontaneous speech, and whether they are the same or closely similar to instances gathered in an interview situation [23, 27]; such informal checking must be done after the actual analysis of elicited data has suggested some structures of interest, because memory for linguistic structure in natural settings is generally not sufficiently reliable. In practice, such observation requires interest in the adventures of friends searching for apartments, and following strangers down the street when their conversation turns to this topic. Such are the exigencies of empirical research.

It is even better to compare interview data with recorded, non-elicited data, to see if they are usably similar. For example, [51] shows that elicited narratives differ from spontaneously produced narratives on a fine level of detail, including use of the historical present tense. This difference arises because *performing* a narrative, so that the addressee can visualise the event, encourages use of the historical present. Performed narratives are much more likely to be produced when the speaker and addressee share characteristics such as age, occupation or ethnicity, or when they are friends. Because these characteristics are not likely to be shared by participants in an interview situation, the tense system will be at least slightly different. Similarly, the form of evaluation (see Section 6.2) in elicited narratives may differ from that of spontaneous narratives, because spontaneous narratives can include negotiations between the primary speaker and other interlocutors that an interviewer may be unwilling to undertake, for fear of biasing the data.

Whether such differences matter depends on the nature of the investigation, and must be determined for each case. If finely detailed data is needed, then elicited narratives cannot be considered identical to spontaneous narratives. But if only less detailed, or higher level structure is needed, then open ended interview data may be adequate.

3.3 Focus and Application Development Groups

The focus group is a kind of group interview, rather widely used in marketing research [42], but less used in pure social science research ([29] gives a favourable review of the potential of focus groups in social science). In this technique, groups are brought together to discuss some topic of interest to the researcher. In market research, this is often done using stimulus materials such as films, story boards, or product mockups as a focus (hence the name), and is commonly used to get the opinions of representative potential customers on new products.

Focus groups have the advantage of allowing more natural interactions between people than questionnaire interviews, or even open ended interviews. However, the groups are usually not natural communities, such as people who eat lunch together, or all the purchasing agents of a particular corporation, but rather are an *ad hoc* collection, constituted for the occasion by the researcher, usually on the basis of demographic considerations. Further, although focus groups may be valuable for eliciting responses to products whose features and trade-offs customers understand (for example, whether they would be willing to pay more for upscale gourmet dog food for their Dobermann Pinschers), they are not useful in eliciting opinions on design issues where the subjects are not experts, and therefore must respond within the categories and structures provided by the researcher.

So called JAD or RAD groups[5] have recently become popular in Requirements Engineering, especially for Information Systems applications, because of their claim to greatly accelerate the development of requirements [1]. This method is closely related to focus groups, and can be expected to suffer from some of the same problems. In particular, participants will certainly be unable to articulate tacit knowledge. Also, even though group facilitators try to avoid imposing their

---

[5]These acronyms stand for Joint Application Development and Rapid Application Development, respectively.

own categories on participants, there is no guarantee that the participants will in fact share categories with each other. Moreover, because participants may have widely different status within the organisation, there is a danger that some will not feel free to say what they really think, especially if it is unpopular. Finally, it will often be difficult for non-technical participants to assess the significance of technical decisions. Although this method appears promising, we believe its potential limitations should be studied empirically.

3.4 Discussion

Interview methods can fail if the interviewer and respondent do not share a category system. For example, because the clients of architects are usually unfamiliar with the conventions of architectural drawings, they can easily agree to a design that fails to satisfy them when built. The Workplace Project[6] [7, 44, 45] found a case where some workers who wanted a space for working together, agreed to a protruding addition to a long tabletop. However, when built, the angle of the protrusion made it harder to view documents jointly than before.

Similar issues arise in requirements elicitation, because requirements engineers often come from communities with different values, assumptions, concerns, etc. from those of users. For example, [6] describes a case where two management information consultants working for a large U.S. university encounter difficulties in promoting schemes to help students, and then explain those difficulties with the theory that the administration is really concerned with "the care and feeding of the faculty," but cannot say so because this conflicts with the university's official mission statement.

Questionnaires, administered either orally or in writing, are often used in Requirements Engineering to determine characteristics or concerns of user populations. They can be useful when the population is large enough, and the issues addressed are clear enough to all concerned. However, they will fail when subjects are asked about topics that they do not have ways to talk about, or do not want to talk about.

4 Protocol Analysis

Protocol analysis asks a subject to engage in some task and concurrently talk aloud, explaining his/her thought process. Proponents claim that this kind of language can be considered a "direct verbalization of specific cognitive processes" ([12], p. 16). Protocol analysis is also used to reflect on problem solving, or some other task, retrospectively, i.e., after it has been accomplished. This section considers concurrent talk-aloud protocols, because they are more common; however, we note that the arguments of previous sections apply to the retrospective approach.

There seem to be two main arguments for talk-aloud protocols: that they are possible, and that they work. The argument for possibility must overcome arguments in psychology about the method of introspection used in the nineteenth and early twentieth centuries. It is

claimed [32] that the arguments against introspection do not apply, because the subject is not introspecting, but rather is emitting a stream of behaviour that does not differ in kind from producing a galvanic skin response or a muscular movement. Therefore, talk-aloud protocols are possible data in the framework of behaviourist psychology.

The argument that protocol analysis works in [12] is based on the apparent success of the GPS (General Problem Solver) system. GPS was originally developed as a research vehicle for problem solving in Artificial Intelligence. It reduces goals to subgoals, and then attempts to solve each subgoal that remains open by reducing it to further subgoals, until all subgoals are solved. In [32], the goals are to deduce certain symbolic logic expressions from others, and the transformations are certain elementary steps of deduction[7].

The results of this research have not stood the test of time. Even within the Artificial Intelligence community, it is hard to find researchers who still believe in top down backtrack problem solving that is driven simply by matching rules to goals to generate subgoals. For example, in motion planning, e.g., for robots, it is becoming increasingly clear that developing a complete plan in advance of execution is difficult, inefficient, inflexible, and does not correspond to how humans carry out actions. For the first point, studies in computational complexity show that producing complete, precise mathematical plans is an intractable problem [9]. For the second, it has been found that inexact, heuristic methods work better; indeed, so called "opportunistic planning," which produces partial plans, and then incrementally replans in response to new information, works much better in practice, because the sensory information and background knowledge available to robots (as to humans) is generally inexact, incomplete, ongoing, and subject to change. For a detailed summary of recent research on human planning, see [43].

Even in mechanical theorem proving, where the difficulties of being embedded in the physical world do not arise, current research uses a variety of heuristics, and also employs techniques that support flexible replanning — as do human mathematicians. No current generation Artificial Intelligence systems bear more than a superficial resemblance to GPS. Prolog [10], which at first glance might seem similar, in fact differs greatly in that it has logical variables, unification, cut, and other non-logical features to force evaluations that are *not* top down. (See [4] for a survey of mechanical theorem proving systems.)

In fact, protocols were *not* used inductively for developing GPS; rather, GPS was developed on the basis of *a priori* principles about mathematical problem solving, and then used as a basis for describing and critiquing the arguments in empirically obtained protocols. Of course, GPS was a significant advance in its time, and indeed, had to be explored thoroughly before moving on. We have no wish to minimise its historical importance in Artificial Intelligence, or its

---

[6]This study, conducted by Xerox Palo Alto Research Center, used as its data an airline operations room that was redesigned for a move to a new terminal.

---

[7]The anthropomorphic language used here is just a convenient shorthand for sketching the design of a computer program.

influence on cognitive psychology, both of which were considerable. However, we *do* wish to point out that its claims about human problem solving were wrong, even allowing a narrow interpretation of its domain, as were its claims about efficient mechanical problem solving. This implies that the experimental method used must have been flawed, and that is our main point: protocol analysis is not a reliable guide to what subjects are thinking, and is open to serious misinterpretation by analysts, who can choose a small sample of protocols (just one was used in [32]!) for an unrealistic problem (both artificially simple and artificially without social context) to impose their preconceptions on the data.

Beyond this demonstration of its fallibility, one can give two further arguments against protocol analysis, one general, and one specific to requirements. The first argument is this: As we have said, the assumption in staging and studying protocols is that people can produce language that gives a trace of autonomous cognitive activity. The problem with this assumption is that language is intrinsically social, created for a partner in conversation. (This property is called *recipient design* in conversation analysis.) When an experimenter asks a person to solve a problem and talk aloud, then that person has to imagine an experimenter with certain desires, and try to provide what the experimenter wants. (Or the subject may be rebellious, and try to frustrate the imagined experimenter.) Thus, protocols are an unnatural discourse form, and moreover, are unnatural in ways that are difficult to specify.

Let us consider the protocol given by Newell and Simon [32], produced by a student doing a problem in elementary symbolic logic:

> Well, looking at the left hand side of the equation, first we want to eliminate one of the sides by using rule 8. It appears to be too complicated to work with first. Now — no, — no I can't do that because I will be eliminating either the Q or the P in that total expression. I won't do that at first. Now I'm looking for a way to get rid of the horseshoe inside the two brackets that appear on the left and right sides of the equation. And I don't see it. Yeh, if you apply rule 6 to both sides of the equation, from there I'm going to see if I can apply rule 7.
>
> I can almost apply rule 7, but one R needs a tilde. So I'll have to look for another rule. I'm going to see if I can change that R to a tilde R. As a matter of fact, I should have used rule 6 on only the left hand side of the equation. So use rule 6, but only on the left hand side.
>
> Now I'll apply rule 7 as it is expressed. Both — excuse me, excuse me, it can't be done because of the horseshoe. So — now I'm looking — scanning the rules here for a second, and seeing if I can change the R to a tilde R in the second equation, but don't see any way of doing it. (Sigh.) I'm just sort of lost for a second.

There are specific linguistic features demonstrating the unnatural provenance of this passage. First, it fluctuates between the language of talking to oneself and the language of talking to an interlocutor who is physically present and involved. One sign of this fluctuation is the shift in pronoun choice: "we," "I," and "you" all appear. "You" seems to be the first choice in language that is specifically produced to be understood by an overhearer as talking to oneself. A first person plural expression like "first we want to eliminate one of the sides by using rule 8" is much more characteristic of a lecturer talking to an audience. Similarly, the use of impersonal constructions, such as "Well, looking at the left hand side" in the first sentence, and "It appears to be" in the second, is characteristic of the language of successful science [20]. Phrases like "excuse me, excuse me, it can't be done because of the horseshoe" are produced for an interlocutor; it is incoherent for a speaker to provide this kind of excuse to him/herself. Finally, a phrase like "I'm just sort of lost for a second" may most naturally be interpreted as an excuse to an interlocutor for a pause. In particular, note that the phrase "for a second" functions as a mitigation of the difficulty, as a kind of excuse for the pause, rather than as a bare description of a mental state.

The most telling argument against protocol analysis is that it *does not* work, as demonstrated by its use to support GPS as a model of human problem solving, once considered a spectacular success, but now seen to be a failure. Moreover, protocol analysis is based on a simplistic cognitivist model of human thinking as essentially computational, involving abstract representations of concepts, and their transformation by algorithms that are precisely specified by computer programs (e.g., see [31]).

Finally, even if it were possible to get a trace of a speaker's autonomous cognitive activity, such an object would be inappropriate for the requirements process, because the client does not have any pre-existing mental model of the desired system. Rather, the client has knowledge about business and organisational needs, while the requirements team has knowledge about technical possibilities. The process of producing requirements from these two different kinds of knowledge is necessarily conversational, because they must be combined. Thus, the requirements problem is intrinsically social, and cannot be solved using only methods that take individual cognition as fundamental.

5 The Question of Social Order

We have now surveyed a number of methods, and discussed some problems that arise from their underlying assumptions. The methods surveyed so far all impose an analyst's order on the social world, with no guarantee that this is the same as the order that members perceive, and with no way of even posing this as a research question. Note that the question of whose social order is assumed can be significant in requirements elicitation, where people from two or more possibly very different communities try to craft an understanding that is workable for all of them. An interesting discussion of some communication difficulties between sociologists and computer scientists is given in [36], based on actual experience at Lancaster University; one source of these difficulties appears to be the very different assumptions made in these two communities about the nature of research.

We have previously asserted the orderliness of the social world as a working principle; we will now examine in detail how certain aspects of social order are produced. Conventional approaches in sociology, anthropology, and the other social sciences assume pre-existing categories, such as social class, norm, rôle, etc., and then explain the observed social order as a reflection of these categories in practice. However, this approach does not explain how pre-given categories can act upon the moment to moment world of practice, to produce the order we observe. This critique of traditional social science is relevant to requirements elicitation because most existing approach are based on it. If we are right, then the results of requirements studies that assume pre-given categories can easily be more inaccurate and misleading than necessary.

Ethnomethodology [13] and conversation analysis (which grew out of ethnomethodology) arose in response to these problems. These fields consider that social order is accomplished by members in their moment by moment activities. For example, consider a seminar. Although the word "seminar" suggests a pre-existing category, it is in fact constructed by the members' furnishing of a room, or choice of a room furnished in a certain way, in the arrangement of chairs, in the orientation of participants towards someone understood to be the speaker, in the allotment of a very long turn to the speaker, etc. It is the work of the participants that makes a seminar, not the category of "seminar" that makes the participants behave in a specified way. The view that social order is constructed by participants' actions, rather than being a pre-existing category that shapes people's actions, may be unfamiliar to many readers, and adopting it may require a different approach to studying social phenomena. This section discusses some fundamental premises that underlie ethnomethodology, using examples from a variety of fields, because the necessary research has not yet been done in the Requirements Engineering setting.

5.1 Natural Setting

To understand social order as an accomplishment of participants, we must study it in natural settings. A laboratory setting is constructed by an experimenter for a particular purpose, and it is considered bad experimental technique to reveal that purpose to the subjects. However, because humans are above all sense-making animals, they do not just sit with blank minds in a white room, passively enduring whatever comes. Rather, they continuously try to construct an understanding of the situation they are in, and then use this understanding to shape their behaviour as participants in the experiment, whether cooperative or subversive. Although the experimenter has control over the experimental setting, this does not determine what kind of sense their subjects make of it. Therefore, we may not get reliable results on the situation the experiment was intended to elucidate, because we do not know what setting the participants think they are in, and their construction may well be very different from the setting that the experimenter had in mind.

For example, early studies of American black children's language argued that these children had a language deficit, and that sound educational policy required teaching them how to speak [3]. This research was based on evidence from experimental settings, in which a single child was brought into a room with an adult experimenter, usually white, shown some toy, like a plastic spaceship, and asked, "Now Johnny, I want you to tell me everything you can about this spaceship." In this context, the children tended to give short, simple, minimal descriptions, with an uncertain intonation, such as [3] "It's red? [Long pause] An' uh [pause] it's pointy?"

Looking at such responses, especially in contrast with the fluent responses of middle class white children, one might well be tempted to say that the black children needed to be taught how to talk. However, a different view was taken by Labov [21]. He went into a classroom with a rabbit and tape recorder, and told the children that the rabbit was shy and needed to be talked to so that it wouldn't be frightened. Then he and the teacher left the room. The language produced in this setting was extensive, fluent, and of startlingly greater complexity and competence than in the artificial test situation described above.

Such findings raise two important questions: "What is the difference between the two settings?" and "What causes the difference between the performance of black and white children in the artificial test setting?" The original test setting is so familiar and unproblematic to academics, who have had a lifetime of dealing with it, that we must pause to consider what it might mean to a black child. The child is asked to describe an object to a questioner who is at least as capable of seeing and describing it, because he owns the object. This is very different from the most common form of question, where the speaker does not know the answer, and has reason to believe that the hearer may. In a situation of such an enormous power differential — black child and white adult — the child in fact shows considerable social understanding in deciding that minimal talk is the least dangerous policy. That is, because the child does not understand the desire of the experimenter, he cannot construct the appropriate response, which in this case is to describe the object as if the experimenter could not see it and had never seen it before. It might be objected that white middle class children of a similar age can do just this kind of task. However, this does not show that their language abilities in general are greater. Rather, there is evidence that middle class white parents train children in just such decontextualised descriptions as a preparation for school: "Look at the kitty. What colour is the kitty?" Because the mother can see the kitty as well as the child, she does not need to be told that it is grey. But she is preparing the child for this kind of school question, which is decontextualised from the relation between speaker and hearer, their relative states of knowledge, etc. ([40], pp. 57–98).

5.2 Member's Categories

Perhaps the most important notion underlying the analysis of social order is that of *member's categories*. This notion comes from ethnomethodology and conversation analysis. The idea is to find the categories that members themselves use to order their social world, rather than to impose an analyst's order on it. For example, it is not useful to approach a given piece of interaction with the assumption that participants are doing a shockingly bad job of whatever it is the analyst decides they are doing. Rather, it is important to determine what the participants are actually doing. The fundamental idea is that the social world is already orderly, and this order is an on-going creation of the participants. Further, we as analysts don't know in advance what the relevant categories are, so we should not come to the data with a pre-given coding scheme.

For example [25], consider a party of eight people at a restaurant after a conference session. An analyst could use any number of category systems, e.g., three Xerox employees and five non-Xerox employees, seven employees of large organisations and one self-employed person, four people who had just given a paper and four who had not, one person who was pregnant, and seven who were not, four with blue eyes and four with brown eyes, six people who drank and two who did not, or one man and seven women. And of course this list could be multiplied indefinitely. The analyst needs to know what categories are relevant, and what relevance might mean. The notion of members' categories implies that the analyst should consider what categories the members themselves use to organise their interaction, that is, what categories they orient to. Thus in this situation, participants oriented to the category of pregnancy or non-pregnancy in deciding whether to take a taxi to the restaurant. They oriented to the nature of the participants' employers in determining what kinds of receipts were required. The waiter oriented to gender (and to recent developments in understanding the economic consequences of gender) in placing the bill in the center of the table facing the one man in the party, but not within his immediate reach. There was no evidence that eye colour was an organising category for any activity.

Let us consider further what it means for a phenomenon to organise an activity. The analyst should state what level of activity is of concern. There are striking phenomena that do not organise interaction at any level we care about. For example, a video of people interacting may clearly reveal particular ways that women with long nails and manicures use their hands, to protect their nail polish, which is easily chipped. But there is no evidence that other participants relate to this way of using the hands, or orient to it in organising their interaction. For example, they do not pass objects to one another differently depending on whether the recipient has a manicure. However, an analysis of this way of using the hands may be very relevant to the design of certain products, particularly packaging.

It is implicit in the notion of members' categories as organising activity that analysts do not reconstruct intentions or mental processes, except in so far as these are evident to those involved in the activity. Thus, if someone starts writing on the upper left corner of a white board, we can say that this action projects that the board will probably be covered.

Another example is body torque: a posture in which and legs face front while the head and shoulders, or head shoulders and trunk, are turned sideways. This posture requires considerable muscular tension to hold for a long period. Therefore, conversations in torque, in which one interlocutor is partially turned towards another, are likely to be short. Thus, if a visitor walks into the office of someone working at a terminal, and the occupant turns his head and neck to greet the visitor while leaving his hands on the keyboard, the visitor can project that a short conversation is likely [18, 39].

This illustrates the demonstration of intention that is needed for this kind of analysis. Analysts cannot simply construct subjects' mental models or intentions. Rather, it is necessary to demonstrate what participants are doing that allows other participants to infer their intentions. Thus, the activity of the analyst in postulating intentions is not different from that of the participants, and proceeds on the same evidence. This leads to the discussion of members' methods.

5.3 Member's Methods

Suppose you are a musician who wishes to study Balinese music. One approach is to transcribe Balinese pieces on Western music paper, based on the modern Western 12 tone equal tempered scale. This would lead you to conclude that Balinese scales are wrong, in that some notes are a little too flat, and others a little too sharp. Similarly, you might conclude that Balinese rhythmic and musical structures are flawed and "primitive." But is this the right method for studying such music? In fact, Balinese musicians are highly accomplished, and have their own methods for teaching their music. They also have their own musical theory, according to which their scales, rhythms, and structures are correct; they do not orient to the twelfth root of two. (See [2] for a discussion of Balinese musical practice.) But in the nineteenth century and before, ethnocentric approaches were the norm, and non-Western culture was systematically devalued by such analyses. This paper suggests that similar things may be going on in much of today's Requirements Engineering.

Much traditional social science is based on a social scientist who stands outside the situation, using methods different from those used by the members of the culture to make sense of their world. To a great extent, this comes from the desire to be as "scientific" as the hard sciences, which are taken as prototypical of how to do science, combined with a fundamentally flawed understanding of how research is conducted in the hard sciences. The naive view of the hard sciences is that they achieve objectivity by banishing the experimenter from the experiment. But it is well known in quantum mechanics that measurements necessarily disturb systems, and it is also widely recognised in the philosophy of science that all measurements are necessarily made in the context of some theory, held by some theorist [22]. Thus the "method" of science that is used by traditional social science as a model does not hold even in the sciences that are taken to be exemplary.

This model of objectivity has always been dubious in social sciences such as anthropology and sociology in which participant observation is a key method. Participant observation is a method in which the observer attempts to become part of the community of interest, by developing a legitimate rôle within that community. For example, researchers have apprenticed as a midwife, jazz musician, waitress, etc. Recently, the postmodern movement in ethnography has studied the process of becoming a member, and the assumptions that underlie the belief that the ethnographer has become a member (e.g., [19]).

The assumption that social science methods differ from those used by the people studied is challenged by ethnomethodology, which argues that social scientists employ the same kinds sense-making activities as members of the culture studied [13]. This argues against scientific objectivity, or at least, against the claim that analysts have a unique access to objectivity.

6 Discourse Analysis

Within linguistics, the phrase "discourse analysis" is used most broadly to describe the study of structures larger than the sentence. This section describes both interactional and linguistic approaches to such structures. The interactional approaches arise from ethnomethodology, and illustrate how social order is reproduced in the particular but very important domain of conversation. The linguistic approaches arise from sociolinguistics, and concern the internal structure of certain discourse forms.

6.1 Conversation Analysis

Conversation Analysis grew out of ethnomethodology (see Section 5). It attempts to describe the underlying social organisation that makes conversation orderly and intelligible. Conversation is one of the most prevalent yet invisible forms of social interaction, and may be considered typical of how people construct their world in an orderly way [16].

Conversation is a folk term for activities that members might describe as sitting around and chatting, just talking, socialising, etc. However, as a technical term in Conversation Analysis, conversation is that interactional system in which turns are not preallocated, i.e., in which the order of interaction is negotiated in real time, as the conversation procedes. By contrast, in forms of interaction such as debates, rituals, and seminars, the order of events, speakers, etc. is prearranged. For example, the order and the orderliness of a church service is not produced by the participants in the course of enacting it; there is no on-the-spot negotiation of whether the sermon shall precede or follow the collection.

6.1.1 Turntaking

Within conversation, turntaking is the basic system for creating social order. The order that it creates is the normative form of conversation: there should be one speaker at a time, with no gaps or overlaps [38]. It is important to note that what counts as a gap or overlap is culturally determined [41]. For example, what sounds like a long pause for a New Yorker may be barely noticeable for a New Englander.

In brief, to achieve turntaking, the current speaker speaks until he/she comes to a possible turn-transition place, i.e., a point which is semantically and syntactically a possible end of sentence. Then he/she may select another speaker, either verbally, by gesture, or by eye gaze, or another participant may self-select as the next speaker, or there may be a gap, i.e., a silence long enough in the particular culture to be noticed as such. The speaker may then continue, so that the possible between-turn gap becomes a within-turn gap. When there are overlaps, i.e., when two speakers speak at once, one drops out.

The important point is that turntaking is achieved in the moment by moment interaction of the participants. It is not the case that there are certain rules that define the set of all possible conversations; rather, the application of rules to particular situations is a matter of on-going work by the participants, who may, for example, negotiate the status of a particular silence.

6.1.2 Adjacency Pairs

While turntaking is an important part of the syntax of conversational organisation, adjacency pairs are a partially syntactic, partially semantic organisational structure. An *adjacency pair* is a pair (or larger set) of utterances "whose central characteristic is the rule that a current action (a 'first pair part' such as a greeting or question) requires the production of a reciprocal action (or 'second pair part') at the first possible opportunity after the completion of the first" ([16], p. 287).

Examples are sequences like question-answer and greeting-greeting, where one speaker's production of a question or greeting projects another speaker's production of an answer or second greeting.

Once a speaker has produced the first part of an adjacency pair, the second pair part can be *noticeably absent*. It is important to distinguish between an absence and a noticeable absence. At any point in a conversation, the range of things that are *not* said is infinite; but because the first pair part projects (or sets up the expectation of) the production of the second pair part, we can notice its absence. In fact, we as analysts can see speakers orienting to such an absence; for example, someone might say, "Don't you say hello?" in response to the absence of a second greeting. Such a response from a speaker shows that adjacency pairs are not merely a construct of the analyst, but in fact are categories that speakers themselves use to organise their conversations.

6.2 Discourse Units

Another approach within linguistics that is relevant for requirements elicitation is the study of the *discourse unit*, the linguistic unit directly above the sentence. Some very common examples of the discourse unit that have been studied extensively are the oral narrative of personal experience [21, 24, 35], the joke [37], the explanation [15], the spatial description [23, 27], and the plan [26]. As a structural unit, the discourse unit has two criterial properties: it has defined boundaries, and a describable internal structure.

The property of *definable boundaries* means that the discourse unit is a *bounded unit*; for example, with some interesting exceptions, we know when a speaker is or is not engaged in telling a narrative. Of course, there may be boundary disputes, either at the beginning, during which a speaker negotiates with hearers whether the narrative will be told, or at the end, where the speaker may negotiate the proper response to the unit with hearers [37, 34, 35]. However, such negotiations do not mean that the unit is not structurally bounded. Rather, they imply that the establishment of boundaries is a social construction, with serious social consequences for how the interaction can proceed.

One important effect of establishing of the boundaries of a discourse unit concerns turntaking. As we have seen, other things being equal, the sentence is the potential unit of turn exchange; i.e., a second speaker may begin to speak when the first speaker has reached a permissible end for his sentence. However, if the first speaker has negotiated permission to produce a recognised discourse unit, such as a joke or a story, then that speaker has the floor until the unit is completed. A second speaker may contribute questions, appreciations, side sequences, etc., but the discourse unit and topic in progress will not be changed until the unit is recognised as completed.

The second important property of the discourse unit is that it has a *precise internal structure* that is just as describable as sentential syntax. The description of this internal structure is necessary for understanding the interactional process of discourse construction, because the task of hearers is quite different, for example, in different sections of a narrative. Moreover, discourse structure can be described with just as much mathematical precision as sentential syntax (see [26, 15] for some appropriate mathematical apparatus).

We expect that narratives will be particularly important for understanding the requirements process, because much of what is communicated between the parties will be framed as stories, e.g., about what our group does, what we hope to accomplish with the new system, what our problems are, etc. For example, a study of experienced photocopy repair personnel [33] shows that they often use narratives for informal training of novices in problems that are not covered in official manuals and training courses. These "war stories" are an important part of the work life of photocopy repair mechanics, although management may see this activity as 'goofing off' rather than as a legitimate part of the job. Also, [14] mentions a case study by the authors of this paper, in which evaluations extracted from jokes and stories were used to reconstruct a value system for an organisation, and where task oriented discourse was used to determine work structure.

6.3 Reproducing Social Order

We have discussed the orderly nature of social interaction, and indicated that this social order is produced by the participants in their moment to moment interactions. We have not yet considered how familiar social orders are reproduced: although participants are continuously producing social order, it always seems to be substantially the *same* order that is reproduced — the relations of class, gender, age, power etc., do not suddenly disappear, and are not suddenly produced in unusual or surprising ways. This observation is a necessary correction to a possible view of members' cate-

gories and members' methods which says that (for example) the structures of gender privilege, or of a ten ton truck bearing down upon you, are just your construction of the world, and if you don't like them, then you can just construct something else. Although few people will take such a naive constructivist attitude towards a truck, some do take it toward social structures, and thus the question must be explored.

There are material artifacts, histories of behaviour, interpretations of behaviour, social expectations of consequences, individual tastes and preferences, etc. that lead participants towards reproducing the same social order. For example, to illustrate the rôle of material artifacts in our example of the construction of a seminar, the social category of seminar is partly constructed by the turntaking behaviour of the participants. It is also constructed by the material artifacts and the ways in which people use them: the arrangement of a table in the room in a position that is understood to be the head, a board and writing materials that one participant uses and the others don't, perhaps a glass of water for one participant.

To illustrate the rôle of the interpretation of behaviour, we consider an example from turntaking, namely interruptions and overlaps, and their relation to gender rôles. A successful interruption is an example of a violation of a speaker's turn in which participant A begins to speak, participant B begins to speak while A is still speaking, and A then drops out. It has been found in U.S. data [52] that interruptions are very rare in same-sex conversations. In cross-sex conversations, from 75% to 90% of successful interruptions involve men interrupting women. (The percentages differ slightly, depending on the situation, and the degree of acquaintance of the conversational partners.)

Why is this? West and Zimmerman [48, 49] suggest that interruption by one's conversation partner is not only a consequence of lesser status, but is also a way of establishing and maintaining a status differential. For this formulation to make sense, it is necessary to understand in detail how participants in an interruption negotiate who is to drop out. When two participants start talking at once, or when one participant begins to speak while another is still speaking, one or both speakers may become louder, and continue to increase volume until the participant who is speaking more softly drops out. This appears to be a gender neutral description of the mechanism. However the social meaning of increasing volume is different for men and women. It is an indication of what kind of a person one is: in the case of men, a person who stands up for his rights, in the case of women, a strident and aggressive person. These different social meanings for the same behaviour ensure that it is almost always the woman who drops out of an overlap.

Some larger scale studies of social reproduction have considered class distinctions among adolescent school children in Britain and the United States [50, 11]. In each case, working class students' attitudes towards the importance of friendship networks and school culture exactly reproduced the kinds of behaviours, attitudes, preferences and skills that led to their being tracked to skilled or unskilled labouring jobs, rather than to higher education or managerial and professional work.

The reproduction of social order is an important issue for Requirements Engineering, because it is necessary to consider the effect of a new system on social structures, as suggested by the following questions: Will the new system reproduce the existing social order? Or will the order be altered in significant ways? Do the existing social structures suggest requirements that would negate the improvements expected from the new system?

7 Discussion

Every method has some limitations. Questionnaire-based interviews are limited by their stimulus-response model of interaction, which assumes that a given question (as stimulus) always has the same meaning to subjects. Moreover, this method excludes the kinds of interaction that could be used to establish shared meaning between the subject and the interviewer. Open ended interviews allow less constrained interaction between the interviewer and the interviewee, who is no longer considered the subject of an experiment. However, this method is still limited by the need for the participants to share basic concepts and methods, without which they will be unable to negotiate shared meanings for the questions asked. Open ended interviews are also more vulnerable to distortion by interviewer bias. These limitations also apply to focus groups, and to their cousins in Requirements Engineering, JAD (or RAD) groups. In addition, these methods are vulnerable to political manipulations by participants. Protocol analysis involves an artificial discourse form, and is based on an incorrect cognitivist model of human thought that entirely ignores social context. None of these methods can elicit tacit knowledge, and all are subject to the say-do problem.

The principles of ethnomethodology, such as members' concepts and members' methods, provide a powerful framework for a deeper consideration of these limitations, and suggest that traditional sociology and its methods are based on faulty assumptions about how social interaction is organised.

Conversation, discourse and interaction analyses are only applicable to situations where there is significant social interaction; conversation and discourse analyses are only applicable to verbal data. But the most important limitation of these methods is that they are very labour intensive. In particular, it can take a highly skilled person a very long time to produce a transcript from a videotape of live interaction. Another limitation is that these methods cannot be (directly) applied to the study of systems that have not yet been built. However, they can be used to obtain tacit knowledge, because they bypass the unreliable explanations of users, and instead examine what they actually do.

Despite their limitations, we do not wish to suggest that any of these methods cannot be useful in requirements elicitation (with the possible exception of protocol analysis). In fact, their strengths seem to some extent complementary, so that combinations of the various methods can be usefully applied to particular problems. In particular, we suggest it is often a good idea to start with an ethnographic study to un-

cover basic aspects of social order, such as the basic category systems used by members, the division into social groups, the goals of various social groups, typical patterns of work, how current technology is used, etc. (see [36] for a review of ethnography in relation to Requirements Engineering). After this, one might use questionnaires or interviews to explore what problems members see as most important, how members place themselves in various classification schemes, etc. Then one might apply conversation, discourse or interaction analysis to get a deeper understanding of selected problematic aspects.

Techniques from discourse analysis can be useful when verbal communication is important to the system being developed; conversation analysis can also help to uncover limitations of other techniques. Some previous joint work of the authors, briefly described in [14], shows how the discourse analysis of stories can be used to explore the value system of an organisation, and how the discourse analysis of explanations can be used for a kind of situated task analysis. Interaction analysis can be used to discover details of non-verbal interaction in real work environments [18]; but the effort required to produce video transcripts suggests that this method should be used very selectively. Ethnography should be used continually to provide context for results obtained by other methods.

To sum up, we recommend a *"zooming"* method of requirements elicitation, whereby the more expensive but detailed methods are only employed selectively for problems that have been determined by other techniques to be especially important. From this point of view, the various techniques based on ethnomethodology can be seen as analoguous to an electron microscope: they provide an instrument that is very accurate and powerful, but that is also expensive, and requires careful preparation to ensure that the right thing is examined.

It is interesting to notice that all of these methods, including zooming, can be used not only for requirements elicitation, but also for studying the system development process itself, including the Requirements Engineering process. In this way, we may hope to develop a scientific methodology for systems development; in fact, we have already tried to do this in a limited way in this paper, by using concepts from ethnomethodology to explore the limitations of more traditional methods.

We close this paper with some research tasks that seem to merit further investigation:

1. Do detailed empirical studies of the entire system lifecycle, including the rôle of planning, management and phases, using ideas of Suchman [43]; in particular, investigate the hypotheses that requirements activities are distributed throughout the lifecycle, and that plans serve at least as much to justify actions as they do to predict them.

2. Do case studies to determine the rôle of political considerations in Requirements Engineering, and how they affect the use of various commercial methods and tools.

3. Do case studies to determine the limitations and strengths of JAD groups, in relation to the entire system lifecycle.

4. Work out detailed guidelines for the zoom method described above, and try it in some case studies. In particular, work out the relationships between discourse, conversation and interaction structures, and when each should be applied.

5. Do detailed empirical studies of the comparative effectiveness of various commercial methods and tools for various purposes.

We believe that if research projects along these lines were completed, then Requirements Engineering would be much closer to having a sound scientific foundation.

References

[1] Dorine C. Andrews. JAD: A crucial demension for rapid applications development. *Journal of Systems Management*, pages 23–31, March 1991.

[2] Judith Becker and Alton Becker. A musical icon: Power and meaning in Javanese gamelan music. In Wendy Steiner, editor, *The Sign in Music and Literature*, pages 203–228. University of Texas, 1981.

[3] Carl Bereiter and Siegfried Engelmann. *Teaching Disadvantaged Children in the Pre-school*. Prentice-Hall, 1966.

[4] Woodrow Wilson Bledsoe and Donald Loveland (editors). *Automated Theorem Proving: After 25 Years*. American Mathematical Society, 1984. Volume 29 of Contemporary Mathematics Series.

[5] Barry Boehm. *Software Engineering Economics*. Prentice-Hall, 1981.

[6] Richard J. Boland. In search of management accounting: Explorations of self and organization. Technical report, Case Western University, January 1991.

[7] Francoise Brun-Cottan. Talk in the workplace: Occupational relevance. *Research on Language and Social Interaction*, 24:277–295, 1990/1991.

[8] Graham Button and Wes Sharrock. Occasioned practises in the work of implementing development methodologies, 1992. Draft, Rank Xerox EuroPARC.

[9] John Canny. *The Complexity of Robot Motion Planning*. MIT, 1988.

[10] William F. Clocksin and Christopher Mellish. *Programming in Prolog*. Springer, 1981.

[11] Penelope Eckert. *Jocks and Burnouts*. Teachers College, 1989.

[12] K. Anders Ericsson and Herbert A. Simon. *Protocol Analysis: Verbal Reports as Data*. MIT, 1984.

[13] Harold Garfinkel. *Studies in Ethnomethodology*. Prentice-Hall, 1967.

[14] Joseph Goguen. The dry and the wet. In Eckhard Falkenberg, Colette Rolland, and El-Sayed El-Sayed, editors, *Information Systems Concepts*, pages 1–17. Elsevier North-Holland, 1992.

[15] Joseph Goguen, James Weiner, and Charlotte Linde. Reasoning and natural explanation. *International Journal of Man-Machine Studies*, 19:521–559, 1983.

[16] Charles Goodwin and John Heritage. Conversation analysis. *Annual Review of Anthropology*, 19:283–307, 1990.

[17] Marina Jirotka. Ethnomethodology and requirements engineering. Technical report, Centre for Requirements and Foundations, Oxford University Computing Lab, 1991.

[18] Adam Kendon. *Conducting Interaction: Patterns of Behavior in Focused Encounters*. Cambridge University, 1990. Studies in Interactional Sociolinguistics Number 7.

[19] D.K. Kondo. *Crafting Selves: Power, Gender and Discourses of Identity in a Japanese Workplace*. Chicago, 1990.

[20] Gunter Kress and Robert Hodges. *Language and Ideology*. Kegan Paul, 1979.

[21] William Labov. The transformation of experience in narrative syntax. In *Language in the Inner City*, pages 354–396. University of Pennsylvania, 1972.

[22] Imre Lakatos. *The Methodology of Scientific Research Programmes*. Cambridge, 1978.

[23] Charlotte Linde. *The Linguistic Encoding of Spatial Information*. PhD thesis, Columbia University, 1974. Department of Linguistics.

[24] Charlotte Linde. Private stories in public discourse. *Poetics*, 15:183–202, 1986.

[25] Charlotte Linde. Personal experience, 1992. Institute for Research on Learning, Palo Alto CA.

[26] Charlotte Linde and Joseph Goguen. Structure of planning discourse. *Journal of Social and Biological Structures*, 1:219–251, 1978.

[27] Charlotte Linde and William Labov. Spatial networks as a site for the study of language and thought. *Language*, 51(4):924–939, 1975.

[28] Paul Luff, David Frohlich, and Nigel Gilbert, editors. *Computers and Conversation*. Academic, 1990.

[29] David L. Morgan. *Focus Groups as Qualitative Research*. Sage, 1988.

[30] Claus Moser and Graham Kalton. *Survey Methods in Social Investigation.* Gower, 1971.

[31] Allen Newell. Physical symbol systems. *Cognitive Science*, 4:135–183, 1980.

[32] Allen Newell and Herbert Simon. GPS, a program that simulates human thought. In Edward Feigenbaum and Julian Feldman, editors, *Computers and Thought*, pages 279–293. McGraw-Hill, 1963.

[33] Julian Orr. Narratives at work: Story telling as co-operative diagnostic activity. In *Proceedings, Conference on Computer Supported Cooperative Work (SIGCHI)*. Association for Computing Machinery, 1986.

[34] Livia Polanyi. So what's the point? *Semiotica*, 25(3–4):208–224, 1978.

[35] Livia Polanyi. *Telling the American Story.* MIT, 1989.

[36] Dave Randall, John Hughes, and Dan Shapiro. Steps twoard a partnership: Ethnography and system design, 1992. Draft, Lancaster University.

[37] Harvey Sacks. An analysis of the course of a joke's telling in conversation. In Richard Baumann and Joel Scherzer, editors, *Explorations in the Ethnography of Speaking*, pages 337–353. Cambridge, 1974.

[38] Harvey Sacks, Emanuel Schegloff, and Gail Jefferson. A simplest systematics of the organization of turn-taking in conversation. *Language*, 504:696–735, 1974.

[39] Emmanuel Schegloff. Body torque, 1990. Paper presented at 89th Annual Meeting of the American Anthropological Association, New Orleans LA, November 1990.

[40] Ron Scollon and Suzanne B.K. Scollon. *Narrative, Literacy and Face in Interethnic Communication.* Ablex, 1981. The Literate Two-year-old: The Fictionalization of Self.

[41] Ron Scollon and Suzanne B.K. Scollon. *Narrative, Literacy and Face in Interethnic Communication.* Ablex, 1981. Chapter 2: Athabaskan-English Interethnic Communication, pp.11–38.

[42] David Stewart and Prem Shamdasani. *Focus Groups: Theory and Practice.* Sage, 1990.

[43] Lucy Suchman. *Plans and Situated Actions: The Problem of Human-machine Communication.* Cambridge University, 1987.

[44] Lucy Suchman. Constituting shared workspaces. In Yrjo Engestrom and David Middleton, editors, *Cognition and Communication at Work.* Cambridge, to appear.

[45] Lucy Suchman. Technologies of accountability: Of lizards and airplanes. In Graham Button, editor, *Technology in Working Order: Studies of Work, Interactioin and Technology.* Routledge, to appear.

[46] Lucy Suchman and Brigitte Jordan. Interactional troubles in face-to-face survey interviews. *Journal of the American Statistical Association*, 85(409):232–241, 1990.

[47] Francisco Varela, Evan Thompson, and Eleanor Rosch, editors. *The Embodied Mind.* MIT, 1991.

[48] Candace West and Don H. Zimmerman. Women's place in everyday talk: Reflections on parent-child interaction. *Social Problems*, 24:521–529, 1977.

[49] Candace West and Don H. Zimmerman. Small insults: A study of interruptions in cross-sex conversations between unacquainted persons. In Barrie Thorne, Cheris Kramarae, and Nancy Henley, editors, *Language, Gender and Society*, pages 102–117. Newbury House (Rowley MA), 1983.

[50] Paul Willis. *Learning to Labor: How Working Class Kids Get Working Class Jobs.* Columbia University, 1977.

[51] Nessa Wolfson. *The Conversational Historical Present in American English Narrative.* Foris, 1982.

[52] Don H. Zimmerman and Candace West. Sex roles, interruptions and silences in conversations. In Barrie Thorne and Nancy Henley, editors, *Langauge and Sex: Difference and Dominance.* Newbury House (Rowley MA), 1975.

Getting started
Using use cases to capture requirements

James Rumbaugh

USER-CENTERED ANALYSIS

What is the most important aspect of a modeling and design methodology? Formal consistency, reusability, efficiency, faithfulness to object-oriented principles? No. None of this matters a bit *if you don't solve the right problem.* There is no internal check that a model or a program is correct. Developers must ask users or domain experts what to do, capture their needs in some form, and then verify that the captured requirements are correct. The requirements must be expressed in some structured way, but they must still be understandable to the users who must verify them.

User-centered analysis is the process of capturing requirements from the user's point of view. The designer must then map the requirements into the computer domain for solution. Don't assume that stating requirements in users' terms will eliminate all problems. In a large system with many interactions, nobody may understand the consequences of each requirement. The purpose of analysis is to explore the consequences of an initial problem statement and come up with a complete, correct model of a problem. You can't just write down all the requirements; you have to start with an initial approximation of them and then refine them while exploring their interactions, implications, and mutual inconsistencies.

Most methodologists now agree that user-centered analysis is the best way to

James Rumbaugh is a computer scientist at General Electric Research and Development Center in Schenectady, NY. Dr. Rumbaugh has been active in object-oriented technology for many years and has taught courses on the OMT methodology around the world. He is co-author of OBJECT-ORIENTED MODELING AND DESIGN (Prentice Hall). He can be reached at GE R&D Center, Bldg. K1-5B42A, P.O. Box 8, Schenectady, NY 12301; 518.387.6358; email: rumbaugh@crd.ge.com

solve the right problem. Capturing the user's needs is a major focus of several methodologies, including Rubin and Goldberg's OBA[1] and Jacobson's Objectory.[2] In particular, Jacobson's *use cases* have been well received by just about every methodologist including us. We feel that use cases fit naturally on the front end of the published OMT process[3] and supplement the existing user-centered features of the method.

USE CASES

An *actor* is an outside entity that interacts directly with a system. Actors include both humans and other quasi-autonomous things, such as machines, computer tasks, and other systems. More precisely, an actor is a role played by such an entity. One person can play several roles and thereby represent several actors such as a computer system operator, a database administrator, and an end user. Objects that are indirectly connected to the system are not actors because their needs must be communicated to the system through an actor.

Each kind of actor uses the system in different ways; otherwise the actors would not be different. A single actor can also use the system in fundamentally different ways. Each way of using the system is called a *use case.*

A use case describes the possible sequences of interactions among the system and one or more actors in response to some initial stimulus by one of the actors. It is not a single scenario (a specific history of specific events exchanged among system and actors) but rather a description of a set of potential scenarios, each starting with some initial event from an actor to the system and following the ensuing transaction to its logical conclusion. Normally each use case focuses on some purpose for the actor. For example, the database administrator might

have a use case for "installing a database" that begins when the DBA starts the installation program and concludes when the installed database is complete. Another use case would be "adding a user to the database," which begins when the DBA runs the "install user" command and concludes when the user is authorized on the database. An end-user use case might be "printing a report," which begins when the user selects a database table and concludes when the report is printed.

A use case involves a sequence of interactions between the initiator and the system, possibly involving other actors. It follows a thread of control in and out of the system, but in the final system it might be interleaved with other threads. The system is considered as a "black box"; we are interested in externally visible behavior. A use case can include choices, iterations, and parameters. It is a description for a set of scenarios, in the same sense that a class is a description for a set of objects. There should be a finite number of use cases for a system, just as there are a finite number of classes, whereas there are usually an infinite number of possible scenarios and objects. You must enumerate all the use cases of a system, otherwise you don't really understand what it does.

In defining a use case, group together all transactions that are "similar" in nature, which a user would think of as being variations on a theme. A typical use case might include a main case, with alternates taken in various combinations and including all possible exceptions that can arise in handling them. For example, a use case for a bank might be "performing a transaction at the counter." Subcases would include making deposits, making withdrawals, and making transfers, in various combinations,

"Getting Started: Using Use Cases to Capture Requirements" by J. Rumbaugh from
J. Object-Oriented Programming, Sept. 1994, pp. 8–12, 23. Reprinted with permission.

together with exceptions such as "overdrawn" or "account closed." These subcases are all similar, in that they require much the same set up and interaction sequences. On the other hand, the use case "applying for a loan" is quite different; the customer will probably deal with different bank personnel, have to fill out a lot of forms, and wait a few days to finish this use case.

Use cases are written as natural language text descriptions expressed informally. The descriptions express what happens from the user's point of view. The details of how the system works internally are irrelevant to a use case. The description includes the events exchanged between objects and the system operations performed by the system, but only those operations visible to the actors.

Table 1 shows a sample use case for "assigning seats" for airline flights. This use case could be used alone (if a passenger calls up for a seat assignment) or as part of a larger use case "check-in for flight." In this use case the system includes the airline computer and the clerk at the counter or on the telephone.

COMBINING USE CASES

Jacobson describes two ways of combining use cases, *extends* and *uses*. *Extends* embeds new behavior into a complete base case. For example, we might have a use case "check-in for flight" in which a traveler hands tickets to a clerk, answers some questions, and ends by receiving a boarding pass. Use case "check baggage" extends the base case "check-in for flight" by having the clerk ask about baggage, collect and tag the baggage, and finally staple a claim check to the customer's ticket. The actual behavior includes both use cases. The base case "check-in for flight" is meaningful and complete in itself, so it is possible to partition out the additional functionality "check baggage."

Uses embeds a fragmentary subsequence as a necessary part of a larger case. The embedded use case is a kind of behavior subroutine. For example, the use cases "process ATM transaction" and "automated telephone bank account inquiry" might both use the subordinate case "validate password," which requests a password and verifies it. The *uses* relationship permits the same behavior to be embedded in many otherwise unrelated use cases. Jacobson identifies *uses* as a kind of inheritance, but I think he has

got it backwards; *extends* should be a kind of inheritance and *uses* a kind of aggregation. In an object model, a subclass inherits base information from its superclass and *extends* it by adding additional information unknown to the superclass, which can stand alone.

I am not convinced that Jacobson's *extends* and *uses* relationships are fundamentally different. Use cases are not active entities that generate behavior; they are more like parsers in that they constrain and interpret behavior sequences imposed from outside. Therefore, it is not meaningful to talk of which use case is "in charge." Both *extends* and *uses* are simply ways of adding an additional subsequence into a base sequence. In the *uses* case, the subsequence is mandatory, an essential part of the entire case, but partitioned out because it may be reusable as part of other base sequences. In the *extends* case, the subsequence is optional and the base sequence may stand alone. Both *extends* and *uses* can be treated as special cases of a directed *adds* association between a base case and an additional case. The multiplicity of the addition is either *one* (for the *uses* case) or *optional* (for the *extends* case). A multiplicity of *many* is also meaningful for the *extends* case, indicating that the extension can occur many times. In either case you have to specify where the subsequence gets added to the base sequence.

In practice, you can think about *extends* and *uses* as different ways to come up with new use cases, but that does not mean that they should not be modeled using a single general form. Figure 1 shows Jacobson's notation contrasted with my unified notation for showing a combination of use cases. Just as an object may get its features from several different classes within a generalization relationship, so a scenario may get its behavior from several different use cases within a combination relationship.

What is the purpose of use cases, given that they are informal and do not carry

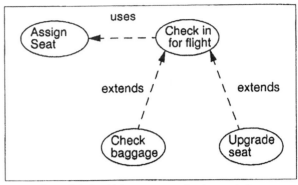

Figure I(a). Combining use cases—Jacobson notation.

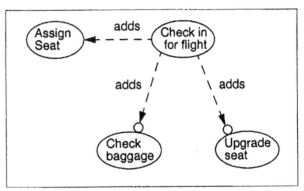

Figure I(b). Combining use cases—unified notation.

strong semantics? They force the analyst to confront the purpose of a system; namely, to implement functionality. Use cases are a way of specifying functionality in a manageable way, organized into categories of functionality from a user's point of view. By trying to enumerate first the actors, then the use cases, there is less chance of forgetting important parts of the system.

USE CASES AND OMT

When should you make up use cases? In our book[3] we recommended making scenarios as part of building a dynamic model, but use cases serve a broader purpose than just control. They provide a first cut at the functionality in an application, so they can be captured right at the beginning of the analysis. I would advise the following approach:

1. Identify the boundary of the proposed application. For example, is a clerk part of a system or is the clerk actually the actor whom the system serves? Identify the objects just outside the boundary that interact directly with the system (objects that send and receive events, including events such as commands, signals, output messages, and output displays).

2. Classify the outside objects by the roles

that they play in the application. Each role defines an actor. Make a list of actors. State the purposes of each actor in using the system.

3. For each actor, think of the fundamentally different ways in which the actor uses the system. Each way of using the system is a use case. Group different scenarios into the same use case if they appear to be variations on a single theme.

4. Make up some specific scenarios for each use case. Plug in actual parameters; don't try to be general. The purpose is to ground your thinking in concrete examples. You can then generalize to the full use case with less danger of forgetting something or violating common sense.

5. Determine the interaction sequences. For each use case, identify the event from the actor that initiates the use case. Determine if there are preconditions that must be true before the use case can begin. Determine the logical conclusion of the transaction: when is the thread of activity complete? There is some judgment about how broadly to define a use case. For example, is "applying for a loan" complete when the application is turned in, when the loan is granted, or when the loan is finally paid off?

6. Write a prose description of the use case. Identify the sequence of interactions that occur in a normal transaction together with the system operations that are invoked. Specify rules for choosing among variations and iteration.

7. Consider all the exceptions that can occur in handling a transaction and specify how they affect the use case.

8. Look for common fragments among different use cases and factor them out into base cases and additions. Determine if the additions are optional or mandatory and specify where they go in the main sequence.

DEGREE OF DETAIL
At the beginning of analysis I would be more concerned about identifying all the different use cases and outlining their main-line behavior rather than describing all the vari-

ant sequences in detail. In complicated situations, I doubt that this informal technique (use cases) can capture all the subtleties of behavior anyway, so treat it as a discovery technique. A more formal specification of behavior comes from the state diagrams in the dynamic model, which must eventually be produced as part of the analysis.

DOMAIN MODELS
Most applications are built on some problem domain that supplies the underlying semantics of the application. A problem domain is an area of real-world expertise, such as mechanical engineering, stock trading, or travel.

Domain classes are classes from a problem domain that are meaningful outside of any application. They carry the semantics of a problem domain in terms meaningful to domain experts. For mechanical engineers, classes such as force, stress, strain, and beam are meaningful; for stockbrokers classes such as stock, bond, trade, and commission schedule; for travel agents, classes such as flight, reservation, and airport. Every field has its own particular terminology, and jargon words usually identify important concepts that are often domain classes. Because domain classes are meaningful by themselves, they can be found and modeled as part of a domain analysis without considering a particular application. *They do not need to be driven by use cases.*

APPLICATION MODELS
An *application model* is a model of a particular application. It goes beyond the real-world domain model to come up with a computer solution to a particular problem. Build an application model on top of a domain model, because the application must ultimately support the underlying semantics of the domain objects while the domain

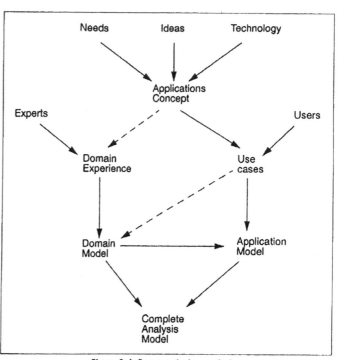

Figure 2. Influences during analysis.

model can stand on its own. Application models contain computer constructs that are not part of the real-world problem domain but are nevertheless visible to users. I described this concept of application classes in an earlier column (JOOP 6[3]). Examples of application classes include graphic images and table views of domain objects, user interfaces, controllers, devices, and external interfaces.

Application classes have no existence apart from an application, so you can't find them in the real world or as part of a domain analysis. They have to be flushed out from the application requirements. They can be identified from the use cases.

TWO-PRONG ANALYSIS
When an application involves real-world expertise (which is normal), it is useful to follow a two-prong analysis approach: first build a domain model by capturing domain knowledge, then build an application model by examining use cases of the particular application. Figure 2 illustrates this two-prong approach to analysis: solid lines indicate strong influences and dashed lines indicate weaker influences.

BUILDING DOMAIN MODELS
Build a domain model by considering the problem domain directly. First build an ob-

ject model by doing one of the following:

1. Think of important real-world concepts, terminology, and jargon in the problem domain. Organize them into a class model showing their relationships. Then think up useful real-world operations on these objects (Bertrand Meyer's "shopping list operations.") This approach requires a good understanding and internal feeling for the problem domain itself but leads to domain models that can be reused many times for different applications.

2. Write a description of the underlying semantics of the particular problem, from the point of view of the domain expert. Don't worry at all about how users will interact with the application; concentrate on the core semantic operations and the objects they affect. A domain expert can prepare this statement. Next, an analyst can extract the classes and their relationships from the statement, but the final model will have to be validated and corrected by the expert. The semantic computations in the statement become the operations on the domain classes. This domain model may be more narrowly drawn to the needs of a particular problem and may not be so reusable unless extra effort is made.

3. Extract the domain objects indirectly from the use cases. This is the most indirect approach, as the domain objects may not appear in the use cases directly and may have to be inferred from their views, which do appear. This approach is probably better as a cross-check for objects that are missed on a more direct approach. Identifying domain operations is also more indirect.

Typically, domain objects do not embody much control; most of them are passive data objects rather than controllers of other objects. It is usually not necessary to build dynamic models of domain objects, although it may be helpful to build a life history model showing the operations that take the object between fundamentally different life states.

BUILDING APPLICATION MODELS

Once the domain model is built, build an application model. Start by listing use cases. Then examine the use cases to identify ap-

Table I. Sample use case.

Use Case:	Assign Seat
Summary:	A passenger with a reservation on a flight requests a seat assignment. The system obtains information from the passenger and then attempts to make an assignment. The assignment is given to the passenger or the passenger is told that no assignment is presently available.
Actors:	Passenger
Preconditions:	The passenger has a reservation on a flight by the given airline
Description:	A passenger requests a seat assignment on a flight. (This may be implicit as part of checking in or may be an explicit request by the passenger.) The system (in the form of the agent) asks for the date of the flight, the flight number, departure airport, and passenger name. The passenger supplies the information. Instead of name, the passenger can supply frequent flyer number with the airline. [Exception: Too early to make assignment.] The system finds the reservation. [Exception: No reservation found.] If the reservation already has a seat assignment, it is given to the passenger who is offered the opportunity of changing the assignment. If there is no assignment or the passenger wants to change, the system requests seat preference (window, aisle) and smoking preference (yes, no). The system uses the information, including frequent flyer level, to try to find a suitable seat assignment subject to previous assignments and the policies of the airline. If necessary, the system asks additional questions: would the passenger accept a bulkhead seat, would the passenger accept a seat in an emergency exit row? The system proposes a seat assignment. If all the passenger's preferences cannot be satisified, then the system proposes the best match it can find. [Exception: No assignment possible.] The passenger can accept the assignment or ask for changes, in which case another assignment is attempted. The use case concludes when an assignment is made and accepted.
Exceptions:	Too early: Raised if the current date is too early, based on an airline algorithm that includes fare category and frequent flyer level. The passenger is advised when seat assignments will be possible and the use case terminates.
	No reservation found: Raised if no reservation can be found. The information is rechecked and searched if necessary for a partial match. If still no reservation can be found, then the passenger is advised to obtain one and the use case terminates.
	No assignment possible: Raised if no assignment is possible based on an airline-dependent formula that includes number of unassigned seats, days until departure, fare category, and frequent flyer level. The passenger is advised to obtain an assignment on check in. If this is part of check in, then the passenger is placed on standby in the order of arrival. The use case terminates.
Postconditions:	If this is part of check in, then the passenger either has a seat assignment or is on the standby queue in order of arrival. Otherwise none (the attempt may fail).

plication objects (plus any domain objects that were overlooked). First determine how underlying domain information will be formatted and presented to the user by visual, aural, mechanical, or other means. Each presentation format is a view class. One domain class may have many views. Also identify devices and interface objects mentioned in the use cases.

Try to separate view classes from the underlying semantic classes that embody the domain information; use the *model-view-controller* framework examined in a previous column (JOOP 7[2]). Examine each view class to see if it is a mapping of some underlying semantic object. Some view classes contain only application information, but presumably the purpose of most applications is to actually do something, so at least some of the view classes should be views of domain objects. If the domain classes have not already been identified from a domain analysis, add them to the domain model.

Continued on page 23

Try to separate domain classes from any particular way of viewing them, and their reusability will be greatly enhanced, even within a single application that may have multiple views of a single domain object.

A *controller* is an object that manages interactions between the system and outside actors to control system objects. It embodies most of the context-dependent decisions in an application, such as user-control options, permitting other reusable objects to be hooked together in flexible ways without having to be modified. The state diagram of the controller defines the allowable sequences of interactions inherent in a use case. Every application needs at least one controller. Start by assuming one controller per use case and later see if you can combine them.

Construct a state diagram for each controller by examining use cases. Go through the use cases, identify events between the outside world and the system, and organize the states of the controller into legal sequences. The state diagram formalizes the interaction sequences stated informally in a use case, so it becomes the definitive statement of behavior.

Many input events trigger the application to perform system operations. Sometimes the operation returns a value to the actor (or another actor) as an output event, sometimes the operation changes the internal state of the application. Identify the system operations from the use cases. Attach each operation on the controller's state diagram to the transition that triggers it, and also assign each operation to the class that handles it. System operations may be domain operations or application operations. Describe each operation (in text at least) in the functional model for the application.

USING USE CASES

This has been a brief overview of using use cases with OMT. I feel that a combination of direct domain analysis and use cases is an effective approach to starting analysis, rather than depending on use cases alone. How do use cases affect the rest of the development effort?

On a large project, use cases can be an effective way to partition the analysis into modules in a top-down manner before discovering all the individual classes. (If you can discover the classes first and then organize them into modules, it is not a large problem!) This is generally equivalent to partitioning the problem by functionality, because each use case normally embodies a certain kind of functionality. If you have a lot of use cases, you may be able to group them at a higher level.

Are use cases still important during design? They are primarily an approach to discovering requirements from a user-centered viewpoint, so the immediate answer is no.

...a combination of direct domain analysis and use cases is an effective approach to starting analysis...

The state diagrams for controllers should incorporate, in a more formal way, the requirements expressed informally in use cases.

Classes and state diagrams describe a system in a reductionist manner, one class at a time. It can be difficult to design a system from such a narrow viewpoint. The design concept of object interaction diagrams (see JOOP 7[3]) is the design-time correlate of use cases: they both follow the flow of a thread of control from object to object within a system for a single holistic transaction, so indirectly use cases are useful even during design.

Acknowledgments

Fred Eddy had valuable suggestions about this column. Thanks also to Phil Magrogan for his version of use cases under the title "layered virtual scenarios." This month's column includes material from the OBJECT-ORIENTED MODELING AND DESIGN TUTORIAL NOTES by James Rumbaugh, Michael Blaha, William Premerlani, and Frederick Eddy. Used by permission of the authors.

References

1. Rubin, K.S. and A. Goldberg. OBJECT BEHAVIOR ANALYSIS. COMMUNICATIONS OF THE ACM 35(9):48–62, 1992.

2. Jacobson, I. OBJECT-ORIENTED SOFTWARE ENGINEERING, Addison-Wesley, Reading, MA, 1992.

3. Rumbaugh, J. et al. OBJECT-ORIENTED MODELING AND DESIGN, Prentice Hall, Englewood Cliffs, NJ, 1991.

Software Requirements: A Tutorial

Stuart R. Faulk

"The hardest single part of building a software system is deciding precisely what to build. No other part of the conceptual work is as difficult as establishing the detailed technical requirements . . . No other part of the work so cripples the resulting system if done wrong. No other part is as difficult to rectify later."

[Brooks 87]

1. Introduction

Deciding precisely what to build and documenting the results is the goal of the requirements phase of software development. For many developers of large, complex software systems, requirements are their biggest software engineering problem. While there is considerable disagreement on how to solve the problem, few would disagree with Brooks' assessment that no other part of a development is as difficult to do well or as disastrous in result when done poorly. The purpose of this tutorial is to help the reader understand why the apparently simple notion of "deciding what to build" is so difficult in practice, where the state of the art does and does not address these difficulties, and what hope we have for doing better in the future.

This paper does not survey the literature but seeks to provide the reader with an understanding of the underlying issues. There are currently many more approaches to requirements than one can cover in a short paper. This diversity is the product of two things: different views about which of the many problems in requirements is pivotal, and different assumptions about the desirable characteristics of a solution. This paper attempts to impart a basic understanding of the requirements problem and its many facets, as well as the trade-offs involved in attempting a solution. Thus forearmed, readers can assess the claims of different requirements methods and their likely effectiveness in addressing the readers' particular needs.

We begin with basic terminology and some historical data on the requirements problem. We examine the goals of the requirements phase and the problems that can arise in attempting those goals. As in Brooks's article [Brooks 87], much of the discussion is moti-

vated by the distinction between the difficulties inherent in what one is trying to accomplish (the "essential" difficulties) and those one creates through inadequate practice ("accidental" difficulties). We discuss how a disciplined software engineering process helps address many of the accidental difficulties and why the focus of such a disciplined process is on producing a written specification of the detailed technical requirements. We examine current technical approaches to requirements in terms of the specific problems each approach seeks to address. Finally, we examine technical trends and discuss where significant advances are likely to occur in the future.

2. Requirements and the Software Life Cycle

A variety of software life-cycle models have been proposed with an equal variety of terminology. Davis [Davis 88] provides a good summary. While differing in the detailed decomposition of the steps (for example, prototyping models) or in the surrounding management and control structure (for example, to manage risk), there is general agreement on the core elements of the model. Figure 1 [Davis 93] is a version of the common model that illustrates the relationship between the software development stages and the related testing and acceptance phases.

When software is created in the context of a larger hardware and software system, system requirements are defined first, followed by system design. System design includes decisions about which parts of the system requirements will be allocated to hardware and which to software. For software-only systems, the life-cycle model begins with software requirements analysis. From this point on, the role of software requirements in the development model is the same whether or not the software is part of a larger system, as shown in Figure 2 [Davis 93]. For this reason, the remainder of our discussion does not distinguish whether or not software is developed as part of a larger system. For an overview of system versus software issues, the reader is referred to Dorfman and Thayer's survey [Thayer 90].

Reprinted from *Software Engineering*, M. Dorfman and R.H. Thayer, eds., 1996, pp. 82–103.

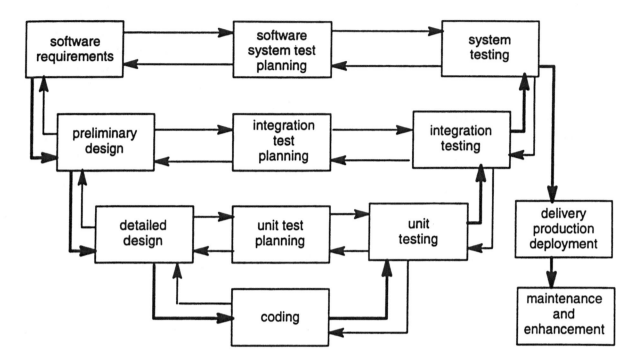

Figure 1. Software life cycle

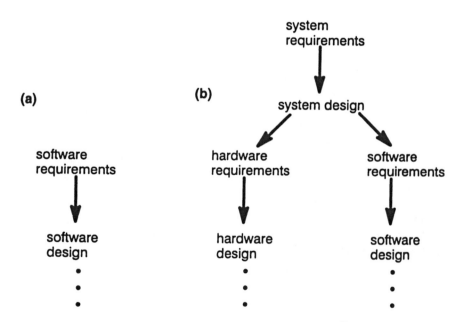

Figure 2. Development paths: (a) software, (b) systems

In a large system development, the software requirements specification may play a variety of roles:

- For customers, the requirements typically document what should be delivered and may provide the contractual basis for the development.

- For managers, it may provide the basis for scheduling and a yardstick for measuring progress.

- For the software designers, it may provide the "design-to" specification.

- For coders, it defines the range of acceptable implementations and is the final authority on the outputs that must be produced.

- For quality assurance personnel, it is the basis for validation, test planning, and verification.

The requirements may also used by such diverse groups as marketing and governmental regulators.

It is common practice (for example, see [Thayer 90]) to classify software requirements as "functional" or "nonfunctional." While definitions vary somewhat in detail, "functional" typically refers to requirements defining the acceptable mappings between system input values and corresponding output values. "Nonfunctional" then refers to all other constraints including, but not limited to, performance, dependability, maintainability, reusability, and safety.

While widely used, the classification of requirements as "functional" and "nonfunctional" is confusing in its terminology and of little help in understanding common properties of different kinds of requirements. The word "function" is one of the most overloaded in computer science, and its only rigorous meaning, that of a mathematical function, is not what is meant here. The classification of requirements as functional and non-functional offers little help in understanding common attributes of different types of requirements since it partitions classes of requirements with markedly similar qualities (for example, output values and output deadlines) while grouping others that have commonality only in what they are not (for example, output deadlines and maintainability goals).

A more useful distinction is between what can be described as "behavioral requirements" and "developmental quality attributes" with the following definitions [Clements 95]:

- *Behavioral requirements*—Behavioral requirements include any and all information necessary to determine if the runtime behavior of a given implementation is acceptable. The behavioral requirements define all constraints on the system outputs (for example, value, accuracy, timing) and resulting system state for all possible inputs and current system state. By this definition, security, safety, performance, timing, and fault tolerance are all behavioral requirements.

- *Developmental quality attributes*—Developmental quality attributes include any constraints on the attributes of the system's static construction. These include properties like testability, changeability, maintainability, and reusability.

Behavioral requirements have in common that they are properties of the runtime behavior of the system and can (at least in principle) be validated objectively by observing the behavior of the running system, independent of its method of implementation. In contrast, developmental quality attributes are properties of the system's static structures (for example, modularization) or representation. Developmental quality attributes have in common that they are functions of the development process and methods of construction. Assessment of developmental quality attributes are necessarily relativistic—for example, we do not say that a design is or is not maintainable but that one design is more maintainable than another.

3. A Big Problem

Requirements problems are persistent, pervasive, and costly. Evidence is most readily available for the large software systems developed for the US government, since the results are a matter of public record. As soon as software became a significant part of such systems, developers identified requirements as a major source of problems. For example, developers of the early Ballistic Missile Defense System noted that:

In nearly every software project that fails to meet performance and cost goals, requirements inadequacies play a major and expensive role in project failure [Alford 79].

Nor has the problem mitigated over the intervening years. A recent study of problems in mission-critical defense systems identified requirements as a major problem source in two thirds of the systems examined [GAO 92]. This is consistent with results of a survey of large aerospace firms that identified requirements as the most critical software development problem [Faulk 92]. Likewise, studies by Lutz

160

[Lutz 92] identified functional and interface requirements as the major source of safety-related software errors in NASA's Voyager and Galileo spacecraft.

Results of industry studies in the 1970s described by Boehm [Boehm 81], and since replicated a number of times, showed that requirements errors are the most costly. These studies all produced the same basic result: The earlier in the development process an error occurs and the later the error is detected, the more expensive it is to correct. Moreover, the relative cost rises quickly. As shown in Figure 3, an error that costs a dollar to fix in the requirements phase may cost $100 to $200 to fix if it is not corrected until the system is fielded or in the maintenance phase.

The costs of such failures can be enormous. For example, the 1992 GAO report notes that one system, the Cheyenne Mountain Upgrade, will be delivered eight years late, exceed budget by $600 million, and have less capability than originally planned, largely due to requirements-related problems. Prior GAO reports [GAO 79] suggest that such problems are the norm rather than the exception. While data from private industry is less readily available, there is little reason to believe that the situation is significantly different.

In spite of presumed advances in software engineering methodology and tool support, the requirements problem has not diminished. This does not mean that the apparent progress in software engineering is illusory. While the features of the problem have not changed, the applications have grown significantly in capability, scale, and complexity. A reasonable conclusion is that the growing ambitiousness of our software systems has outpaced the gains in requirements technology, at least as such technology is applied in practice.

4. Why Are Requirements Hard?

It is generally agreed that the goal of the requirements phase is to establish and specify precisely what the software must do without describing how to do it. So simple seems this basic intent that it is not at all evident why it is so difficult to accomplish in practice. If what we want to accomplish is so clear, why is it so hard? To understand this, we must examine more closely the goals of the requirements phase, where errors originate, and why the nature of the task leads to some inherent difficulties.

Most authors agree in principle that requirements should specify "what" rather than "how." In other words, the goal of requirements is to understand and specify the *problem* to be solved rather than the *solution*. For example, the requirements for an automated teller system should talk about customer accounts, deposits, and withdrawals rather than the software algorithms and data structures. The most basic reason for this is that a specification in terms of the problem captures the actual requirements without overconstraining the subsequent design or implementation. Further, solutions in software terms are typically more complex, more difficult to change, and harder to understand (particularly for the customer) than a specification of the problem.

Unfortunately, distinguishing "what" from "how" itself represents a dilemma. As Davis [Davis 88], among others, points out, the distinction between what and how is necessarily a function of perspective. A specification at any chosen level of system decomposition can be viewed as describing the "what" for the next level. Thus customer needs may define the "what" and the decomposition into hardware and software the corresponding "how." Subsequently, the behavioral requirements allocated to a software component define its "what," the software design, the "how," and so on. The upshot is that requirements cannot be effectively discussed at all without prior agreement on which system one is talking about and at what level of decomposition. One must agree on what constitutes the problem space and what constitutes the solution space—the analysis and specification of requirements then properly belongs in the problem space.

Stage	Relative Repair Cost
Requirements	1–2
Design	5
Coding	10
Unit test	20
System test	50
Maintenance	200

Figure 3: Relative cost to repair a software error in different stages

In discussing requirements problems, one must also distinguish the development of large, complex systems from smaller efforts (for example, developments by a single or small team of programmers). Large system developments are multiperson efforts. They are developed by teams of tens to thousands of programmers. The programmers work in the context of an organization typically including management, systems engineering, marketing, accounting, and quality assurance. The organization itself must operate in the context of outside concerns also interested in the software product, including the customer, regulatory agencies, and suppliers.

Even where only one system is intended, large systems are inevitably multiversion as well. As the software is being developed, tested, and even fielded, it evolves. Customers understand better what they want, developers understand better what they can and cannot do within the constraints of cost and schedule, and circumstances surrounding development change. The results are changes in the software requirements and, ultimately, the software itself. In effect, several versions of a given program are produced, if only incrementally. Such unplanned changes occur in addition to the expected variations of planned improvements.

The multiperson, multiversion nature of large system development introduces problems that are both quantitatively and qualitatively different from those found in smaller developments. For example, scale introduces the need for administration and control functions with the attendant management issues that do not exist on small projects. The quantitative effects of increased complexity in communication when the number of workers rises are well documented by Brooks [Brooks 75]. In the following discussion, it is this large system development context we will assume, since that is the one in which the worst problems occur and where the most help is needed.

Given the context of multiperson, multiversion development, our basic goal of specifying what the software must do can be decomposed into the following subgoals:

1. Understand precisely what is required of the software.

2. Communicate the understanding of what is required to all of the parties involved in the development.

3. Provide a means for controlling the production to ensure that the final system satisfies the requirements (including managing the effects of changes).

It follows that the source of most requirements errors is in the failure to adequately accomplish one of these goals, that is:

1. The developers failed to understand what was required of the software by the customer, end user, or other parties with a stake in the final product.

2. The developers did not completely and precisely capture the requirements or subsequently communicate the requirements effectively to other parties involved in the development.

3. The developers did not effectively manage the effects of changing requirements or ensure the conformance of down-stream development steps including design, code, integration, test, or maintenance to the system requirements.

The end result of such failures is a software system that does not perform as desired or expected, a development that exceeds budget and schedule or, all too frequently, failure to deliver any working software at all.

4.1 Essential Difficulties

Even our more detailed goals appear straightforward; why then do so many development efforts fail to achieve them? The short answer is that the mutual satisfaction of these goals, in practice, is inherently difficult. To understand why, it is useful to reflect on some points raised by Brooks [Brooks 87] on why software engineering is hard and on the distinction he makes between essential difficulties—those inherent in the problem, and the accidental difficulties—those introduced through imperfect practice. For though requirements are inherently difficult, there is no doubt that these difficulties are many times multiplied by the inadequacies of current practice.

The following essential difficulties attend each (in some cases all) of the requirements goals:

- *Comprehension*. People do not know what they want. This does not mean that people do not have a general idea of what the software is for. Rather, they do not begin with a precise and detailed understanding of what functions belong in the software, what the output must be for every possible input, how long each operation should take, how one decision will affect another, and so on.

Indeed, unless the new system is simply a reconstruction of an old one, such a detailed understanding at the outset is unachievable. Many decisions about the system behavior will depend on other decisions yet unmade, and expectations will change as the problem (and attendant costs of alternative solutions) is better understood. Nonetheless, it is a precise and richly detailed understanding of expected behavior that is needed to create effective designs and develop correct code.

- *Communication.* Software requirements are difficult to communicate effectively. As Brooks points out, the conceptual structures of software systems are complex, arbitrary, and difficult to visualize. The large software systems we are now building are among the most complex structures ever attempted. That complexity is arbitrary in the sense that it is an artifact of people's decisions and prior construction rather than a reflection of fundamental properties (as, for example, in the case of physical laws). To make matters worse, many of the conceptual structures in software have no readily comprehensible physical analogue so they are difficult to visualize.

In practice, comprehension suffers under all of these constraints. We work best with regular, predictable structures, can comprehend only a very limited amount of information at one time, and understand large amounts of information best when we can visualize it. Thus the task of capturing and conveying software requirements is inherently difficult.

The inherent difficulty of communication is compounded by the diversity of purposes and audiences for a requirements specification. Ideally, a technical specification is written for a particular audience. The brevity and comprehensibility of the document depend on assumptions about common technical background and use of language. Such commonality typically does not hold for the many diverse groups (for example, customers, systems engineers, managers) that must use a software requirements specification.

- *Control.* Inherent difficulties attend control of software development as well. The arbitrary and invisible nature of software makes it dif-

ficult to anticipate which requirements will be met easily and which will decimate the project's budget and schedule if, indeed, they can be fulfilled at all. The low fidelity of software planning has become a cliche, yet the requirements are often the best available basis for planning or for tracking to a plan.

This situation is made incalculably worse by software's inherent malleability. Of all the problems bedeviling software managers, few evoke such passion as the difficulties of dealing with frequent and arbitrary changes to requirements. For most systems, such changes remain a fact of life even after delivery. The continuous changes make it difficult to develop stable specifications, plan effectively, or control cost and schedule. For many industrial developers, change management is the most critical problem in requirements.

- *Inseparable concerns.* In seeking solutions to the foregoing problems, we are faced with the additional difficulty that the issues cannot easily be separated and dealt with, piecemeal. For example, developers have attempted to address the problem of changing requirements by baselining and freezing requirements before design begins. This proves impractical because of the comprehension problem—the customer may not fully know what he wants until he sees it. Similarly, the diversity of purposes and audiences is often addressed by writing a different specification for each. Thus there may be a system specification, a set of requirements delivered to customer, a distinct set of technical requirements written for the internal consumption of the software developers, and so on. However, this solution vastly increases the complexity, provides an open avenue for inconsistencies, and multiplies the difficulties of managing changes.

These issues represent only a sample of the inherent dependencies between different facets of the requirements problem. The many distinct parties with an interest in a system's requirements, the many different roles the requirements play, and the interlocking nature of software's conceptual structures, all introduce dependencies between concerns and impose conflicting constraints on any potential solution.

The implications are twofold. First we are constrained in the application of our most effective strategy for dealing with complex problems—divide and conquer. If a problem is considered in isolation, the solution is likely to aggravate other difficulties. Effective solutions to most requirements difficulties must simultaneously address more than one problem. Second, developing practical solutions requires making difficult trade-offs. Where different problems have conflicting constraints, compromises must be made. Because the trade-offs result in different gains or losses to the different parties involved, effective compromises require negotiation. These issues are considered in more detail when we discuss the properties of a good requirements specification.

4.2 Accidental Difficulties

While there is no doubt that software requirements are inherently difficult to do well, there is equally no doubt that common practice unnecessarily exacerbates the difficulty. We use the term "accidental" in contrast to "essential," not to imply that the difficulties arise by chance but that they are the product of common failings in management, elicitation, specification, or use of requirements. It is these failings that are most easily addressed by improved practice.

- *Written as an afterthought.* It remains common practice that requirements documentation is developed only after the software has been written. For many projects, the temptation to rush into implementation before the requirements are adequately understood proves irresistible. This is understandable. Developers often feel like they are not really doing anything when they are not writing code; managers are concerned about schedule when there is no visible progress on the implementation. Then too, the intangible nature of the product mitigates toward early implementation. Developing the system is an obvious way to understand better what is needed and make visible the actual behavior of the product. The result is that requirements specifications are written as an afterthought (if at all). They are not created to guide the developers and testers but treated as a necessary evil to satisfy contractual demands.

Such after-the-fact documentation inevitably violates the principle of defining what the system must do rather than the how since it is a specification of the code as written. It is produced after the fact so it is not planned or managed as an essential part of the development but is thrown together. In fact, it is not even available in time to guide implementation or manage development.

- *Confused in purpose.* Because there are so many potential audiences for a requirements specification, with different points of view, the exact purpose of the document becomes confused. An early version is used to sell the product to the customer, so it includes marketing hype extolling the product's virtues. It is the only documentation of what the system does, so it provides introductory, explanatory, and overview material. It is a contractual document, so it is intentionally imprecise to allow the developer latitude in the delivered product or the customer latitude in making no-cost changes. It is the vehicle for communicating decisions about software details to designers and coders, so it incorporates design and implementation. The result is a document in which it is unclear which statements represent real requirements and which are more properly allocated to marketing, design, or other documentation. It is a document that attempts to be everything to everyone and ultimately serves no one well.

- *Not designed to be useful.* Often, in the rush to implementation, little effort is expended on requirements. The requirements specification is not expected to be useful and, indeed, this turns out to be a self-fulfilling prophecy. Because the document is not expected to be useful, little effort is expended on designing it, writing it, checking it, or managing its creation and evolution. The most obvious result is poor organization. The specification is written in English prose and follows the author's stream of consciousness or the order of execution [Heninger 80].

The resulting document is ineffective as a technical reference. It is unclear which statements represent actual requirements. It is unclear where to put or find particular requirements. There is no effective procedure for ensuring that the specification is consistent or complete. There is no systematic way to manage requirements changes. The specification is difficult to use and difficult to maintain. It quickly becomes out of date and loses whatever usefulness it might originally have had.

- *Lacks essential properties.* Lack of forethought, confusion of purpose, or lack of careful design and execution all lead to requirements that lack properties critical to good technical specifications. The requirements, if documented at all, are redundant, inconsistent, incomplete, imprecise, and inaccurate.

Where the essential difficulties are inherent in the problem, the accidental difficulties result from a failure to gain or maintain intellectual control over what is to be built. While the presence of the essential difficulties means that there can be no "silver bullet" that will suddenly render requirements easy, we can remove at least the accidental difficulties through a well thought out, systematic, and disciplined development process. Such a disciplined process then provides a stable foundation for attacking the essential difficulties.

5. Role of a Disciplined Approach

The application of discipline in analyzing and specifying software requirements can address the accidental difficulties. While there is now general agreement on the desirable qualities of a software development approach, the field is insufficiently mature to have standardized the development process. Nonetheless, it is useful to examine the characteristics of an idealized process and its products to understand where current approaches are weak and which current trends are promising. In general, a complete requirements approach will define:

- *Process*: The (partially ordered) sequence of activities, entrance and exit criteria for each activity, which work product is produced in each activity, and what kind of people should do the work.

- *Products*: The work products to be produced and, for each product, the resources needed to produce it, the information it contains, the expected audience, and the acceptance criteria the product must satisfy.

Currently, there is little uniformity in different author's decomposition of the requirements phase or in the terminology for the activities. Davis [Davis 88] provides a good summary of the variations. Following Davis's integrated model and terminology [Davis 93],

the requirements phase consists of two conceptually distinct but overlapping activities corresponding to the first two goals for requirements enumerated previously:

1. *Problem analysis*: The goal of problem analysis is to understand precisely what problem is to be solved. It includes identifying the exact purpose of the system, who will use it, the constraints on acceptable solutions, and the possible trade-offs between conflicting constraints.

2. *Requirements specification*: The goal of requirements specification is to create a document, the Software Requirements Specification (SRS), describing exactly what is to be built. The SRS captures the results of problem analysis and characterizes the set of acceptable solutions to the problem.

In practice, the distinction between these activities is conceptual rather than temporal. Where both are needed, the developer typically switches back and forth between analysis of the problem and documentation of the results. When problems are well understood, the analysis phase may be virtually nonexistent. When the system model and documentation are standardized or based on existing specifications, the documentation paradigm may guide the analysis [Hester 81].

5.1 Problem Analysis

Problem analysis is necessarily informal in the sense that there is no effective, closed-end procedure that will guarantee success. It is an information-acquiring, -collating, and -structuring process through which one attempts to understand all the various parts of a problem and their relationships. The difficulty in developing an effective understanding of large, complex software problems has motivated considerable effort to structure and codify problem analysis.

The basic issues in problem analysis are:

- How to effectively elicit a complete set of requirements from the customer or other sources?

- How to decompose the problem into intellectually manageable pieces?

- How to organize the information so it can be understood?

- How to communicate about the problem with all the parties involved?

- How to resolve conflicting needs?
- How to know when to stop?

5.2 Requirements Specification

For substantial developments, the effectiveness of the requirements effort depends on how well the SRS captures the results of analysis and how useable the specification is. There is little benefit to developing a thorough understanding of the problem if that understanding is not effectively communicated to customers, designers, implementors, testers, and maintainers. The larger and more complex the system, the more important a good specification becomes. This is a direct result of the many roles the SRS plays in a multiperson, multiversion development [Parnas 86]:

1. The SRS is the primary vehicle for agreement between the developer and customer on exactly what is to be built. It is the document reviewed by the customer or his representative and often is the basis for judging fulfillment of contractual obligations.

2. The SRS records the results of problem analysis. It is the basis for determining where the requirements are complete and where additional analysis is necessary. Documenting the results of analysis allows questions about the problem to be answered only once during development.

3. The SRS defines what properties the system must have and the constraints on its design and implementation. It defines where there is, and is not, design freedom. It helps ensure that requirements decisions are made explicitly during the requirements phase, not implicitly during programming.

4. The SRS is the basis for estimating cost and schedule. It is management's primary tool for tracking development progress and ascertaining what remains to be done.

5. The SRS is the basis for test plan development. It is the tester's chief tool for determining the acceptable behavior of the software.

6. The SRS provides the standard definition of expected behavior for the system's maintainers and is used to record engineering changes.

For a disciplined software development, the SRS is the primary technical specification of the software and the primary control document. This is an inevitable result of the complexity of large systems and the need to coordinate multiperson development teams. To ensure that the right system is built, one must first understand the problem. To ensure agreement on what is to be built and the criteria for success, the results of that understanding must be recorded. The goal of a systematic requirements process is thus the development of a set of specifications that effectively communicate the results of analysis.

Requirement's accidental difficulties are addressed through the careful analysis and specification of a disciplined process. Rather than developing the specification as an afterthought, requirements are understood and specified before development begins. One knows what one is building before attempting to build it. The SRS is the primary vehicle for communicating requirements between the developers, managers, and customers, so the document is designed to be useful foro that purpose. A useful document is maintained.

6. Requirements for the Software Requirements Specification

The goals of the requirements process, the attendant difficulties, and the role of the requirements specification in a disciplined process determine the properties of a "good" requirements specification. These properties do not mandate any particular specification method but do describe the characteristics of an effective method.

In discussing the properties of a good SRS, it is useful to distinguish semantic properties from packaging properties [Faulk 92]. Semantic properties are a consequence of what the specification says (that is, its meaning or semantics). Packaging properties are a consequence of how the requirements are written—the format, organization, and presentation of the information. The semantic properties determine how effectively an SRS captures the software requirements. The packaging properties determine how useable the resulting specification is. Figure 4 illustrates the classification of properties of a good SRS.

An SRS that satisfies the semantic properties of a good specification is:

- *Complete*. The SRS defines the set of acceptable implementations. It should contain all the information needed to write software that is acceptable to the customer and no more. Any implementation that satisfies every statement in the requirements is an acceptable product. Where information is not available before development begins, areas of incompleteness must be explicitly indicated [Parnas 86].

SRS Semantic Properties	SRS Packaging Properties
Complete	Modifiable
Implementation independent	Readable
Unambiguous and consistent	Organized for reference and review
Precise	
Verifiable	

Figure 4. Classification of SRS properties

- *Implementation independent.* The SRS should be free of design and implementation decisions unless those decisions reflect actual requirements.

- *Unambiguous and consistent.* If the SRS is subject to conflicting interpretation, the different parties will not agree on what is to be built or whether the right software has been built. Every requirement should have only one possible interpretation. Similarly, no two statements of required behavior should conflict.

- *Precise.* The SRS should define exactly the required behavior. For each output, it should define the range of acceptable values for every input. The SRS should define any applicable timing constraints such as minimum and maximum acceptable delay.

- *Verifiable.* A requirement is verifiable if it is possible to determine unambiguously whether a given implementation satisfies the requirement or not. For example, a behavioral requirement is verifiable if it is possible to determine, for any given test case (that is, an input and an output), whether the output represents an acceptable behavior of the software given the input and the system state.

An SRS[1] that satisfies the packaging properties of a good specification is:

- *Modifiable.* The SRS must be organized for ease of change. Since no organization can be equally easy to change for all possible changes, the requirements analysis process must identify expected changes and the relative likelihood of their occurrence. The specification is then organized to limit the effect of likely changes.

- *Readable.* The SRS must be understandable by the parties that use it. It should clearly relate the elements of the problem space as understood by the customer to the observable behavior of the software.

- *Organized for reference and review.* The SRS is the primary technical specification of the software requirements. It is the repository for all the decisions made during analysis about what should be built. It is the document reviewed by the customer or his representatives. It is the primary arbitrator of disputes. As such, the document must be organized for quick and easy reference. It must be clear where each decision about the requirements belongs. It must be possible to answer specific questions about the requirements quickly and easily.

To address the difficulties associated with writing and using an SRS, a requirements approach must provide techniques addressing both semantic and packaging properties. It is also desirable that the conceptual structures of the approach treat the semantic and packaging properties as distinct concerns (that is, as independently as possible). This allows one to change the presentation of the SRS without changing its meaning.

In aggregate, these properties of a good SRS represent an ideal. Some of the properties may be unachievable, particularly over the short term. For example, a common complaint is that one cannot develop complete requirements before design begins because the customer does not yet fully understand what he wants or is still making changes. Further, different SRS "requirements" mitigate toward conflicting solutions. A commonly cited example is the use of English prose to express requirements. English is readily understood but notoriously ambiguous and imprecise. Conversely, formal languages are precise and unambiguous, but can be difficult to read.

Although the ideal SRS may be unachievable, possessing a common understanding of what constitutes

---

1. Reusability is also a packaging property and becomes an attribute of a good specification where reusability of requirements specifications is a goal.

an ideal SRS is important [Parnas 86] because it:

- provides a basis for standardizing an organization's processes and products,

- provides a standard against which progress can be measured, and,

- provides guidance—it helps developers understand what needs to be done next and when they are finished.

Because it is so often true that (1) requirements cannot be fully understood before at least starting to build the system, and (2) a perfect SRS cannot be produced even when the requirements are understood, some approaches advocated in the literature do not even attempt to produce a definitive SRS. For example, some authors advocate going directly from a problem model to design or from a prototype implementation to the code. While such approaches may be effective on some developments, they are inconsistent with the notion of software development as an engineering discipline. The development of technical specifications is an essential part of a controlled engineering process. This does not mean that the SRS must be entire or perfect before anything else is done but that its development is a fundamental goal of the process as a whole. That we may currently lack the ability to write good specifications in some cases does not change the fact that it is useful and necessary to try.

7. State of the Practice

Over the years, many analysis and specification techniques have evolved. The general trend has been for software engineering techniques to be applied first to coding problems (for example, complexity, ease of change), then to similar problems occurring earlier and earlier in the life cycle. Thus the concepts of structured programming led eventually to structured design and analysis. More recently, the concepts of object-oriented programming have led to object-oriented design and analysis. The following discussion characterizes the major schools of thought and provides pointers to instances of methods in each school. The general strengths and weaknesses of the various techniques are discussed relative to the requirements difficulties and the desirable qualities of analysis and specification methods.

It is characteristic of the immature state of requirements as a discipline that the more specific one gets, the less agreement there is. There is not only disagreement in terminology, approach, and the details of different methods, there is not even a commonly accepted classification scheme. The following general groupings are based on the evolution of the underlying concepts and the key distinctions that reflect paradigmatic shifts in requirements philosophy.

7.1 Functional Decomposition

Functional decomposition was originally applied to software requirements to abstract from coding details. Functional decomposition focuses on understanding and specifying what processing the software is required to do. The general strategy is to define the required behavior as a mapping from inputs to outputs. Ideally, the analysis proceeds top down, first identifying the function associated with the system as a whole. Each subsequent step decomposes the set of functions into steps or sub-functions. The result is a hierarchy of functions and the definitions of the functional interfaces. Each level of the hierarchy adds detail about the processing steps necessary to accomplish the more abstract function above. The function above controls the processing of its subfunctions. In a complete decomposition, the functional hierarchy specifies the "calls" structure of the implementation. One example of a methodology based on functional decomposition is Hamilton and Zeldin's Higher Order Software [Hamilton 76].

The advantage of functional decomposition is that the specification is written using the language and concepts of the implementors. It communicates well to the designers and coders. It is written in terms of the solution space so the transition to design and code is straightforward.

Common complaints are that functional specifications are difficult to communicate, introduce design decisions prematurely, and difficult to use or change. Because functional specifications are written in the language of implementation, people who are not software or systems experts find them difficult to understand. Since there are inevitably many possible ways of decomposing functions into subfunctions, the analyst must make decisions that are not requirements. Finally, since the processing needed in one step depends strongly on what has been done the previous step, functional decomposition results in components that are closely coupled. Understanding or changing one function requires understanding or changing all the related functions.

As software has increased in complexity and become more visible to nontechnical people, the need for methods addressing the weaknesses of functional decomposition has likewise increased.

7.2 Structured Analysis

Structured analysis was developed primarily as a

means to address the accidental difficulties attending problem analysis and, to a lesser extent, requirements specification, using functional decomposition. Following the introduction of structured programming as a means to gain intellectual control over increasingly complex programs, structured analysis evolved from functional decomposition as a means to gain intellectual control over system problems.

The basic assumption behind structured analysis is that the accidental difficulties can be addressed by a systematic approach to problem analysis using [Svoboda 90]:

- a common conceptual model for describing all problems,
- a set of procedures suggesting the general direction of analysis and an ordering on the steps,
- a set of guidelines or heuristics supporting decisions about the problem and its specification, and
- a set of criteria for evaluating the quality of the product.

While structured analysis still contains the decomposition of functions into subfunctions, the focus of the analysis shifts from the processing steps to the data being processed. The analyst views the problem as constructing a system to transform data. He analyzes the sources and destinations of the data, determines what data must be held in storage, what transformations are done on the data, and the form of the output.

Common to the structured analysis approaches is the use of data flow diagrams and data dictionaries. Data flow diagrams provide a graphic representation of the movement of data through the system (typically represented as arcs) and the transformations on the data (typically represented as nodes). The data dictionary supports the data flow diagram by providing a repository for the definitions and descriptions of each data item on the diagrams. Required processing is captured in the definitions of the transformations. Associated with each transformation node is a specification of the processing the node does to transform the incoming data items to the outgoing data items. At the most detailed level, a transformation is defined using a textual specification called a "MiniSpec." A MiniSpec may be expressed in several different ways including English prose, decision tables, or a procedure definition language (PDL).

Structured analysis approaches originally evolved for management information systems (MIS). Examples of widely used strategies include those described by DeMarco [DeMarco 78] and Gane and Sarson [Gane

79]. "Modern" structured analysis was introduced to provide more guidance in modeling systems as data flows as exemplified by Yourdon [Yourdon 89]. Structured analysis has also been adapted to support specification of embedded control systems by adding notations to capture control behavior. These variations are collectively known as structured analysis/real-time (SA/RT). Major variations of SA/RT have been described by Ward and Mellor [Ward 86] and Hatley and Pirbhai [Hatley 87]. A good summary of structured analysis concepts with extensive references is given by Svoboda [Svoboda 90].

Structured analysis extends functional decomposition with the notion that there should be a systematic (and hopefully predictable) approach to analyzing a problem, decomposing it into parts, and describing the relationships between the parts. By providing a well-defined process, structured analysis seeks to address, at least in part, the accidental difficulties that result from ad hoc approaches and the definition of requirements as an afterthought. It seeks to address problems in comprehension and communication by using a common set of conceptual structures—a graphic representation of the specification in terms of those structures—based on the assumption that a decomposition in terms of the data the system handles will be clearer and less inclined to change than one based on the functions performed.

While structured analysis techniques have continued to evolve and have been widely used, there remain a number of common criticisms. When used in problem analysis, a common complaint is that structured analysis provides insufficient guidance. Analysts have difficulty deciding which parts of the problem to model as data, which parts to model as transformations, and which parts should be aggregated. While the gross steps of the process are reasonably well defined, there is only very general guidance (in the form of heuristics) on what specific questions the analyst needs to answer next. Similarly, practitioners find it difficult to know when to stop decomposition and addition of detail. In fact, the basic structured analysis paradigm of modeling requirements as data flows and data transformations requires the analyst to make decisions about intermediate values (for example, form and content of stored data and the details of internal transformations) that are not requirements. Particularly in the hands of less experienced practitioners, data flow models tend to incorporate a variety of detail that properly belongs to design or implementation.

Many of these difficulties result from the weak constraints imposed by the conceptual model. A goal of the developers of structured analysis was to create a very general approach to modeling systems; in fact, one that could be applied equally to model human enterprises, hardware applications, software applications of different kinds, and so on. Unfortunately, such generality can be achieved only by abstracting away any semantics that are not common to all of the types of systems potentially being modeled. The conceptual model itself can provide little guidance relevant to a particular system. Since the conceptual model applies equally to requirements analysis and design analysis, its semantics provide no basis for distinguishing the two. Similarly, such models can support only very weak syntactic criteria for assessing the quality of structured analysis specifications. For example, the test for completeness and consistency in data flow diagrams is limited to determining that the transformations at each level are consistent in name and number with the data flows of the level above.

This does not mean one cannot develop data flow specifications that are easy to understand, communicate effectively with the user, or capture required behavior correctly. The large number of systems developed using structured analysis show that it is possible to do so. However, the weakness of the conceptual model means that a specification's quality depends largely on the experience, insight, and expertise of the analyst. The developer must provide the necessary discipline because the model itself is relatively unconstrained.

Finally, structured analysis provides little support for producing an SRS that meets our quality criteria. Data flow diagrams are unsuitable for capturing mathematical relations or detailed specifications of value, timing, or accuracy so the detailed behavioral specifications are typically given in English or as pseudocode segments in the MiniSpecs. These constructs provide little or no support for writing an SRS that is complete, implementation independent, unambiguous, consistent, precise, and verifiable. Further, the data flow diagrams and attendant dictionaries do not, themselves, provide support for organizing an SRS to satisfy the packaging goals of readability, ease of reference and review, or reusability. In fact, for many of the published methods, there is no explicit process step, structure, or guidance for producing an SRS, as a distinct development product, at all.

7.3 Operational Specification

The operational[2] approach focuses on addressing two of the essential requirements dilemmas. The first is that we often do not know exactly what should be built until we build it. The second is the problem inherent in moving from a particular specification of

requirements (what to build) to a design that satisfies those requirements (how to build it). The closer the requirements specification is to the design, the easier the transition, but the more likely it is that design decisions are made prematurely.

The operational approach seeks to address these problems, among others, by supporting development of executable requirements specifications. Key elements of an operational approach are: a formal specification language and an engine for executing well-formed specifications written in the language. Operational approaches may also include automated support for analyzing properties of the formal specification and for transforming the specification into an equivalent implementation. A good description of the operational approach, its rationale, and goals is given by Zave [Zave 82].

The underlying reasoning about the benefits of the operational approach is as follows:

- Making the requirements specification itself executable obviates the dilemma that one must build the system to know what to build. The developer writes the requirements specification in a formal language. The specification may then be executed to validate that the customer's needs have been captured and the right system specified (for example, one can apply scenarios and test cases). The approach is presumed to require less labor and be more cost-effective than conventional prototyping because a separate requirements specification need not be produced; the specification and the "prototype" are the same thing.

- Operational specifications allow the developer to abstract from design decisions while simplifying the transition from requirements to design and implementation. Transition to design and implementation is both simple and automatable because the behavioral requirements are already expressed in terms of computational mechanisms. During design, one makes decisions concerning efficiency, resource management, and target language realization that are abstracted from the operational specification.

For general applications, operational approaches have achieved only limited success. This is at least in part due to the failure to achieve the necessary semantic distinction between an operational computational model and conventional programming. The benefits of the approach are predicated on the assumption that the

---

2. We use the term "operational" here specifically to denote approaches based on executable specifications in the sense of Zave [Zave 82]. The term is sometimes used to contrast with axiomatic specification–that is not the meaning here.

operational model can be written in terms of the problem domain, without the need to introduce conceptual structures belonging to the solution domain. In practice, this goal has proven elusive. To achieve generality, operational languages have typically had to introduce implementation constructs. The result is not a requirements specification language but a higher-level programming language. As noted by Parnas [Parnas 85b] and Brooks [Brooks 87], the specification ends up giving the solution method rather than the problem statement. Thus, in practice, operational specifications do not meet the SRS goal of implementation independence.

The focus of operational specification is on the benefits of early simulation rather than on the properties of the specification as a reference document. Since executability requires formality, operational specifications necessarily satisfy the SRS semantic properties of being unambiguous, consistent, precise, and verifiable. The ability to validate the specification through simulation also supports completeness. However, as discussed, these properties have not been achieved in concert with implementation independence. Further, the methods discussed in the literature put little emphasis on the communication or packaging qualities of the specification, except as these qualities overlap with desirable design properties. Thus, there may be some support for modifiability but little for readability or organizing an SRS for reference and review.

7.4 Object Oriented Analysis (OOA)

There is currently considerable discussion in the literature, and little agreement, on exactly what should and should not be considered "object oriented." OOA has evolved from at least two significant sources: information modeling and object oriented design. Each has contributed to current views of OOA, and the proponents of each emphasize somewhat different sets of concepts. For the purposes of this tutorial, we are not interested in which method is by some measure "more object oriented" but in the distinct contributions of the object-oriented paradigm to analysis and specification. For an overview of OOA concepts and methods, see Balin's article [Balin 94]; Davis's book [Davis 93] includes both discussion and examples. Examples of recent approaches self-described as object oriented include work by Rumbaugh [Rumbaugh 91], Coad and Yourdon [Coad 91], Shlaer and Mellor [Shlaer 88], and Selic, Gullekson, and Ward [Selic 94].

OOA techniques differ from structured analysis in their approach to decomposing a problem into parts and in the methods for describing the relationships between the parts. In OOA, the analyst decomposes the problem into a set of interacting objects based on the entities and relationships extant in the problem domain. An object encapsulates a related set of data, processing, and state (thus, a significant distinction between object-oriented analysis and structured analysis is that OOA encapsulates both data and related processing together). Objects provide externally accessible functions, typically called services or methods. Objects may hide information about their internal structure, data, or state from other objects. Conversely, they may provide processing, data, or state information through the services defined on the object interface. Dynamic relationships between objects are captured in terms of message passing (that is, one object sends a message to invoke a service or respond to an invocation). The analyst captures static relationships in the problem domain using the concepts of aggregation and classification. Aggregation is used to capture whole/part relationships. Classification is used to capture class/instance relationships (also called "is-a" or inheritance relationships).

The structural components of OOA (for example, objects, classes, services, aggregation) support a set of analytic principles. Of these, two directly address requirements problems:

1. From information modeling comes the assumption that a problem is easiest to understand and communicate if the conceptual structures created during analysis map directly to entities and relationships in the problem domain. This principle is realized in OOA through the heuristic of representing problem domain objects and relationships of interest as OOA objects and relationships. Thus an OOA specification of a vehicle registration system might model vehicles, vehicle owners, vehicle title, and so on [Coad 90] as objects. The object paradigm is used to model both the problem and the relevant problem context.

2. From early work on modularization by Parnas [Parnas 72] and abstract data types, by way of object-oriented programming and design, come the principles of information hiding and abstraction. The principle of information hiding guides one to limit access to information on which other parts of the system should not depend. In an OO specification of requirements, this principle is applied to hide details of design and implementation. In OOA, behavior requirements are specified in terms of the data and services provided on the object interfaces; how those services are implemented is encapsulated by the object.

The principle of abstraction says that only the relevant or essential information should be presented. Abstraction is implemented in OOA by defining object interfaces that provide access only to essential data or state information encapsulated by an object (conversely hiding the incidentals).

The principles and mechanisms of OOA provide a basis for attacking the essential difficulties of comprehension, communication, and control. The principle of problem-domain modeling helps guide the analyst in distinguishing requirements (what) from design (how). Where the objects and their relationships faithfully model entities and relationships in the problem, they are understandable by the customer and other domain experts; this supports early comprehension of the requirements.

The principles of information hiding and abstraction, with the attendant object mechanisms, provide mechanisms useful for addressing the essential problems of control and communication. Objects provide the means to divide the requirements into distinct parts, abstract from details, and limit unnecessary dependencies between the parts. Object interfaces can be used to hide irrelevant detail and define abstractions providing only the essential information. This provides a basis for managing complexity and improving readability. Likewise objects provide a basis for constructing reusable requirements units of related functions and data.

The potential benefits of OOA are often diluted by the way the key principles are manifest in particular methods. While the objects and relations of OOA are intended to model essential aspects of the application domain, this goal is typically not supported by a corresponding conceptual model of the domain behavior. As for structured analysis, object-modeling mechanisms and techniques are intentionally generic rather than application specific. One result is insufficient guidance in developing appropriate object decompositions. Just as structured analysis practitioners have difficulty choosing appropriate data flows and transformations, OOA practitioners have difficulty choosing appropriate objects and relationships.

In practice, the notion that one can develop the structure of a system, or a requirements specification, based on physical structure is often found to be oversold. It is true that the elements of the physical world are usually stable (especially relative to software details) and that real-world-based models have intuitive appeal. It is not, however, the case that everything that must be captured in requirements has a physical analog. An obvious example is shared state information. Further, many real-world structures are themselves arbitrary and likely to change (for example, where two hardware functions are put on one physical platform to reduce cost). While the notion of basing requirements structure on physical structure is a useful heuristic, more is needed to develop a complete and consistent requirements specification.

A further difficulty is that the notations and semantics of OOA methods are typically based on the conceptual structures of software rather than those of the problem domain the analyst seeks to model. Symptomatic of this problem is that analysts find themselves debating about object language features and their properties rather than about the properties of the problem. An example is the use of message passing, complete with message passing protocols, where one object uses information defined in another. In the problem domain it is often irrelevant whether information is actively solicited or passively received. In fact there may be no notion of messages or transmission at all. Nonetheless one finds analysts debating about which object should initiate a request and the resulting anomaly of passive entities modeled as active. For example, to get information from a book one might request that the book "read itself" and "send" the requested information in a message. To control an aircraft the pilot might "use his hands and feet to 'send messages' to the aircraft controls which in turn send messages to the aircraft control surfaces to modify themselves" [Davis 93]. Such decisions are about OOA mechanisms or design, not about the problem domain or requirements.

A more serious complaint is that most current OOA methods inadequately address our goal of developing a good SRS. Most OOA approaches in the literature provide only informal specification mechanisms, relying on refinement of the OO model in design and implementation to add detail and precision. There is no formal basis for determining if a specification is complete, consistent, or verifiable. Further, none of the OOA techniques discussed directly address the issues of developing the SRS as a reference document. The focus of all of the cited OOA techniques is on problem analysis rather than specification. If the SRS is addressed at all, the assumption is that the principles applied to problem understanding and modeling are sufficient, when results are documented, to produce a good specification. Experience suggests otherwise. As we have discussed, there are inherent trade-offs that must be made to develop a specification that meets the needs of any particular project. Making effective trade-offs requires a disciplined and thoughtful approach to the SRS itself, not just the problem. Thus, while OOA provide the means to address packaging issues, there is typically little methodological emphasis on issues like modifiability or organization of a specification for reference and review.

7.5 Software Cost Reduction (SCR) Method

Where most of the techniques thus far discussed focus on problem analysis, the requirements work at the US Naval Research Laboratory (NRL) focused equally on issues of developing a good SRS. NRL initiated the Software Cost Reduction (SCR) project in 1978 to demonstrate the feasibility and effectiveness of advanced software engineering techniques by applying them to a real system, the Operational Flight Program (OFP) for the A-7E aircraft. To demonstrate that (then-academic) techniques such as information hiding, formal specification, abstract interfaces, and cooperating sequential processes could help make software easier to understand, maintain, and change, the SCR project set out to reengineer the A-7E OFP.

Since no existing documentation adequately captured the A-7E's software requirements, the first step was to develop an effective SRS. In this process, the SCR project identified a number of properties a good SRS should have and a set of principles for developing effective requirements documentation [Heninger 80]. The SCR approach uses formal, mathematically based specifications of acceptable system outputs to support development of a specification that is unambiguous, precise, and verifiable. It also provided techniques for checking a specification for a variety of completeness and consistency properties. The SCR approach introduced principles and techniques to support our SRS packaging goals, including the principle of separation of concerns to aid readability and support ease of change. It also includes the use of a standard structure for an SRS specification and the use of tabular specifications that improve readability, modifiability, and facilitate use of the specification for reference and review.

While other requirements approaches have stated similar objectives, the SCR project is unique in having applied software engineering principles to develop a standard SRS organization, a specification method, review method [Parnas 85a], and notations consistent with those principles. The SCR project is also unique in making publicly available a complete, model SRS of a significant system [Alspaugh 92].

A number of issues were left unresolved by the original SCR work. While the product of the requirements analysis was well documented, the underlying process and method were never fully described. Since the original effort was to reengineer an existing system, it was not clear how effective the techniques would be on a new development. Since the developers of the A-7E requirements document were researchers, it was also unclear whether industrial developers would find the rather formal method and notation useable, readable, or effective. Finally, while the A-7E

SRS organization is reasonably general, many of the specification techniques are targeted to real-time, embedded applications. As discussed in the following section, more recent work by Parnas [Parnas 91], NRL [Heitmeyer 95a,b], and others [Faulk 92] has addressed many of the open questions about the SCR approach.

8. Trends and Emerging Technology

While improved discipline will address requirement's accidental difficulties, addressing the essential difficulties requires technical advances. Significant trends, in some cases backed by industrial experience, have emerged over the past few years that offer some hope for improvement:

- *Domain specificity*: Requirements methods will provide improved analytic and specification support by being tailored to particular classes of problems. Historically, requirements approaches have been advanced as being equally useful to widely varied types of applications. For example, structured analysis methods were deemed to be based on conceptual models that were "universally applicable" (for example, [Ross 77]); similar claims have been made for object-oriented approaches.

Such generality comes at the expense of ease of use and amount of work the analyst must do for any particular application. Where the underlying models have been tailored to a particular class of applications, the properties common to the class are embedded in the model. The amount of work necessary to adapt the model to a specific instance of the class is relatively small. The more general the model, the more decisions that must be made, the more information that must be provided, and the more tailoring that must be done. This provides increased room for error and, since each analyst will approach the problem differently, makes solutions difficult to standardize. In particular, such generality precludes standardization of sufficiently rigorous models to support algorithmic analysis of properties like completeness and consistency.

Similar points have been expressed in a recent paper by Jackson [Jackson 94]. He points out that some of the characteristics separating real engineering disciplines from what is euphemistically described as "software engineering" are well-understood procedures, mathematical models, and standard designs specific to narrow classes of applications. Jackson points out the need for software methods based on the conceptual structures and mathematical models of behavior inherent in a given problem domain (for example, publication, command and control, accounting, and so on). Such common underlying constructs can provide the engineer guidance in developing the specification for a particular system.

- *Practical formalisms*: Like so many of the promising technologies in requirements, the application of formal methods is characterized by an essential dilemma. On one hand, formal specification techniques hold out the only real hope for producing specifications that are precise, unambiguous, and demonstrably complete or consistent. On the other, industrial practitioners widely view formal methods as impractical. Difficulty of use, inability to scale, readability, and cost are among the reasons cited. Thus, in spite of significant technical progress and a growing body of literature, the pace of adoption by industry has been extremely slow.

In spite of the technical and technical transfer difficulties, increased formality is necessary. Only by placing behavioral specification on a mathematical basis will we be able to acquire sufficient intellectual control to develop complex systems with any assurance that they satisfy their intended purpose and provide necessary properties like safety. The solution is better formal methods—methods that are practical given the time, cost, and personnel constraints of industrial development.

Engineering models and the training to use them are de rigueur in every other discipline that builds large, complex, or safety-critical systems. Builders of a bridge or skyscraper who did not employ proven methods or mathematical models to predict reliability and safety would be held criminally negligent in the event of failure. It is only the relative youth of the software discipline that permits us to get away with less. But, we cannot expect great progress overnight. As Jackson [Jackson 94] notes, the field is sufficiently immature that "the prerequisites for a more mathematical approach are not in place." Further, many of those practicing our craft lack the background required of licensed engineers in other disciplines [Parnas 89]. Nonetheless, sufficient work has been done to show that more formal approaches are practical and effective in industry. For an overview of formal methods and their role in practical developments, refer to Rushby's summary work [Rushby 93].

- *Improved tool support*: It remains common to walk into the office of a software develop-

ment manager and find the shelves lined with the manuals for CASE tools that are not in use. In spite of years of development and the contrary claims of vendors, many industrial developers have found the available requirements CASE tools of marginal benefit.

Typically, the fault lies not so much with the tool vendor but with the underlying method or methods the tool seeks to support. The same generality, lack of strong underlying conceptual model, and lack of formality that makes the methods weak limits the benefits of automation. Since the methods do not adequately constrain the problem space and offer little specific guidance, the corresponding tool cannot actively support the developer in making difficult decisions. Since the model and SRS are not standardized, its production eludes effective automated support. Since the underlying model is not formal, only trivial syntactic properties of the specification can be evaluated. Most such tools provide little more than a graphic interface and requirements database.

Far more is now possible. Where the model, conceptual structures, notations, and process are standardized, significant automated support becomes possible. The tool can use information about the state of the specification and the process to guide the developer in making the next step. It can use standardized templates to automate rote portions of the SRS. It can use the underlying mathematical model to determine to what extent the specification is complete and consistent. While only the potential of such tools has yet been demonstrated, there are sufficient results to project the benefits (for example, [Heitmeyer 95b], [Leveson 94]).

- *Integrated paradigms*: One of the Holy Grails of software engineering has been the integrated software development environment. Much of the frustration in applying currently available methods and tools is the lack of integration, not just in the tool interfaces, but in the underlying models and conceptual structures. Even where an approach works well for one phase of development, the same techniques are either difficult to use in the next phase or there is no clear transition path. Similarly tools are either focused on a small subset of the many tasks (for example, analysis but not documentation) or attempt to address the entire life cycle but support none of it well. The typical development employs a hodgepodge of software engineering methodologies and ad hoc techniques. Developers often build their own software to bridge the gap between CASE platforms.

In spite of a number of attempts, the production of a useful, integrated set of methods and supporting environment has proven elusive. However, it now appears that there is sufficient technology available to provide, if not a complete solution, at least the skeleton for one.

The most significant methodological trend can be described as convergent evolution. In biology, convergent evolution denotes a situation where common evolutionary pressures lead to similar characteristics (morphology) in distinct species. An analogous convergence is ongoing in requirements. As different schools of thought have come to understand and attempt to address the weaknesses and omissions in their own approaches, the solutions have become more similar. In particular, the field is moving toward a common understanding of the difficulties and common assumptions about the desired qualities of solutions. This should not be confused with the bandwagon effect that often attends real or imaginary paradigm shifts (for example, the current rush to object-oriented everything). Rather, it is the slow process of evolving common understanding and changing conventional practices.

Such trends and some preliminary results are currently observable in requirements approaches for embedded software. In the 1970s, the exigencies of national defense and aerospace applications resulted in demand for complex, mission-critical software. It became apparent early on that available requirements techniques addressed neither the complexity of the systems being built nor the stringent control, timing, and accuracy constraints of the applications. Developers responded by creating a variety of domain-specific approaches. Early work by TRW for the US Army on the Ballistic Missile Defense system produced the Software Requirements Engineering Method (SREM) [Alford 77] and supporting tools. Such software problems in the Navy led to the SCR project. Ward, Mellor, Hatley, and Pirbhai ([Ward 86], [Hatley 87]) developed extensions to structured analysis techniques targeted to real-time applications. Work on the Israeli defense applications led Harel to develop statecharts [Harel 87] and the supporting tool Statemate.

The need for high-assurance software in mission-

and safety-critical systems also led to the introduction of practical formalisms and integrated tools support. TRW developed REVS [Davis 77] and other tools as part of a complete environment supporting SREM and other phases of the life cycle. The SCR project developed specification techniques based on mathematical functions and tabular representations [Heninger 80]. These allowed a variety of consistency and completeness checks to be performed by inspection. Harel introduced a compact graphic representation of finite state machines with a well-defined formal semantics. These features were subsequently integrated in the Statemate tool that supported symbolic execution of statecharts for early customer validation and limited code generation. All of these techniques began to converge on an underlying model based on finite state automata.

More recent work has seen continuing convergence toward a common set of assumptions and similar solutions. Recently, Ward and colleagues have developed the Real-Time Object-Oriented Modeling (ROOM) method [Selic 94]. ROOM integrates concepts from operational specification, object-oriented analysis, and statecharts. It employs an object-oriented modeling approach with tool support. The tool is based on a simplified statechart semantics and supports symbolic execution and some code generation. The focus of ROOM currently remains on problem modeling and the transition to design, and execution rather than formal analysis.

Nancy Leveson and her colleagues have adapted statecharts to provide a formally based method for embedded system specification [Jaffe 91]. The approach has been specifically developed to be useable and readable by practicing engineers. It employs both the graphical syntax of statecharts and a tabular representation of functions similar to those used in the SCR approach. Its underlying formal model is intended to support formal analysis of system properties, with an emphasis on safety. The formal model also supports symbolic execution. These techniques have been applied to develop a requirements specification for parts of the Federal Aviation Administration's safety-critical Traffic Alert and Collision Avoidance System (TCAS) [Leveson 94].

Extensions to the SCR work have taken a similar direction. Parnas and Madey have extended the SCR approach to create a standard mathematical model for embedded system requirements [Parnas 91]. Heitmeyer and colleagues at NRL have extended the Parnas/Madey work by defining a corresponding formal model for the SCR approach [Heitmeyer 95b]. This formal model has been used to develop a suite of prototype tools supporting analysis of requirements properties like completeness and consistency [Heitmeyer

95a]. The NRL tools also support specification-based simulation and are being integrated with other tools to support automated analysis of application-specific properties like safety assertions. Concurrent work at the Software Productivity Consortium by Faulk and colleagues [Faulk 92] has integrated the SCR approach with object-oriented and graphic techniques and defined a complete requirements analysis process including a detailed process for developing a good SRS. These techniques have been applied effectively in development of requirements for Lockheed's avionics upgrade on the C-130J aircraft [Faulk 94]. The C-130J avionics software is a safety-critical system of approximately 100K lines of Ada code.

Other recent work attempts to increase the level of formality and the predictability of the problem analysis process and its products. For example, Potts and his colleagues are developing process models and tools to support systematic requirements elicitation that include a formal structure for describing discussions about requirements [Potts 94]. Hsia and his colleagues, among others, are investigating formal approaches to the use of scenarios in eliciting and validating requirements [Hsia 94]. Recent work by Boehm and his colleagues [Boehm 94] seeks to address the accidental difficulties engendered by adversarial software procurement processes.

While none of the works mentioned can be considered a complete solution, it is clear that (1) the work is converging toward common assumptions and solutions, (2) the approaches all provide significantly improved capability to address both accidental and essential requirements difficulties, and (3) the solutions can be effectively applied in industry.

9. Conclusions

Requirements are intrinsically hard to do well. Beyond the need for discipline, there are a host of essential difficulties that attend both the understanding of requirements and their specification. Further, many of the difficulties in requirements will not yield to technical solution alone. Addressing all of the essential difficulties requires the application of technical solutions in the context of human factors such as the ability to manage complexity or communicate to diverse audiences. A requirements approach that does not account for both technical and human concerns can have only limited success. For developers seeking new methods, the lesson is caveat emptor. If someone tells you his method makes requirements easy, keep a hand on your wallet.

Nevertheless, difficulty is not impossibility and the inability to achieve perfection is not an excuse for surrender. While all of the approaches discussed have significant weaknesses, they all contribute to the attempt to make requirements analysis and specification a controlled, systematic, and effective process. Though there is no easy path, experience confirms that the use of *any* careful and systematic approach is preferable to an ad hoc and chaotic one. Further good news is that, if the requirements are done well, chances are much improved that the rest of the development will also go well. Unfortunately, ad hoc approaches remain the norm in much of the software industry.

A final observation is that the benefits of good requirements come at a cost. Such a difficult and exacting task cannot be done properly by personnel with inadequate experience, training, or resources. Providing the time and the means to do the job right is the task of responsible management. The time to commit the best and brightest is before, not after, disaster occurs. The monumental failures of a host of ambitious developments bear witness to the folly of doing otherwise.

10. Further Reading

Those seeking more depth on requirements methodologies than this tutorial can provide should read Alan Davis' book *Software Requirements: Objects, Functions, and States* [Davis 93]. In addition to a general discussion of issues in software requirements, Davis illustrates a number of problem analysis and specification techniques with a set of common examples and provides a comprehensive annotated bibliography.

For a better understanding of software requirements in the context of systems development, the reader is referred to the book of collected papers edited by Thayer and Dorfman, *System and Software Requirements Engineering* [Thayer 90]. This tutorial work contains in one volume both original papers and reprints from many of the authors discussed above. The companion volume, *Standards, Guidelines, and Examples on System and Software Requirements Engineering* [Dorfman 90] is a compendium of international and US government standards relating to system and software requirements and provides some illustrating examples.

For enjoyable reading as well as insightful commentary on requirements problems, methods, and a host of requirements-related issues, the reader is referred to Michael Jackson's recent book, *Software Requirements and Specifications: A Lexicon of Practice, Principles, and Prejudice.* [Jackson 95]

Acknowledgments

C. Colket at SPAWAR, E. Wald at ONR and A. Pyster at the Software Productivity Consortium supported the development of this report. The quality of this paper has been much improved thanks to thoughtful reviews by Paul Clements, Connie Heitmeyer, Jim Kirby, Bruce Labaw, Richard Morrison, and David Weiss.

References

[Alford 77] Alford, M., "A Requirements Engineering Methodology for Real-Time Processing Requirements," *IEEE Trans. Software Eng.*, Vol. 3, No. 1, Jan. 1977, pp. 60–69.

[Alford 79] Alford, M. and J. Lawson, "Software Requirements Engineering Methodology (Development)," *RADC-TR-79-168*, U.S. Air Force Rome Air Development Center, June 1979.

[Alspaugh 92] Alspaugh, T. et al., *Software Requirements for the A-7E Aircraft*, NRL/FR/5530-92-9194, Naval Research Laboratory, Washington, D.C., 1992.

[Balin 94] Balin, S., "Object-Oriented Requirements Analysis," in *Encyclopedia of Software Engineering*, J. Marciniak ed., John Wiley & Sons, New York, N.Y., 1994, pp. 740–756.

[Basili 81] Basili, V. and D. Weiss, "Evaluation of a Software Requirements Document by Analysis of Change Data," *Proc. 5th Int'l Conf. Software Eng.*, IEEE CS Press, Los Alamitos, Calif., 1981, pp. 314–323.

[Boehm 81] Boehm, B., *Software Engineering Economics*, Prentice-Hall, Englewood Cliffs, N.J., 1981.

[Boehm 94] Boehm, B. et al., "Software Requirements as Negotiated Win Conditions," *Proc. 1st Int'l Conf. Requirements Eng.*, IEEE CS Press, Los Alamitos, Calif., 1994, pp. 74–83.

[Brooks 75] Brooks, F., *The Mythical Man-Month*, Addison-Wesley, Reading, Mass., 1975.

[Brooks 87] Brooks, F., "No Silver Bullet: Essence and Accidents of Software Engineering," *Computer*, Apr. 1987, pp. 10–19.

[CECOM 89] *Software Methodology Catalog: Second Edition*, Technical report C01-091JB-0001-01, US Army Communications-Electronics Command, Fort Monmouth, N.J., Mar. 1989.

[Clements 95] Clements, P., private communication, May 1995.

[Coad 90] Coad, P. and E. Yourdon, *Object Oriented Analysis*, Prentice-Hall, Englewood Cliffs, N.J., 1990.

[Davis 77] Davis, C. and C. Vick, "The Software Development System," *IEEE Trans. Software Eng.*, Vol. 3, No. 1, Jan. 1977, pp. 69–84.

[Davis 88] Davis, A., "A Taxonomy for the Early Stages of the Software Development Life Cycle," *J. Systems and Software*, Sept. 1988, pp. 297–311.

[Davis 93] Davis, A., *Software Requirements (Revised): Objects, Functions, and States*, Prentice-Hall, Englewood Cliffs, N.J., 1993.

[DeMarco 78] DeMarco, T., *Structured Analysis and System Specification*, Prentice-Hall Englewood Cliffs, N.J., 1978.

[Dorfman 90] Dorfman, M. and R. Thayer, eds., *Standards, Guidelines, and Examples on System and Software Requirements Engineering*, IEEE CS Press, Los Alamitos, Calif., 1990.

[Faulk 92] Faulk, S. et al., "The Core Method for Real-Time Requirements," *IEEE Software*, Vol. 9, No. 5, Sept. 1992.

[Faulk 93] Faulk, S. et al., *Consortium Requirements Engineering Guidebook*, Version 1.0, SPC-92060-CMC, Software Productivity Consortium, Herndon, Virginia, 1993.

[Faulk 94] Faulk, S. et al., "Experience Applying the CoRE Method to the Lockheed C-130J," *Proc. 9th Ann. Conf. Computer Assurance*, IEEE Press, Piscataway, N.J., 1994, pp. 3–8.

[GAO 79] US General Accounting Office, *Contracting for Computer Software Development—Serious Problems Require Management Attention to Avoid Wasting Additional Millions*, Report FGMSD-80-4, November 1979.

[GAO 92] US General Accounting Office, *Mission Critical Systems: Defense Attempting to Address Major Software Challenges*, GAO/IMTEC-93-13, December 1992.

[Gane 79] Gane, C. and T. Sarson, *Structured Systems Analysis*, Prentice-Hall, New Jersey, 1979.

[Hamilton 76] Hamilton, M. and S. Zeldin, "Higher Order Software-A Methodology for Defining Software," *IEEE Trans. Software Eng.*, Vol. 2, No. 1, Jan. 1976, pp. 9–32.

[Harel 87] Harel, D., "Statecharts: a Visual Formalism for Complex Systems," *Science of Computer Programming 8*, 1987, pp. 231–274.

[Hatley 87] Hatley, D. and I. Pirbhai, *Strategies for Real-Time Specification*, Dorset House, New York, N.Y., 1987.

[Heitmeyer 95a] Heitmeyer, C., B. Labaw, and D. Kiskis, "Consistency Checking of SCR-Style Requirements Specifications," *Proc. 2nd IEEE Int'l Symp. Requirements Eng.*, IEEE CS Press, Los Alamitos, Calif., 1995, pp. 56–63.

[Heitmeyer 95b] Heitmeyer, C., R. Jeffords, and B. Labaw, *Tools for Analyzing SCR-Style Requirements Specifications: A Formal Foundation*, NRL Technical Report NRL-7499, U.S. Naval Research Laboratory, Washington, DC, 1995.

[Heninger 80] Heninger, K., "Specifying Software Requirements for Complex Systems: New Techniques and Their Application," *IEEE Trans. Software Eng.*, Vol. 6, No. 1, Jan. 1980.

[Hester 81] Hester, S., D. Parnas, and D. Utter, "Using Documentation as a Software Design Medium," *Bell System Technical J.*, Vol. 60, No. 8, Oct. 1981, pp. 1941–1977.

[Hsia 94] Hsia, P. et al., "Formal Approach to Scenario Analysis," *IEEE Software*, Mar. 1994, pp. 33–41.

[Jackson 83] Jackson, M., *System Development*, Prentice-Hall, Englewood Cliffs, N.J., 1983.

[Jackson 94] Jackson, M., "Problems, Methods, and Specialization," *IEEE Software*, Nov. 1994, pp. 57–62.

[Jackson 95] Jackson, M., *Software Requirements and Specifications: A Lexicon of Practice, Principles, and Prejudice*, ACM Press/Addison Wesley, Reading, Mass., 1995.

[Jaffe 91] Jaffe, M. et al., "Software Requirements Analysis for Real-Time Process-Control Systems," *IEEE Trans. Software Eng.*, Vol. 17, No. 3, Mar. 1991, pp. 241–257.

[Leveson 94] Leveson, N. et al., "Requirements Specification for Process-Control Systems," *IEEE Trans. Software Eng.*, Vol. 20, No. 9, Sept. 1994.

[Lutz 93] Lutz, R., "Analyzing Software Requirements Errors in Safety-Critical Embedded Systems," *Proc. IEEE Int'l Symp. Requirements Eng.*, IEEE CS Press, Los Alamitos, Calif., 1993, pp. 126–133.

[Parnas 72] Parnas, D., "On the Criteria to be Used in Decomposing Systems into Modules," *Comm. ACM*, Vol. 15, No. 12, Dec. 1972, pp. 1053–1058.

[Parnas 85a] Parnas, D. and D. Weiss, "Active Design Reviews: Principles and Practices," *Proc. 8th Int'l Conf. Software Eng.*, IEEE CS Press, Los Alamitos, Calif., 1985.

[Parnas 85b] Parnas, D. "Software Aspects of Strategic Defense Systems," *American Scientist*, Sept. 1985, pp. 432–440.

[Parnas 86] Parnas, D. and P. Clements, "A Rational Design Process: How and Why to Fake It," *IEEE Trans. Software Eng.*, Vol. 12, No. 2, Feb. 1986, pp. 251–257.

[Parnas 89] Parnas, D., *Education for Computing Professionals*, Technical Report 89-247, Department of Computing and Information Science, Queens University, Kingston, Ontario, 1989.

[Parnas 91] Parnas, D. and J. Madey, *Functional Documentation for Computer Systems Engineering* (Version 2), CRL Report No. 237, McMaster University, Hamilton, Ontario, Canada, Sept. 1991.

[Potts 94] Potts, C., K. Takahashi, and A. Anton, "Inquiry-Based Requirements Analysis," *IEEE Software*, Mar. 1994, pp. 21–32.

[Shlaer 88] Shlaer, S. and S. Mellor, *Object-Oriented Systems Analysis: Modeling the World in Data*, Prentice-Hall, Englewood Cliffs, N.J., 1988.

[Ross 77] Ross, D. and K. Schoman Jr., "Structured Analysis for Requirements Definitions," *IEEE Trans. Software Eng.*, Vol. 3, No. 1, Jan. 1977, pp. 6–15.

[Rumbaugh 91] Rumbaugh, M. Blaha et al, *Object-Oriented Modeling and Design*, Prentice-Hall, Englewood Cliffs, N.J., 1991.

[Rushby 93] Rushby, J., *Formal Methods and the Certification of Critical Systems*, CSL Technical Report SRI-CSL-93-07, SRI International, Menlo Park, Calif., Nov., 1993.

[Selic 94] Selic, B., G. Gullekson, and P. Ward, *Real-Time Object-Oriented Modeling*, John Wiley & Sons, New York, N.Y., 1994.

[Svoboda 90] Svoboda, C., "Structured Analysis," in *Tutorial: System and Software Requirements Engineering*, R. Thayer and M. Dorfman, eds., IEEE CS Press, Los Alamitos, Calif., 1990, pp. 218–237.

[Thayer 90]   Thayer, R. and M. Dorfman, eds., *Tutorial: System and Software Requirements Engineering*, IEEE CS Press, Los Alamitos, Calif., 1990.

[Ward 86]   Ward, P. and S. Mellor, *Structured Development for Real-Time Systems*, Vols. 1, 2, and 3, Prentice-Hall, Englewood Cliffs, N.J., 1986.

[Yourdon 89]   Yourdon, E., *Modern Structured Analysis*, Yourdon Press/Prentice-Hall, Englewood Cliffs, N.J., 1989.

[Zave 82]   Zave, P., "An Operational Approach to Requirements Specification for Embedded Systems," *IEEE Trans. Software Eng.*, Vol. 8, No. 3, May 1982, pp. 250–269.

Requirements engineering with viewpoints

by Gerald Kotonya and Ian Sommerville

The requirements engineering process involves a clear understanding of the requirements of the intended system. This includes the services required of the system, the system users, its environment and associated constraints. This process involves the capture, analysis and resolution of many ideas, perspectives and relationships at varying levels of detail. Requirements methods based on global reasoning appear to lack the expressive framework to adequately articulate this distributed requirements *knowledge structure*. The paper describes the problems in trying to establish an adequate and stable set of requirements and proposes a viewpoint-oriented requirements definition (VORD) method as a means of tackling some of these problems. This method structures the requirements engineering process using viewpoints associated with sources of requirements. The paper describes VORD in the light of current viewpoint-oriented requirements approaches and shows how it improves on them. A simple example of a bank auto-teller system is used to demonstrate the method.

1   Introduction

Requirements constitute the earliest phase of the software development life-cycle. They are statements of need intended to convey understanding about a desired result, independent of its actual realisation. The main objective of the requirements engineering process is to provide a model of what is needed in a clear, consistent, precise and unambiguous statement of the problem to be solved. The model is incomplete unless the environment with which the component interacts is also modelled. If the environment is not well understood, it is unlikely that the requirements as specified will reflect the actual needs the component must fulfil. Moreover, as the environment affects the complexity of the component design, con-straining the environment can reduce the component complexity.

Studies by Boehm [1, 2] and others have shown that the potential impact of poorly formulated requirements is substantial. Boehm suggested that requirements, specification and design errors are the most numerous in a system, averaging 64% compared to 36% for coding errors. Most of these errors are not found during the development stage but at the testing and delivery stages. The resulting cost to correct these bugs increases with the time lag in finding them. A requirements error found at the requirements stage costs only about one-fifth of what it would if found at the testing stage, and one-fifteenth of what it would cost after the system is in use.

It has been observed that many of the problems of software engineering are difficulties with the requirements specification. It is natural for the developer to interpret an ambiguous requirement so that its realisation is as cheap as possible. Often, however, this is not what the client wants and it usually results in the system being reworked.

Discrepancies between a delivered system and the needs it must fulfil are common and incur very high costs [4]. In some extreme cases, these discrepancies may make the entire system useless. An example of these extreme cases is illustrated by the findings of a survey conducted by the US Government Accounting Office [5]. This survey reviewed nine software development projects that had recently been completed. Although the size of the projects was quite small (the total sum of the nine contracts was $7 million), the findings showed that 47% of the money was spent on software that was never used. 29% of the money was spent on software that was never delivered and 19% resulted in software that was either reworked extensively after delivery or abandoned after delivery but before the GAO study was conducted. The GAO report indicated that of the $317 000 spent on 'successful' projects, some additional modifications were required to be about $198 000 of it, and only $119 000 worth of software could be used as delivered. This implies that less than 2% of the amount spent resulted in software that completely met its requirements.

Requirements fall into two main categories: functional and non-functional [6]. Functional requirements capture the nature of interaction between the component and its environment. Non-functional requirements constrain the solutions that might be considered. An ideal notation for requirements engineering should cover all aspects of functionality, performance, interface design constraints and the broader context in which the system will be placed [4, 7, 8].

The failure of software to satisfy the real needs of customers is the most visible manifestation of the problems of establishing an adequate set of requirements for a software system. Some of these problems are listed below.

- In most cases, the requirements engineer is not an expert in the application domain being addressed. Many problems in formulating requirements can be traced to misunderstandings on the parts of the requirements engineers and software engineers, and implicit assumptions by potential users.
- There is often inadequate communication between the requirements engineer and the system's potential users due to the differences in their experience and education. Specifically this means that the analyst and the users do not have a common understanding of the terms used [9].
- The notion of 'completeness' in requirements definition is problematic. There is no simple analytical procedure for determining when the users have told the developers everything that they need to know in order to produce the system required.
- Requirements are never stable. Changes in the environment in which the system has to work may change even before the system is installed, due to change in its operational environment.
- Natural languages are often used to describe system requirements. Although they aid users in understanding the system, they have inherent ambiguities that can lead to misinterpretations.
- No one requirements approach or technique can adequately articulate all the needs of a system. More than one specification language may be needed to represent the requirements adequately.
- There is a general lack of *appropriate* tools for supporting the requirements engineering process. There is a need for tools that can help the requirements engineer to collect, structure and formulate requirements in an efficient and consistent manner.

We believe that any requirements engineering method intended to solve these problems must have certain necessary properties. These properties are discussed below.

2 Properties of a requirements engineering method

Requirements reflect the needs of customers and users of a system. They should include a justification for the system, what the system is intended to accomplish, and what design constraints are to be observed.

A *software requirements specification* (SRS) is a document containing a complete description of what the software will do, independent of implementation details. The process of producing the requirements specification, including analysis, is denoted *requirements definition* [10].

The process of eliciting, structuring and formulating requirements may be guided by a requirements engineering method. Notations are associated with the method and

provide a means of expressing the requirements. We believe that the following attributes are a necessary part of an effective requirements engineering method.

1. The precision of definition of its notation: this indicates the extent to which requirements may be checked for consistency and correctness using the notation. Imprecise notations may lead to errors and misunderstanding. It should be possible to check the requirements both internally and against a description of the real world.

2. Suitability for agreement with the end-user: this indicates the extent to which the notation is understandable (as opposed to 'writeable') by someone without formal training. A problem with formally expressed specifications and their notations is that they cannot be easily understood without special training. One solution to this problem may be to integrate both informal and formal descriptions of the system requirements.

3. Assistance with formulating requirements: this can be viewed in terms of two aspects:

- how the notation organises the requirements *knowledge structure* for the system; understanding a system, the services required of it and its environment involves the capture, analysis and resolution of many ideas, perspectives and relationships at varying levels of detail; the requirements definition process should be guided by a problem analysis techniques that takes all these viewpoints and their requirements into account.
- how the notation affords the separation of concerns; ideally, this means that readers of the requirements specification should need to find only those parts of the requirements specification that are relevant to their own area of interest.

4. Definition of the system's environment: the requirements model is incomplete unless the environment is modelled with which the component interacts. If the environment is not well understood, it is unlikely that the requirements as specified will reflect the actual needs the component must fulfil.

5. The scope for evolution: it must be recognised that requirements are built gradually over long periods of time and continue to evolve throughout the component's lifecycle. The specification must be tolerant of temporary incompleteness and adapt to changes in the nature of the needs being satisfied by the component. In essence, whatever the method or approach used to formulate the requirements, it must be able to accommodate changes without the need to rework the entire set of requirements.

6. Scope for integration: this can be viewed in terms of requirements approaches and types of requirements:

- There is no single requirements approach that can adequately articulate all the requirements of a system both from the developers' and the users' viewpoints; for example, a data-flow model does not adequately reflect control requirements of a system and a formal language may not be able to express non-functional requirements properly.
- non-functional requirements tend to be related to one or more functional requirements; expressing functional and non-functional requirements separately obscures the correspondence between them, whereas

stating them together may make it difficult to separate the functional and non-functional considerations.

7. Scope for communication: the requirements process is a human endeavour, and so the requirements method or tool must be able to support the need for people to communicate their ideas and obtain feedback.

8. Tool support: although notations and methods can provide much conceptual help with the process of defining requirements, it is their incorporation into, or support by, tools which makes the biggest contribution to improving our ability to manage complexity on large projects. Tools impose consistency and efficiency on the requirements process. It lets the requirements engineer collect, structure and formulate requirements in an efficient and consistent manner.

It is probably impossible for a single requirements engineering method to completely satisfy all of the above requirements. Method designers, however, should be aware of these desirable properties and should make explicit decisions about which are most important to them.

3   Viewpoints for requirements definition

The notion of viewpoints as a means of organising and structuring the requirements engineering activity is now well known. Viewpoints are implicitly present in SADT [11] and were first made explicit in the CORE method [12]. Since then there have been various other viewpoint-based approaches and proposals [13–16]. We have summarised these methods and described our own work on viewpoints for interactive system design elsewhere [17].

In our initial work, the model adopted for viewpoints was a service-oriented model, where viewpoints are analogous to clients in a client-server system. The system delivers services to viewpoints, and the viewpoints pass control information and associated parameters to the system. Viewpoints map to classes of end-users of a system or with other systems interfaced to it.

This approach can be used to support a user-centred design process [18]. Like user-centred design, it tends to focus the RE process on the user issues rather than organisational concerns. This leads to incomplete system requirements. To allow organisational requirements and concerns to be taken into account, we have extended the concept of viewpoints to consider other inputs apart from direct clients of the system. Viewpoints fall into two classes:

1. *Direct viewpoints*: these correspond directly to clients, in that they receive services from the system and send control information and data to the system. Direct viewpoints are either system operators/users or other subsystems which are interfaced to the system being analysed.
2. *Indirect viewpoints*: indirect viewpoints have an 'interest' in some or all of the services which are delivered by the system but do not interact directly with it. Indirect viewpoints may generate requirements which constrain the services delivered to direct viewpoints.

Although the concept of a direct viewpoint is fairly clear, the notion of indirect viewpoints is necessarily diffuse. Indirect viewpoints vary radically, from engineering viewpoints

(i.e. those concerned with the system design and implementation) through organisational viewpoints (those concerned with the system's influence on the organisation) to external viewpoints (those concerned with the system's influence on the outside environment). Therefore, if we take a simple example of a bank teller system, some indirect viewpoints might be

☐   a security viewpoint concerned with general issues of transaction security.
☐   a systems planning viewpoint concerned with future delivery of banking services.
☐   a trade-union viewpoint concerned with the effects of the system introduction on staffing levels and bank staff duties.

Indirect viewpoints are very important as they often have significant influence within an organisation. If their requirements go unrecognised, they often decide that the system should be abandoned or significantly changed after delivery. This is particularly true for some classes of safety-related systems which must be certified by an external regulator. If certification requirements are not met, the system will not be allowed to go into service.

Note that the notion of viewpoint which we have adopted is distinct from the ideas used in other methods of requirements engineering, although it has something in common with Greenspan's SOS approach [19] and the requirements elicitation approach proposed by Leite [14]. In methods such as SADT and in the practical application of CORE, viewpoints are seen as sources or sinks of data flows. In the VOSE method [15], viewpoints are akin to what we would call engineering viewpoints; they recognise that there are many system models used by different engineers involved in system specification and design. These models often conflict, and the method proposed is geared to exposing and reconciling these conflicts.

Fig. 1 summarises the notion of viewpoints advanced by current approaches. Several features are summarised. Fig. 1 looks at whether some form of classifying mechanism is adopted in structuring viewpoints; we believe this is important as viewpoints may have similar characteristics but differing requirements. It also summarises viewpoint orientation adopted by these methods. Most approaches have an intuitive notion of a viewpoint and do not extend the viewpoint analysis beyond the data sink/source orientation.

Functional requirements do not exist in isolation. They are related to other requirements of the system, for example, non-functional requirements and control requirements. There is a need in a requirements method to provide a basis for integrating these requirements to expose this correspondence [17]. Fig. 1 shows that this kind of broad integration is lacking in most of the viewpoint-oriented methods. This is particularly true of the integration of functional and non-functional requirements. It is also useful if specifications can be expressed in several different representations. This aids the understanding of the requirements and promotes communication between the user and the software developers.

More than one specification may be needed to represent the requirements adequately. Fig. 1 shows that only VOSE and Leite's approach support multiple representations. We

182

feature	approach				
	SRD	SADT [11]	CORE [12]	VOSE [15]	Leite [14]
notation of viewpoint	intuitive	intuitive	weak	defined	defined
viewpoint classification	no	no	no	no	yes
viewpoint orientation	data sink/source	data sink/source	process	role/responsibility	role
integration of functional and non-functional requirements	no	no	no	no	no
provision for multiple representations	no	no	no	yes	no
support for event scenarios/control requirements	no	yes	yes	not explicit	no
support for object-oriented development	no	no	no	not explicit	no
support for indirect viewpoints	no	no	limited	no	no
tool support	no	yes	limited	yes	yes

Fig. 1   Summary of current viewpoint approaches

have already discussed the notion of an *indirect* viewpoint; we believe the requirements engineering process is incomplete unless these viewpoints are considered. With the exception of CORE, this notion is largely lacking in the methods discussed. The CORE notion of an indirect viewpoint is synonymous with an external entity that provides inputs to processes and receives outputs from processes. However, CORE focuses its main analysis on defining viewpoints, which are processes that transform the inputs to outputs. Each defining viewpoint forms the basis for further decomposition.

3.1   VORD viewpoints

Many viewpoint-oriented approaches consider viewpoints as data sinks or sources, sub-system processes or internal perspectives. Our proposed notion of viewpoint is based on the entities whose requirements are responsible for, or may constrain, the development of the intended system. These *requirements sources* comprise the end-users, stake-holders, systems interfacing with the proposed system and other entities in the environment of the intended system that may be affected by its operation. Each requirements source (*viewpoint*) has a relationship with the proposed system based on its needs and interactions with the system. It is therefore important that the techniques used should adequately capture and organise not only global, but also the specific requirements of the different viewpoints into a cohesive knowledge structure that is both complete and visible. Fig. 2 shows our proposed viewpoint structure. The notion is discussed below.

4   Viewpoints-oriented requirements definition (VORD)

Based on the foregoing notion of viewpoints, we have developed a method for requirements engineering called VORD (Viewpoint-Oriented Requirements Definition) which covers the RE (requirements engineering) process from initial requirements discovery through to detailed system modelling. For the purposes of this paper, the latter modelling stages of the method are not important. This dis-

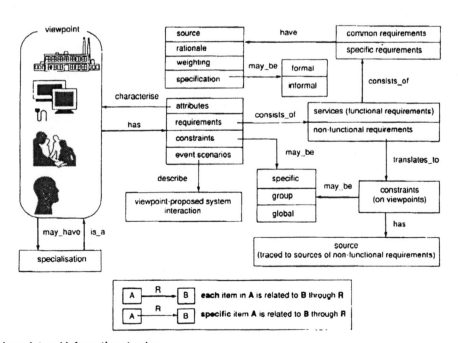

Fig. 2   VORD viewpoint and information structure

183

cussion therefore concentrates on the first three iterative steps in VORD:

- viewpoint identification and structuring.
- viewpoint documentation.
- viewpoint requirements analysis and specification.

Fig. 3 shows the VORD process model. The first step, viewpoint identification and structuring, is concerned with identifying relevant viewpoints in the problem domain and structuring them. The starting point for viewpoint identification is with abstract statements organisational needs and abstract viewpoint classes. This step is described in Section 4.2.

The second step is concerned with documenting the viewpoints identifed in the first step. Viewpoint documentation consists of documenting the viewpoint name, requirements, constraints on its requirements and its requirements source. Viewpoint requirements comprise a set of required services, control requirements and set of non-functional requirements. This step is described in Section 4.3.

The last step is concerned with specifying the functional and non-functional viewpoint requirements in an appropriate form. The notation used depends on the viewpoint, the requirements and requirements source associated with the viewpoint. Appropriate notations range from natural language (if the requirements source is concerned with non-technical requirements), through equations (e.g. if the requirements source is a physicist), to system models expressed in formal or structured notations.

Viewpoints and their requirements are collected into a central repository that serves as input to the requirements analysis process. The objective of the analysis process is to establish the correctness of the documentation and to expose conflicting requirements across all viewpoints.

4.1 ATM example

We use the example of an automated teller machine (ATM) to illustrate the VORD process model. The ATM contains an embedded software system to drive the machine hardware and to communicate with the bank's customer database. The system accepts customer requests and produces cash, account information, provides for limited message passing and funds transfer. The ATM is also required to make provisions for major classes of customers, the home customer and foreign customer. Home customers are defined as people with accounts in any of the branches of the bank to which the ATM

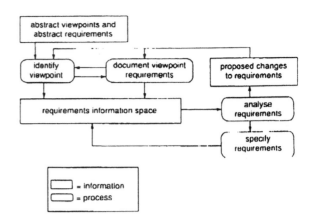

Fig. 3   VORD process model

belongs. These customers receive all the services provided by the ATM. Foreign customers are people with accounts in other banks affiliated to the bank concerned. Apart from providing services to its users, the ATM is also required to update the customer account database each time there is a cash withdrawal or funds transfer.

All the services provided by the ATM are subject to certain conditions, which can be considered at different levels. The top level sets out conditions necessary for accessing the services. These include a valid ATM cash-card and correct personal identification number (PIN). The level is concerned with service requests and is subject to the availability of particular services. Beyond this level, all services provided by the ATM are subject to specific conditions set out for their provision.

4.2   Viewpoint identification

All structured methods must address the basic difficulty of identifying the relevant problem domain entities for the system being specified or designed. The majority of methods provide little or no active guidance for this, and rely on the method user's judgement and experience in identifying these entities. We cannot claim that we have solved the problem of identifying relevant problem domain entities. However, our method provides some help to the analyst in the critical step of viewpoint identification.

The process of understanding the system under analysis, its environment, requirements and constraints places a lot of reliance on the 'system authorities'. These are people or documents with an interest in or specialist knowledge of the application domain. They include system

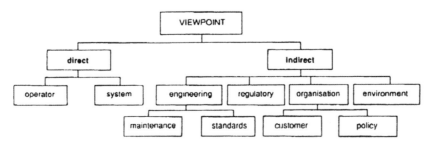

Fig. 4   Abstract viewpoint classes

184

end-users, system procurers, system engineers and documentation of existing system(s).

We have generalised these 'system authorities' into a set of viewpoint classes, which can be used as a starting point for finding viewpoints specific to the problem domain. Fig. 4 shows part of the tree diagram of the abstract viewpoint classes. Normally, the indirect viewpoints would be decomposed to greater depth than shown here. The organisation viewpoint, for example, would have policy, customer and training viewpoints as sub-classes, and the environment viewpoint may have people and others systems in the environment.

The root of the tree represents the generation notion of a viewpoint. Information can be inherited by viewpoint sub-classes, and so global requirements are represented in the more abstract classes and inherited by sub-classes. In the direct viewpoint class, the sub-system viewpoint represents the abstract class of systems within an organisation that may interact directly with the proposed system. These include shared databases and other sub-systems. The operator class represents the abstract class of people who will interact with the system directly.

Under the indirect viewpoint class, the customer viewpoint represents the requirements and policy of the organisation which is purchasing the system, the regulatory viewpoint represents legal and regulatory requirements associated with the system, the engineering viewpoint represents the engineering requirements for the system, and the environment viewpoint represents environment issues affecting the system development.

Of course, this class hierarchy is not generic. Each organisation must establish its own hierarchy of viewpoint classes based on its needs and the application domain of the systems which it develops. The information encapsulated in this class hierarchy is an important organisational resource.

The method of viewpoint identification that we propose involves a number of stages.

☐ Prune the viewpoint class hierarchy to eliminate viewpoint classes that are not relevant for the specific system being specified. In the ATM example, let us assume that there is no external certification authority and no environmental effect. We therefore do not need to look for viewpoints under these headings.

☐ Consider the system stake-holders, i.e. those people who will be affected by the introduction of the system. If these stake-holders fall into classes which are not part of the organisational class hierarchy, add these classes to it.

☐ Using a model of the system architecture, identify subsystem viewpoints. This model may either be derived from the existing models or may have to be developed as part of the RE process. In the ATM example, we can identify one main sub-system, the *customer database*. We note that architectural models of systems almost always exist because new systems must be integrated with existing organisational systems.

☐ Identify system operators who use the system on a regular basis, who use the system on an occasional basis and who request others to use the system for them. All of these are potential viewpoints. We can identify three instances of direct viewpoint in this example; the *bank customer* (regular), *ATM operator* (occasional), the *bank manager* (occasional).

☐ For each indirect viewpoint class that has been identified, consider the roles of the principal individual who might be associated with that class. For example, under the viewpoint class 'customer', we might be interested in the roles of 'regulations officer', 'maintenance manager', 'operations manager' etc. There are often viewpoints associated with these roles. In the ATM example, there are many possible indirect viewpoints but we confine our analysis to a security officer, a system developer and a bank policy viewpoint.

Based on this approach, the viewpoints that might be considered when developing an ATM specification are shown in Fig. 5. Home customer and foreign customer viewpoints are specialisations of the customer viewpoint and as such inherit its requirements and attributes. Likewise the bank manager, bank teller and ATM operator viewpoints are specialisations of bank employee.

4.3 Documenting viewpoint requirements

Viewpoints have an associated set of requirements, sources and constraints. Viewpoint requirements are made up of a set of services (functional requirements), a set of non-functional requirements and control requirements. Control requirements describe the sequence of events involved in the interchange of information between a direct viewpoint and the intended system. Constraints describe how a viewpoint's requirements are affected by non-functional requirements defined by other viewpoints.

We do not have space to look at the detailed requirements of each viewpoint here. However, Fig. 6 shows examples of initial requirements which might apply to an auto-teller system. The ATM operator and customer database viewpoints are concerned with providing control information to the proposed system. The ATM operator is concerned with stocking the ATM with cash and starting and stopping its operation. The operator needs to be alerted whenever the cash dispenser is empty. The customer database stores the customer account information which is used by the system to process transactions.

Each viewpoint has an associated template, which is a collection of structured forms for documenting detailed viewpoint requirements. This template includes

● the requirements associated with the viewpoint; these may be either functional or non-functional requirements.

● associated sources for viewpoint requirements.

● a rationale for the proposed requirement

● constraints on viewpoint requirements and their sources

● viewpoint events; viewpoint events describe the interaction between the viewpoint and the intended system in terms of viewpoint events, system responses and exceptions.

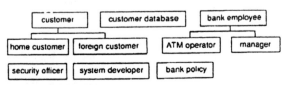

Fig. 5 ATM viewpoints

viewpoint	service	non-functional requirements
bank manager	transaction reports	1. reports must be provided on a daily basis 2. reports should comprise the account name, transaction, date and time 3. failure rate of this service should not exceed 1 in 1000 requests 4. system must be operational within 6 months
ATM operator	operator paging	1. failure rate of this service should not exceed 1 in 10 000 attempts
home customer	1. cash withdrawal 2. balance enquiry 3. funds transfer 4. message passing 5. last five transactions	1. cash withdrawal service should be available 999/1000 requests 2. cash withdrawal service should have a response time of no more than 1 minute 3. cash withdrawal service should permit withdrawal in a choice of denominations 4. balance enquiry should not fail more than 1 in 1000 requests 5. funds transfer service should be reliable with a maximum failure rate of no more than 1 in 100 000 attempts 6. message passing should include request for cheque books and complaints on erroneous cash withdrawals
customer database		
foreign customer	1. cash withdrawal 2. balance enquiry	
security officer		1. all system security risks must be explicitly identified, analysed and minimised according to the ALARP principle 2. bank standard encryption algorithms must be used 3. system must print paper record of all transactions
system developer		system must be developed using standards defined in 'System Quality Plan xxx'
bank policy		1. cash withdrawal service should be available for 9 out of 10 requests 2. cash withdrawal service should have a response time of no more than 2 minutes 3. balance enquiry service should not have a failure rate of more than 1 in 50 requests

Fig. 6   Initial distilled list of viewpoint requirements

Certain items of the template are optional and need not have entries for all viewpoints. For example, an indirect viewpoint such as a government regulating body may not require services from the intended system, but may have certain non-functional requirements which place constraints on the system.

4.3.1 Viewpoint templates: as we do not have space to develop the complete requirements analysis for ATM here, we confine our analysis to two viewpoints; the *home customer* and *foreign customer.* For the most part our example is the *cash withdrawal* service. We believe this particular service has sufficient diversity associated with it in terms of usage and constraints to adequately demonstrate the usefulness of our approach. Fig. 7 shows the general viewpoint template for the customer viewpoint. The customer viewpoint represents the most abstract description of the home and foreign customer classes. Attributes and services described at the customer level are inherited by its two specialisations. The service template

illustrates the provision of the *cash withdrawal* service to the home customer viewpoint.

Fig. 8 shows the detailed viewpoint template for the home customer and foreign customer viewpoints in relation to the cash withdrawal service. Event scenarios and service specifications are described in Sections 4.3.2. It is important to note that VORD provides the user with a framework for formulating very detailed requirements specification, yet maintains a clear separation of concerns. For example, the cash withdrawal service (Fig. 8) is intended for both the home and foreign customer viewpoints, but the source of, rationale for and constraints on the service differ in each instance. In the case of the home customer, the source of the requirement is the viewpoint itself, whereas in the case of the foreign customer, the source of the requirement is the bank policy viewpoint. Similar constraints (e.g. availability) on the service are less stringent for the foreign customer than for the home customer viewpoint. The template also shows that certain constraints can be specific, whereas others can be group or global con-

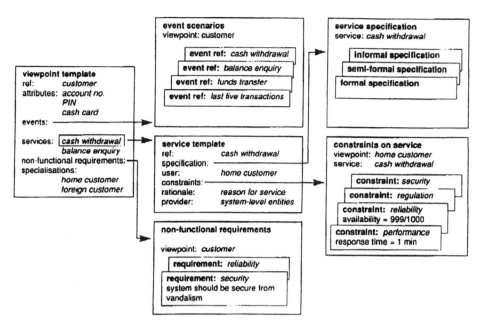

Fig. 7   Structure of ATM customer and service distribution

straints. Group constraints are associated with constraints affecting similar requirements across several viewpoints. Global constraints affect all system requirements.

4.3.2   Event scenarios and control: control requirements define how a system controls its environment and how the environment controls the system. Control influences occur not only between the environment and the system, but also between the elements of the environment themselves. Control relationships between the proposed system and its environment are largely due to the need to conform to, enforce or assist control relationships between elements of the environment. In essence, control can be viewed as a distributed layered process through levels of the environment culminating in the system as the service provider at the lowest level.

Several models have been proposed for extending current requirements definition approaches to incorporate control requirements. These models are typified, in structured analysis, by the Ward–Mellor [20] and Hartley–Pirbhai [21] extensions to the basic structured analysis notation, and in object-oriented analysis by the Rumbaugh dynamic model [22], the Shlaer–Mellor object state model [23], and Harel statecharts [24]. These models offer insights into the representation of control requirements.

The provision of a viewpoint service is the culmination of a series of events arising from the viewpoint layer and filtering through levels of control to entities that are ultimately responsible for its provision. Fig. 9 illustrates a simple event trace diagram involving a single viewpoint. Normally the provision of a service involves the participation of several viewpoints; each bringing its control influences to bear on the service. It is important in documenting a viewpoint service to identify other viewpoints affecting or participating in the provision of a service. This provides a means of tracing the impact of later modification in the requirements of one viewpoint on others.

Viewpoint events are a reflection of the control requirements as perceived by the user. System-level events reflect

the realisation of control at the system level. Distinguishing between the two levels of control provides us with a mechanism for

☐ addressing control requirements from the user perspective.
☐ tracing system-level control to viewpoints.
☐ exposing conflicting control requirements.
☐ capturing the distributed and layered nature of control.

We have devised a simple mechanism to do the above, based on event scenarios. An event scenario is defined as a sequence of events together with exceptions that may arise during the exchange of information between the viewpoint and the system. A normal sequence of events may have exceptions at various points in the event sequence. At the system level, exceptions cause a transfer of control to exception-handlers. As exception-handlers describe alternative courses of action, they are treated as separate event scenarios. The top layer of an event scenario is referred to as the *normal scenario*; it represents the 'normal' sequence of events. Event scenarios can therefore be thought of as layered, with each subsequent layer comprising events that describe exceptions in the previous layer.

There are three steps in describing viewpoint events:

● describing isolated viewpoint event scenarios.
● tracing events and predicates to viewpoints.
● identifying viewpoints participating in a service provision.

Fig. 10 shows the event scenario associated with the service *cash withdrawal* of the customer viewpoint. The normal event scenario is shown in bold transitions. We use an extended state transition model, based on a model proposed by Rumbaugh [22], to represents the event scenarios.

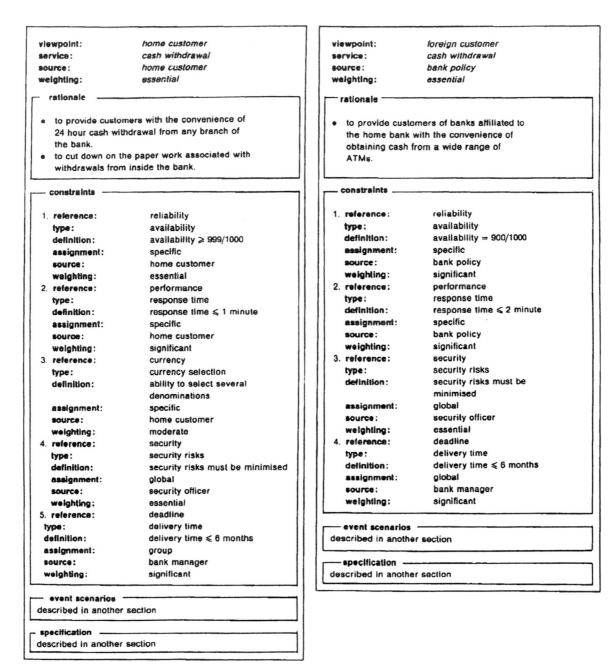

viewpoint:	home customer
service:	cash withdrawal
source:	home customer
weighting:	essential

┌─ rationale ──────────────────────────

- to provide customers with the convenience of 24 hour cash withdrawal from any branch of the bank.
- to cut down on the paper work associated with withdrawals from inside the bank.

┌─ constraints ──────────────────────────

1. reference:	reliability
type:	availability
definition:	availability $\geqslant$ 999/1000
assignment:	specific
source:	home customer
weighting:	essential
2. reference:	performance
type:	response time
definition:	response time $\leqslant$ 1 minute
assignment:	specific
source:	home customer
weighting:	significant
3. reference:	currency
type:	currency selection
definition:	ability to select several denominations
assignment:	specific
source:	home customer
weighting:	moderate
4. reference:	security
type:	security risks
definition:	security risks must be minimised
assignment:	global
source:	security officer
weighting:	essential
5. reference:	deadline
type:	delivery time
definition:	delivery time $\leqslant$ 6 months
assignment:	group
source:	bank manager
weighting:	significant

┌─ event scenarios ──────────────────────────
described in another section

┌─ specification ──────────────────────────
described in another section

viewpoint:	foreign customer
service:	cash withdrawal
source:	bank policy
weighting:	essential

┌─ rationale ──────────────────────────

- to provide customers of banks affiliated to the home bank with the convenience of obtaining cash from a wide range of ATMs.

┌─ constraints ──────────────────────────

1. reference:	reliability
type:	availability
definition:	availability = 900/1000
assignment:	specific
source:	bank policy
weighting:	significant
2. reference:	performance
type:	response time
definition:	response time $\leqslant$ 2 minute
assignment:	specific
source:	bank policy
weighting:	significant
3. reference:	security
type:	security risks
definition:	security risks must be minimised
assignment:	global
source:	security officer
weighting:	essential
4. reference:	deadline
type:	delivery time
definition:	delivery time $\leqslant$ 6 months
assignment:	global
source:	bank manager
weighting:	significant

┌─ event scenarios ──────────────────────────
described in another section

┌─ specification ──────────────────────────
described in another section

Fig. 8   Viewpoint template for the home and foreign customers

Each transition has a triggering event, preconditions which must be satisfied before that transition can take place and actions which are associated with the transition.

Tracing events to viewpoints is usually straightforward. In most cases, the events can be traced to the viewpoint requesting the service. For example, the insert (card) event in an ATM is associated with initiating all customer services, and so is traced to the customer viewpoint. The preconditions can be traced to viewpoints by analysing the various states of the predicate variable (left-hand side of Fig. 10) to determine whether any external events are associated with causing the transitions. If no external events are involved, the variable is probably an internally generated value and may be traced to a database or data dictionary.

4.3.3 Service specification:
the orientation of a service makes it easy to specify it using a variety of notations. We consider this important for two reasons.

☐   One of the major problems associated with software development is a lack of adequate communication

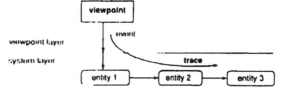

Fig. 9   Simple event trace diagrams

188

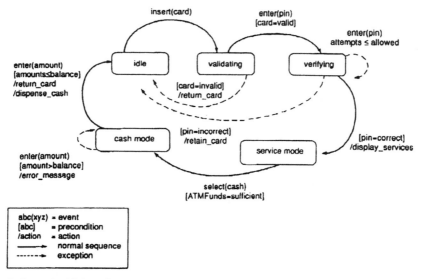

Fig. 10 Event scenario for cash withdrawal

between the requirements engineer and the system's potential users due to the differences in their experience and education. The ability to represent the same requirement in different notations that are familiar to different people enhances communication and aids understanding.

☐ No single requirements notation can adequately articulate all the needs of a system. More than one specification language may be needed to represent the requirement adequately.

This aspect of a service provides us with a basis for replicating approaches such as VOSE [15], whose notion of a viewpoint is associated with different representation schemes.

We illustrate these aspects of a service by specifying a simplified version of the ATM's cash withdrawal service using a formal and informal notation. We use a simplified form of the formal notation Z and an informal notation to specify the service. In both cases, we assume that the customer has a valid cash card and has entered the correct personal identification number (PIN).

Fig. 11 shows an informal specification of the cash withdrawal service.

There are clearly a number of ambiguities in this description, but it is expressed at a level which could easily be understood by non-technical staff. A more precise specification can be developed and linked to this informal description (as shown in Fig. 7). Of course, we recognise that the problem with multiple representations of a service is the demonstration that these representations are equiva-

lent. We have tried to address this problem. Finkelstein *et al.* [15] have identified a comparable problem, the VOSE approach, and discuss methods of equivalence demonstration.

More precisely, the cash withdrawal service can be specified as a disjunction (OR) of two Z schemas; *PermitWithdrawal* and *RefuseWithdrawal* (Fig. 12). This is based on the following free types:

```
FundStatus : : = adequate | inAdequate
AccountStatus : : = overdrawn | goodStanding
criticalLevel = 1000
accountNumber: 0..10⁶
```

FundStatus represents the stock of the ATM funds. An *inAdequate status* indicates that the ATM funds have fallen below 1000, represented by *criticalLevel*. AccountStatus represents the status of the customer account.

For a cash withdrawal to be permitted (Fig. 13), two conditions must be fulfilled.

● The customer account must be in good standing (i.e. not overdrawn).
● The ATM must contain adequate funds.

After a cash withdrawal, the customer account is updated. This is illustrated in the separate specification of PermitWithdrawal and RefuseWithdrawal.

5 Viewpoint analysis

The purpose of viewpoint analysis is to establish that viewpoint requirements are correct and 'complete'. There are two stages to this analysis.

```
Customer requests cash withdrawal
If any of the following conditions is true refuse withdrawal:
    condition1: The requested amount exceeds customer balance.
    condition2: The funds in ATM are less than request amount
else do the following:
    dispense cash
    update customer account
endif
```

Fig. 11 Informal specification of simplified cash withdrawal service

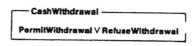

Fig. 12 Specification for cash withdrawal

189

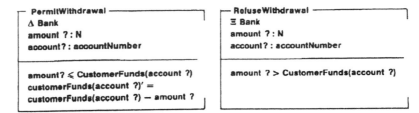

Fig. 13 Specification of PermitWithdrawal and RefuseWithdrawal

☐ correctness of viewpoint documentation; the view-point documentation must be checked to ensure that it is consistent and that there are no omitted sections.

☐ conflict analysis; conflicting requirements from different viewpoints must be exposed.

Analysis is a complex subject, which we cannot discuss in detail here. Frankly, we are sceptical about the usefulness of automated semantic analysis. Conflict analysis in VORD is performed by the requirements engineer with the help of the toolset. The VORD toolset has provisions for detecting a number of conflicting requirements and generating reports. Our checking facilities are therefore based on ensuring that information can be presented to the requirements engineer in such a way that manual analysis is simplified. We briefly describe the support for analysis below.

5.1 Viewpoint documentation checking

Checking the correctness of a viewpoint documentation involves verifying that it has been correctly entered and it is complete. We have defined a viewpoint as an entity consisting of a set of attributes, requirements, constraints and even scenarios. Although all viewpoints have attributes that characterise them, other viewpoint information may be omitted, depending on whether the viewpoint is a direct or indirect viewpoint. For example, an indirect viewpoint does not receive services or provide control information to the system, but may have non-functional requirements. Direct viewpoints may receive services, have non-functional requirements or provide control information to the system. Both classes of viewpoints may have constraints.

A detailed description of the viewpoint template, its contents and their inter-relationships is provided in Section 3.1. We have built into the VORD toolset a mechanism to analyse all these aspects of the viewpoint template for completeness and correctness.

5.2 Conflict analysis

Viewpoints have differing stakes in and interactions with the intended system and have requirements that are closely aligned with these interests. Conflicts may arise from contradictions among individual viewpoint requirements. Some related work in this area includes the work on domain-independent conflict resolution by EasterBrook [25] and the work on rule-based software quality engineering by Hausen [26].

In Section 2, we discussed how non-functional requirements tend to conflict and interact with the other system requirements. This kind of conflict may be quite specific,

as in the following two cases:

● where the provision of a service across viewpoints is associated with different constraints of the same general type; for example, a conflict is reported in the case where the reliability of a service is specified in terms of its availability in one viewpoint, and in terms of its probability of failure on demand (POFOD) in another viewpoint.

● where the provision of a service across viewpoints is associated with similar constraints, but differing constraint values; for example, a conflict is reported in the case where the reliability of a service, specified in terms of its availability, has a value of 999/1000 in one viewpoint and a value of 900/1000 in another viewpoint.

It may also be the case that a requirement in one viewpoint contradicts a requirement in another viewpoint; for example, the security officer viewpoint requirement that the system must be maintained regularly conflicts with the availability requirements for the home customer and bank manager viewpoints. The home customer requires that the cash withdrawal service is available for 999/1000 requests, and the bank manager requires that transaction reports are provided daily with a failure rate of less than 1 in 1000.

These type of conflicts can be exposed by analysing the constraints associated with a particular service, for consistency, and by analysing one viewpoint's requirements against other viewpoint requirements for contradictions.

In addition to these specific viewpoint requirements are high-level organisational and other global requirements against which all requirements must be analysed. At this level, we are interested in establishing whether specific viewpoint requirements augment or contradict general organisational and global requirements.

Viewpoints place varying levels of importance on their requirements. It is important to characterise these varying levels of importance in order to sift the essential requirements from the non-essential and to resolve conflicts. One way of characterising requirements is to weigh them in order of importance. The weighing of non-functional requirements is especially important as they translate to constraints on services, which are reusable across viewpoints and may therefore have differing constraints placed on them that may conflict. Another important reason for characterising constraints is that it provides the designer with a basis on which to trade-off the less important constraints.

VORD incorporates a mechanism for weighting requirements that takes into account the viewpoint-requirement relationship, thereby accommodating differing perceptions and stakes. This mechanism can be used in conjunction with the stated rationales to resolve conflicting requirements or to suggest improvements. The VORD process diagram in Fig. 3 shows that the result from analysis feeds back into the main requirements process through the proposed changes.

6   VORD toolset

Tools make a significant contribution to the requirements formulation process [10]. Their incorporation or support in methods improves the engineer's ability to manage the complexity associated with information collection, structuring, verification, consistency checking and integrity preservation. VORD is based on an extensible toolset whose framework lends itself to tailoring and component reuse. We would like to emphasise that the use of tools in VORD is an integral part of the method and is intended to provide support from the initial requirements formulation through to detailed specification.

The underlying philosophy of the VORD toolset is to afford users scope for creativity and experimentation in arriving at an expression of requirements, while enforcing the method. We believe the ability of a tool to accommodate potentially conflicting information without unduly restricting the user is very important. To this end, the VORD toolset incorporates interactive conflict report generation at all stages of requirements formulation.

Fig. 14 shows the general architecture of the toolset. The toolset has eight main components: the viewpoint editor, requirements space, constraint library, specification editor, proposed changes log, analysis process, entity identification process and mapping process. Straddling these six components are a report generation and method guidance tools.

The viewpoint editor facilitates the creation and structuring of viewpoint information collection. The requirements space is a central requirements repository; it maintains an updated record of all requirements, their sources, rationale, constraints, events scenarios, specifications and users. It serves as a source for reusable services as well as a reference point for other components of the toolset. The entity identification process (Fig. 14), for example, uses the requirements space to derive entities responsible for the provision of services and the viewpoint editor sees it as repository for reusable services.

The constraint library is a collection of user-defined non-functional requirements that can be associated with services. It comprises a tool for defining non-functional requirement templates, a constraint library browser and a facility for previewing and testing defined constraints. Both formal and informal constraints can be described using the tool.

The specification editor facilitates the definition of notation templates and the specification of services in various notations. The proposed changes log maintains a list of proposed changes to the requirements, and the analysis process tool provides a means of managing the analysis process.

The mapping process is concerned with mapping viewpoint-level information to system-level information and verifying that system-level information is consistent with the viewpoint-level requirements.

7   Limitations of VORD

A possible criticism of the method is that it does not explicitly support the analysis of the interaction across and within the viewpoints. This criticism is based on the fact that viewpoint interactions are addressed only in the context of services, i.e. a viewpoint is analysed for its role in the provision of a service. This is a reasonable criticism. We believe this type of analysis may provide system developers with additional information that may need to be taken into account in formulating the system requirements. Consider the example of direct interaction between the bank customer and bank manager resulting in the manager authorising cash withdrawal, even though the customer balance is less than the minimum prescribed level. It may be that the system requires this kind of flexibility built into it.

Currently, the model of control requirements adopted by VORD does not explicitly address control issues associated with concurrency. However, the method supports a framework that allows the engineer to reason about concurrency in relation to service provision. As services are explicitly identified with entities at the system level, it is possible to argue about possibilities of providing services concurrently, i.e. if they do not share similar entities.

One aspect of control that is usually ignored in many requirements methods is the flow of time. In structured analysis, the belief is that so long as data flows and data constraints are fully defined, time flow is not necessary because it follows as a property of the data flow/constraint information. This could be true only if you could guarantee a complete definition of the data flows and corresponding constraints. In practice, this is very difficult. In VORD we have not attempted to address the time issue beyond defining it as a constraint on system services.

VORD has been deliberately restricted to a service-oriented view of systems. A criticism of the method therefore is that it is difficult to apply to those systems which do not fit neatly into the service-oriented systems (SOS) paradigm. Service-oriented systems can be viewed as service-

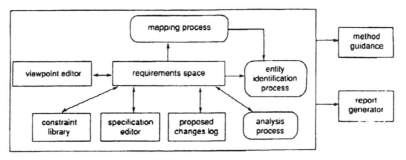

Fig. 14   VORD toolset architecture

191

providing enterprises; they employ systems composed of people, computer hardware and software, and other mechanisms to perform service actions in the customer environment [19].

We do not, however, consider this to be a serious limitation as we believe that most systems can be regarded as providing services of some kind to their environment. The intuitive end-user orientation of a service provides us with the ability to clearly distinguish between user needs on the one hand what is required (at system level) to meet those needs on the other. Secondly, the notion of a service also finds parallels in real life. Thus, for example, we can talk of the reliability of a service, the efficiency of a service and the cost of providing a service, all of which correspond to non-functional requirements. Thirdly, a service is a reusable commodity that is provided to many users, all (potentially) imposing differing constraints on it.

Issues relating to change control and the interface with existing software tools have not been explicitly addressed in VORD. The issue of change control is important as it may take several years to analyse requirements and to develop a large system and it must be expected that requirements changes will be identified during that time. It is therefore important that the inevitability of this is recognised and anticipated when producing a requirements document. A commercial version of VORD would need to incorporate a mechanism to support change control. It is important that VORD is able to interface with existing software tools, as this would allow inter-operability which would enhance the process of formulating requirements.

8 Conclusions

The notion of viewpoints proposed in VORD offers several added advantages over other viewpoint-oriented approaches to requirements engineering.

☐ Most existing viewpoint approaches lack any obvious framework for distinguishing between various user classes, types of user-system interaction and specific user requirements. Our proposed solution to this problem has been to address requirements from the user perspective (viewpoint), thereby creating a framework for distinguishing between user classes and specific user requirements. The intuitive end-user orientation of a service provides us with the ability to clearly distinguish between user needs on the one hand and what is required (at the system level) to meet those needs on the other hand.

☐ Unlike most viewpoint approaches whose concept of a viewpoint is largely intuitive, VORD is based on a clearly defined concept of viewpoints. Existing approaches have also failed to analyse viewpoints beyond considering them as data sources, data sinks or sub-system processes. These approaches focus most on their analysis on what are essentially internal perspectives of the proposed system. A VORD viewpoint is clearly defined by its attributes, services, events and specialisations.

☐ We have demonstrated the importance of incorporating indirect viewpoints into the requirements engineering process. Indirect viewpoints are very important because people associated with them are often very influential in an organisation and can make decisions on whether the system goes into service. The notion of indirect viewpoints is largely lacking in current approaches.

☐ The explicit identification of viewpoints with services in VORD has made it possible to create a framework where several related aspects can be encapsulated. It is possible, for example, to encapsulate within a viewpoint its rationale for a service and various constraints that it imposes on the service. This is a very useful attribute of VORD, as it improves the potential reusability of services and promotes incremental development.

☐ A lack of understanding of the terms used in requirements formulation, and hence a lack of communication between requirements engineers and systems users, has been cited as a major stumbling block to developing successful software systems (Section 2.1). A partial solution to this problem is to construct a framework that supports the integration of various formal and informal notations. Developing such a framework within existing requirement methods is difficult because they are usually associated with specific notations and are not based on extensible frameworks.

In VORD, there is no predefined notation for expressing service specifications. VORD allows an organisation to define a library of templates, based on different specification notations, and to use these in the specification of services. A template is intended to act as a guideline to the user by partitioning the specification into logical subsections. The tools allow the user to construct both whole and modular notation templates.

• Many methods do not address non-functional requirements explicitly, and those that address them have tended to address them as secondary to the 'central' issue of functional requirements. Existing methods lack support for the broad integration of functional and non-functional requirements. There is also a general lack of notations and tools that are flexible enough to accommodate the great diversity of non-functional requirements. VORD has addressed the issue of both global and specific non-functional requirements in relation to the system. Defined services may be associated with non-functional requirements that are derived from different viewpoints. Indirect viewpoints serve as a vehicle for collecting system-level non-functional requirements, and the viewpoint hierarchy allows these to be propagated to all services.

• VORD provides a framework that is amenable to requirements traceability.

In summary, we believe that VORD is a useful contribution to the field of requirements engineering. We have demonstrated that a method can be developed which takes into account both end-user and organisational considerations. The service orientation of the method ensures that system requirements, rather than high-level system specifications or designs, are derived by applying the method. We have developed a comprehensive toolset for VORD. Of course, the method is still being developed to address some of the problems identified earlier, but we would like to mention that an earlier version of the method was used to specify a fairly complex transactions-related system with some notable success. Suggestions arising from this early trial have been invaluable in the development of the current model. Other user trials are underway, including the development of detailed requirements for an autonomous excavator.

9 References

[1] BOEHM, B.: 'Model and metrics for software management and engineering' (IEEE Computer Society Press, 1984), pp. 4–9

[2] BOEHM, B.: 'Industrial software metrics top 10 list', *IEEE Softw.*, 1987, **4**, (5), pp. 84–85

[3] SOMMERVILLE, I.: 'Software engineering' (Addison Wesley, 1992)

[4] ROMAN, G.C.R.: 'A taxonomy of current issues in requirements engineering', *IEEE Computer*, 1985, **18**, (4), pp. 14–21

[5] U.S. Government Accounting Office. Contracting for Computer Software Development: 'Serious problems require management attention to avoid wasting additional millions'. Report FGMSD-80-4, 1979

[6] RZEPKA, W.: 'Requirements engineering environment: software tools for modelling user needs', *IEEE Computer*, 1985, **18**, (4), pp. 9–12

[7] BORGIDA, A., GREENSPAN, S., and MYLOPOULOS, J.: 'Knowledge representation as a basis for requirements specifications', *IEEE Comput.*, 1985, **18**, (4), pp. 71–85

[8] DAVIS, A.M.: 'Software requirements analysis and specification' (Prentice-Hall International, 1990)

[9] BROWN, A.W., EARL, N.A., and McDERMID, J.: 'Software engineering environments: automated support for software engineering' (McGraw-Hill, 1992)

[10] DORFMAN, M., and THAYER, R.H.: 'Requirements definition guidelines, and examples on system and software requirements engineering' (IEEE Computer Society Press, 1991)

[11] ROSS, D., and SCHOMAN, K.E.: 'Structured analysis for requirements definition', *IEEE Trans.*, 1977, **3**, (1), pp. 6–15

[12] MULLERY, G.P.: 'A method for controlled requirements specifications'. 4th IEEE Computer Society Int. Conf. on Software Engineering, pp. 126–135, Munich, Germany, 1979

[13] FICKAS, S., VAN LAMSWEERDE, A., and DARDENNE,: 'Goal-directed concept acquisition in requirements elicitation. 6th Int. IEEE Computer Society Press Workshop on Software Specification and Design, Como, Italy, 1991, pp. 14–21

[14] LEITE, J.C.P.: 'Viewpoints analysis: a case study', *ACM Softw. Eng. Notes*, 1989, **14**, (3), pp. 111–119

[15] FINKELSTEIN, A., KRAMER, J., NUSEIBEH, B., and GOEDICKE, M.: 'Viewpoints: a framework for integrating multiple perspectives in system development', *Int. J. Softw. Eng. Knowl. Eng.*, 1992, **2**, (10), pp. 31–58

[16] KOTONYA, G.: 'A viewpoint-oriented method for requirements definition'. PhD Thesis, Lancaster University, UK, 1994

[17] KOTONYA, G., and SOMMERVILLE, I.: 'Framework for integrating functional and non-functional requirements'. IEE Int. Workshop on Systems Engineering for Real-Time Applications, Cirencester, UK, 1993, pp. 148–153

[18] NORMAN, and DRAPER,: 1986

[19] GREENSPAN, S., and FEBLOWITZ, M.: 'Requirements engineering using the SOS paradigm'. RE '93 IEEE Int. IEEE Society Press Requirements Symp. on Requirements Engineering, San Diego, California, 1993, pp. 260–263

[20] WARD, P., and MELLOR, S.: 'Structured development for real-time systems' (Prentice-Hall, Englewood Cliffs, New Jersey, 1985)

[21] HARTLEY, D., and PIRBHAI, I.: 'Strategies for real-time systems specifications' (Dorset House, New York, 1987)

[22] RUMBAUGH, J., BLAHA, M., PREMERLANI, W., EDDY, F., and LORENSEN, W.: 'Object-oriented modelling and design' (Prentice-Hall International, 1991)

[23] SHLAER, S., and MELLOR, S.J.: 'Object-oriented systems analysis: modelling the world in data' (Yourdon Press, Prentice Hall, Englewood Cliffs, New Jersey, 1988)

[24] HAREL, D., LACHOVER, D., NAAMAD, A., PNUELI, A., POLITI, M., SHERMAN, R., and SHTULTRAURING, A.: 'STATEMATE: a working environment for development of complex reactive systems'. Tenth IEEE Int. IEEE Computer Society Press Conf. on Software Engineering, Washington, DC, 1988, pp. 396–406

[25] EASTERBROOK, S.M.: 'Resolving conflicts between domain descriptions with computer-supported negotiation', *Knowl. Acquisition*, 1991, **43**, (3), pp. 255–289

[26] HAUSEN, H.L.: 'A notion of rule-based software quality engineering'. Symp. on Applied Computing, Kansas City, USA, April 1991
FINKELSTEIN, A., KRAMER, J., and GOEDICKE, M.: 'Viewpoints oriented software specification'. 3rd Int. IEEE Computer Society Workshop on Software Engineering and its Applications, Toulouse, France, 1990, pp. 337–351

The paper was first received on 28 February and in revised form on 10 October 1995.

The authors are with the Department of Computing, Lancaster University, School of Engineering, Computing and Mathematical Sciences, Lancaster LA1 4YR, UK.

Identifying and Measuring Quality
in a Software Requirements Specification

Alan Davis, Scott Overmyer, Kathleen Jordan, Joseph Caruso,
Fatma Dandashi, Anhtuan Dinh, Gary Kincaid, Glen Ledeboer,
Patricia Reynolds, Pradip Sitaram, Anh Ta, and Mary Theofanos

Abstract

Numerous treatises exist that define appropriate qualities that should be exhibited by a well written software requirements specification (SRS). In most cases these are vaguely defined. This paper explores thoroughly the concept of quality in an SRS and defines attributes that contribute to that quality. Techniques for measuring these attributes are suggested.

I. Introduction

Software metrics may be used to measure attributes of software process or intermediate or final products of software development. One early intermediate product of software development is the software requirements specification. A *software requirements specification* (SRS) is a document that describes all the externally observable behaviors and characteristics expected of a software system. Generally, a *quality* SRS is one that contributes to successful, cost-effective creation of software that solves real user needs. Specifically, a *quality* SRS is one that exhibits the following qualities:

1. Unambiguous	13. Electronically Stored
2. Complete	14. Executable/Interpretable
3. Correct	15. Annotated by Relative Importance
4. Understandable	16. Annotated by Relative Stability
5. Verifiable	17. Annotated by Version
6. Internally Consistent	18. Not Redundant
7. Externally Consistent	19. At Right Level of Detail
8. Achievable	20. Precise
9. Concise	21. Reusable
10. Design Independent	22. Traced
11. Traceable	23. Organized
12. Modifiable	24. Cross-Referenced

The purpose of this paper is to provide the beginnings for definitions of metrics suitable for these qualities.

This work was supported in part by a grant from the El Pomar Foundation. Affiliations: Davis: U. of Colorado at Colorado Springs, Colorado Springs, CO 80933-7150; Overmyer: Minot State U.; Jordan: Institute for Defense Analyses; Caruso, Dandashi, Dinh, Ledeboer: George Mason University.; Kincaid: Calspan; Reynolds, Ta: Mitre; Sitaram: STX Hughes; Theofanos: Oak Ridge Lab.

There are many errors being introduced into SRS's. In 1981, Basili's requirements specification team reported 88 errors in the 400 page A-7E Operational Flight Program software requirements specification [BAS81]. And that SRS was written by a group of requirements writing experts. Also in the late 1970's, Celko reported that applying requirements checking tools to an SRS for an existing Army management information system revealed the presence of many hundreds of errors [CEL81]. DeMarco, as quoted by Tavolato and Vincena [TAV84], reports that 56% of all errors ever made on a software development effort can be traced to errors in the SRS. Boehm reports that 45% of all errors made on software development efforts at TRW can be traced to either requirements or preliminary design [BOE75]. Obviously, if we can better understand how to recognize and measure quality in an SRS, we will be better equipped to detect errors in the SRS.

To make matters worse, SRS errors need to be detected during the requirements phase, or the cost to repair them will grow significantly. Three analyses [DAL77, BOE76, FAG74] provide conclusive evidence that the later in the life cycle an error is detected and repaired, the more it will cost. These show a 200:1 ratio between detecting and repairing an error during requirements vs. maintenance phases. It is only with data from Boehm [BOE75] that we can also see that the reason for the cost increase is that errors are remaining latent. That is, if we detect an SRS error when writing it, all we do is fix it. If we detect that same SRS error during design, we must fix both the design as well as the SRS. If we detect the same SRS error during coding, we must fix the code, design, and SRS, etc. [MIZ83]. If we can better understand how to recognize SRS quality, we will be better equipped to detect SRS errors and thus prevent them from remaining, and thus costing more to detect and repair. Let us not fail to recognize that there are two different general classes of requirements errors: knowledge errors and specification errors. *Knowledge errors* are caused by not knowing what the true requirements are. *Specification errors* are caused by not

Reprinted from *Proc 1st Int'l Software Metrics Symp.*, 1993, pp. 141–152.

knowing how to adequately specify requirements. Knowledge errors can be reduced through prototyping [AND89, DAV92]. However, there may exist knowledge errors that cannot be found until after the system is deployed. There is little excuse for specification errors.

The above list of SRS qualities is a compilation of lists made by others. See Figure 1. These authors however have not attempted to provide useful ways of measuring SRS quality. The implications if we ignore SRS quality are [DAV93]:

- The resulting software may not satisfy user needs
- Multiple interpretations may cause disagreements between customers and developers
- It may be impossible to thoroughly test [DAV90a]
- The wrong system might be built.

As attempts are made to achieve quality in an SRS, one must be careful to recognize that although quality is attainable, perfection is not. Any of the above 24 quality attributes can be achieved, but often at the expense of other attributes. On any one given project, requirements writers need to agree as to which quality attributes are most important, and strive for those.

II. SRS Quality Attributes

A quality SRS is one that exhibits the 24 attributes listed in the introduction, i.e., is devoid of any errors that would violate these attributes. The following 24 sub-sections (1) define each attribute, (2) provide ideas on measuring the attribute, (3) provide the attribute with a recommended weight relative to other attributes, and (4) describe types of activities that can be used to optimize presence of that attribute. In all cases, we assume there are n_r requirements in the SRS, and the set of all these requirements is denoted as R. In addition, we assume that there are n_f functional requirements (R_f) and n_{nf} non-functional (i.e., ilities) requirements (R_{nf}) in the SRS, where $n_r = n_f + n_{nf}$, and $R = R_f \cup R_{nf}$.

2.1 Unambiguous

An SRS is *unambiguous* if and only if every requirement stated therein has only one possible interpretation [IEE84]. Ambiguity is a function of the backgrounds of the reader. For example, "generate a dial tone" may be ambiguous to non-telephony people because they do not realize that standards exist that demand a dial tone be of a specific frequency. Due to these standards, telephony people in domestic systems may see the term as totally unambiguous. Strangely, telephony people in domestic and international systems would once again find it ambiguous due to conflicting standards.

Certain languages are inherently more ambiguous than other languages. Perhaps there is a measure of inherent ambiguity of various languages. Deterministic finite state machines (FSM), Petri nets (PN), decision trees (DT), propositional calculus, predicate calculus and many others all have well defined semantics and thus suffer from no inherent ambiguity. Natural language or any formalism that includes natural language (e.g., structured English) has much inherent ambiguity. Once you choose to use less ambiguous forms of expression, the specific choice will be driven primarily by expressive power and suitability for the aspect of the system, than by its inherent ambiguity. Since ambiguity is primarily in the eyes of the reader, one way to measure it is via review, i.e., as the percentage of requirements that have been interpreted in a unique manner by all its reviewers, i.e.,

$$Q_1 = \frac{n_{ui}}{n_r}$$

where n_{ui} is the number of requirements for which all reviewers presented identical interpretations. This ranges from 0 (every requirement has multiple interpretations) to 1 (every requirement has a unique interpretation). Because unambiguity is so critical to project success, we recommend a weight of 1, i.e., $W_1 = 1$.

Replacing natural language with formal notations, e.g., FSMs, PNs, DTs, greatly decreases ambiguity in the SRS but almost always at the expense of understandability[1]. A better approach is to *augment* natural language with more formal models. That way, the advantages of both natural and formal languages are preserved.

2.2 Complete

An SRS is *complete* if:

o Everything that the software is supposed to do is included in the SRS [DAV93]

o Responses of the software to all realizable classes of input data in all realizable classes of situations is included [IEE84]

o All pages numbered; all figures and tables numbered, named, and referenced; all terms defined; all units of measure provided; and all referenced material present [IEE84]

o No sections marked "To Be Determined" [DAV93].

---

[1] Decision trees are one of the few exceptions. When applicable, they can be used with no explanation and can be easily understood by the layperson.

Requirements Quality Factor	BOE 74	ALF 76	BEL 76	DAV 79	BAS 81	ZAV 81	CEL 83	IEC 84	NCC 87	ESA 87	DOD 88	JPL 88	CAR 90	DAV 90	ROM 90	DAV 93
Unambiguous		X	X	X	X	X	X	X	X	X		X		X	X	X
Complete	X	X	X	X	X	X	X	X	X	X		X		X	X	X
Correct		X	X		X							X		X	X	X
Understandable		X		X			X	X	X	X	X			X	X	X
Verifiable		X	X				X		X	X	X	X		X	X	X
Consistent (Internal)	X	X	X	X	X	X	X	X	X	X	X	X		X	X	X
Consistent (External)		X							X	X	X	X			X	X
Achievable		X	X							X					X	
Concise													X			X
Design Independent		X	X	X		X						X				X
Traceable	X	X						X		X		X		X	X	X
Modifiable		X			X	X		X						X	X	X
Electronically Stored									X							
Interpretable/ Prototypable						X								X		
Annotated by Relative Importance										X		X		X		X
Annotated by Relative Stability										X					X	X
Annotated by Version																
Not Redundant		X	X	X			X			X				X		X
At Right Level of Detail															X	
Precise						X			X	X					X	
Reusable																
Traced		X					X	X			X	X		X		X
Organized		X							X						X	X
Cross-Referenced																

Figure 1. Attributes of an SRS

Obviously, if an SRS is incomplete by the first meaning, users will not be satisfied when the system is deployed. If an SRS is incomplete by any other definition, developers are likely to make assumptions about intended behavior, and those assumptions may be false, leading once again to unsatisfied users.

Given the first definition, completeness is extremely difficult to measure; it is generally agreed that the more requirements we include in an SRS (or see in a system),

196

the more new requirements we will think of. We are thus trying to measure a moving target. However, using the second definition, there are some metrics that do make sense. For example, completeness implies that the function *f(state, stimulus) --> (state, response)* is defined for all elements in the cross product *state x stimulus*. Assuming we count numbers of inputs, i.e., stimuli (n_i) specified in the SRS, and numbers of states (n_s) defined in or implied by the SRS, then we know their product ($n_i \times n_s$) is the total number of function values that must be specified. If we now count the actual unique functions (n_u) specified (Note that $n_u <= n_f$ because some of the n_f functions could be redundant), we can measure completeness by the equation,

$$Q_2 = \frac{n_u}{n_i \times n_s}.$$

This measures percentage of necessary functions specified. It may be useful in well understood, bounded, problem domains. It does not address completeness of non-functional requirements. Jaffe, et al. [JAF91] have a done a remarkable job of delineating all types of requirements that must be present in a FSM-based SRS in order to declare it complete.

In less understood, less bounded, problem domains, it is likely that stimuli and states specified in the SRS are themselves incomplete. Alexander [ALE90] provided ideas that may be of help here. Figure 2 provides an omniscient view of all requirements for a system, i.e., assume we are able to look to the future and ascertain all requirements that users will ever need. Block A represents requirements that we know, and that we know are applicable to this problem; these are the requirements typically captured in an SRS. Block B represents requirements that we know, but have not really thought about or verbalized; these are typically uncovered during interviews or brainstorming. Of course, once uncovered, they move to block A. Block C represents requirements that we know we need, but don't understand them well enough to describe them; these are typically uncovered during prototyping. Once uncovered, they move to block A. Block D represents potential requirements that we don't know, and that we don't even know we don't know. Prototyping may help uncover these because sometimes seeing one feature makes us aware of another. Once uncovered, they tend to move to block B. Arrows in Figure 2 show requirements migration. Notice the trend is all requirements moving to block A. All requirements in block A is equivalent to the first definition of completeness. A measure of the percentage of requirements that are in block A could be an effective measure of completeness, i.e.,

$$\frac{n_A}{n_A + n_B + n_C + n_D}$$

where n_A, n_B, n_C, and n_D are numbers of requirements in blocks A, B, C, and D, respectively. Values range from 0 (totally incomplete) to 1 (complete). Since we do not know how to measure the areas of blocks C or D, an alternative might be:

$$Q_{2'} = \frac{n_A}{n_A + n_B}.$$

Once again, values range from 0 (totally incomplete) to 1 (complete).

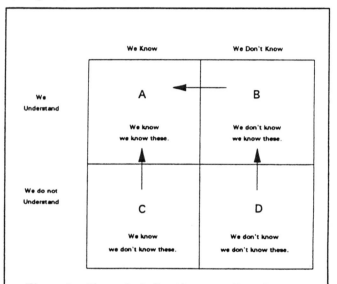

Figure 2. Alexander's Requirements Completeness Model

Another alternative is to measure local completeness, i.e., percentage of all recognized requirements that have been documented in the SRS. Figure 3 is a variation of Figure 2 where the vertical axis represents whether or not a requirement appears in the SRS, and the vertical axis represents the degree to which a requirement is understood. Block A represents requirements that we know, and that we have captured. Block B represents requirements that have been documented, but are either poorly specified, abstractly stated, or not yet validated. Once firm, they move to block A. Block C represents requirements that we know we need, but have not yet specified. Once documented, they move to block A. Block D represents potential requirements that we don't understand well enough to document. If we choose to specify them abstractly (as a place holder), they move to block B. If we choose to investigate their validity first, say via a prototype, and we grow to understand them, then they move to block C. Arrows in Figure 3 show

197

requirements migration. Notice the trend is all requirements moving to block A. Given this model, we could measure completeness as the percentage of requirements in the SRS that are well understood, i.e.,

$$Q_{2''} = \frac{n_A}{n_r}$$

or alternatively as the percentage of known requirements that have been documented in the SRS, i.e.,

$$Q_{2'''} = \frac{n_r}{n_A + n_B + n_C + n_D}$$

where n_A, n_B, n_C, and n_D are numbers of requirements in A, B, C, and D, respectively. In both cases, $n_r = n_A + n_B$ and values range from 0 (totally incomplete) to 1 (complete). Regardless of which is used, we recommend a weight of approx. .7, i.e., $W_2 = .7$ because completeness is critical to project success but difficult to measure.

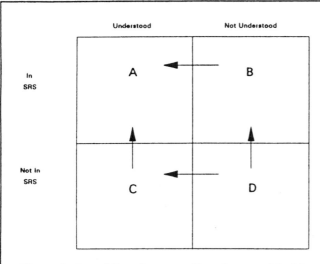

Figure 3. Local Requirements Completeness Model

To achieve completeness by any definition, reviews of the SRS by customer or user are essential. Prototypes also help raise awareness of new requirements and help us better understand poorly or abstractly defined requirements [AND89, DAV92].

2.3. Correct

An SRS is *correct* if and only if every requirement represents something required of the system to be built [DAV93], i.e., every requirement in the SRS contributes to the satisfaction of some need.

Since the term correctness applies to an individual requirement and an entire SRS, one convenient way of measuring correctness of an SRS might be to measure the percentage of individually correct requirements, i.e.,

$$\frac{n_C}{n_C + n_I}$$

where n_C and n_I are the numbers of correct and incorrect requirements, respectively, and $n_r = n_C + n_I$. Values range from 0 (totally incorrect) to 1 (totally correct). Ironically, if we could measure correctness by the above formula, we would have to know which requirements were incorrect, and we would remove them, making it 100% correct! Thus applying the above formula will always result in a score of 1. A more practical, but less theoretically satisfying, is to measure percentage of requirements in the SRS that have been validated. We arrive at a more practical measure of completeness:

$$Q_3 = \frac{n_C}{n_C + n_{NV}} = \frac{n_C}{n_r}$$

where n_C and n_{NV} are numbers of correct and not (yet) validated requirements, respectively, and once again, $n_r = n_C + n_{NV}$. Because correctness is so critical to project success, we recommend a weight of 1, i.e., $W_3 = 1$.

There is no oracle against which to validate correctness of a requirement. The only technique is to involve people who have the problem or mission. In effect, they serve as oracles. They can read and study the SRS, or can witness or manipulate a prototype.

2.4 Understandable

An SRS is *understandable* if all classes of SRS readers can easily comprehend the meaning of all requirements with a minimum of explanation. Readers include customers, users, project managers (PM), software developers, and testers. In general, the first three desire ease of reading, and thus natural language is ideal. Obviously, if users and customers cannot understand the SRS, they cannot intelligently approve it, leaving success of the product outcome to chance. In general, the last two desire to ascertain precisely what the system is expected to do, and thus formal language is ideal. Obviously, if designers and testers cannot understand the SRS, it is impossible to build or test the system. The burden of creating an understandable SRS falls on the shoulders of the writers; it is not the readers' responsibility to learn everything writers know in order to digest the SRS.

Measuring understandability is difficult. If we could measure the degree of understandability on a scale, we have a graph like Figure 4. A point reflects the degree to which an SRS is understandable by two categories of readers. Use of a technique may contribute to moving this point, e.g., adding DTs (which appear regularly in common literature without semantic explanation) to an

SRS in an appropriate manner would move the point toward the northeast, i.e., increased understandability by both parties. Adding PNs to an SRS in an appropriate manner would move the point toward the southeast, i.e., increased understandability by developers and testers, but decreased understandability by customers, users, and PMs. The only measure we can conceive of is

$$Q_4 = \frac{n_{ur}}{n_r}$$

where n_{ur} is the number of requirements for which all reviewers thought they understood. This ranges from 0 (every requirement understood) to 1 (no requirement understood). Because understandability is so critical to project success, we recommend a weight of 1, i.e., $W_4 = 1$.

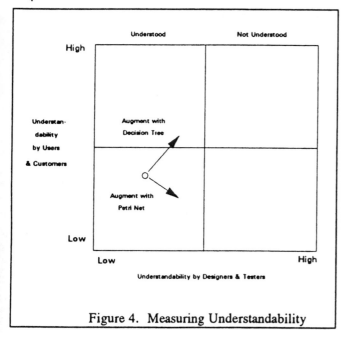

Figure 4. Measuring Understandability

A variety of techniques are available to determine and/or improve SRS understandability. First is to let representatives of all reader classes read it and comment. Assuming this is done repeatedly, and the SRS is revised accordingly, it may converge upon understandability. Augmentation with a prototype can improve effective understandability because it is often easier to see a prototype's behavior than to read a document.

2.5 Verifiable

An SRS is *verifiable* if there exist finite, cost effective techniques that can be used to verify that every requirement stated therein is satisfied by the system as built. Some requirements are easy to test: WHENEVER THE BUTTON X IS BEING PRESSED, THE LIGHT L SHALL BE LIT. Others are difficult to test: THE SOFTWARE SHALL

EXHIBIT A FRIENDLY EASY-TO-USE INTERFACE WITH THE USER. There are a variety of reasons why a requirement may be difficult to verify:

a. Ambiguous. Any requirement with ambiguity will fare poorly for verifiability. If multiple interpretations exist for a requirement, there is no way to verify it [DAV90a].

b. Undecideable. Any requirement that is equivalent to the halting problem renders it unverifiable. Thus the requirement THE SYSTEM SHALL NEVER HALT is not verifiable.

c. Not worth cost (financial or life). For example, the requirement, IN THE CASE OF A REACTOR MELT-DOWN, THE SYSTEM SHALL REDUCE THE DEATHS OF PERSONNEL WITHIN A 20 MILE RADIUS BY AT LEAST 80% is not worth the cost to test.

Measurement of verifiability is difficult. When verifiability is related to ambiguity, we have already seen it is impossible to adequately measure (see Section 2.1). When verifiability is related to the halting problem, the requirement either is or is not verifiable. A measure of percentage of requirements whose verification is unde-cideable is not helpful. There are some measurement avenues for cost-effectiveness or finiteness of the verification approach. If $c(r_i)$ and $t(r_i)$ are the cost and time necessary to verify presence of requirement r_i, then

$$Q_5 = \frac{n_r}{n_r + \sum_i c(r_i) + \sum_i t(r_i)}$$

measures inherent SRS verifiability where 0 means very poor verifiability, and 1 means very good verifiability. Verifiability is relative important to project success, so we recommend a weight of .7, i.e., $W_5 = .7$.

Techniques to help verifiability are (1) all techniques described above for ambiguity, (2) knowledge of unde-cideability and review for its presence, and (3) review of SRS by experienced testers who can determine high cost or schedule testing implications.

2.6. Internally Consistent

An SRS is *internally consistent* if and only if no subset of individual requirements stated therein conflict [IEE84].

Measuring internally consistency is easier if we think of the SRS as defining a function that maps inputs and states into outputs and states, i.e,. treat it as an FSM. A consistent SRS is now one that can be described as a deterministic FSM. Any nondeterminism implies the SRS defines two different system responses or next states in identical situations. Assuming that we enumerate all stimuli (n_i) specified and all states (n_s) defined in or implied by the SRS, then we know there should be exactly $(n_i \times n_s)$ total function values that must be specified to be complete, consistent and non-redundant. We now count the actual unique functions (n_u) specified (Note: $n_u <= n_f$), and we count how many of them are nondeterministic (n_n), i.e., how many of them map the same point in the domain into different points in the range. Then a measure of internal consistency is the percentage of unique functions that are deterministic:

$$Q_6 = \frac{n_u - n_n}{n_u}.$$

Values range from 0 (100% internally inconsistent) to 1 (100% internally consistent). Internal consistency is critical to project success, so we recommend a weight of 1, i.e., $W_6 = 1$.

Internal consistency is most easily achieved with tools like RLP [DAV79a] or REVS [ALF85]. Both provide consistency error reports for SRSs specified using multiple FSMs. Most CASE tools do consistency checking for data flow diagrams (DFD) and rudimentary consistency checking among DFDs and FSMs.

2.7 Externally Consistent

An SRS is *externally consistent* if and only if no requirement stated therein conflicts with any already baselined project documentation. These baselined documents include system-level requirements specifications (RS), statements of work (SOW), white papers, an earlier version of the SRS to which this new SRS must be upward compatible, and RSs for other systems to which this system must interface.

Measuring external consistency is more difficult than internal consistency. The best measure we can arrive at is the percentage of requirements that are consistent with all other documents, i.e.,

$$Q_7 = \frac{n_{EC}}{n_{EC} + n_{EI}} = \frac{n_{EC}}{n_r}$$

where n_{EC} is the number of requirements in the SRS that are consistent with all other documents and n_{EI} is the number that is not. Note that $n_r = n_{EC} + n_{EI}$. External consistency is critical to project success, so we recommend a weight of 1, i.e., $W_7 = 1$.

To ensure external consistency one must create and maintain full cross-references between all requirements and relevant statements made in other documents (see Section 2.22). However, maintaining external consistency may entail more than this. For example, it might be that a software development plan (SDP) or a development contract states that development effort must

consume no more than \$1M or last no more than 18 months, but the SRS defines so many requirements that it is impossible to meet cost or schedule. Here the problem is not individual requirements but the combined effect of all requirements. The SRS must be reviewed simultaneously with all possible conflicting documents, including SOW, development contract, and SDP.

2.8 Achievable

An SRS is *achievable* if and only if there could exist at least one system design and implementation that correctly implements all the requirements stated in the SRS. Achievability, Q_8, is a measure of the existence of a single system and thus has a discrete value of 1 or 0, i.e., a set of requirements are either achievable or given acceptable development resources they are not. A weight of $W_8 = 1$ is appropriate. The best way to ensure achievability is to construct a working prototype of parts of the system where achievability may be in doubt.

2.9 Concise

An SRS is *concise* if it is as short as possible without adversely affecting any other quality of the SRS. Thus if we have two SRS's that describe the identical system, with identical measures of qualities for the 23 other quality attributes, then the shorter one is better.

One way to measure conciseness is to count pages. However, comparative SRS sizes are only important after we are sure they describe identical systems. In general, determining if two SRSs describe identical systems is undecideable. The ultimate in conciseness is the null SRS; this should earn a 1. The worst case of conciseness is an SRS of infinite size; and score zero. One metric that exhibits these properties is the hyperbole:

$$Q_9 = \frac{1}{size + 1}$$

where *size* is the number of pages. An appropriate weight is probably $W_9 = .2$.

Major reductions in SRS size are rarely possible without adversely effecting other qualities. The primary exception is when writers are prone to baroque writing, e.g., THE CHECK PRINTING FUNCTION OF THE PAYROLL SYSTEM SHALL PROVIDE THE CAPABILITY TO VALIDATE CHECK AMOUNTS can be shortened to THE PAYROLL SYSTEM SHALL VALIDATE CHECK AMOUNTS and score higher for conciseness *and* understandability.

2.10 Design-Independent

An SRS is *design independent* if and only if there exist more than one system design and implementation that correctly implements all requirements stated in the SRS. The purpose of the SRS is to express desired external behavior to a degree that user satisfaction is guaranteed and a maximum number of designs exist to satisfy those needs and behaviors. It is okay to describe external behavior of a solution system using an FSM as long as it is clearly stated that the solution system must behave externally the same way that the FSM behaves externally. It is not okay to include an FSM and imply that the solution system must be designed as an FSM.

Let us assume that the requirements in the SRS include some (R_E) that describe pure external behavior, and some (R_I) that directly address architecture or algorithms of the solution (Note that $R = R_E \cup R_I$). Then there exists some number of actual solution system designs $(D(R_E \cup R_I))$ that satisfy all requirements, and some number of actual solution system designs $(D(R_E))$ that satisfy only those external behavior requirements. Design independence can be measured as the percentage of possible solution systems that are eliminated by adding the overly constraining requirements:

$$Q_{10} = \frac{D(R_E \cup R_I)}{D(R_E)}.$$

Values range from 0 (highly design dependent) to 1 (design independent). Projects can still succeed with poor design independence, but their success becomes hampered. For that reason, we give it weight $W_{10} = .5$.

One effective technique to ensure design independence is to have designers review the SRS. In general, designers take pride in their ability to synthesize an optimal design. Therefore they are likely to have a tremendous ego investment in finding ways to reduce design dependence of the SRS.

2.11 Traceable

An SRS is *traceable* if and only if it is written in a manner that facilitates the referencing of each individual requirement [DAV93]. During design and test it is essential to know which requirements are being supported by the component or verified by the test. Without this, it is impossible to design or test in a quality manner.

An SRS is either traceable or it is not. An SRS could contain some traceable requirements and some not traceable. However, this should render the entire document untraceable. Traceability, Q_{11}, earns a score of 1 if it exhibits any of the qualities described below, or 0 if it does not. There are a variety of effective techniques for achieving traceability [DAV93]:

o Number every paragraph hierarchically. You can later refer to any by a paragraph and sentence number, e.g., requirement 2.3.2.4s3 refers to the requirement in sentence 3 of paragraph 2.3.2.4.

o Number every paragraph hierarchically and include only one requirement in any paragraph. You can refer to any by a paragraph number.

o Number every requirement with a unique number in parentheses immediately after the requirement.

o Use a convention for indicating a requirement, e.g., always use the word *shall* in a sentence containing a requirement; then use a simple *shall*-extraction tool to extract and number all sentences with *shall*.

2.12 Modifiable

An SRS is *modifiable* if its structure and style are such that any changes can be made easily, completely, and consistently [IEE84]. There are two primary reasons for modifiability: (1) needs always evolve, and (2) the SRS, like all complex software-related documents, will contain errors. As needs evolve, the SRS will be modified to capture new, record changes to old, or delete obsolete requirements. Obviously, modifiability is enhanced if the SRS is also traceable (see Section 2.11), in machine readable form (see Section 2.13), traced (see Section 2.22), organized (see Section 2.23), and cross-referenced (see Section 2.24). Modifiability is also enhanced if it includes a table of contents and index.

Since most factors are already included in other metrics, we will measure modifiability, Q_{12}, here as: 1 if table of contents and index are present and 0 otherwise. Its weight is highly dependent on the application.

We know that inherent modifiability of a *program* is related to the degrees of cohesion exhibited by its components and coupling existent between components [YOU79]. As defined by Yourdon and Constantine, these measures make no sense for requirements, but perhaps similar measures can be developed for SRSs so we can measure cohesion of an SRS section or degree of interrelatedness between two SRS sections.

2.13 Electronically Stored

An SRS is *electronically stored* if and only if the entire SRS is in a word processor, it has been generated from a requirements database or has been otherwise synthesized from some other form. Usually, an SRS is either stored electronically or it is not. However, one could measure the percentage of the volume of the SRS that has been electronically stored and call it Q_{13}. Its weight is application dependent.

2.14 Executable/Interpretable/Prototypable

An SRS is *executable, interpretable,* or *prototypable* if and only if there exists a software tool capable of inputting the SRS and providing a dynamic behavioral model. This might be achieved by the SRS being written in a language that (1) is directly understood by a computer, or (2) is translatable into a language directly understood by a computer, or (3) can be interpreted by a software tool and thus simulated.

SRSs may be partially written in an executable, interpretable, or prototypable language. Therefore the metric Q_{14} ranges from 0 (entirely not executable) to 1 (entirely executable). Its weight is highly dependent on the application.

The best technique to ensure executability is to use any commercially available tool that provides such execution of requirements: PAISLey [ZAV86], RAPID [WAS86], and STATEMATE [HAR88]. Dozens of DFD-based CASE tools claim to also provide such executability, but execution is limited to DFDs where behavior of each bubble is defined using some behavioral model (e.g., FSMs, DTs), and the semantics of the DFDs are augmented with execution precedence rules. These CASE tools can also be used but power, versatility, and requirements orientation of behavioral models are superior to DFD-based specifications.

2.15 Annotated by Relative Importance

An SRS is *annotated by relative importance* if a reader can easily determine which requirements are of most importance to customers, which are next most important, etc. This is needed to allocate dollars sensibly, and determine priorities when budgets are inadequate.

Typically, an SRS is either annotated by relative importance or not. Obviously we can calculate the percentage of requirements that are annotated and use that as a measure, Q_{15}. Its weight is application dependent.

One way to achieve this is to suffix every requirement with (M), (D) and (O) to denote that this requirement is mandatory, desirable, or optional.

2.16 Annotated by Relative Stability

An SRS is *annotated by relative stability* if a reader can easily determine which requirements are of most likely to change, which are next most likely, etc. Designers need this to help determine where to build in flexibility. Knowing the relative stability can help a team decide whether or not to build in that flexibility.

Typically, an SRS is either annotated by relative stability or not. Obviously we can calculate the percentage of requirements that are annotated and use that as a measure, Q_{16}. Its weight is application dependent.

One way to achieve this is to suffix every requirement with (H), (M) and (L) to denote whether the probability of change is high, medium, or low.

2.17 Annotated by Version

An SRS is *annotated by version* if a reader can easily determine which requirements will be satisfied in which versions of the product. Both customers and designers obviously need to know this.

Like the previous two annotations, and SRS is either annotated by version or not. The percentage of requirements annotated by version is a reasonable measure, Q_{17}. It is assumed that an SRS written for just one version of the software is fully annotated (by default) and thus scores a 1. Its weight is application dependent.

The most common way of annotating requirements by version is to add a column in the margin for each version of software to be produced. "X"s are placed beside each requirement in the respective columns.

2.18 Not Redundant

An SRS is *redundant* if the same requirement is stated more than once. Unlike the other 23 attributes, redundancy is not necessarily bad. Often redundancy can be used to increase readability of the SRS significantly. The only problem that redundancy causes is when an SRS is revised. If all occurrences of a redundant requirement are not changed then the SRS becomes inconsistent.

If we count the actual functions (n_f) specified, and the actual unique functions (n_u) specified, then a measure of nonredundancy in an SRS is the percentage of unique functions that are not repeated, i.e.,

$$Q_{18} = \frac{n_f}{n_u}.$$

Values range from 0 (completely redundant) to 1 (no redundancy). Weight will usually be 0.

Since redundancy is not necessarily bad, no technique should be applied specifically. There are techniques that reduce the risks involved in using redundancy. These include incorporation of an index and cross references among any redundant requirements.

2.19 At Right Level of Abstraction/Detail

Requirements can be stated at many levels of abstraction. These examples of requirements range from most abstract to most detailed, but all are in the requirements domain:

a. SYSTEM SHALL PROVIDE COMMUNICATIONS.
b. SYSTEM SHALL PROVIDE VOICE COMMUNICATIONS.
c. TELEPHONE SYSTEM SHALL PROVIDE VOICE COMMUNICATIONS.
d. TELEPHONE SYSTEM SHALL PROVIDE LOCAL CALLS, CALL FORWARDING, LONG DISTANCE CALLS....

e. TELEPHONE SHALL PROVIDE LONG DISTANCE CALLS WHERE USER LIFTS IDLE PHONE, DIAL TONE IS HEARD WITHIN 3 SECONDS, USER DIALS NINE, DISTINCTIVE DIAL TONE IS HEARD WITHIN 2 SECONDS, ETC.

The right level of detail is a function of how the SRS is being used. Generally, the SRS should be specific enough that any system built that satisfies the requirements in the SRS satisfies all user needs, and abstract enough that all systems that satisfy all user needs also satisfy all requirements. Thus, an SRS being used for a contract between customer and developer should be relatively specific to ensure the customer knows what is being acquired, and there are a minimum of surprises.

We can certainly develop ways to subjectively measure the abstraction level of an SRS. All we do is assign a number to each of the five above examples, examine a requirement, decide which example it is closest to, and assign it that value. The level of abstraction of the SRS, Q_{19}, is then the average of the values of each of its constituent requirements. The problem with this is that our goal is not to measure the *level* of abstraction of the SRS but to measure the *appropriateness* of the level of abstraction. This is highly scenario dependent and cannot be measured.

2.20 Precise

An SRS is *precise* if and only if (a) numeric quantities are used whenever possible, and (b) the appropriate levels of precision are used for all numeric quantities. Thus, THE SYSTEM SHALL EXHIBIT FAST RESPONSE TIME is not precise as THE SYSTEM SHALL FULLY RESPOND TO EVERY REQUEST WITHIN 2 SECONDS. Also, THE SYSTEM SHALL DISPLAY THE WAIT TIMES is not as good as THE SYSTEM SHALL DISPLAY THE WAIT TIMES TO THE NEAREST TENTH OF A SECOND. Also, assuming that the nearest tenth of a second is all that is needed, this requirement exhibits inappropriate levels of precision: THE SYSTEM SHALL DISPLAY THE WAIT TIMES TO THE NEAREST NANOSECOND.

2.21 Reusable

An SRS is *reusable* if and only if its sentences, paragraphs and sections can be easily adopted or adapted for use in a subsequent SRS. Much research is underway concerning reuse of design and code. Little extends to the requirements domain.

Ideally, reusability should be measured on results rather than potential. Thus a score of 1 should be given to an SRS whose contents have been fully reused by later SRSs and 0 to an SRS none of whose contents have been. Unfortunately, metrics are more useful if they can be established at the time of SRS creation rather than many years later. An alternative is to measure SRS reusability as the potential for SRS reuse. In the case of reuse of design and code, research results have helped us recognize what makes a component reusable, although results are not consistent or conclusive. In the case of requirements reuse, no research results are available. The next paragraph will introduce some experimental requirements reuse properties. When more information becomes known, a reusability metric of "percentage of paragraphs that exhibit reuse properties" can be used. However, it will have the same problems as for design and code. Given a software system, the percentage of components that are data abstractions (or have any of the many other qualities that increase potential reuse) does not yield a reasonable reusability metric because there exist data abstractions that are not reusable.

Little is known about techniques to optimize potential reuse of requirements specifications. Here are some avenues from the most to the least understood:

1. Write SRS sections using "symbolic constants," e.g., in the performance section, use a word processor symbolic constant for key response times. Then, later applications with similar functionality but with different response times can simply change the value in the symbolic constant.

2. Use formal models. The specific FSMs, DTs, PNs, and statecharts are unlikely to be reusable, but their presence will likely cause the next SRS writer to reuse the concept of employing such models.

3. Create library of *abstract requirements types*. These are generic requirements paragraphs that are instantiated by providing tailoring information about characteristics of a particular application. The actual SRS becomes a series of instantiations.

2.22 Traced

An SRS is *traced* if and only if the origin of each of its requirements is clear [DAV93]. This implies that every requirement that has a basis is cross-referenced to that basis. Typical bases include: system-level RSs, system-level design documents, hardware RSs, SOWs, contracts, white papers/research reports, and SDPs. Any of these documents may hold a clue as to the reason why a particular requirement exists. For example, a requirement THE SYSTEM SHALL REPORT THE CURRENT POSITION OF ALL SHIPS NO LESS OFTEN THAN EVERY SECOND may exist because an earlier white paper reported the maximum possible ship speed, and an earlier system-level RS reported the resolution and scale of the display medium. In this case, the above requirement should be cross-referenced to both of the earlier documents.

Measuring the level of traced-ness is impossible. Ideally, we want to measure the following:

$$\frac{Number\ of\ requirements\ traced\ to\ their\ origins}{Number\ of\ requirements\ that\ have\ origins}$$

Unfortunately, the only way to measure the denominator is to examine the SRS for such cross-references! Thus, the above fraction will always have a value of 1.

There are two techniques to record traces. First is to include explicit cross-references in parentheses following each requirement in the SRS. Second is to record all requirements in a database. Each requirement is a record. A field is used for cross-references. The SRS becomes a retrieval of the database and might include or exclude the cross-references.

2.23 Organized

An SRS is *organized* if and only if its contents are arranged so that readers can easily locate information and logical relationships among adjacent sections is apparent. One way is to follow any of the many SRS standards [DOR90]. Certainly boiler plate sections of all SRS standards are roughly equivalent. Primary differences concern organization of detailed requirements. There are many ways to organize these. However, given any particular system, there are probably only a few right ways. Some alternatives are [DAV93] (in all cases assume that detailed requirements are in Section 3):

1. group the functional requirements by *class of user*. For example, an elevator control system SRS might include a Section 3.1 for all passenger requirements, 3.2 for all fireperson requirements, and 3.3 for all maintenance person requirements.

2. group the functional requirements by *common stimulus*. For example, an automated helicopter landing system SRS might include a Section 3.1 for all requirements relating to gusts of wind, 3.2 for all relating to being out of fuel, 3.3 for all relating to breakage of landing gear, etc.

3. group the functional requirements by *common response*. For example, a payroll system SRS might include a Section 3.1 for all requirements relating to generation of paychecks, 3.2 for all relating to generation of a report of all current employees with their monthly salaries, etc.

4. group the functional requirements by *feature*. For example, a payroll system SRS might include a Section 3.1 for all requirements relating to local calls, 3.2 for all relating to long distance calls, 3.3 for all relating to conference calls, etc.

5. group the functional requirements by *object*. For example, an airline reservation system SRS might include a Section 3.1 for all requirements relating to seats, 3.2 for all relating to flight segments, 3.3 for all relating to travel agents, 3.4 for all relating to tickets, etc.

Organization is purely subjective; we do not believe it can be measured.

To achieve useful organization, (1) follow a standard, and (2) use one of the above five organizational models which renders the SRS most easily understood.

2.24 Cross-Referenced

An SRS is *cross referenced* if and only if cross-references are used in the SRS to relate sections containing requirements to other sections containing:

o identical (i.e., redundant) requirements
o more abstract or more detailed descriptions of the same requirements
o requirements that depend on them or on which they depend (see related discussion of coupling in Section 2.12).

Any well-written SRS will describe requirements at a variety of levels, usually from the most abstract to the most detailed. To increase understandability many SRSs include redundancy. All SRSs will include requirements with interdependency. Thus, all SRSs should include cross-references. Like traced (see Section 2.22), there is no way to determine how many cross references are appropriate in an SRS. For this reason, any attempt to measure cross-references is fallacious.

The same techniques that work for traced (see Section 2.22) work for cross-references. Either use explicit in-text cross-references or preferably store all requirements in a database and use specific fields to store the three above types of cross references.

III. SRS Quality: A Compromise

A perfect SRS is impossible. For example, if we remove all ambiguity, we will add so much formality that it would no longer be understandable by a non-computer expert. If we remove all redundancy, it becomes difficult to read. If we go overboard with completeness, we lose conciseness. There are some qualities for which we can strive without adversely affecting others: correct, internally consistent, externally consistent, achievable, design-independent, organized, traced, traceable, all annotations, electronically stored and cross-referenced.

There may be some value in an overall rating of the quality of an SRS. The presence of some of SRS qualities appears to be essential for all applications and thus have been given weights of 1. Others seem less important in general and have lower weights. The actual weights for all the attributes must be assigned by each project to be meaningful. To have an overall quality on a scale from 0 to 1, we have:

$$Q = \frac{\sum_{i=1}^{18} W_i Q_i}{\sum_{i=1}^{18} W_i}$$

The above equation is a gross simplification; it is useful primarily for people who need to see just one number that states the quality of an SRS. More meaningful are the values for the entire vector Q_i.

IV. Summary

In summary, this paper defined 24 qualities that SRSs should exhibit. In 18 cases, it has provided a metric. It is hoped that in the future, we (or others) will be able to more fully expand the list of qualities, and will provide more complete measures for all qualities.

Acknowledgments

The authors thank P. Aiken, F. Armour, C. Gorski, S. Paey, S. Park, M. Ricker, G. Santacruz, and R. Sonnemann for many hours of stimulating discussion on the subject of this paper, J. Berdon and T. Nakajima for helpful feedback on the paper's contents, and K. Baugh for typing it.

References

[ALE90] Alexander, L., *Selection Criteria for Alternative Software Life-Cycle Process Models*, Software Engineering M. S. Thesis, Fairfax, Virginia: George Mason University, 1990.

[ALF76] Alford, M., and I. Burns, "R-nets: A Graph Model for Real-Time Software Requirements," *Symposium on Computer Software Engineering*, New York: Polytechnic Press, 1976, pp. 97-108.

[ALF85] Alford, M., "SREM at the Age of Eight: *The Distributed Computing Design System.*" *IEEE Computer, 18*, 4 (April 1989), pp. 36-46.

[AND89] Andriole, S., *Storyboard Prototyping*, Wellesley, Massachusetts: QED, 1989.

[BAS81] Basili, V., and D. Weiss, "Evaluation of a Software Requirements Document by Analysis of Change Data," *Fifth IEEE Int'l Conf. on Software Eng.*, 1981, pp. 314-323.

[BOE75] Boehm, B., et al., "Some Experience with Automated Aids to the Design of Large-Scale Reliable Software," *IEEE Trans. Software Eng., 1*, 1 (March 1975), pp. 125-133.

[BOE76] Boehm, B., "Software Engineering," *IEEE Trans. Computers, 25*, 12 (December 1976), pp. 1226-1241.

[CAR90] Caruso, J., private communication, Fairfax, Virginia, Fall 1990.

[CEL83] Celko, J., et al., "A Demonstration of Three Requirements Language Systems," *ACM SIGPLAN Notices, 18*, 1 (January 1983), pp. 9-14.

[DAL77] Daly, E., "Management of Software Development," *IEEE Trans. Computers, 3*, 3 (May 1977), pp. 229-242.

[DAV79] Davis, A., and T. Rauscher, "Formal Techniques and Automated Processing to Ensure Correctness in Requirements Specifications," *IEEE Specifications of Reliable Software Conf.*, 1979, pp. 15-35.

[DAV79a] Davis, A., et al., "RLP: An Automated Tool for the Processing of Requirements." *IEEE COMPSAC '79*, 1979.

[DAV90] Davis, A., *Software Requirements: Analysis and Specification*, Englewood Cliffs, New Jersey: Prentice Hall, 1990.

[DAV90a] Davis, A., "System Testing: Implications of Requirements Specifications," *Information and Software Technology, 32*, 6 (July/August 1990), pp. 407-414.

[DAV92] Davis, A., "Operational Prototyping: A New Development Approach," *IEEE Software, 9*, 5 (September 1992), pp. 70-78.

[DAV93] Davis, A., *Software Requirements: Objects, Functions, and States* (Second Edition), Englewood Cliffs, New Jersey: Prentice Hall, 1993.

[DOD88] Department of Defense, *Military Standard: Defense System Software Development*, DOD-STD-2167A, Washington, D.C., 1988.

[DOR90] Dorfman, M., and R. Thayer, *Standards, Guidelines, and Examples on System and Software Requirements Engineering*, Washington D.C.: IEEE Computer Society Press, 1990.

[ESA87] European Space Agency, *ESA Software Engineering Standards*, Noordwijk, Netherlands: ESA Publications Division, 1987.

[FAG74] Fagan, M., *Design and Code Inspections and Process Control in the Development of Programs*, IBM Report IBM-SDD-TR-21-572, December 1974.

[HAR88] Harel, D., et al., "STATEMATE: A Working Environment for the Development of Complex Reactive Systems." *IEEE Tenth Int'l Conf. on Software Eng.*, 1988.

[IEE84] Institute for Electrical and Electronics Engineers, *IEEE Guide to Software Requirements Specifications*, Standard 830-1984, New York: IEEE Computer Society Press, 1984.

[JAF91] Jaffe, M., et al., "Software Requirements Analysis for Real-Time Process-Control Systems," *IEEE Trans. Software Engineering, 17*, 3 (March 1991), pp. 241-258.

[JPL88] Jet Propulsion Laboratory, *Software Requirements Analysis Phase*, JPL-D-4005, Pasadena, California, 1988.

[MIZ83] Mizuno, Y., "Software Quality Improvement," *IEEE Computer, 15*, 3 (March 1983), pp. 66-72.

[NCC87] National Computer Centre Ltd., *The STARTS Guide*, Manchester, England, 1987.

[ROM90] Rombach, H., *Software Specifications: A Framework*, Curriculum Module SEI-CM-11-2.1, Pittsburgh, Pennsylvania: Software Engineering Institute, January 1990.

[TAV84] Tavolato, P., and K. Vincena, "A Prototyping Methodology and its Tool," in *Approaches to Prototyping*, R. Budde, ed., Berlin: Springer-Verlag, 1984, pp. 434-446.

[WAS86] Wasserman, A., et al., "Developing Interactive Information System with the User Software Engineering Methodology." *IEEE Trans. Software Eng., 12*, 2 (February 1986), pp. 325-345.

[WEB86] *Webster's Third New International Dictionary*, Springfield, Massachusetts: Merriam-Webster, Inc., 1986.

[YOU79] Yourdon, E., and l. Constantine, *Structured Design*, Englewood Cliffs, New Jersey: Prentice-Hall, 1979.

[ZAV81] Zave, P., and R. Yeh, "Executable Requirements for Embedded Systems," *Fifth IEEE Int'l Conf. on Software Eng.*, 1981, pp. 295-304.

IEEE Std 830-1998
(Revision of
IEEE Std 830-1993)

IEEE Recommended Practice for Software Requirements Specifications

Sponsor

**Software Engineering Standards Committee
of the
IEEE Computer Society**

Approved 25 June 1998

IEEE-SA Standards Board

Abstract: The content and qualities of a good software requirements specification (SRS) are described and several sample SRS outlines are presented. This recommended practice is aimed at specifying requirements of software to be developed but also can be applied to assist in the selection of in-house and commercial software products. Guidelines for compliance with IEEE/EIA 12207.1-1997 are also provided.
Keywords: contract, customer, prototyping, software requirements specification, supplier, system requirements specifications

Introduction

(This introduction is not a part of IEEE Std 830-1998, IEEE Recommended Practice for Software Requirements Specifications.)

This recommended practice describes recommended approaches for the specification of software requirements. It is based on a model in which the result of the software requirements specification process is an unambiguous and complete specification document. It should help

a) Software customers to accurately describe what they wish to obtain;

b) Software suppliers to understand exactly what the customer wants;

c) Individuals to accomplish the following goals:

　　1) Develop a standard software requirements specification (SRS) outline for their own organizations;

　　2) Define the format and content of their specific software requirements specifications;

　　3) Develop additional local supporting items such as an SRS quality checklist, or an SRS writer's handbook.

To the customers, suppliers, and other individuals, a good SRS should provide several specific benefits, such as the following:

— *Establish the basis for agreement between the customers and the suppliers on what the software product is to do.* The complete description of the functions to be performed by the software specified in the SRS will assist the potential users to determine if the software specified meets their needs or how the software must be modified to meet their needs.

— *Reduce the development effort.* The preparation of the SRS forces the various concerned groups in the customer's organization to consider rigorously all of the requirements before design begins and reduces later redesign, recoding, and retesting. Careful review of the requirements in the SRS can reveal omissions, misunderstandings, and inconsistencies early in the development cycle when these problems are easier to correct.

— *Provide a basis for estimating costs and schedules.* The description of the product to be developed as given in the SRS is a realistic basis for estimating project costs and can be used to obtain approval for bids or price estimates.

— *Provide a baseline for validation and verification.* Organizations can develop their validation and verification plans much more productively from a good SRS. As a part of the development contract, the SRS provides a baseline against which compliance can be measured.

— *Facilitate transfer.* The SRS makes it easier to transfer the software product to new users or new machines. Customers thus find it easier to transfer the software to other parts of their organization, and suppliers find it easier to transfer it to new customers.

— *Serve as a basis for enhancement.* Because the SRS discusses the product but not the project that developed it, the SRS serves as a basis for later enhancement of the finished product. The SRS may need to be altered, but it does provide a foundation for continued production evaluation.

The readers of this document are referred to Annex B for guidelines for using this recommended practice to meet the requirements of IEEE/EIA 12207.1-1997, IEEE/EIA Guide—Industry Implementation of ISO/IEC 12207: 1995, Standard for Information Technology—Software life cycle processes—Life cycle data.

Participants

This recommended practice was prepared by the Life Cycle Data Harmonization Working Group of the Software Engineering Standards Committee of the IEEE Computer Society. At the time this recommended practice was approved, the working group consisted of the following members:

Leonard L. Tripp, *Chair*

Edward Byrne	Dennis Lawrence	Terry Rout
Paul R. Croll	David Maibor	Richard Schmidt
Perry DeWeese	Ray Milovanovic	Norman F. Schneidewind
Robin Fralick	James Moore	David Schultz
Marilyn Ginsberg-Finner	Timothy Niesen	Basil Sherlund
John Harauz	Dennis Rilling	Peter Voldner
Mark Henley		Ronald Wade

The following persons were on the balloting committee:

Syed Ali	David A. Gustafson	Indradeb P. Pal
Theodore K. Atchinson	Jon D. Hagar	Alex Polack
Mikhail Auguston	John Harauz	Peter T. Poon
Robert E. Barry	Robert T. Harley	Lawrence S. Przybylski
Leo Beltracchi	Herbert Hecht	Kenneth R. Ptack
H. Ronald Berlack	William Hefley	Annette D. Reilly
Richard E. Biehl	Manfred Hein	Dennis Rilling
Michael A. Blackledge	Mark Heinrich	Andrew P. Sage
Sandro Bologna	Mark Henley	Helmut Sandmayr
Juris Borzovs	Debra Herrmann	Stephen R. Schach
Kathleen L. Briggs	John W. Horch	Hans Schaefer
M. Scott Buck	Jerry Huller	Norman Schneidewind
Michael Caldwell	Peter L. Hung	David J. Schultz
James E. Cardow	George Jackelen	Lisa A. Selmon
Enrico A. Carrara	Frank V. Jorgensen	Robert W. Shillato
Lawrence Catchpole	William S. Junk	David M. Siefert
Keith Chan	George X. Kambic	Carl A. Singer
Antonio M. Cicu	Richard Karcich	James M. Sivak
Theo Clarke	Ron S. Kenett	Richard S. Sky
Sylvain Clermont	Judith S. Kerner	Nancy M. Smith
Rosemary Coleman	Robert J. Kierzyk	Melford E. Smyre
Virgil Lee Cooper	Dwayne L. Knirk	Harry M. Sneed
W. W. Geoff Cozens	Shaye Koenig	Alfred R. Sorkowitz
Paul R. Croll	Thomas M. Kurihara	Donald W. Sova
Gregory T. Daich	John B. Lane	Luca Spotorno
Geoffrey Darnton	J. Dennis Lawrence	Julia Stesney
Taz Daughtrey	Fang Ching Lim	Fred J. Strauss
Bostjan K. Derganc	William M. Lively	Christine Brown Strysik
Perry R. DeWeese	James J. Longbucco	Toru Takeshita
James Do	Dieter Look	Richard H. Thayer
Evelyn S. Dow	John Lord	Booker Thomas
Carl Einar Dragstedt	Stan Magee	Patricia Trellue
Sherman Eagles	David Maibor	Theodore J. Urbanowicz
Christof Ebert	Harold Mains	Glenn D. Venables
Leo Egan	Robert A. Martin	Udo Voges
Richard E. Fairley	Tomoo Matsubara	David D. Walden
John W. Fendrich	Mike McAndrew	Dolores Wallace
Jay Forster	Patrick D. McCray	William M. Walsh
Kirby Fortenberry	Christopher McMacken	John W. Walz
Eva Freund	Jerome W. Mersky	Camille SWhite-Partain
Richard C. Fries	Bret Michael	Scott A. Whitmire
Roger U. Fujii	Alan Miller	P. A. Wolfgang
Adel N. Ghannam	Celia H. Modell	Paul R. Work
Marilyn Ginsberg-Finner	James W. Moore	Natalie C. Yopconka
John Garth Glynn	Pavol Navrat	Janusz Zalewski
Julio Gonzalez-Sanz	Myrna L. Olson	Geraldine Zimmerman
L. M. Gunther		Peter F. Zoll

210

When the IEEE-SA Standards Board approved this recommended practice on 25 June 1998, it had the following membership:

Richard J. Holleman, *Chair*   **Donald N. Heirman,** *Vice Chair*

Judith Gorman, *Secretary*

Satish K. Aggarwal	James H. Gurney	L. Bruce McClung
Clyde R. Camp	Jim D. Isaak	Louis-François Pau
James T. Carlo	Lowell G. Johnson	Ronald C. Petersen
Gary R. Engmann	Robert Kennelly	Gerald H. Peterson
Harold E. Epstein	E. G. "Al" Kiener	John B. Posey
Jay Forster*	Joseph L. Koepfinger*	Gary S. Robinson
Thomas F. Garrity	Stephen R. Lambert	Hans E. Weinrich
Ruben D. Garzon	Jim Logothetis	Donald W. Zipse
	Donald C. Loughry	

*Member Emeritus

Valerie E. Zelenty
IEEE Standards Project Editor

211

Contents

IEEE Recommended Practice for Software Requirements Specifications

1. Overview

This recommended practice describes recommended approaches for the specification of software requirements. It is divided into five clauses. Clause 1 explains the scope of this recommended practice. Clause 2 lists the references made to other standards. Clause 3 provides definitions of specific terms used. Clause 4 provides background information for writing a good SRS. Clause 5 discusses each of the essential parts of an SRS. This recommended practice also has two annexes, one which provides alternate format templates, and one which provides guidelines for compliance with IEEE/EIA 12207.1-1997.

1.1 Scope

This is a recommended practice for writing software requirements specifications. It describes the content and qualities of a good software requirements specification (SRS) and presents several sample SRS outlines.

This recommended practice is aimed at specifying requirements of software to be developed but also can be applied to assist in the selection of in-house and commercial software products. However, application to already-developed software could be counterproductive.

When software is embedded in some larger system, such as medical equipment, then issues beyond those identified in this recommended practice may have to be addressed.

This recommended practice describes the process of creating a product and the content of the product. The product is an SRS. This recommended practice can be used to create such an SRS directly or can be used as a model for a more specific standard.

This recommended practice does not identify any specific method, nomenclature, or tool for preparing an SRS.

2. References

This recommended practice shall be used in conjunction with the following publications.

ASTM E1340-96, Standard Guide for Rapid Prototyping of Computerized Systems.[1]

IEEE Std 610.12-1990, IEEE Standard Glossary of Software Engineering Terminology.[2]

IEEE Std 730-1998, IEEE Standard for Software Quality Assurance Plans.

IEEE Std 730.1-1995, IEEE Guide for Software Quality Assurance Planning.

IEEE Std 828-1998, IEEE Standard for Software Configuration Management Plans.[3]

IEEE Std 982.1-1988, IEEE Standard Dictionary of Measures to Produce Reliable Software.

IEEE Std 982.2-1988, IEEE Guide for the Use of IEEE Standard Dictionary of Measures to Produce Reliable Software.

IEEE Std 1002-1987 (Reaff 1992), IEEE Standard Taxonomy for Software Engineering Standards.

IEEE Std 1012-1998, IEEE Standard for Software Verification and Validation.

IEEE Std 1012a-1998, IEEE Standard for Software Verification and Validation: Content Map to IEEE/EIA 12207.1-1997.[4]

IEEE Std 1016-1998, IEEE Recommended Practice for Software Design Descriptions.[5]

IEEE Std 1028-1997, IEEE Standard for Software Reviews.

IEEE Std 1042-1987 (Reaff 1993), IEEE Guide to Software Configuration Management.

IEEE P1058/D2.1, Draft Standard for Software Project Management Plans, dated 5 August 1998.[6]

IEEE Std 1058a-1998, IEEE Standard for Software Project Management Plans: Content Map to IEEE/EIA 12207.1-1997.[7]

IEEE Std 1074-1997, IEEE Standard for Developing Software Life Cycle Processes.

IEEE Std 1233, 1998 Edition, IEEE Guide for Developing System Requirements Specifications.[8]

---

[1]ASTM publications are available from the American Society for Testing and Materials, 100 Barr Harbor Drive, West Conshohocken, PA 19428-2959, USA.

[2]IEEE publications are available from the Institute of Electrical and Electronics Engineers, 445 Hoes Lane, P.O. Box 1331, Piscataway, NJ 08855-1331, USA.

[3]As this standard goes to press, IEEE Std 828-1998; IEEE Std 1012a-1998; IEEE Std 1016-1998; and IEEE Std 1233, 1998 Edition are approved but not yet published. The draft standards are, however, available from the IEEE. Anticipated publication date is Fall 1998. Contact the IEEE Standards Department at 1 (732) 562-3800 for status information.

[4]See Footnote 3.

[5]See Footnote 3.

[6]Upon approval of IEEE P1058 by the IEEE-SA Standards Board, this standard will be integrated with IEEE Std 1058a-1998 and published as IEEE Std 1058, 1998 Edition. Approval is expected 8 December 1998.

[7]As this standard goes to press, IEEE Std 1058a-1998 is approved but not yet published. The draft standard is, however, available from the IEEE. Anticipated publication date is December 1998. Contact the IEEE Standards Department at 1 (732) 562-3800 for status information. See Footnote 6.

[8]See Footnote 3.

3. Definitions

In general the definitions of terms used in this recommended practice conform to the definitions provided in IEEE Std 610.12-1990. The definitions below are key terms as they are used in this recommended practice.

3.1 contract: A legally binding document agreed upon by the customer and supplier. This includes the technical and organizational requirements, cost, and schedule for a product. A contract may also contain informal but useful information such as the commitments or expectations of the parties involved.

3.2 customer: The person, or persons, who pay for the product and usually (but not necessarily) decide the requirements. In the context of this recommended practice the customer and the supplier may be members of the same organization.

3.3 supplier: The person, or persons, who produce a product for a customer. In the context of this recommended practice, the customer and the supplier may be members of the same organization.

3.4 user: The person, or persons, who operate or interact directly with the product. The user(s) and the customer(s) are often not the same person(s).

4. Considerations for producing a good SRS

This clause provides background information that should be considered when writing an SRS. This includes the following:

a) Nature of the SRS;
b) Environment of the SRS;
c) Characteristics of a good SRS;
d) Joint preparation of the SRS;
e) SRS evolution;
f) Prototyping;
g) Embedding design in the SRS;
h) Embedding project requirements in the SRS.

4.1 Nature of the SRS

The SRS is a specification for a particular software product, program, or set of programs that performs certain functions in a specific environment. The SRS may be written by one or more representatives of the supplier, one or more representatives of the customer, or by both. Subclause 4.4 recommends both.

The basic issues that the SRS writer(s) shall address are the following:

a) *Functionality.* What is the software supposed to do?
b) *External interfaces.* How does the software interact with people, the system's hardware, other hardware, and other software?
c) *Performance.* What is the speed, availability, response time, recovery time of various software functions, etc.?
d) *Attributes.* What are the portability, correctness, maintainability, security, etc. considerations?
e) *Design constraints imposed on an implementation.* Are there any required standards in effect, implementation language, policies for database integrity, resource limits, operating environment(s) etc.?

The SRS writer(s) should avoid placing either design or project requirements in the SRS.

For recommended contents of an SRS see Clause 5.

4.2 Environment of the SRS

It is important to consider the part that the SRS plays in the total project plan, which is defined in IEEE Std 610.12-1990. The software may contain essentially all the functionality of the project or it may be part of a larger system. In the latter case typically there will be an SRS that will state the interfaces between the system and its software portion, and will place external performance and functionality requirements upon the software portion. Of course the SRS should then agree with and expand upon these system requirements.

IEEE Std 1074-1997 describes the steps in the software life cycle and the applicable inputs for each step. Other standards, such as those listed in Clause 2, relate to other parts of the software life cycle and so may complement software requirements.

Since the SRS has a specific role to play in the software development process, the SRS writer(s) should be careful not to go beyond the bounds of that role. This means the SRS

    a)   Should correctly define all of the software requirements. A software requirement may exist because of the nature of the task to be solved or because of a special characteristic of the project.

    b)   Should not describe any design or implementation details. These should be described in the design stage of the project.

    c)   Should not impose additional constraints on the software. These are properly specified in other documents such as a software quality assurance plan.

Therefore, a properly written SRS limits the range of valid designs, but does not specify any particular design.

4.3 Characteristics of a good SRS

An SRS should be

    a)   Correct;
    b)   Unambiguous;
    c)   Complete;
    d)   Consistent;
    e)   Ranked for importance and/or stability;
    f)   Verifiable;
    g)   Modifiable;
    h)   Traceable.

4.3.1 Correct

An SRS is correct if, and only if, every requirement stated therein is one that the software shall meet.

There is no tool or procedure that ensures correctness. The SRS should be compared with any applicable superior specification, such as a system requirements specification, with other project documentation, and with other applicable standards, to ensure that it agrees. Alternatively the customer or user can determine if the SRS correctly reflects the actual needs. Traceability makes this procedure easier and less prone to error (see 4.3.8).

4.3.2 Unambiguous

An SRS is unambiguous if, and only if, every requirement stated therein has only one interpretation. As a minimum, this requires that each characteristic of the final product be described using a single unique term.

In cases where a term used in a particular context could have multiple meanings, the term should be included in a glossary where its meaning is made more specific.

An SRS is an important part of the requirements process of the software life cycle and is used in design, implementation, project monitoring, verification and validation, and in training as described in IEEE Std 1074-1997. The SRS should be unambiguous both to those who create it and to those who use it. However, these groups often do not have the same background and therefore do not tend to describe software requirements the same way. Representations that improve the requirements specification for the developer may be counterproductive in that they diminish understanding to the user and vice versa.

Subclauses 4.3.2.1 through 4.3.2.3 recommend how to avoid ambiguity.

4.3.2.1 Natural language pitfalls

Requirements are often written in natural language (e.g., English). Natural language is inherently ambiguous. A natural language SRS should be reviewed by an independent party to identify ambiguous use of language so that it can be corrected.

4.3.2.2 Requirements specification languages

One way to avoid the ambiguity inherent in natural language is to write the SRS in a particular requirements specification language. Its language processors automatically detect many lexical, syntactic, and semantic errors.

One disadvantage in the use of such languages is the length of time required to learn them. Also, many non-technical users find them unintelligible. Moreover, these languages tend to be better at expressing certain types of requirements and addressing certain types of systems. Thus, they may influence the requirements in subtle ways.

4.3.2.3 Representation tools

In general, requirements methods and languages and the tools that support them fall into three general categories—object, process, and behavioral. Object-oriented approaches organize the requirements in terms of real-world objects, their attributes, and the services performed by those objects. Process-based approaches organize the requirements into hierarchies of functions that communicate via data flows. Behavioral approaches describe external behavior of the system in terms of some abstract notion (such as predicate calculus), mathematical functions, or state machines.

The degree to which such tools and methods may be useful in preparing an SRS depends upon the size and complexity of the program. No attempt is made here to describe or endorse any particular tool.

When using any of these approaches it is best to retain the natural language descriptions. That way, customers unfamiliar with the notations can still understand the SRS.

4.3.3 Complete

An SRS is complete if, and only if, it includes the following elements:

a) All significant requirements, whether relating to functionality, performance, design constraints, attributes, or external interfaces. In particular any external requirements imposed by a system specification should be acknowledged and treated.

b) Definition of the responses of the software to all realizable classes of input data in all realizable classes of situations. Note that it is important to specify the responses to both valid and invalid input values.

c) Full labels and references to all figures, tables, and diagrams in the SRS and definition of all terms and units of measure.

4.3.3.1 Use of TBDs

Any SRS that uses the phrase "to be determined" (TBD) is not a complete SRS. The TBD is, however, occasionally necessary and should be accompanied by

a) A description of the conditions causing the TBD (e.g., why an answer is not known) so that the situation can be resolved;

b) A description of what must be done to eliminate the TBD, who is responsible for its elimination, and by when it must be eliminated.

4.3.4 Consistent

Consistency refers to internal consistency. If an SRS does not agree with some higher-level document, such as a system requirements specification, then it is not correct (see 4.3.1).

4.3.4.1 Internal consistency

An SRS is internally consistent if, and only if, no subset of individual requirements described in it conflict. The three types of likely conflicts in an SRS are as follows:

a) The specified characteristics of real-world objects may conflict. For example,
   1) The format of an output report may be described in one requirement as tabular but in another as textual.
   2) One requirement may state that all lights shall be green while another may state that all lights shall be blue.

b) There may be logical or temporal conflict between two specified actions. For example,
   1) One requirement may specify that the program will add two inputs and another may specify that the program will multiply them.
   2) One requirement may state that "A" must always follow "B," while another may require that "A and B" occur simultaneously.

c) Two or more requirements may describe the same real-world object but use different terms for that object. For example, a program's request for a user input may be called a "prompt" in one requirement and a "cue" in another. The use of standard terminology and definitions promotes consistency.

4.3.5 Ranked for importance and/or stability

An SRS is ranked for importance and/or stability if each requirement in it has an identifier to indicate either the importance or stability of that particular requirement.

Typically, all of the requirements that relate to a software product are not equally important. Some requirements may be essential, especially for life-critical applications, while others may be desirable.

Each requirement in the SRS should be identified to make these differences clear and explicit. Identifying the requirements in the following manner helps:

a) Have customers give more careful consideration to each requirement, which often clarifies any hidden assumptions they may have.

b) Have developers make correct design decisions and devote appropriate levels of effort to the different parts of the software product.

4.3.5.1 Degree of stability

One method of identifying requirements uses the dimension of stability. Stability can be expressed in terms of the number of expected changes to any requirement based on experience or knowledge of forthcoming events that affect the organization, functions, and people supported by the software system.

4.3.5.2 Degree of necessity

Another way to rank requirements is to distinguish classes of requirements as essential, conditional, and optional.

a) *Essential.* Implies that the software will not be acceptable unless these requirements are provided in an agreed manner.

b) *Conditional.* Implies that these are requirements that would enhance the software product, but would not make it unacceptable if they are absent.

c) *Optional.* Implies a class of functions that may or may not be worthwhile. This gives the supplier the opportunity to propose something that exceeds the SRS.

4.3.6 Verifiable

An SRS is verifiable if, and only if, every requirement stated therein is verifiable. A requirement is verifiable if, and only if, there exists some finite cost-effective process with which a person or machine can check that the software product meets the requirement. In general any ambiguous requirement is not verifiable.

Nonverifiable requirements include statements such as "works well," "good human interface," and "shall usually happen." These requirements cannot be verified because it is impossible to define the terms "good," "well," or "usually." The statement that "the program shall never enter an infinite loop" is nonverifiable because the testing of this quality is theoretically impossible.

An example of a verifiable statement is

Output of the program shall be produced within 20 s of event × 60% of the time; and shall be produced within 30 s of event × 100% of the time.

This statement can be verified because it uses concrete terms and measurable quantities.

If a method cannot be devised to determine whether the software meets a particular requirement, then that requirement should be removed or revised.

4.3.7 Modifiable

An SRS is modifiable if, and only if, its structure and style are such that any changes to the requirements can be made easily, completely, and consistently while retaining the structure and style. Modifiability generally requires an SRS to

a) Have a coherent and easy-to-use organization with a table of contents, an index, and explicit cross-referencing;

b) Not be redundant (i.e., the same requirement should not appear in more than one place in the SRS);

c) Express each requirement separately, rather than intermixed with other requirements.

Redundancy itself is not an error, but it can easily lead to errors. Redundancy can occasionally help to make an SRS more readable, but a problem can arise when the redundant document is updated. For instance, a requirement may be altered in only one of the places where it appears. The SRS then becomes inconsistent. Whenever redundancy is necessary, the SRS should include explicit cross-references to make it modifiable.

4.3.8 Traceable

An SRS is traceable if the origin of each of its requirements is clear and if it facilitates the referencing of each requirement in future development or enhancement documentation. The following two types of traceability are recommended:

a) *Backward traceability (i.e., to previous stages of development).* This depends upon each requirement explicitly referencing its source in earlier documents.

b) *Forward traceability (i.e., to all documents spawned by the SRS).* This depends upon each requirement in the SRS having a unique name or reference number.

The forward traceability of the SRS is especially important when the software product enters the operation and maintenance phase. As code and design documents are modified, it is essential to be able to ascertain the complete set of requirements that may be affected by those modifications.

4.4 Joint preparation of the SRS

The software development process should begin with supplier and customer agreement on what the completed software must do. This agreement, in the form of an SRS, should be jointly prepared. This is important because usually neither the customer nor the supplier is qualified to write a good SRS alone.

a) Customers usually do not understand the software design and development process well enough to write a usable SRS.

b) Suppliers usually do not understand the customer's problem and field of endeavor well enough to specify requirements for a satisfactory system.

Therefore, the customer and the supplier should work together to produce a well-written and completely understood SRS.

A special situation exists when a system and its software are both being defined concurrently. Then the functionality, interfaces, performance, and other attributes and constraints of the software are not predefined, but rather are jointly defined and subject to negotiation and change. This makes it more difficult, but no less important, to meet the characteristics stated in 4.3. In particular, an SRS that does not comply with the requirements of its parent system specification is incorrect.

This recommended practice does not specifically discuss style, language usage, or techniques of good writing. It is quite important, however, that an SRS be well written. General technical writing books can be used for guidance.

4.5 SRS evolution

The SRS may need to evolve as the development of the software product progresses. It may be impossible to specify some details at the time the project is initiated (e.g., it may be impossible to define all of the screen formats for an interactive program during the requirements phase). Additional changes may ensue as deficiencies, shortcomings, and inaccuracies are discovered in the SRS.

Two major considerations in this process are the following:

a) Requirements should be specified as completely and thoroughly as is known at the time, even if evolutionary revisions can be foreseen as inevitable. The fact that they are incomplete should be noted.

b) A formal change process should be initiated to identify, control, track, and report projected changes. Approved changes in requirements should be incorporated in the SRS in such a way as to

   1) Provide an accurate and complete audit trail of changes;
   2) Permit the review of current and superseded portions of the SRS.

4.6 Prototyping

Prototyping is used frequently during the requirements portion of a project. Many tools exist that allow a prototype, exhibiting some characteristics of a system, to be created very quickly and easily. See also ASTM E1340-96.

Prototypes are useful for the following reasons:

a) The customer may be more likely to view the prototype and react to it than to read the SRS and react to it. Thus, the prototype provides quick feedback.

b) The prototype displays unanticipated aspects of the systems behavior. Thus, it produces not only answers but also new questions. This helps reach closure on the SRS.

c) An SRS based on a prototype tends to undergo less change during development, thus shortening development time.

A prototype should be used as a way to elicit software requirements. Some characteristics such as screen or report formats can be extracted directly from the prototype. Other requirements can be inferred by running experiments with the prototype.

4.7 Embedding design in the SRS

A requirement specifies an externally visible function or attribute of a system. A design describes a particular subcomponent of a system and/or its interfaces with other subcomponents. The SRS writer(s) should clearly distinguish between identifying required design constraints and projecting a specific design. Note that every requirement in the SRS limits design alternatives. This does not mean, though, that every requirement is design.

The SRS should specify what functions are to be performed on what data to produce what results at what location for whom. The SRS should focus on the services to be performed. The SRS should not normally specify design items such as the following:

a) Partitioning the software into modules;
b) Allocating functions to the modules;
c) Describing the flow of information or control between modules;
d) Choosing data structures.

4.7.1 Necessary design requirements

In special cases some requirements may severely restrict the design. For example, security or safety requirements may reflect directly into design such as the need to

a) Keep certain functions in separate modules;
b) Permit only limited communication between some areas of the program;
c) Check data integrity for critical variables.

Examples of valid design constraints are physical requirements, performance requirements, software development standards, and software quality assurance standards.

Therefore, the requirements should be stated from a purely external viewpoint. When using models to illustrate the requirements, remember that the model only indicates the external behavior, and does not specify a design.

4.8 Embedding project requirements in the SRS

The SRS should address the software product, not the process of producing the software product.

Project requirements represent an understanding between the customer and the supplier about contractual matters pertaining to production of software and thus should not be included in the SRS. These normally include items such as

a) Cost;
b) Delivery schedules;
c) Reporting procedures;
d) Software development methods;
e) Quality assurance;
f) Validation and verification criteria;
g) Acceptance procedures.

Project requirements are specified in other documents, typically in a software development plan, a software quality assurance plan, or a statement of work.

5. The parts of an SRS

This clause discusses each of the essential parts of the SRS. These parts are arranged in Figure 1 in an outline that can serve as an example for writing an SRS.

While an SRS does not have to follow this outline or use the names given here for its parts, a good SRS should include all the information discussed here.

```
┌─────────────────────────────────────────────────────────────┐
│ Table of Contents                                           │
│ 1. Introduction                                             │
│     1.1 Purpose                                             │
│     1.2 Scope                                               │
│     1.3 Definitions, acronyms, and abbreviations           │
│     1.4 References                                         │
│     1.5 Overview                                          │
│ 2. Overall description                                     │
│     2.1 Product perspective                                │
│     2.2 Product functions                                  │
│     2.3 User characteristics                               │
│     2.4 Constraints                                       │
│     2.5 Assumptions and dependencies                       │
│ 3. Specific requirements (See 5.3.1 through 5.3.8 for       │
│    explanations of possible specific requirements. See also│
│    Annex A for several different ways of organizing         │
│    this section of the SRS.)                               │
│ Appendixes                                                 │
│ Index                                                      │
└─────────────────────────────────────────────────────────────┘
```

Figure 1—Prototype SRS outline

5.1 Introduction (Section 1 of the SRS)

The introduction of the SRS should provide an overview of the entire SRS. It should contain the following subsections:

a) Purpose;
b) Scope;
c) Definitions, acronyms, and abbreviations;
d) References;
e) Overview.

5.1.1 Purpose (1.1 of the SRS)

This subsection should

a) Delineate the purpose of the SRS;
b) Specify the intended audience for the SRS.

5.1.2 Scope (1.2 of the SRS)

This subsection should

a) Identify the software product(s) to be produced by name (e.g., Host DBMS, Report Generator, etc.);

b) Explain what the software product(s) will, and, if necessary, will not do;

c) Describe the application of the software being specified, including relevant benefits, objectives, and goals;

d) Be consistent with similar statements in higher-level specifications (e.g., the system requirements specification), if they exist.

5.1.3 Definitions, acronyms, and abbreviations (1.3 of the SRS)

This subsection should provide the definitions of all terms, acronyms, and abbreviations required to properly interpret the SRS. This information may be provided by reference to one or more appendixes in the SRS or by reference to other documents.

5.1.4 References (1.4 of the SRS)

This subsection should

a)   Provide a complete list of all documents referenced elsewhere in the SRS;
b)   Identify each document by title, report number (if applicable), date, and publishing organization;
c)   Specify the sources from which the references can be obtained.

This information may be provided by reference to an appendix or to another document.

5.1.5 Overview (1.5 of the SRS)

This subsection should

a)   Describe what the rest of the SRS contains;
b)   Explain how the SRS is organized.

5.2 Overall description (Section 2 of the SRS)

This section of the SRS should describe the general factors that affect the product and its requirements. This section does not state specific requirements. Instead, it provides a background for those requirements, which are defined in detail in Section 3 of the SRS, and makes them easier to understand.

This section usually consists of six subsections, as follows:

a)   Product perspective;
b)   Product functions;
c)   User characteristics;
d)   Constraints;
e)   Assumptions and dependencies;
f)   Apportioning of requirements.

5.2.1 Product perspective (2.1 of the SRS)

This subsection of the SRS should put the product into perspective with other related products. If the product is independent and totally self-contained, it should be so stated here. If the SRS defines a product that is a component of a larger system, as frequently occurs, then this subsection should relate the requirements of that larger system to functionality of the software and should identify interfaces between that system and the software.

A block diagram showing the major components of the larger system, interconnections, and external interfaces can be helpful.

This subsection should also describe how the software operates inside various constraints. For example, these constraints could include

a) System interfaces;
b) User interfaces;
c) Hardware interfaces;
d) Software interfaces;
e) Communications interfaces;
f) Memory;
g) Operations;
h) Site adaptation requirements.

5.2.1.1 System interfaces

This should list each system interface and identify the functionality of the software to accomplish the system requirement and the interface description to match the system.

5.2.1.2 User interfaces

This should specify the following:

a) *The logical characteristics of each interface between the software product and its users.* This includes those configuration characteristics (e.g., required screen formats, page or window layouts, content of any reports or menus, or availability of programmable function keys) necessary to accomplish the software requirements.

b) *All the aspects of optimizing the interface with the person who must use the system.* This may simply comprise a list of do's and don'ts on how the system will appear to the user. One example may be a requirement for the option of long or short error messages. Like all others, these requirements should be verifiable, e.g., "a clerk typist grade 4 can do function X in Z min after 1 h of training" rather than "a typist can do function X." (This may also be specified in the Software System Attributes under a section titled Ease of Use.)

5.2.1.3 Hardware interfaces

This should specify the logical characteristics of each interface between the software product and the hardware components of the system. This includes configuration characteristics (number of ports, instruction sets, etc.). It also covers such matters as what devices are to be supported, how they are to be supported, and protocols. For example, terminal support may specify full-screen support as opposed to line-by-line support.

5.2.1.4 Software interfaces

This should specify the use of other required software products (e.g., a data management system, an operating system, or a mathematical package), and interfaces with other application systems (e.g., the linkage between an accounts receivable system and a general ledger system). For each required software product, the following should be provided:

— Name;
— Mnemonic;
— Specification number;
— Version number;
— Source.

For each interface, the following should be provided:

— Discussion of the purpose of the interfacing software as related to this software product.
— Definition of the interface in terms of message content and format. It is not necessary to detail any well-documented interface, but a reference to the document defining the interface is required.

5.2.1.5 Communications interfaces

This should specify the various interfaces to communications such as local network protocols, etc.

5.2.1.6 Memory constraints

This should specify any applicable characteristics and limits on primary and secondary memory.

5.2.1.7 Operations

This should specify the normal and special operations required by the user such as

a) The various modes of operations in the user organization (e.g., user-initiated operations);
b) Periods of interactive operations and periods of unattended operations;
c) Data processing support functions;
d) Backup and recovery operations.

NOTE—This is sometimes specified as part of the User Interfaces section.

5.2.1.8 Site adaptation requirements

This should

a) Define the requirements for any data or initialization sequences that are specific to a given site, mission, or operational mode (e.g., grid values, safety limits, etc.);
b) Specify the site or mission-related features that should be modified to adapt the software to a particular installation.

5.2.2 Product functions (2.2 of the SRS)

This subsection of the SRS should provide a summary of the major functions that the software will perform. For example, an SRS for an accounting program may use this part to address customer account maintenance, customer statement, and invoice preparation without mentioning the vast amount of detail that each of those functions requires.

Sometimes the function summary that is necessary for this part can be taken directly from the section of the higher-level specification (if one exists) that allocates particular functions to the software product. Note that for the sake of clarity

a) The functions should be organized in a way that makes the list of functions understandable to the customer or to anyone else reading the document for the first time.
b) Textual or graphical methods can be used to show the different functions and their relationships. Such a diagram is not intended to show a design of a product, but simply shows the logical relationships among variables.

5.2.3 User characteristics (2.3 of the SRS)

This subsection of the SRS should describe those general characteristics of the intended users of the product including educational level, experience, and technical expertise. It should not be used to state specific requirements, but rather should provide the reasons why certain specific requirements are later specified in Section 3 of the SRS.

5.2.4 Constraints (2.4 of the SRS)

This subsection of the SRS should provide a general description of any other items that will limit the developer's options. These include

a) Regulatory policies;
b) Hardware limitations (e.g., signal timing requirements);
c) Interfaces to other applications;
d) Parallel operation;
e) Audit functions;
f) Control functions;
g) Higher-order language requirements;
h) Signal handshake protocols (e.g., XON-XOFF, ACK-NACK);
i) Reliability requirements;
j) Criticality of the application;
k) Safety and security considerations.

5.2.5 Assumptions and dependencies (2.5 of the SRS)

This subsection of the SRS should list each of the factors that affect the requirements stated in the SRS. These factors are not design constraints on the software but are, rather, any changes to them that can affect the requirements in the SRS. For example, an assumption may be that a specific operating system will be available on the hardware designated for the software product. If, in fact, the operating system is not available, the SRS would then have to change accordingly.

5.2.6 Apportioning of requirements (2.6 of the SRS)

This subsection of the SRS should identify requirements that may be delayed until future versions of the system.

5.3 Specific requirements (Section 3 of the SRS)

This section of the SRS should contain all of the software requirements to a level of detail sufficient to enable designers to design a system to satisfy those requirements, and testers to test that the system satisfies those requirements. Throughout this section, every stated requirement should be externally perceivable by users, operators, or other external systems. These requirements should include at a minimum a description of every input (stimulus) into the system, every output (response) from the system, and all functions performed by the system in response to an input or in support of an output. As this is often the largest and most important part of the SRS, the following principles apply:

a) Specific requirements should be stated in conformance with all the characteristics described in 4.3.
b) Specific requirements should be cross-referenced to earlier documents that relate.
c) All requirements should be uniquely identifiable.
d) Careful attention should be given to organizing the requirements to maximize readability.

Before examining specific ways of organizing the requirements it is helpful to understand the various items that comprise requirements as described in 5.3.1 through 5.3.7.

5.3.1 External interfaces

This should be a detailed description of all inputs into and outputs from the software system. It should complement the interface descriptions in 5.2 and should not repeat information there.

It should include both content and format as follows:

a) Name of item;
b) Description of purpose;
c) Source of input or destination of output;
d) Valid range, accuracy, and/or tolerance;
e) Units of measure;
f) Timing;
g) Relationships to other inputs/outputs;
h) Screen formats/organization;
i) Window formats/organization;
j) Data formats;
k) Command formats;
l) End messages.

5.3.2 Functions

Functional requirements should define the fundamental actions that must take place in the software in accepting and processing the inputs and in processing and generating the outputs. These are generally listed as "shall" statements starting with "The system shall…"

These include

a) Validity checks on the inputs
b) Exact sequence of operations
c) Responses to abnormal situations, including
    1) Overflow
    2) Communication facilities
    3) Error handling and recovery
d) Effect of parameters
e) Relationship of outputs to inputs, including
    1) Input/output sequences
    2) Formulas for input to output conversion

It may be appropriate to partition the functional requirements into subfunctions or subprocesses. This does not imply that the software design will also be partitioned that way.

5.3.3 Performance requirements

This subsection should specify both the static and the dynamic numerical requirements placed on the software or on human interaction with the software as a whole. Static numerical requirements may include the following:

a) The number of terminals to be supported;
b) The number of simultaneous users to be supported;
c) Amount and type of information to be handled.

Static numerical requirements are sometimes identified under a separate section entitled Capacity.

Dynamic numerical requirements may include, for example, the numbers of transactions and tasks and the amount of data to be processed within certain time periods for both normal and peak workload conditions.

All of these requirements should be stated in measurable terms.

For example,

> *95% of the transactions shall be processed in less than 1 s.*

rather than,

> *An operator shall not have to wait for the transaction to complete.*

NOTE—Numerical limits applied to one specific function are normally specified as part of the processing subparagraph description of that function.

5.3.4 Logical database requirements

This should specify the logical requirements for any information that is to be placed into a database. This may include the following:

a) Types of information used by various functions;
b) Frequency of use;
c) Accessing capabilities;
d) Data entities and their relationships;
e) Integrity constraints;
f) Data retention requirements.

5.3.5 Design constraints

This should specify design constraints that can be imposed by other standards, hardware limitations, etc.

5.3.5.1 Standards compliance

This subsection should specify the requirements derived from existing standards or regulations. They may include the following:

a) Report format;
b) Data naming;
c) Accounting procedures;
d) Audit tracing.

For example, this could specify the requirement for software to trace processing activity. Such traces are needed for some applications to meet minimum regulatory or financial standards. An audit trace requirement may, for example, state that all changes to a payroll database must be recorded in a trace file with before and after values.

5.3.6 Software system attributes

There are a number of attributes of software that can serve as requirements. It is important that required attributes be specified so that their achievement can be objectively verified. Subclauses 5.3.6.1 through 5.3.6.5 provide a partial list of examples.

5.3.6.1 Reliability

This should specify the factors required to establish the required reliability of the software system at time of delivery.

5.3.6.2 Availability

This should specify the factors required to guarantee a defined availability level for the entire system such as checkpoint, recovery, and restart.

5.3.6.3 Security

This should specify the factors that protect the software from accidental or malicious access, use, modification, destruction, or disclosure. Specific requirements in this area could include the need to

a) Utilize certain cryptographical techniques;
b) Keep specific log or history data sets;
c) Assign certain functions to different modules;
d) Restrict communications between some areas of the program;
e) Check data integrity for critical variables.

5.3.6.4 Maintainability

This should specify attributes of software that relate to the ease of maintenance of the software itself. There may be some requirement for certain modularity, interfaces, complexity, etc. Requirements should not be placed here just because they are thought to be good design practices.

5.3.6.5 Portability

This should specify attributes of software that relate to the ease of porting the software to other host machines and/or operating systems. This may include the following:

a) Percentage of components with host-dependent code;
b) Percentage of code that is host dependent;
c) Use of a proven portable language;
d) Use of a particular compiler or language subset;
e) Use of a particular operating system.

5.3.7 Organizing the specific requirements

For anything but trivial systems the detailed requirements tend to be extensive. For this reason, it is recommended that careful consideration be given to organizing these in a manner optimal for understanding. There is no one optimal organization for all systems. Different classes of systems lend themselves to different organizations of requirements in Section 3 of the SRS. Some of these organizations are described in 5.3.7.1 through 5.3.7.7.

5.3.7.1 System mode

Some systems behave quite differently depending on the mode of operation. For example, a control system may have different sets of functions depending on its mode: training, normal, or emergency. When organizing this section by mode, the outline in A.1 or A.2 should be used. The choice depends on whether interfaces and performance are dependent on mode.

5.3.7.2 User class

Some systems provide different sets of functions to different classes of users. For example, an elevator control system presents different capabilities to passengers, maintenance workers, and fire fighters. When organizing this section by user class, the outline in A.3 should be used.

5.3.7.3 Objects

Objects are real-world entities that have a counterpart within the system. For example, in a patient monitoring system, objects include patients, sensors, nurses, rooms, physicians, medicines, etc. Associated with each object is a set of attributes (of that object) and functions (performed by that object). These functions are also called services, methods, or processes. When organizing this section by object, the outline in A.4 should be used. Note that sets of objects may share attributes and services. These are grouped together as classes.

5.3.7.4 Feature

A feature is an externally desired service by the system that may require a sequence of inputs to effect the desired result. For example, in a telephone system, features include local call, call forwarding, and conference call. Each feature is generally described in a sequence of stimulus-response pairs. When organizing this section by feature, the outline in A.5 should be used.

5.3.7.5 Stimulus

Some systems can be best organized by describing their functions in terms of stimuli. For example, the functions of an automatic aircraft landing system may be organized into sections for loss of power, wind shear, sudden change in roll, vertical velocity excessive, etc. When organizing this section by stimulus, the outline in A.6 should be used.

5.3.7.6 Response

Some systems can be best organized by describing all the functions in support of the generation of a response. For example, the functions of a personnel system may be organized into sections corresponding to all functions associated with generating paychecks, all functions associated with generating a current list of employees, etc. The outline in A.6 (with all occurrences of stimulus replaced with response) should be used.

5.3.7.7 Functional hierarchy

When none of the above organizational schemes prove helpful, the overall functionality can be organized into a hierarchy of functions organized by either common inputs, common outputs, or common internal data access. Data flow diagrams and data dictionaries can be used to show the relationships between and among the functions and data. When organizing this section by functional hierarchy, the outline in A.7 should be used.

5.3.8 Additional comments

Whenever a new SRS is contemplated, more than one of the organizational techniques given in 5.3.7.7 may be appropriate. In such cases, organize the specific requirements for multiple hierarchies tailored to the specific needs of the system under specification. For example, see A.8 for an organization combining user class and feature. Any additional requirements may be put in a separate section at the end of the SRS.

There are many notations, methods, and automated support tools available to aid in the documentation of requirements. For the most part, their usefulness is a function of organization. For example, when organizing by mode, finite state machines or state charts may prove helpful; when organizing by object, object-oriented analysis may prove helpful; when organizing by feature, stimulus-response sequences may prove helpful; and when organizing by functional hierarchy, data flow diagrams and data dictionaries may prove helpful.

In any of the outlines given in A.1 through A.8, those sections called "Functional Requirement i" may be described in native language (e.g., English), in pseudocode, in a system definition language, or in four subsections titled: Introduction, Inputs, Processing, and Outputs.

5.4 Supporting information

The supporting information makes the SRS easier to use. It includes the following:

a) Table of contents;
b) Index;
c) Appendixes.

5.4.1 Table of contents and index

The table of contents and index are quite important and should follow general compositional practices.

5.4.2 Appendixes

The appendixes are not always considered part of the actual SRS and are not always necessary. They may include

a) Sample input/output formats, descriptions of cost analysis studies, or results of user surveys;
b) Supporting or background information that can help the readers of the SRS;
c) A description of the problems to be solved by the software;
d) Special packaging instructions for the code and the media to meet security, export, initial loading, or other requirements.

When appendixes are included, the SRS should explicitly state whether or not the appendixes are to be considered part of the requirements.

Annex A

(informative)

SRS templates

A.1 Template of SRS Section 3 organized by mode: Version 1

```
3. Specific requirements
3.1      External interface requirements
         3.1.1    User interfaces
         3.1.2    Hardware interfaces
         3.1.3    Software interfaces
         3.1.4    Communications interfaces
3.2      Functional requirements
         3.2.1    Mode 1
                  3.2.1.1  Functional requirement 1.1
                  .
                  .
                  .
                  3.2.1.n  Functional requirement 1.n
         3.2.2    Mode 2
         .
         .
         .
         3.2.m    Mode m
                  3.2.m.1  Functional requirement m.1
                  .
                  .
                  .
                  3.2.m.n  Functional requirement m.n
3.3      Performance requirements
3.4      Design constraints
3.5      Software system attributes
3.6      Other requirements
```

A.2 Template of SRS Section 3 organized by mode: Version 2

```
3. Specific requirements
3.1. Functional requirements
         3.1.1    Mode 1
                  3.1.1.1  External interfaces
                           3.1.1.1.1  User interfaces
                           3.1.1.1.2  Hardware interfaces
                           3.1.1.1.3  Software interfaces
                           3.1.1.1.4  Communications interfaces
                  3.1.1.2  Functional requirements
                           3.1.1.2.1  Functional requirement 1
                  .
                  .
                  .
```

             3.1.1.2.*n* Functional requirement *n*

             3.1.1.3   Performance

     3.1.2   Mode 2

       .

       .

       .

     3.1.*m*   Mode *m*

3.2   Design constraints

3.3   Software system attributes

3.4   Other requirements

A.3 Template of SRS Section 3 organized by user class

3. Specific requirements

3.1   External interface requirements

     3.1.1   User interfaces

     3.1.2   Hardware interfaces

     3.1.3   Software interfaces

     3.1.4   Communications interfaces

3.2   Functional requirements

     3.2.1   User class 1

             3.2.1.1   Functional requirement 1.1

             .

             .

             .

             3.2.1.*n*   Functional requirement 1.*n*

     3.2.2   User class 2

       .

       .

       .

     3.2.*m*   User class *m*

             3.2.*m*.1 Functional requirement *m*.1

             .

             .

             .

             3.2.*m*.*n* Functional requirement *m.n*

3.3   Performance requirements

3.4   Design constraints

3.5   Software system attributes

3.6   Other requirements

A.4 Template of SRS Section 3 organized by object

3. Specific requirements

3.1   External interface requirements

     3.1.1   User interfaces

     3.1.2   Hardware interfaces

     3.1.3   Software interfaces

     3.1.4   Communications interfaces

3.2   Classes/Objects

     3.2.1   Class/Object 1

     3.2.1.1 Attributes (direct or inherited)
       3.2.1.1.1 Attribute 1

        .

        .

        .

       3.2.1.1.n Attribute n
     3.2.1.2 Functions (services, methods, direct or inherited)
       3.2.1.2.1 Functional requirement 1.1

        .

        .

        .

       3.2.1.2.m Functional requirement 1.m
     3.2.1.3 Messages (communications received or sent)
   3.2.2 Class/Object 2

    .

    .

    .

   3.2.p Class/Object p
3.3 Performance requirements
3.4 Design constraints
3.5 Software system attributes
3.6 Other requirements

A.5 Template of SRS Section 3 organized by feature

3. Specific requirements
3.1 External interface requirements
   3.1.1 User interfaces
   3.1.2 Hardware interfaces
   3.1.3 Software interfaces
   3.1.4 Communications interfaces
3.2 System features
   3.2.1 System Feature 1
     3.2.1.1 Introduction/Purpose of feature
     3.2.1.2 Stimulus/Response sequence
     3.2.1.3 Associated functional requirements
       3.2.1.3.1 Functional requirement 1

        .

        .

        .

       3.2.1.3.n Functional requirement n
   3.2.2 System feature 2

    .

    .

    .

   3.2.m System feature m

    .

    .

    .

3.3 Performance requirements
3.4 Design constraints
3.5 Software system attributes
3.6 Other requirements

A.6 Template of SRS Section 3 organized by stimulus

3. Specific requirements
3.1   External interface requirements
      3.1.1   User interfaces
      3.1.2   Hardware interfaces
      3.1.3   Software interfaces
      3.1.4   Communications interfaces
3.2   Functional requirements
      3.2.1   Stimulus 1
            3.2.1.1   Functional requirement 1.1
            .
            .
            .
            $3.2.1.n$ Functional requirement $1.n$
      3.2.2   Stimulus 2
      .
      .
      .
      $3.2.m$ Stimulus m
            $3.2.m.1$ Functional requirement $m.1$
            .
            .
            .
            $3.2.m.n$ Functional requirement $m.n$
3.3   Performance requirements
3.4   Design constraints
3.5   Software system attributes
3.6   Other requirements

A.7 Template of SRS Section 3 organized by functional hierarchy

3. Specific requirements
3.1   External interface requirements
      3.1.1   User interfaces
      3.1.2   Hardware interfaces
      3.1.3   Software interfaces
      3.1.4   Communications interfaces
3.2   Functional requirements
      3.2.1   Information flows
            3.2.1.1   Data flow diagram 1
                 3.2.1.1.1 Data entities
                 3.2.1.1.2 Pertinent processes
                 3.2.1.1.3 Topology
            3.2.1.2   Data flow diagram 2
                 3.2.1.2.1 Data entities
                 3.2.1.2.2 Pertinent processes
                 3.2.1.2.3 Topology
            .
           .
           .
           $3.2.1.n$ Data flow diagram n

3.3   Performance requirements
3.4   Design constraints
3.5   Software system attributes
3.6   Other requirements

A.8 Template of SRS Section 3 showing multiple organizations

3. Specific requirements
3.1   External interface requirements
       3.1.1   User interfaces
       3.1.2   Hardware interfaces
       3.1.3   Software interfaces
       3.1.4   Communications interfaces
3.2   Functional requirements
       3.2.1   User class 1
             3.2.1.1   Feature 1.1
                   3.2.1.1.1 Introduction/Purpose of feature
                   3.2.1.1.2 Stimulus/Response sequence
                   3.2.1.1.3 Associated functional requirements
             3.2.1.2   Feature 1.2
                   3.2.1.2.1 Introduction/Purpose of feature
                   3.2.1.2.2 Stimulus/Response sequence
                   3.2.1.2.3 Associated functional requirements

           .
           .
           .

             3.2.1.*m* Feature 1.*m*
                   3.2.1.*m*.1 Introduction/Purpose of feature
                   3.2.1.*m*.2 Stimulus/Response sequence
                     3.2.1.*m*.3 Associated functional requirements
       3.2.2   User class 2

        .
        .
        .

       3.2.*n*   User class *n*

        .
        .
        .

3.3   Performance requirements
3.4   Design constraints
3.5   Software system attributes
3.6   Other requirements

Annex B

(informative)

Guidelines for compliance with IEEE/EIA 12207.1-1997

B.1 Overview

The Software Engineering Standards Committee (SESC) of the IEEE Computer Society has endorsed the policy of adopting international standards. In 1995, the international standard, ISO/IEC 12207, Information technology—Software life cycle processes, was completed. The standard establishes a common framework for software life cycle processes, with well-defined terminology, that can be referenced by the software industry.

In 1995 the SESC evaluated ISO/IEC 12207 and decided that the standard should be adopted and serve as the basis for life cycle processes within the IEEE Software Engineering Collection. The IEEE adaptation of ISO/IEC 12207 is IEEE/EIA 12207.0-1996. It contains ISO/IEC 12207 and the following additions: improved compliance approach, life cycle process objectives, life cycle data objectives, and errata.

The implementation of ISO/IEC 12207 within the IEEE also includes the following:

— IEEE/EIA 12207.1-1997, IEEE/EIA Guide for Information Technology—Software life cycle processes—Life cycle data;

— IEEE/EIA 12207.2-1997, IEEE/EIA Guide for Information Technology—Software life cycle processes—Implementation considerations; and

— Additions to 11 SESC standards (i.e., IEEE Stds 730, 828, 829, 830, 1012, 1016, 1058, 1062, 1219, 1233, 1362) to define the correlation between the data produced by existing SESC standards and the data produced by the application of IEEE/EIA 12207.1-1997.

NOTE—Although IEEE/EIA 12207.1-1997 is a guide, it also contains provisions for application as a standard with specific compliance requirements. This annex treats 12207.1-1997 as a standard.

B.1.1 Scope and purpose

Both IEEE Std 830-1998 and IEEE/EIA 12207.1-1997 place requirements on a Software Requirements Description Document. The purpose of this annex is to explain the relationship between the two sets of requirements so that users producing documents intended to comply with both standards may do so.

B.2 Correlation

This clause explains the relationship between IEEE Std 830-1998 and IEEE/EIA 12207.0-1996 and IEEE/EIA 12207.1-1997 in the following areas: terminology, process, and life cycle data.

B.2.1 Terminology correlation

Both this recommended practice and IEEE/EIA 12207.0-1996 have similar semantics for the key terms of software, requirements, specification, supplier, developer, and maintainer. This recommended practice uses the term "customer" where IEEE/EIA 12207.0-1996 uses "acquirer," and this recommended practice uses "user" where IEEE/EIA 12207.0-1996 uses "operator."

B.2.2 Process correlation

IEEE/EIA 12207.0-1996 uses a process-oriented approach for describing the definition of a set of requirements for software. This recommended practice uses a product-oriented approach, where the product is a Software Requirements Description (SRD). There are natural process steps, namely the steps to create each portion of the SRD. These may be correlated with the process requirements of IEEE/EIA 12207.0-1996. The difference is that this recommended practice is focused on the development of software requirements whereas IEEE/EIA 12207.0-1996 provides an overall life cycle view and mentions Software Requirements Analysis as part of its Development Process. This recommended practice provides a greater level of detail on what is involved in the preparation of an SRD.

B.2.3 Life cycle data correlation

IEEE/EIA 12207.0-1996 takes the viewpoint that the software requirements are derived from the system requirements. Therefore, it uses the term, "description" rather that "specification" to describe the software requirements. In a system in which software is a component, each requiring its own specification, there would be a System Requirements Specification (SRS) and one or more SRDs. If the term Software Requirements Specification had been used, there would be a confusion between an SRS referring to the system or software requirements. In the case where there is a stand-alone software system, IEEE/EIA 12207.1-1997 states "If the software is a stand-alone system, then this document should be a specification."

B.3 Content mapping

This clause provides details bearing on a claim that an SRS complying with this recommended practice would also achieve "document compliance" with the SRD described in IEEE/EIA 12207.1-1997. The requirements for document compliance are summarized in a single row of Table 1 of IEEE/EIA 12207.1-1997. That row is reproduced in Table B.1 of this recommended practice.

Table B.1—Summary of requirements for an SRD excerpted from Table 1 of IEEE/EIA 12207.1-1997

Information item	IEEE/EIA 12207.0-1996 Clause	Kind	IEEE/EIA 12207.1-1997 Clause	References
Software Requirements Description	5.1.1.4, 5.3.4.1, 5.3.4.2	Description (See note for 6.22.1 of IEEE/EIA 12207.1-1997.)	6.22	IEEE Std 830-1998; EIA/IEEE J-STD-016, F.2.3, F.2.4; MIL-STD 961D. Also see ISO/IEC 5806, 5807, 6593, 8631, 8790, and 11411 for guidance on use of notations.

The requirements for document compliance are discussed in the following subclauses:

— B.3.1 discusses compliance with the information requirements noted in column 2 of Table B.1 as prescribed by 5.1.1.4, 5.3.4.1, and 5.3.4.2 of IEEE/EIA 12207.0-1996.

— B.3.2 discusses compliance with the generic content guideline (the "kind" of document) noted in column 3 of Table B.1 as a "description". The generic content guidelines for a "description" appear in 5.1 of IEEE/EIA 12207.1-1997.

— B.3.3 discusses compliance with the specific requirements for a Software Requirements Description noted in column 4 of Table B.1 as prescribed by 6.22 of IEEE/EIA 12207.1-1997.

— B.3.4 discusses compliance with the life cycle data objectives of Annex H of IEEE/EIA 12207.0-1996 as described in 4.2 of IEEE/EIA 12207.1-1997.

B.3.1 Compliance with information requirements of IEEE/EIA 12207.0-1996

The information requirements for an SRD are those prescribed by 5.1.1.4, 5.3.4.1, and 5.3.4.2 of IEEE/EIA 12207.0-1996. The requirements are substantively identical to those considered in B.3.3 of this recommended practice.

B.3.2 Compliance with generic content guidelines of IEEE/EIA 12207.1-1997

According to IEEE/EIA 12207.1-1997, the generic content guideline for an SRD is generally a description, as prescribed by 5.1 of IEEE/EIA 12207.1-1997. A complying description shall achieve the purpose stated in 5.1.1 and include the information listed in 5.1.2 of IEEE/EIA 12207.1-1997.

The purpose of a description is:

IEEE/EIA 12207.1-1997, subclause 5.1.1: Purpose: Describe a planned or actual function, design, performance, or process.

An SRD complying with this recommended practice would achieve the stated purpose.

Any description or specification complying with IEEE/EIA 12207.1-1997 shall satisfy the generic content requirements provided in 5.1.2 of that standard. Table B.2 of this recommended practice lists the generic content items and, where appropriate, references the clause of this recommended practice that requires the same information.

Table B.2—Coverage of generic description requirements by IEEE Std 830-1998

IEEE/EIA 12207.1-1997 generic content	Corresponding clauses of IEEE Std 830-1998	Additions to requirements of IEEE Std 830-1998
a) Date of issue and status	—	Date of issue and status shall be provided.
b) Scope	5.1.1 Scope	—
c) Issuing organization	—	Issuing organization shall be identified.
d) References	5.1.4 References	—
e) Context	5.1.2 Scope	—
f) Notation for description	4.3 Characteristics of a good SRS	—
g) Body	5. The parts of an SRS	—
h) Summary	5.1.1. Overview	—
i) Glossary	5.1.3 Definitions	—
j) Change history	—	Change history for the SRD shall be provided or referenced.

B.3.3 Compliance with specific content requirements of IEEE/EIA 12207.1-1997

The specific content requirements for an SRD in IEEE/EIA 12207.1-1997 are prescribed by 6.22 of IEEE/EIA 12207.1-1997. A compliant SRD shall achieve the purpose stated in 6.22.1 of IEEE/EIA 12207.1-1997.

The purpose of the SRD is:

> IEEE/EIA 12207.1-1997, subclause 6.22.1: Purpose: Specify the requirements for a software item and the methods to be used to ensure that each requirement has been met. Used as the basis for design and qualification testing of a software item.

An SRS complying with this recommended practice and meeting the additional requirements of Table B.3 of this recommended practice would achieve the stated purpose.

An SRD compliant with IEEE/EIA 12207.1-1997 shall satisfy the specific content requirements provided in 6.22.3 and 6.22.4 of that standard. Table B.3 of this recommended practice lists the specific content items and, where appropriate, references the clause of this recommended practice that requires the same information.

An SRD specified according the requirements stated or referenced in Table B.3 of this recommended practice shall be evaluated considering the criteria provided in 5.3.4.2 of IEEE/EIA 12207.0-1996.

Table B.3—Coverage of specific SRD requirements by IEEE Std 830-1998

IEEE/EIA 12207.1-1997 specific content	Corresponding clauses of IEEE Std 830-1998	Additions to requirements of IEEE Std 830-1998
a) Generic description information	See Table B.2	—
b) System identification and overview	5.1.1 Scope	—
c) Functionality of the software item including: – Performance requirements – Physical characteristics – Environmental conditions	5.3.2 Functions 5.3.3 Performance requirements	Physical characteristics and environmental conditions should be provided.
d) Requirements for interfaces external to software item	5.3.1 External interfaces	—
e) Qualification requirements	—	The requirements to be used for qualification testing should be provided (or referenced).
f) Safety specifications	5.2.4 Constraints	—
g) Security and privacy specifications	5.3.6.3 Security	—
h) Human-factors engineering requirements	5.2.3 User characteristics 5.2.1.2 User interfaces	—
i) Data definition and database requirements	5.3.4 Logical data base requirements	—
j) Installation and acceptance requirements at operation site	5.2.1.8 Site adaptation requirements	Installation and acceptance requirements at operation site
k) Installation and acceptance requirements at maintenance site	—	Installation and acceptance requirements at maintenance site
l) User documentation requirements	—	User documentation requirements
m) User operation and execution requirements	5.2.1.7 Operations	User execution requirements

Table B.3—Coverage of specific SRD requirements by IEEE Std 830-1998 (continued)

IEEE/EIA 12207.1-1997 specific content	Corresponding clauses of IEEE Std 830-1998	Additions to requirements of IEEE Std 830-1998
n) User maintenance requirements	5.3.6.4 Maintainability	—
o) Software quality characteristics	5.3.6 Software system attributes	—
p) Design and implementation constraints	5.2.4 Constraints	—
q) Computer resource requirements	5.3.3 Performance requirements	Computer resource requirements
r) Packaging requirements	—	Packaging requirements
s) Precedence and criticality of requirements	5.2.6 Apportioning of requirements	—
t) Requirements traceability	4.3.8 Traceable	—
u) Rationale	5.2.5 Assumptions and dependencies	—
Items a) through f) below are from 6.22.4 a) Support the life cycle data objectives of Annex H of IEEE/EIA 12207.0-1996	—	Support the life cycle data objectives of Annex H of IEEE/EIA 12207.0-1996
b) Describe any function using well-defined notation	4.3 Characteristics of a good SRS	—
c) Define no requirements that are in conflict	4.3 Characteristics of a good SRS	—
d) User standard terminology and definitions	5.1.3 Definition	—
e) Define each unique requirement one to prevent inconsistency	4.3 Characteristics of a good SRS	—
f) Uniquely identify each requirement	4.3 Characteristics of a good SRS	—

B.3.4 Compliance with life cycle data objectives

In addition to the content requirements, life cycle data shall be managed in accordance with the objectives provided in Annex H of IEEE/EIA 12207.0-1996.

B.4 Conclusion

The analysis suggests that any SRS complying with this recommended practice and the additions shown in Table B.2 and Table B.3 also complies with the requirements of an SRD in IEEE/EIA 12207.1-1997. In addition, to comply with IEEE/EIA 12207.1-1997, an SRS shall support the life cycle data objectives of Annex H of IEEE/EIA 12207.0-1996.

To order IEEE standards...

Call 1. 800. 678. IEEE (4333) in the US and Canada.

Outside of the US and Canada:
1. 732. 981. 0600

To order by fax:
1. 732. 981. 9667

IEEE business hours: 8 a.m.–4:30 p.m. (EST)

For on-line access to IEEE standards information...

Via the World Wide Web:
http://standards.ieee.org/

Via ftp:
stdsbbs.ieee.org

ISBN 0-7381-0332-2

IEEE Std 1233, 1998 Edition
(Includes IEEE Std 1233-1996
and IEEE Std 1233a-1998)

IEEE Guide for Developing System Requirements Specifications

Sponsor

**Software Engineering Standards Committee
of the
IEEE Computer Society**

IEEE Std 1233-1996 Approved 17 April 1996
IEEE Std 1233a-1998 Approved 8 December 1998
by the

IEEE-SA Standards Board

Abstract: Guidance for the development of the set of requirements, System Requirements Specification (SyRS), that will satisfy an expressed need is provided. Developing an SyRS includes the identification, organization, presentation, and modification of the requirements. Also addressed are the conditions for incorporating operational concepts, design constraints, and design configuration requirements into the specification. This guide also covers the necessary characteristics and qualities of individual requirements and the set of all requirements.
Keywords: requirement, SyRS, system, system requirements specification

The Institute of Electrical and Electronics Engineers, Inc.
345 East 47th Street, New York, NY 10017-2394, USA

Copyright © 1998 by the Institute of Electrical and Electronics Engineers, Inc.
All rights reserved. Published 22 December 1998. Printed in the United States of America.

Print: ISBN 0-7381-0337-3 SH94659
PDF: ISBN 0-7381-1515-0 SS94659

Introduction

(This introduction is not a part of IEEE Std 1233, 1998 Edition, IEEE Guide for Developing System Requirements Specifications.)

The purpose of this guide is to provide guidance for capturing system requirements. This guide serves the analyst by providing a clear definition for identifying well-formed requirements and ways of organizing them.

This guide should be used to help the analyst capture requirements at the beginning of the system requirements phase. It should be used to clarify what constitutes a good requirement and provide an understanding of where to look to identify different requirement sources.

The readers of this guide are referred to Annex C for guidelines for using this guide to meet the requirements of IEEE/EIA 12207.1-1997, IEEE/EIA Guide for Information Technology—Software life cycle processes—Life cycle data.

Participants

IEEE Std 1233-1996 was prepared by a working group chartered by the Software Engineering Committee of the IEEE Computer Society. At the time it was approved, the working group consisted of the following members:

Louis E. Miller, *Chair* **William N. Sabor,** *Secretary*

Bakul Banerjee	P. Michael Guba	Jim Longbucco
David Byrch	James R. Hughes	Donald F. Parsons
Kim A. Cady	Joe Iaquinto	Eric Peterson
Larry Diehr	Marybeth A. Jupina	John Sheckler
Charles A. Droz	Thomas M. Kurihara	Jess Thompson
Larry C. Forrest	Richard C. Lee	Eva D. Williams

Other contributors included

Geoff Cozens	Kristin Dittmann	Virginia Nuckolls
Paul Davis	Christof Ebert	Anne O'Neill
	Don McCash	

The following persons balloted IEEE Std 1233-1996:

H. Ronald Berlack	Eitan Froumine	J. Dennis Lawrence
Mark Bilger	Yair Gershkovitch	Ben Livson
William J. Boll	Adel N. Ghannam	Harold Mains
Fletcher Buckley	Julio Gonzalez-Sanz	Roger Martin
Edward R. Byrne	Patrick J. Griffin	James W. McClean
François Coallier	David A. Gustavson	Sue McGrath
Christopher Cooke	John Harauz	Louis E. Miller
Geoff Cozens	Derek J. Hatley	Dennis E. Nickle
Alan M. Davis	William Hefley	Indradeb P. Pal
Robert E. Dwyer	Umesh P. Hiriyannaiah	Joseph A. Palermo
Sherman Eagles	Jody Howard	Stephen R. Schach
Leo G. Egan	Eiichi Kaneko	Norman Schneidewind
Caroline L. Evans	Jerry Kickenson	Wolf A. Schnoege
Richard L. Evans	Janet Kintner	Gregory D. Schumacher
John W. Fendrich	Thomas M. Kurihara	Carl S. Seddio
Peter Fillery	Renee Lamb	David M. Siefert
Larry Forrest	John B. Lane	Richard S. Sky
Eugene P. Friedman	Boniface Lau	Alfred R. Sorkowitz

Robert N. Sulgrove	Leonard L. Tripp	Dolores Wallace
Tanehiro Tatsuta	Tom Vaiskunas	William M. Walsh
Richard H. Thayer	Thomas E. Vollman	Paul R. Work
George D. Tice	Ronald L. Wade	Janusz Zalewski

IEEE Std 1233a-1998 was prepared by the Life Cycle Data Harmonization Working Group of the Software Engineering Standards Committee of the IEEE Computer Society. At the time it was approved, the working group consisted of the following members:

Leonard L. Tripp, *Chair*

Edward Byrne	Dennis Lawrence	Terry Rout
Paul R. Croll	David Maibor	Richard Schmidt
Perry DeWeese	Ray Milovanovic	Norman F. Schneidewind
Robin Fralick	James Moore	David Schultz
Marilyn Ginsberg-Finner	Timothy Niesen	Basil Sherlund
John Harauz	Dennis Rilling	Peter Voldner
Mark Henley		Ronald Wade

The following persons balloted IEEE Std 1233a-1998:

Syed Ali	Julio Gonzalez-Sanz	Lawrence S. Przybylski
Robert E. Barry	L. M. Gunther	Kenneth R. Ptack
Leo Beltracchi	David A. Gustafson	Annette D. Reilly
H. Ronald Berlack	Jon D. Hagar	Dennis Rilling
Richard E. Biehl	John Harauz	Helmut Sandmayr
Michael A. Blackledge	Herbert Hecht	Stephen R. Schach
Sandro Bologna	William Hefley	Norman Schneidewind
Kathleen L. Briggs	Mark Heinrich	David J. Schultz
M. Scott Buck	Debra Herrmann	Lisa A. Selmon
Michael Caldwell	John W. Horch	Robert W. Shillato
James E. Cardow	Jerry Huller	David M. Siefert
Enrico A. Carrara	Peter L. Hung	Carl A. Singer
Antonio M. Cicu	George Jackelen	Richard S. Sky
Theo Clarke	Frank V. Jorgensen	Alfred R. Sorkowitz
Sylvain Clermont	Vladan V. Jovanovic	Donald W. Sova
Rosemary Coleman	William S. Junk	Luca Spotorno
Virgil Lee Cooper	George X. Kambic	Julia Stesney
W. W. Geoff Cozens	Ron S. Kenett	Fred J. Strauss
Paul R. Croll	Judith S. Kerner	Toru Takeshita
Gregory T. Daich	Robert J. Kierzyk	Richard H. Thayer
Geoffrey Darnton	Thomas M. Kurihara	Booker Thomas
Taz Daughtrey	John B. Lane	Patricia Trellue
Bostjan K. Derganc	J. Dennis Lawrence	Leonard L. Tripp
Perry R. DeWeese	Randal Leavitt	Theodore J. Urbanowicz
Evelyn S. Dow	Fang Ching Lim	Glenn D. Venables
Carl Einar Dragstedt	John Lord	Udo Voges
Sherman Eagles	Stan Magee	David D. Walden
Christof Ebert	Harold Mains	Dolores Wallace
Leo Egan	Robert A. Martin	William M. Walsh
Richard E. Fairley	Tomoo Matsubara	John W. Walz
John W. Fendrich	Patrick D. McCray	Scott A. Whitmire
Jay Forster	Bret Michael	P. A. Wolfgang
Kirby Fortenberry	Alan Miller	Paul R. Work
Eva Freund	James W. Moore	Natalie C. Yopconka
Barry L. Garner	Pavol Navrat	Janusz Zalewski
Marilyn Ginsberg-Finner	Alex Polack	Geraldine Zimmerman
John Garth Glynn	Peter T. Poon	Peter F. Zoll

When the IEEE-SA Standards Board approved IEEE Std 1233a-1998 on 8 December 1998, it had the following membership:

Richard J. Holleman, *Chair*   **Donald N. Heirman,** *Vice Chair*

Judith Gorman, *Secretary*

Satish K. Aggarwal	James H. Gurney	L. Bruce McClung
Clyde R. Camp	Jim D. Isaak	Louis-François Pau
James T. Carlo	Lowell G. Johnson	Ronald C. Petersen
Gary R. Engmann	Robert Kennelly	Gerald H. Peterson
Harold E. Epstein	E. G. "Al" Kiener	John B. Posey
Jay Forster*	Joseph L. Koepfinger*	Gary S. Robinson
Thomas F. Garrity	Stephen R. Lambert	Hans E. Weinrich
Ruben D. Garzon	Jim Logothetis	Donald W. Zipse
	Donald C. Loughry	

*Member Emeritus

Valerie E. Zelenty
IEEE Standards Project Editor

Contents

IEEE Guide for Developing System Requirements Specifications

1. Overview

1.1 Scope

This guide provides guidance for the development of a set of requirements that, when realized, will satisfy an expressed need. In this guide that set of requirements will be called the System Requirements Specification (SyRS). Developing an SyRS includes the identification, organization, presentation, and modification of the requirements. This guide addresses conditions for incorporating operational concepts, design constraints, and design configuration requirements into the specification. This guide also addresses the necessary characteristics and qualities of individual requirements and the set of all requirements.

This guide does not specify industry-wide system specification standards nor state a mandatory System Requirements Specification. This guide is written under the premise that the current state of the art of system development does not warrant or support a formal standards document.

2. References

This guide shall be used in conjunction with the following publications:

IEEE Std 100-1996, IEEE Standard Dictionary of Electrical and Electronics Terms.[1]

IEEE Std 610.12-1990, IEEE Standard Glossary of Software Engineering Terminology.

IEEE Std 730-1998, IEEE Standard for Software Quality Assurance Plans.

IEEE Std 828-1998, IEEE Standard for Software Configuration Management Plans.

IEEE Std 830-1998, IEEE Recommended Practice for Software Requirements Specifications.

IEEE Std 1074-1997, IEEE Standard for Developing Software Life Cycle Processes.

---

[1]IEEE publications are available from the Institute of Electrical and Electronics Engineers, 445 Hoes Lane, P.O. Box 1331, Piscataway, NJ 08855-1331, USA (http://www.standards.ieee.org/).

IEEE Std 1220-1998, IEEE Standard for Application and Management of the Systems Engineering Process.

ISO 9000-1: 1994, Quality management and quality assurance standards—Part 1: Guidelines for selection and use.[2]

ISO 9126: 1991, Information technology—Software product evaluation—Quality characteristics and guidelines for their use.

MIL-STD-490A, Specification Practices.[3]

MIL-STD-498, Software Development and Documentation.

3. Definitions

The definitions listed below establish meaning in the context of this guide. Terms not defined in this guide are included in IEEE Std 610.12-1990.[4]

3.1 analyst: A member of the technical community (such as a systems engineer or business analyst, developing the system requirements) who is skilled and trained to define problems and to analyze, develop, and express algorithms.

3.2 annotation: Further documentation accompanying a requirement such as background information and/or descriptive material.

3.3 baseline: A specification or system that has been formally reviewed and agreed upon, that thereafter serves as the basis for further development and can be changed only through formal change control procedures. (IEEE Std 610.12-1990)

3.4 constraint: A statement that expresses measurable bounds for an element or function of the system. That is, a constraint is a factor that is imposed on the solution by force or compulsion and may limit or modify the design changes.

3.5 customer(s): The entity or entities for whom the requirements are to be satisfied in the system being defined and developed. This can be an end-user of the completed system, an organization within the same company as the developing organization (e.g., System Management), a company or entity external to the developing company, or some combination of all of these. This is the entity to whom the system developer must provide proof that the system developed satisfies the system requirements specified.

3.6 derived requirement: A requirement deduced or inferred from the collection and organization of requirements into a particular system configuration and solution.

3.7 element: A component of a system; may include equipment, a computer program, or a human.

3.8 end user: The person or persons who will ultimately be using the system for its intended purpose.

[2]ISO publications are available from the ISO Central Secretariat, Case Postale 56, 1 rue de Varembé, CH-1211, Genève 20, Switzerland/Suisse (http://www.iso.ch/). ISO publications are also available in the United States from the Sales Department, American National Standards Institute, 11 West 42nd Street, 13th Floor, New York, NY 10036, USA (http://www.ansi.org/).
[3]MIL publications are available from Customer Service, Defense Printing Service, 700 Robbins Ave., Bldg. 4D, Philadelphia, PA 19111-5094, USA.
[4]Information on references can be found in Clause 2.

3.9 environment: The circumstances, objects, and conditions that will influence the completed system; they include political, market, cultural, organizational, and physical influences as well as standards and policies that govern what the system must do or how it must do it.

3.10 function: A task, action, or activity that must be accomplished to achieve a desired outcome.

3.11 model: A representation of a real world process, device, or concept.

3.12 prototype: An experimental model, either functional or nonfunctional, of the system or part of the system. A prototype is used to get feedback from users for improving and specifying a complex human interface, for feasibility studies, or for identifying requirements.

3.13 raw requirement: An environmental or customer requirement that has not been analyzed and formulated as a well-formed requirement.

3.14 representation: A likeness, picture, drawing, block diagram, description, or symbol that logically portrays a physical, operational, or conceptual image or situation.

3.15 requirement: (A) A condition or capability needed by a user to solve a problem or achieve an objective. **(B)** A condition or capability that must be met or possessed by a system or system component to satisfy a contract, standard, specification, or other formally imposed document. **(C)** A documented representation of a condition or capability as in definition (A) or (B). (IEEE Std 610.12-1990)

3.16 system: An interdependent group of people, objects, and procedures constituted to achieve defined objectives or some operational role by performing specified functions. A complete system includes all of the associated equipment, facilities, material, computer programs, firmware, technical documentation, services, and personnel required for operations and support to the degree necessary for self-sufficient use in its intended environment.

3.17 System Requirements Specification (SyRS): A structured collection of information that embodies the requirements of the system.

3.18 testability: The degree to which a requirement is stated in terms that permit establishment of test criteria and performance of tests to determine whether those criteria have been met. (IEEE Std 610.12-1990)

3.19 traceability: The degree to which a relationship can be established between two or more products of the development process, especially products having a predecessor-successor or master-subordinate relationship to one another; e.g., the degree to which the requirements and design of a given system element match. (IEEE Std 610.12-1990)

3.20 validation: The process of evaluating a system or component during or at the end of the development process to determine whether a system or component satisfies specified requirements. (IEEE Std 610.12-1990)

3.21 verification: The process of evaluating a system or component to determine whether the system of a given development phase satisfies the conditions imposed at the start of that phase. (IEEE Std 610.12-1990)

3.22 well-formed requirement: A statement of system functionality (a capability) that can be validated, and that must be met or possessed by a system to solve a customer problem or to achieve a customer objective, and is qualified by measurable conditions and bounded by constraints.

4. System requirements specification

A System Requirements Specification (SyRS) has traditionally been viewed as a document that communicates the requirements of the customer to the technical community who will specify and build the system. The collection of requirements that constitutes the specification and its representation acts as the bridge between the two groups and must be understandable by both the customer and the technical community. One of the most difficult tasks in the creation of a system is that of communicating to all of the subgroups within both groups, especially in one document. This type of communication generally requires different formalisms and languages.

4.1 Definition

The SyRS presents the results of the definition of need, the operational concept, and the system analysis tasks. As such, it is a description of what the system's customers expect it to do for them, the system's expected environment, the system's usage profile, its performance parameters, and its expected quality and effectiveness. Thus it presents the conclusions of the SyRS development process described in Clause 5.

This guide suggests a distinction between this structured collection of information and the way in which it is presented to its various audiences. The presentation of the SyRS should take a form that is appropriate for its intended use. This can be a paper document, models, prototypes, other non-paper document representations, or any combination. All of these representations can be derived from this one SyRS to meet the needs of a specific audience. However, care should be taken to ensure that each of these presentations is traceable to a common source of system requirements information. The audience should be made aware that this structured collection of information remains the one definitive source for resolving ambiguities in the particular presentation chosen.

This guide makes a clear distinction between the system requirements (what the system must do) contained in the SyRS and process requirements (how to construct the system) that should be contained in contract documents such as a Statement of Work.

4.2 Properties

The collection of requirements should have the following properties:

a) *Unique set.* Each requirement should be stated only once.

b) *Normalized.* Requirements should not overlap (i.e, they shall not refer to other requirements or the capabilities of other requirements).

c) *Linked set.* Explicit relationships should be defined among individual requirements to show how the requirements are related to form a complete system.

d) *Complete.* An SyRS should include all the requirements identified by the customer, as well as those needed for the definition of the system.

e) *Consistent.* SyRS content should be consistent and noncontradictory in the level of detail, style of requirement statements, and in the presentation of material.

f) *Bounded.* The boundaries, scope, and context for the set of requirements should be identified.

g) *Modifiable.* The SyRS should be modifiable. Clarity and nonoverlapping requirements contribute to this.

h) *Configurable.* Versions should be maintained across time and across instances of the SyRS.

i) *Granular.* This should be the level of abstraction for the system being defined.

4.3 Purpose

The purpose of the SyRS is to provide a "black-box" description of what the system should do, in terms of the system's interactions or interfaces with its external environment. The SyRS should completely describe all inputs, outputs, and required relationships between inputs and outputs. The SyRS organizes and communicates requirements to the customer and the technical community.

4.3.1 Organizing requirements

The purpose of the SyRS can best be achieved by organizing the system requirements into conceptual categories. In practice, it is difficult to identify and separate requirements from other aspects of the customer's perception of the system that are often included in documents that define "requirements." Often, traditional user procedures or user or technical community assumptions about the implementation cloud the fundamental statement of need. The analyst should capture and state the fundamental needs of the customer and the technical community, properly form requirements, and organize or group these needs and requirements into meaningful categories.

While organizing the unstructured users' statements into a structured set of requirements, the analyst should identify technical requirements without being diverted into stating an implementation approach. To be distracted into implementation issues before a clear understanding of the requirements is achieved may lead to both an inadequate statement of requirements and a faulty implementation. Discerning between technical requirements and technical implementations is a constant challenge to the analyst.

The description of the system should be stated in operational and logistical terms. Issues addressed include the system's desired operational capabilities; physical characteristics; performance parameters and expected values; interfaces and interactions with its environment; documentation requirements; reliability requirements; logistical requirements; and personnel requirements.

These requirements should be communicated in a structured manner to ensure that the customer and technical community are able to do the following:

a) Identify requirements that are derived from other requirements;

b) Organize requirements of different levels of detail into their appropriate levels;

c) Verify the completeness of the set of requirements;

d) Identify inconsistencies among requirements;

e) Clearly identify the capabilities, conditions, and constraints for each requirement;

f) Develop a common understanding with the customer of the purpose and objectives of the set of requirements;

g) Identify requirements that will complete the SyRS.

It is important that structure be added to the set of requirements by the analysts, and that representations of the SyRS communicate the requirements in a structured manner. Clause 6 provides guidelines for explicitly defining the requirements.

4.3.2 Communicating to two audiences

The SyRS has two primary audiences and essentially serves to document an agreement between the customer and the technical community.

4.3.2.1 Customer

Customer is a collective term that may include the customer of the proposed system, the funding agency, the acceptor who will sign-off delivery, and the managers who will be responsible for overseeing the implementation, operation, and maintenance of the system.

All customers will have vested interests and concerns that should be resolved in the SyRS. In addition, some customers may not understand the process of establishing requirements or the process of creating a system. Although competent in their areas of responsibility and in the application for which the system is being defined, they generally may not be familiar with the vocabulary and representation techniques that are often used to specify requirements. Since one of the primary goals of system requirements analysis is to ensure that the SyRS is understood, it will be necessary to provide the customers with a representation of the SyRS in a language that the customer understands and that is complete, concise, and clear.

4.3.2.2 Technical community

The SyRS should also communicate the customer's requirements to the technical community. The technical community includes analysts, estimators, designers, quality assurance officers, certifiers, developers, engineers, integrators, testers, maintainers, and manufacturers. For this audience the representation of the SyRS should be technically precise and presented in a formalism from which they can design, build, and test the required system.

4.4 Intended use

The recommended uses of the SyRS, which vary as the development cycle progresses, are as follows:

a) During systems design, requirements are allocated to subsystems, hardware, software, operations, and other major components of the system.

b) The SyRS is utilized in constructing the resulting system. The SyRS is also used to write appropriate system verification plans. If the system contains hardware and software, then the hardware test plan and software test plan are also generated from the system requirements.

c) During the implementation phase, test procedures will be defined from the SyRS.

d) During the validation process, validation procedures based on the SyRS are used to provide the customer with a basis for acceptance of the system.

If any changes to the SyRS baseline are to be made, they should be controlled through a formal change management process. This process should include appropriate negotiation among parties affected by the change and should trigger pertinent risk assessments (e.g., schedules or costs).

4.5 Benefits

A properly written SyRS benefits all subsequent phases of the life cycle in several different ways. The SyRS documents the complete set of system capabilities and provides the following benefits:

a) Assurance to the customer that the technical community understands the customer's needs and is responsive to them;

b) An early opportunity for bidirectional feedback between the customer and the technical community;

c) A method for the customer and the technical community to identify problems and misunderstandings while relatively inexpensive to correct;

d) A basis for system qualification to establish that the system meets the customer's needs;

e) Protection for the technical community, providing a baseline for system capabilities and a basis of determining when the construction of the system is complete;

f) Support for the developer's program planning, design, and development efforts;

g) Aid in assessing the effects of the inevitable requirement changes;

h) Increased protection against customer and technical community misunderstandings as development progresses.

4.6 Dynamics of system requirements

Requirements are rarely static. Although it is desirable to freeze a set of requirements permanently, it is rarely possible. Requirements that are likely to evolve should be identified and communicated to both customers and the technical community. A core subset of requirements may be frozen early. The impact of proposed new requirements must be evaluated to ensure that the initial intent of the requirements baseline is maintained or that changes to the intent are understood and accepted by the customer.

5. SyRS development process overview

This clause provides an overview of the steps in the SyRS development process. The system requirements development process, in general, interfaces with three external agents—the customer, the environment, and the technical community. Each of the external agents is described in the text below. Figure 1 shows the interactions among the various agents necessary to develop an SyRS.

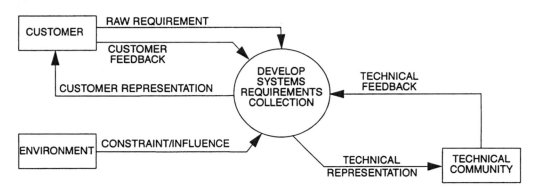

Figure 1—Context for developing an SyRS

5.1 Customer

Customers are the keystone element of the SyRS context. They are prime system drivers providing their objectives, needs, or problems to the SyRS process. The exchange between customers and SyRS developers is discussed below.

5.1.1 Raw requirements

Prior to the SyRS process the customer has an idea for a system, for a process improvement, or for a problem to be solved. At this point, any initial concept for a system may be imprecise and unstructured. Requirements will often be intermingled with ideas and suggestions for potential designs. These raw requirements are often expressed in initiating documents similar to the following:

a) *Concept of operations.* This type of document focuses on the goals, objectives, and general desired capabilities of the potential system without indicating how the system will be implemented to actually achieve the goals.

b) *System concept.* This type of document includes concept of operations information, but will also include a preliminary interface design for the system and other explicit requirements.

c) *Marketing specification.* This type of document includes a features list (often in bullet format) for a new system or systems and will identify the scope of the features and their priority (which are mandatory or highly desirable) to provide an edge in the marketplace. It also includes a context or boundary defining how the new system must interact with existing systems. A cost/benefit analysis and required delivery schedule may be provided.

d) *Request for proposal (RFP).* In some instances an RFP will be prepared. This may include one or more of the above initiating documents. Its purpose will be to solicit bids for consideration from several sources to construct a system, or may simply require assistance to generate system initiating documents.

e) *External system interfaces.* The definition of all interfaces external to the system, literally or by reference, is one of the most important (yet most often overlooked) activities to be accomplished prior to the generation of the SyRS. An approved definition of the system's external universe reasonably bounds or restricts what the system is required to do internally. All known elements of each separately defined interface should be described. This information may be included in the SyRS if it is not too voluminous. However, in most cases it is better to have a System External Interface Control Document (ICD). There are many types of possible interfaces external to the system and a single system may have several interfaces of differing types. The following list provides some examples:

— Operational;
— Computer to computer;
— Electrical;
— Data links and protocols;
— Telecommunications lines;
— Device to system, system to device;
— Computer to system, system to computer;
— Environmental sense and control interfaces.

5.1.2 Customer representation

Feedback to the customer includes SyRS representations and technical interchange or communications clarifying and/or confirming requirements.

5.1.3 Customer feedback

Customer feedback includes information updating the customer's objectives, problems, or needs; modifying requirements concerning technical interchange communications; and identifying new requirements.

5.2 Environment

In addition to the analyst and the customer, the environment can implicitly or explicitly influence or place a constraint on the system requirements. The analyst should be aware of these influences on system capabilities. In cases where systems are sensitive to environmental influences, the customers and analyst will specify environmental influences that affect system requirements. Environmental influences can be classified into overlapping categories, as follows:

a) Political;
b) Market;

    c)   Standards and technical policies;
    d)   Cultural;
    e)   Organizational;
    f)   Physical.

These categories are described below. Although these descriptions represent factors that should be considered, this list is not to be construed as exhaustive.

5.2.1 Political influence

International, federal, state, and local governmental agencies have laws and regulations that influence system requirements. Some governmental agencies may have enforcement organizations that check for compliance with their laws and regulations. Examples of governmental laws are copyright, patent, and trademark laws. Examples of governmental regulations are zoning, environmental hazards, waste, recycling, system safety, and health.

Political influence changes as a function of political boundaries. What affects system requirements in one environment may be completely different in another. Therefore, it is important to conduct research in the political environment where the system will be manufactured and/or used to ensure that the system conforms to all of the governmental laws and regulations.

5.2.2 Market influence

There are three types of market conditions that influence the development of the systems specification. The first matches the customer's needs to the systems by using marketing research or by developing markets to match technical research. Matching the customer's needs to systems affects the system requirements up front and becomes part of the customer requirements.

The second market influence is the demand-fulfilling influence. This influence is part of the environmental inputs as shown in Figure 1. The demand-fulfilling influence must be considered because it affects system distribution and accessibility, which adds to the system requirements (e.g., the system should be lightweight to reduce shipping cost, or the system must be of small size to fit into vending machines). Distribution and accessibility requirements must be identified during system development and before the system is manufactured and/or integrated to allow these requirements to be incorporated into the system. Without easy access to the system, system success will be limited. Therefore, it is important to consider the market segments for which the system is targeted and to consider how marketing information can be used to derive system requirements.

The third market influence is competition. Knowing a competitor's systems will help define requirements. To stay competitive, the following should be considered:

    a)   Functionality;
    b)   Price;
    c)   Reliability;
    d)   Durability;
    e)   Performance;
    f)   Maintainability;
    g)   System safety and security.

Analyzing the competitive market is a continuous process and will affect requirements for both new and existing systems. Systems can evolve into completely new systems that may have little resemblance to the customer's original concepts.

5.2.3 Standards and technical policies influence

System requirements are influenced directly by customers who have to conform to standards and technical policies issued by government or industries. Technical policies and associated standards and guidelines help ensure the following:

a)   System consistency;
b)   System safety;
c)   System reliability and maintainability.

System consistency standards and guidelines prescribe specific requirements by providing details about how a particular system should be implemented.

Industrial safety standards are generally imposed to help prevent safety hazards and potential legal problems. Safety compliance requirements should be clearly identified in a system requirements document [i.e., safety requirements for the toy manufacturing industry, UL certifications, or National Electrical Code® requirements].

The customer and technical community may require that the system should pass certain reliability criteria as prescribed in technical standards. Reliability and maintainability requirements should be identified in the SyRS. These requirements can come in many forms. For instance, they may be directly system oriented and may require specifications of maximum outage time and minimum mean time between failure, or minimum mean time to repair.

5.2.4 Cultural influence

Culture is the integrated human behavior patterns that are transmitted from generation to generation. It is a learned experience that originates from religious beliefs, country of origin, ethnic group, socioeconomic level, language, media, place of employment, and immediate family. To understand the culture of a region or market segment, the values and beliefs of the people must be known. Cultural influence should be considered when developing a system because it will affect the system requirements.

5.2.5 Organizational influence

System requirements are influenced by the organization in which the requirements are developed. Company organizational influence can take the form of marketing, internal politics, technical policies, and internal standards. The company's influences on system requirements are similar to those of the other spheres of influence, plus it has its own unique set (i.e., every company has its own culture, purposes, values, and goals that can and will influence the system that it develops, manufactures, and/or delivers).

5.2.6 Physical influence

Physical influence includes natural and man-made influences such as temperature, radiation, moisture, pressure, and chemicals.

5.3 Technical community

The technical community, represented in Figure 1, is composed of those involved in the activities of system design, implementation, integration, test, manufacturing, deployment, operations, and maintenance. All elements of the technical community should be involved in the SyRS development process as early as possible. Early inclusion of the technical community provides a mechanism for the SyRS developers to reduce the possibility that new requirements or changes to the original requirements may be discovered later in the system life cycle.

5.3.1 Technical representation

Representations of the requirement collection, prepared for the technical community, may include technical interchange or communications that clarify and/or confirm requirements.

5.3.2 Technical feedback

The technical community provides feedback during various activities that can cause modification, additions, and/or deletions to the requirement collection. The SyRS is refined as necessary to support subsequent life cycle phases of the system. For example, following the requirement phase, a system test plan is developed where individual requirements are allocated to specific tests. This process can reveal requirements that are non-testable, resulting in modification of the SyRS to ensure testability.

Other feedback from the technical community may provide customers with the most recent system features, upcoming technologies, and insight into advanced implementation methods.

6. Well-formed requirements

This clause explains the properties of a well-formed requirement, provides an example of a well-formed requirement, and points out requirement pitfalls.

6.1 Definition of a well-formed requirement

As previously defined, a well-formed requirement is a statement of system functionality (a capability) that can be validated, that must be met or possessed by a system to solve a customer problem or to achieve a customer objective, and that is qualified by measurable conditions and bounded by constraints.

This definition helps in the classification of general customer requirements. Requirements can be taken from customer needs and can be derived from technical analysis. The definition provides a means for distinguishing between requirements as capabilities and the attributes of those requirements (conditions and constraints). Constraints may be functional or nonfunctional. An example of a nonfunctional constraint might be that the system is to be painted a particular shade of blue solely for nonrequired decorative purposes.

This guide recommends that system implementation process requirements, such as mandating a particular design methodology, not be included in an SyRS. Process requirements should be captured in other system controlling technical documentation such as quality plans, contracts, or statements of work.

6.1.1 Capabilities

Capabilities are the fundamental requirements of the system and represent the features or functions of the system needed or desired by the customer. A capability should usually be stated in such a way that it describes what the system should do. The capability should also be stated in a manner that is solution independent. This will permit consideration of different ways of meeting the need or of providing the feature or function. For example, capabilities of a high-speed rail system between Los Angeles and New York could include the ability to start, accelerate, cruise, decelerate, stop, load passengers, and unload passengers. However, the brand of the computer operating system is not considered to be a capability of the high-speed rail system.

6.1.2 Conditions

Conditions are measurable qualitative or quantitative attributes and characteristics that are stipulated for a capability. They further qualify a capability that is needed, and provide attributes that permit a capability to be formulated and stated in a manner that can be validated and verified. For example, in the high-speed rail system mentioned above, a condition of the capability to cruise may be a cruise range of 0 km/hr to 300 km/hr or an optimal cruise rate of 200 km/hr.

It makes sense to include conditions (measurable attributes) only if they apply to something to be measured, such as a capability. For example, it is meaningless to have a system requirement that states 0–200 km/hr in the abstract. This range can qualify a cruising speed for a high-speed rail link but not the speed at which an elevator should lift passengers.

Conditions may limit the options open to a designer. It is important to identify conditions as attributes of capabilities, not as primary capabilities, to ensure that the requirements clearly define the need without imposing unnecessary bounds on the solution space.

6.1.3 Constraints

Constraints are requirements that are imposed on the solution by circumstance, force, or compulsion. Constraints limit absolutely the options open to a designer of a solution by imposing immovable boundaries and limits. For example, the high-speed rail link mentioned above will be constrained by the need to get people to their destination alive (a safety constraint could be mandatory seatbelts) and could be constrained by technology (the customer may require that all train control software be written in Ada).

A list of constraints can include interfaces to already existing systems (e.g., format, protocol, or content) where the interface cannot be changed, physical size limitations (e.g., a controller must fit within a limited space in an airplane wing), laws of nature, laws of a particular country, available time or budget, priority (e.g., mandatory or optional), or a pre-existing technology platform.

Constraints may apply across all requirements or be specified in a relationship to a specific capability or set of capabilities.

Constraints may be identified as stand-alone requirements (i.e., not bounding any specific capability), or as constraints upon individual capabilities. Many constraints, such as the choice of technology (e.g., the type of operating system), will apply to the entire set of capabilities. Other constraints will apply to only a single or a few capabilities. For example, there will be safety constraints imposed on acceleration for a high-speed rail system that will not apply to the passenger loading functions.

6.1.4 Example

The purpose of this example is to state a well-formed requirement and its associated conditional and capability requirements, as follows:

Move people from New York to California at a maximum speed of 5300 km/hr.

Capability:	Move people between Los Angeles and New York
Condition:	Cruising speed of 2500 km/hr
Constraint:	Maximum speed of 5300 km/hr

6.2 Properties of a requirement

Each requirement should possess the following properties:

a) *Abstract.* Each requirement should be implementation independent.
b) *Unambiguous.* Each requirement should be stated in such a way so that it can be interpreted in only one way.

c) *Traceable.* For each requirement it should be feasible to determine a relationship between specific documented customer statement(s) of need and the specific statements in the definition of the system given in the SyRS as evidence of the source of a requirement.

d) *Validatable.* Each requirement should have the means to prove that the system satisfies the requirements.

6.3 Categorization

To support the analysis of requirements, the requirements should be categorized by their identification, priority, criticality, feasibility, risk, source, and type. Each of these categories is described in more detail below.

a) *Identification.* Each requirement should be uniquely identified (i.e., number, name tag, mnemonic, buttons, hypertext). Identification can reflect linkages and relationships, if needed, or they can be separate from identification.

b) *Priority.* The customer should identify the priority of each requirement. This may be established through a consensus process among potential customers. As appropriate, a scale such as 1:10 or a simple scheme such as High, Medium, Low, Out, could be used for identifying the priority of each requirement.

c) *Criticality.* The analyst, working with the customer, should define the criticality of each requirement. Some requirements could have a low priority from the user's perspective, but nevertheless be essential for the success of the system. For example, a requirement to measure external ambient temperature could be essential to provide support to other requirements such as the maintenance of internal cabin temperature. This relationship should be identified so that if the primary requirement is removed by the customer, the supporting requirement can also be eliminated.

d) *Feasibility.* The customer and analyst working together should identify the feasibility of including each particular requirement in the system, and classify each requirement by types of feasibility appropriate to the system domain. Feasibility could be based upon an understanding of such things as the current state of technology (e.g., commercially available components vs. original research), the customer's environment (e.g., readiness or capability to accept change), and the risk or cost associated with a particular requirement.

e) *Risk.* Risk analysis techniques can be used to determine a grading for system requirements. In terms of their consequences or degree of risk avoidance, major risks are related to potential financial loss, environmental impact, safety and health issues, and national standards or laws.

f) *Source.* Each requirement should be further classified by a label that indicates the originator. There may be multiple sources that can all be considered creators of the requirement. It is useful to identify the creator(s) of each requirement so that if requirements are unclear, conflict, or need to be modified or deleted, it will be possible to identify the individual(s) or organization(s) to be consulted.

g) *Type.* Requirements can also be categorized by one or more of the following types:

   —Input (e.g., receive EDI data);
   —Output (e.g., export a particular format);
   —Reliability (e.g., mean time to failure);
   —Availability (e.g., expected hours of operation);
   —Maintainability (e.g., ease with which components can be replaced);
   —Performance (e.g., response time);
   —Accessibility (e.g., different navigation paths for novice and experienced users);
   —Environmental conditions (e.g., dust levels that must be tolerated);
   —Ergonomic (e.g., use of particular colors to reduce eye strain);
   —Safety (e.g., below specified limits for electrical magnetic radiation);
   —Security (e.g., limits to physical, functional, or data access, by authorized or unauthorized users);

—Facility requirements (e.g., use of domestic electrical current);
—Transportability (e.g., weight limits for portability);
—Training (e.g., includes tutorials or computer-based training);
—Documentation (e.g., on-line help facility);
—External interfaces (e.g., support for industry standard communication mode/format);
—Testing (e.g., support for remote diagnostics);
—Quality provisions (e.g., minimum required calibration intervals);
—Policy and regulatory (e.g., environmental protection agency policies);
—Compatibility to existing systems (e.g., uses analog telephone system as default mode);
—Standards and technical policies (e.g., products to conform to ASME codes);
—Conversion (e.g., will accept data produced by older versions of system);
—Growth capacity (e.g., will support an additional number of users);
—Installation (e.g., ability to put a new system into service).

6.4 Pitfalls

Some pitfalls to avoid when building well-formed requirements are as follows:

a) *Design and implementation.* There is a tendency on the part of analysts and customers who are defining requirements to include design and implementation decisions along with the requirements statements. Such information may still be important. In this case, the information should be documented and communicated in some other form of documentation in order to aid in design and implementation.

b) *Overspecification.*

  1) Requirements that express an exact commercial system set or a system that can be bought rather than made (these are not an expression of what the system should do);

  2) Requirements that state tolerances for items deep within the conceptual system (frequently stated as error requirements at very low levels);

  3) Requirements that implement solutions (requirements state a need).

c) *Overconstrained.* Requirements with unnecessary constraints. (For example, if a system must be able to run on rechargeable batteries, a derived requirement might be that the time to recharge should be less than 3 h. If this time is too restrictive and a 12 h recharge time is sufficient, potential solutions are eliminated.)

d) *Unbounded.*

  1) Requirements making relative statements. (These requirements cannot be verified and may only need to be restated. For example, the requirement to "minimize noise" may be restated as "noise levels should not exceed...")

  2) Requirements that are open-ended (frequently stated as "including, but not limited to..." or lists ending in "etc.").

  3) Requirements making subjective or vague statements (frequently contain terms such as "user friendly," "quick response time," or "cost effective").

e) *Assumptions.*

  1) Requirements based on undocumented assumptions. (The assumption should be documented as well as the requirement.)

  2) Requirements based on the assumption that a particular standard or system undergoing development will reach completion. (The assumption and an alternative requirement should be documented.)

7. SyRS development

System requirements specification development, as shown in Figure 1, is an iterative process. The four subprocesses are shown in Figure 2. These subprocesses are as follows:

a) Identify requirements from the customer, the environment, and the experience of the technical community;
b) Build well-formed requirements;
c) Organize the requirements into an SyRS;
d) Present the SyRS in various representations for different audiences.

The purpose of decomposing the system requirements specification development process into subprocesses is to aid in the full and accurate development of the SyRS. The subprocesses below are presented as occurring sequentially. However, there will often be a degree of subprocess overlap or iteration.

The iterative application of this process results in the ongoing modification of the SyRS. Modifications are usually applied against the SyRS baseline, and managed under change control procedures. See IEEE Std 1220-1998 for change control procedures.

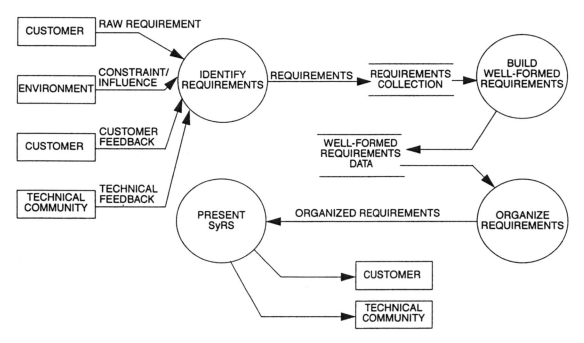

Figure 2—SyRS development process

7.1 Identify requirements

Working with customers, analysts filter the various inputs identified in Figure 2 and extract a set of requirements, establish necessary derived requirements, and create requirements. Requirements may be extracted from initiating documents and through analytical exercises conducted with the customer. The goal of this iterative process is to solicit all system requirements, ensure that each requirement is stated once, and ensure that none are missed.

There are a variety of approaches that can be followed in the identification of customer requirements. In practice, each organization will have its own approach to identifying requirements and initiating the process of creating a system solution. In some organizations, customers will undertake the entire process in-house. In this case the identification and specification of requirements will be driven by the customer. In other organizations, customers will identify a preliminary set of requirements and will request assistance from an analyst within their organization or through a contract with an external consultant or systems integrator.

The analyst, whether from within the organization or external, will work with the customer to identify and structure the requirements. In some organizations the analyst will work directly with the customer. In other organizations, the analyst will not be given direct access to the customer and will have to work through one or more layers of intermediaries (technical, legal, administrative) who represent the customer.

Because of the dynamics involved in identifying requirements, it is important that the customer and analyst agree on the process. The analyst needs to prepare a plan to guide the process, define representations of the SyRS that will be produced for different audiences, and identify the tools and techniques that will be used.

The process should move forward toward the goal of developing the SyRS database and provide customers with a system that will meet their needs. The analyst should ensure that the identification of requirements uses all appropriate techniques within this process.

A requirements management process should be used to ensure the following:

a)   The process is goal-directed and aimed at the production of a set of requirements.

b)   The system boundaries are defined.

c)   All requirements are solicited, fairly evaluated, and documented.

d)   Requirements are specified as capabilities, and qualifying conditions and bounding constraints are identified distinctly from capabilities.

e)   Requirements are validated, or purged, if invalid, from the requirements set.

f)   Consideration is given to consistency when many individuals ("authors") may be contributing to the development of the requirements set.

g)   The developing requirements set is understood, at an appropriate level of detail, by all individuals participating in the process.

7.1.1 Techniques for identifying requirements

Requirements begin as ideas or concepts that may originate from a response to a perceived threat to security or market share, from an imposition of legislation or regulation, from a desire to create a new or better system or process, from the need to replace an existing system, or from some other actual or perceived need. Although the ideas or concepts may originate with one individual, a set of requirements usually is best obtained from the interaction of a group where ideas are shared and shaped.

There are a number of techniques for identifying requirements, including the following:

a)   Structured workshops;
b)   Brainstorming or problem-solving sessions;
c)   Interviews;
d)   Surveys/questionnaires;
e)   Observation of work patterns (e.g., time and motion studies);
f)   Observation of the system's organizational and political environment (e.g., sociogram);
g)   Technical documentation review;
h)   Market analysis;
i)   Competitive system assessment;
j)   Reverse engineering;
k)   Simulations;
l)   Prototyping;
m)   Benchmarking processes and systems.

7.1.2 Interaction between customers and analysts

In a situation where an analyst has been hired to work with a customer, it will be necessary to establish an effective process of interaction between the two parties. To make this interaction effective, each party needs to understand that they have a role in educating the other party and that they should work together to jointly define the requirements.

7.1.2.1 Mutual education

Education must be a two-way process. First, the analysts need to learn about the customer's environment, current systems (if any), and requirements. Time and effort need to be allocated on both sides to accommodate this education process.

Second, customers may also need education. They may need education from the analysts during the process of identifying and specifying requirements. In addition, the analysts may be needed to educate customers with respect to the requirements themselves and contribute requirements from their experience.

7.1.2.2 Joint definition of requirements

There are multiple ways in which the customer and analysts may interact in the process of defining requirements. For example, analysts may simply conduct interviews to solicit input and then organize and present the requirements for review by the customer.

The analysts' experience is very important, but it should not bias or stifle the customer's involvement in any way. As they work with the customer, their primary objective should be to solicit and organize requirements derived from the customer. They should add requirements from their own experience or from previously defined system solutions only when these additional requirements have been missed by the customer, clearly add value for the customer to the system being specified, and have been approved by the customer.

As another example, personnel from the customer may be involved in workshop sessions with the analysts. At these workshops there can be a significant amount of brainstorming and interactive definition of requirements. These sessions are usually driven and directed by the analysts. The results of the workshop are documented by the analysts.

A more cooperative (joint definition) approach may involve the customer even more directly in the definition of requirements. Customer personnel may participate in the definition of the requirements to the extent that they also author the SyRS.

Whatever techniques are used, the objective is to define the requirements while building consensus and a common level of understanding. The customer and the analysts need to come to a point where they have a common understanding of the requirements and can represent these consistently as an SyRS, to the satisfaction of the customer.

7.2 Build a well-formed requirement

The analysts carry out this subphase by doing the following:

a) Ensuring that each requirement is a necessary, short, definitive statement of need (capability, constraints);

b) Defining the appropriate conditions (quantitative or qualitative measures) for each requirement and avoiding adjectives such as "resistant" or "industry wide;"

c) Avoiding requirements pitfalls (see 6.4);

d) Ensuring the readability of requirements, which entails the following:
   1) Simple words/phrases/concepts;
   2) Uniform arrangement and relationship;
   3) Definition of unique words, symbols, and notations;
   4) The use of grammatically correct language and symbology.
e) Ensuring testability.

The following is an example of how to generate a well-formed requirement from an initial customer statement. The customer statement "Move people between Los Angeles and New York" is a statement of a raw requirement and is the basis of a well-formed requirement. Further information from the customer includes: "speed should be no greater than 300 km/hr and cruising speed should be 200 km/hr." These conditions and constraints can be applied to the following raw requirement:

Capability:	Move people between Los Angeles and New York
Condition:	Cruising speed of 200 km/hr
Constraint:	Maximum speed of 300 km/hr
Well-formed requirement:	This system should move people between Los Angeles and New York at an optimal cruising speed of 200 km/hr with a maximum speed of 300 km/hr.

With a single capability, there can be multiple conditions and constraints. However, additional conditions and/or additional constraints on a capability may necessitate the definition of additional well-formed requirements.

7.3 Organize requirements

In this subprocess, analysts add structure to the set of requirements by relating the requirements to one another according to some comparative definition method. Certain tasks in this process can be supported by automation.

This activity is characterized by the following:

— Searching for patterns around which to group requirements;
— Utilizing experience and judgment to account for appropriate technical approaches;
— Utilizing creativity and intuition to generate alternative approaches and to prioritize requirements based on customer inputs;
— Defining the requirements properties;
— Defining the requirement attributes.

Requirement attributes can be assigned to each well-formed requirement. For example:

<identification> = 2.1.3.6
<priority> = high
<criticality> = low
<feasibility> = high
<risk> = medium
<source> = customer
<type> = performance

There are various schemes for organizing specifications into an ordered set. The most often used scheme is to assemble requirements into a hierarchy of capabilities where more general capabilities are decomposed into subordinate requirements. Another scheme is to use network links (e.g., hypertext) showing the relationship between all the lowest-level requirements. Whatever scheme is used, the SyRS should indicate the relationships among the requirements. The specific relationships will depend on the methods, techniques, and tools used to capture, record, and store the requirements. Some of the relationships among the requirements that can be maintained in an SyRS include the following hierarchical dependencies:

a) Events;
b) Information/data;
c) Physical or abstract objects;
d) Functions.

7.4 Present requirements

In this subprocess, analysts working with the customer identify the best means of communicating the requirements to all individuals who need to understand, review, accept, or use the SyRS. A single representation is not always suitable because

a) The customer and technical community usually have different cultures and languages; thus, the same system requirements may have to be presented differently to the technical or customer communities;

b) Retrieval of specific information is difficult in some representations;

c) Presentation of interactions can be difficult to do in some methods of representations;

d) Relating information in one place to information in another place can be difficult in some representations.

Therefore, it is important that the analysts, working with the customer, identify the best means of communicating the requirements to all individuals who need to understand, review, accept, or use the SyRS. To accomplish this, different representations should be prepared from the SyRS. These representations should not be separately maintained; rather, they should be representations derived from, and generated from, the SyRS. For example, an overview document may be produced for customer management that contains annotation narrative and a selected subset of the high-level requirements. For the individual who is responsible for accepting the requirements on behalf of the customer, a more detailed document, including formal models, may be generated. For the design team, a complete set of formal models may be generated. Automated tools could be used productively both to maintain the SyRS and to generate different representations.

7.4.1 Methods of representation

Methods of representation may be one or a combination of the following so that they allow appropriate views of the requirements depending on the needs of the audience:

a) Textual
   1) Paper
   2) Electronic
b) Model
   1) Physical
   2) Symbolic
   3) Graphical
   4) Prototype

The writing of requirements generally continues beyond the approval of the SyRS. In large and complicated systems, there is a high probability that the first approved version of the SyRS will contain errors of omission or distortion. In addition, many systems will evolve with the addition of new features. This necessitates the repeat or iteration of this process to correct the initial requirements errors or to add new requirements to enhance the system's features. Formal control of the SyRS is critical to manage changes to the SyRS.

Annex A

(informative)

System Requirements Specification outline

This guide recognizes and endorses a wide variety of techniques and media to communicate requirements, including text and models. The purpose of this outline is to help focus on the technical content of an SyRS. See IEEE Std 1220-1998 for process requirements for developing an SyRS. The representation and content can be expanded or contracted for the customer or technical community. There are many possible representations of an SyRS and the following is merely one example.

An SyRS Outline

Table of contents
List of figures
List of tables

1.   Introduction

    1.1 System purpose
    1.2 System scope
    1.3 Definitions, acronyms, and abbreviations
    1.4 References
    1.5 System overview

2.   General system description

    2.1 System context
    2.2 System modes and states
    2.3 Major system capabilities
    2.4 Major system conditions
    2.5 Major system constraints
    2.6 User characteristics
    2.7 Assumptions and dependencies
    2.8 Operational scenarios

3.   System capabilities, conditions, and constraints

    NOTE—System behavior, exception handling, manufacturability, and deployment should be covered under each capability, condition, and constraint.

    3.1 Physical
        3.1.1 Construction
        3.1.2 Durability
        3.1.3 Adaptability
        3.1.4 Environmental conditions
    3.2 System performance characteristics
    3.3 System security
    3.4 Information management
    3.5 System operations
        3.5.1 System human factors
        3.5.2 System maintainability
        3.5.3 System reliability
    3.6 Policy and regulation
    3.7 System life cycle sustainment

4.   System interfaces

Outline explanation

For those items that are not self-explanatory, the following information is provided:

1.2 System scope

This subclause should

    a)   Identify the system to be produced by name.

    b)   Refer to and state the results of the earlier finalized needs analysis, in the form of a brief but formal expression of the customer's problem(s). Explain what the system will and will not do to satisfy those needs.

    c)   Describe the application of the system being specified. As a portion of this, it should describe all relevant top-level benefits, objectives, and goals as precisely as possible.

2.1 System context

Appropriate diagrams and narrative should be included in this subclause, to provide an overview of the context of the system, defining all significant interfaces crossing the system's boundaries.

2.2 System modes and states

If the system can exist in various modes or states, this subclause should describe these and, as appropriate, use diagrams.

2.3 Major system capabilities

This subclause should provide diagrams and accompanying narrative to show major capability groupings of the requirements.

2.6 User characteristics

This subclause should identify each type of user of the system (by function, location, type of device), the number in each group, and the nature of their use of the system.

2.8 Operational scenarios

This subclause should provide descriptive examples of how the system will be used.

3. System capabilities, conditions, and constraints

3.1 Physical

3.1.1 Construction

The environmental (mechanical, electrical, chemical) characteristics of where the system will be installed should be included. For example, the weight limits of the system, moments of inertia, dimensional and volume limitations, crew space, operator station layout, ingress, egress, and access for maintenance should be specified here. Requirements for materials to be used in the item or service covered by this specification should be stated. Requirements covering nameplates and system markings, interchangeability of equipment, and workmanship should be covered in this subclause.

3.1.3 Adaptability

Growth, expansion, capability, and contraction should be included in this subclause. For example, if the system will require future network bandwidth, the hardware rack should be specified with extra slots to accommodate new network cards as demand increases.

3.1.4 Environmental conditions

This subclause should include environmental conditions to be encountered by the system. The following subjects should be considered for coverage: natural environment (wind, rain, temperature); induced environment (motion, shock, noise); and electromagnetic signal environment.

3.2 System performance characteristics

This subclause should be used to highlight the critical performance conditions and their associated capabilities. As a general guide, include such considerations as

a) Dynamic actions or changes that occur (e.g., rates, velocities, movements, and noise levels).
b) Quantitative criteria covering endurance capabilities of the equipment required to meet the user needs under stipulated environmental and other conditions, including minimum total life expectancy. Indicate required operational session duration and planned utilization rate.
c) Performance requirements for the operational phases and modes.

3.3 System security

System security requirements related to both the facility that houses the system and operational security requirements should be given in this subclause. One example of security requirements might be to specify the security and privacy requirements, including access limitations to the system, such as existence of log-on procedures and passwords, and of data protection and recovery methods. This could include the factors that would protect the system from accidental or malicious access, use, modification, destruction, or disclosure. Especially in safety-critical embedded systems this should incorporate a distributed log or history of data sets, the assignment of certain functions to different single systems, or the restriction of communications between some areas of the system.

3.5.1 System human factors

This subclause should reference applicable documents and specify any special or unique requirements, e.g., constraints on allocation of functions to personnel and communications and personnel/equipment interactions. Included should be those specific areas, stations, or equipment that would require concentrated human engineering attention due to the sensitivity of the operation or criticality of the task (i.e., those areas where the effects of human error would be particularly serious).

3.5.2 System maintainability

This subclause should specify the quantitative maintainability requirements. The requirements should apply to maintenance in the planned maintenance and support environment and should be stated in quantitative terms. Examples are as follows:

a) Time (e.g., mean and maximum downtime, reaction time, turnaround time, mean and maximum times to repair, mean time between maintenance actions)
b) Rate (e.g., maintenance staff hours per specific maintenance action, operational ready rate, maintenance time per operating hour, frequency of preventative maintenance)
c) Maintenance complexity (e.g., number of people and skill levels, variety of support equipment)
d) Maintenance action indices (e.g., maintenance costs per operating hour, staff hours per overhaul)

3.5.3 System reliability

This subclause should specify the system reliability requirements in quantitative terms, and should define the conditions under which the reliability requirements are to be met. The system reliability subclause may include the reliability apportionment model to support allocation of reliability values assigned to system functions for their share in achieving desired system reliability.

3.6 Policy and regulation

This subclause should detail any relevant organizational policies that will affect the operation or performance of the system as well as any relevant external regulatory requirements, or constraints imposed by normal business practices. Examples of requirements include multilingual support, labor policies, protection of personnel information, and reports to a regulatory agency.

Health and safety criteria, including those basic to the design of the system, with respect to equipment characteristics, methods of operation, and environmental influences, should be specified in this subclause.

Requirements covering toxic systems and electromagnetic radiation should be covered in this subclause.

3.7 System life cycle sustainment

This subclause should outline quality activities, such as review, and measurement collection and analysis, to help realize a quality system.

4. System interfaces

This clause contains the specification of requirements for interfaces among different components and their external capabilities, including all its users, both human and other systems. The characteristics of interfaces to systems under development, or future systems, should also be included. Any interdependencies or constraints associated with the interfaces should also be identified (e.g., communication protocols, special devices, standards, fixed formats). Each interface may represent a bidirectional flow of information. A graphic representation of the interfaces should be used when appropriate for the sake of clarity.

NOTE—This outline does not include all capability categories pertinent to all fields. For example, it does not cover communications, storage, distribution, sensors, or instrumentation. Also, the above clauses can be organized in any way the reader sees fit.

Annex B

(informative)

Bibliography

[B1] Blanchard, Benjamin S. *System Engineering Management.* Wiley-Interscience, 1991.

[B2] Blanchard, Benjamin S., and Walter J. Fabrycsky, *Systems Engineering & Analysis.* International Series and Industrial & Systems Engineering, Prentice Hall, 1990.

[B3] Gause, Donald C., and Gerald M. Weinberg. *Exploring Requirements: Quality Before Design.* New York: Dorset House Publishing, 1989.

Annex C

(informative)

Guidelines for compliance with IEEE/EIA 12207.1-1997

C.1 Overview

The Software Engineering Standards Committee (SESC) of the IEEE Computer Society has endorsed the policy of adopting international standards. In 1995, the international standard, ISO/IEC 12207, Information technology—Software life cycle processes, was completed. The standard establishes a common framework for software life cycle processes, with well-defined terminology, that can be referenced by the software industry.

In 1995 the SESC evaluated ISO/IEC 12207 and decided that the standard should be adopted and serve as the basis for life cycle processes within the IEEE Software Engineering Collection. The IEEE adaptation of ISO/IEC 12207 is IEEE/EIA 12207.0-1996. It contains ISO/IEC 12207 and the following additions: improved compliance approach, life cycle process objectives, life cycle data objectives, and errata.

The implementation of ISO/IEC 12207 within the IEEE also includes the following:

— IEEE/EIA 12207.1-1997, IEEE/EIA Guide for Information Technology—Software life cycle processes—Life cycle data;

— IEEE/EIA 12207.2-1997, IEEE/EIA Guide for Information Technology—Software life cycle processes—Implementation considerations; and

— Additions to 11 SESC standards (i.e., IEEE Stds 730, 828, 829, 830, 1012, 1016, 1058, 1062, 1219, 1233, 1362) to define the correlation between the data produced by existing SESC standards and the data produced by the application of IEEE/EIA 12207.1-1997.

NOTE—Although IEEE/EIA 12207.1-1997 is a guide, it also contains provisions for application as a standard with specific compliance requirements. This annex treats 12207.1-1997 as a standard.

In order to achieve compliance with both this guide and IEEE/EIA 12207.1-1997, it is essential that the user review and satisfy the data requirements for both standards.

When this guide is directly referenced, the precedence for conformance is based upon this standard alone. When this guide is referenced with the IEEE/EIA 12207.x standard series, the precedence for conformance is based upon the directly referenced IEEE/EIA 12207.x standard, unless there is a statement that this standard has precedence.

C.1.1 Scope and purpose

Both this guide and IEEE/EIA 12207.1-1997 place requirements on a System Requirements Specification. The purpose of this annex is to explain the relationship between the two sets of requirements so that users producing documents intended to comply with both standards may do so.

C.2 Correlation

This clause explains the relationship between this guide and IEEE/EIA 12207.0-1996 in the following areas: terminology, process, and life cycle data.

C.2.1 Terminology correlation

Both this guide and IEEE/EIA 12207.0-1996 have similar semantics for the key terms of system, requirements, and specification. This guide further clarifies the semantics for a requirement by defining the concept of a "well-formed requirement."

C.2.2 Process correlation

Both this guide and IEEE/EIA 12207.0-1996 use a process-oriented approach for describing the definition of a set of requirements for a system. The difference is that this guide is focused on the development of systems requirements whereas IEEE/EIA 12207.0-1996 provides an overall life cycle view. This guide does not use the activity and task model for a process used by IEEE/EIA 12207.0-1996. This guide provides a discussion about the various audiences that are involved in either the definition or implementation of a System Requirements Specification. This guide provides a greater level of detail about what is involved in the preparation of a System Requirements Specification.

C.2.3 Life cycle data correlation for System Requirements Specifications

The information required in a System Requirements Specification by this guide and the information required in a System Requirements Specification by IEEE/EIA 12207.1-1997 are similar. It is reasonable to expect that a single document could comply with both standards. Both documents use a process-oriented approach to describe the content of a System Requirements Specification.

C.2.4 Life cycle data correlation between other data in IEEE/EIA 12207.1-1997 and IEEE Std 1233, 1998 Edition

Table C.1 correlates the life cycle data other than System Requirements Specification between IEEE/EIA 12207.1-1997 and this guide. It provides information to users of both standards.

**Table C. 1—Life cycle data correlation between other data in
IEEE/EIA 12207.1-1997 and IEEE Std 1233, 1998 Edition**

Information item	IEEE/EIA 12207.0-1996 subclauses	Kind of documentation	IEEE/EIA 12207.1-1997 subclause	IEEE Std 1233, 1998 Edition subclause
System architecture and requirements allocation description	5.3.3.1, 5.3.3.2	Description	6.25	7.3
System requirements evaluation record	5.3.2.2	Record	6.6	6.0

C.3 Document compliance

This clause provides details bearing on a claim that a System Requirements Specification complying with this guide may achieve "document compliance" with a System Requirements Specification as prescribed in

IEEE/EIA 12207.1-1997 provided that the additional information listed in the third column of Table C.3 and Table C.4 of this guide is present. The requirements for document compliance are summarized in a single row of Table 1 of IEEE/EIA 12207.1-1997. That row is reproduced in Table C.2 of this guide.

Table C.2—Summary of requirements for a System Requirements Specification excerpted from Table 1 of IEEE/EIA 12207.1-1997

Information item	IEEE/EIA 12207.0-1996 subclauses	Kind of documentation	IEEE/EIA 12207.1-1997 subclause	References
System requirements specification	5.1.1.2, 5.3.2.1, 5.3.2.2	Specification	6.26	IEEE Std 1220-1998 IEEE Std 1233, 1998 Edition EIA/IEEE J-Std-016-1995, F.2.2 MIL-STD-961D Also see ISO/IEC 5806, 5807, 6593, 8631, 8790, and 11411 for guidance on use of notations.

The requirements for document compliance are discussed in the following subclauses:

— C.3.1 discusses compliance with the information requirements noted in column 2 of Table C.2 as prescribed by 5.1.1.2, 5.3.2.1, and 5.3.2.2 of IEEE/EIA 12207.0-1996.

— C.3.2 discusses compliance with the generic content guideline (the "kind" of document) noted in column 3 of Table C.2 as a "specification." The generic content guidelines for a "specification" appear in 5.7 of IEEE/EIA 12207.1-1997.

— C.3.3 discusses compliance with the specific requirements for a System Requirements Specification noted in column 4 of Table C.2 as prescribed by 6.26 of IEEE/EIA 12207.1-1997.

— C.3.4 discusses compliance with the life cycle data objectives of Annex H of IEEE/EIA 12207.0-1996 as described in 4.2 of IEEE/EIA 12207.1-1997.

C.3.1 Compliance with information requirements of IEEE/EIA 12207.0-1996

The information requirements for a System Requirements Specification are prescribed by 5.1.1.2, 5.3.2.1, and 5.3.2.2 of IEEE/EIA 12207.0-1996. Most of these requirements are inherited from 6.26.3 of IEEE/EIA 12207.1-1997, and dealt with in C.3.3. The only exceptions are testing requirements, compliance standards, procedures (required by 5.1.1.2 of IEEE/EIA 12207.0-1996), and capabilities (required by 5.3.2.1 of IEEE/EIA 12207.0-1996). Capabilities are extensively treated in this guide, thus granting compliance with IEEE/EIA 12207.0-1996. Although the specification of testing requirements, compliance standards, and procedures is not covered in this guide, they do constitute additional requirements that a document compliant with this guide shall satisfy in order to comply also with IEEE/EIA 12207.0-1996.

C.3.2 Compliance with generic content guidelines of IEEE/EIA 12207.1-1997

The generic content guidelines for a "specification" in IEEE/EIA 12207.1-1997 are prescribed by 5.7 of IEEE/EIA 12207.1-1997. A complying specification shall achieve the purpose stated in 5.7.1 and include the information listed in 5.7.2 of that standard.

The purpose of a specification is as follows:

IEEE/EIA 12207.1-1997, subclause 5.7.1: Purpose: Specify a required function, performance, or process (e.g., requirements specification).

A System Requirements Specification complying with this guide would achieve the stated purpose.

Any specification complying with IEEE/EIA 12207.1-1997 shall satisfy the generic content requirements provided in 5.7.2 of that standard. Table C.3 of this guide lists the generic content items and, where appropriate, references the clause of this guide that requires the same information.

Table C.3—Coverage of generic specification requirements by IEEE Std 1233, 1998 Edition

IEEE/EIA 12207.1-1997 generic content	Corresponding clauses of 1233, 1998 Edition, Annex A	Additions to requirements of 1233, 1998 Edition, Annex A
a) Date of issue and status	—	Date of issue and status shall be provided.
b) Scope	1.2 System scope	—
c) Issuing organization	—	Issuing organization shall be identified.
d) References	1.4 References	—
e) Approval authority	—	Approval authority shall be identified.
f) Body	2. General system description 3. System capabilities, conditions, and constraints 4. System interfaces	—
g) Delivery instructions	—	Delivery instructions shall be provided as specified by the customer.
h) Assurance requirements	—	Assurance requirements shall be provided as specified by the customer.
i) Conditions, …	2.4 Major system conditions	—
… constraints, and …	2.5 Major system constraints	—
… characteristics	2.6 User characteristics	—
i) Glossary	1.3 Definitions, acronyms, and abbreviations	—
j) Change history	—	Change history for the System Requirements Specification shall be provided or referenced.

C.3.3 Compliance with specific content requirements of IEEE/EIA 12207.1-1997

The specific content requirements for a System Requirements Specification in IEEE/EIA 12207.1-1997 are prescribed by 6.26 of IEEE/EIA 12207.1-1997. A complying System Requirements Specification shall achieve the purpose stated in 6.26.1 and include the information listed in 6.26.3 of that standard.

The purpose of the System Requirements Specification is as follows:

IEEE/EIA 12207.1-1997, subclause 6.26.1: Purpose: Specify the requirements for a system or subsystem and the methods to be used to ensure that each requirement has been met. The

System Requirements Specification is used as the basis for design and qualification testing of a system or subsystem.

A System Requirements Specification complying with this guide and meeting the additional requirements of Table C.3 and Table C.4 of this guide would achieve the stated purpose.

A System Requirements Specification complying with IEEE/EIA 12207.1-1997 shall satisfy the specific content requirements provided in 6.26.3 of that standard. Table C.4 of this guide lists the specific content items and, where appropriate, references the clause of this guide that requires the same information.

Table C.4—Coverage of specific System Requirements Specification requirements by IEEE Std 1233, 1998 Edition

IEEE/EIA 12207.1-1997 specific content	Corresponding clauses of 1233, 1998 Edition, Annex A	Additions to requirements of 1233, 1998 Edition, Annex A
a) Generic specification information	See Table C.3	—
b) System identification and ...	1.2 System scope	—
... overview	1.5 System overview	—
c) Required states and modes	2.2 System modes and states	—
d) Requirements for the functions ... of the system and;	2.8 Operational scenarios	Requirements for the functions of the system shall be provided.
... performance of the system	3.2 System performance characteristics	—
e) Business requirements ...	3.6 Policy and regulation	—
... organizational requirements...	3.6 Policy and regulation	—
... and user requirements;	3.5.1 System human factors	—
f) Safety requirements, ...	3.6 Policy and regulation	—
... security requirements, ...	3.3 System security 3.6 Policy and regulation	—
... privacy protection requirements	3.6 Policy and regulation	—
g) Human factors engineering (ergonomics) requirements	3.5.1 System human factors	—
h) Operations requirements and ...	3.5 System operations	—
... maintenance requirements	3.7 System life cycle sustainment	—
i) System external interface requirements	4. System interfaces	—
j) System environmental requirements	3.1.4 Environmental conditions 3.6 Policy and regulation	—
k) Design constraints ...	2.5 Major system constraints 3.6 Policy and regulation	—
... and qualification requirements	—	System qualification requirements shall be provided as specified by the customer.
l) Computer resource requirements	3.2 System performance characteristics	—
l) (i) Computer hardware requirements	—	Computer hardware requirements shall be provided.
l) (ii) Computer hardware resource requirements, including utilization requirements	—	Computer hardware resource requirements, including utilization requirements, shall be provided.
l) (iii) Computer software requirements	—	Computer software requirements shall be provided.

Table C.4—Coverage of specific System Requirements Specification requirements by IEEE Std 1233, 1998 Edition (continued)

IEEE/EIA 12207.1-1997 specific content	Corresponding clauses of 1233, 1998 Edition, Annex A	Additions to requirements of 1233, 1998 Edition, Annex A
1) (iv) Computer communications requirements	—	Computer communications requirements shall be provided.
m) System quality characteristics	—	System quality characteristics shall be provided.
n) Internal data requirements	—	Internal data requirements shall be provided.
o) Installation-dependent data requirements	—	Installation-dependent requirements shall be provided.
p) Physical requirements	3.1 Physical	—
q) Personnel requirements,	3.5.1 System human factors	—
... .training requirements, ...	—	Training requirements shall be provided.
... and logistics requirements	3.5.2 System maintainability	—
r) Packaging requirements	—	Packaging requirements shall be provided as specified by the customer.
s) Precedence and criticality of requirements	—	Precedence and criticality of requirements shall be provided.
t) Rationale	—	Rationale for system requirements shall be provided.

C.3.4 Compliance with life cycle data objectives

In addition to the content requirements, life cycle data shall be managed in accordance with the objectives provided in Annex H of IEEE/EIA 12207.0-1996.

NOTE—The information items covered by this guide include plans and provisions for creating software life cycle data related to the basic type "requirements data" in H.4 of IEEE/EIA 12207.0-1996. It provides for the following requirements data: expected functionality, operational context, performance constraints and expectations, basis for qualification testing, and key decision rationale.

C.4 Conclusion

The analysis documented in this annex suggests that any System Requirements Specification prepared using this guide and complying with the content requirements specified in Table C.3 and Table C.4 of this guide would comply with the requirements of a System Requirements Specification in IEEE/EIA 12207.1-1997. In addition, to comply with IEEE/EIA 12207.1-1997, a System Requirements Specification shall support the life cycle data objectives of Annex H of IEEE/EIA 12207.0-1996.

Chapter 4

Software Requirements Methodologies and Tools

1. Introduction to Chapter

A *software development methodology* can be defined as (1) an integrated set of software engineering methods, policies, procedures, rules, standards, techniques, tools, languages, and other methodologies for analyzing, designing, implementing, and testing software; and (2) a set of rules for selecting for use the correct methodology, process, or tools.

One of the major problems in the past was our inability to represent or document software requirements; therefore, the only alternative was to represent the requirements for a software system with the code that was going to implement it. This problem is what fueled the desire to "rush into code."

In the last 15 years numerous software requirements methodologies have been developed that can aid a software engineer in establishing and documenting the software requirements—in other words, representing the requirements. Many of these tools and techniques receive widespread use, for example *structured analysis*. Others are reasonably new, such as *real-time structured analysis, object-oriented analysis,* and *formal specification methods*.

A *software tool* is a software system or software package used by programmers or software engineers in the performance of their tasks. Examples are software systems used to help develop, test, analyze, or maintain another software system or its documentation (for example, automated design tools, compilers, test tools, maintenance tools, word processors, and so on).[1] Software requirements engineering tools would then be software tools that help analyze a user's requirements and/or develop a requirements specification. *Not all tools are automated.*

In the mid-1980s many of the techniques and methodologies described in Chapter 4 became targets for automation. Many of these new tools run only on personal computers (PCs) or workstations such as Sun or H-P or in a few cases general-purpose machines like IBM and DEC. The techniques or methodologies most commonly automated are real-time and non-real-time structured analysis and design.

This large chapter is the first chapter to contain articles on ways to analyze and document software requirements. It reflects the current interest in tools and methodologies. It examines "manual" software requirements methods and representations that can be used both to analyze requirements and "document" them for the benefit of both the customer and the designer. The chapter contains articles on both formal and informal approaches for developing a requirements specification. Many of these methodologies can be used in system engineering as well as software engineering.

Articles in this chapter are selected because of their tutorial nature in describing what are, in many cases, the most popular methodologies and tools.

The initial article by Davis paves the way by explaining the different types of representation methods such as natural language and formal methods. The editors identified four major requirement analysis methodologies and found articles to represent them (see Table 1). The article by Patrick Loy compares structured analysis to object-oriented analysis.

Also included in this chapter are an article on computer-aided software engineering (CASE) tools and an article on traceability as a tool for requirements engineering.

2. Description of Articles

The first article, by Dr. Alan Davis, takes the position that natural language alone is an inadequate means of representation for the requirements specification of a large system. To avoid misunderstandings due to ambiguity, inconsistency, or incompleteness, it is necessary to use other, more formal techniques along with or instead of natural language. Davis describes the application of a number of methods of differing formality to some elementary problems.

The second article, by Cy Svoboda, provides an up-to-date tutorial on structured analysis, including real-time structured analysis (RT-SA) and non-real-time structured analysis (SA) methodologies. Most of the articles that describe structured analysis are old and in many cases are outdated in that they:

- Do not reflect the way structured analysis is done today

- Do not present structured analysis the way the "standard" reference/text books do

- Present only one way of doing structured analysis, for example SADT[TM] (Structured Requirements and Design Technique) or the Gane and Sarson method

In contrast, Svoboda's article:

- Discusses and illustrates "conventional" SA

- Compares the variations of SA—SADT[2] and Gane and Sarson[3]—to other methodologies.

- Discusses and illustrates RT-SA

- Compares Hatley and Pirbhai[4] and Ward and Mellor[5] to other methodologies and representation methods

- Discusses some of the automated tools that implement SA and RT-SA

- Discusses some of the changes on the horizon for SA and RT-SA

Table 1. Major Requirement Analysis Methodologies.

Methodology	Representative Paper(s)
Structured analysis	C.P. Svoboda, "Structured Analysis"
Entity-relationship diagrams	John Reilly, "Entity-Relationship Approach to Data Modeling"
Object-oriented requirements analysis	S.C. Bailin, "Object Oriented Requirements Analysis"
Formal Methods	Robert Vienneau, "A Review of Formal Methods"
	H. Saiedian, "Formal Methods in Information Systems Engineering"

The article "Entity-Relationship Approach to Data Modeling" by John P. Reilly was written specifically for this tutorial. Again, there was a lack of basic articles on one of the most effective and mature software analysis methodologies in existence. This article describes the components of a data model and steps the reader through a process for building a business model. The article discusses entity types, the relationships between entity types, entity attributes, and data models.

"Object-Oriented Requirements Analysis," by Sidney C. Bailin, is an original article based on his article of the same title in the *Encyclopedia of Software Engineering*.[6] This article provides a very good overview of object-oriented requirements analysis as a method of formulating the requirements for a software system in terms of objects and their interactions. In addition, the article describes the fundamentals of object-oriented design and programming and their relationships to object-oriented analysis.

The article discusses the initial problems with structured analysis and the difficulty in transitioning from structured analysis to object-oriented design or even from structured analysis to structured design. The article discusses several object-oriented techniques such as those developed by Coad and Yourdon, Rumbaugh and co-workers, Shlaer and Mellor, Wirfs-Brock and co-workers, R. Smith, and Seidewitz and Stark. The article discusses objects, classes, relationships between objects, attributes of an object class, inheritance, polymorphism, information hiding, and interaction among objects (that is, message passing).

Next, the article discusses the management and technical risks involved in transitioning to object-oriented methods.

Finally, the author concludes that object-oriented analysis reduces the amount of restructuring needed to create an object-oriented design from a requirements specification. The author also believes that by encouraging the specification of self-contained systems and subsystems the use of object-oriented partitioning criteria should improve the reusability of requirement analysis products.

In "A Comparison of Object-Oriented and Structured Development Methods," Patrick Loy seeks a perspective on the two approaches. He summarizes the history and attributes of object-oriented methods, considers and rejects the idea that the object-oriented approach is a more natural (or less natural) approach to system analysis than is a functional approach, and presents a plan for evaluating a transition to object-oriented development.

The sixth article in this chapter is "A Review of Formal Methods" by Robert Vienneau of the Kaman Sciences Corporation. This article is an extract from a longer report with the same title.[7] The author defines a formal method in software development as a method that provides a formal language describing a software artifact (such as specification, design, source code) such that formal proofs are possible in principle about properties of the artifacts so expressed. Formal methods support precise and rigorous specification of those aspects of a computer system capable of being expressed in the language. Formal methods are considered to be an alternative to requirements analysis methods such as structured analysis and object-oriented analysis. The article says that formal methods can provide more precise specifications, better communications, and higher quality and productivity.

There is a range of opinion on the proper scope of validity for formal methods with the current state of technology. The Vienneau article agrees with the editors' views that claims of reduced errors and improved reliability through the use of formal methods remain unproved. This point of view is also expressed by Fenton et al.[8] However, there is a body of opinion that takes the more expansive view that, in critical systems such as microcode, secure systems, and perhaps safety applications, the use of formal methods to specify requirements is an important aid in detecting flaws in the requirements. This opinion is represented in Gerhart et al.[9] and Bowen et al.,[10] but even this view recognizes that the use of formal methods is expensive and there are very few applications willing to pay the cost.

Representative of the view that formal methods are underutilized is the original article, "Formal Methods in Information Systems Engineering," by Prof. Hossein Saiedian of the University of Nebraska at Omaha. Saiedian begins with an overview of formal methods, defined as methods that use formal tools or notations. Formal tools and notations, in turn, are defined as those that involve precise mathematical semantics.

Saiedian uses a simple airline reservation system as an example of the use of the Z (pronounced "zed") approach to requirements analysis and specification. He shows how states are defined in Z and how operations may change the state. He addresses what he regards as misconceptions about formal methods, for example, that they are only for verification and that they are not applicable to real projects. He notes that a lack of easily used tools limits the practical use of formal methods and addresses approaches to increasing the use of the methods in industry.

The next article, by Alfonso Fuggetta, is on the classification of CASE technology. The purpose of this article is to provide a survey and a classification system to help categorize CASE tools. Some of the tools looked at by the author are editing tools, programming tools, configuration management tools, verification/validation tools, project management tools, metrics and measurement tools, and some miscellaneous tools.

The ninth and last article, on traceability, was written for this tutorial and the *Software Engineering* tutorial by James Palmer, recently retired from George Mason University. Palmer defines *traceability* and a number of other related terms. He notes that traceability should be established among requirements, design, code, test, and implementation. He then describes the state of the practice, and the benefits of establishing and maintaining traceability during system development. He notes that, even with tool support, establishment of traceability is a labor-intensive process, because it is necessary to read and understand the system documents (requirements, design, test plans, and so on) in order to define those elements that trace to each other.

Palmer describes an ideal process for establishing traceability, and explains why the actual process used in practice is different. He states that it is difficult or impossible to establish the "return on investment" of traceability. While the cost is easy to determine, the benefit in errors or rework avoided is difficult to identify and credit to traceability.

He describes the current state of tool support for traceability. Most tools require the user to establish traceability; the tools then manage the resulting database and provide information conveniently. Some tools, however, provide semi-automated approaches that assist the user in establishing traceability. Palmer concludes with a summary of current research and a projection of future tools and technology for traceability.

References

1. Adapted from *IEEE Standard Glossary of Software Engineering Terminology,* ANSI/IEEE Std 729-1983, IEEE, Inc., NY, 1983.

2. Ross, D.T., "Applications and Extensions of SADT," *Computer,* Apr. 1985, pp. 25–34.

3. Gane, C. and T. Sarson, *Structured Systems Analysis: Tools and Techniques,* Prentice-Hall, Englewood Cliffs, N.J., 1979.

4. Hatley, D.J. and I.M. Pirbhai, *Strategies for Real-Time System Specification,* Dorset House Publishing, New York, N.Y., 1987.

5. Ward, P.T. and S.J. Mellor, *Structured Development for Real-Time Systems,* Vol. 1: *Introduction & Tools;* Vol. 2: *Essential Modeling Techniques;* Vol. 3: *Implementation Modeling Techniques,* Yourdon Press, New York, N.Y., 1986. (Note: The principal author for Volume 3 is S.J. Mellor.)

6. Marciniak, J.J., Editor-in-Chief, *Encyclopedia of Software Engineering,* John Wiley & Sons, New York, N.Y., 1994.

7. Vienneau, R., *A Review of Formal Methods,* Kaman Science Corporation, Utica, N.Y., May 26, 1993, pp. 3–15, 27–33.

8. Fenton, N., S. Lawrence Pfleeger, and R.L. Glass, "Science and Substance: A Challenge to Software Engineers," *IEEE Software,* Vol. 11, No. 4, July 1994, pp. 86–95.

9. Gerhart, S., D. Craigen, and T. Ralston, "Experience with Formal Methods in Critical Systems," *IEEE Software,* Vol. 11, No. 1, Jan. 1994, pp. 21–29.

10. Bowen, J.P. and M.G. Hinchley, "Ten Commandments of Formal Methods," *Computer,* Vol. 28, No. 4, Apr. 1995, pp. 56–63.

Edgar H. Sibley
Panel Editor

The elimination of ambiguity, inconsistency, and incompleteness in a
Software Requirements Specification (SRS) document is inherently difficult,
due to the use of natural language. The focus here is a survey of available
techniques designed to reduce these negatives in the documentation of a
software product's external behavior.

A COMPARISON OF TECHNIQUES FOR THE SPECIFICATION OF EXTERNAL SYSTEM BEHAVIOR

ALAN M. DAVIS

During the requirements specification phase of the software development life cycle, it is necessary to describe in detail the expected external behavior of the system to be built. This behavior is recorded in a document commonly called the Software Requirements Specification (SRS). Currently, most SRSs are written in natural language. Unfortunately, natural language is inherently ambiguous, resulting in documents that are ambiguous, inconsistent, and incomplete. With software being used in more and more life-critical applications, it becomes increasingly important to find ways of reducing the ambiguity, inconsistency, and incompleteness in SRSs.

Software Engineering is the application of scientific principles to: (1) the orderly transformation of a problem into a working software solution, and (2) the subsequent maintenance of that software through the end of its useful life. People and projects that follow an engineered approach to software development generally pass through a series of phases. Royce [48] was the first to coin the phrase *waterfall model* to characterize the

series of software engineering phases. Figure 1 shows the original model that Royce presented. This model, however, fails to show the symmetry that exists between the earlier and later phases of the development life cycle. For this reason, the symmetrical view of the development process, as shown in Figure 2, is generally more useful. In this model, the path indicated by a series of bold arrows is the primary path, consisting of the following steps:

- *Software Requirements.* The activity that includes analysis of the software problem at hand and concludes with a complete specification of the expected external behavior of the software system to be built.
- *Preliminary Design.* The activity that decomposes the software system into its actual constituent (architectural) components and then iteratively decomposes these components into successively smaller subcomponents.
- *Detailed Design.* The activity of defining and documenting algorithms for each component that will be realized as code.
- *Coding.* The activity of transforming the algorithms defined during the detailed design stage into a computer-understandable language.
- *Unit Testing.* The activity of checking each coded module for the presence of bugs.

Some of the material in this paper has been excepted from a forthcoming book by the author, entitled *Software Requirements: Analysis and Specification.* Prentice-Hall, Englewood Cliffs, New Jersey.

- *Integration Testing.* The activity that interconnects sets of previously tested modules to ensure that the sets behave as well as their independently tested module components did.
- *System Testing.* The activity of checking that the entire software system (i.e., fully integrated) embedded in its actual hardware environment behaves according to the SRS.
- *Delivery, Production, Deployment.* After final system testing, the software and its surrounding hardware become operational.
- *Maintenance and Enhancement.* Maintenance is the continued detection and repair of bugs after deployment, and enhancement is the addition of new capabilities.

The remaining three boxes in Figure 2 are present as it is best to figure out how you are going to test before the testing stage. Starting from the top and working down:

- *Software System Test Planning.* The activity whose primary purpose is to assess how the software system will be tested for conformity to the software requirements. Another purpose of software system test plan-

ning is the thorough examination of the SRS to determine whether it is verifiable, i.e., whether or not it is written in a manner that makes it possible to verify that the software meets the requirements.
- *Integration Test Planning.* The activity whose purpose is to generate and document plans and procedures to effect an orderly system integration.
- *Unit Test Planning.* The activity whose purpose is to generate and document plans and procedures to thoroughly test each module independently.

As determined in Figure 1, the requirements phase is of extreme importance. During this phase, an SRS is written whose purpose is to:

- contain a complete description of *what* the software will do without describing *how* it will do it (i.e., it will contain a complete description of the software product's external behavior but not any information concerning the software product's internal structure).
- serve as *the* basis for all design activities; and
- serve as *the* basis for all system test planning.

Various terms are used to denote the writing of an SRS [25]: requirements [2, 9, 32, 49], specification [16], system design [47], functional specification [8], external design [56], software requirements specification [37, 45], and input/output perspective [39].

Errors in SRSs are common [5, 14], often not detected until after product delivery [10], and cost far more to fix the later they are detected [9, 18, 30]. Therefore, it is of extreme importance to find ways to reduce the most common types of errors in SRSs: incorrect facts, omissions, inconsistencies, and ambiguities [5]. The use of formal models to specify a product's external behavior reduces the number of errors that may remain latent in the SRS because the associated techniques and tools can alert the SRS writers to many potential errors.

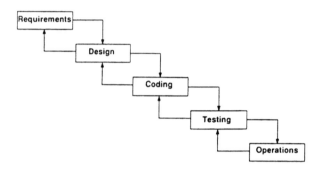

FIGURE 1. Standard Waterfall Life Cycle Model

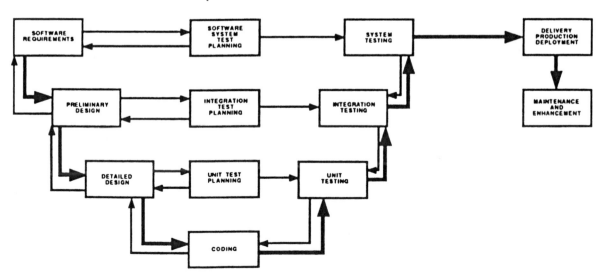

FIGURE 2. A Software Engineering Life Cycle

286

A SURVEY OF TECHNIQUES

Maintaining One's Perspective

Most requirements specifications today are written in natural language and range in length from a few pages to 5,000 pages or more. The size of the document rarely has any relationship to the complexity of the problem. The larger documents are usually created by organizations that are attempting more "completeness." In this attempt to create a comprehensive document, they often create monsters. The larger the natural language document becomes, the more impossible consistency and maintenance become. The fear of ruining a document becomes a major deterrent to the evolution of the product! While I am not opposed to large SRSs, I *am* opposed to large SRSs written in natural language. This is analogous to building a 100-story skyscraper. I am not opposed to 100-story office buildings, just to those constructed entirely of wood.

The solution to the skyscraper problem is simple: use steel. The solution to the SRS problem is also simple: use a formal technique. Nevertheless, wood does have its proper place, even in a 100-story building. And natural language does have its proper place in an SRS. Where do you apply a formal technique and where do you apply something else? The answer is: *use a formal technique when you cannot afford to have the requirement misunderstood.*

Criteria for Evaluating a Technique

The following subsections discuss a variety of behavioral requirements specification techniques and their underlying models. So they can be fairly judged, here are the traits that we would like to see a behaviorable specification technique exhibit:

(1) When the technique is properly used, the resulting SRS should be helpful and understandable to non-computer-oriented customers and users.

(2) When the technique is properly used, the resulting SRS should be able to serve effectively as the basis for design and testing.

(3) The technique should provide automated checks for ambiguity, incompleteness, and inconsistency.

(4) The technique should encourage the requirements writer to think and write in terms of external product behavior, not internal product components.

(5) The technique should help organize the information in the SRS.

(6) The technique should provide a basis for automated prototype generation.

(7) The technique should provide a basis for automated system test generation.

(8) The technique should be suitable to the particular application.

Finite State Machines

A *finite state machine* (FSM) is a hypothetical machine that can be in only one of a given number of states at any specific time. In response to an input, the machine generates an output and changes state. Both the output and the new state are purely functions of the current state and the input.

There are two notations commonly used to define FSMs: state transition diagrams (STD) and state transition matrices (STM). When STDs are used, a circle denotes a state, a directed arc connecting two states denotes the potential to transition between the two indicated states, and the label on the arc (which has two parts separated by a slash) denotes the input that triggers the transition and the output with which the sys-

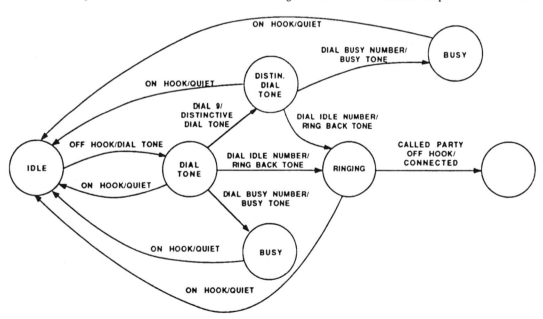

FIGURE 3. State Transition Diagram Example

STIMULUS / STATE	LIFT PHONE	DIAL 9	DIAL 1-8	DIAL 0	HANG UP PHONE	SEVENTH DIGIT COLLECTED	OUTPUTS
IDLE	DIAL TONE STATE	–	–	–	–	–	QUIET
DIAL TONE STATE	–	DISTINCTIVE DIAL TONE	COLLECTING 7 DIGITS	OPERATOR	IDLE	–	DIAL TONE TO CALLING PARTY
DISTINCTIVE DIAL TONE STATE	–	COLLECTING 7 DIGITS	COLLECTING 7 DIGITS	OPERATOR	IDLE	–	DISTINCTIVE DIAL TONE TO CALLING PARTY
OPERATOR STATE	–	–	–	–	IDLE	–	CONNECT CALLING PARTY TO OPERATOR
COLLECTING 7 DIGITS STATE	–	COLLECTING 7 DIGITS	COLLECTING 7 DIGITS	COLLECTING 7 DIGITS	IDLE	IF CALLED PARTY BUSY, BUSY STATE; OTHERWISE, RINGING STATE	NO TONE TO CALLING PARTY
RINGING STATE	–	–	–	–	–	–	RINGING SIGNAL TO CALLED PARTY; RINGBACK TONE TO CALLING PARTY
BUSY STATE	–	–	–	–	–	–	BUSY TONE TO CALLING PARTY

FIGURE 4. Finite State Machine Telephony Example

tem responds. For example, Figure 3 shows a small fragment of the specification of the external behavior of a telephone switching system. Starting with the IDLE state on the left, there is exactly one arc emanating out of it. It is labeled "OFF HOOK/DIAL TONE" and terminates at the DIAL TONE state. That means that when the system is in IDLE and receives the stimulus OFF HOOK, it will generate a DIAL TONE and enter the DIAL TONE state. There are four arcs emanating from the DIAL TONE state, and the path taken will be a function of whether the system receives an ON HOOK (system will generate QUIET and return to the IDLE state), a "9" (system will generate a DISTINCTIVE DIAL TONE and enter the DISTINCTIVE DIAL TONE state), a DIAL IDLE NUMBER (system will generate a RING BACK TONE and enter the RINGING state), or a DIAL BUSY NUMBER (system will generate a BUSY TONE and enter the BUSY state). It *is* possible to describe the behavior shown in Figure 3 in natural language. We just have. As soon as you stop talking however, in terms of states, inputs, and outputs, the behavioral description becomes extremely hard to create or understand without ambiguity.

Remember that Figure 3 is part of an SRS; it is not a design. The implication to the designer reading Figure 3 in the SRS is:

Dear Designer: I don't care how you design the system, but when it is all done and I observe it as a black box, I want it to behave externally as if it were designed as the finite state machine shown. Signed, the Requirements Writer.

The second way to describe the behavior of a finite state machine is the STM. In an STM, a table is drawn with all the possible states labeling the rows and all the possible stimuli labeling the columns. In the Mealy model, the next state and the required system response

appear in each intersection. In the Moore model, the intersections of columns and rows contain only the name of the next state, and a separate column is drawn to indicate the system response associated with each state. The choice between Mealy and Moore should be guided by which one is most expressive and understandable for the particular application. Figure 4 shows a small subset of a telephone switching system's external behavior using a Moore STM.

Finite state machines have been used effectively for requirements specifications for telephony applications [38, 58]. They also serve as the underlying model of many of the techniques that follow.

Decision Tables and Decision Trees

Sometimes there is a need to describe the required external behavior of some aspect of a system when the FSM approach makes no sense. For example, if we want to specify the external behavior of a software-controlled elevator door on an elevator control system, we would easily agree that:

- If the elevator is stopped at a floor and the OPEN DOOR button is pressed, the elevator doors should open.
- If the CLOSE DOOR button is pressed, the elevator doors should close.
- If the time limit is exceeded, the elevator doors should close.

We would agree that the SRS should include these three statements, yet what if a combination of the conditions is true? For example, what do we do when the time limit is exceeded and the OPEN DOOR button is pressed? In general, the required system responses to all combinations of these stimuli are difficult to describe using a finite state machine, and even more difficult to describe in English. One simple solution is the

One column for every combination of condition outcomes

		RULE #1	RULE #2	RULE #3	RULE #4	RULE #5	RULE #6	RULE #7	RULE #8
List all conditions that influence decisions	CONDITION #1	Y	Y	Y	Y	N	N	N	N
	CONDITION #2	Y	Y	N	N	Y	Y	N	N
	CONDITION #3	Y	N	Y	N	Y	N	Y	N
List all the possible decisions	ACTION #1	X	X	X				X	
	ACTION #2		X	X	X				
	ACTION #3						X		
	ACTION #4	X			X	X			

All combinations of answers

Fill in with the actual required system behavior

FIGURE 5. Decision Table

decision table. Decision tables and decision trees have been known for decades. Their uses and capabilities were recently explored thoroughly by Chvalovsky [17] and Moret [41].

To construct a *decision table* (see Figure 5), first draw a row for each condition (or stimulus) that will be used in the process of making a decision. Next draw a column for every possible combination of outcomes of those conditions (if there are n conditions and each has a binary result, then there will be 2^n columns). Finally, add rows at the bottom of the table for each action (or response) that you may want the system to perform (or generate), and fill in the boxes to reflect which actions you want performed for each combination of conditions. Figure 6 shows a decision table for a software-controlled elevator door problem. Although it has

64 columns, it is easier to create and understand than an STD or STM and is considerably easier to understand than the corresponding English!

A *decision tree* captures the same information as a decision table but is graphical rather than tabular. Basically it is a flow chart without loops and without fan-in (i.e., two arrows pointing to the same node). The decision tree often takes up more room than the corresponding decision table because of the blank space required between the nodes, but because the decision tree captures the order of evaluating the conditions, it is possible to save considerable space on some problems due to the all-encompassing effect of some conditions. For example, the decision tree in Figure 7 shows the same behavior as the decision table in Figure 6.

Decision tables can easily be "automated" with any

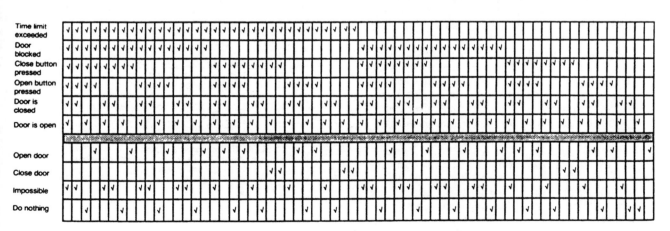

FIGURE 6. A Decision Table for an Elevator Door Control

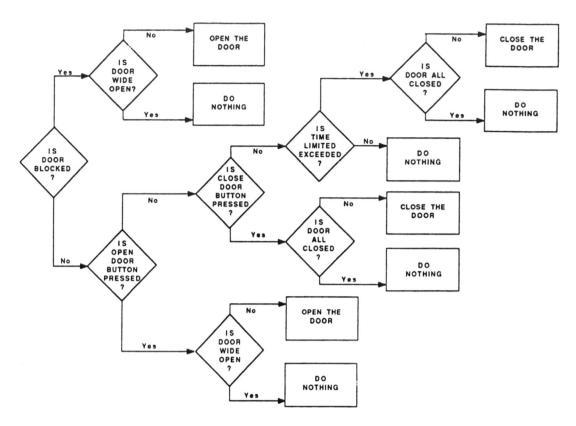

FIGURE 7.   A Decision Tree for an Elevator Door Control

standard spreadsheet package. The external behavior of at least one large product was specified using decision tables [11].

Program Design Language

Program Design Language (PDL) is now the de facto standard for specifying detailed designs for software modules. PDL, also called structured English and pseudocode, is simply free-form English with special meanings for certain key words. The most commonly used PDL today is processed by a tool called PDL [12].

Many people who see PDL in SRSs claim that the requirements writers have overstepped their bounds and fallen into design. One reason for this may be that these people are voicing an objection because they are so familiar with seeing PDL during design that they may not even read the SRS PDL to find out what it says. It is not the format that makes something appropriate for the requirements or the design phase; it is the content.

For example, let us return to the elevator door control problem. We indicated that it is important during the requirements phase to specify completely the doors' desired *external* behavior resulting from all possible combinations of *external* stimuli that may be present. Figure 8 shows a PDL specification that exhibits the same behavior as Figures 6 and 7. One of the biggest problems with using PDL during the requirements

phase is the incredible ease with which one can fall into design. The best advice to help one stay out of design is to initially select all the nouns, verbs, and adjectives to be used in the SRS to represent things that can be seen, smelled, felt, heard, or tasted by somebody who is an external observer of the final system. This approach of preselection was demonstrated for telephony by Casey [13] and Davis [27] and for a flight control application by Heninger [36].

```
IF door blocked
THEN IF door not wide-open
        THEN open door
        ENDIF
ELSE IF open_door_button pressed
      THEN IF door not wide-open
            THEN open door
            ENDIF
      ELSE IF close_door_button pressed
           THEN IF door not completely-closed
                 THEN close door
                 ENDIF
           ELSE IF time-limit exceeded
                THEN IF door not completely-closed
                      THEN close door
                      ENDIF

          ENDIF
        ENDIF
    ENDIF
ENDIF
```

FIGURE 8.   A PDL for an Elevator Door Control

Structured Analysis/Real-Time

Two extensions of Structured Analysis (SA) [29] were recently proposed by Hatley [35] and Ward [54]. These extensions have been termed *Structured Analysis/Real-Time* (SA/RT). Hatley's extensions add control diagrams and control specs to their data counterparts. For example, in addition to the standard Data Flow Diagram (DFD), he adds the Control Flow Diagram (CFD). In addition to the process spec (DeMarco, et al., also called this the "mini-spec" [29]), he adds the control spec. Since Hatley appreciates the unique difference between requirements and design, he defines the requirements dictionary as the repository for all the processes, data, and controls present in the set of diagrams. The CFD looks just like a DFD but all arrows are drawn dotted, and the arrows denote control rather than data. Control implies either a command or a report of an occurrence of something happening. DFDs and CFDs are usually at the same level of abstraction. Thus, CFDs are associated with a corresponding DFD and are *slaves* (in the electrical engineering sense) of their DFD. Control specs are Mealy or Moore model state transition diagrams or matrices for finite state machines corresponding to a CFD. Hatley has applied his extensions to a commercial flight management computer system.

Ward's extensions are very similar to Hatley's. Rather than two types of diagrams, the DFD and the CFD, Ward allows the introduction of control information in the standard DFD. Thus, in addition to the usual processes (i.e., data transformations), data flows, and data stores (i.e., data bases) in a DFD, he allows for control transformations, event flows, and buffers. Furthermore, Ward differentiates between two types of data flows:

(1) *Discrete Data.* A single item of data (e.g., current floor in an elevator control example); and

(2) *Continuous Data.* A source of constantly available and perhaps continuously changing data (e.g., current position of doors where 0 is open and 1 is closed and all values in between are possible);

and three types of event flows:

(1) *Signal.* Reporting of an event (e.g., doors have reached their full open position);

(2) *Activation.* A direct overt action to initiate control process (e.g., the elevator control system activating the elevator door control process upon arrival at a floor); and

(3) *Deactivation.* A direct overt action to stop another process (e.g., the elevator control system deactivating the usual elevator dispatching process upon detecting a fire in the building).

In addition, Ward has given the SRS writer the ability to specify a Mealy model finite state machine description for each control transformer in the DFD. Notationally, rectangles are used for the states in the STD to prevent accidentally mistaking it for a DFD, as shown in Figure 9 [54]. Ward's final extension provides for the hierarchical definition of transformation schemas, that is, hierarchical finite state machines. His brief description falls far short of the elegance and rigor of state-charts, which we will discuss next.

Statecharts

Statecharts, extensions to Finite State Machines (FSM), were recently proposed by Harel [33]. Statecharts make it even easier to model complex real-time system behavior without ambiguity. The extensions provide a notation and set of conventions that facilitate the hierarchical decomposition of FSMs and a mechanism for communication between concurrent FSMs. The first extension to FSMs suggested by Harel allows a transition that is a function not only of an external stimulus but also of the truth of a particular condition. As shown in Figure 10, the condition becomes a convenient notation in telephony, for example, to specify that the new state (BUSY TONE or RING BACK TONE) is a function of whether or not the party being called (i.e., the CALLEE) is busy.

The next simple extension is the *superstate*. The superstate can be used to aggregate sets of states with common transitions. For example, let us assume that we have a situation in which two states, S_1 and S_2, both transition to state S_3 upon the same stimulus, i. Using regular STDs, Figure 11(a) would result. With the superstate concept, however, we can use the shorthand notation shown in Figure 11(b). Telephony, once again, provides an excellent example. In particular, the caller going on-hook causes a transition from most call states back to the idle state. Figure 12 demonstrates this application of the superstate. It is apparent that superstates can be conceptualized and defined before they are decomposed into subordinate states; thus superstates pro-

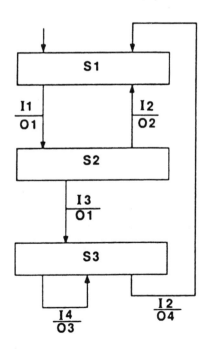

FIGURE 9. Ward-style State Transition Diagram

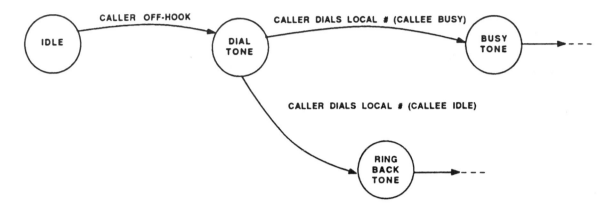

FIGURE 10. Using the Condition Transition Extension for a Local Telephone Call

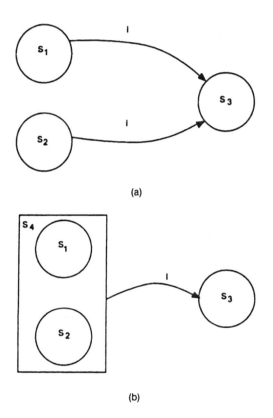

FIGURE 11. The Superstate Extension to FSMs

vide us with a formal basis for iterative refinement and successive decomposition of FSMs.

Harel also introduces the concept of the default entry state. This is the subordinate state of a superstate into which the FSM enters if no other subordinate state is specified as the next state. One specifies such a default entry state with a small arrow as shown in Figure 13. Thus, if state S_{21} were defined as the default entry state of state S_2, Figure 13 would imply that we move transitionally from state S_1 to state S_{21} in the event of stimulus, i.

Earlier, we described the process of decomposing a state (e.g., S_2) into subordinate states (e.g., S_{21} and S_{22}). The implied semantics of this refinement are that of an *or* function; namely, that when we are in state S_2 at the higher level of abstraction, we are really in either state S_{21} or state S_{22} at the lower level of abstraction. Harel also introduces a different type of state refinement: the *and* function. The *and* decomposition in statecharts is represented by splitting a box using dashed lines. For example, Figure 14(a) shows a simple STD. Figure 14(b) shows the refinement of state S_2 into its two subordinate states, S_{21} and S_{22}. The semantics behind this notation are well defined. In particular, when we are in state S_2, we are in states S_{21} *and* S_{22}. This becomes more meaningful when states S_{21} and S_{22} are further refined as shown in Figure 14(c). On receipt of stimulus i_1, in state S_1, we enter both states S_{211} and S_{222} simultaneously. If stimulus i_4 now arrives, we transition from states S_{211} and S_{222} simultaneously into states S_{212} *and* S_{223}. On the other hand, if stimulus i_6 arrives while we are in states S_{211} and S_{222}, only the S_{22} machine changes state from state S_{222} to S_{221}, leaving us in both S_{211} and S_{221}. Harel uses the term *orthogonal* to describe this type of decomposition and to emphasize the independence of state machines S_{21} and S_{22}. The simplicity, applicability, and elegance of Harel's orthogonal decomposition becomes most apparent when one compares equivalent behavioral descriptions using conventional state transition diagrams. Figure 15 shows the equivalent to Figure 14(c) using conventional STDs. Not only has the number of states increased (which makes STDs tenuous at best for describing complex system behavior), but also the monolithic structure of Figure 15 makes it extremely hard to understand in comparison to the statechart of Figure 14(c).

Earlier, we discussed the ability to specify the triggering of a transition not only on the arrival of a stimulus, but also on the truth of a condition. In concert with the orthogonality refinement, Harel has also defined the ability to specify a transition based on whether an FSM is in a particular state. For example, Figure 16 shows a modification of Figure 14(c) in order to specify that the

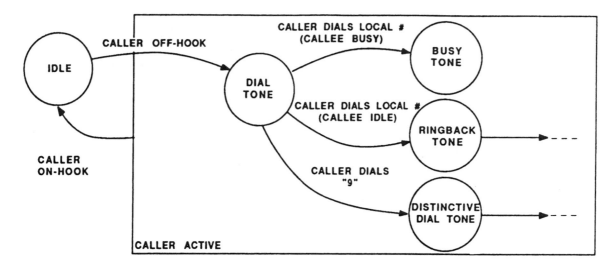

FIGURE 12. Using the Superstate Extension in Telephony

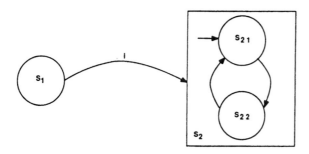

FIGURE 13. Default Entry State Example

transition from state S_{213} to state S_{211} will only occur if machine (superstate) S_{22} is in state S_{222}.

In summary, Harel's statecharts provide natural extensions to FSMs to make them more suitable for the specification of external behavior of real-time systems. These extensions provide for the hierarchical decomposition of states and the specification of transitions dependent on global conditions and on being in particular states.

Requirements Engineering Validation System

The *Requirements Engineering Validation System* (REVS) [28] is a set of tools that analyzes requirements written in the Requirements Statement Language (RSL) [6] developed using the Software Requirements Engineering Methodology (SREM) [2]. The tools, language, and methodology were developed by TRW, Inc., for the U.S. Army Ballistic Missile Defense (now called the Strategic Defense Command) Advanced Technology Center in Huntsville, Alabama. RSL and its corresponding graphical notation, R-nets [4], represent an extension to conventional FSMs. In particular, for some large, complex, real-time systems, it may not make sense to describe the external behavior of the entire system as one huge finite state machine.

As described earlier, Harel's extensions, which provide the hierarchical decomposition of FSMs, may not be easy or straightforward to apply. In particular, some applications are *stimulus rich*. Stimulus rich implies that customers view the system they want to buy or build in terms of its rich set of stimuli. For such systems, it is easier for customers to think of their requirements for the solution system's external behavior as organized into a set of units, each describing all required system responses to a single stimulus, R-nets. One can think of

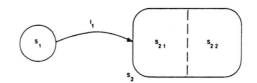

(a) The Highest Level Statechart

(b) The Refinement of State S_2

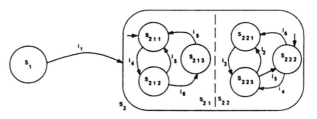

(c) The Refinement Of States S_{21} and S_{22}

FIGURE 14. Refinement Using the "And" Function

293

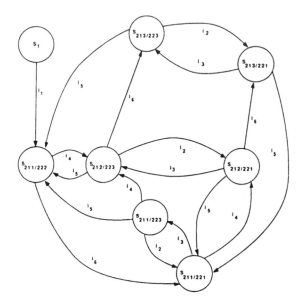

FIGURE 15. An Equivalent Conventional STD

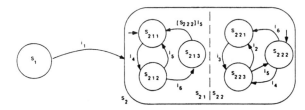

FIGURE 16. Specifying Transitions Dependent on States

an R-net as a column of the state transition matrix, and thus the R-net is simply an organizational piece of a full FSM. R-net notation is shown in Figure 17. Figure 18 shows an example of an R-net for the "Dial 9" column of Figure 4. Figure 19 defines the same behavior in RSL.

REVS has been operational since 1977. Originally hosted on a Texas Instruments Advanced Scientific Computer and on a CDC 7600, and later rewritten in PASCAL and rehosted on VAX, REVS has most recently been rewritten in Ada. TRW in Huntsville and Ascent Logic Corporation in San Jose have extended SREM and REVS to encompass earlier development phases, such as a system level requirements and system design. The new support tool is called the Distributed Computing Design System (DCDS), and the methodology is called the System Level Requirements Methodology (SYSREM) [3].

Requirements Language Processor
The Requirements Language Processor (RLP) [20, 26] is part of an overall Requirements Processing System (RPS) developed by GTE Laboratories in Waltham, Massachusetts. The motivation for developing RLP was similar to that of REVS: namely that monolithic FSMs seemed to be too unwieldy for the requirements specification of complex, real-time systems. Whereas REVS

uses the R-net as the organizational unit of the SRS, RLP uses the *stimulus-response sequence*. In essence, a stimulus-response sequence is a trace of a two-way dialog between the system under specification and its environment. The selection of which sequences to use is simple: use sequences that define *typical* dialogs. These typical dialogs should correspond to actual user-oriented, user-known, external system features. Figure 20 shows a complete example of the external behavior of a local call [23].

The decision of whether or not to use RLP on a particular application should be based on the types of questions a typical customer or user would ask about

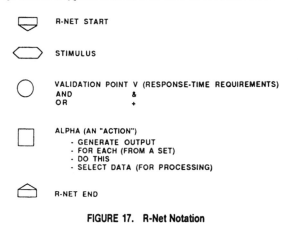

FIGURE 17. R-Net Notation

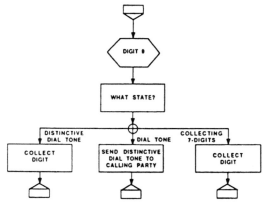

FIGURE 18. An R-Net Example

```
R Net: Process__digit__nine
    Structure:
            Input__interface digit__9__dialed__by__calling__party
            What__state
            Do (state = dial tone)
                        Send__distinctive__dial__tone__to__calling__party
                (state = collecting 7 digits)
                        Collect__digit
                        Terminate
                (distinctive dial tone)
                        Collect__digit
                        Terminate
        End
    End
```

FIGURE 19. An RSL Example

294

```
FEATURE:  local to local call
    IN Idle state
     WAIT FOR calling party to go off hook
     IN receiving dial tone state
     WAIT FOR calling party to go on hook OR dial local no.
    IF calling party Is on hook
    THEN IN Idle state
    ELSE IF called party Is busy
       THEN IN receiving busy tone state
           WAIT FOR calling party to go on hook
           IN Idle state
       ELSE IN receiving ringback tone state
           WAIT FOR calling party to go on hook OR
               called party to go off hook
           IF calling party Is on hook
           THEN IN Idle state
           ELSE
               DO WHILE (called party Is off hook)
                 Connect (called party, calling party)
                 WAIT FOR called party to go on hook OR
                     calling party to go on hook
                 IF called party Is on hook
                 THEN WAIT FOR called party to go off hook OR
                     calling party to go on hook
                 ELSE IN disconnected calling party state
                     WAIT FOR called party to go on hook
               END DO
END FEATURE
```

FIGURE 20. Stimulus-Response Sequence Example

the product. If the questions are about features (e.g., long-distance calls, call-forwarding) rather than particular stimuli (e.g., dialing 0, dialing 9), then RLP may be the answer.

Also, RLP is *multilingual* [23, 52], which means that it supports a wide variety of requirements languages, each tailored to a specific application. For example, it might be desirable to use RLP for four different applications: battlefield command and control, patient monitoring, ballistic missile defense, and nuclear reactor control. The four languages used would be defined in the "Language definition tables" as shown in Figure 21 (adapted from [21]). Once these tables existed, requirements writers would select an appropriate language, write requirements using that language, and run RLP. RLP would check the requirements for correct syntax and semantics; detect and report violations; detect and report any inconsistency, ambiguity, and incompleteness in the requirements; and generate a requirements

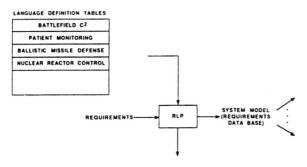

REPORTS
• ERRORS (INCONSISTENT, INCOMPLETE, AMBIGUOUS)
• FORMATTED OUTPUTS

FIGURE 21. The Requirements Language Processor Architecture

database. This database can later be used to drive automatic system test generation [15, 19, 21], automated requirements simulation [22], and automatic program synthesis [24]. RLP also has the capability of generating SDL charts from textual requirements languages.

The Specification and Description Language

The *Specification and Description Language* (SDL) [46] was developed in the late 1970s by CCITT for the external behavior and internal design of telephone switching systems. SDL is a superset of STDs. Figure 22 shows the SDL for the identical segment of an SRS as was shown in Figure 20 using RLP.

PAISLey

The *Process-oriented*, *Applicative* and *Interpretable Specification Language* (PAISLey) was developed by Pamela Zave while at the University of Maryland and later at AT&T Bell Laboratories. PAISLey [60, 62] is a language for the requirements specification of embedded systems using an operational approach. *Operational* means that the resulting specification can be executed (or interpreted), and the resulting behavior would mimic the behavior required of the system to be built. From that perspective, statecharts, REVS, and RLP all provide operational approaches to requirements specification.

What makes PAISLey unique is that it is a simple language, with rigor and formality adopted from the disciplines of asynchronous processes and functional programming. *Asynchronous processes*, exemplified by the cooperating "and" FSMs of Harel, are independently operating autonomous abstractions of computations that usually communicate with each other via some protocol, such as interrupts, messages, handshakes, etc. *Functional programming* is a technique that describes behavior through the definition of functions that map inputs into outputs rather than through the definition of procedures that, when executed, transform inputs into outputs.

When using PAISLey, the requirements writer decomposes both the system under specification and its environment into sets of asynchronous interacting processes. For example, Figure 23 shows a decomposition of a patient monitoring system into five processes and its environment into four processes (adapted from [60]). Once this is accomplished, each process must be defined. This is accomplished by defining the range of possible states in which the process may enter (i.e., the state space) and by declaring and defining sets of functions that define how the processes change state (successor functions) and how the processes interact (exchange functions). Processes that are part of the environment are treated no differently than processes that are part of the system. Figure 24 shows a small subset of some of these definitions and declarations of processes and functions. Figure 24 is only a partial specification of the behavior of the patient monitoring system shown in Figure 23. Still necessary are descriptions of the update of the acceptable vital sign tolerances for

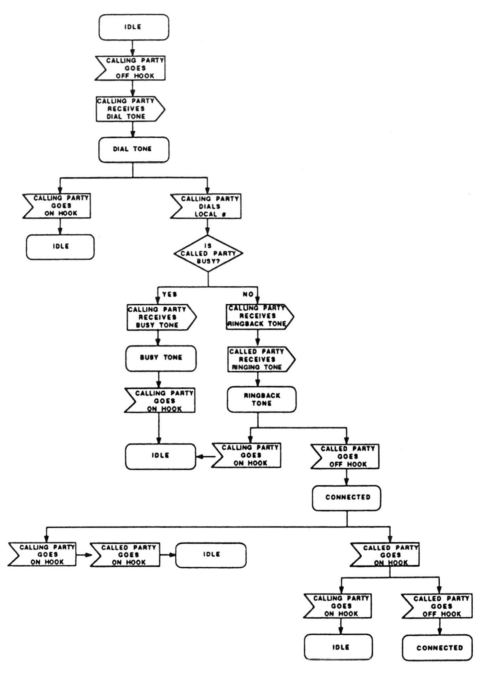

FIGURE 22. An SDL Example

patients, the action of the real-time clock as an initiator of the "patient-check-cycle" and as a source of the current time for the database storage, and many other functions.

Some critics of PAISLey claim that the resulting specification is a design specification, not a requirements specification. Two primary reasons for this claim are that the resulting specification is difficult, if not impossible, for the typical customer or user to understand, and that writing in PAISLey requires a lot of rigorous,

detailed thought. Zave defends PAISLey against this claim [60] by saying that customers and users need not view the same representation of the requirements and that the difference between requirements and design is subtle. Further she claims that the software synthesis process is a series of iterations in which each level implies the requirements for the next level.

A set of PAISLey tools has recently been implemented to find and report syntactic or semantic violations, perform static analysis, and provide interactive execution of PAISLey specifications [61]. A recent experiment in using PAISLey on a real system development effort is reported in [7].

Petri-nets

Petri-nets were first introduced in 1962 by Petri [44] and later described by Peterson [43]. Like the finite state machines described earlier, Petri-nets are abstract virtual machines with a very well-defined behavior. They have been used for many years to specify process synchrony during the design phase of time-critical applications. There has only recently been interest in their application during the requirements phase.

Petri-nets are usually represented as a graph composed of two types of nodes: circles (called places) and lines (called transitions). Arrows (directed arcs) interconnect places and transitions. Black dots (called tokens) move from place to place according to a specific rule. The rule is that tokens may pass through a transition only when (a) a clock pulse has arrived (i.e., the Petri-net is synchronized) and (b) all the arrows entering that transition are emanating from places that contain tokens.

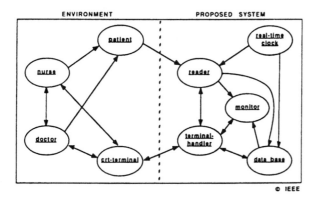

FIGURE 23. Asynchronous Processes for a System and Its Environment

```
(patient-cycle:  PATIENT-STATE  ———➤  PATIENT-STATE,
patient-check-cycle:  ALERT-STATUS  ———➤  ALERT-STATUS
retrieve:  DATABASE x REQUEST  ———➤  DATABASE x VITAL-SIGN-TOLERANCE
sense:  PATIENT-STATE  ———➤  ACTUAL-VITAL-SIGNS
check:  VITAL-SIGN-TOLERANCE x ACTUAL-VITAL-SIGNS  ———➤  ALERT-STATUS
update:  DATABASE x ACTUAL-VITAL-SIGNS  ———➤  DATABASE)
```

(a) Partial Declaration of Processes and their Successor Functions

```
patient-check-cycle[n] =

    proj-2-1[(check[(sense[n], retrieve[patient-database,n])]),
            update[(patient-database, sense[n])])]
```

(b) Definition of the Primary Patient Monitoring System Function

FIGURE 24. Sample PAISLey Statements

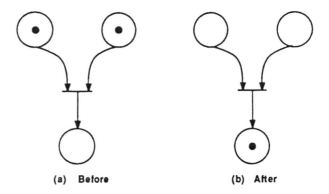

(a) Before   (b) After

FIGURE 25. Token Merging in Petri Nets

Let us assume that only one token is permitted at any one place.[1] The arrival of a clock pulse at Figure 25(a) will result in Figure 25(b). Also, let us assume that, in the cases of a fan-out, the token will be replicated and a copy will follow every path that it can.

Let us now observe the behavior of a Petri-net through a series of clock pulses over a period of time. The initial state of the Petri-net is shown in Figure 26(a). Figures 26(b) through (e) show the movements of the tokens as each clock pulse is processed.

Let us now look at a specific application in which a Petri-net could be helpful during the requirements phase: the automation of a warehouse. Figure 27(a) shows a Petri-net that captures the timing requirements of this application. At place P_1, a truck arrives at the loading dock. At place P_2, the paperwork is processed and inventory is checked. At place P_3, all the conveyor belts are moving from the loading dock to the warehouse. The belts are transporting people, robots, and forklifts. At place P_4, the conveyor belts are moving from the warehouse to the loading dock with all the requisite merchandise. At place P_5, the goods are loaded onto the truck.

This is a fine use of a Petri-net and at first glance explicitly shows how more than one truck can be handled at a time. On closer examination, however, there is a problem: if one truck is being processed at P_4 and the next truck is being processed at P_3, the conveyor belts would need to be going in both directions at once—an obvious impossibility. The solution is to introduce three new places, as shown in Figure 27(b). In particular, place P_7 prevents P_3 and P_4 from being active simultaneously. I call the token in P_7 the *escort token*, because it escorts tokens representing trucks (i.e., those on the P_1 to P_5 track) along the critical region of P_3 and P_4. As soon as the conveyor belts have completed the return of all the merchandise to the loading dock, not only does the token at P_4 move to the next step, P_5, but P_7 becomes reactivated and ready to escort the next token through the critical region. P_6 and P_8

---

[1] This is not the case with pure Petri-nets, but is an extension put forth by Patil [59].

297

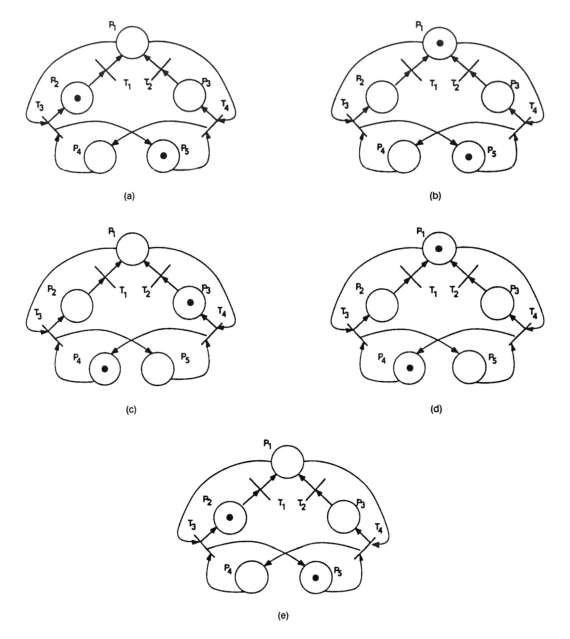

FIGURE 26. A Petri Net Sequence Example

serve similar functions for single steps; they prevent two tokens from accidentally falling into the same station.

Presumably, this entire Petri-net would also need places corresponding to physical buttons (see Figure 27(c)): the P_9 button would be pressed by the order taker when paperwork was complete, the P_{10} button would be pressed by the loaders when the conveyor belt was fully loaded with merchandise, and the P_{11} button would be pressed by the unloaders when the conveyor belt was completely unloaded.

Once again, Petri-nets are relatively simple to understand and are best used to describe pieces of intended system behavior where ambiguity cannot be tolerated

and precise process synchrony is important. One of the best descriptions of how Petri-nets can be used for real applications is given in [1]. Extensive examples of applying Petri-nets for the requirements specification of real-time systems are found in [59].

COMPARISON OF TECHNIQUES

In an earlier section, eight criteria were defined for the evaluation of requirements specification techniques. The techniques will now be analyzed, compared, and contrasted using each of the eight criteria. Figure 28 summarizes the results and scores each approach and criteria on a scale from 0 (poor) to 10 (excellent).

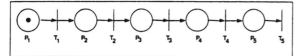

(a)   Version 1

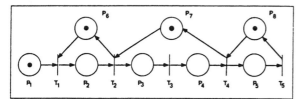

(b)   Version 2

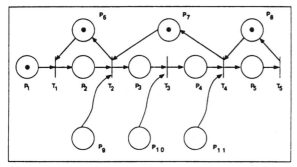

(c)   Version 3

FIGURE 27.   A Petri Net Example for a Warehouse

Understandable to Computer-naive Personnel

The ability of a computer-naive customer to understand an SRS is a subjective determination. On the other hand, understandability appears to be inversely proportional to the level of complexity and formality present [23]. Obviously, PDL, which is primarily natural language, is almost as easy to read as natural language. Decision trees appear in the non-technical literature regularly with no explanation, so they too are extremely understandable. Finite state machines, SA/RT, REVS, RLP, and SDL all require about the same amount of instruction to computer-naive people to enable them to read and comprehend SRS sections written using those approaches.

I have successfully taught hundreds of non-computer-oriented personnel to comprehend at least the basics of all these approaches in less than an hour per approach. Statecharts, PAISLey, and Petri-nets appear to be much more difficult to comprehend than the others for three unrelated reasons. In particular, statecharts are probably difficult because of their semantic richness. The concepts that statecharts add to basic FSMs provide expressive power and reduce the size of the resulting specification; many of the new concepts, however, are not intuitive to the non-computer scientist (albeit 100 percent intuitive to any computer scientist with even basic skills in automata theory and asynchronous processes). Conceptually, PAISLey suffers from the same problem that statecharts do. Practically, however, PAISLey has one additional problem: language that is a difficult to understand for the noncomputer scientist. Petri-nets are difficult to understand by an applications-oriented non-computer expert.

Basis for Design and Test

For a technique to make an SRS more useful to designers and system testers, its ambiguity level must be lowered and its understandability to the computer-oriented people who design and test must be increased. The former issue has already been discussed. For the latter issue, computer-oriented people prefer formal, precise documents. I contend that the very reasons why some techniques received low points for ambiguity are the same for why they received low points for understandability from testers and designers.

Automated Checking

Miller and Taylor [40] define three distinct levels of errors detectable in an SRS:

(1) *Static Structural.* Signals transmitted through inappropriate ports, or signals received by an entity but not sent by any entity;

(2) *Behavioral.* Two requirements conflict; a specification is ambiguous, incomplete, or redundant (see Davis [27] for further discussion of this class of error); and

(3) *Protocol.* Deadlocks between subsystems (see Sunshine [51] for further discussion of this class of error).

Natural language does not provide for automatic checking of any of these. PDL will be capable of detecting static structural errors. Finite state machines (using an automated tool, such as the Transition Diagram Editor [55–57]), SA/RT, REVS, and RLP all provide automatic checking of behavioral and static structural errors. Statecharts (using an automated tool such as STATEMATE1[2] [34, 50]) and PAISLey both provide full protocol error checking in addition to behavioral and static structural checking. Pure Petri-nets show synchrony very well, but one needs the Yoeli and Barzelai extensions [59] to fully specify protocols between asynchronous entities. Unfortunately, to my knowledge Petri-nets have not been automated, and thus suffer somewhat in their ability to automatically check for protocol violations. Decision trees and decision tables do not provide the ability to specify protocol and, although they are used to specify behavior, I do not know of any tools that automatically check for consistency. Finally, SDL can be used to specify protocol. To my knowledge, however, SDL has not been automated to any degree.

[2] STATEMATE1 is a trademark of I-Logix, Inc.

FIGURE 28. A Comparison of SRS Approaches

Criterion	Natural Language	FSM's	DT's	PDL	SA/RT	Statecharts	REVS	RLP	SDL	PAISLey	Petri-nets
1 Understandable to computer-naive personnel	10 — Obviously understandable to computer-naive personnel	10 — Requires an hour or two of instruction to facilitate understanding by computer-naive personnel	10 — Appear in literature regularly without explanation	10 — Almost as easy to read as natural language because most of it is natural language	7 — See FSM's	5 — Many FSM extensions not intuitive to the noncomputer scientist	7 — See FSM's	7 — See FSM's	7 — See FSM's	2 — Many concepts are not intuitive to the noncomputer scientist; hard-to-understand language for same audience	4 — Synchrony and Petri-nets appear to be difficult for noncomputer scientists to grasp
2 Basis For Design and Test	0 — With no formality there is no basis	7 — The formal model enables one to unambiguously define intended product behavior and thus serve as a basis for both design and test	7 — See FSM's	2 — Being little more than natural language, the lack of formality provides no basis	7 — The static data-oriented view of a system is helpful for data-intensive applications. See also FSM's	9 — With the additional expressive power over FSM's, there is less potential for ambiguity and thus a more formal basis for design and test	9 — See statecharts	9 — See statecharts	7 — See FSM's	9 — See statecharts	7 — See FSM's
3 Automated Checking	0 — No processor is available to perform any checking	7 — Static structural and behavioral errors can be detected	0 — See natural language	1 — Static structural errors can be detected	7 — See FSM's	9 — Static structural, behavioral, and protocol errors can be detected	7 — See FSM's	7 — See FSM's	0 — See natural language (potential exists for static structural and behavioral error checking)	0 — See statecharts	0 — See natural language (potential exists for protocol error checking)
4 External View, Not Internal View	0 — No help provided	3 — Needs human discipline in defining the external entities up front	3 — See FSM's	0 — No help provided	2 — For many applications, the data view is the design of the software	5 — Structural view provided explicitly and independent of behavioral views	7 — Same as RLP, but slightly lower because R-Net is more design oriented than stimulus-response sequence	9 — Once external entities are defined, specifier stays naturally in the requirements domain	8 — See RLP	2 — A common criticism of PAISLey is its design orientation. Save is not concerned if design is performed during requirements	2 — Very difficult to use Petri-nets in the application domain. Many people versed in Petri-nets are designers
5 SRS Organizational Assistance	1 — Paragraph and Chapter	2 — The machine	2 — The table or tree	2 — The module	8 — Hierarchical definition of transforms and machines	8 — See SA/RT; plus more semantic richness; hierarchical alternatives; multiple viewpoints	8 — The R-Net plus hierarchy of alphas	7 — The stimulus-response sequence; the feature	7 — The stimulus-response sequence; the feature	8 — See statecharts	7 — The net
6 Prototype Generation	0 — None	10 — Yes, using IDE tools	0 — None	0 — None	0 — None	10 — Yes, using i-logix tools	7 — Yes, using TRW tools plus auxiliary coding	2 — Feasibility demonstrated, but not implemented	0 — None	10 — Yes, using Bell Labs tools	0 — None
7 Automatic Test Generation	0 — None	0 — None	0 — None	0 — None	0 — None	0 — None	0 — None	10 — Yes, using GTE tools	0 — None	0 — None	0 — None
8 Appropriate Applications	Any application where misinterpretation of requirements is acceptable, or at least non-critical	Any real-time application that is small enough to not warrant statecharts, REVS or RLP. For example: small process-control applications	Those particular parts of any application which are decision-intensive	See natural language	Applications with strong data intensity or a need to identify cooperation between FSM's; for example: Most business applications; many process-control applications	Any complex real-time application; especially those with sufficient complexity and criticality to warrant the multiple viewpoints and extra expressive power	Real-time applications that are stimulus-oriented; for example: many defense systems	Real-time applications that are feature-oriented; for example: telephony	SDL was specifically developed for telephone switching system, but is probably applicable to all RLP applications	PAISLey was developed for complex real-time systems	Those particular parts of any application in which synchrony is critical to the specification of external behavior

External View, Not Internal View

PDL does not provide help for the requirements writer who needs to remain at the requirements level and not proceed into design. Due to its genealogy (i.e., structured analysis, which is one of the worst offenders in this regard), SA/RT, must also score low. Finite state machines, decision tables, and decision trees require a considerable amount of human discipline to first define the external entities and then use the approach to describe the attributes of and existent relationships between those entities. Statecharts are slightly better as they provide the structural viewpoint independent from the behavioral and data-flow viewpoints. The methodology, however, does not encourage one to specifically define the requirements for an entity before defining that entity's internal structure. Finally, REVS, RLP, and SDL provide much better assistance due to their requirement to deal only with previously defined explicit external signals, although all three can be easily misused. REVS probably scores slightly lower than RLP and SDL because the view of "what will the system do in response to this input signal" is somewhat more of an inside-out view than the "what do I have to do to make the system perform this function" view exhibited by RLP and SDL.

SRS Organizational Assistance

Finite state machines, decision tables, decision trees, PDL, and Petri-nets all provide rudimentary SRS organizational assistance. In particular, the FSM and Petrinet approaches offer the underlying machine model as the only organizational entity. Decision tables and trees provide the table and tree, respectively. PDL provides a module that can be used for anything. REVS enables SRS writers to organize the behavioral requirements into R-nets, each corresponding to a system stimulus. SDL and RLP enable SRS writers to organize the behavioral requirements into user-oriented features. SA/RT, statecharts, and PAISLey all provide at least two levels of organization because of their ability to separately model synchrony, data flow, and external behavior.

Automatic Prototype and Test Generation

Automatic generation of prototypes is possible with FSMs (e.g., when using TDE [55–57]), statecharts (e.g., when using STATEMATE1 [34, 50]), and PAISLey, without much intervention other than defining the requirements in their respective languages. REVS provides prototype generation capability, but it requires considerable auxiliary coding effort on the user's part [31]. The feasibility of automatic prototype generation using RLP has been explored but not implemented [22, 53]. None of the other approaches support prototype generation. RLP has the capability to automatically generate system-level tests directly from the requirements [15].

Appropriate Applications

Each technique is suitable to a particular subset of applications. The bottom row of Figure 28 describes the appropriate applications for each technique.

Acknowledgments. Dr. Edward Bersoff deserves special recognition for his faith, financial support, and moral support. Also, my thanks to Kathy Brown, Judy Israel, Marcia Lewis, Jere Milburn, and Lee Price for helping to make this a professional product.

REFERENCES

1. Agerwala, T. Putting Petri-nets to work. *IEEE Comput. 12,* 12 (Dec. 1979), 85–94.
2. Alford, M. A requirements engineering methodology for real-time processing requirements. *IEEE Trans. Softw. Eng. 3,* 1 (Jan. 1977), 60–69.
3. Alford, M. SREM at the age of eight; The distributed design system. *IEEE Comput. 18,* 4 (Apr. 1985), 36–46.
4. Alford, M., and Burns, I. R-nets: A graph model for real-time software requirements. In *Proceedings of the Symposium on Computer Software Engineering.* Polytechnic Press, New York, 1976, pp. 97–108.
5. Basili, V., and Weiss, D. Evaluation of a software requirements document by analysis of change data. In *Proceedings of the 5th International Conference on Software Engineering* (San Diego, CA. March 9–12). pp. 314–323, IEEE Press, Wash., D.C., 1981.
6. Bell, T., and Bixler, D. A flow oriented requirements statement language. In *Proceedings of the Symposium on Computer Software Engineering.* Polytechnic Press, New York, 1976, pp. 109–122.
7. Berliner, E., and Zave, P. An experiment in technology transfer: PAISLey specification of requirements for an undersea lightwave cable system. In *Proceedings of the 9th IEEE International Conference on Software Engineering* (Monterey, CA, March 30–April 2), pp. 42–50. IEEE Press, Wash., D.C., 1987.
8. Berzins, V., and Gray, M. Analysis and design in MSG 84: Formalizing functional specifications. *IEEE Trans. Softw. Eng. 11,* 8 (Aug. 1985), 657–670.
9. Boehm, B. Software engineering. *IEEE Trans. Comput. 25,* 12 (Dec. 1976), 1226–1241.
10. Boehm, B., et al. Some experience with automated aids to the design of large-scale reliable software. *ACM SIGPLAN Not. 10,* 6 (June 1975), 105–113.
11. Buhrke, R., et al. Design choices for a large PCM switch with multiprocessor control. In *Proceedings of the International Switching Symposium* (May 1979).
12. Caine, S., and Gordon, E. PDL—A tool for software design. In *Proceedings of the AFIPS National Computer Conference,* Vol. 44 (Anaheim, CA, 1975). AFIPS Press, Montvale, New Jersey, pp. 271–276.
13. Casey, B., and Taylor, B. Writing requirements in English: A natural alternative. In *Proceedings of the IEEE Software Engineering Standards Workshop* (San Francisco, California, August). IEEE Press, Wash., D.C., 1981. pp. 95–101.
14. Celko, J., et al. A demonstration of three requirements language systems. *SIGPLAN Not. 18,* 1 (Jan. 1983). 9–14.
15. Chandrasekharan, M., et al. Requirements-based testing of real-time systems: Modeling for testability. *IEEE Comput. 18,* 4 (Apr. 1985), 71–80.
16. Charette, R. *Software Engineering Environments.* McGraw Hill, New York, 1986.
17. Chvalovsky, V. Decision tables. *Softw. Pract. Exper. 13* (1983), 423–429.
18. Daly, E. Management of software development. *IEEE Trans. Softw. Eng. 3,* 3 (May 1977), 230–242.
19. Dasarathy, B. Test plan generation for the requirements validation of real-time systems. In *Proceedings of the IEEE Workshop on Automatic Test Program Generation* (Philadelphia, PA, April). IEEE Press, Wash., D.C., 1986.
20. Davis, A. Requirements language processing for the effective testing of real-time software. *ACM Softw. Eng. Notes 3,* 5 (Nov. 1978), 61–66.
21. Davis, A. Automating the requirements phase: Benefits to later phases of the software life-cycle. In *Proceedings of IEEE COMPSAC '80* (Chicago, Ill., October 27–31), pp. 42–48. IEEE Press, Wash., D.C., 1980.
22. Davis, A. Rapid prototyping using executable requirements specifications. *ACM Softw. Eng. Notes 7,* 5 (Dec. 1982), 39–44.
23. Davis, A. The design of a family of applications-oriented requirements languages. *IEEE Comput. 15,* 5 (May 1982), 21–28.
24. Davis, A. The role of requirements in the software synthesis of real-time systems. In *Proceedings of the International Symposium on Current Issues in Requirements Engineering Environments* (Kyoto, Japan, Sept. 20–21) North-Holland, Amsterdam, The Netherlands, 1982, pp. 151–158.
25. Davis, A. A taxonomy for the early stages of the software development life cycle. *J. Syst. Softw. 8,* 4 (Sept. 1988).

26. Davis, A., et al. RLP: An automated tool for the processing of requirements. In *Proceedings of IEEE COMPSAC '79* (Chicago, Ill., November 5–8)), pp. 289–299, IEEE Press, Wash., D.C., 1979.

27. Davis, A., and Rauscher, T. Formal techniques and automatic processing to ensure correctness in requirements specifications. In *Proceedings of the IEEE Specifications of Reliable Software Conference* (Cambridge, Mass., April), pp. 15–35, IEEE Press, Wash., D.C., 1979.

28. Davis, C., and Vick, C. The software development system. *IEEE Trans. Softw. Eng. 3*, 1 (Jan. 1977), 69–84.

29. DeMarco, T. *Structured Analysis and System Specification*. Prentice Hall, Englewood Cliffs, New Jersey, 1979.

30. Fagan, M. Design and code inspections and process control in the development of programs. IBM Report IBM-SDD-TR-21.572. Dec. 1974, IBM, Bethesda, Maryland.

31. Furia, N. A comparative evaluation of RSL/REVS and PSL/PSA applied to a digital flight control system. In *Proceedings of the AIAA 2nd Computers in Aerospace Conference*, pp. 330–337, American Institute of Aeronautics and Astronautics, New York, NY, 1979.

32. Glaseman, S., and Davis, M. Software requirements for embedded computers: A preliminary report. U.S. Air Force Document R-2567-AF. Mar. 1980.

33. Harel, D. Statecharts: A visual formalism for complex systems. *Sci. Comput. Prog. 8* (1987).

34. Harel, D., et al. STATEMATE1: a working environment for the development of complex reactive systems. In *Proceedings of the Tenth International Conference on Software Engineering* (Singapore, April). IEEE Press, Wash. D.C., 1988.

35. Hatley, D. The use of structured methods in the development of large software-based avionics systems. In *Proceedings of the AIAA/IEEE 6th Digital Avionics Systems Conference* (Baltimore, MD), pp. 6–15, IEEE Press, Wash., D.C., 1984.

36. Heninger, K. Specifying software requirements for complex systems: New techniques and their application. *IEEE Trans. Softw. Eng. 6*, 1 (Jan. 1980), 2–13.

37. IEEE A guide for software requirements specifications. IEEE/ANSI Standard 830-1984. Institute of Electrical and Electronics Engineers, New York, 1984.

38. Kawashima, H., et al. Functional specification of call processing by state transition diagram. *IEEE Trans. Commun. 19*, 5 (Oct. 1971), 581–587.

39. Kerola, P., and Freeman, P. A comparison of life cycle models. In *Proceedings of the 5th International Conference on Software Engineering* (San Diego, CA, March 9–12), pp. 90–99, IEEE Press, Wash., D.C., 1981.

40. Miller, T., and Taylor, B. A system requirements methodology. In *Proceedings of the IEEE Electro '81 Conference* (New York, Apr.), pp. 18.5.1–18.5.5, IEEE Press, Wash., D.C. 1981.

41. Moret, B. Decision trees and diagrams. *ACM Comput. Surv. 14*, 4 (Dec. 1982), 593–623.

42. Patil, S. Coordination of asynchronous events. Ph.D. dissertation. MIT, Cambridge, Massachusetts, 1970.

43. Peterson, J. Petri-nets. *ACM Comput. Surv. 9*, 3 (Sept. 1977), 223–252.

44. Petri, C. Kommunikation mit automation. *Schriften des Reinsch-Westfalischen Inst. fur Instrumentelle Mathematik an der Universitat Bonn*, Bonn, West Germany, 1962.

45. Pressman, R. *Software Engineering: A Practitioner's Guide*. McGraw Hill, New York, 1982.

46. Rockstrom, A., and Saracco, R. SDL—CCITT specification and description language. *IEEE Trans. Commun. 30*, 6 (June 1982), 1310–1318.

47. Roman, G.-C., et al. A total system design framework. *IEEE Comput. 17*, 5 (May 1984), 15–26.

48. Royce, W. Managing the development of large software systems: Concepts and techniques. Reprinted in *Proceedings of the Ninth International Conference on Software Engineering* (Monterey, Calif., March 30–April 2), pp. 328–338, IEEE Press, Wash., D.C., 1987.

49. Searle, L. An air force guide to the system specification. U.S. Air Force Document TM-5772/010/00. Jan. 1981.

50. *STATEMATE1: The STATEMATE1 Working Environment for System Development*. AD CAD, Inc., Cambridge, Massachusetts, 1985.

51. Sunshine, C. Formal methods for communication protocol specification and verification. ARPA Order 3460/3681. Nov. 1979.

52. Taylor, B. A method for expressing functional requirements of real-time systems. In *Proceedings of the IFAC/IFIP Workshop on Real-Time Programming* (Leibnitz, Austria, April), Pergamon Press, New York, 1980.

53. Wang, Y. A distributed specification model and its prototyping. In *Proceedings of IEEE COMPSAC '86* (Chicago, Ill., October 8–10), pp. 130–137, IEEE Press, Wash., D.C., 1986.

54. Ward, P. The transformation schema: An extension of the data flow diagram to represent control and timing. *IEEE Trans. Softw. Eng. 12*, 2 (Feb. 1986), 198–210.

55. Wasserman, A. User software engineering and the design of interactive systems. In *Proceedings of the Fifth IEEE International Conference on Software Engineering* (San Diego, March 9–12), pp. 387–393, IEEE Press, Wash., D.C., 1981.

56. Wasserman, A. Extending state transition diagrams for the specification of human–computer interaction. *IEEE Trans. Softw. Eng. 11*, 8 (Aug. 1985), 699–713.

57. Wasserman, A., et al. Developing interactive information systems with the user software engineering methodology. *IEEE Trans. Softw. Eng. 12*, 2 (Feb. 1986), 326–345.

58. Whitis, V., and Chiang, W. A state machine development method for call processing software. In *Proceedings of the IEEE Electro 81* (Apr.) IEEE Press, Wash., D.C., 1981.

59. Yoeli, M., and Barzilai, Z. Behavioural descriptions of communication switching systems using extended Petri-nets. *Digital Processes 3*, 4 (1977), 307–320.

60. Zave, P. An operational approach to requirements specification for embedded systems. *IEEE Trans. Softw. Eng. 8*, 3 (May 1982), 250–269.

61. Zave, P., and Shell, W. Salient features of an executable specification language and its environment. *IEEE Trans. Softw. Eng. 12*, 2 (Feb. 1986), 312–325.

62. Zave, P., and Yeh, R. Executable requirements for embedded systems. In *Proceedings of the 5th IEEE International Conference on Software Engineering* (San Diego, CA, March 9–12), pp. 285–304, IEEE Press, Wash., D.C., 1981.

CR Categories and Subject Descriptors: D.2.1 [**Software Engineering**]: Requirements/Specifications; D.3.2 [**Programming Languages**]: Language Classifications

General Terms: Requirements Tools, Software Engineering Tools, Software Requirements Specifications

Additional Key Words and Phrases: Decision tables, decision trees, finite state machines, PAISLey, PDL, Petri nets, REVS, RPL, SDL, statecharts, structured analysis

Received 11/87; accepted 3/88

Structured Analysis

Cyril P. Svoboda, Ph.D.
Advanced Systems Technology Corp. (ASTEC)
9111 Edmonston Road, Suite 404
Greenbelt, Maryland 20770
(301) 441-9036

1: Why a Methodology?

1.1: The Undisciplined Human Mind

Developing an information system can be considered a form of problem-solving. Someone has determined to move from a current state of affairs, i.e., the way a system is presently functioning, to some desired state of affairs, i.e., the way a system needs to function for the forseeable future. The gap between the two is closed by planning the project; analyzing the basic requirements for the system and incorporating desired new functionality; creating a design that uses pertinent new technology; and writing the programs that will implement the design. To solve such a complex problem, developers need to move carefully. The potential for costly errors is great.

Research in problem-solving shows that use of an appropriate strategy provides better solutions faster than use of no strategy. But use of a strategy assumes discipline: We have to expend the effort to plan for using a strategy and for staying with a strategy when we encounter difficulties. Yet philosophers have told us that the human mind is not by nature disciplined. Human beings do not come into this world gifted with a set of problem-solving strategies. Therefore, if we are faced with such a large, complex problem as building an information system, we need to adopt some disciplined, strategic method to guide our efforts. Without the help of some form of discipline, the human mind will approach the task of developing an information system in a random, reactive manner.

1.2: The Components of a Methodology

Those who want to develop an information system strategically, in a disciplined manner, employ a methodology, i.e., a body of rules, postulates, and procedures guiding their activity. Some of these methodologies support work in different phases of the system development life cycle, e.g., planning, analysis, design and programming. Others purport to cover the whole development life cycle.

Whatever its scope or application area, a methodology should contain at least four components: (1) a conceptual model of constructs essential to the problem, (2) a set of procedures suggesting the direction and order to proceed, (3) a series of guidelines identifying things to be avoided, and (4) a collection of evaluative criteria for assessing the quality of the product.

The conceptual model in a methodology should help developers distinguish things of importance from those that are irrelevant to the present activity. Without such guidance, developers may spend time and energy studying the wrong aspect of a system.

The set of procedures in a methodology lets both management and technicians know where the task should begin and what activities they need to follow. Without procedural direction, developers run the risk of "getting wrapped around the axle," suffering a series of "false starts," confusing different levels of detail, or decomposing only certain processes while stubbing others.

Evaluative criteria in a methodology give those involved in a system development project a handle on how well they are doing their jobs. Without such standards, developers have no way of knowing whether what they have done is complete, consistent, or traceable.

1.3: A History of System Development Methodologies

Methodologies to support information system development appeared in great number and variety in the 1970s. One of the earliest, "stepwise refinement" [1], covered the programming phase. Shortly thereafter, McGowan and Kelly [2] offered "structured programming," while Warnier [3] suggested the "logical construction of programs." Yourdon and Constantine [4] offered help with "structured design" and Jackson [5] proposed "principles of program design."

Eventually authors realized that something came before programming and design of programs. In quick succession

Reprinted from *System and Software Requirements Engineering*, M. Dorfman and R.H. Thayer, eds., 1990, pp. 218–237.

they proposed some form of "structured analysis" for the development of business-oriented management information systems (MIS). These variants are discussed in more detail in Section 3. Doug Ross [6] and colleagues at SofTech, Inc. developed a composite: Structured Analysis and Design Technique (SADT). DeMarco [7] showed how "structured analysis" as practiced in Yourdon's firm could be used to produce a "system specification." Gane and Sarson [8] produced a variant of the Yourdon-DeMarco method with distinct graphic notation. Orr [9] adapted the ideas of Warnier and made available strategies for "structured systems development."

In 1971, Teichroew and Sayani [10] introduced the Problem Statement Language/Problem StatementAnalyzer (PSL/PSA™) as a tool for automating the system-building process. With PSL the system developer could capture information about the target system gathered during any phase of the life cycle. This formalized information could then be handed to PSA for examination (by means of display reports) and evaluation (by means of analysis reports). Later, Sayani [11] developed the Automated Documentation System (ADS) for incorporating PSA reports as part of documents that conform to any selected or mandated documentation standard.

Carnap [12] had shown that any system could be expressed in terms of its major components (objects), their distinctive characteristics (properties), and the associations (relationships) that link them systemically. In a similar vein, Chen [13] suggested that system analysts develop a "unified view of data" by identifying a system's data (entities), their distinctive properties (attributes), and the associations (relationships) that link any pairs of entities. Using the entity-relationship-attribute (ERA) model, system developers produce one or more ERA diagrams that show the major data components of a system, their data composition, and how they are linked to any other entities in the system. Flavin [14] built on these ideas to produce an analysis methodology called "information modeling." Following this approach, a study team examines the target system from the functional, data, and control points of view against the context of organization regulations and produces an extended ER diagram that forms the basis for a logical design of the system's database.

In 1977, Bell, Bixler, and Dyer [15] discussed a Software Requirements Engineering Methodology (SREM) which, though similar to PSL/PSA, bypassed system requirements to deal immediately at a much lower level with primitive processing requirements. For several years Alford [16] was intimately involved with the refinement of SREM and its technology. He has shown that, while SREM has a specification language and a software package for checking consistency and traceability (as does PSL/PSA), only with the introduction of SYSREM does the technique adequately address requirements at all levels of a system. Possibly because SREM is based on a finite-state-machine model of a system, it has proved most useful for the specification of real-time, embedded systems [17].

As methodologies and tools for handling requirements analysis were cropping up, authors inside IBM [18] turned to the planning phase, offering support for creating an information architecture of "business systems." This effort also gave birth to a number of variants. Since the introduction of Business Systems Planning, various authors have produced refinements of these different planning methodologies, and software vendors are beginning to offer automated support for them.

In the last few years authors [19, 20] have returned to the analysis phase and have offered extensions to structured analysis that make it applicable to the development of real-time, embedded information systems. Ward and Mellor [21] published the first set of strategies for the "structured development of real-time systems." Hatley and Pirbhai [22] followed that with their own approach for the development of a "real-time system specification." These four and other interested parties have lately banded together to produce a standard real-time system modeling language to be used by developers of real-time systems [23].

2: The Components of Structured Analysis

2.1: A Definition

Analysis is a development phase typically performed after planning and before design. The analyst assumes that the questions pertinent to the planning phase have been asked and seeks to begin analysis with the information contained in the answers to those questions. As a term, "structured analysis" applies to a number of methodological approaches that guide the practitioner in the analysis (i.e., identification of system requirements and phase of the development life cycle). Typically the structured analyst is concerned with answers to the question "What?": What must the system do? What must the system produce? What can the system expect as input? What are sources and destinations of the data with which the system interacts? What data must the system hold in storage? What is the structure and composition of data held in storage? What are the components of high-level system constructs? If the system is "real-time," what are the events to which the system must be responsive? What are the triggers that cause a transition from one operational phase to another? What are the resultant actions that must be carried out upon state transition?

While all systems have the three major construct-types of data, activity, and control, different types of systems will place different emphases on them. For data-oriented or activity-oriented systems, structured analysis proceeds in a top-down fashion. Attention is first focused on the system at its "top level" and then it is studied progressively through more detailed levels until a primitive level is reached. Since any lower level is an elaboration or explosion of its immediate superior, each "child" level must be balanced with its "parent" level. When analysts have completed this top-down, leveled analysis of a system, they will have created a hierarchy of system activities in which no activity has more than a single parent. For control-oriented systems, Hatley and Pirbhai also suggest a top-down, leveled, hierarchical approach. On the other hand, Ward and Mellor suggest that analysis begin at whatever level the system is responsive to the environment, proceeding to decompose further to the primitive level and, eventually, organizing the overall system into a hierarchical structure.

2.2: The Models of Structured Analysis

Analysis asks "What?"; design asks "How?" During analysis, the developer studies the different components of the system in varying levels of detail, *without trying to create any particular arrangement of these components.* Ideally, the analyst begins with a model of the "current physical" system (as it actually operates today) and proceeds to create models of the system free of any implementation constraints. Attaining this ideal requires intense discipline, because the human mind deals much more easily with the concrete, physical aspects of a problem than with its abstract, logical aspects.

The process of moving the system in its "current physical" state to the system in its "new physical" state is not direct. Beginning with the information describing the system as it now exists, the analyst must first build a "current logical" model of the system by abstracting from the "current physical" information what McMenamin and Palmer [24] call the system's "essential requirements." Then, taking into account the new objectives desired for the system and what new requirements these entail, the analyst builds a "new logical" model of the system under development. With this phase completed, the work of analysis is finished, and the "new logical" model can be turned over to the designers and programmers for implementation.

While this is the ideal path for redesigning a system (whether it is computer-based or not), it is not always chosen by organizations developing a system. As Yourdon [25] notes, political dynamics have killed many a development project that took too long to build a model of a system that was soon to be obsolete. Projects are likely to fall into this trap if the current system is poorly understood and documented within the organization. Information about the "current physical" system should not be an end in itself, but a means to develop by abstraction a model of the "current logical" system. Without this latter model, the analyst has to uncover for the first time both the essential require-

ments of the current system and those of the desired system, instead of working from the "current logical" model to the "new logical" model. The purpose of creating models is twofold: (1) to account for the functionality of the existing system and (2) to provide a means for making the transition from the current to the newly developed system.

2.3: MIS Constructs of the Structured Analysis Conceptual Model

After encountering several problems of the same type, the human mind forms a conceptual model of that type of problem. A conceptual model consists of three components: (1) major constructs (object-types) generic to the problem being modeled, (2) relationships that associate any one construct with others in the model, and (3) properties that either define or describe an object-type. Structured analysis methodologists, with the exception of Doug Ross, have identified six object-types of business-oriented MIS (not real-time) systems. These are the major constructs of importance to the structured analyst:

1. *Process:* Functions or activities in the system that transform or manipulate data in some way. Processes exchange data either with other processes, stores of data, or sources/destinations outside the boundaries of the system.

2. *Data flow:* Data that pass from some source, either internal or external to the system, to destinations, either internal or external to the system. Data flows relate not only to their sources and destinations, but also to data objects of which they are either a part or a composite.

3. *Data store:* A place where data are held for later transformation or for reference. Data stores relate to the data flows that are either stored within or drawn from them. Data stores can also relate to their components.

4. *External entity (alias, terminator):* Some activity outside the boundary and control of the target system that interacts with the system by means of data. This object-type is of interest only insofar as it enables the analyst to identify specific sources and destinations of data with which the target system interacts. Externals, therefore, interact with processes by means of data, but never with data stores.

5. *Data group:* A cluster of data, identified as a component of one or more data flows. Data groups can be visualized as data flows, but are included in the data structure of higher-level data objects. A data group can consist of lower-level data groups or elemental units of data.

6. *Data element:* A basic unit of data which, with data group, forms the components of higher-level data

flows. Data elements are of interest only insofar as they help us to understand the elemental details of higher-level data objects.

The task of the structured analyst is to identify the many different instances of these six object-types and show how each relates to others within an MIS system. Section 4 shows the constructs that have been added to accommodate the analysis of real-time systems.

2.4: The Support Media of Structured Analysis

Traditional structured analysis (of business-oriented systems), with the exception of SADT, offers the practitioner four major tools to identify the requirements of the system under development. Each tool has a specific purpose and makes a specific contribution to the overall analysis of a system.

2.4.1: Data Flow Diagram

A data flow diagram (DFD) is a visualization of the data interaction that the overall system or some lower-level part of it has with other activities, whether internal or external to the system. On a DFD a reader will find graphic representations of external entities, processes, data flows, and data stores interconnected to show the progressive transformation of data. The disciplined analyst will create DFDs that are not overly cluttered, but are adequate representations of data interaction for the particular level of detail being visualized.

The first DFD to be created represents the target system at its context level. In a diagram such as that in Figure 1, the system is left as an unexplored "black box." The emphasis, instead, is on the types of data flows with which the system

interacts: both those that enter the system from their source and those that travel from the system to their destination. The creation of the context level DFD permits the developer to sketch the boundaries of the target system, so that both client and developer can agree on the scope of the system to be developed. Not surprisingly, this first view of the system can take a disproportionately long time to complete because it exposes arguments of ownership, boundaries, rights, etc.

Once client and developer reach consensus on the scope of the target system, the developer can proceed to identify the data-process interaction in progressively finer detail. Each resulting DFD, at what are called the "intermediate levels," is an elaboration or explosion of data-process interaction at the prior level. For instance, the single process in the context level DFD shown in Figure 1, is now exploded into a diagram, such as that shown in Figure 2 that visualizes its inner workings. On this diagram the main functional areas of the system under development are represented as processes that accept or produce the data flows identified on the context level. Note that the external entities shown on the context level DFD are not repeated on lower-level diagrams, lest these become too cluttered. Instead, the reader is expected to read a child diagram in the context of its parent. In addition to data that flow from sources or to destinations external either to the diagram or to the system itself, processes on a diagram may produce data flows that they send to one or more of the other processes on the same diagram, and they may interact with one or more data stores as required.

Before proceeding with an explosion of each of these processes, the analyst must balance the child diagram against the parent. To do so, the analyst must make sure both that the "data in" at the child level (**Figure 2**) is identical with or adds up to the "data in" at the parent level (**Figure 1**) and

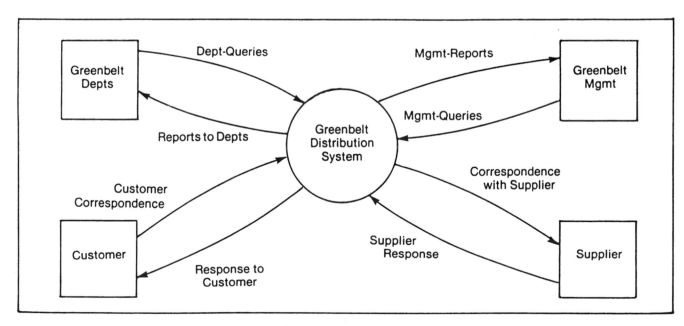

Figure 1: Context level data flow diagram

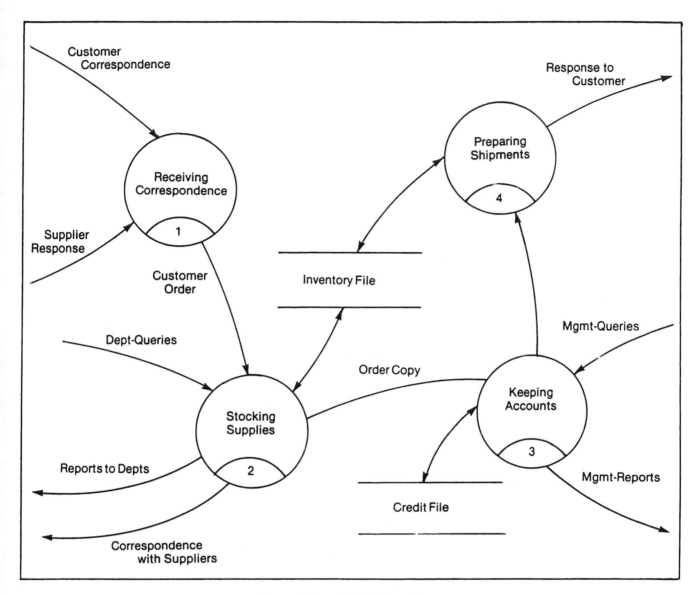

Figure 2: Level 0 data flow diagram

that the "data out" at the child level is identical with or adds up to the "data out" at the parent level. The data that pass between the processes on the child DFD do not enter into this evaluation because they were internal to the process at the parent level.

After completing "level balancing," the analyst explores each process on the balanced diagram into its own DFD, showing the inner workings of each. For instance, the process called "Receiving Correspondence" is explored in Figure 3. When any DFD is completed and balanced with its parent, the analyst continues to explore each of the processes on the just-completed DFD.

Analysts are often tempted to bypass these intermediate-level DFDs, thinking that the information represented

thereon is trivial and merely gets in the way of the "good stuff," i.e., the information found on the lowest level of detail. However, without doing the intermediate-level DFDs, the analyst would have no way of ensuring that information has not been lost "through the cracks" or that spurious information has not entered the analysis.

Eventually the analyst reaches a level of detail at which it is no longer useful to decompose the functions and the data with which they interact. This level, called the "functional primitive," is not common across all system processes; the process hierarchy need not be symmetrical. The analyst knows that the functional primitive level has been reached when the process to be further explored is a single (not a compound) function producing only a single kind of data flow. An example of functional primitive processes is

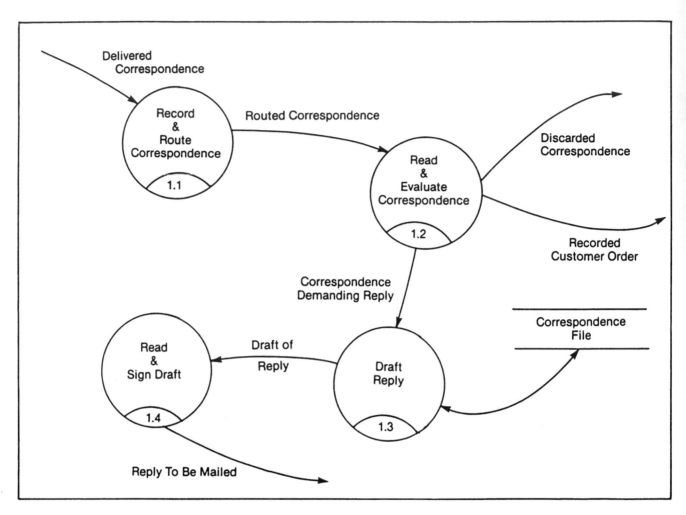

Figure 3: Intermediate-level DFD: Receiving correspondence

shown in Figure 4. When the analyst has explored all system processes to their functional primitive level and has completed level balancing, no further DFDs are needed.

2.4.2: Data Dictionary

As the analyst completes each data flow diagram, hc/she should employ a second tool of structured analysis, the data dictionary. As envisioned by the original developers of structured analysis, the data dictionary is a repository, manual or computer-based, containing information about the various data objects appearing on each DFD. It should in-clude an entry for each data object identified. For instance, for each data store there will be an entry that specifies its name, all of its aliases, narrative text describing it, its contents, and the names of all processes that access it. For each data flow there will be an entry, such as that in Figure 5, that specifies its name, all of its aliases, narrative text describing it, and its composition. When specifying the composition of a data flow, the analyst will show not only the names of its component data, but will indicate by means of Backus-Naur Form symbols whether any of the components are optional (surrounded by parentheses (. .)), alternates (surrounded by brackets [. .] with alternate components

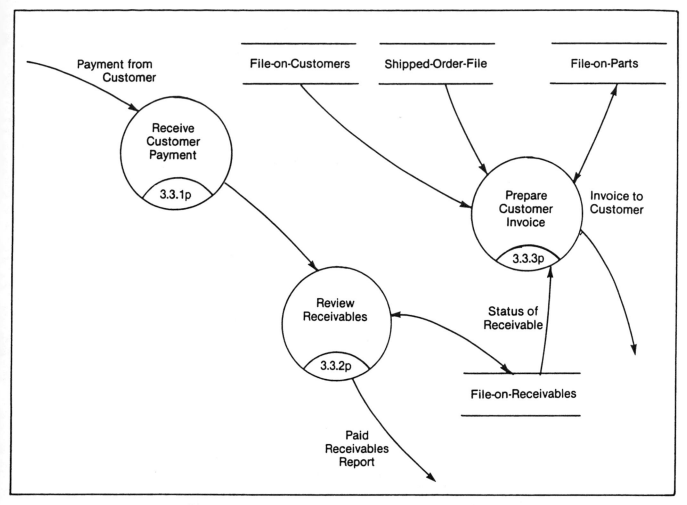

Figure 4: Functional primitive DFD: Accounts receivable

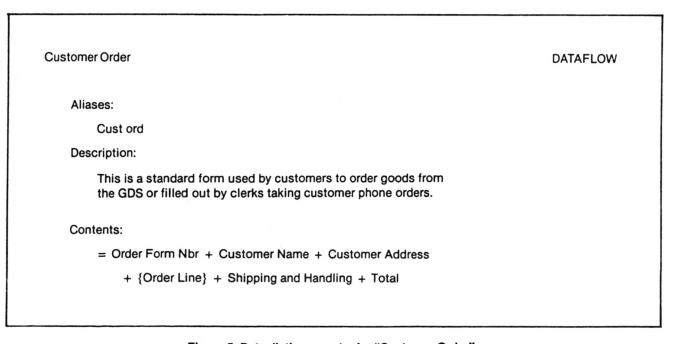

Figure 5: Data dictionary entry for "Customer Order"

Table 1: Backus-Naur Form symbols

BNF

Symbol	Meaning
=	"is composed of"
+	"and," "as well as," "together with"
{name}	"repetitions of"
[name/name]	"choice between," "alternates are"
(name)	"optional," "may not be present"
{order-line}	"repetitions of order-line"
1 {order-line}n	"one-through-n repetitions of order-line"

Mailing Label Information   DATA GROUP
     = customer-name + customer-address
Customer-name   DATA GROUP
     = customer-last-name + customer-first-name
         + customer-middle-initial
Customer-Address   DATA GROUP
     = Local-address + community-address + zip-code
Local-address   DATA GROUP
     = House-number + street-name + (apt-number)
Community-address   DATA GROUP
     = city-name + [state-name/province-name]

Figure 6: Dictionary entries for data group

separated by a bar |), or repeating data (surrounded by braces { . . }). These symbols are explained in Table 1.

Data flows need not decompose immediately to data elements. Very often the components of a data flow may be what was called above a data group, i.e., named clusters of other data groups and/or data elements. Each data group will have an entry in the data dictionary showing its name, all of its aliases, narrative text describing it, and its composition.

For instance, a data flow called "Mailing Label Information" could decompose into such components as "Customer Name" and "Customer Address." "Customer Name" could be a data group consisting of "Last Name," "First Name," and "Middle Initial." "Customer Address," shown in Figure 6, might be modeled as a data group consisting of the data groups "Local Address" and "Community Address" and the data element "Zip Code." "Local Address" could consist of "House Number," "Street Name," and an optional "Apartment Number." "Community Address" could consist of "City Name" and either "State Name" or "Province Name."

Each data element identified will also have an entry in the data dictionary. In addition to its name, all of its aliases, and narrative text describing it, the data element entry might include any of its special characteristics (e.g., its format, type, length, etc.) and its set of legal values.

The pioneers of structured analysis suggested that each data dictionary entry be made on a separate 3 × 5 card kept in a box or on pages in a three-ring binder. These manual information storage means have been abandoned in favor of various computer-aided database management systems. Currently developers seem to feel that information about all system objects, not just the data objects, should reside in the dictionary.

This position is basic to the work done by the X3H4 technical committee of the American National Standards through the 1980s to provide the federal government with a data dictionary system standard that is flexible, user-friendly, and able to support all phases of the system development life cycle. In 1989, the Information Resource Dictionary System became a Federal Information Processing Standard and will likely become the criterion against which other dictionary systems will be judged.

2.4.3: The Primitive Process Specification ("MiniSpec")

As the analyst identifies functional primitive processes in any DFD, he/she can explore each, not into a lower-level DFD, but into its primitive process specification or "MiniSpec." This third tool of structured analysis is usually a linguistic statement of the essential procedural steps necessary to carry out the action of a primitive process. The information contained herein might be a narrative statement of relevant business policies or a formal listing of "condition-action" definitions. Ultimately a "MiniSpec" should express the actual component tasks required to carry out a function called for by some verifiable business policy; it should not be a collection of the "neat things" some developer could make it do. The process specification can be kept in the repository, as part of the description of the primitive process of which it is an explosion.

A "MiniSpec" may be expressed in various ways. During an interview with a client, an analyst may capture the steps of an identified primitive process in the client's English narrative. However, it is possible to use some formal notation, as shown in Figure 7, that expresses the same three major action types found in programming: sequence, decision, and iteration. Whether structured English, a decision tree, a decision table, or even some procedure definition language (PDL) is used, the emphasis in writing a process specification should be on *what* steps the process must carry out, not on *how* it will do them. The actual means of expression chosen should represent a compromise between the client's ease of understanding or expressing the steps and the rigor required for expressing them with precision. The choice will vary from organization to organization, from project to project, or from process to process.

2.4.4: Structured Walkthrough

A fourth tool of structured analysis is not so much a product as a process. The structured walkthrough is a formal meeting, ideally held periodically through the life of a development project, during which some part of the analysis is presented and critiqued. Participants are usually given formal roles (e.g., moderator, presenter, secretary, etc.) and responsibilities. For instance, the presenter has the responsibility of showing and explaining what and how the work being presented was done. The moderator has the responsibility of shepherding the communication processes and controlling the group dynamics active during the meeting. The secretary has the responsibility of documenting what items were called into question, what suggestions for change were made, and whether the moderator assigned any "action items" requiring resolution prior to final approval of that part of the analysis.

In addition to these participatory roles, other individuals ought to be invited to attend the structured walkthrough, at least as observers. If the emphasis of the analysis has been on the process side, someone involved in database design should bring a data orientation. Someone should represent the quality assurance department. A representative from the programming or maintenance team should be invited. In fact, any interested party in either the client or developer organization (if they are different) should be encouraged to attend.

There are various reasons for conducting structured walkthroughs:
- to gain as many perspectives on the target system as possible
- to elicit critical comments and suggestions to enhance the developing understanding of the target system
- to invest as many representatives from the organization as possible (to defuse an adversary atmosphere)

Development projects may call this step an inspection, in-process review, or milestone review.

3: Varieties of a Structured Approach to Analysis

Different individuals have suggested different ways to approach analysis in a structured manner. Common across these various approaches are the goals of improving understanding of the system under development and communication of that understanding to the client and others in the development process. Whichever structured analysis approach an organization adopts, it is encouraged to adapt the methodology to its own situation and culture.

3.1: Structured Analysis and Design Technique

Doug Ross and his colleagues at SofTech, Inc., proposed an early version called "Structured Analysis and Design

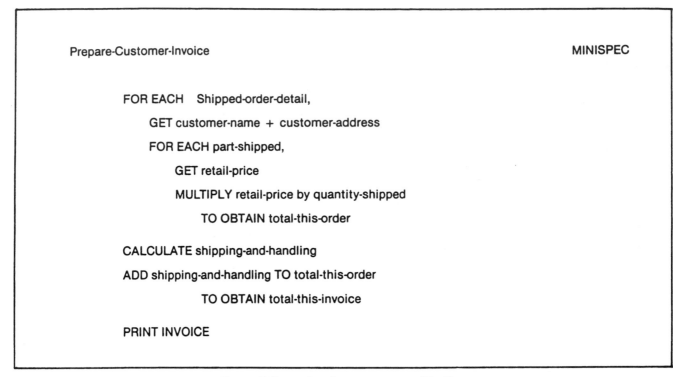

FOR EACH   Shipped-order-detail,

    GET customer-name + customer-address

    FOR EACH part-shipped,

      GET retail-price

      MULTIPLY retail-price by quantity-shipped

        TO OBTAIN total-this-order

CALCULATE shipping-and-handling

ADD shipping-and-handling TO total-this-order

      TO OBTAIN total-this-invoice

PRINT INVOICE

Figure 7: Example of a process specification

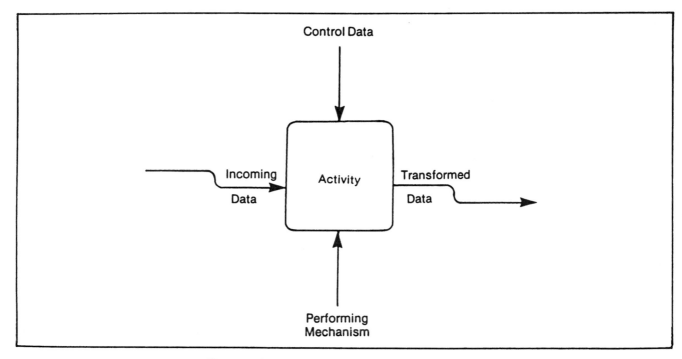

Figure 8: Constructs of a SADT activity diagram

Technique" (SADT) [6] that encourages the analyst to begin by asking about the objectives of a system (the "why?" questions) before progressing to the major components of a system (the "what?" questions) and eventually determining the implementation techniques (the "how?" questions). This technique has been used for planning as well as for analysis and design.

Like all versions of structured analysis, SADT suggests that to understand a system you begin at the top and pro-gress through the many layers from conceptual abstractions to concrete components. This top-down approach views data and activity as two sides of a coin. In a diagrammatic tool called the activity diagram, the analyst pictures the interaction of data and activities by means of the graphic symbols shown in Figure 8. Data are classified as "consumed" (i.e., data tranformed by the activity) and "non-consumed" (i.e., data that contol the activity but are not transformed). The analyst is also expected to identify the "mechanism"

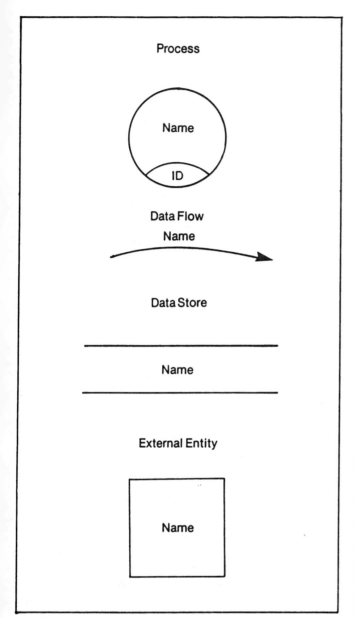

Figure 9: Constructs of Yourdon-DeMarco

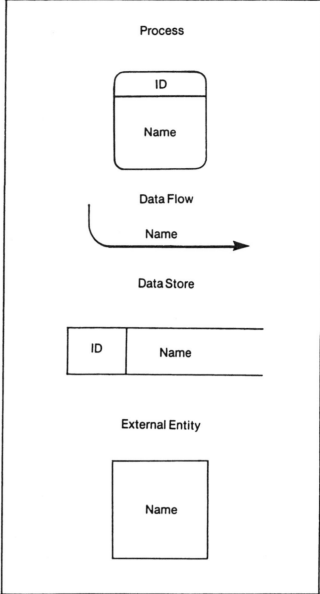

Figure 10: Constructs of Gane and Sarson

that will perform each activity. Using this approach at different milestones throughout a project, analysts are encouraged to develop "kits" of documents, such as activity diagrams, written records of decisions made and alternatives considered, etc., and present them to different individuals playing such roles as reader, commentator, technical expert, or project manager.

3.2: Yourdon-DeMarco

Yourdon founded a firm of consultants who developed and have taught a generic form of structured analysis to organizations throughout the world. DeMarco wrote one of the most popular books on their approach [7]. The technique advocates a top-down approach in which the analyst is led to decompose the system and its functions through levels of increasing detail. Other consultants of this firm

have produced articles and books explaining and popularizing this approach.

The six object types discussed earlier and their graphic notation, presented in Figure 9, were first delineated by this approach, as were the four tools of structured analysis presented earlier. While it was initially process-oriented, more recent proponents [26] of this approach have introduced the technique of information modeling to provide a better balance between the aspects of data and activity.

3.3: Gane and Sarson

This pair co-wrote a study [8] of a version of structured analysis that suggests a slightly different emphasis from the Yourdon-DeMarco approach and a different graphic notation, shown in Figure 10, for the data flow diagram. This approach pays more attention than does the Yourdon-

313

DeMarco approach to the identification of the data components of a system. What we have called in this paper a data group, Gane and Sarson call a data structure. The two terms have the same meaning.

In addition to the four tools already presented, Gane and Sarson suggest the use of a data access diagram to describe the structure and contents of data stores in the system. Each data store is viewed as collecting several entity-types, each of which is related in some way to one or more of the other entities in the data store. The data access diagram pictorially presents the different entities in a data store and the access paths that link them.

4: Real-Time Extensions to Structured Analysis

Traditional structured analysis, with the exception of SADT, led practitioners to devote most of their energies to the identification of the activity and data aspects of the target system, to the exclusion of the control aspect. It was felt that the latter was actually a construct in the design phase and should not enter into analysis of a system. While this may have been true for MIS-type systems, it placed intolerable constraints on the analysis of systems in which process activation or deactivation, issues of deadlock, etc., are important. Recently methodologists have offered extensions to the traditional conceptual model of structured analysis that begin to fill that void.

4.1: Ward and Mellor

Ward and Mellor were the first to publish their techniques for the analysis of "real-time, embedded" systems [21]. To the six object-types presented in Section 2.3, they added the following constructs:

1. *Control transform:* An activity that coordinates the functioning of the processes (also called data transforms) in a real-time system. Such a process does not deal with value-bearing data, but only with signals declaring that important events have occurred or that monitored conditions have reached a critical point calling for determined action.

2. *Control flow:* Either a nonvalue-bearing signal denoting the occurrence of some event of importance to the system or a prompt given by a control transform commanding that other processes "turn on" or "turn off" their predefined activity.

3. *Control store:* A store for holding control flows for later sampling or polling. Data flows cannot be held in control stores, nor can control flows be held in data stores.

4. *State:* An operational mode in which some parts of the target system behave in a predetermined manner until triggered to change to a different state.

5. *Transition:* The actual movement or change from one operational mode to another.

6. *Condition:* A simple or compound stimulus that causes the transition from one state to another.

7. *Action:* A response made by some part of the target system as a result of a transition from one state to another.

8. *Entity:* A thing about which the system must keep information in memory. This thing can be a physical entity, such as an aircraft, or an informational entity, such as a flight plan.

9. *Relationship:* An association that links two or more entities. A relationship is often expressed as a verb with one of the entities playing the role of subject and the other playing the role of object.

Ward and Mellor advocate building a series of models during the analysis and design phases of real-time system development. Since real-time systems must be responsive to the environment, the analyst using their approach would first concentrate on building an essential model of the target system. This model consists of two subparts: the environmental model and the behavior model. The environmental model consists of a list of important events to which the target system must respond and a system context diagram that describes the high-level interaction of the target system with the outside world. The behavior model consists of three subparts: the information model, the process model, and the control model of the target system.

Ward and Mellor base their information model on a version of the ERA model, referenced in Section 1.3, and produce entity-relationship diagrams that identify the major entities about which information must be kept in the system and the associations that link any one entity with others in the model. A portion of such a model is shown in Figure 11.

Ward and Mellor's process model is visualized by means of a transformation schema, a data flow diagram that contains both traditional DFD constructs and real-time con-

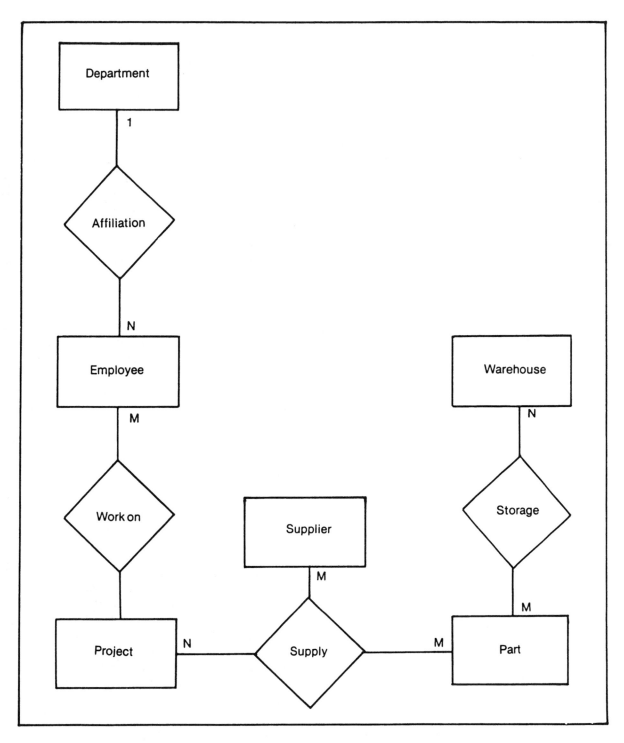

Figure 11: Portion of an information model

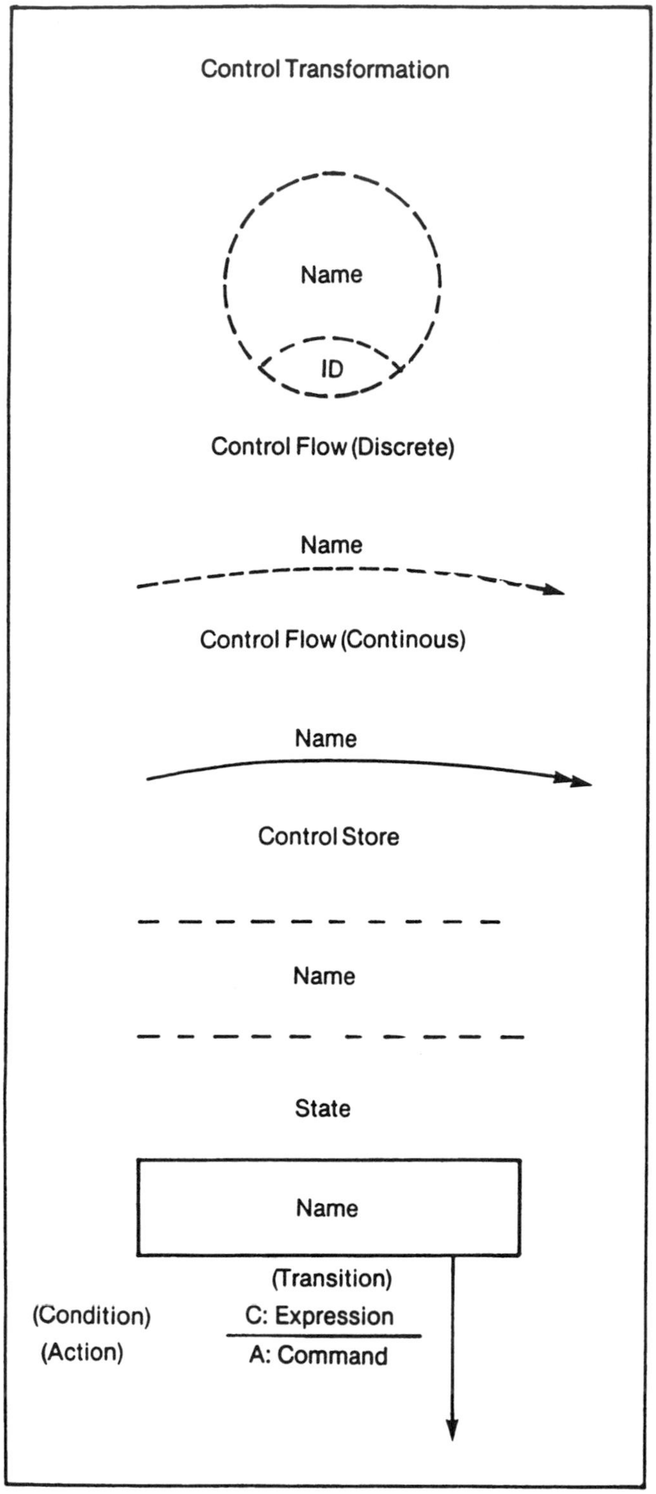

Figure 12: Real-time constructs (Ward and Mellor)

structs discussed earlier in 1-3, the graphic symbols of which are shown in Figure 12.

On the data flow diagram an analyst can show the interactions of both those processes that transform data and those that react to events in the environment and exercise control over other processes. Figure 13 presents an example of a transformation schema. Data processes explode to lower-level transformation schemas, which can contain both data and control objects.

However, the explosion of control processes contributes to the control model of the system under development. System developers visualize this model by means of either a state transition diagram (for sequential finite machines) or a state transition matrix (for combinational finite machines). Figure 14 is an example of a state transition diagram, showing states of an operation (oblong boxes), transitions from one state to another (vectors between boxes), conditions that trigger the transition ("C: <expression>"), and actions taken as a result of the transition ("A: <expression>").

Having completed the behavior model of the system, the designer following the Ward and Mellor technique proceeds to build an implementation model comprising a processor model, a task model, and a module model. The processor model captures the allocation of essential model constructs to different processors that will do the work. The task model determines the different activity units assigned to each processor identified in the processor model. The module model is built by designers employing Constantine and Yourdon's [4] structured design methodology. Designers translate the transformation schemas identified in the behavior model into structure charts that show the particular arrangement of modules required to carry out any task, as well as the data and status flags exchanged by the modules.

4.2: Hatley and Pirbhai

In 1987, Hatley and Pirbhai [22] published a study that presents a slightly different set of extensions for real-time system analysis and design. The constructs are much the same as those suggested by Ward and Mellor (see Figure 12); but the major difference is in the tools Hatley and Pirbhai suggest. The analyst uses not only the data flow diagrams of traditional structured analysis, but creates parallel control flow diagrams (CFDs) containing the processes of the DFD, devoid of data flows, but with control flows. Figure 15 presents an example of parallel data flow and control flow diagrams produced by following this approach.

Below the primitive-level DFD are process specifications or "MiniSpecs" (PSPECS). Any interaction between the DFDs and CFDs is captured in control specifications (CSPECS) which describe the logic of either sequential or combinational finite-state machines. These CSPECS can combine various diagrams (e.g., a state transition diagram), matrices (e.g., a state transition matrix), or tables (e.g., decision table, timing requirements table, or process activation tables). The authors advise against using CSPECS too liberally, lest analysts fall out of analysis and into design.

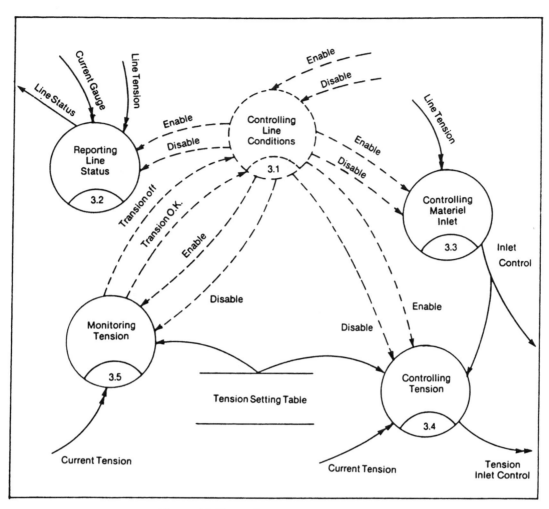

Figure 13: Example of transformation schema

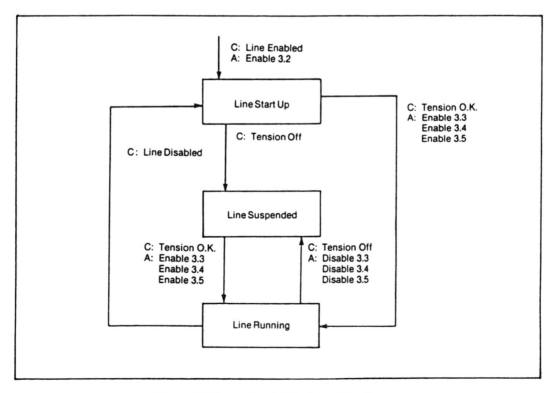

Figure 14: Example of state transition diagram

317

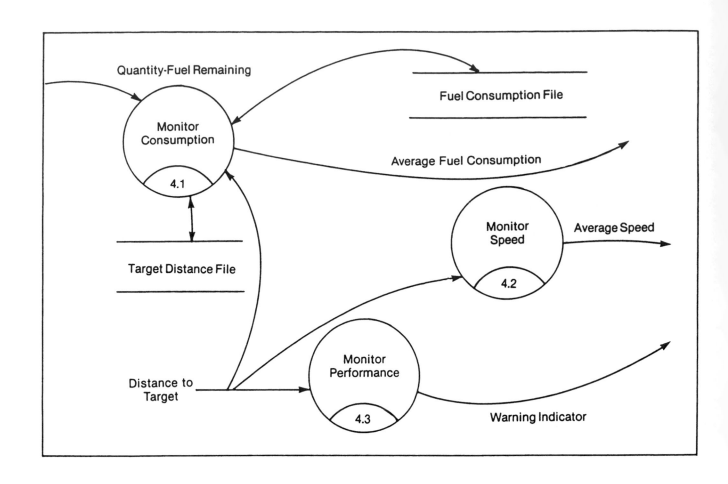

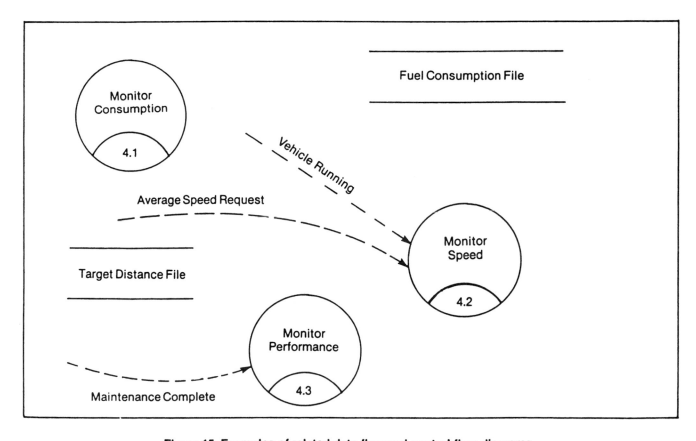

Figure 15: Examples of related data flow and control flow diagrams

In the Hatley and Pirbhai approach, the analyst constructs a requirements model of the target system and the designer produces an architectural model of the same. The requirements model consists of a context level DFD and CFD, intermediate-level DFDs and CFDs, primitive-process DFDs and their PSPECS, CSPECS, timing requirements, and a requirements dictionary.

In the view of these authors, design of a real-time system will produce an architecture model, comprising architectural flow diagrams, architectural interconnect diagrams, lower-level specifications of both, and an architectural dictionary showing the allocation of the requirements to implementation components.

4.3: Extended System Modeling Language

Ward and Hatley have worked with other methodologists to devise a compromise graphic notation for expressing components of a real-time system. Bruyn, Jensen, Keskar, and Ward [23] publicized an extended system modeling language (ESML) as having "a broad range of mechanisms for describing both combinatorial and sequential control logic." At present, the real-time constructs to be identified during the analysis phase have been agreed upon and are shown inFigure 16. Currently a committee is working on the constructs of the design phase.

5: Case Tools to Support Structured Analysis

The original creators of structured analysis presented developers with a strictly manual methodology. As practitioners found it increasingly cumbersome to maintain the mass of paper used to capture DFDs, MiniSpecs, and a data dictionary, they began to look for some automated support.

5.1: Linguistic Dictionaries

One of the first computer-aided tools to support structured analysis was PSL/PSA [27]. Commercial firms and government agencies have used PSL to capture the information on the DFDs, MiniSpecs, and in the data dictionary and then have entered it into the PSA database. From this database, these organizations have derived display reports for use in structured walkthroughs. They have used PSA's analysis reports to evaluate the quality of the information captured. By means of a related tool, the report specification interface, many of these organizations have been able to incorporate this information into documentation that conformed to mandated standards, such as Department of Defense (DoD) 7935.S or DoD 2167A.

5.2: Graphics Packages

In the last six years, computer-aided software engineering (CASE) has burst on the scene. Several different vendors have produced graphics packages that give developers vari-

ous forms of support. In the past year, Rinaldi [28] reviewed some 75 CASE tools that support system developers in some phase(s) of the development life cycle. Chikofsky and Rubenstein [29] examined CASE tools as a means for achieving reliability when engineering an information system. Wasserman and Pircher [30] have discussed the capabilities of an integrated environment that assists software developers graphically. Martin [31] has diagnosed the less-than-complete acceptance of CASE tools by the development community. He maintains that these tools have certain inherent limits (e.g., lack of adaptability to different methodologies, a dearth of administrator tools, difficulty in producing user-formatted hard-copy documentation, and cumbersome diagram production).

Organizations are exploring the use of these graphics packages to draw DFDs, ER diagrams, structure charts, and state transition diagrams, as well as various forms of data model diagrams. Developers are able to store in the dictionary underlying any of these packages both information related to the visual icons on the diagrams and supplementary information. Most of these packages have both report writing and analysis capabilities to assist developers in reflecting on the information captured and evaluating it against various quality standards. In the last two years, several of these packages have added graphic support for the real-time extensions discussed above.

In the experience of the author, organizations enjoy the most success when adopting these tools if they view them as instruments or means to an end, not as solutions in themselves. Merely learning the mechanics of using these tools does not replace knowing the principles of the methodologies that they are intended to support. Knowing how to do something does not imply knowing what ought to be done or why.

6: Technology Transfer Issues

Organizations deciding to adopt some structured approach to analysis expose themselves to a number of problems bundled under the heading "technology transfer." Technology transfer refers both to the time that it takes for technology to be adopted and to the dynamics that militate against its effective adoption. Possibly because our business milieu focuses on the short term, we grow impatient with the learning curve that any new technology demands. The author has heard managers proclaim, "If my people can't become proficient with a tool in a day or two, it isn't worth it." This forces such individuals into "waiting for Godot," i.e., ignoring available technology while waiting for a technology that is cheap, painless, and universally applicable.

More important than the technology to be adopted is the process of introducing whatever technology is selected into the workplace. Before examining what technology is available, an organization would do well to understand the

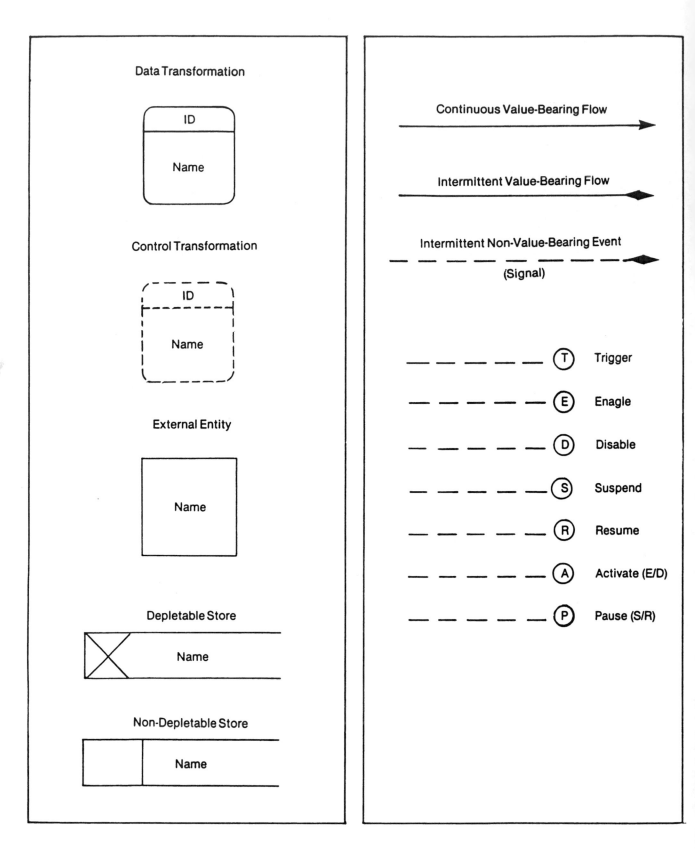

Figure 16: Real-time constructs (ESML)

specific characteristics of its business culture, lest it choose technology that runs counter to the culture and is rejected by the developers. Merely adopting a technology not only does not solve problems, but can create difficulties of its own. Mosley [32] argues that the introduction of technology into a development process that is not clearly defined, founded on sound development principles, or mature can be very disruptive and can lead to lower productivity and quality.

Two evaluative criteria have proved to be vital when considering the adoption of a methodology or support tool: (1) how well the technology can be adapted to the organization's culture or to a project's special situation and (2) how easily the products of the prior development phase can become the inputs for the subsequent phase. Having decided on some methodology and support tool, developers need to establish, disseminate, and enforce a set of standards and conventions as organizational guidelines for developing a system. Svoboda [33] has been arguing for several years that, without project standards and conventions, an organization has not "gotten its act together before putting the show on the road." The blame for the disaster that will follow should not be placed on the technology used, but on its improper introduction, usage, and support.

7: Conclusions and Future Directions

Human beings need methodologies to guide them in carrying out complex tasks on large problems. Structured analysis is a methodology that helps developers in the analysis phase of the system development life cycle. As computer support for this phase becomes not only available but increasingly sophisticated, more organizations will probably adopt computerized tools, thinking that they will automatically enforce a methodology. Eventually these organizations will discover that they need first to learn and commit to using the methodology, and then they may find that the tools can support their use and commitment quite well.

Organizations should examine the "real-time" extensions to structured analysis and realize that even their system includes some, admittedly limited, control aspect and that a complete analysis requires paying attention not only to activity, but to control. Finally, the work done on information (data) modeling should lead practitioners of structured analysis to complete the triad and build models for all three components of any information system: the data, the activities, and the controls.

Users of a methodology find that they have to make trade-offs: while the methodology does constrain their creativity, it will help to keep them from losing their way in developing a system. Use of the methodology can greatly reduce trial and error. Following a methodology requires an act of faith in its creator, but doing so guides technicians through a puzzling territory and enables managers to determine whether the work done is well done. To derive the full benefits of using a methodology, an organization must be able to adapt it to its own situation and culture.

8: References

[1] Wirth, N., "Program Development by Stepwise Refinement," *Communications of ACM,* Vol. 14, No. 4, 1971, pp. 221-227.

[2] McGowan, C. and Kelly, J., *Top Down Structured Programming.* New York: Petrocelli, 1975.

[3] Warnier, J., *Logical Construction of Programs.* New York: Van Nostrand Reinhold, 1974.

[4] Yourdon, E. and Constantine, L., *Structured Design.* Englewood Cliffs, N.J.: Prentice-Hall, 1979.

[5] Jackson, M., *Principles of Program Design.* London, England: Academic Press, 1975.

[6] Ross, D., "Structured Analysis (SA): A Language for Communicating Ideas," *IEEE Transactions on Software Engineering,* Vol. SE-3, No. 1, 1977.

[7] DeMarco, T., *Structured Analysis and System Specification.* New York: Yourdon Press, 1978.

[8] Gane, C. and Sarson, T., *Structured Systems Analysis: Tools and Techniques.* Englewood Cliffs, N.J.: Prentice-Hall, 1979.

[9] Orr, K., *Structured Systems Development.* New York: Yourdon Press, 1977.

[10] Teichroew, D. and Sayani, H., "Automation of System Building," *Datamation,* August 15, 1971, pp. 25-30.

[11] Sayani, H., "The Automated Documentation System," Paper presented at Seventeenth Annual Technical Symposium, National Bureau of Standards, Gaithersburg, Md., June 15, 1978.

[12] Carnap, R., *The Logical Structure of the World.* Berkeley, Cal.: University of California Press, 1967.

[13] Chen, P., "The Entity-Relationship Model—Toward a Unified View of Data," *ACM Transactions on Database Systems,* Vol. 1, No. 1, March 1976.

[14] Flavin, M., *Fundamental Concepts of Information Modeling.* Englewood Cliffs, N.J.: Prentice-Hall, 1981.

[15] Bell, T., Bixler, D., and Dyer, M., "An Extendable Approach to Computer-Aided Software Requirements Engineering," *IEEE Transactions on Software Engineering.* Vol. SE-3, No. 1, January 1977.

[16] Alford, M., "SREM at the Age of Eight: The Distributed Computing Design System," *IEEE Computer,* Vol. 18, No. 4, May 1985.

[17] Alford, M., "A Requirements Engineering Methodology for Real-Time Processing Requirements," *IEEE Transactions on Software Engineering,* Vol. SE-3, No. 1, January 1977.

[18] Staff, International Business Machines Corp., *Business Systems Planning—Information Systems Planning Guide,* 3rd ed., White Plains, N.Y.: IBM Corp., 1981.

[19] Hatley, D., "The Use of Structured Methods in the Development of Large Software-Based Avionics Systems," *AIAA/IEEE Sixth Digital Avionics Systems Conference*, 1984.

[20] Ward, P., "The Transformation Schema: An Extension of the Data Flow Diagram to Represent Control and Timing," *IEEE Transactions on Software Engineering*, Vol. SE-12, No. 2, February 1986.

[21] Ward, P. and Mellor, S., *Structured Development for Real-Time Systems*. Englewood Cliffs, N.J.: Prentice-Hall, 1985.

[22] Hatley, D. and Pirbhai, I., *Strategies for Real-Time System Specification*. New York: Dorset House, 1987.

[23] Bruyn, W., Jensen, R., Keskar, D., and Ward, P., "ESML: An Extended Systems Modeling Language Based on the Data Flow Diagram." *ACM SIGSOFT—Software Engineering Notes*, Vol. 13, No. 1, January 1988.

[24] McMenamin, S. and Palmer, J., *Essential Systems Analysis*. New York: Yourdon Press, 1984.

[25] Yourdon, E., "Whatever Happened to Structured Analysis?", *Datamation*, June 1, 1986, pp. 133-138.

[26] Stehle, G., "Data Modeling," paper presented at CASE Studies 1988, Ann Arbor, MI. Shows that data modeling is an integral part of structured systems analysis course given by Keith London Associates, Hertfordshire, Great Britain.

[27] Teichroew, D. and Heshey, A., "PSL/PSA: A Computer-Aided Technique for Structured Documentation and Analysis of Information Processing Systems," *IEEE Transactions on Software Engineering*, Vol. SE-3, No. 1, January 1977.

[28] Rinaldi, D., "Getting Beyond Drawings," *Software Magazine*, Vol. 8, No. 5, April 1988, pp. 51-58.

[29] Chikofsky, E. and Rubenstein, B., "CASE: Reliability Engineering for Information Systems," *IEEE Software*, Vol. 5, No. 2, March 1988.

[30] Wasserman, A. and Pircher, P., "A Graphic, Extensible Integrated Environment for Software Development," *ACM SIGPLAN Notices*, New York: Association for Computing Machinery, Inc., January 1987.

[31] Martin, C., "Second-Generation CASE Tools: A Challenge to Vendors," *IEEE Software*, March 1988, pp. 46-49.

[32] Mosley, D., "Are We Ready for CASE?," *American Programmer*, Vol. 2, No. 3, March 1989, pp. 20-25.

[33] Svoboda, C., "Setting Up Project Standards and Conventions," paper presented at Second Annual Excelerator Users Group Conference, San Diego, Calif., September 10, 1986.

Note: For a current, comprehensive view of this topic, read Yourdon, E., *Modern Structured Analysis*. Englewood Cliffs, N.J.: Prentice-Hall, 1989.

Entity-Relationship Approach to Data Modeling

John P. Reilly

A Collaborative Approach to Modeling

Gone are the days when developers collected requirements from users and then scurried back to their workplace to normalize data and construct user interfaces. Automated development tools possessing features that enable rapid prototyping have transformed application development. Today users and developers collaborate to build applications.

This transformation has also changed the way in which the data model is constructed. Today, while the basic components of the data model have not changed, the data model evolves throughout the development process as progressively lower levels of detail are discovered. The search for the "perfect" data model at the end of analysis is over.

This article describes the components of the data model, then steps you through a proven process and techniques that can be used to build today's business models.

Components of the Data Model

The primary goal of data modeling is to depict accurately the data requirements of all or part of an enterprise. The requirements include:

- things with which the business deals, called **entity types**
- associations between these things, called **relationships**
- characteristics that describe each of these things, called **attributes**Entity Types

Definition

An **entity type** describes a collection of entities, which are fundamental things of relevance to the enterprise about which data may be kept. Consider an insurance company that offers both home and automobile insurance policies. These policies are offered to individuals and businesses. POLICY and CUSTOMER are both entity types in this example, while home and automobile are entities of POLICY, and individual and business are entities of CUSTOMER.

An entity type is the description of all entities to which a common definition and common relationships and attributes apply. In the example above the definition of POLICY is "an agreement with a customer to provide insurance coverage." Entity type definitions are important for identifying the scope and qualifying all entities of the type. Definitions are also useful in identifying other entity types and relationships that exist between the entity type being defined and the identified entity types. In this example, CUSTOMER and COVERAGE are identified as other entity types related to POLICY.

Classifications of Entity Types

Entity types are the fundamental building blocks of the data model. Entity types are graphically depicted in an entity relationship diagram (ERD) as shown in Figure 1.

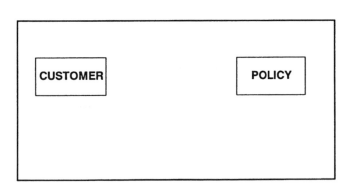

Figure 1. Two entity types in an entity relationship diagram.

Entity types can be classified in a number of ways. Each classification assists in the discovery of entity types that belong in the data model. One classification is used to categorize entity types. There are three categories: **tangible**, **active,** and **conceptual**. Tangible entity types represent things like people, places, things, organizations, and so forth. Active entity types are usually associated with business events and capture information about the activities associated with an event. Conceptual entity types represent ideas or principles that are used to organize and control activities or communications. Being intangible, conceptual entity types take on meaning when they are viewed, like on a report or window.

A data model typically has each of these types. In our example CUSTOMER is a tangible entity type while POLICY is a conceptual entity type. These entity types capture and document data about one tangible object (CUSTOMER) and one intangible object (POLICY) that are of interest to the business. Another entity type that may be in our insurance example is POLICY CLAIM. This is an example of an active entity type.

Another classification describes a dominance relationship between entity types. This classification assists in structuring the data model and in determining when entity types are discovered during the development process. Entity types may be **independent** or **dependent**. CUSTOMER and POLICY are both examples of independent entity types. An independent entity type's entities are not dependent on the existence of any other entities, while a dependent entity type's entities are dependent on the existence of other entities. POLICY CLAIM is an example of a dependent entity type since it depends on entity occurrences of POLICY.

Independent entity types are usually found first during data modeling, followed by dependent entity types, which are considered a lower level of detail. For example, the entity type CLAIM STATUS, which contains the history of a POLICY CLAIM, adds further detail, or information, about another dependent entity type. When constructing the entity relationship diagram independent entity types should occupy the upper left quadrant. This simplifies construction of the diagram and makes it easier to "read" because all relationships "emanate" from the independent entity types.

Dependent entity types can be further classified into type groups: **characteristic** or **associative**. Characteristic entity types add further detail to the entity type on which it depends. For example, CUSTOMER ADDRESS further describes a CUSTOMER. An associative entity type further describes the association between two entity types. In our example, we may add the entity type CUSTOMER POLICY to describe the role that a CUSTOMER carries out for a POLICY, such as payer, insured, guarantor, and so forth.

Relationships

Definition

A **relationship** is a reason for associating two entity types. These relationships are sometimes called **binary** relationships because they involve two entity types. Some forms of data models allow more than two entity types to be associated. Relationships like this, called **n-ary**, are outside the scope of this article. A CUSTOMER is *insured by* a POLICY. A POLICY CLAIM is *made against* a POLICY. Relationships are represented in the entity relationship diagram as shown in Figure 2. A special kind of relationship can exist between an entity type and itself. It is called an involuted or recursive relationship. The association EMPLOYEE *supervises* EMPLOYEE is an example of an involuted relationship.

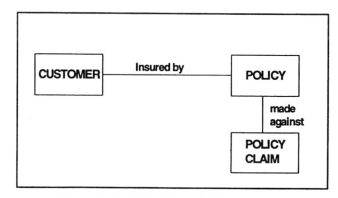

Figure 2. Relationships added to the ERD.

Cardinality and Optionality

The concept of a relationship can be extended to include additional facts about the association between entity types.

The first fact deals with the membership each entity type has in a relationship. It describes how many entities of an entity type can be associated with one occurrence of the other entity type in a relationship. This is called the **cardinality** of a relationship membership. In our example, a CUSTOMER can be *insured by* many POLICYs. Similarly, a POLICY can *cover* many CUSTOMERs. Each of the cardinalities for this relationship is referred to as many. One POLICY can be *impacted by* many POLICY CLAIMs. A POLICY CLAIM is *made against* one POLICY; this is called a one cardinality. The first relationship is called a many-to-many relationship. The second is called a one-to-many relationship. There is a third combination called a one-to-one, for example a COUNTRY *flies* one FLAG and a FLAG is *flown by* one COUNTRY.

The second fact defines whether all entities must participate in the relationship. This is called **optionality**. It effectively extends the concept of cardinality to include zero. In our example a POLICY may not have any POLICY CLAIMs filed against it.

This means that this relationship membership is optional. An updated entity relationship diagram is shown in Figure 3. The "crows foot" represents the many POLICY CLAIMs that can be related to a POLICY. The "o" means that there can be POLICYs without a CLAIM (optionality). The single bar means that each CLAIM can be related to only one POLICY.

Types of Relationships

Just as classifications of entity types assist in the identification of entity types and the construction of the ERD, types of relationships can be used to help identify relationships between entity types and to quality assure the data model. The types of relationships are grouped by the three different combination of relationships and the optionality possible within each group. Figure 4 shows the ten different types of relationships that can occur in a data model.

The most common combination is the one-to-many. Approximately 80–90 percent of the relationships in a data model are of this type. Within this combination the most frequently occurring are shown from top to bottom. One-to-many relationships are the easiest relationships to identify and not much time should be spent on them when quality assuring a model.

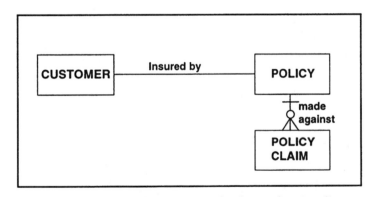

Figure 3. ERD updated with cardinality and optionality.

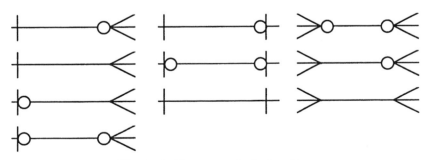

Figure 4. Ten types of relationships.

The last two one-to-many relationships do not occur very often and are usually refined as the data model evolves. The reason that they do not occur very often is that they both represent "unnatural" business situations. Ambiguity of the data model increases as the optionality of relationships increases. The rules that govern whether or not one entity is related to the other are not very apparent. These types of relationships are not favored by database analysts because they can introduce a large number of null foreign key columns in a database if they are implemented. Each typically represents a loss of data that further describes the relationship and removes ambiguity. This loss can be made up by introducing another entity type.

The optional one-to-many mandatory relationship can be viewed as many occurrences of one entity type not being paired with another at some point in time. For example, suppose a PROJECT TEAM MEMBER *may be assigned to* a WORK GROUP as shown in Figure 5. Some of the data that could be missing as a result of using this type of relationship is the date the PROJECT TEAM MEMBER was assigned to the WORK GROUP, the responsibility within the work group, how long the assignment will last, and so forth. The resolution of this loss is shown in Figure 6. The

data model is much easier to understand with the addition of the WORK GROUP ASSIGNMENT entity type. The null foreign key column is removed from the PROJECT TEAM MEMBER entity type. The resolution also results in a one-to-one relationship, which is not very common. This enables the questions "Does a project team member belong to only one work group?" and "Is the history of a project team member's assignments to work groups not of interest?" to be raised. The answers to these questions will help determine the correct cardinality for this newly added relationship. If the answer to both questions is "yes" then the one-to-one relationship can stand as it is. The other rare type of relationship can be resolved using a similar technique. The only difference is that the one-to-many fully mandatory relationship becomes a mandatory-one-to-optional-many relationship.

The next most common are the one-to-one combinations. They should total the remaining 10–20 percent of the relationships. To illustrate the relative low frequency of this type of relationship, try to give an example of a fully mandatory one-to-one relationship. Remember, occurrences of each entity type involved in the relationship must always exist at the same time, and each entity type must have a different definition. Give up yet? Figure 7 is an example.

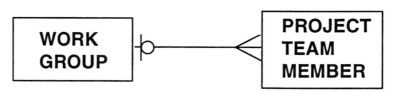

Figure 5. Rare one-to-many relationship.

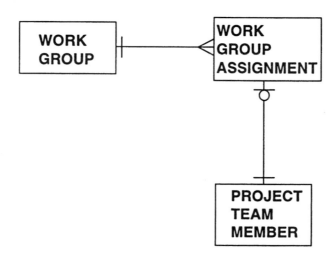

Figure 6. Resolution of rare relationship.

A partially optional one-to-one relationship does not have to be resolved and is the most common of this type of relationship. This type is commonly used to depict an alternative method of subtyping or to depict the relationship between an entity type and additional optional facts about that entity type stored in another entity type. An example is shown in Figure 8.

An attempt should be made to resolve all fully optional one-to-one relationships. Fully optional one-to-one relationships can hide information just as fully optional one-to-many relationships can. Figures 9 and 10 show how this type of relationship is resolved. In Figure 9 the model does not permit attributes to be kept about the installation of a motor in a boat. They could be kept in either BOAT or MOTOR, but would be invisible unless the properties of the entity type were investigated. Doing this also does not conform to the rules of normalization. The information about the installation is dependent on both BOAT and MOTOR. Figure 10 depicts the resolution of this relationship. The benefits gained from resolving a partially optional or fully optional one-to-many relationship are also gained when resolving a fully optional one-to-one relationship.

Figure 7. One-to-one fully mandatory relationship.

Figure 8. One-to-one partially optional.

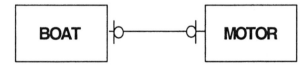

Figure 9. One-to-one fully optional.

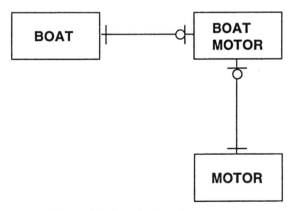

Figure 10. Resolution of one-to-one.

The many-to-many combinations occur in the early stages of data model development, but these types of relationships are usually refined as the model evolves. Missing information that results in associative entity types is the typical resolution. Figure 12 shows the resolution of the many-to-many relationship in Figure 11.

Attributes

Definition

An enterprise needs to know certain facts about each entity of a certain type. For example, CUSTOMER is described by a number, name, date established, date of birth, and so forth. Each of these facts is called an **attribute**. As attributes take on values they describe a single entity type. For example, CUSTOMER number 100932, name Joe E. Lyle, established on 12/23/1995, date of birth 11/05/49 describes one occurrence of CUSTOMER.

Attributes can be optional, just like relationship memberships. An **optional attribute** is one that does not have to have a value assigned to it. For example, suppose POLICY is described by the attribute date discontinued. POLICYs that are still active would not have a value assigned to this attribute. That means that it is optional.

Entity Type Identifiers

Attributes serve one other purpose in the data model. They are used to identify individual occurrences of entity types. For example, CUSTOMER is identified by number; POLICY is identified by number. They can be used in combination with other attributes and relationships to serve as the **entity type identifier**.

When a relationship is used for an identifier, its foreign key is actually used as part of the identifier. For example, suppose POLICY CLAIM *consists of* many CLAIM ITEMs. CLAIM ITEM is identified by the relationship to POLICY CLAIM and the attribute CLAIM ITEM number. This means that the identifier of POLICY CLAIM, number, a foreign key of CLAIM ITEM, is part of CLAIM ITEM's identifier.

Entity Subtypes

Sometimes we may find that entities of the same type have different attributes and/or relationships. But, they still share some attributes and/or relationships. To handle situations like this entity subtypes can be used.

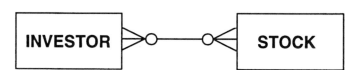

Figure 11. Many-to-many relationship.

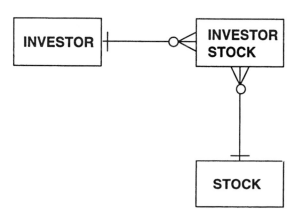

Figure 12. Resolved many-to-many relationship.

Definition

An **entity subtype** is a further refinement of the same entity type to which additional attributes and/or relationships apply. In the insurance example we have been using, CUSTOMERs can be individuals or businesses. There may be attributes that are unique to an individual, like spousal information. There may be relationships that are unique to a business, like a relationship to another entity type that describes the organizational structure of the business.

Subtype Partitioning

In the example above an attribute, such as customer type, partitions the entity type CUSTOMER into two entity subtypes, INDIVIDUALS and BUSINESS. These two subtypes belong to a **partitioning** of the entity type. It is possible to partition an entity type into multiple partitionings. For example, there may be additional attributes and/or relationships that describe a foreign customer versus a domestic customer. It is important to note that some data modeling techniques that employ partitioning allow the subtypes in a partition to overlap, while other techniques require them to be mutually exclusive.

Improving on the Collaboration

In working with users to construct data models an interesting phenomenon occurred over and over again during modeling sessions. Users lost interest in the process of data modeling once fairly large-grained data objects were discovered. As data modelers moved from the task of discovering entity types and attributes to normalizing the attributes, determining cardinality and optionality of relationships, and so forth, users could not quite grasp what was going on. Unless, perhaps, they were expert data modelers.

Today, rather than have users continually present during modeling sessions, they participate in information gathering and confirmation sessions. Data modelers concentrate on structuring the results of gathered information and identifying gaps in the structures. Filling the gaps forms the focus of further information gathering sessions with users.

Subject Areas

Subject areas began their life as a way to aggregate files into subject area databases in the days of distributed processing during the early 1980s. They are also useful in aggregating entity types.

Definition

A **subject area** is a grouping of entity types or other subject areas that are focused on the same general area of interest, such as a major resource or activity. A subject area that contains only entity types is called a **primitive subject area**. It has important implications when working with users (as is explained later in this section). A primitive subject area contains six to ten entity types, each described by an average of five attributes. Figure 13 depicts a partially developed subject area for the insurance example we have been using.

Data Decomposition

Subject areas are an effective way to group entity types together and effectively organize the data model, focus discussion, and make the data model easier to understand. There are a few simple rules that help make the identification of subject areas and their decomposition repeatable.

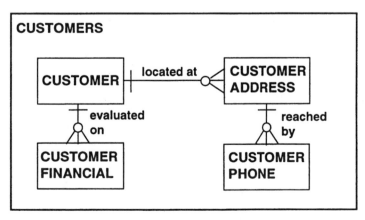

Figure 13. Partial CUSTOMERS subject area.

First, let's borrow some guidelines from programming best practice. Subject areas should exhibit a high degree of cohesion and a low degree of coupling. Cohesion is measured by the number of relationships between entity types within the same subject area. Coupling is measured by the number of relationships between entity types in different subject areas. Therefore the goal should be to minimize the number of relationships between subject areas (low coupling) and maximize the number of relationships between entity types within a subject area (high cohesion).

Second, we've borrowed some best practice from functional decomposition to help guide the decomposition process. These rules focus on beginning decomposition by identifying areas of specialization and proceeding on to decomposition by life cycle. A **data decomposition diagram** illustrating decomposition best practice is shown for the insurance example (Figure 14).

The first level of the diagram is based on specialized areas of the enterprise (*Note:* it is not complete). The second level begins to move away from specialization toward a life-cycle approach. For example, there must be Customers before there are Policies.

Business Objects

Within the last few years the collaboration between modelers and users has evolved further. The advent of the business object concept has facilitated this advance. Now aspects of both data and process are analyzed together.

Definition

A **business object (type)** is some type of thing that the business needs to keep track of during its operation. The representation includes both data and process, including business rules governing the process. Business objects are occurrences of the type, but to avoid confusing users and others the terms are typically used interchangeably.

Examples of business objects are CUSTOMERS, POLICIES, POLICY CLAIMS, QUOTATIONS, PROSPECTS. They are very similar to the concept of a primitive subject area, except a business object has process information associated with it.

Business Object Modeling

Business object modeling is performed throughout the development process, from analysis through testing and implementation. There is no recognized standard established yet on how to carry out or represent the business object model. A simple convention is used in this chapter. Figure 15 represents a business object from a modeling standpoint. As a project progresses, attributes are identified, and business logic, user interfaces, and data manipulation logic are added to the process components of the business object. Business objects become the focus of application and database design. Finally, the business object becomes operating software units.

Insurance
 Marketing
 Sales
  Customers
  Policies
 Product Development
 Customer Service
  Policy Claims
 Human Resources
 Procurement

Figure 14. Data decomposition diagram.

330

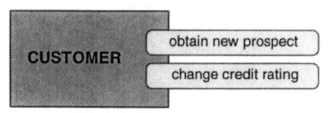

Figure 15. Customer business object.

Impact on the Data Model

What impact have these advances made on the entity-relationship approach to data modeling? We look at each of these advances in turn.

Subject Areas

Subject areas help organize the data model, focus discussion, and make the data model easier to understand. Organizationally, subject areas can be "contracted" to hide the entity types and relationships it contains. Fewer things in a diagram facilitate focused discussion. A diagram like the data decomposition diagram makes the data model easier to understand by presenting data in an indented list format. The decomposition concept also allows data to be broken down, subject area by subject area. This means that data modeling progresses from higher to lower degrees of granularity in a stepwise, repeatable process.

Business Objects

Modeling business objects has dramatically changed the concept of data modeling in a number of ways. First, both data and process modeling are performed concurrently when building a business object model. Second, the internal structure of the data is "hidden" from the user. It becomes the purview of physical data modelers. All the user needs to fully understand is the list of attributes that describe the business object and the function of the processes, or operations, that act on the business object.

The use of business objects continues on into application design. Business objects can be the focal point of application design as depicted in Figure 16.

Not all enterprises have all nine functions. Additionally, the complexity of the functions may vary from enterprise to enterprise. Once the initial scope of the model has been identified the techniques described in the next section can be used to continue development of the model.

Requirements Gathering Techniques

The three techniques presented in this section represent only a sample of those available to the modeler. Two of them have been time-proven: one is the context diagram (the old level zero data flow diagram), and the other is the event consequence diagram. The third technique employs Use Cases.

A context diagram puts the entire application to be developed into the proper perspective. It identifies the functional scope of the application and the interfaces for the application. In Figure 17 three business objects are evident: Borrowers, Loan Applications, and Credit Bureaus. More may be found as the project progresses, but this is a good place to start.

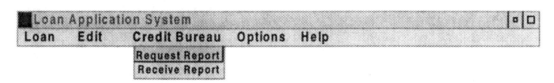

Figure 16. Application design on the basis of business objects.

Figure 17. Context diagram.

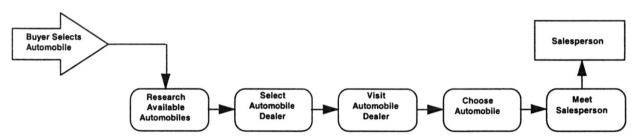

Figure 18. Event consequence diagram.

Event analysis, which originally surfaced in the 1970s, is also an effective technique to use. When employing it, events that occur relative to the business and the business response to them are analyzed. Figure 18 illustrates an event and the business objects that are identified by employing it.

Here the candidate business objects, Buyer, Salesperson, Automobile, and Dealer, have been identified. Use Cases have evolved from the efforts of I. Jacobson et al. in the object-oriented arena.[1] They describe the interaction of objects with a system. In a manner very similar to event analysis, they look at the roles played in the interaction with business processes, such as how a prospective buyer interacts with a real estate agent. Here, two candidate business objects are Buyer and Agent

Building the Model

Once requirements have been gathered the next step is

to employ modeling techniques to organize and structure the model. The techniques described above can continue to be used to extend and detail the model. One additional technique that has been used successfully to organize and structure the model is discussed in the next section. The final section in this article describes how modeling has been recognized as an evolutionary process that continues throughout the development process.

Modeling Techniques

For years a battle has raged on between process-focused and data-focused techniques used to perform business modeling. The technique presented here serves as a compromise between the two camps by performing data and process modeling in parallel. **Parallel decomposition** develops both data and process concurrently from the outset of a project. The results of data modeling confirm the results of process modeling, and the results of process modeling confirm the results of data modeling. This fits in well with the concept of business object modeling.

M. Porter's value chain or some similar structure

---

[1]Jacobson, Ivar, et al., *Object-Oriented Software Engineering: A Use Case-Driven Approach*, Addison-Wesley/ACM Press, Reading, Mass., 1992.

can be used to begin business object modeling. It continues until primitive subject areas, or business objects, are identified. Then both the data and process aspects of business objects are studied and recorded. As previously stated in the section on business objects, no standard for business object modeling has emerged. Companies that develop application development tools, such as Texas Instruments, are on the forefront of bringing a standard to bear.

Evolutionary Modeling

The use of these techniques crosses the traditional boundaries of analysis and design. The model evolves through analysis, design, and test with lower levels of detail being found as the project progresses. For example, finding additional attributes while designing a user interface is perfectly acceptable. And, by keeping the physical structure out of specifications for user interfaces and logic there is little impact to project deliverables. Mapping to physical data structures is a job left until late in the development cycle and should be done in I/O modules, not in user interfaces or logic.

Summary

Using entity-relationship diagramming to represent data is still an important technique today. It should not, however, be used in isolation, but together with other techniques that fully represent the business objects we encounter every day.

Suggested Reading

Coad, P., *Object Models: Strategies, Patterns, and Applications,* Prentice-Hall, Englewood Cliffs, N.J., 1995.

Jennison, L. et al., *Business Objects: Software Solutions,* John Wiley & Sons, New York, N.Y., 1994.

McMenamin, S. et al., *Essential Systems Analysis*, Prentice-Hall, Englewood Cliffs, N.J., 1984.

Reilly, J., *Rapid Application Prototyping: Moving to Business-Centric Development*, International Thompson Computer Press, Boston, Mass., 1996.

Sims, O., *Business Objects: Delivering Cooperative Objects for Client/Server,* McGraw-Hill, New York, N.Y., 1994.

Vaskevitch, D., *Client/Server Strategies: A Survival Guide for Corporate Engineers,* IDG Books Worldwide, San Mateo, Calif., 1993.

Yourdon, E., *Techniques of Program Structure and Design,* Prentice-Hall, Englewood Cliffs, N.J., 1975.

Object-Oriented Requirements Analysis

Sidney C. Bailin
Knowledge Evolution, Inc.
Washington, DC

1. Introduction

Object-oriented requirements analysis (OORA) is a method of formulating the requirements for a software system in terms of objects and their interactions. The discipline was started by practitioners of object-oriented design who found that conventional process-oriented requirements analysis methods, such as structured analysis (Gane and Sarsen, 1978; DeMarco, 1979) or structured analysis and design technique (SADT; SofTech, 1978), did not flow well into an object-oriented design. The difficulties in proceeding from structured analysis to object-oriented design stem from differences in the criteria for decomposing a system into subsystems and lower-level components. Converting a process-oriented decomposition—the result of a structured analysis—into an object-oriented decomposition frequently requires a great deal of reorganization.[1] Object-oriented requirements analysis seeks to decompose a system into interacting parts that represent the user's requirements as faithfully as conventional analysis methods, but to do so in a way that is compatible with object-oriented design.

Compatibility with object-oriented design facilitates the transition from the requirements analysis to the design phase. It also simplifies the traceability of requirements throughout the development life cycle, and makes less disruptive the process of iterating over requirements and design (that is, backtracking to the requirements analysis if the design implications are discovered to be infeasible).

Historically, OORA arose for these reasons. Some proponents of the approach argue that the object-oriented framework provides a more robust and accurate description of user requirements than the conventional approaches, and is therefore to be preferred intrinsically over process-oriented analysis.

Distinguishing Characteristics of Object-Oriented Requirements Analysis. Object-oriented requirements analysis differs from conventional process-oriented methods in two major respects: (1) the way in which a system is partitioned into subsystems and components, and (2) the way in which the interaction between subsystems or components is described.

Partitioning a System into Objects. In a process-oriented approach, a system is described as a set of interacting processes. In the object-oriented approach, a system is described as a set of interacting objects. The first question that any newcomer to this approach will ask is, therefore, "What is an object?"

The question of what constitutes an object is a difficult one. Determining what the objects are is one of the fundamental tasks of an object-oriented requirements analysis, and later of object-oriented design. Most simple answers tend to beg the question by saying that an object is a "real-world entity" or a "thing" as opposed to an "action." These answers may be suggestive, but all they really do is replace one word (*object*) with another (*entity* or *thing*).

Despite the difficulty in defining precisely what an object is, there are frequently many obvious candidates during the requirements analysis phase. These are the major "things" about which one finds oneself talking when discussing the system. For example, in an air-traffic control system, one frequently refers to aircraft, sectors, controllers, and weather. Each of these is a candidate object. But there is no simple algorithm for identifying or selecting these and precisely defining their interfaces. That is the task of the requirements analysis process.

As shown in Figure 1, each object encapsulates a set of services (also called *functions* or *methods*) and a *state* to which the services have read and write access. A fundamental goal in defining objects is to group data items together with the functions that read or write to those items. This kind of grouping makes each object a cohesive set of functions and data.

This approach to partitioning contrasts with the conventional functional or process-oriented approach, in which a system is decomposed into the primary services that it performs. We discuss this difference in more detail in Section 2.

---

[1] An early example of this may be found in Section 5 of Seidewitz and Stark (1986).

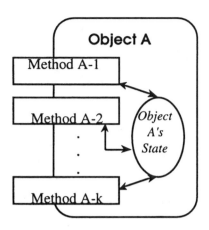

Figure 1. The structure of an object.

Describing Interaction. The basic idea in OORA is to represent system requirements in terms of interacting objects. Objects interact by sending messages to each other; this typically results in the receiving object performing some service for the sending object. Messages may have both input and output arguments, through which data can be passed between the sender and the receiver of the message: input arguments specify the parameters of the service being requested, and output arguments return the results. The basic paradigm is illustrated in Figure 2.

What is most significant about this paradigm is that each object provides a well-defined interface to its clients. The clients are all other objects that send messages to this object. The interface describes exactly what form of messages the object will accept. Another way to view the interface is that it describes what *services* the object provides, or what *operations* it is capable of performing. Thus, an object encapsulates a set of services. The services provided by all the objects, taken together, represent the functional requirements of the system. The primary goal of the analysis process is to determine how these services should be encapsulated, that is, to determine what the objects are, what services they should provide, and how they should interact.

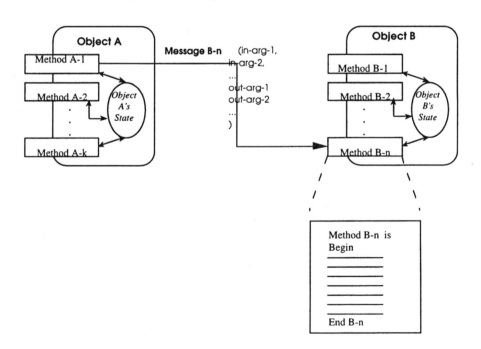

Figure 2. The object interaction paradigm.

In contrast to the well-defined interfaces of the object-oriented approach, functional or process-oriented methods tend to rely on less precise dataflow representations of system interfaces. The ambiguities of dataflow models are well known. For example, when two flows are shown to enter a process, does this mean that they arrive at the same time (as distinct arguments passed to an operation that the process must perform), or that they are independent, alternative means of activating the process? Through its more precise models, the object-oriented approach forces the analyst (and later the designer) to address important questions that might otherwise go unnoticed until implementation.

Outline. In Section 2 of this article we present the most important concepts of object-oriented requirements analysis in (what we hope is) a notationally and methodologically open fashion—that is, without trying to induce the reader to think in terms of a specific notation or a specific set of steps to be followed. In addition to the fundamental object-oriented concepts, we also introduce the most typical models that are used to describe system requirements in an object-oriented manner. These models are found in most of the published OORA methods, although the notations and the specific information captured may vary. Also in Section 2 we discuss the criteria for deciding when an object-oriented requirements analysis is (tentatively) complete.

In Section 3 we show how several specific OORA methods apply the concepts previously discussed. The methods discussed are those of Coad and Yourdon (1991), Shlaer and Mellor (1992), Wirfs-Brock et al. (1990), the fusion method (Coleman et al., 1994), and the unified method (Booch et al., 1995). In addition to showing how the common concepts appear in these methods, we point out some of the unique aspects of each approach. The intention here is to provide the reader with a sense of what each approach can offer, as a basis for choosing between them or incorporating aspects of them in a hybrid method.

In Section 4 we discuss the risks involved in an organization transitioning to OORA. These include methodological traps that are easy to fall into, technology acceptance issues, and issues concerning the relationship between system and software engineering.

In Section 5 we summarize the main areas of impact of object-oriented requirements analysis on software engineering practice.

2. Fundamental Concepts

The basic concepts of OORA are also those of object-oriented design and object-oriented programming:

- Objects
- Classes
- Methods (also known as *services* or *functions*)
- Variables (also known as *attributes*)
- Inheritance
- Polymorphism
- Information hiding
- Message passing (and the related issue of binding)

What distinguishes OORA from object-oriented design is the fact that OORA is concerned with *problem-domain objects* and *problem-domain classes*. In the design process, one is still concerned with these, but also with solution-domain objects and classes. In object-oriented programming, one is concerned with ways of representing the objects and classes within a given programming language.

Objects. We begin by stating what we mean by "problem-domain objects." Commonly offered phrases such as "entities that play a role in the problem to be solved" are suggestive, but do not provide clear criteria for identifying objects. At the expense of some of this suggestiveness, we can define an object precisely as follows:

An object is a data structure together with a collection of functions that act on, or refer to, that data structure.

The data structure represents the current *state* of an object, or the current *attributes* of the object. The functions—which are called *methods* in object-oriented jargon—provide the means for setting or changing the object's state, for retrieving the current values that make up its state, for computing values derived from the current state, and for performing operations that require access (read, write, or both) to the current state.

An object is a *problem-domain* object if its data and functions are intrinsic to the problem that the software is intended to solve. An object is a *solution-domain* (design) object if its data and/or functions represent ways of solving the problem. Thus, whether an object belongs to the problem domain or the solution domain is not so much a property of the object itself as of one's conception of the problem to be solved. Again, there are no ready-made answers: the boundaries between the problem and solution domains may be well defined; if they are not, then it is part of the requirements analysis process to decide where the boundaries lie.[2] Typically considered as design objects are those whose sole purpose is to support the distribution of data between other objects, or to schedule the activation of other objects' services. Design objects also include those that provide low-level services, such as communication or input/ output, which are needed by other objects.

More on Objects and System Partitioning. The goal of cohesively grouping functions and data leads to criteria for partitioning a system (into objects) that are quite different from the traditional functional criteria. In the functional approach, a system is partitioned into the principal high-level functions that it performs. Each of these functions is then decomposed into subfunctions, that is, the constituent steps or actions through which the high-level function is achieved. Each subfunction can then be decomposed into sub-subfunctions, and so on.

Thus, in the functional approach, the analyst begins by asking, "What does the system have to do?" This leads to a set of functions $F_1...F_n$. For each such identified function F_i, the analyst then asks, "What needs to be done in order to accomplish F_i?" This process of functional decomposition continues until the lowest level of identified functions is considered to be well enough defined to permit a straightforward design and implementation.

A process-oriented approach to system partitioning follows the same overall criteria of functional decomposition, the only difference being that decomposing a process P into subprocesses $P_1...P_n$ does not necessarily mean that $P_1...P_n$ are performed successively. Instead, some or all of them may be performed in parallel.

In the object-oriented approach to analysis, we start by asking "What are the key objects that play a role in this system?" Some objects may suggest themselves immediately. As a means of identifying other objects, we may ask the functional question "What does the system have to do?"[3] From the resulting

identification of the top-level services or functions, we might then ask "What state information or data items do these functions act on or reference?" We can then begin to identify key objects by grouping the top-level functions with the state information or data items to which they "belong." It is this grouping process that makes the approach object-oriented.

Classes. Classes are a means of organizing objects in terms of their similarities and differences. We can group similar objects into a *class* that represents the shared aspects of those objects. For example, animals who share the characteristic that their body temperature remains near constant, regardless of changes in the environmental temperature, are grouped by zoologists into the class of "warm-blooded animals."

In a software system it is useful to identify a class when there will be several objects that we expect to behave similarly. By defining a class, we are able to specify—and eventually to implement—requirements for the entire class; these requirements will then implicitly apply to each object in the class. We therefore have two criteria for the identification of classes:

- Multiple objects
- Similar behavior

In other words, it does not make sense to define a class containing only a single object. Nor does it make sense to define a class of objects whose behaviors, within the system being developed, will be dissimilar from each other. In a software system, the behavior of an object is characterized by the services it provides and by its intrinsic attributes. Objects are "similar" to each other if they perform some of the same services, or if they have some of the same attributes. For example, in an airline reservation system, one of the services (in fact, the key service) performed by an airplane might be *passenger flight.* Since this is a similarity in the behavior of all the airplanes represented in the reservation system, it makes sense to define a class of airplanes. In an air-traffic control system, not all of the airplanes represented will perform *passenger flight,* so it might make sense to distinguish the class of passenger airplanes from the class of commercial transport airplanes.

It is important to realize that the "right" classes may not be immediately apparent. There are usually many ways to organize objects into classes and subclasses, depending on what similarities and what differences are considered to be important. It is the task of the analyst to consider these alternatives and to choose among them according to the following criterion: which organization best represents the similarities and differences that are significant for this appli-

---

[2] The purpose of distinguishing between problem and solution domains is to prevent the analyst from prematurely ruling out useful alternative approaches to building the system. This does not imply that one "finishes" defining requirements before considering design. Throughout the analysis process, the design implications of the requirements (e.g., the feasibility of realizing them) should be considered. This may involve performing design in parallel with requirements analysis. Nevertheless, the distinction between the two activities, and their respective roles, should be maintained.

[3] In fact, we argue in Section 4 of this article that this question *must* be asked during the requirements analysis process, whether one's approach is object-oriented or not.

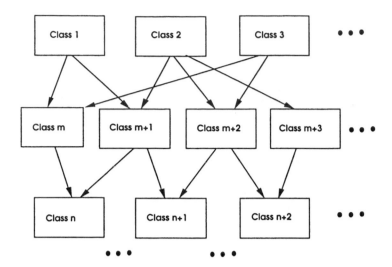

Figure 3. Lattice of classes and subclasses.

cation? This process is sometimes called *abstraction analysis,* and it is fundamental to the object-oriented approach in requirements analysis as well as in design and implementation.

Parent Classes and Subclasses. Classes themselves are organized into a structure of generalization and specialization: thus, warm-blooded animals are a special type of animal—we say that warm-blooded animals are a *subclass* of the class of animals, which is in turn a subclass of the class of all living beings (consisting of animals and plants).

The structure of classes and subclasses can be understood in terms of the predicate "is-a." Every warm-blooded animal *is an* animal; every animal *is a* living being.[4] It follows that a class can have several subclasses (for instance, warm-blooded animals, cold-blooded animals), and also that a class can be a subclass of several "parent" classes (animals are living beings, animals are also mobile entities). In its most general form, the structure of classes and subclasses is a lattice of the form shown in Figure 3, in which the an arrow from *A* to *B* means that *B* is a subclass of *A*.

Describing Objects and Classes. If an object belongs to a class, it is described implicitly through the description of that class. We describe a class in terms of the services provided by, and the attributes inherent in, the objects of that class. A singular object—one that plays a unique role in the system, and does not

belong to any class (other than the universal class of all objects)—is described in terms of the services *it* provides, and the attributes that *it* possesses.

Methods or Functions of an Object Class. The methods of a class are the things that objects in the class can do. They are operations that an object in the class performs when called on to do so. These calls are made by the methods of other objects, or by other processing elements in the system (for example, system event handlers, or a system main procedure that does not "live" inside any object).

It is in the methods of a system's classes that the functional capabilities of the system are realized. The methods can, therefore, consist of whatever kind of processing is needed. There are, however, certain standard types of methods that a class will frequently possess:

* Constructors and destructors
* Set and get

A constructor for the class *C* is a method whose job is to create instances of—that is, new objects in—class *C*. Constructors are used when objects must be created dynamically during system operation. A destructor for class *C* is a method that discards an instance of class *C* when it is no longer needed (for instance, in implementation terms, freeing up the memory that the object occupied). A constructor typically returns a reference to the new object that has been created. A destructor requires that a reference to the object being destroyed be passed as an input argument.

Set and get methods are used to update and access the state of an object. An object's state is determined by the values of its internal variables or

---

[4] This is true in object-oriented requirements analysis, but is not always true in object-oriented programming. In object-oriented programming languages like C++, in which one can distinguish between *public* and *private* subclasses, the latter may be used to represent the predicate "is implemented by means of" rather than the predicate "is a."

attributes. For each such variable, there can be a *set* method, which allows users of the object to *change* the value of the variable, and a *get* method, which allows users of the object to *read* the value of the variable. Access to either or both of these methods may be restricted, and the methods need not be provided at all. Determining which variables should have set and/or get methods and how access to them should be controlled is the question of information hiding, discussed below.

Variables or Attributes of an Object Class. Typically, the state of an object is represented as a set of values that are assigned to the object's *variables* (sometimes called *attributes*). We described an object as consisting of a data structure together with a set of functions associated with the data structure. The object's variables constitute its data structure (Figure 4).

Unlike methods, each object in a class has its own set of variables, which are used to represent the object's current state. It is also possible for certain variables to be associated with the class as a whole, rather than with any particular object in the class. Such variables, which represent the state of the class itself, are known as *class variables*.

Just as with a class's methods, there are various levels of detail at which we can describe a class's variables. At the most general level, they can simply be named, together with a short description of what each variable represents. More detail can be given by specifying the data type of each variable. Finally, the visibility and modifiability of each variable can be specified in terms of which other objects in the system can read and/or update it.

Inheritance. We described the lattice of classes and subclasses in terms of the relation *is-a*. Each member of a subclass *is-a* member of the parent class as well. In object-oriented systems, the *is-a* relation is realized through *inheritance*. Each member of a subclass inherits some of its characteristics from the parent class.

Specifically, members of a subclass inherit the methods and variables of the parent class. That is, if method M is defined for class C_p, and class C_s is a subclass of class C_p, then every member of class C_s with have a method called M. The reason for this is clear: members of class C_s are also members of class C_p; since all members of class C_p provide method M, the members of C_s must also provide method M.

The method M that is provided by all members of class C_s will have the same name and the same signature (that is, input and output arguments) as the method M which is provided by class C_p. However, the method M provided by class C_p may be left undefined ("virtual") so that it can be replaced, in each subclass of C_p (such as C_s), by one that is appropriate specifically to that subclass. This is because members of a subclass C_s may have additional characteristics, not found among other members of class C_p, which require special processing. For example, suppose C_p is the class of Documents, and C_s is a subclass of Documents that may contain embedded graphics. All members of class C_p might provide a Print method, but the specific capabilities of the Print method may vary depending on the type of document. The subclass C_s would, therefore, provide a print routine that can handle embedded graphics, while other subclasses might provide print routines that handle other types of documents. The process of replacing a virtual method M with a specific version is called *specialization*. The capabilities of the parent class are *specialized* to reflect the additional characteristics of the subclass (see Figure 5).

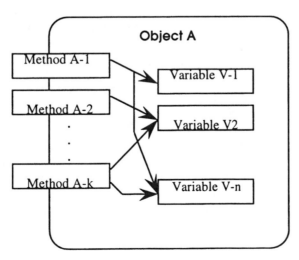

Figure 4. The variables of an object.

339

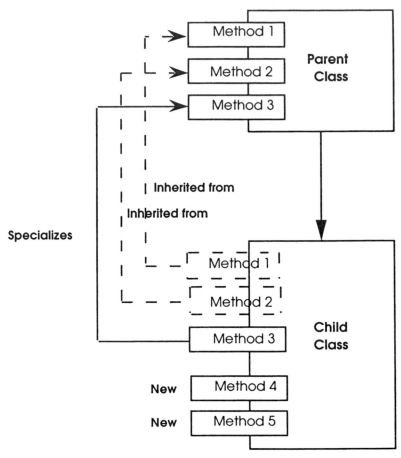

Figure 5. Specialization of a method from parent to child class.

In principle, the parent class could provide a default version of the Print method (say, one that handles pure text documents), and this version could be overridden by subclasses that handle different types of documents. However, this has come to be viewed as bad practice among object-oriented practitioners because it compromises the *is-a* relationship between parent class and subclass.

When a subclass has several parents, as in Figure 3, it inherits the methods and variables of all its parents. This is known as *multiple inheritance*. Multiple inheritance can be a powerful tool for modeling real-world problems. Different properties of objects in the real-world can be separated into different classes: for example, airborne objects might be in class C_a, while objects belonging to foreign countries might be in class C_f. An airplane belonging to France would then be a member of both of these classes. More generally, an object with certain properties would be a member of the classes that provide those properties. Multiple inheritance should be used with caution because it can be difficult to implement successfully. The difficulties tend to arise during the programming phase of development. An awareness of the potential difficulties is

appropriate during requirements analysis, however, in order to keep the transition to the later phases of development as smooth as possible. There are often other less risky ways of representing the same information.

Polymorphism. When different classes provide an identically named method, such as our Print example above, the system is said to support polymorphism. Polymorphism means that a function—which is thought of as a single function at a conceptual level—takes different forms depending on the type of object on which it is acting. The benefit of polymorphism is that the users of this function need not be concerned with the different behaviors required by the different types of objects.

Information Hiding. We have mentioned that the description of a class requires decisions about which variables or attributes will be visible to users of the class, and which are solely for internal use by the class's own methods. Similarly, update-access to some variables may be provided to users of the class via a "set" or "put" function. More generally, for each method of a class, there is a choice between allowing the method to be called by users of the class or only by other methods in the same class. These decisions determine how much information about the class is available to the class's users. The decisions should be based on the concept that the class represents. It is helpful to think of the objects in a class as *virtual machines* that provide a set of well-defined services to their users. The methods made available to users of a class should be those that provide these services. Additional methods, which are needed only as supporting functions in order to implement the services, should be kept private within the class. During the analysis phase, one is less interested in these supporting functions since they describe "how" the services of the virtual machine are to be implemented, rather than "what" the services of the virtual machine are.

Interaction among Objects: Message Passing. Now that we have discussed how classes and objects are described, we can return to the issue of how they interact with each other. As we mentioned in the Introduction, objects interact by sending messages to each other. The messages that an object can accept correspond to the services that the object provides (refer back to Figure 2). How does an object send a message to another object? We have seen that all the activity of an object is carried out by its methods. Thus, it is the *methods* of an object that will send messages to other objects, thereby invoking methods within those other objects. How, then, do things get started? Typically, some initiating event—such as system startup, or the occurrence of an interrupt—will cause the activation of some method in some object. From that point on, the objects interact via message passing.

We have mentioned polymorphism as the ability of a system to execute what is conceptually one function in different ways, depending on the object on which the function is acting. Thus, printing a textual document at a laser printer is different from printing a graphic at a color monitor, but polymorphism can allow us to treat these operations similarly, as manifestations of the single conceptual function *print*. In an object-oriented system, polymorphism is achieved by having different classes provide an identically named method. The "decision" as to which class should process a polymorphic function call—for example, which class's Print function should be activated—is equivalent to deciding on the *destination* of the message requesting the Print. This decision process is called *binding*: the message, or service request, is *bound* to a specific class. In an implementation of an object-oriented system, binding may occur at execution time (this is called dynamic binding), or at compile time (static binding). Although this distinction is an implementation issue, it may have implications for performance and/or fault tolerance, and it is therefore something that the analyst should understand.

2.1. Models Commonly Used in Object-Oriented Requirements Analysis

We now discuss the ways in which the concepts described above are used to capture system requirements. Typically, some or all of the basic concepts are applied to create a *model*, which expresses certain required aspects of the system to be built. The following types of models are commonly used in OORA:

- Whole–part (aggregation, assembly)
- Classification (is-a, inheritance)
- Class/object definition
- Object interaction (communication, message flow, usage)
- State machine

Whole–Part Model. This is a way of describing how objects are composed of simpler objects (see Figure 6). For example, a car consists of a body, an engine, a transmission, an exhaust system, and so on. Each of these, in turn, consists of lower-level objects. The ability to describe complex objects as a structure of interacting simpler objects is one of the key benefits of the object-oriented approach. The whole–part model can be represented in a hierarchy diagram in which the boxes represent classes, and an arrow from A to B means that each object of type A (that is, in class A) contains an object of type B. The whole–part model is sometimes known as the *aggregation* model, or the *assembly* model.

Classification Model. This type of model describes the inheritance relationships between classes. We discussed these relationships above, under *Classes*. A classification model can be represented by a lattice diagram such as Figure 3. Alternatively, aggregation and inheritance relationships can both be shown in the same diagram, by using a different type of arc to represent the two different relations. Whatever notation is used, it is important to keep in mind the distinction between these relations. Aggregation refers to the situation when one object *is a part of* another object. Classification refers to the situation when the objects of one class *are a kind of* the objects of a more inclusive class.

Class/Object Definition. At some point in the analysis process, we must specify what services are provided by the objects in each class. This effectively defines each class within the system. There are various levels of detail at which a class's services, or

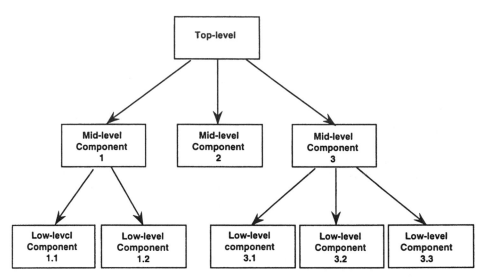

Figure 6: Whole–part model.

methods, can be specified. At the most general level they can simply be named: with each class, we associate a list of the methods provided by that class. At a slightly greater level of detail, we can identify the input and output arguments of each method, and provide a concise description of what each method does. A more formal approach is to be precise about the *types* of the input and output arguments. Still more formal detail can be provided by specifying the preconditions and postconditions of the method: the relationship between the object's state before and after the method is executed. Finally, a pseudocode or minispec presentation of the method's procedural logic can be provided. Choosing among these approaches must take into account the novelty of the class (classes that perform standard, well-understood functions may not need to be described as fully as more novel ones), its importance in the system (how much risk is entailed by not specifying the details), and the completion criteria that we discuss in Section 2.2.

Object Interaction Model. An object-oriented

model of a system must describe the way the objects interact. As discussed above, objects interact by sending messages to each other. Thus, an object interaction model shows the message flow between objects. There are several ways that message flow can be shown, corresponding to different levels of detail. The analyst must choose which level of detail is appropriate to the current task (see *Completion Criteria*, below).

A detailed object interaction model would show each message that flows between each object, together with the method that each message activates in the receiving object. Thus it might look something like Figure 7a.

A slightly less detailed representation (Figure 7b) would show each message, but would not explicitly show the methods that are activated.

A still less detailed form (Figure 7c) of this model would only show which objects send messages to other objects, without explicitly showing each message as a unique arc in the diagram.

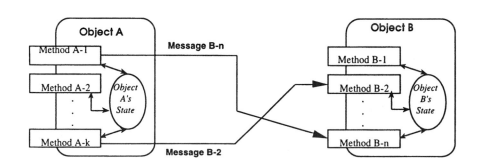

Figure 7a. Object interaction model.

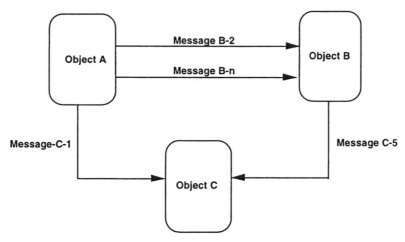

Figure 7b. Less detailed object interaction model.

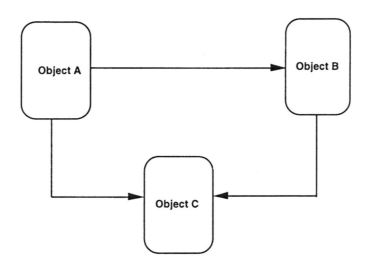

Figure 7c. Still less detailed object interaction model.

State Model. In this type of model, each object is modeled as a state machine. This is a form of behavioral modeling in which an object's behavior is described as a passage through different states. In dynamic systems, the creation of an object and its eventual disappearance from the system may also be modeled; the passage of the object from its creation, through its various states, to its destruction is called the object's life cycle (see the discussion of the Shlaer–Mellor approach, in Section 3.2).

Objects are typically modeled as *finite* state machines. This means that there are only a finite number of states in which the object can exist. For most systems, such a model will be a significant abstraction from the actual behavior of the constituent objects. For example, an object that has *heat* as an attribute may eventually be implemented so that its

heat is represented by a floating-point number. Thus there are virtually an infinite number of possible states, corresponding to the continuous range of possible temperatures.[5] For the purpose of modeling system requirements, it may suffice to describe the object as being in one of the following three states at any point in time:

- Temperature acceptable
- Too hot (temperature above some limit)
- Too cold (temperature below some limit)

---

[5] We say "virtually" because in any computer implementation the accuracy of floating-point numbers is limited, so that really only a finite—but very large—range of numbers can be represented.

The state model describes the conditions under which the object passes from one state to another. These are called *state transitions*. In the case of an object with a heat attribute, for example, the transition from "acceptable" to "too hot" occurs when its heat rises above a maximum acceptable temperature T_{max}.

State models are usually specified in either a graphical or a tabular form. The graphical form is typically a state transition diagram (STD; Figure 8a). Nodes in an STD represent possible states of the object. An arrow between two nodes represents a transition between those two states.

An arrow is typically labeled with the name of the event, or condition, that causes the change in state. More detailed STDs may specify an action that the object performs when entering a state, or after it has entered the state, or when it is leaving a state. These actions are typically specified by means of a descriptive label (such as "Notify Controller of Excessive Temperature"). The label may in turn refer to a more detailed description of the activity, in the form of pseudocode (or, in structured analysis terminology, a minispec).

The tabular form of the state model is called a transition matrix, and it is equivalent in expressive power to a state transition diagram. In a transition matrix, each row corresponds to one of the object's states, and so does each column. The entry in the jth row and kth column represents the transition from the jth state to the kth state. Figure 8b shows the transition matrix that corresponds to the state transition diagram of Figure 8a.

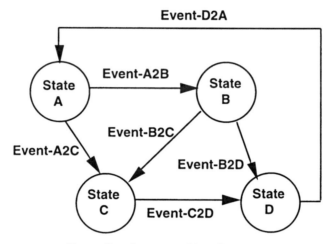

Figure 8a. State transition diagram.

| | After Event | | | |
Before Event	State A	State B	State C	State D
State A		Event A2B	Event A2C	
State B			Event B2C	Event B2D
State C				Event C2D
State D	Event D2A			

Figure 8b. Transition matrix.

344

2.2. Completion Criteria for an Object-Oriented Requirements Analysis

In fact, requirements analysis is never complete until the system has been retired. Until then, there is a continual need to reassess, or at least to reconfirm, the users' requirements. What we mean by "completion criteria" is more modest—namely, the conditions under which one decides to proceed with building (or modifying) a system that conforms to the requirements models. This represents the point at which the analyst's job is, for the time being, done. While there may have been design activity during the analysis phase for purposes of understanding the implications of various requirements, the design activity now becomes primary: it begins the process of realizing the requirements by transforming the models into software.

The question is when this should happen. As in any transition from requirements analysis to design, we can answer the question with two considerations:

- Traceability
- Absence of significant ambiguity

The analysis process is complete when (1) all specified requirements can be traced to the models, and (2) the models themselves are precise enough so that *any* realization of them will be acceptable.

The second item is a tall order. This is one reason why requirements must be continually revisited. Just as some design activity is necessary in the analysis phase—in order to explore the implications of the requirements—it is also true that some analysis activity is invariably needed during the design phase. This is because ambiguities that had not been previously recognized in the models may later appear, as one tries to "build to" the models.

Let us look at what traceability and absence of ambiguity mean in the object-oriented approach. The initial requirements specification for a system is typically formulated in terms of *function* and *performance*—that is, what the system must do, and how quickly, accurately, and under what workload conditions it must do it. Traceability therefore requires that all functional capabilities identified in the initial specification must be mapped to objects. In the most straightforward cases, we can map a required function to the object that provides that function as a method. Because of the encapsulated nature of objects, however, it is not always the case that a single object will suffice to perform an entire system-level function. There might, instead, be a chain of successive method invocations, involving several objects, that *together* perform the required function. This is the primary reason that modeling a system's end-to-end behavior is an important aspect of OORA (see Section 4).

One way to facilitate traceability is to structure the system so that every required function corresponds to an *interface method*. In this approach, the system itself is modeled as a "large" object providing certain services to the system's environment (which may consist of users and/or other systems). The required functional capabilities can be directly mapped to these system-level services. The system-level services can then be allocated to lower-level objects using the standard method of object decomposition/aggregation. This approach is illustrated Figure 9. The reader should note that even using this approach, end-to-end behavioral modeling is still necessary in order to guarantee that performance requirements will be met.

Absence of ambiguity means that the contents of the initially specified requirements have been sufficiently clarified so that any implementation of them will be acceptable. There is no easy way to ascertain this. Extensive discussion with the prospective users of the system, and prototypes of key features that can be tried out for user feedback, still form the foundation of a successful requirements analysis. The object-oriented approach does help in one respect: because there is a more direct relationship between the form of the OORA products and the eventual design and implementation, there is less of a chance of intentions becoming lost in the translation from requirements to design, or from design to implementation. Because the requirements and design representations are similar in form, it is easier to iterate the analysis process if ambiguities are discovered during design.

3. Comparison of Five Different Approaches

The models we described in Section 2.1 form the basis of all of the approaches that we now discuss. Thus, the various methods have a lot in common. They differ from each other in several respects:

- Emphasis (that is, their view of which models are most important)
- Specific notations (for example, additional information that can be provided in the models)
- Recommended steps to be followed in developing the models

In this section we concentrate on the differences—particularly the differences in emphasis, and the kinds of information that each approach suggests putting into the models. The notational differences are fairly arbitrary, and the reader should recognize that elements of the different methods can be combined, as appropriate, for modeling the most important information about a particular system's requirements.

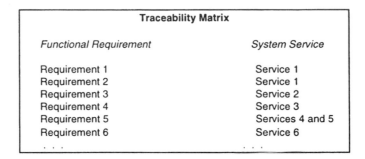

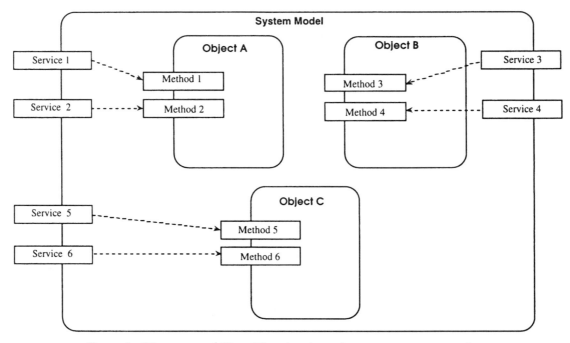

Figure 9. Direct traceability of functional requirements to system services.

3.1. The Coad–Yourdon Approach

Coad and Yourdon present an object-oriented analysis as consisting of five "layers." These layers are not layers of the system being described, but rather layers of the analysis itself. The development of each layer adds certain information to the resulting specification, and the analysis is complete when all five layers have been specified. The layers are as follows:

- Class–object
- Structure
- Subject
- Attribute
- Service

The *class–object* layer consists of identifying the key classes and objects in the application. The *structure* layer consists of describing the whole–part (aggregation) and generalization–specialization (inheritance) relations between classes and objects. In

the Coad–Yourdon notation, the whole–part and generalization–specialization relations can be presented together in a single diagram: different arc shapes are used to indicate the two different relations, as shown in Figure 10.

The *subject* layer consists of identifying what Coad and Yourdon call "subjects." These are high-level groupings of objects and/or classes into major areas, and are similar to what have conventionally been called "subsystems." The criteria for grouping objects and classes into subjects are less well defined than those that govern the definition of classes (namely, strong internal coupling and well-defined service-based interfaces). The purpose of the subjects is to provide an easily comprehended top-level view of a system that is compatible with the more detailed enumeration of classes and objects.

The attribute and service layers are where the classes and objects of a system are described in detail. Also, in these layers, the analyst explores relationships between classes other than specialization and aggregation.

346

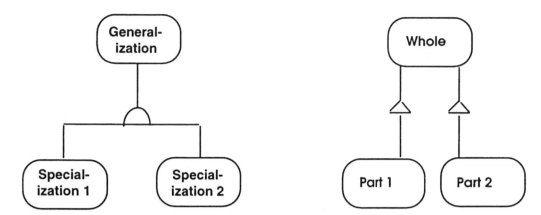

Figure 10. Coad–Yourdon notation for whole–part and generalization–specialization relations.

Coad and Yourdon suggest a number of questions that can help one identify a class's (or an object's) attributes. Once the attributes have been identified, they recommend identifying *instance connections* between objects. An instance connection is an association between two objects—essentially the same as a relationship in an entity-relationship model. Associations have cardinality constraints such as one-to-one, one-to-many, many-to-many, and optional. After the instance connections have been identified, Coad and Yourdon recommend checking for certain "suspect" connections; these are connections that "hide" additional classes, which should then be explicitly defined. Instance connections may be used to eliminate attributes with *repeating values*—for example, the attribute "car" of the class "owner" (an owner can have many cars). Such attributes can be replaced by classes in their own right—in our example, the class "car." An instance connection (such as "owner has car") can then be used to represent the relationship between the original class and what used to be the repeating attribute.

Finally, in the service layer, the analyst identifies the services that each class (or object) provides. The most notable feature of this step is the order in which Coad and Yourdon recommend describing system dynamics: first model each object as a *state machine*, then identify the *services* that each object provides, and then identify *message connections* between objects. Thus, the behavior of an object as a state machine provides a basis for identifying services. The elaboration of each service, in turn, provides a basis for identifying messages that flow between objects.

Services are classified into two high-level categories: *algorithmically simple* and *algorithmically complex*. Within the simple category, four types of services are identified: *create, connect, access,* and *release*. Within the complex category, there are two types of services: *calculate* and *monitor*. A *service diagram*, which is essentially a structured form of flow chart, is used to specify the procedural logic of each service.

3.2. The Shlaer–Mellor Approach

The Shlaer–Mellor approach differs from Coad–Yourdon in placing more emphasis on information modeling and state modeling, and less emphasis on modeling object interfaces. The approach is also distinguished by its view of the development process and the role of analysis models within that process. Shlaer–Mellor analysis models are intended to be sufficiently detailed to permit automatic generation of application code. Code generation is accomplished by combining the application-specific information represented in the analysis model with a selected design approach, which is represented in an *architecture*. The two types of models—analysis and architecture—are treated as orthogonal, so that a given application may be implemented in a variety of ways by choosing the corresponding architectures (Shlaer and Mellor, 1996).

Shlaer and Mellor discuss three basic analysis models, and several supplementary models. The basic three are as follows:

- The *information model* involves identifying and describing the *objects* of a system, the *relationships* between objects, and the *attributes* of the objects and relationships. This is essentially an entity-relationship-attribute model, borrowing ideas that were originally developed for database systems (Chen, 1976).[6]

- *The state model* in the Shlaer–Mellor approach is treated in more depth and detail than in other OORA methods.

---

[6] In the context of OORA, Shlaer and Mellor speak of objects rather than entities.

- The *process model* is a dataflow representation of each method of an object; it describes the processing performed by each method.[7]

In the following paragraphs we discuss some of the highlights of these and the supplementary models.

Information Model. Shlaer and Mellor identify three types of attributes: descriptive, naming, and referential. *Descriptive* attributes identify the relevant properties of an object. The descriptive attributes of a physical object might, for example, include weight, heat, color, or speed. *Naming* attributes are identifiers that are used to locate specific objects; they include the names with which a system user would identify objects, as well as internal identifiers used by the system itself. A *referential* attribute is a reference within an object to another object. For example, in a vehicle registration system, the object type *car* might have the attribute *owner*. This is a referential attribute because it refers to another object in the system, namely the owner of the car.

Shlaer and Mellor specify a handful of rules for structuring the information model—these are derived from the standard rules for normalizing databases, and help to ensure the integrity of the system's data throughout its operation (Codd, 1970).

Relationships in the information model are classified as unconditional, conditional, and biconditional. An unconditional relationship is one that holds throughout the lifetime of the objects involved. A conditional relationship between objects arises dynamically when certain conditions are met. A biconditional relationship is one in which either object may or may not be involved. For example, the relationship *Driver owns Car* arises when a car is purchased. Since both a Driver and a Car can exist without being in such a relationship, this is a biconditional relation.

The Shlaer–Mellor approach supports the notion of *associative* objects, that is, objects that represent specific relationships. For example, a *Title* object can be defined to represent the relationship *Driver owns Car*. Representing relationships as objects in their own right provides considerable flexibility to the information model. An associative object can, for example, enter into relationships with other objects. In particular, by identifying the "is-a" relationships between associative objects, the analyst can define a hierarchy of relationship types. For example, a hierarchy of purchase types may be defined by introducing the associative objects *Title, House Title,* and *Car Title,* where a *House Title* is-a *Title,* and similarly a *Car Title* is-a *Title.*

State Model. Shlaer and Mellor introduce the notion of an *object life cycle* to describe the sequence of states that an object passes through from its creation to its disappearance. Certain life-cycle paradigms are described—for example, a *circular life cycle* is one in which an object repeatedly passes through the same sequence of states, indefinitely. A *born-and-die life cycle* is one in which an object is dynamically created during the system's operation, passes through a series of states, and then disappears from the system. In the Shlaer–Mellor approach, actions are associated with object states: that is, when an object is in a given state it will perform a specific action associated with that state.[8] This implies the *same data rule:* all events that cause a transition into a particular state must carry the same event data.

The Shlaer–Mellor state model includes some unique constructs, such as:

- *Timer objects:* These are objects that generate events at specific time intervals. Shlaer and Mellor provide a generic state model for such objects.
- *Subtype migration:* This occurs when an object, through a change of state, also changes its type (that is, the class that it belongs to). Subtype migration is not explicitly supported by any of the mainstream object-oriented programming languages. It is, however, consistent both with the object-oriented paradigm and with the concept of objects as state machines: in different states, an object will accept different messages, or will process the same messages differently. One way to represent such differences is to place the object in different subclasses when it is in these different states.

The Shlaer–Mellor approach is particularly strong in its treatment of *relationship dynamics.* It introduces the concepts of assignor objects and monitor objects for modeling competitive relationships—that is, relationships in which several objects compete for access to a limited set of resources. An *assignor object* is one whose purpose is to mediate such competition by serializing requests for resources and assigning resources to the requesting objects as they become available. A *monitor object* is a simple form of assignor: the monitor repeatedly cycles through the states "waiting for request," "waiting for resource," "assigning resource to request." More complex forms of assignor

---

[7] Shlaer and Mellor speak of an object's *actions* rather than its methods.

[8] The alternative, which is supported in the Rumbaugh approach described below, is to associate actions with transitions between states.

life cycle are sometimes necessary: Shlaer and Mellor go into quite a bit of detail about different forms of competitive relationships and the kinds of assignor objects that are needed to mediate them.

System dynamics are described by means of an *object communication model* (OCM), which is essentially the object interaction model that we showed in Figure 7b: individual messages between objects are shown as arcs, but the services that they cause to be invoked are not explicitly shown. The OCM implies a layering of objects, wherein top-level objects issue messages, lowest-level objects receive messages, and middle-layer objects do both. Shlaer and Mellor adhere to the accepted wisdom that top-level objects are responsible for control, lowest-level objects perform common services, and middle level objects carry out functions specific to the application.

An important part of the Shlaer–Mellor approach is the dynamic modeling of individual *threads* in a system—a thread being the sequence of actions, across all objects, that occur in response to a given event. The thread-of-control chart is a graphical model of this behavior. Each object's sequence of states is shown in a column—one object per column. Interactions between objects in specific states are shown as arrows between the respective columns. This model is especially important because, as we discuss in Section 4, end-to-end modeling of system behavior is often ignored in the practice of OORA.

Process Model. The third basic model in the Shlaer–Mellor approach represents the processing performed by each object action (that is, method). The decomposition of an action into subprocesses is shown by means of a dataflow diagram, enhanced with a notation for showing control flow and conditional outputs. In their discussion of the process model they identify several types of processes:

- Accessors, which access an object's data store (that is, the object's variables)

- Event generators, which signal other processors

- Transformations, which operate on input data and make the results available as output data

- Tests, which check whether specific conditions hold and then cause control to be transferred appropriately

Finally, the *object access model* is an abstraction of the process model: it shows dataflow between objects, and is thus complementary to the object communication model.

3.3. The Wirfs-Brock et al. Approach

Wirfs-Brock et al. originally offered their approach as a way of doing object-oriented design, but it has evolved to encompass analysis as well. The most recent version of this method, known as responsibility-driven design, places a great deal of emphasis on "system description," which is a form of requirements analysis. This process involves understanding the stakeholders of a system to be built, describing the actors (human or external system) that drive the system, developing system operation scenarios, and constructing "conversations" between the system and the actors. Following the system description phase come the *exploratory* phase and the *refinement* phase. The exploratory phase consists of identifying classes, responsibilities, and collaborations, which historically have formed the kernel of the method. In the refinement phase, the emphasis is on developing an inheritance hierarchy and providing greater detail about contractual relationships between classes.

From an object-oriented viewpoint, the salient characteristic of this approach is its emphasis on *responsibilities*, *collaborations*, and *contracts*. The responsibilities of a class are the functions that it is intended to perform. Collaborations are the uses that one class—the client—makes of another class—the server—in performing its responsibilities. Contracts are the "agreements" or "protocols" that govern a collaboration between client and server. Ultimately a contract will be implemented by means of one or more messages between the classes.

The emphasis in the Wirfs-Brock et al. approach is on clarifying each class's responsibilities, identifying the collaborations necessary to meet those responsibilities, and defining the contracts that will govern those collaborations. In studying the interaction between classes—specifically from the point of view of meeting the functional requirements of the system—this approach goes into more depth than the others considered here. The theme of collaborations is closely related to the object interaction graphs of the fusion method and the object message and message trace diagrams of the unified method (see Sections 3.4 and 3.5). It is also manifested in Shlaer–Mellor's thread-of-control diagrams. In the Wirfs-Brock et al. approach, however, the theme of responsibilities, collaborations, and contracts takes center stage.

A *collaborations graph* is similar to the object interaction model shown in Figure 7a, in that each contract is shown as an arc between a port in the client class and a port in the server class. Wirfs-Brock et al. also recommend the use of a *hierarchy graph,* which is similar to the classification model shown in Figure 3, and also *Venn diagrams* as a means of expressing common responsibilities of classes, as shown in Figure 11.

The emphasis on collaborations shows up in the Wirfs-Brock et al. template for class specifications. As

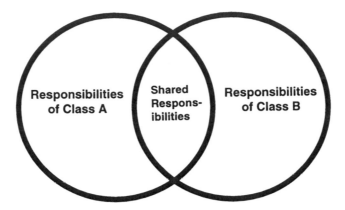

Figure 11. Venn diagram showing shared responsibilities.

in the Coad–Yourdon and Rumbaugh approaches, these specifications identify the services performed by the class—that is, its contracts. Unlike Coad–Yourdon and Rumbaugh, the Wirfs-Brock et al. description of each contract includes a list of required collaborations—that is, collaborations that this class needs in order to meet its responsibility as defined by the contract. Thus, the class specification includes not only a list of services *provided* by the class, but also of services *used* by the class (and provided by other classes).

3.4 The Fusion Method

Fusion is a "second generation" object-oriented development method that combines aspects of several "first generation" methods, specifically the object modeling technique (Rumbaugh et al., 1991), the class responsibility collaborator technique (exemplified in Wirfs-Brock et al.), the Booch method (Booch 1991), objectory method (Jacobson 1992), and formal methods (pre- and postconditions). Its goal is to package the most useful elements of these earlier methods in a simple and adaptable form.

Fusion divides the development process into three phases: analysis, design, and implementation. The analysis phase consists of developing three main models:

- Object model—Essentially an entity-relationship model, with emphasis on class aggregation and *is-a* subtyping, similar to the Shlaer–Mellor information model

- Operation model—A combined informal text and formal declaration of the system's operations, including (for each operation): data items read, data items changed, messages sent, preconditions assumed, and resulting postconditions

- Life-cycle model—Specification, in the form of regular expressions, of the admissible se-

quences of interactions that the system may have with its environment (people and external systems)

The operation model and life-cycle model together form what fusion calls the interaction model. It is a model of the system's behavior as a black box. In addition to these models, a data dictionary is created during the analysis phase and is maintained throughout the development process.

The fusion method recommends the development of *scenarios* as an initial step toward creating the interaction model. Scenarios may be represented by time-line diagrams, which show the exchange of messages and events between the system and the components of its environment. Figure 12 shows an example of a time-line diagram.

In fusion, several aspects of an object-oriented model are explicitly deferred until the design phase: these include messaging between objects, the specification of each class's methods, and decisions about class inheritance. Although the object model in the analysis phase does describe *is-a* relationships between classes, they are viewed as representing the intrinsic relationships between the classes as a model of the "real world," without implying that inheritance should be used to implement the relationships. The decision to use inheritance to implement any of these relationships is deferred until the design phase.

Although it is outside the strict purvue of this article, we mention the fusion design phase models because they are similar to some of the models discussed in Section 2. Object interaction graphs (OIGs) in fusion are similar to the type of model illustrated in Figure 7b, above, in that specific messages between objects are identified. The OIGs go further, however, by specifying the arguments of the messages, the sequence in which they occur, and any dynamic creation of objects that they may cause. Object interaction graphs also provide a means of distinguishing when messages are sent to all members in a collection of

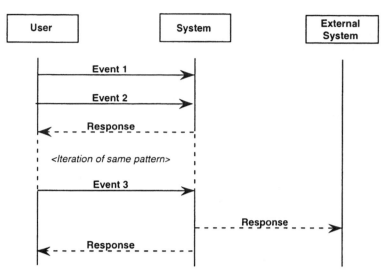

Figure 12. Example of a fusion time-line diagram.

objects or, rather, to a subset of a collection. Finally, the notion of a Controller object is introduced: this is the unique object in an OIG that receives a message from the environment.

A visibility graph in fusion specifies the dynamics of an object's visibility to other objects, that is, it addresses the issue of when a given "server" object is available to receive messages from a "client" object, and whether servers are shared between clients or dedicated to a single client. This information is reminiscent of some of the object life-cycle material developed as part of the Shlaer–Mellor analysis model, but in fusion it is treated during the design phase.

The fusion method suggests informal procedures for developing each of the models in the appropriate phase, including criteria with which to evaluate the resulting models. The criteria are for the most part heuristic rather than prescriptive, and the procedures themselves are relatively simple to communicate. The thinking required in building the model is, of course, not trivial. By keeping both the notation and the recommended procedures relatively simple, however, and by providing heuristics to guide their application, the authors of the method have achieved an approach that can be learned relatively quickly.

3.5. The Unified Method

The unified method (UM) is a "third generation" object-oriented modeling approach which, like fusion, seeks to build on and unify the most useful aspects of previously defined methods. The principal authors of the UM are G. Booch, J. Rumbaugh, and I. Jacobson. The UM represents, in particular, an attempt to amalgamate the methods previously developed independently by these authors. The definition of the UM is ongoing; the specification is currently in Version 0.9 (Booch and Rumbaugh, 1996).

The unified method, despite its name, is primarily a modeling *language* rather than a set of recommended procedures for building object-oriented models. Considerable effort is being put into selecting and structuring the elements of this language in the hope that it can become (or evolve into) a standard, thereby eliminating the confusing proliferation of object-oriented notations.

Like fusion, the UM spans the analysis, design, and implementation phases. Unlike fusion, there is no explicit allocation of certain types of models to each phase. This reflects the intention that the UM be usable in a variety of contexts (for example, domain analysis, system design, and software specification) by a variety of types of users, and that it be both comprehensible to humans and processable by machines.

The UM is distinguished from all the other approaches discussed in this article by containing a formally specified metamodel—that is, a formal definition of the UM language. The language also provides for uninterpreted constructs so that it can be used in conjunction with, for example, domain-specific methods.

The core of the UM consists of seven types of diagrams:

- Class diagram
- Use case diagram
- Message trace diagram
- Object message diagram
- State diagram
- Module diagram
- Platform diagram

351

Class Diagrams (CDs) correspond to the information model in Shlaer–Mellor and the object model in fusion: they are an enriched form of entity-relationship diagrams. One of the precursors of the UM, Rumbaugh's object modeling technique (OMT), was distinguished from other object-oriented methods by the richness of the types of relations and constraints that could be modeled. This feature is inherited by the class diagrams in the UM. For example, class nodes in a CD can be decorated or qualified with the following types of information:

- Stereotypes—User-defined qualifications indicating different "kinds" of classes

- Attributes and operations—Including types, initialization, derived values, arguments, and scope

- Template (parameterized) classes and their instantiations

- Utilities—Global attributes and operations, grouped for convenience into classes

- Individual objects (instances of classes)

Relationships between classes are known as *associations* in the UM, and they may be represented by *association classes* themselves. Associations may be *constrained* by formally specified conditions; constraints are interpreted to mean that the condition must hold at all times. Associations may also be combined by the logical operators *and* and *or*. Conventionally we think of subclassing and an "or" relationship and aggregation as an "and" relationship, but the UM notation allows one to specify other situations. For example, *and*'d subclasses can be used to represent mixins: these are independent aspects of a class that are combined to form instances of the class. The *or* operator may be inclusive or exclusive.

Class diagrams also support two higher-level constructs: categories and composites. Categories are high-level groupings of classes: they are essentially subsystems, but they have precisely defined interfaces derived from the public interfaces of the classes they contain. Composites are essentially patterns: they are aggregations of classes and associations that recur or are useful enough to be added to the modeling language in a specific context.

Use cases are adopted from the objectory method (Jacobson, 1992). They represent the end-to-end processing of the different types of transactions that a system can handle. They are similar in intention to the life-cycle model in fusion. The use case diagram is a notation for summarizing, in a single diagram, all of the use cases (transaction types) and the external agents that participate in them.

Message trace diagrams (MTDs) are similar to fusion time-line diagrams with the following important difference: the participants (vertical bars) in an MTD can be objects *within* a system; in fusion, the system being developed is represented by a *single* bar, and the other bars represent components of the external environment. The notation itself is roughly the same, but the intended use in the UM is more general.

Object message diagrams (OMDs) are similar to the object interaction graphs in fusion. Like the fusion diagrams, they can express the sequential flow of messages between several objects. They can also express concurrent operations.

State diagrams are an adaptation of D. Harel's Statecharts (Harel, 1987), which in turn are a hierarchical form of state transition diagram (discussed in Section 2). The fundamental idea in statecharts—hierarchically grouping low-level states into more abstract higher-level states—is a key technique for controlling complexity when representing the behavior of a large system.

Module diagrams represent the system as a set of interrelated developmental items, such as source code files. Platform diagrams represent the physical topology of a system. These views are not the primary concern of requirements analysis, although they are not entirely irrelevant either: for example, the physical topology of the surrounding system environment could be important in analyzing requirements for a new system.

4. Risks in Transitioning to Object-Oriented Requirements Analysis

As a relatively new approach to software engineering, the transition of an organization to OORA carries with it several risks. In this section, we discuss the following risk areas:

Management risks

- Acceptance
- Interface with systems engineering
- Need for domain analysis

Technical risks

- Identifying objects
- Ignoring behavioral modeling
- Ignoring dataflows

Acceptance. This is an issue in all technology transfer. In the case of object-oriented methods, the situation is muddied by the sheer popularity of the term "object-oriented" and the myths associated with it. Education in the basic concepts, as presented in Section 2 of this article, is essential in combating the resistance that stems from ignorance or misconceptions. The *reasons* for object-oriented partitioning criteria—their impact on maintainability and reusability—should be emphasized and illustrated with examples. It may also be useful to point out that the underlying issues addressed by the object-oriented approach—such as cohesion, coupling, and information hiding—are not new, nor are the answers particularly surprising. Object-oriented development makes explicit the issues that the best engineers have always tackled. Thus, OORA can be presented not as a radically new approach being imposed by fiat or because of fashion, but rather as a sharpening of the basic principles of software engineering, which have long been known.

Interface with Systems Engineering. In the conventional organization of a large development project, the systems engineering group produces a system design that allocates functions to software and hardware, and from which software requirements are derived. The allocation of functions to software frequently involves the identification of major software blocks, sometimes known as computer software configuration items, or sometimes (less formally) as software subsystems. There is a tremendous risk to this approach if the system design process has followed the traditional method of functional decomposition: the major blocks of software will not represent good object-oriented partitions, and the system design will force the software development team to compromise its application of object-oriented criteria. This in turn can lead to confused and poorly justified software design decisions, and eventually to disillusionment with object-oriented methods on the part of the software team ("we tried it and it didn't work").

There are two measures that can prevent such situations: (1) integrate object-oriented partitioning principles into the system design process, and (2) ensure early and ongoing interaction between the system design team and the software development team. The latter may be an easier measure to implement in the short term, but a commitment to object-oriented system development is probably necessary, in the long term, if the full benefits of object-oriented software development are to be realized.

Need for Domain Analysis. Although reuse and object orientation are not synonymous, the culture of object orientation is largely a culture of reuse, for two reasons: (1) objects, with their well-defined interfaces and encapsulated functionality, provide an effective vehicle for reuse, and (2) good objects and classes are hard to define, and arriving at them requires a significant investment (abstraction analysis). If this second point is not recognized by management, there will be unrealistic expectations for an early return on investment in object-oriented development.

A commitment to object-oriented development entails a commitment to a serious and ongoing analysis of what the "right" objects and classes are. This is nothing but domain analysis. If an organization practices object-oriented development on a regular basis, it will be doing domain analysis whether it is aware of this fact or not. Awareness of the fact will enable an organization to employ, to its advantage, the methods and techniques that are now being developed for domain analysis.

Identifying Objects. This is the technical counterpart to the risk area just discussed. Practitioners should not expect that their first attempt to identify the objects of an application will be optimal. The identification and definition of objects and classes involves tradeoffs, the answers to which are not always clear until negative lessons have been learned through experience. A number of books on object-oriented programming provide guidance in this area (for example, Meyer, 1992; Cargill, 1992), but the OORA literature is still fairly shallow on this point, probably because the field is new.

Ignoring Behavioral Modeling. With its emphasis on data encapsulation and information hiding, the early literature on OORA tended to emphasize static modeling: the definition of objects, classes, and their interfaces. Dynamic modeling, to the extent that it was addressed, tended to be limited to the behavior of individual objects, that is, describing them as state machines or specifying each method in pseudocode. Interactions between objects were described in terms of the individual messages that flow between them. There was frequently an implicit assumption that if a system were implemented to meet such specifications, it could be assured to behave correctly.

This assumption is ill-founded, and carries with it the risk that the required end-to-end behavior of the system—that is, the behavior of the system as a whole—will not be sufficiently analyzed. A thorough requirements analysis must include some consideration of end-to-end processing, starting with the occurrence of an event that activates some system processing, following the succession of messages and activations of objects' services that occur in response to the event, and ending with a description of the system's steady state at the conclusion of this processing and of any output that results. The models described in Section 2.1 must be verified against such scenarios; and the scenarios themselves must be checked for completeness with respect to the system requirements and operations concept. The time-line diagrams in fusion and the use cases and message trace diagrams in the unified method are effective ways of representing end-to-end behavior.

Ignoring Dataflows. A related risk is the tendency in object-oriented development to ignore the functional aspects of a system, and of the objects within a system. Although OORA leads us away from functional decomposition as a method of *structuring* a system, it does not relieve us of the obligation to analyze what the system is supposed to do! In the object-oriented approach, inputs and outputs are passed as arguments within messages exchanged between objects. This view tends to downplay their importance in comparison to the messages themselves. Nevertheless, it is through the conversion of inputs to outputs that the proper operation of each object, and of the system as a whole, will eventually be assessed. It is, therefore, necessary to describe the functional relationships between system-level inputs and outputs, and between the input and output arguments of each object's methods. The dataflow view can be useful in this connection, as long as (1) its purpose is understood (namely, to describe the functional properties of a system), (2) its limitations are recognized (that is, the need to complement it with the models described in Section 2.1), and (3) a well-defined relationship between the dataflow models and the other models is established (that is, it must be possible to map the dataflow model into the others, for example by considering dataflow between *objects* rather than between less well-defined *processes*).

5. Conclusion: Impact on the Software Engineering Practice

The use of OORA reduces the amount of restructuring needed to create an object-oriented design from the requirements analysis products. In doing so, it improves the ability of developers and verifiers to trace requirements to designs. The emphasis on precise interface definitions should lead to more manageable development "in the large," and facilitate the eventual integration of independently developed blocks of software. Finally, by encouraging the specification of relatively self-contained subsystems, the use of object-oriented partitioning criteria in the requirements analysis phase should improve the reusability of requirements analysis products from one system to the next.

Little, if any, numerical evidence has been collected in support of these expectations, and it is perhaps not unfair to argue that the verdict on OORA is still out. Nevertheless, its practice appears to be growing, and its use in the successful development of operational (as opposed to prototype) systems has made it a serious competitor to the more process- or function-oriented approaches.

References

Arnold, P. et al. "An Evaluation of Five Object-Oriented Development Methods," Technical Report HPL-91-52, Information Management Laboratory, Hewlett-Packard Laboratories, Bristol, June 1991.

Bailin, S., "An Object-Oriented Requirements Specification Method," *Comm. ACM,* Vol. 32, No. 5, May 1989.

Booch, G. and Rumbaugh, J., *Unified Method for Object-Oriented Development: Documentation Set,* Rational Software Corporation, Santa Clara, Calif., 1996.

Booch, G., *Object-Oriented Design with Applications,* Benjamin/Cummings, Menlo Park, Calif., 1991.

Cargill, T., *C++ Programming Style.* Addison-Wesley, Reading, Mass., 1992.

Chen, P., "The Entity-Relationship Model—Towards a Unified View of Data," *ACM Trans. Database Systems,* Vol. 1, No. 1, Mar. 1976.

Coad, P., "Object-Oriented Patterns," *Comm. ACM,* Vol. 35, No. 9, Sept. 1992.

Coad, P. and Yourdon, E., *Object-Oriented Analysis,* 2nd Ed., Yourdon Press, Prentice-Hall, Englewood Cliffs, N.J., 1991.

Codd, E., "A Relational Model of Data for Large Shared Data Banks," *Comm. ACM,* Vol. 13, No. 6, June 1970.

Coleman, D. et al., *Object-Oriented Development: The Fusion Method,* Prentice-Hall, Englewood Cliffs, N.J., 1994.

DeChampeaux, D., "Object-Oriented Analysis and Top-Down Software Development," Technical Report HPL-91-21, Software and Systems Laboratory, Hewlett-Packard Laboratories, Palo Alto, Calif., Feb. 1991.

DeChampeaux, D., "A Comparative Study of Object-Oriented Analysis Methods," Technical Report HPL-91-41, Software and Systems Laboratory, Hewlett-Packard Laboratories, Palo Alto,Calif., Apr. 1991.

DeMarco, T., *Structured Analysis and Systems Specification.* Prentice-Hall, Englewood Cliffs, N.J., 1979.

Embly, D., Kurtz, B., and Woodfield, S., *Object-Oriented Systems Analysis: A Model-Driven Approach,* Yourdon Press, Prentice-Hall, Englewood Cliffs, N.J., 1992.

Fayad, M.E. et al. "Using the Shlaer–Mellor Object-Oriented Analysis Method," *IEEE Software,* Vol. 10, No. 2, Mar. 1993.

Fichman, R.G. and Kemerer, C.F., "Object-Oriented and Conventional Analysis and Design Methodologies," *Computer,* Vol. 25, No. 10, Oct. 1992.

Firesmith, D.G., *Object-Oriented Requirements Analysis and Logical Design: A Software Engineering Approach,* John Wiley & Sons, New York, 1993.

Gane, C. and Sarsen, T., *Structured Systems Analysis: Tools and Techniques,* Prentice-Hall, Englewood Cliffs, N.J., 1978.

Harel, D., "Statecharts: A Visual Formalism for Complex Systems," *Science of Computer Programming*, Vol. 8, 1987, pp. 231–274.

Jacobson, I., *Object-Oriented Software Engineering,* Addison-Wesley, Reading, Mass., 1992.

Lang, N., "Shlaer–Mellor Object-Oriented Analysis Rules," *Software Engineering Notes*, Vol. 18, No. 1, Jan. 1993.

Meyers, S., *Effective C++: 50 Specific Ways to Improve Your Programs and Designs,* Addison-Wesley, Reading, Mass., 1992.

Monarchi, D.E. and Puhr, G.I., "A Research Typology for Object-Oriented Analysis and Design," *Comm. ACM,* Vol. 35, No. 9, Sept. 1992.

Nelson, J.-M., "Applying Object-Oriented Analysis and Design," *Comm. ACM,* Vol. 35, No. 9, Sept. 1992.

Rubin, K.S. and Goldberg, A., "Object Behavior Analysis," *Comm. ACM,* Vol. 35, No. 9, Sept. 1992.

Rumbaugh, J. et al., *Object-Oriented Modeling and Design,* Prentice-Hall, Englewood Cliffs, N.J., 1991.

Seidewitz, E. and Stark, M., *Principles of Object-Oriented Software Development with Ada,* Millenium Systems, Inc., Rockville, Md., 1992.

Seidewitz, E. and Stark, M., *General Object-Oriented Software Development, Software Engineering Laboratory Series,* SEL-86-002, NASA/Goddard Space Flight Center, Greenbelt, Md., August 1986.

Shlaer, S. and Mellor, S., "A Systematic Approach to Developing an Application-Independent Architecture Using Object Methods and Patterns," Internal Report, Project Technology, Inc., Berkeley, Calif., 1996.

Shlaer, S. and Mellor, S., *Object Lifecycles: Modeling the World in States,* Yourdon Press, Prentice-Hall, Englewood Cliffs, N.J., 1992.

Shlaer, S. and Mellor, S., *Object-Oriented Systems Analysis: Modeling the World in Data.* Prentice-Hall, Englewood Cliffs, N.J., 1988.

SofTech, Inc., "An Introduction to SADT Structured Analysis and Design Technique," Technical Report 9022-78R, SofTech, Inc., Waltham Mass., 1978.

Starr, L., *How to Build Shlaer–Mellor Object Models*, Prentice-Hall, Englewood Cliffs, N.J., 1996.

Wirfs-Brock, R., "Responsibility-Driven Development: An Adaptable Object-Oriented Software Development Method," Draft White Paper, ParcPlace-Digitalk, Inc., Tualatin, Ore.

Wirfs-Brock, R., *Tutorial Notes for Responsibility-Driven Design.* OOPSLA '95.

Wirfs-Brock, R., Wilkerson, B., and Wiener, L., *Designing Object-Oriented Software,* Prentice-Hall, Englewood Cliffs, N.J., 1990.

Yourdon, E. and Constantine, L., *Structured Design: Fundamentals of a Discipline of Computer Programs and Systems,* Prentice-Hall, Englewood Cliffs, N.J., 1979.

A COMPARISON OF OBJECT-ORIENTED AND STRUCTURED DEVELOPMENT METHODS

Patrick H. Loy
Loy Consulting, Inc.
P.O. Box 24648
Baltimore, MD 21214
(410) 426-1996
Internet: 76326.3275@compuserve.com

ABSTRACT

The significance of "object-oriented" as a development method, and the current confusion over the term are addressed. A set of characteristics is proposed as a basis for agreement on a definition of the term. Object-oriented development is compared to the "structured techniques," and work in progress on integrating the two methods is reviewed. Practical recommendations on assessing the importance of object-oriented development are given.

BIOGRAPHICAL SKETCH

Patrick Loy is the president of Loy Consulting, Inc., a firm that provides training and consulting services for system developers. He also serves part-time on the faculty of The Johns Hopkins University. He has 19 years of experience in the computing industry, mainly focused in the areas of software requirements analysis, design, and process improvement. He consults and teaches seminars in these areas throughout the U.S. and Europe, and trains software acquisition managers for a U.S. defense agency.

Mr. Loy is the author of several seminars offered by his firm, and by the Addison-Wesley Publishing Company. He is a member of the IEEE, ACM, and Computer Professionals for Social Responsibility. He received his M.S. degree in computer science from The Johns Hopkins University, and his B.S. degree in mathematics from the University of Oregon.

1. INTRODUCTION

It is an undeniable truism that the methods and tools used during software development can have a significant impact on the quality of the final product. Over the past 15 years or so, the "structured techniques" have gained a great deal of acceptance as being methods that can assist the developer in the task of engineering quality into the system as it is being developed. These methods are based on a functional view of the system, with the system being partitioned according to its functional aspects.

Recently a new approach to system modeling has been gaining popularity, and many would say that it is the current state-of-the-art method for system development. This new approach, called "object-oriented," is supported by several programming languages, and several familiar names in the field of computer science endorse it as being the most advanced abstract modeling technique. Moreover, the religious zeal of some proponents of this approach has engendered an expectation that we may be heralding the arrival of the long-awaited "silver bullet " for software development.

Consequently, the subject of object-oriented development (OOD) has generated a great deal of interest among practitioners, with many dp professionals asking the questions, "what exactly is OOD?"; "how does it compare to the structured techniques?"; "is it a partial or complete life cycle method?"; and, "should we adopt it in our organization?"

Unfortunately, these questions have been very difficult to answer. Two areas of confusion lie at the heart of the problem. First, there is no universally agreed upon definition of what constitutes the OOD approach to system modeling. There are some OOD advocates, for example, who, with great conviction, tout Ada as being an object-oriented language, or even as the *premier* object-oriented language. There are others, however, who adamantly dispute that notion, declaring with equal conviction that Ada is decidedly not an object-oriented language.

The second area of confusion, which is closely related to the first, is on the differences between OOD and the structured methods. Some authors have suggested that there is a high degree of compatibility between at least some of the structured techniques and OOD. Others disagree with that notion, claiming that the differences in the modeling perspectives preclude any meaningful compatibility between the methods. Some advocates of OOD claim that it involves a more "natural" way to think than the functional approach. Some proponents of the structured techniques, on the other hand, insist that it is just as "natural" to think about functions as it is to think about objects.

This paper will address itself to the task of cutting through some of the fog surrounding this debate in an attempt to gain some clarity and perspective on the matter.

2. WHY THE ISSUE IS IMPORTANT

Many new software development methods have appeared over the past several years. Consequently, there can be a tendency to view object-oriented development as "just another method" for the developer's toolbox. However, this new approach, as evidenced by its rising popularity and the fact that the concept has matured to the point that it now encompasses a full life cycle approach, represents something more profound. In this author's opinion, OOD embodies a unique, coherent theory of knowledge for system development. As such, it describes a cognitive process for capturing, organizing, and communicating the essential knowledge of the system's "problem space," and, for the model thereby formed, gives guidance on using specific techniques to map this problem space model to a "solution space" model.

The challenge of conceptual models has always been much more than just increasing the number of tools in the developers toolbox. To say "here is a bunch of tools to choose from" is very different from being able to say "here is a coherent theory of knowledge for system development *and* here is a bunch of tools to choose from that can be applied consistent with the theory." The theory gives guidance on what tool is most applicable for a particular situation. Herein lies a danger in the toolbox metaphor: it can be vulgarized to omit the critical need for a corresponding theory of knowledge on the use of the tools. It is nice for the carpenter to have many screwdrivers in the toolbox, but just as important is to *know* when it is appropriate to use the Phillips screwdriver and when to use the standard screwdriver.

Thus, a theory of knowledge is more comprehensive than a particular method for a particular life cycle phase. The work being done on object-oriented analysis (OOA)[1,4] signals the fact that OOD has gone from being a partial to a full life cycle approach, which means that OOD is much broader than just a "method." The emerging OOD paradigm promotes a particular mode of thought, a particular system viewpoint, which has far-reaching implications.

In the context of our discussion, a theory of knowledge for system development must give guidance on how to cope with complexity. Many of today's systems are exceedingly complex, and it is impossible to consider equally all of their attributes. Consequently, to understand such a system an *abstraction* must be used, whereby the most important attributes of the system are illuminated, and the others are suppressed. But, of course, this involves making assumptions about which aspects are more important, and which are less important. OOD is an abstraction that makes different assumptions than structured development (SD) about what to illuminate and what to suppress. Thus, OOD offers a unique and different perspective on what point of view best guides the thinking of the system modeler.

3. TOWARD A DEFINITION OF "OBJECT-ORIENTED"

3.1 Clearing the "Semantic Thicket"

Why is there so much confusion over what "object-oriented" means? To address this question, consider the origins of the term. "Object -oriented programming" emerged as a term associated with the development of Smalltalk, the original object-oriented language, and the one most often regarded as a pure object-oriented language.

Smalltalk drew heavily from Simula, ultimately incorporating the notion of *class* as the sole structural unit, with instances of classes or *objects*, being the concrete units which inhabit the world of the Smalltalk system. To a lesser degree, Smalltalk was influenced by LISP.

Rentsch has provided an interesting history of the origins of object-oriented programming and Smalltalk, and, in 1982, predicted the confusion that would accompany its growing popularity: "My guess is that object oriented programming will be in the 1980's what structured programming was in the 1970's. Everyone will be in favor of it. Every manufacturer will promote his products as supporting it. Every manager will pay lip service to it. Every programmer will practice it (differently). And no one will know just what it is."[2]

To get to the heart of the confusion surrounding OOD, it may be helpful to consider the following points. First, OOD as a development philosophy has its roots in object-oriented *programming*, and evolved bottom up, i.e., from programming to design to requirements analysis. Thus, it is helpful to be familiar with object-oriented programming to grasp the OOD paradigm.

Second, OOD involves an unfamiliar way of thinking to most software developers, and in this respect some confusion is to be expected. Our training has not taught us to think in object-oriented terms. This dynamic can be seen when people are introduced to any new manner of thought. When the structured development techniques were first introduced, they also involved a new way of thinking about software development, and this led inevitably to some confusion. As another example, programmers often state that their first exposure to the simulation language GPSS V "blows their minds" because it involves a way of thinking that is radically different from the procedural languages they are used to.

Beyond these two factors, however, OOD has faced an even deeper problem in being understood. Early on in the history of object-oriented programming, bits and pieces of the concept were supported in various languages, and these languages became erroneously regarded as "object-oriented." Ada is the main example of this. As Ada was taking form in the late 1970's, it was widely understood that it was, in large part, based on features found in Pascal and ALGOL. Later, as Ada became touted as an object-oriented language, people who had experience with Pascal or ALGOL naturally made the connection in their minds that "object-oriented" was somehow a souped up extension of a Pascal-type procedural language. As Cox said, in commenting on the confusion surrounding the object-oriented buzzword, "It is hard to imagine two languages more different than Smalltalk-80 and Ada, yet both are sometimes called object-oriented languages."[3]

In addition, probably due to the heritage of Simula, some modeling techniques that utilize classification have been advertised as being object-oriented. The book by Shlaer and Mellor, *Object-Oriented Systems Analysis*,[4] has been criticized by some as being little more than an approach to semantic data modeling.[5,1] (Interestingly, apart from its title, the term "object-oriented" hardly ever appears in the book.) However, while this author generally agrees with the above cited criticisms as to the incompleteness of the method presented, the book does provide useful guidance for the front-end activities of an object-oriented approach, specifically in the critical task of identifying the "objects," which will be discussed below.

So, object-oriented has become a term that means different things to different people. It is this author's opinion that a uniform definition of object-oriented is possible and desirable, at least in terms of the *characteristics* of an object-oriented approach. Moreover, the literature on the subject is completely adequate in this respect. In coalescing around a definition we should be primarily guided by the original intent of the term, especially in its connection to Smalltalk, and by the development of the theory that has built upon that original meaning, which extended the notion to design and analysis.

3.2 Comparing Development Paradigms

Structured analysis, structured design, and structured programming are collectively known as structured development (SD). The ideas behind these methods are found in the writings of Yourdon and Constantine,[19] Dijkstra,[20] DeMarco,[21] Myers,[22] and many others. Although there are several versions of SD in existence today, all of them are based on a philosophy of system development that analyzes the system from a functional point of view. In describing this viewpoint, Constantine says "the main features of software that are of interest to the analyst, designer, or programmer are the functional aspects: what functions or tasks the software must perform, what subfunctions or subtasks are needed to complete the overall functions, what pieces or component parts will perform various functions, how those functions will be performed."[23] Constantine calls this way of thinking the "functional paradigm."

Constantine points out that "this focus is so embedded in our thinking about computer programming that we are scarcely aware of it. We do not think of it as constituting a particular way of viewing programs or consider the possibility of alternative views."[23]

Given that this is the current conventional way of thinking, Constantine provides a concise comparison of the functional and object-oriented viewpoints:

> In the functional paradigm, function and procedure are primary, data are only secondary. Functions and related data are either conceived of as independent, or data are associated with or attached to the functional components.
>
> The antithesis of this viewpoint is the object-oriented paradigm. In this paradigm, data are considered primary and procedures are secondary; functions are associated with related data. Problems and applications are looked at as consisting of interrelated classes of real objects characterized by their common attributes, the rules they obey, and the functions or operations defined on them. Software systems consist of structured collections of abstract data structures embodying those object classes that model the interrelated objects of the real-world problem.
>
> From this it should be clear that the object-oriented paradigm is based on a new way of looking at the old dichotomy of procedure and data. [23]

The SD techniques are generally associated with a top-down development strategy, whereas OOD is essentially a bottom-up approach. The "top" of a system structure contains control modules representing the activation of large chunks of the overall capabilities. At the "bottom" are the basic facilities for defining and manipulating the data, and for hiding its structure from the rest of the system. These concepts are embodied in the idea of the "object," as will be discussed later. OOD thus facilitates a natural bottom-up organization of the software.

3.3 Characterizing Object-Oriented Systems

With this overview of the two development paradigms as a framework, below are brief descriptions of the characteristics of object-oriented development. The following discussion is not meant to be a tutorial on the subject, but is presented to help formulate a definition. For more complete discussions of specific object-oriented methods, the reader is referred to the references, especially Coad,[1] Booch,[7] Cox,[3] Rentsch,[2] and Meyer.[26]

Objects
At the heart of OOD is the idea of the "object." An object is an entity defined by a set of common attributes, and the services or operations associated with it. Objects are the major actors, agents, and servers in the problem space of the system, and can be identified by carefully analyzing this domain. Whatever form of system requirements that is provided by the user or client can be used as a starting point for this task. Objects can be found among devices that the system interacts with (e.g., sensors), other systems that interface with the system under study, organizational units (departments, divisions, etc.), things that must be remembered over time (e.g., details about events occurring in

the system's environment), physical locations or sites, and specific roles played by humans (clerk, pilot, etc.).

The central problem in OOD turns out to be "finding the objects." As mentioned above, Shlaer and Mellor have made a contribution in this area, providing tools and concepts for enumerating various categories of potential object classes.[4]

In characterizing the object concept it is important to discuss the viewpoint associated with objects. OOD is interested in how an object appears (an outside view), rather than what an object is (an inside view). This shift in viewpoint is critical to the concept of OOD. It enables the system modeler to think not only about objects as classification entities, but also about the intrinsic behavior associated with objects. This intrinsic behavior embodied within an object provides the visibility of the object in relation to other objects.

For example, consider the object called "policeman." The object called "ordinary citizen" is not much interested in exactly what a policeman *is* (inside view) but is *very* interested in the *intrinsic behavior* (outside view) of the object (issues speeding tickets, etc.) Also the ordinary citizen object is interested in what *services* it can invoke from policeman (give directions when lost, etc.), which are also part of the intrinsic behavior of the object.

The term *encapsulation* has come to represent this central notion of OOD, and is based on the concept of *information hiding*, as espoused by David Parnas.[27] Rentsch stresses the importance of this viewpoint for OOD, saying

> The shift in viewpoint from inside to outside is itself an essential part of object oriented programming. In my experience this shift occurs as a quantum leap, the "aha!" that accompanies a flash of insight. In spite of this, I am convinced that the view from outside is the natural one - only my years of training and experience as a programmer conditioned me to "normally" view objects from inside ... The first principle of object oriented programming might be called *intelligence encapsulation:* view objects from outside to provide a natural metaphor of intrinsic behavior.[2]

Nonhierarchic Object Model
Developers accustomed to using structured techniques usually think of the system-structure model as a hierarchy of functions, which maps to a set of nested subroutines. (It should be noted that, at least in the case of structured design, this is a manifestation of the way the method is practiced, not in the method itself. Yourdon and Constantine explicitly allowed for nonhierarchic module collections, as discussed in chapter 18 of their book, *Structured Design*.[19]) The object model, on the other hand, is a nonhierarchic topology of objects. This topology forms an abstract view of the problem space, which is meant to map naturally to a nonhierarchic model of the solution space. As Booch says, "a program that implements a model of reality may be viewed as a set of objects that interact with each other."[7]

Processing and Communication
In the OOD model, processing takes place inside objects. "An object, far from being inert matter, is an active, alive, intelligent entity, and is responsible for providing its own computational behavior. Thus processing capability is not only inside the object, it is everpresent within and inseparable from the object."[2]

While an object contains processing capability, it is not always self sufficient in this respect, and may need to interact with other objects. The "ordinary citizen" object, for example, can do many things for itself (eat, read, write), but may at times need to invoke the services of the "policeman" object (get directions). Thus communication between objects is needed.

The model being nonhierarchic, objects communicate with other objects by a mechanism of "message passing," which is similar to the concept of "coroutines" as discussed by Yourdon and Constantine.[19] Thus, an invocation of one module by another is not necessarily associated with a hierarchical relationship in the organization of the objects. "Message sending serves as the uniform metaphor for communication in the same way that objects serve as the uniform metaphor for processing capability and synthesis. ... all processing is accomplished by message sending. ... A message serves to initiate processing and request information."[2]

Inheritance
Basic to the idea of OOD is a framework of classing, subclassing, and superclassing, that allows individuals within a collection to *share* common attributes, as needed. This framework is collectively referred to as *inheritance*. If the class "tree," for example, contains the attribute "leafy branches," then members of the tree subclasses (oak, elm, maple, etc.) can inherit this attribute, and it need not be redefined.

Object-Oriented Software Organization
There are several variations of object-oriented methods, all of them being somewhat sketchy. Booch, for example, has offered the skeleton of a step-by-step approach for object-oriented design,[7] and other writers have made similar gestures. Consequently, it is impossible to describe *the* object-oriented method, or to be very specific in discussing exactly what *the* end product of OOD looks like. However, it is possible to discuss a general object-oriented concept that refers to a way of structuring software systems that is language independent.

Object-oriented software organization refers to a structuring approach that makes it possible to organize a system by object-oriented concepts and implement it as a set of "object modules" in conventional procedural languages as well as in object-oriented languages. Constantine has this to say about this concept:

> Object-oriented organization is a form of modular structure in which a program is designed as a structured collection of "object modules" implementing data abstractions. An object module encapsulates the implementation of a class of data structures and their related services, exporting specific services (and sometimes attributes) as features of the "official" external interface of the module. Object modules are interrelated by their usage of the attributes and services of other modules, just as in conventional functional structures, as well as by feature inheritance. An object module is thus an organizing concept that groups together a collection of functions (services) based on their association with a well-defined class of data structures. Object modules are, in effect, multi-function packages that group functions based on principles of strong association with common data structures, with groups interrelated and defined as classes and subclasses of abstract data. [23]

3.4 Deciding if an Approach is Truly Object-Oriented

The preceding discussion can be summarized to say that an object-oriented method contains at least these basic ideas: *classification* of data abstractions, *inheritance* of common attributes, and *encapsulation* of attributes, operations and services.
If these characteristics form the basis for a definition of "object-oriented," then it is clear that some languages and methods which are often cited as being object-oriented are something less. According to Peter Coad and Edward Yourdon:

> One can look at different languages, environments, methods, and books and ask "Are you really Object-Oriented?" Unfortunately, many times the answer is "no"; Object-Oriented suffers from being a catchy marketing word, used at times to mean "the good stuff."

> Is Ada an Object-Oriented language? No. Genericity, that is, typed parameters, is convenient, but no substitute for inheritance.

> Is an information modeling approach Object-Oriented (e.g., Object-Oriented Systems Analysis [Shlaer and Mellor, 1988], a book better titled "making Semantic Data Modeling Practical")? No. Services are missing. Classification is missing. Inheritance is missing. [1]

Coad and Yourdon offer this equation for recognizing an object-oriented approach:

Object-Oriented =
    Objects
        (an encapsulation of Attributes and exclusive Services;
        an abstraction of the something in the problem space, with
        some number of instances in the problem space)
    + Classification & Inheritance.[1]

The importance of a clear, consistent definition of OOD is that the *essence* of this paradigm for system development not be watered-down, or completely lost in the shuffle, by a loose use of the term. As discussed earlier, OOD represents a theory of knowledge, a mode of thought, that is decidedly unique in its own right. Our use of the term should be directed toward that uniqueness, not toward certain specific *features* of OOD. However, this does not mean that languages or methods that contain certain of those features are of no use. Many of them are, but we should be careful not to characterize them as being "object-oriented," lest we continue to foster the confusion over the term.

4. IS OOD BETTER THAN SD?

A great deal of hopeful enthusiasm has accompanied many of the writings on OOD. According to Cox, "It is time for a revolution in how we build systems ... The revolution is object-oriented programming."[3] From Booch, "[OOD] leads to improved maintainability and understandability of systems."[7] From Danforth and Tomlinson, "[object-oriented programming] represents a positive step toward the design and implementation of complex software systems."[8]

The proponents of OOD usually cite two reasons for their excitement about the approach. One is the claim that the thinking process inherent in OOD is more "natural" than that of SD, i.e., in building an abstract model of reality it is more natural to think in terms of objects than in terms of functions. The other is that the modeling of the problem space maps more directly to the solution space in OOD than it does in SD.

Let us consider the latter argument first. Anyone involved with SD knows that the transition from the analysis model to the design model can be tricky. For example, in moving from a data flow diagram view of the system to creating design structure charts the modeler is forced to make a significant shift in perspective. There are strategies to assist in the matter (transform analysis, transaction analysis, etc.), but it remains a difficult task because the mapping is not truly isomorphic. The proponents of OOD often claim that with OOD the mapping *is* truly isomorphic, or at least far more isomorphic than in SD, which, if true, would offer a great advantage. Coad and Yourdon make this claim, and stress that the singular abstraction medium is a key: "It's a matter of using the same underlying representation in analysis and design. This is a bedrock concept of the [object-oriented analysis] approach."[1]

But is this claim true? Unfortunately, there is little evidence of this in the writings on the subject, a fact which, in part, reflects the relative newness of the field. In fact there are those that refute the notion completely. Constantine says "The mapping from analysis model to design model is every bit as 'not isomorphic' in OOD as in SD once you get beyond textbook and toy examples" (his emphasis). [24] It seems the jury is still out on this question, and the matter will not be resolved until there is some published hard evidence.

Part of the difficulty in resolving this matter is that the overall development environment seems to be largely inadequate to exploit the paradigm fully. Stroustrup has compared several languages in terms of their support for OOD, and points out that if the proper language support is missing the paradigm will be of limited value.[9] And Williams says, "Due to the informality of the approach, lack of adequate language support, and lack of experience with large systems, the potential of the object model in software engineering remains largely unexplored."[6] As might be expected, there is much on-going research in this area.[10] But, the potential emergence of a more isomorphic mapping of problem space to solution space in the OOD paradigm is itself an important reason for software professionals to stay abreast of the developments in the OOD world.

Now to the argument that thinking in terms of objects is more "natural" than thinking in terms of functions. As cited earlier, Rentsch is "convinced that the [OOD] view is the natural one," and as evidence he posits that "children learn Smalltalk very quickly."[2] Coad and Yourdon state that object-oriented analysis "is based upon concepts which we first learned in kindergarten: objects and attributes, classes and members, wholes and parts." They further assert that for today's modern systems "an object-oriented approach... is a more natural way of dealing with such systems."[1]

It is enticing to think that we have stumbled upon a more natural way of thinking after all these years, but does the evidence really support this notion? It is true that kindergarten children readily learn to classify objects, and it may be true that they learn Smalltalk quickly. But they *also* readily ("naturally?") think in terms of functions, and they learn function-oriented procedural languages quickly. Ask a child to tell you about his or her school, and then try to predict if the response will be primarily in functional terms, or in classification terms (but don't bet on it being one or the other). Is one way of thinking really more "natural" than the other?

Constantine doesn't think so, saying, "there are no 'object classes' in the real physical universe, as these are constructs that exist only in the mind of the viewer... 'objects' are no more real or natural than 'functions.'"[23]

Interestingly, this same type of debate exists in other fields of study. In fact some variation of the "form vs. function" controversy is part of every field. In general, it involves how one views the relative importance of the structural vs. the functional aspects of knowledge. In developmental psychology it is the debate between Piaget and the Gestaltists, and then later between Piaget and the new functionalists;[11,12] in epistemology the debate focuses on the relation between the knower and the object known ;[13] in cognitive anthropology the issue revolves around how a grouping of people synthesizes structure and function as they form their own model of reality in pursuing an understanding of the world they live in.

Two Anthropologists, Dr. George Brandon of the University of Maryland, and Dr. Elliot Fratkin of Duke University were interviewed by the author for the purposes of this paper. Both of them were intrigued that such an issue was being argued in the software field, and saw the clear connection to the debate in their own discipline. Both believe it is a manifestation of a universal question, and were decisive in their opinions that the matter is not resolved, and probably never will be resolved.

Obviously, the details of these various debates is beyond the scope of this paper; but the important finding is that there is no final resolution to the matter. The struggle is ongoing. There is very little that you can say with much confidence about a "most natural" way that people think about the realities of their universe. Thus, to say that the object model is a more natural way to think involves a rather sizeable leap of faith.

Undoubtedly, the truth of the matter is that both paradigms are "natural," and that the proper synthesis of the two, in relation to a particular problem, is what should be striven for. In fact, this is part of the challenge for the next period. OOD has helped to crystallize a way of analyzing systems that brings into sharp relief the fact that we have been limited and one-sided in our approach to the matter up to this time. But we must be careful not to throw the baby out with the bath water. Functional partitioning is a very valuable analytical approach. The task ahead is to move the debate to a higher level - not arguing about which is more "natural" - but exploring how we best take advantage of both approaches.

In this author's view, Ward and Mellor were on the right track when they suggested that the system modeler must determine which modeling approach should play a dominant role, based on the particular type of system being modeled.[14] As the methods mature, guidelines need to be developed and refined to help the modeler determine whether the perspective of OOD or SD should dominate in a particular situation.

5. TOWARD AN INTEGRATION OF THE METHODS

Over the past few months, several papers have addressed the synthesis question mentioned above. Ward has recently written a brief tutorial showing that there is no inherent conflict between the two approaches, and that "real-time structured analysis / structured design can, with modest extensions to the notation and to the model-building heuristics, adequately express an object-oriented design."[15] Jalote proposes an "extended object-oriented design methodology," which incorporates a top-down, step-wise refinement approach.[16] Bailin describes a method for combining structured analysis with the object-oriented approach for requirements specifications.[17] Constantine has recently written two papers that address the topic of the integration of the methods.[23,25] In one he stresses that we must get beyond the "madness of methods," and get "back to basics" by agreeing on a set of fundamental principles independent of methods. With sound principles being recognized as more important than specific methods the groundwork will be laid for a coherent integration of the methods. He points out that there are "a number of common principles [that] are revered by almost all the sundry gurus and acolytes," which can form a basis for what he calls "convergent design methods."[25]

This type of work is highly significant on two counts. First, it is useful to begin exploring these areas of compatibility for purely pragmatic reasons: contractual and/or documentation requirements may make it necessary. Second, and more important, it pushes the theory of knowledge for system development to a higher level, and facilitates the evolution of more coherent and useable methods.

6. RECOMMENDATIONS FOR PROJECT LEADERS

Every software development organization should begin figuring out where they stand in relation to OOD and SD. For shops already engaged with the structured methods, this means having a *plan* for assessing if, and how, OOD might be used to advantage. Ideally, such a plan should be part of a technology transfer program of the organization, as proposed by Loy,[18] and should proceed with both bottom-up and top-down activities being done concurrently.

A suggested plan outline is the following:

1. Have at least two, and preferably three or more, senior software engineers start playing around with Smalltalk. If Smalltalk is not an available option, pick another language that incorporates the features mentioned in section 3 above. It is important that some experienced people begin learning the paradigm at the programming level by getting experience with an object-oriented language. This activity can be done part-time in conjunction with other ongoing assignments. But they should keep at it on a regular basis.

2. Concurrent with the above task, start tracking the literature on the subject. Have an organized effort to do this, with different people assigned specific responsibilities in this respect. For example, one person might be assigned to monitor the articles that appear in one periodical. Much has been written in the past year, especially, and the trend will undoubtedly increase. Continually assess how the experience in other shops relates to your situation. The references cited in section 5 above could be a good starting point.

3. After a few weeks, provide some of the folks involved in the above two tasks with some "formal" OOD training, e.g., a seminar in OOD. This should help to quickly broaden their perspective on the potential of OOD.

4. Get continual, systematic feedback from all people who are involved in the above tasks about their views on OOD. Do they feel it might play a role in your environment? How significant does its value appear to be? How should it be incorporated into your development plans? Their views on these matters may change over time, so it is important that the feedback mechanism be regular and systematic.

5. Based on the results of the above activities, begin to formulate options for integrating OOD into your environment. This will involve considering the whole spectrum of trade-offs specific to your situation.

7. SUMMARY AND CONCLUSIONS

Object-oriented development is bound to have a major influence on the manner in which systems are built. It has matured to where it must be viewed as a theory of knowledge that embodies a unique perspective for capturing, organizing, and communicating the essential features of a system. The OOD paradigm is derived ultimately from object-oriented programming, an understanding of which is helpful to grasp the essence of OOD.

The software engineering community has been sloppy in its use of the term "object-oriented," and there is currently confusion over the meaning of it. The term should refer collectively to the concepts of *classification, encapsulation,* and *inheritance.*

While some contend that OOD involves a more "natural" way to think than does SD, there is little evidence of this. In fact, both approaches are based on modes of thought that might be called "natural." OOD and SD are not incompatible, and much recent work has been devoted to exploring the potential synthesis and integration of the two. Research in this area should help crystallize the contribution of OOD to our field, and push the quest for a theory of knowledge for systems development to a higher level.

Project leaders should have a plan for investigating the worth of OOD to their shops. This plan, a sample of which was offered, should be part of an ongoing technology transfer program.

Acknowledgements

Many people reviewed the first draft of this paper and provided very helpful, constructive criticisms. Many thanks are due, especially, to Larry Constantine, Jack Bond, Merlin Dorfman, Sally Shlaer, Stephen Mellor, and Bruce Blum for their insightful feedback.

REFERENCES

1 Peter Coad and Edward Yourdon, "An Introduction to OOA - Object-Oriented Analysis," (May 30, 1989), *Tutorial: Systems and Software Requirements Engineering,* Vol. 1, edited by Merlin Dorfman and Richard Thayer, IEEE Press, 1989.

2 Tim Rentsch, "Object Oriented Programming," *SIGPLAN Notices,* Vol.17, No. 9, pp. 51-57, 1982.

3 Brad Cox, *Object-Oriented Programming,* Addison-Wesley, 1986.

4 Sally Shlaer and Stephen Mellor, *Object-Oriented Systems Analysis: Modeling the World in Data,* Yourdon Press, 1988.

5 T.L. (Frank) Pappas, "Object-oriented analysis is flawed," *IEEE Software,* January, 1989.

6 Lloyd Williams, *The Object Model in Software Engineering,* Software Engineering Research, 1986.

7 Grady Booch, "Object-Oriented Development," *IEEE Transactions on Software Engineering,* February, 1986.

8 Scott Danforth and Chris Tomlinson, *Type Theories and Object-Oriented Programming,* ACM Computing Surveys, March, 1988.

9 Bjarne Stroustrup, "What is Object-Oriented Programming?", *IEEE Software,* May 1988.

10 *Research Directions in Object-Oriented Programming,* edited by Bruce Shriver and Peter Wegner, MIT Press, 1987.

11 Herbert Ginsburg and Sylvia Opper, *Piaget's Theory of Intellectual Development,* Prentice-Hall, 1969.

12 *New Trends in Conceptual Representation: challenges to Piaget's Theory?,* edited by Ellin Kofsky Scholnick, Lawrence Erlbaum Associates, 1983.

13 *Academic American Encyclopedia,* vol. 7, 1981.

14 Paul Ward and Stephen Mellor, *Structured Development for Real-Time Systems,* Yourdon Press, 1985.

15 Paul Ward, "How to Integrate Object Orientation with Structured analysis and Design," *IEEE Software,* March, 1989.

16 Pankaj Jalote, "Functional Refinements and Nested Objects for Object-Oriented Design," *IEEE Transactions on Software Engineering,* March, 1989.

17 Sidney Bailin, "An Object-Oriented Requirements Specification Method," *Communications of the ACM,* May, 1989.

18 Patrick Loy, "Five Components of a Software Quality Assurance Paradigm", *Proceedings of the Sixth Annual Pacific Northwest Software Quality Conference,* September, 1988.

19 Edward Yourdon and Larry L. Constantine, *Structured Design,* Yourdon Press, 1975.

20 E.W. Dijkstra, *A Discipline of Programming,* Prentice-Hall, 1976.

21 Tom DeMarco, *Structured Analysis and System Specification,* Yourdon Press, 1978.

22 Glenford J. Myers, *Composite/Structured Design,* Van Nostrand Reinhold , 1978.

23 Larry L. Constantine, Object-Oriented and Structured Methods: Toward Integration, *American Programmer,* vol. 2, no. 7/8, August, 1989.

24 Larry L. Constantine, letter to the author (unpublished), July 3, 1989.

25 Larry L. Constantine, "Beyond the Madness of Methods: System Structure Modeling and Convergent Design," *Software Development '89: Proceedings*, Miller-Freeman Publishing Co., 1989.

26 Meyer, Bertrand, *Object-Oriented Software Construction,* Prentice-Hall, 1988.

27 Parnas, David, "On the Criteria to be Used in Decomposing Systems into Modules," *Communications of the ACM,* December, 1972.

A Review of Formal Methods

Prepared for:
Rome Laboratory
RL/C3C
Griffiss AFB, NY 13441-5700

Prepared by:
Robert Vienneau
Kaman Sciences Corporation
258 Genesee Street
Utica, New York 13502-4627

Introduction

The seventies witnessed the structured programming revolution. After much debate, software engineers became convinced that better programs result from following certain precepts in program design. Recent imperative programming languages provide constructs supporting structured programming. Achieving this consensus did not end debate over programming methodology. Quite the contrary, a period of continuous change began, with views on the best methods of software development mutating frequently. Top-down development, modular decomposition, data abstraction, and, most recently, object oriented design are some of the jargon terms that have arisen to describe new concepts for developing large software systems. Both researchers and practitioners have found it difficult to keep up with this onslaught of new methodologies.

There is a set of core ideas that lies at the base of these changes. Formal methods have provided a unifying philosophy and central foundation upon which these methodologies have been built. Those who understand this underlying philosophy can more easily adopt these and other programming techniques. This report provides the needed understanding of formal methods to guide a software manager in evaluating claims related to new methodologies. It also provides an overview for the software engineer and a guide to the literature. Ample examples are provided to fully convey the flavor of using formal methods.

The underlying philosophy for formal methods has not changed in over two decades. Nevertheless, this approach is a revolutionary paradigm shift from conventional notions about computer programming. Many software engineers have adopted the new methodologies that grew out of this work without understanding or even being aware of the root concepts.

The traditional notion of programming looks at the software engineer's task as the development of code to instruct a physically existing machine to compute a desired result. Existing computers possess many idiosyncrasies reflecting hardware engineering concerns. Likewise user interfaces and the desired function can be expected to introduce additional complexities. In the traditional view of programming, these details can be expected to appear in a design, or even a specification, at all levels of abstraction. The engineer's job is seen as the introduction of more details and tricks to get the utmost in speed and performance out of computers. Since software development is therefore a "cut and fit" process, such complex systems can be expected to be full of bugs. A careful testing process is seen as the means of detecting and removing these bugs.

The mindset behind formal methods is directly opposite to the traditional view. It is the job of the hardware engineer, language designer, and compiler writer to provide a machine for executing code, not the reverse:

> Originally I viewed it as the function of the abstract machine to provide a truthful picture of the physical reality. Later, however, I learned to consider the abstract machine as the 'true' one, because that is the only one we can "think" it is the physical machine's purpose to supply "a working model," a (hopefully!) sufficiently accurate physical simulation of the true, abstract machine...It used to be the program's purpose to instruct our computers; it became the computer's purpose to execute our programs. [Dijkstra 76]

The software engineer's task is to produce several models or descriptions of a system for an abstract machine, with accompanying proofs that models at lower levels of abstraction correctly implement higher-level models. Only this design process can ensure high levels of quality, not testing. Edsger Dijkstra has asserted that testing can demonstrate the presence of faults, not their absence. Since software engineers must be able to read and reason about designs, implementation details must be prevented from influencing the expression of designs as long as possible. A separation of concerns exists here, and if microefficiency concerns are allowed to dominate, produced code will reflect a design that cannot be convincingly demonstrated correct by anyone.

The contrast between these views is controversial (for example, see the discussion engendered in the ACM Forum by [DeMillo 79], [Fetzer 88], [Dijkstra 89], or [Gries 91]). Advocates of formal methods argue that many have adopted structured programming and top-down development without really understanding the underlying formalism [Mills 86]. A concern with formal methods can produce more rigorous specifications, even if they are expressed in English [Meyer 85]. Designs and code will be easier to reason about, even if fully formal proofs are never constructed. Critics focus on the difficulties in scaling up to large systems, the impracticalities of formalizing many inherently complex aspects of systems (for example, user interactions and error- checking code), and the radical retraining needed for the large population of already existing software engineers.

This report's purpose is not to advocate one or another position on formal methods. Rather, it overviews the technical basis for formal methods, while critically noting weaknesses. Polemics are avoided, but enough information is reviewed to allow the reader to form an informed judgment on formal methods. Formal methods are beginning to see more widespread industrial use, especially in Europe. Their use is characteristic of organizations with a Defined (Level 3) process or better, as specified in the process maturity framework developed by the Software Engineering Institute [Humphrey 88]. Formal methods have the potential of engendering further revolutionary changes in practice and have provided the underlying basis of past changes. These reasons make it imperative that software managers and engineers be aware of the increasingly widespread debate over formal methods.

Definition and Overview of Formal Methods

Wide and narrow definitions of formal methods can be found in the literature. For example, Nancy Leveson states:

A broad view of formal methods includes all applications of (primarily) discrete mathematics to software engineering problems. This application usually involves modeling and analysis where the models and analysis procedures are derived from or defined by an underlying mathematically- precise foundation. [Leveson 90]

A more narrow definition, however, better conveys the change in practice recommended by advocates of formal methods. The definition offered here is based on that in [Wing 90], and has two essential components. First, formal methods involve the essential use of a formal language. A formal language is a set of strings over some well-defined alphabet. Rules are given for distinguishing those strings, defined over the alphabet, that belong to the language from strings that do not.

Second, formal methods in software support formal reasoning about formulae in the language. These methods of reasoning are exemplified by formal proofs. A proof begins with a set of axioms, which are to be taken as statements postulated to be true. Inference rules state that if certain formulas, known as premises, are derivable from the axioms, then another formula, known as the consequent, is also derivable. A set of inference rules must be given in each formal method. A proof consists of a sequence of well-defined formulae in the language in which each formula is either an axiom or derivable by an inference rule from previous formulae in the sequence. The last axiom in the sequence is said to be proven. The following definition summarizes the above discussion:

A formal method in software development is a method that provides a formal language for describing a software artifact (for instance, specifications, designs, or source code) such that formal proofs are possible, in principle, about properties of the artifact so expressed.

Often, the property proven is that an implementation is functionally correct, that is, it fulfills its specification. Thus, either the formal language associated with a method permits a system to be described by at least two levels of abstraction or two languages are provided for describing a specification and its implementation. The method provides tools with which an implementation can be proven to satisfy a specification. To be practically useful, the method should also provide heuristics and guidelines for developing elegant specifications and for developing implementations and proofs in parallel.

The concept of formalism in formal methods is borrowed from certain trends in 19th and 20th century mathematics. The development of consistent non-Euclidean geometries, in which supposedly parallel lines may intersect, led mathematicians to question their methods of proof and to search for more rigorous foundations. Eventually, these foundations came to be seen as describing numbers, sets, and logic. Leading mathematicians in this movement included Karl Weierstrass, Gottlob Frege, Giuseppe Peano, and David Hilbert. By the turn of the century, a foundation seemed to be in place, but certain strange examples and antinomies caused mathematicians to question the security of their foundations and even their own intuition on fundamental matters. A mechanical method of manipulating symbols was thus invented to investigate these questions. Due to fundamental discoveries of Kurt Godel, Thoralf Skolem, and Leopold Lowenheim, the results of using this method were ambiguous. Nevertheless, the axiomatic method became widely used in advanced mathematics, especially after impetus was added to this tendency by an extremely influential group of French mathematicians writing around World War II under the pseudonym of Nicholas Bourbaki [Kline 80].

Formal methods are merely an adoption of the axiomatic method, as developed by these trends in mathematics, for software engineering. In fact, Edsger Dijkstra has suggested, somewhat tongue-in-cheek, that computer science be renamed Very Large Scale Application of Logic (VLSAL) [Dijkstra 89]. Mastery of formal methods in software requires an understanding of this mathematics background. Mathematical topics of interest include formal logic, both the propositional calculus and predicate logic, set theory, formal languages, and automata such as finite state machines. The full flavor of the relevant mathematics cannot be conveyed here.

Use of Formal Methods

How are the mathematics of formal languages applied in software development? What engineering issues have been addressed by their application? Formal methods are of global concern in software engineering. They are directly applicable during the requirements, design, and coding phases and have important consequences for testing and maintenance. They have influenced the development and standardization of many programming languages, the programmer's most basic tool. They are important in ongoing research that may change standard practice, particularly in the areas of specifications and design methodology. They are entwined with lifecycle models that

may provide an alternative to the waterfall model, namely rapid prototyping, the Cleanroom variant on the spiral model, and "transformational" paradigms.

What Can be Formally Specified

Formal methods support precise and rigorous specifications of those aspects of a computer system capable of being expressed in the language. Since defining what a system should do and understanding the implications of these decisions are the most troublesome problems in software engineering, this use of formal methods has major benefits. In fact, practitioners of formal methods frequently use formal methods solely for recording precise specifications, not for formal verifications ([Hall 90] and [Place 90]).

Some of the most well-known formal methods consist of or include specification languages for recording a system's functionality. These methods include:

- Z (pronounced "Zed")
- Communicating Sequential Processes (CSP)
- Vienna Development Method (VDM)
- Larch
- Formal Development Methodology (FDM).

Formal methods can be used to specify aspects of a system other than functionality. The emphasis of this report is on functionality since such techniques are currently the most well-known, developed, and of general interest. Software safety and security are other areas where formal methods are sometimes applied in practice. The benefits of proving that unsafe states will not arise, or that security will not be violated, can justify the cost of complete formal verifications of the relevant portions of a software system. Formal methods can deal with many other areas of concern to software engineers but, other than in research organizations, have not been much used for dealing with issues unrelated to functionality, safety, and security. Areas in which researchers are exploring formal methods include fault tolerance, response time, space efficiency, reliability, human factors, and software structure dependencies [Wing 90].

Formal methods can include graphical languages. Data Flow Diagrams (DFDs) are the most well-known graphical technique for specifying the function of a system. DFDs can be considered a semi-formal method, and researchers have explored techniques for treating DFDs in a completely formal manner. Petri nets provide another well-known graphical technique, often used in distributed systems [Peterson 77]. Petri nets are a fully formal technique. Finally, finite state machines are often presented in tabular form. This does not decrease the formalism in the use of finite state machines. So the definition of formal methods provided earlier is quite encompassing.

Software engineers produce models and define the properties of systems at several levels of abstraction. Formal methods can be employed at each level. A specification should describe what a system should do, but not how it is done. More details are provided in designs, with the source code providing the most detailed model. For example, Abstract Data Types (ADTs) frequently are employed at intermediate levels of abstraction. ADTs, being mathematical entities, are perfect candidates for formal treatment and are often so treated in the literature.

Formal methods are not confined to the software components of large systems. System engineers frequently use formal methods. Hardware engineers also use formal methods, such as VHSIC Hardware Description Language (VHDL) descriptions, to model integrated circuits before fabricating them.

Reasoning about a Formal Description

Once a formal description of a system has been produced, what can be done with it? Usable formal methods provide a variety of techniques for reasoning about specifications and drawing implications. The completeness and consistency of a specification can be explored. Does a description imply a system should be in several states simultaneously? Do all legal inputs yield one and only one output? What surprising results, perhaps unintended, can be produced by a system? Formal methods provide reasoning techniques to explore these questions.

Do lower level descriptions of a system properly implement higher level descriptions? Formal methods support formal verification, the construction of formal proofs that an implementation satisfies a specification. The possibility of constructing such formal proofs was historically the principle driver in the development of formal methods. Prominent technology for formal verification includes Edsger Dijkstra's "weakest precondition" calculus ([Dijkstra 76] and [Gries 81]) and Harlan Mills' "functional correctness" approach [Linger 79].

Tools and Methodology

Developments in supporting tools and methodologies have accompanied the development of technology for formalizing software products. The basic idea is that the ultimate end-product of development is not solely a working system. Of equal importance are specifications and proofs that the program meets its specification. A proof is very hard to develop after the fact. Consequently, proofs and programs should be developed in parallel, with close interconnections in the development history. Since programs must be proven correct, only those constructions that can be clearly understood should be used. This is the primary motivation that many early partisans had for advocating structured programming.

A challenge is to apply these ideas on large scale projects. Formal specifications seem to scale up much easier than formal verifications. Nevertheless, ideas relating to formal verifications are applicable to projects of any size, particularly if the level of formality is allowed to vary. David Gries recommends a design methodology incorporating certain heuristics that support more reliable and provable designs [Gries 81]. Harlan Mills has spent considerable effort developing the Cleanroom approach, a lifecycle in which formal methods, inspections, and reliability modeling and certification are integrated in a social process for producing software ([Mills 87] and [Dyer 92]).

Formal methods have also inspired the development of many tools. These tools may bring formal methods into more widespread practice, although interestingly enough, many advocates of formal methods are not strong believers in tools. An obvious example of such tools are program provers. Some tools animate specifications, thereby converting a formal specification into an executable prototype of a system. Other tools derive programs from specifications through various automated transformations. Under some approaches a program is found as a solution to an equation in a formal language. Transformational implementation suggests a future in which many software systems are developed without programmers, or at least with more automation, higher productivity, and less labor ([Agresti 86] and [KBSE 92]).

In some sense, no programmer can avoid formal methods, for every programming language is, by definition, a formal language. Ever since Algol 60 was introduced, standards defining programming languages have used a formal notation for defining language syntax, namely Backus-Naur Form (BNF). Usually, standards do not formally define the semantics of programming languages, although, in principle, they could. The convention of using natural language descriptions for defining language semantics is due to not having yet developed settled techniques for defining all constructs included in large languages. Nevertheless, formal methods have resulted in one widely agreed criterion for evaluating language features: how simply can one formally reason about a program with a proposed new feature? The formal specification of language semantics is a lively area of research. In particular, formal methods have always been an interest of the Ada community, even before standardization ([London 77], [McGettrick 82] and [Preston 88]).

Limitations of Formal Methods

Given the applicability of formal methods throughout the lifecycle, and their pervasive possibilities for almost all areas of software engineering, why are they not more widely visible? Part of the problem is educational. Revolutions are not made by conversion, but by the old guard passing away. More recent university graduates tend to be more willing to experiment with formal methods.

On the other hand, the only barrier to the widespread transition of this technology is not lack of knowledge on the part of practitioners. Formal methods do suffer from certain limitations. Some of these limitations are inherent and will never be overcome. Other restrictions, with research and practice, will be removed as formal methods are transitioned into wider use.

The Requirements Problem

The inherent limitations in formal methods are neatly summarized in the oft-repeated aphorism, "You cannot go from the informal to the formal by formal means." In particular, formal methods can prove that an implementation satisfies a formal specification, but they cannot prove that a formal specification captures a user's intuitive informal understanding of a system. In other words, formal methods can be used to verify a system, but not to validate a system. The distinction is that validation shows that a product will satisfy its operational mission, while verification shows that each step in the development satisfies the requirements imposed by previous steps [Boehm 81].

The extent of this limitation should not be underemphasized. One influential field study, [Curtis 88], found that the three most important problems in software development are:

- The thin spread of application domain knowledge
- Changes in and conflicts between requirements
- Communication and coordination problems.

Successful projects were often successful because of the role of one or two key exceptional designers. These designers had a deep understanding of the applications domain and could map the applications requirements to computer science concerns. These findings suggest the reduction of informal application knowledge to a rigorous specification is a key problem area in the development of large systems.

Empirical evidence does suggest, however, that formal methods can make a contribution to the problem of adequately capturing requirements. The discipline of producing a formal specification can result in fewer specification errors. Furthermore, implementors without an exceptional designer's knowledge of the application area commit less errors when implementing a formal specification than when relying on hazy knowledge of the application [Goel 91]. These benefits may exist even when the final specification is expressed in English, not a formal language [Meyer 85]. A specification acts as a "contract" between a user and a developer. The specification describes the system to be delivered. Using specifications written in a formal language to complement natural language descriptions can make this contract more precise. Finally, developers of automated programming environments, which use formal methods, have developed tools to interactively capture a user's informal understanding and thereby develop a formal specification [Zeroual 91].

Still, formal methods can never replace deep application knowledge on the part of the requirements engineer, whether at the system or the software level. The application knowledge of the exceptional designer is not limited to one discipline. For example, an avionics application might require knowledge of flight control, navigation, signal processing, and electronic countermeasures. Whether those drawing on interdisciplinary knowledge in developing specifications come to regard formal methods as just another discipline making their life more complicated, or an approach that allows them to simply, concisely, and accurately record their findings, will only be known with experience and experimentation.

Physical Implementations

The second major gap between the abstractions of formal methods and concrete reality lies in the nature of any actual physically existing computer. Formal methods can verify that an implementation satisfies a specification when run on an idealized abstract machine, but not when run on any physical machine.

Some of the differences between typical idealized machines and physical machines are necessary for humanly-readable correctness proofs. For instance, an abstract machine might be assumed to have an infinite memory, while every actual machine has some upper limit. Similarly, physical machines cannot implement real numbers, as axiomatically described by mathematicians, while proofs are most simply constructed assuming the existence of mathematically precise reals. No reason in principle exists why formal methods cannot incorporate these limitations. The proofs will be much messier and less elegant, and they will be limited to a particular machine.

A limitation in principle, however, does exist here. Formal proofs can show with certainty, subject to mistakes in calculation, that given certain assumptions, a program is a correct implementation of a specification. What cannot be formally shown is that those assumptions are correct descriptions of an actual physical system. A compiler may not correctly implement a language as specified. So a proof of a program in that language will fail to guarantee the execution behavior of the program under that compiler. The compiler may be formally verified, but this only moves the problem to a lower level of abstraction. Memory chips and gates may have bugs. No matter how thoroughly an application is formally verified, at some point one must accept that an actual physical system satisfies the axioms used in a proof. Explanations must come to an end sometime.

Both critics [Fetzer 88] and developers ([Dijkstra 76] and [Linger 79]) of formal methods are quite aware of this limitation, although the critics do not always seem to be aware of the developers' explicit statements on this point. This limitation does not mean formal methods are pointless. Formal proofs explicitly isolate those locations where an error may occur. Errors may arise in providing a machine that implements the abstract machine, with sufficient accuracy and efficiency, upon which proofs are based. Given this implementation, a proof vastly increases confidence in a program [Merrill 83].

Although no prominent advocate of formal methods recommends testing be avoided entirely, it is unclear what role testing can play in increasing confidence in the areas not addressed by formal methods. The areas addressed by testing and formal methods may overlap, depending on the specific methodologies employed. From an abstract point of view, the question of what knowledge or rational belief can be provided by testing is the riddle of the rational basis for induction. How can an observation that some objects of a given type have a certain property ever convince anyone that all objects of that type have the property? Why should a demonstration that a program produces the correct outputs for some inputs ever lead to a belief that the program is likely to produce the correct output for all inputs? If a compiler correctly processes certain programs, as defined by a syntactical and semantic standard, why should one conclude that any semantic axiom in the standard can be relied upon for a formal proof of the correctness of a program not used in testing the compiler? Over two centuries ago, the British philosopher David Hume put related questions at the center of his epistemology.

Two centuries of debate have not reached a consensus on induction. Still, human beings are inclined to draw these conclusions. Software developers exhibit the same inclination in testing computer programs. Formal methods will never entirely supplant testing, nor do advocates intend them to do so. In principle, a gap always exists between physical reality and what can be formally verified. With more widespread use of formal methods, however, the role of testing will change.

Implementation Issues

The gaps between users' intentions and formal specifications and between physical implementations and abstract proofs create inherent limitations to formal methods, no matter how much they may be developed in the future. There are also a host of pragmatic concerns that reflect the current state of the technology.

The introduction of a new technology into a large-scale software organization is not a simple thing, particularly a technology as potentially revolutionary as formal methods. Decisions must be made about whether the technology should be completely or partially adopted. Appropriate accompanying tools need to be acquired. Current personnel need to be retrained, and new personnel may need to be hired. Existing practices need to be modified, perhaps drastically. All of these issues arise with formal methods. Optimal decisions depend on the organization and the techniques for implementing formal methods. Several schemes exist, with various levels of feasibility and impact.

The question arises, however, whether formal methods are yet suitable for full-scale implementation. They are most well-developed for addressing issues of functionality, safety, and security, but even for these mature methods, serious questions exist about their ability to scale up to large applications. In much academic work, a proof of a hundred lines of code was seen as an accomplishment. The applicability of such methods to a commercial or military system, which can be over a million lines of code, is seriously in doubt. This issue of scaling can be a deciding factor in the choice of a method. Harlan Mills claims his program function approach applies easier on large systems than Dijkstra's competing predicate calculus method [Mills 86]. Likewise, the languages considered in academic work tend to be extremely simplified compared to real-world programming languages.

One frequently adopted scheme for using formal methods on real-world projects is to select a small subset of components for formal treatment, thus finessing the scalability problem. These components might be selected under criteria of safety, security, or criticality. Components particularly amenable to formal proof might be specifically selected. In this way, the high cost of formal methods is avoided for the entire project, but only incurred where project requirements justify it. Under this scheme, the issue of scaling is avoided, for formal methods are never applied on a large scale.

Decisions about tool acquisition and integration need to be carefully considered. Advocates of formal methods argue that they should be integrated into the design process. One does not develop a specification and an implementation and then attempt to prove the implementation satisfies the specification. Rather, one designs the implementation and proof in parallel, with continual interaction. Sometimes discussion about automated verifiers suggests that the former approach, not the latter, provides an implementation model ([DeMillo 79] and [Merrill 83]). Selective implementation of formal methods on small portions of large projects may make this integration difficult to obtain.

Another approach can have much more global impacts. Perhaps the entire waterfall lifecycle should be scrapped. An alternate approach is to develop formal specifications at the beginning of the lifecycle and then automatically derive the source code for the system. Maintenance, enhancements, and modifications will be performed on the specifications, with this derivation process being repeated. Programmers are replaced by an intelligent set of integrated tools, or at least given very strong guidance by these tools. Knowledge about formal methods then becomes embodied in the tools, with Artificial Intelligence techniques being used to direct the use of formal methods. This revolutionary programmerless methodology is not here yet, but it is providing the inspiration for many tool developers. For example, this vision is close to that of Rome Laboratory's Knowledge-Based Software Engineering project [KBSE 92].

A third alternative is to partially introduce formal methods by introducing them throughout an organization or project, but allowing a variable level of formality. In this sense, informal verification is an argument meant to suggest that details can be filled in to provide a completely formal proof. The most well-known example of this alternative is the Cleanroom methodology, developed by Harlan Mills [Mills 87]. Given varying levels of formality, tools are much less useful under this approach. The Cleanroom methodology involves much more than formal methods, but they are completely integrated into the methodology. Other technologies involved include the spiral lifecycle, software reliability modeling, a specific testing approach, reliability certification, inspections, and statistical process control. Thus, although this approach allows partial experimentation with formal methods, it still requires drastic changes in most organizations.

No matter to what extent an organization decides to adopt formal methods, if at all, training and education issues arise. Most programmers have either not been exposed to the needed mathematical background, or do not use it in their day-to-day practice. Even those who thoroughly understand the mathematics may have never realized its applicability to software development. Set theory is generally taught in courses in pure mathematics, not computer programming. Even discrete mathematics, a standard course whose place in the university curriculum owes much to the impetus of computer science professional societies, is often not tied to software applications. Education in formal methods should not be confined to degreed university programs for undergraduates newly entering the field. Means need to be found, such as seminars and extension courses, for retraining an existing workforce. Perhaps this educational problem is the biggest hurdle to the widespread transition of formal methods.

Specification Methods

Formal methods were originally developed to support verifications, but higher interest currently exists in specification methods. Several methods and languages can be used for specifying the functionality of computer systems. No single language, of those now available, is equally appropriate for all methods, application domains, and aspects of a system. Thus, users of formal specification techniques need to understand the strength and weaknesses of different methods and languages before deciding on which to adopt. This section briefly describes characteristics of different methods now available.

The distinction between a specification method and a language is fundamental. A method states what a specification must say. A language determines in detail how the concepts in a specification can be expressed [Lamport 89]. Some languages support more than one method, while most methods can be used in several specification languages. Some methods are more easily used with certain languages.

Semantic Domains

A formal specification language contains an alphabet of symbols and grammatical rules that define well-formed formulae. These rules characterize a language's "syntactic domain." The syntax of a language shows how the symbols in the language are put together to form meaningless formulae. Neither the nature of the objects symbolized nor the meanings of the relationships between them are characterized by the syntax of a language.

Meanings, or interpretations of formulae, are specified by the semantics of a language. A set of objects, known as the language's "semantic domain," can provide a model of a language. The semantics are given by exact rules which state what objects satisfy a specification. For example, Cartesian Geometry shows how theorems in Euclidean Geometry can be modeled by algebraic expressions. A language can have several models, but some will seem more natural than others.

A specification is a set of formulae in a formal language. The objects in the language's semantic domain that satisfy a given specification can be nonunique. Several objects may be equivalent as far as a particular specification is concerned. Because of this nonuniqueness, the specification is at a higher level of abstraction than the objects in the semantic domain. The specification language permits abstraction from details that distinguish different implementations, while preserving essential properties. Different specification methods defined over the same semantic domain allow for specifying different aspects of specified objects. These concepts can be defined more precisely using mathematics. The advantage of this mathematics is that it provides tools for formal reasoning about specifications. Specifications can then be examined for completeness and consistency.

Specification languages can be classified by their semantic domains. Three major classes of semantic domains exist [Wing 90]:

- Abstract Data Type specification languages
- Process specification languages
- Programming languages.

ADT specification languages can be used to specify algebras. An ADT 'defines the formal properties of a data type without defining implementation features' [Vienneau 91]. Z, the Vienna Development Method, and Larch are examples of ADT specification languages. Process specification languages specify state sequences, event sequences, streams, partial orders, and state machines. C.A.R. Hoare's Communicating Sequential Processes (CSP) is the most well-known process specification language.

Programming languages provide an obvious example of languages with multiple models. Predicate transformers provide one model, functions provide another model, and the executable machine instructions that are generated by compiling a program provide a third model. Formal methods are useful in programming because programs can be viewed both as a set of commands for physical machines and as abstract mathematical objects as provided by these alternative models.

Operational and Definitional Methods

The distinction between operational and definitional methods provides another important dimension for classifying formal methods [Avizienis 90]. Operational methods have also been described as constructive or model-oriented [Wing 90]. In an operational method, a specification describes a system directly by providing a model of the system. The behavior of this model defines the desired behavior of the system. Typically, a model will use abstract mathematical structures, such as relations, functions, sets, and sequences. An early example of a model-based method is the specification approach associated with Harlan Mills' functional correctness approach. In this approach, a computer program is defined by a function from a space of inputs to a space of outputs. In effect, a model-oriented specification is a program written in a very high-level language. It may actually be executed by a suitable prototyping tool.

Definitional methods are also described as property-oriented [Wing 90] or declarative [Place 90]. A specification provides a minimum set of conditions that a system must satisfy. Any system that satisfies these conditions is functionally correct, but the specification does not provide a mechanical model showing how to determine the output of the system from the inputs. Two classes of definitional methods exist, algebraic and axiomatic. In algebraic methods, the properties defining a program are restricted to equations in certain algebras. Abstract Data Types are often specified by algebraic methods. Other types of axioms can be used in axiomatic methods. Often these axioms will be expressed in the predicate calculus. Edsger Dijkstra's method of specifying a program's function by preconditions and postconditions is an early example of an axiomatic method.

Use of Specification Methods

Different specification methods are more advantageous for some purposes than others. In general, formal methods provide for more precise specifications. Misunderstandings and bugs can be discovered earlier in the lifecycle. Since the earlier a fault is detected, the cheaper it can be removed; formal specification methods can dramatically improve both productivity and quality. Cost savings can only be achieved if formal methods are used appropriately. How to best use them in a specific environment can only be determined through experimentation.

Formal specifications should not be presented without a restatement of the specification in a natural language. In particular, customers should be presented with the English version, not a formal specification. Very few sponsors of a software development project will be inclined to read a specification whose presentation is entirely in a formal language.

Whether an ADT or process specification language should be adopted depends on the details of the project and the skills of the analysts. Choosing between operational and definitional methods also depends on project-specific details and experience. Generally, programmers are initially more comfortable with operational methods since they are closer to programming. Operational specifications may lead to over-specification. They tend to be larger than definitional specifications. Their complexity thus tends to be greater, and relationships among operations tend to be harder to discern.

Definitional specifications are generally harder to construct. The appropriate axioms to specify are usually not trivial. Consistency and completeness may be difficult to establish. Usually completeness is more problematic than consistency. Intuition will tend to prevent the specification of inconsistent axioms. Whether some axioms are redundant, or more are needed, is less readily apparent. Automated tools are useful for guidance in answering these questions [Guttag 77].

Conclusions

This report has briefly surveyed various formal methods and the conceptual basis of these techniques. Formal methods can provide:

- More precise specifications
- Better internal communication
- An ability to verify designs before executing them during test
- Higher quality and productivity.

These benefits will come with costs associated with training and use. Hard and fast rules do not exist on how to properly vary the level of formalism on a project or on how to transition the use of formal methods into an organization. Their enthusiastic use certainly depends on the organization's members perceiving a need that formal methods can fill. No change is likely to be achievable in an organization that is satisfied with its current practice.

Even if formal methods are not integrated into an organization's process, they can still have positive benefits. Consider a group whose members have been educated in the use of formal methods, but are not encouraged to use formal methods on the job. These programmers will know that programs can be devel-oped to be fault-free from the first execution. They will have a different attitude to both design and testing, as contrasted to programmers who have not been so exposed to formal methods. They will be able to draw on a powerful set of intellectual tools when needed. They will be able to use formal methods on a personal basis and, to a limited extent, to communicate among one another. If management provides the appropriate milieu, this group can be expected to foster high quality attitudes with consequent increases in both productivity and quality.

To get their full advantages, formal methods should be incorporated into a software organization's standard procedures. Software development is a social process, and the techniques employed need to support that process. How to fully fit formal methods into the lifecycle is not fully understood. Perhaps there is no universal answer, but only solutions that vary from organization to organization.

The Cleanroom as a Lifecycle with Integrated Use of Formal Methods

Harlan Mills has developed the Cleanroom methodology [Mills 87], which is one approach for integrating formal methods into the lifecycle. The Cleanroom approach combines formal methods and structured programming with Statistical Process Control (SPC), the spiral lifecycle and incremental releases, inspections, and software reliability modeling. It fosters attitudes, such as emphasizing defect prevention over defect removal, that are asociated with high quality products in non-software fields.

Cleanroom development begins with the requirements phase. Ideally, specifications should be developed in a formal language, although the Cleanroom approach allows the level of formality to vary. The Cleanroom lifecycle uses incremental releases to support SPC. Cleanroom-developed specifications include:

- Explicit identification of functionality to be included in successive releases
- Failure definitions, including levels of severity
- The target reliability as a probability of failure-free operation
- The operational profile for each increment, that is, the probability distribution of user inputs to the system
- The reliability model that will be applied in system test to demonstrate reliability.

The design and coding phases of Cleanroom development are distinctive. Analysts must develop proofs of correctness along with designs and codes. These proofs use functional correctness techniques and are meant to be human-readable. They serve a social role and are not intended to be automatically checked by automated verification tools. Inspections are emphasized for reviewing designs, proofs, and code. The design process is intended to prevent the introduction of defects. In keeping with this philosophy, the Cleanroom methodology includes no unit or integration test phase. In fact, coders are actually forbidden to compile their programs. Cleanroom development takes its name from just this aspect of the methodology. Testing is completely separated from the design process, and analysts are not permitted to adopt the attitude that quality can be tested in. Instead, they must produce readable programs which can be convincingly shown correct by proof.

Testing does play a very important role in Cleanroom development. It serves to verify that reliability goals are being attained. Given this orientation, testing is organized differently than in traditional methods. Unit and integration testing do not exist. Functional methods, not structural testing methods, are employed. Furthermore, the testing process is deliberately designed to meet the assumptions of the chosen software reliability model. Test cases are statistically chosen from the specified operational profile. Although faults are removed when detected, the testing group's responsibility is not to improve the product to meet acceptable failure-rate goals. Rather, the testing group exists to perform reliability measurement and certification.

When testing fails to demonstrate the desired reliability goal is met, the design process is altered. The level of formality may be increased, or more inspections may be planned. Testing and incremental builds are combined to provide feedback into the development process under a Statistical Process Control philosophy as tailored for software. Formal methods are embodied in an institutional structure designed to foster a "right the first time" approach. The Cleanroom methodology draws upon evolving concepts of the best practice in software, including formal methods. The Cleanroom approach is beginning to generate interest and experimentation in organizations unassociated with Harlan Mills and International Business Machines [Selby 87].

Technologies Supported by Formal Methods

Researchers are drawing on formal methods in developing tools and techniques that may not be state-of-the-practice for several years. Lifecycle paradigms that rely on automatically transforming specifications to executable code are necessarily formal. Many soft-

ware development tools, whether standalone or integrated into a common environment, draw on formal methods. Consequently, as software development becomes more tool intensive, formal methods will be more heavily used. Inasmuch as these formal methods are embodied in the tools, tool users may not be fully aware of the embedded formalism. Tool users who are trained in formal methods will be able to wield some of these tools more effectively. Formal methods, through their use in tools, have the promise of being able to transform the software development lifecycle from a labor-intensive error-prone process to a capital-intensive high quality process.

Emerging technologies that are increasingly widespread today also draw on formal methods. A knowledge of formal methods is needed to completely understand these popular technologies and to use them most effectively. These technologies include:

- Rapid prototyping
- Object Oriented Design (OOD)
- Structured programming
- Formal inspections.

Rapid prototyping depends on the ability to quickly construct prototypes of a system to explore their ability to satisfy user needs. Using executable specifications to describe a system at a high level is a typical approach. The tool that compiles the specification fills in the details. Specifications constructed under a rapid prototyping methodology, if executable, are by definition in a formal language. Often the languages used in prototyping tools involve the same set theoretical and logical concepts used in formal specification methods not intended for prototyping.

OOD is another increasingly well-known technology that is based on formal methods. Abstract Data Types provide a powerful basis for many classes in Object Oriented systems. Furthermore, at least one pure object oriented language, Eiffel, has assertions, preconditions, postconditions, and loop invariants built into the language to a certain extent. Simple boolean expressions are checked during execution of an Eiffel program, but not all assertions, such as those with existential and universal quantifiers, can be expressed in the language [Meyer 88]. Thus, formal methods can be usefully combined with object oriented techniques.

The connection between formal methods and structured programming is very close. Structured programming is a set of heuristics for producing high quality code. Only a limited set of constructs should be used. Programs should be developed in a top-down fashion. The historical source for these heuristics lies in formal methods. Programs developed with these precepts will be capable of being rigorously proven correct. Consequently, they will also be capable of being understood intuitively and nonrigorously. Structured programming cannot be completely understood without understanding the rigorous mathematical techniques associated with formal methods. Adopting formal methods is a natural progression for software development teams who employ structured programming techniques.

Inspections throughout the lifecycle have been shown to increase both productivity and quality. A rigorous methodology has been defined for inspections [Fagan 76]. Those participating in inspections play specified roles: moderator, author, coder, tester, and so on. Inspections should be organized to include representatives from specified departments (for example, Quality Assurance) within a software organization. Fault data is collected during inspections and analyzed to ensure the development process is under control. Inspections rely on the ability of individuals to reason about software products and to convince others of the correctness of their reasoning. Training in formal methods provides inspection team members with a powerful language to communicate their trains of reasoning. Formal and semi-formal verifications can lead to more effective inspections. The Cleanroom methodology demonstrates the potential synergy between formal methods and inspections.

Summary

Formal methods promise to yield benefits in quality and productivity. They provide an exciting paradigm for understanding software and its development, as well as a set of techniques for use by software engineers. Over the last 20 years, researchers have drawn on formal methods to develop certain software technologies that are currently becoming increasingly popular and are dramatically altering software development and maintenance. Further revolutionary advances based on formal methods are highly likely considering research currently in the pipeline.

Many organizations have experience with the use of formal methods on a small scale. Formal methods are typically used in organizations attaining a Level 3 rating and above on the Software Engineering Institute's process maturity framework. Increasingly, recently trained software engineers have had some exposure to formal methods. Nevertheless, their full scale use and transition is not fully understood. An organization that can figure out how to effectively integrate formal methods into their current process will be able to gain a competitive advantage.

References

[Agresti 86] W.W. Agresti, *New Paradigms for Software Development*, IEEE Computer Society Press, Los Alamitos, Calif., 1986.

[Aho 86] A.V. Aho, R. Sethi, and J.D. Ullman, *Compilers: Principles, Techniques, and Tools*, Addison-Wesley, Reading, Mass., 1986.

[Avizienis 90] A. Avizienis and C.-S. Wu, "A Comparative Assessment of Formal Specification Techniques," *Proc. 5th Ann. Knowledge-Based Software Assistant Conf.*, 1990.

[Baber 91] R.L. Baber, *Error-Free Software: Know-how and Know-why of Program Correctness*, John Wiley & Sons, New York, N.Y., 1991.

[Backus 78] J. Backus, "Can Programming Be Liberated from the von Neumann Style? A Functional Style and Its Algebra of Programs," *Comm. ACM*, Vol. 21, No. 8, Aug. 1978.

[Boehm 81] B.W. Boehm, *Software Engineering Economics*, Prentice-Hall, Inc., Englewood Cliffs, N.J., 1981.

[Curtis 88] B. Curtis, H. Krasner, and N. Iscoe, "A Field Study of the Software Design Process for Large Systems," *Comm. ACM*, Vol. 31, No. 11, Nov.1988.

[DeMillo 79] R. DeMillo, R. Lipton, and A. Perlis, "Social Processes and Proofs of Theorems and Programs," *Comm. ACM*, Vol. 22, No. 5, May 1979.

[DeRemer 76] F. DeRemer and H.H. Kron, "Programming-in-the-Large Versus Programming-in-the-Small," *IEEE Trans. Software Eng.*, Vol. SE-2, No. 2, June 1976, pp. 312–327.

[Dijkstra 76] E.W. Dijkstra, *A Discipline of Programming*, Prentice Hall, Englewood Cliffs, N.J., 1976.

[Dijkstra 89] E.W. Dijkstra, "On the Cruelty of Really Teaching Computer Science," *Comm. ACM*, Vol. 32, No. 12, Dec. 1989.

[Dyer 92] M. Dyer, *The Cleanroom Approach to Quality Software Development*, John Wiley & Sons, New York, N.Y., 1992.

[Fagan 76] M.E. Fagan, "Design and Code Inspections to Reduce Errors in Program Development," *IBM Systems J.*, Vol. 15, No. 3, 1976.

[Fetzer 88] J.H. Fetzer, "Program Verification: The Very Idea," *Comm. ACM*, Vol. 31, No. 9, Sept. 1988.

[Goel 91] A.L. Goel and S.N. Sahoo, "Formal Specifications and Reliability: An Experimental Study," *Proc. Int'l Symp. Software Reliability Eng.* IEEE Computer Society Press, Los Alamitos, Calif., 1991, pp. 139–142.

[Gries 81] D. Gries, *The Science of Programming*, Spring-Verlag, New York, N.Y., 1981.

[Gries 91] D. Gries, "On Teaching and Calculation," *Comm. ACM*, Vol. 34, No. 3, Mar. 1991.

[Guttag 77] J. Guttag, "Abstract Data Types and the Development of Data Structures," *Comm. ACM*, Vol. 20, No. 6, June 1977.

[Hall 90] A. Hall, "Seven Myths of Formal Methods," *IEEE Software*, Vol. 7, No. 5, Sept. 1990, pp. 11–19.

[Hoare 85] C.A.R. Hoare, *Communicating Sequential Processes*, Prentice-Hall International, 1985.

[Hoare 87] C.A.R. Hoare, "Laws of Programming," *Comm. ACM*, Vol. 30, No. 8, Aug. 1987.

[Humphrey 88] W.S. Humphrey, "Characterizing the Software Process: A Maturity Framework," *IEEE Software*, Vol. 5, No. 2, Mar. 1988, pp. 73–79.

[KBSE 92] *Proc. 7th Knowledge-Based Software Eng. Conf.*, 1992.

[Kline 80] M. Kline, *Mathematics: The Loss of Certainty*, Oxford University Press, 1980.

[Lamport 89] L. Lamport, "A Simple Approach to Specifying Concurrent Systems," *Comm. ACM*, Vol. 32, No. 1, Jan. 1989.

[Leveson 90] N.G. Leveson, "Guest Editor's Introduction: Formal Methods in Software Engineering," *IEEE Trans. Software Eng.*, Vol. 16, No. 9, Sept. 1990, pp. 929–931.

[Linger 79] R.C. Linger, H.D. Mills, and B.I. Witt, *Structured Programming: Theory and Practice*, Addison-Wesley Publishing Company, Reading, Mass., 1979.

[London 77] R.L. London, "Remarks on the Impact of Program Verification on Language Design," in *Design and Implementation of Programming Languages*, Springer-Verlag, New York, N.Y., 1977.

[Lyons 77] J. Lyons, *Noam Chomsky*, Penguin Books, Revised Edition 1977.

[McGettrick 82] Andrew D. McGettrick, *Program Verification using Ada*, Cambridge University Press, 1982.

[Merrill 83] G. Merrill, "Proofs, Program Correctness, and Software Engineering," *SIGPLAN Notices*, Vol. 18, No. 12, Dec. 1983.

[Meyer 85] B. Meyer, "On Formalism in Specifications," *IEEE Software*, Vol. 2, No. 1, Jan. 1985, pp. 6–26.

[Meyer 88] B. Meyer, *Object-Oriented Software Construction*, Prentice-Hall, Englewood Cliffs, N.J., 1988.

[Mills 86] H.D. Mills, "Structured Programming: Retrospect and Prospect," *IEEE Software,* Vol. 3, No. 6, Nov. 1986, pp. 58–66.

[Mills 87] H.D. Mills, Michael Dyer, and Richard C. Linger, "Cleanroom Software Engineering," *IEEE Software*, Vol. 4, No. 5, Sept. 1987, pp. 19–25.

[Peterson 77] J.L. Peterson, "Petri Nets," *Computing Surveys*, Vol. 9, No. 3, Sept. 1977.

[Place 90] P.R.H. Place, W. Wood, and M. Tudball, *Survey of Formal Specification Techniques for Reactive Systems*, Software Engineering Institute, CMU/SEI-90-TR-5, May 1990.

[Preston 88] D. Preston, K. Nyberg, and R. Mathis, "An Investigation into the Compatibility of Ada and Formal Verification Technology," *Proc. 6th Nat'l Conf. Ada Technology*, 1988.

[Selby 87] R.W. Selby, V.R. Basili, and F.T. Baker, "Cleanroom Software Development: An Empirical Evaluation," *IEEE Trans. Software Eng.*, Vol. SE-13, No. 9, Sept. 1987, pp. 1027–1037.

[Spivey 88] J.M. Spivey, *Understanding Z: A Specification Language and its Formal Semantics*, Cambridge University Press, 1988.

[Stolyar 70] A.A. Stolyar, *Introduction to Elementary Mathematical Logic*, Dover Publications, 1970.

[Suppes 72] P. Suppes, *Axiomatic Set Theory*, Dover Publications, 1972.

[Terwilliger 92] R.B. Terwilliger, "Simulating the Gries/Dijkstra Design Process," *Proc. 7th Knowledge-Based Software Eng. Conf.,* IEEE Computer Society Press, Los Alamitos, Calif., 1992, pp. 144–153.

[Vienneau 91] R. Vienneau, *An Overview of Object Oriented Design,* Data & Analysis Center for Software, Apr. 30, 1991.

[Wing 90] J.M. Wing, "A Specifier's Introduction to Formal Methods," *Computer*, Vol. 23, No. 9, Sept. 1990, pp. 8–24.

[Zeroual 91] K. Zeroual, "KBRAS: A Knowledge-Based Requirements Acquisition System," *Proc. 6th Ann. Knowledge-Based Software Eng. Conf.,* IEEE Computer Society Press, Los Alamitos, Calif., 1991, pp. 38–47.

Formal Methods in Information Systems Engineering

Hossein Saiedian, PhD
Department of Computer Science
College of Information Science and Technology
University of Nebraska at Omaha
Omaha, NE 68182-0500

Abstract

The objective of this article is to promote the interests of information systems developers in formal methods. We discuss the role of formal methods in the context of an engineering approach to information systems development. The importance of formalism during the early stages of information systems development is discussed. An example in Z is given. Some misconceptions about formal methods and challenges in transferring formal methods technology into industrial practice are presented.

Keywords: Formal Methods, Engineering Paradigm, Information Systems Development, Language Z

1. Introduction

Computer-based systems are built in areas such as air traffic control, on-line hospital patient record management, stock transaction control systems, and so forth. These systems play important roles in our daily lives. As such systems evolve from being merely "information systems," and are used more and more in increasingly sensitive and sometimes life-critical environments, operating over distributed platforms and with strict requirements on response times, inadvertent errors in their specification, design, and implementation could have a major impact on our safety and well-being. Some of these systems will consist of millions of lines of code and their complexity may eventually supersede the complexity of any artifact ever built by mankind.

It is important that the developers of such systems employ those methods that can offer a high assurance that a system will operate as desired. Thus, it is essential that such developers seek assurance that the system requirements accurately capture the users' critical requirements, that the system design correctly reflects the system requirements, and that an implementation in software (or hardware) is an accurate realization of the system design. In fact, one of the most challenging tasks in the development of an information system is to assure reliability, that is, for the system to perform its functions as expected. Providing such assurance is especially important as these systems are used in increasingly sensitive and often life-critical environments.

The reliability of software, although the primary concern, has not been the only one. Another major concern of the computing industry has been the increased cost of developing and maintaining software. In the mid-1950s, software cost was less than 20 percent of total computing cost, but now it exceeds 80 percent. Precise and up-to-date figures representing the actual cost are either not available or are not easy to establish. Boehm [1] suggested that in 1985 worldwide software cost exceeded $140 billion and was growing at a rate of 12 percent per year. According to these figures, software cost will reach $600 billion by the year 2000. Small improvements in software development can, therefore, result in a substantial reduction in this high cost. A large portion of software cost is due to its maintenance. The maintenance of existing software systems can account for more than 70 percent of all efforts expended by a software organization. This percentage continues to rise. Researchers have indicated that a lack of rigorous practice to eliminate residual errors in specification and produce precise and unambiguous specification in software development activities has translated into a large portion of these maintenance costs.

The above-described characteristics of information systems imply that the specification, design, implementation, and validation of these systems represent an engineering process of considerable difficulty comparable to other complex engineering products. The question is, are our future information system specialists prepared for the design and maintenance of such systems? Will they be concerned with the efficiency, reliability, safety, ease of use, and robustness of their information system products, just as engineers have been concerned with their products?

If we are to use traditional engineering disciplines as guides for our information system design, we must understand the engineering methods and the process by which engineers have achieved their goals. (Note that the emphasis here is not necessarily on what engineering is but on what engineers do.) Although these methods are many and varied, we like to emphasize the application of science and by extension mathematics in the activities of practicing engineers. By doing so, we like to assert that *formal methods* may mirror these activities in the area of information systems. By combining the investigation into engineering uses of mathematics with our taxonomy of formal methods, we hope to establish the important place of formal methods in information system development, point to the parallel between mathematics/engineering and formal methods/information systems, and emphasize the importance of introducing the concept of formal methods to the information systems curriculum.

There are a number of excellent references on what constitutes an engineering process. One such reference is Koen [13]. According to Koen, the engineering method is "the strategy for causing the best change in a poorly understood or uncertain situation within the available resources"; Koen further explains that engineers base their work on the choosing of the best heuristics from a pool of given heuristics. Indeed, what distinguishes an engineering practice is its assessment of a body of heuristics that succeed more often than they fail. However, the most important aspect of Koen's thesis and the one that we emphasize is his emphasis on the use of science and, by extension, the mathematics part of the engineering process. The information system also has its own heuristics, for example, avoid `goto`, limit modules to one page, avoid excessive global data definition, etc. It is important to use information system heuristics that have proven effective. Our goal is to emphasize the more important thesis of Koen, that of the application of mathematics.

Although space does not permit detailed discussion of Koen's thesis and its implications, the overall theme, that is, the emphasis on the role of science and mathematics, provides a framework for judging the place of formal methods, which in our opinion play a role in information systems analogous to the role of mathematics in engineering. Great achievements in past chemical, electrical, industrial, civil, and mechanical engineering have been firmly based on an understanding and application of formal methods. The time has come to use formal methods for information system development and to construct a pragmatic framework for teaching the basic concepts to newcomers.

Our objective is not to instruct the readers in the theoretical world of formal methods, but rather in the importance of their application in developing informa-

tion systems. The organization of this article is as follows: We first discuss formal methods and then discuss the effectiveness of specifications that are *formal*, that is, based on a mathematical approach. We will then give an example to show how a formal system, called Z, can be used to formally describe the functionality of an information system. This example is a simplified version of a library system; nevertheless, the effectiveness of formalism is illustrated. We then examine the roots of some common misconceptions about formal methods. Finally, the article ends with a discussion of how to transfer the formal methods technology into the workplace and focuses on further research areas for making formal methods more widely used.

2. Formalism in Modeling and Specification

The development of any large system must be preceded by a specification of what is required. Without such a specification, the system's developers will have no firm statement of the needs of the would-be users of the system. The need for precise specification is accepted in most engineering disciplines. Information systems are in no less need of precision than other engineering tasks.

We place special importance on the requirement analysis and specification phase since we believe that precise and concise specifications are an essential prerequisite to the successful development and evolution of a system. If the system is not precisely specified, the design process could become chaotic, resulting in a system that is complicated, error-prone, and difficult to maintain.

Many aspects of an information system must be specified, including its functionality, performance, and cost. In this article attention is focused on a system's functionality. The requirements specification phase, that is, when the functions of an software are specified, plays a critical role. Its role is so critical that failure to carry out this phase properly is historically known to cause great financial losses. Hence requirements specification has been the subject of a great deal of attention in recent years. The existence of workshops and conferences devoted to this subject, for example, the *International Workshop on Software Specification and Design*, bear witness to the importance of this field.

Requirements can be specified informally via a natural language. Informal specifications alone are certainly not appropriate because they are normally inconsistent, inaccurate, and ambiguous and they rapidly become bulky, and it would be very difficult to check for their completeness. Semiformal approaches to specification have been developed since the 1970s to improve the practices used in software development. A particular emphasis in semiformal approaches (for example, dataflow diagrams) is on graphical representation of the software being built. Major problems with semi-formal methods include:

- Their lack of precise semantics that can be used to reason about or verify the properties of the software, and
- Their generally "free" interpretation

To overcome the limitations of informal and semiformal approaches, we emphasize using *formal methods* to produce precise and unambiguous specifications (known as *formal specifications*).

A method is defined as a set of *procedures* (or guidelines) for *selecting* and applying *tools* and techniques to *construct* a (reliable) artifact (in this case, an information system). A tool is formal if it can be mechanically manipulated according to some well-defined, mathematically based rules. That is, the tool should have precise mathematical semantics. (Note that a notation is a form of tool.) If a method uses formal tools (or notations), then it is called formal. The objective of formal methods is to achieve rigor in reasoning as well as mechanical support.

Formal methods of software development use a mathematical notation. By mathematics, we do not mean derivations, integration, differential equations, and such. Most popular formal methods employ only a limited branch of mathematics consisting of set theory and logic. The elements of both set theory and logic (which are taught in discrete mathematics classes) are easily understood. Such a notation is used to describe the properties of a software *precisely,* without unduly constraining the way in which these properties are to be realized. In other words, they describe *what* the system must do without saying *how* it is to be done. This abstraction is very useful in developing software since it allows questions about the properties of the system to be answered *confidently* without speculating about the meaning of certain phrases in an imprecisely worded prose description. Furthermore, formal methods provide a basis for logical reasoning about the artifacts produced. (These artifacts may be abstract in terms of specifications, or they may be concrete, in terms of programming code.) We believe that it is important to build an (abstract) mathematical description of an information system, using formal methods, before building the system itself. The reason for doing so is to achieve more precision in the descriptions and to explore the validity of the design by reasoning about the descriptions.

A formal approach is also needed to achieve precise communication among various users and developers of a system. Precise communication is critical because in large projects a group of people must arrive at a consistent understanding of the proposed system in order to construct it successfully.

We do not assert that informal (for example, natural language descriptions) and semiformal specifications are useless. Clear use of a natural language obviously has a place in describing systems. In fact, they may be very useful as a first introduction to a software and as comments to enhance the readability of formal specifications. Thus formal and informal specifications must not be regarded as the only alternatives but rather as complementary. To achieve *precision*, however, a specification must be formal.

In addition to precision in specifications, formal methods enable the designer to use *rigorous mathematical reasoning* to prove the properties of the software. Thus design errors (for example, inconsistencies, incompleteness, contradictions) can be detected at an early stage of development.

Formal methods can be applied during the specification, design, and implementation phases of information systems development. Some formal systems, such as Z [7], are considered to be modeling and specification tools while a system like the VDM [12] emphasizes design. Dijkstra's "weakest precondition" approach can be used during the implementation to prove the correctness of a program. Most formal methods support both system modeling and reasoning. (Of course, the degree to which emphasis is shifted from modeling to reasoning is varied in different approaches.) A formal system like Z can be used to produce a clear and concise model of an information system. This by itself is of sufficient value to encourage and warrant the use of formal methods. This, in fact, is our emphasis. That is, we emphasize the use of formal methods for specification and modeling. Of course, a formal model of a system produced by a method like Z can be used in conjunction with verified design by a series of refinements during which abstract descriptions are transformed into more concrete design structures. While this transformation is being done, *inference rules* can be used to uncover inconsistencies.

3. An Example: A Simple Library System

We mentioned that formal methods can be used both during early stages of software development for modeling and specification purposes and in later stages for verification, formal walkthrough, or to show the equivalence of different implementations. For this example, the use of formal methods for specification is emphasized. We provide an example in Z to show the effectiveness of formal methods in the specification of an information system.

An important feature of Z is that it provides a framework within which a specification of a system can be constructed incrementally. The main building block of this framework is a two-dimensional graphical structure called a *schema*. Schemas group all the relevant information that belongs to a system, and describe its static aspects (for example, the states it occupies) and the dynamic properties (for example, the operations that are possible on the state). A complete Z specification is constructed from schemas that themselves can be expressed in terms of other schemas. (This is similar to construction of a program by a series of program modules that can be read and understood in isolation.) Figure 1 shows the structure of a schema.

The signature introduces variables that define the state and is analogous to the declaration part of a Pascal program. The predicate of a schema refers to variables (both local and "global"—those that are defined in other schemas) and relates the values of these variables to each other. (To reduce unnecessary clutter, entries of declaration and conjuncts of predicate are placed on separate lines. However, it is possible to place more than one declaration entry, separated by a semicolon, on each line. Similarly, conjuncts of predicate can be placed on a single line and explicitly connected by an "and" connective.) The signature and predicate part of a schema are separated by a horizontal bar, which is pronounced as "such that." There is an equivalent *linear* notation for schemas shown as [*Signature | Predicate*].

To illustrate the specification approach in Z, we will specify a simple book library system that manages available books that library users (or borrowers) may want to check out. The system allows operations such as checking out and returning a book and maintains which users have borrowed which books. (This example is based on the storage manager problem given in Woodcock and Loomes [20]; a more elaborate example of a library system is provided as a case study in Diller [7].)

The requirements of the library system can be stated as follows:

1. No book can simultaneously be borrowed by more than one user

2. There is no limit on how many books a library user may borrow

3. Some books may never be borrowed by a user (this requirement is "unconsciously" made ambiguous)

4. Some library users may wish never to borrow a book

We present the specifications in four simple steps.

Step 1: Present Given, User-Defined, and Global Definitions

Given sets (types) are normally presented in all uppercase letters inside brackets. For the library system, the given types are as follows:

[USER; BOOK]

In other words, at an abstract level, the details of users and books are not of any interest; that is why we assume they are given types.

There are several ways to introduce user-defined sets (or types). One way is by means of enumeration. For our library system, we can use the following enumerated type:

MESSAGE ::= 'OK' | 'Book not available' | 'Invalid return'

Note that the above specification may suggest forward-referencing. For a user-defined set such as *MESSAGE*, the constituting elements are actually introduced as the specifications are developed. For example, if the specification of the library is expanded, we may discover the need for additional elements such as `Invalid user`, etc.

$$\boxed{\begin{array}{l} \underline{\quad SchemaName}\underline{} \\ Signature \\ \underline{} \\ Predicate \\ \end{array}}$$

Figure 1. A Z schema.

Step 2: Define an Abstract State

The next step is to present the abstract state of the library system. The state is composed of at least two objects:

1. *available:* Representing the set of all books available in the library; this object is of type *BOOK*

2. *borrowed:* A many-to-many relation from books to borrowers representing which books have been borrowed by which users. Note that:

    a. The *borrowed* relation needs to be *functional* because each book can be borrowed by one user at a time

    b. The functional relation *borrowed* need not be *injective* since a user may borrow more than one book

    c. The functional relation *borrowed* need not be *surjective* since some users may never wish to borrow a book, and

    d. The functional relation *borrowed* should be *partial*. Although all books are borrowable, some may never be borrowed because of a lack of interest

The Z symbol for representing a partial function as described above is $\nrightarrow$ (Z provides unique symbols for the partial and total versions of each type of a function.) The formal definition and meaning of $\nrightarrow$ is sufficient to guarantee unique interpretation and thus the unintentional ambiguity introduced earlier would be eliminated.

The Z schema representing the state of the library system is as shown in Figure 2.

The $\mathbb{P}$ symbol is the power set symbol. The keyword dom is short for domain. The predicates of the *LibSys* represent invariant expressions that state the following two facts:

1. The union of available books and books borrowed represents all books owned by the library

2. No book can be both available and borrowed at the same time

Normally at this step, the Δ and Ξ versions of the abstract state, shown, respectively, as Δ*LibSys* and Ξ*LibSys*, are also formally introduced. We introduce them informally later.

Step 3: Define the Initial State

The next step, shown in Figure 3, is to present the initial state of the *LibSys*, showing that at least one initial state exists.

$$
\begin{array}{|l}
\hline
\_LibSys \underline{\hspace{8cm}} \\
available : \mathbb{P}\ BOOK \\
borrowed : BOOK \nrightarrow USER \\
\hline
available \cup \mathrm{dom}\ borrowed = BOOK \\
available \cap \mathrm{dom}\ borrowed = \varnothing \\
\hline
\end{array}
$$

Figure 2. State schema for the library system.

$$
\begin{array}{|l}
\hline
\_InitLibSys \underline{\hspace{8cm}} \\
LibSys' \\
\hline
available' = BOOK \\
borrowed' = \varnothing \\
\hline
\end{array}
$$

Figure 3. The initial state of the library system.

388

Step 4: Presenting the State Transition Operations

Next, we present operations that result in state transitions. The successful case for each operation is given, followed by its error cases, followed by a total operation.

The first operation is that of checking out a book. Input to this operation includes a borrower (shown as *user?*) and the book to be checked out (shown as *book?*). The output is a reply message (shown as *reply!*). The symbols ? and ! are used for decorating input and output items, respectively. The successful case of the check-out operation is as shown in Figure 4.

The declaration Δ*LibSys* alerts us to the fact that the schema is describing a state change and transition; the state of the *LibSys* will be modified by this operation to effect the next state. There are four expressions in the predicate part:

- The first expression is essentially a *precondition*, requiring that the requested book be available for check-out

- The other three expressions are *postconditions*. The prime symbol is used for decorating the after-operation values (or values after the state change). Thus the value of *available* after the operation should be the same as the value before the operation minus the checked-out book; the value of *borrowed* after the operation will be a union of borrowed before the operation and a new entry. (The maplet symbol $\mapsto$ shows the mapping or association between the elements of a relation.)

To strengthen the specification of an operation, one must specify what is to happen if and when the precondition(s) are not fulfilled. In the case of *CheckOutOK* operation, the precondition is *book?* $\in$ *available*. When the book to be checked out is not available, some special message is to be displayed. We show this by means of the *BookNotAvailable* schema (Figure 5).

$$\begin{array}{|l}
\underline{\;CheckOutOK\;} \underline{\hspace{8cm}} \\
\Delta LibSys \\
user? : USER \\
book? : BOOK \\
reply! : MESSAGE \\
\hline
book? \in available \\
available' = available \setminus \{book?\} \\
borrowed' = borrowed \cup \{book? \mapsto user?\} \\
reply! = \text{`OK'} \\
\end{array}$$

Figure 4. Z schema to model a checkout operation.

$$\begin{array}{|l}
\underline{\;BookNotAvailable\;} \underline{\hspace{8cm}} \\
\Xi LibSys \\
book? : BOOK \\
reply! : MESSAGE \\
\hline
book? \notin available \\
reply! = \text{`Book not available'} \\
\end{array}$$

Figure 5. Z schema representing an error case.

Note that once an error occurs (such as attempting to check out a book that is unavailable), the state of the *LibSys* should not be altered. The declaration Ξ*LibSys* represents this fact.

It is now possible to construct a total (or robust) version of the check-out operation. We use the operators of Z's schema calculus:

$$CheckOut \; \hat{=} \; CheckOutOK \vee BookNotAvailable$$

The above notation introduces a new schema called *CheckOut* obtained by combining two existing schemas. The signature of *CheckOut* contains all variables of *CheckOutOK* and *BookNotAvailable*. Likewise, its predicate part is a disjunction of expressions in *CheckOutOK* and *BookNotAvailable*. If expanded, *CheckOut* will appear as in Figure 6.

We now give the specification of an operation for handling book returns in Figure 7.

The precondition of the *ReturnOK* states that the entry to be removed from the *borrowed* relation must in fact be a valid existing entry. If this precondition is not satisfied, it means an invalid return is to be recorded. The following schema in Figure 8 handles that error case.

_ CheckOut _____

Δ*LibSys*
user? : *USER*
book? : *BOOK*
reply! : *MESSAGE*

$(book? \in available$
$available' = available \setminus \{book?\}$
$borrowed' = borrowed \cup \{book? \mapsto user?\}$
$reply! = \text{`OK'})$
$\vee$
$(book? \notin available$
$available' = available$
$borrowed' = borrowed$
$reply! = \text{`Book not available'})$

Figure 6. A complete checkout operation.

_ ReturnOK _____

Δ*LibSys*
user? : *USER*
book? : *BOOK*
reply! : *MESSAGE*

$(book? \mapsto user?) \in borrowed$
$available' = available \cup \{book?\}$
$borrowed' = borrowed \setminus \{book? \mapsto user?\}$
$reply! = \text{`OK'}$

Figure 7. Z schema to model a return operation.

$$
\begin{array}{|l}
\underline{\quad InvalidReturn\quad\rule{0pt}{0pt}}\\
\Xi LibSys \\
user? : USER \\
book? : BLOCK \\
reply! : MESSAGE \\
\hline
(book? \mapsto user?) \notin borrowed \\
reply! = \text{`Invalid return'} \\
\end{array}
$$

Figure 8. Z schema to model an invalid return.

We can now construct a total (robust) operation for returning a book:

$$Return \;\; \widehat{=} \;\; ReturnOK \vee InvalidReturn$$

The *LibSys* can be queried in many ways. One example is to find out the number and title of books checked out by a user. The output of this operation includes *books!* and *count!* (of type integer, shown as Z symbol):

The range restriction operator, $\triangleright$, produces a new set containing those entries in the *borrowed* relation that have *user?* as a range value. The dom operator subsequently produces the book titles and the size operator, #, gives the size.

3.1. Observations

As can be observed from the above, formal specifications can aid in arriving at the *most useful abstract* description of a system because they *highlight* the relevant details of a system. Formal specifications given in a language like Z allow one interpretation and, unlike programming languages, they are not required to contain efficiently implementable constructs and thus eliminate unnecessary details. This attribute contributes to the readability, minimality, and precision of specifications. The advantages of formal modeling and specifications, as evident from the above example, can be summarized as follows:

- Preciseness—Formal specifications allow requirements of an information system to be recorded accurately
- Unambiguous—Different interpretations are avoided because the constructs used have well-defined meaning
- Conciseness—A mathematical notation is capable of expressing complex facts about information systems in a short space

$$
\begin{array}{|l}
\underline{\quad CheckedOutBooks\quad\rule{0pt}{0pt}}\\
\Xi LibSys \\
user? : USER \\
books! : \mathbb{P}\,BOOK \\
count! : \mathbb{Z} \\
\hline
books! = \text{dom}(borrowed \triangleright \{user?\}) \\
count! = \#(borrowed \triangleright \{user?\}) \\
\end{array}
$$

Figure 9. Z schema to model a query.

3.2. Comments on the Z Approach

The design of Z illustrates that informal (English) descriptions are complementary to formal specifications. As can be seen from the above example, small chunks of formal descriptions, framed in schema boxes, are surrounded by informal prose, explaining the relationship between the formal expressions and reality, thus motivating discussion and subsequently decisions that are captured by formalism. Note that in the above example, the English statements were used primarily to explain the Z notation. For a real project, the English description should complement the formal expressions. Z also allows us to begin the specification with a simple description of the overall structures of an information system (with as few variables/operations as possible) and then expand the descriptions (while leaving the initial descriptions unchanged). This is done by:

1. Embedding the initial general schema inside other schemas
2. Forming new schemas by connecting existing schemas through schema connective operators

Such an approach encourages and facilitates modularity: Individual requirements are defined separately and then they are joined together by connective operators. The schema calculus of Z is based on simple connective operators (such as $\wedge$, $\vee$, $\Rightarrow$).

4. Concerns about Formal Methods

There are a number of common concerns (misconceptions) about the uses of formal methods. For example, it is argued that formal methods are difficult to use, are too mathematical, are only applicable to trivial academic problems, and are not widely used. In this section, we examine a number of such misconceptions. Many of these and other misconceptions are discussed in greater detail in the context of "myths of formal methods" by Hall [9]. (A more recent article addresses seven more myths of formal methods [3].)

4.1. Inapplicability to Large Projects

A concern of misconception is that formal methods are not used in industry for real projects. A survey of industrial usage on both sides of the Atlantic has become widely quoted, and should play a major role in highlighting the benefits of formal methods [6]. Hinchey and Bowen [10] attempt to consolidate much of this information in an industrially useful manner. It includes a summary of the findings of the aforemen-tioned survey, and contains contributions relating to a number of the systems addressed in that survey, the contributions being written by the actual developers.

The case studies relate to a wide range of formal methods (B, CCS, VDM, Z, etc.) and to a wide range of applications (such as high-integrity systems in avionics, nuclear projects, atomic energy control, railway industries, security-critical systems, etc.). The use of Z and B in CICS, often cited as a prime example of the successful industrialization of formal methods, is also discussed as well as more unusual applications such as a voting system.

Concerns for a lack of mathematical techniques in industry is also evident from a recently completed report by the Computer Science and Technology Board [15] in the United States. This report points to the need for strengthened mathematical foundations in information systems and related areas. For example, the report warns that as the software developers begin to envision information systems that require many thousands of person-years, current pragmatic or heuristic approaches begin to appear less adequate to meet application needs. Therefore, the developers may have to call for more systematic approaches. More mathematics, science, and engineering are needed to meet their call. For an international survey on industrial applications of formal methods see Craigen et al. [6] This report evaluates international industrial experience in using formal methods, provides an authoritative record on the practical experience of formal methods to date, and suggests areas where future research and technology development are needed.

Of course, "inapplicability" is different from technology transfer. There are many issues to be addressed for making the formal methods technology transition more effective. Many of these issues are discussed in Saiedian [17.]

4.2. The Notation is Too Mathematical

Another concern is that formal methods are too mathematical and too complicated, requiring extensive mathematical background to understand and use them. Formal methods are based on mathematics. However, the mathematics of formal methods are not difficult to learn. Using them requires some training, but experience has shown that such training is not difficult and that people with only high school math can develop the skills to write good formal specifications. Most popular formal methods languages (for example, Z and VDM) employ only a limited branch of mathematics consisting of set theory and logic. The elements of both set theory and logic are easily understood and are taught early in high school these days. Certainly, anyone who can learn a programming language can learn a specification language like Z. In fact, learning a specification language such as Z should be easier than a programming language like COBOL. Z is smaller; it is abstract, and is implementation independent. (For example, the data types used in Z are sets, rather than implementation-dependent types used in programming language. This kind of representation captures the essence of what is required better than the corresponding implementation structures.) The specification of a problem in Z is shorter and much easier to understand than its expression in a programming language like COBOL.

The negative perception of the role of mathematical techniques in requirements specification is very unfortunate. When problems become very large and complex in other engineering disciplines, they normally turn to mathematics for help. Unfortunately, some software developers feel that formal methods and mathematical tools are of academic interest only and that real problems are too large and complex to be handled by formal methods and mathematical tools.

The need for a broader use of mathematical techniques and concerns about lack of rigor and accountability in software development are not felt just by the academicians. Consider, for example, a recent report released by the Subcommittee and Oversight of the U.S. House of Representatives Committee on Science, Space and Technology [11]. This report addresses the problem of software reliability and quality and criticizes universities for not providing adequate education for software engineers. In an article summarizing this congressional report, Cherniavksy [5] writes:

> "[there is] a fundamental difference between software engineers and other engineers. Engineers are well trained in the mathematics necessary for good engineering. Software engineers are not trained in the disciplines necessary to assure high-quality software ..."

4.3. Specification versus Verification

One misconception is that formal methods are for program verification only. A lot of work, especially in academic institutions, has concentrated on using formal methods for program verification. Program verification makes formal methods seem very difficult and technical. In fact, one reason that formal methods are unpopularly perceived is that they are often confused with proving programs corrects. Program verification, however, is only one aspect of formal methods and perhaps the *least significant*. Program verification is normally applied to the later stages of development well after the system has been modeled and specified. The primary use of formal methods is for writing specifications that precisely define what a system is intended to do.

5. Technology Transfer Challenges

Numerous pragmatic challenges are still ahead in order to transfer formal methods technology into the actual workplace and make them more popular. We will give our guidelines and suggestions in this section. Most importantly, professionals and students must be trained and educated in the use of formal methods. Training and education guidelines are given at the end of this section. (A much more detailed discussion of these and other guidelines is given by Saiedian and Hinchey [18].)

Large-Scale Case Studies. As mentioned earlier, most practitioners perceive formal methods as academic tools that are difficult to use. They are reluctant to use them despite their considerable advantage over traditional methods. A study needs to be done to discover what it will take to move formal methods from this unfair perception into a wider acceptability within the information systems community. Case studies must be developed to demonstrate the applicability of formal methods, with the intention of convincing the practitioners that the benefits outweigh the difficulties of transition; the results of these case studies should be disseminated widely. To demonstrate that formal methods pay off, more realistic, large-scale examples performed in conjunction with industry (for example, IBM's CICS) are necessary. These industrial case studies not only are necessary for advancing the technology and demonstrating the potential benefits; they also help identify the needs of companies that adopt formal methods and enhance the integration of formal methods with current software engineering practices. In general, formal methods tend to address semantic issues rather than pragmatic issues of a software. Managers and practitioners are, however, most concerned with pragmatics issues. This understanding would help researchers delineate more precisely where formal methods are most useful.

Case studies also assist in identifying the limits of formal methods. Formal methods have proven very useful for the specification of functional properties of a system. Nonfunctional properties of a software system such as reliability, cost, performance, portability, man–machine interfaces, and resource consumption of running programs are difficult, perhaps even impossible, to specify by means of formal methods. Research needs to be done to find out if formal methods can in fact be used for such purposes. It is only in practical applications that the limits or constraints of formal methods are revealed.

Debora Weber-Wulff [19] addresses some of the typical questions in attempting to introduce formal methods into industry, elaborates on other marketing aspects of formal methods, and offers 10 propositions for industrial strength formal methods. Some of these propositions include:

1. An industrial formal method should be confinable, that is, restricted to just one aspect of a large software project, so that it will not disrupt the rest

2. The uses of formal methods should be reversible so that if it were decided to drop the use of these methods, it would be possible to revert to the previous status in development

3. A formal method should allow interchangeability of software components or allow the use of different tools

4. A formal method should not be coercive or overly concerned with imposing and enforcing restrictions on trivial aspects of software development

5. A formal method should be teachable

6. A formal method should be inexpensive

7. There must be adequate documentation for an industrial formal methods technique

Automated Tools. One factor limiting the use of formal methods is the lack of investment in automated tools and support structures to reduce the efforts of applying these methods. In fact, lack of support tools is often seen as a major barrier to using formal methods. A key factor in the acceptance of high-level languages has been the presence of a comprehensive set of tools to support the user. If formal method languages are to achieve the same level of acceptance, they too require extensive automated support. Support tools may reduce the learning time, thereby aiding their widespread use. In our opinion, automated tools may include:

- Special editing environment
- Syntax checkers
- Animation tool
- Refinement and proof tools

In addition to the above, good interface to specification languages, transformation tools for taking popular methods and converting them into formal methods, and tools for inferencing from specifications to assist software validation are needed.

Furthermore, a specification is and should be considered a major reference document for the customer as well as the developer. It is impractical, however, to expect a customer to read mathematical expressions. A large amount of work needs to be done in this area for developing tools, for example, to animate the mathematical expressions in a specification document so that a customer may understand them more easily. It should be noted that a number of very useful tools have already been developed for Z, including ZTC, FUZZ, and CADiZ. Similarly, automated toolboxes for VDM-SL support formal development as well as type and semantic checkers as well as a pretty-printer that produces L^{A}T$_E$X code. Certain formal models incorporate tool support directly. For example, OBJ includes an executable subset while Larch supports a theorem prover. More tools have recently been reported [3].

When to Use Formal Methods. An important responsibility of the proponents of formal methods is to clarify when in the development process formal methods should be applied. As full formal development is rarely employed, thus far the greatest benefits of formal methods have been demonstrated at the early stages of development for the purposes of modeling and specification.

What normally discourages practitioners is the mathematics involved in proving programs correct (program verification). Program verification, however, is carried out at the later phases of development when actual programs have been coded. Program coding is not necessarily the most error-prone part of development, especially if the overall structure of the system under development has been properly designed and well conceived. The need for complicated programs and, by extension, program verification, is in fact a sign of poor design.

The greatest benefit of formal methods emerges when they are employed during the specification and modeling stages, early in the development process. During these stages, formal methods can be applied profitably to develop clear and concise specifications. The simple act of precise specification and modeling often provides the greatest benefit, although reasoning about specifications can also provide considerable additional advantages. Consider, for example, one of the better known real-life applications of formal methods—the application of SCR (software cost reduction) techniques to the Darlington Nuclear Facility in Canada.

That application is often cited as a major argument in favor of formal methods. Indeed, the work involved highlighting several errors in the existing code that would have gone undetected by testing. Specifications and models derived from the implementation were amenable to formal examination and analysis. The application is also often cited, however, as a means of highlighting the extreme cost of formal methods. It is true that the project cost several million dollars, although the software consisted of just 2000 lines of code.

Nevertheless, the project stands as one of the great success stories of formal methods, and it is our contention (and that of David Parnas, who acted as a consultant in establishing the Ontario Hydro standards [14]) that the costs would have been significantly less had formal methods been used in the initial stages of development (rather than used to "backfit" the existing code).

Although Darlington was expensive, and many might dispute such a high investment, we believe that (in this case) the investment was warranted, owing to the catastrophic destruction and loss of human life that would have ensued as a result of a system failure. However, that is not to say that formal methods are justified in all system development, and one must clarify *when* formal methods should be applied.

Applying formal methods blindly to *all* aspects of a system would certainly not be cost-effective. Most successful applications of formal methods have concentrated on *critical components*, and indeed the use of formal methods is justified in all high-integrity systems, or components of systems that are required to meet the highest integrity standards [2], that is, where "correctness" is of the essence.

Toward a Reusable Framework. Traditional efforts on formal methods have been for functional specification of a software system and have largely focused on abstraction techniques (and refining abstractions into some implementation). To make formal methods an integral part of industrial software development, the use of these methods must be as cost-effective as possible. One way of achieving such cost-effectiveness is through development of a framework for reuseability of already developed formal specifications. Such a framework has numerous benefits [8]:

1. If a single specification can serve a number of products, its development cost can be amortized over those products

2. The development of several products from the same specification can lead to uniformity across those products as well as their development

3. Reusability in specification may lead to correspondingly reusable products

4. The fact that a specification can serve as a framework for several products may cause its developers to strive for particularly elegant abstractions. This in turn may lead to cleaner

definitions of the fundamental concepts behind related applications

5. The job of defining specifications for the framework may be delegated to a small team of highly skilled engineers

6. Libraries of formally specified software components that form the basic design repertoire of software developers may gradually be produced

The fact that formal specifications may be reused is also likely to encourage greater rigor in their derivation and documentation, as developers consciously consider that greater effort at this stage may in future result in faster and cheaper development with less effort.

Such factors are likely to increase the acceptability of formal methods in industrial development. In fact, while potential reuse might be a justification for the adoption of formal methods, it has been argued that reuse cannot exist without formal methods, as without a formal specification a program is neither adaptable nor portable, and thus not even *potentially* reusable [4].

Training for Professionals. Since the job of software developers is product oriented, they require a different kind of education than that typically taught by research institutions and computer science departments. The ideal approach for educating the practitioners is to develop a curriculum for a graduate professional degree (analogous to an MBA degree but perhaps with less course work). Such a curriculum would cover the necessary background for using formal methods (for example, discrete mathematics courses covering sets and logic) and would present a variety of principles, tools, and skills in applying formal methods during software development. Such a professional curriculum is, unfortunately, not very practical now but should be considered for the near future.

The professional degree is not the only approach. A good deal of knowledge of formal methods for software development can be found in professional workshops in industry and can be attained through apprenticeship. Typical workshops on formal methods present concepts and comparisons of various types of specifications for different software components (for example, data structures, files, single procedures, composite objects, and programs). Examples are developed and the relationships between formal specifications and other topics such as logic programming, program verification, and "clean-room development" are illustrated. We suggest the following hints for the information systems professional:

- Training in discrete mathematics covering elementary set theory and logic should be the first step. For those who have a mathematical background but are unfamiliar with the basic concepts of set theory and propositional logic 1 or at most 2 days suffice to introduce the ideas. For others 1 week of training is required

- Training in a particular formal method such as Z or VDM should be the next step. Such training typically takes 3 to 5 weeks, once the participant has the necessary mathematical background

- Tutoring and consultation in a real project is helpful, as is participation in workshops where one can study a problem and describe it formally with the help of a tutor

Tools for Students. A glance at the structure of most popular formal methods (for example, Z and VDM) will show that elementary set theory and mathematical logic are of prime importance in these systems and are heavily used in the context of software development. Students need to be familiar with these concepts and with how they provide a basis for precise definition of the entities we perceive in an information system. Both of these concepts are covered in *discrete mathematics* course. (It is called discrete mathematics to distinguish it from the continuous mathematics of real numbers that include differential and integral calculus.) Discrete mathematics is the study of calculations involving a finite number of steps and is the foundation for much of computing science. It focuses on the understanding of concepts and provides invaluable tools for thinking and problem solving. Discrete mathematics is especially important when a student is not required to study much of ancillary mathematics [16]. Students should be taught the skills for formalizing problems and behaviors and adjusting the level of rigor to fit software development processes. (In the United States, the Software Engineering Institute has initiated such teaching programs.)

Students learn more by active participation than just by observing. Theoretical concepts (such as discrete mathematics) should be reinforced with hands-on experience in laboratories. Since such courses should be taught early in college (to provide necessary background for high-level courses), educators must ensure that the students learn the concepts well. As is often the case, the students have difficulty with theoretical concepts that are described in books using definitions, theorems, and proofs. A tool that visualizes theoretical concepts and allows a student to experiment with these concepts creates a creative environment. Such a tool is helpful in solving various discrete math problems that would be tedious to work by hand. Freed from the mechanical aspects of these calculations, the students can focus their attention on the concepts that form the basis of the material being studied.

6. Conclusions

Formal methods are mathematically based techniques that can be used for rigorous modeling, analysis, specification, and design of information systems. This article discusses the role of formal methods in the context of an engineering paradigm and how they apply to information systems development. An introduction to the precise, concise, and unambiguous description of information systems using a formal method is provided. An example is given to illustrate the effectiveness of formal methods in describing an information system. The overall aim of the article is to introduce formal methods, address some misconceptions and concerns, and narrow the gap between the results of academia and the pragmatic concerns of the information systems industry.

We believe that methods can be particularly useful during the early stages of software engineering, and enable the software developer to discover and correct errors that otherwise might go undetected, increasing the quality of the software and its maintainability, while decreasing its failure rate as well as its maintenance costs. Although such ideas are the objectives of all software development methods, the use of formal methods results in a much higher likelihood of achieving them.

Acknowledgment

Collaborative research work with Mike Hinchey (for example, see Saiedian and Hinchey [18]) has influenced this article.

References

[1] B. Boehm, "Improving Software Engineering Production," *Computer*, Vol. 20, No. 9, Sept. 1987, pp. 43–58.

[2] J.P. Bowen and M.G. Hinchey, "Formal Methods and Safety-Critical Standards," *Computer*, Vol. 27, No. 8, Aug. 1994, pp. 68–71.

[3] J.P. Bowen and M.G. Hinchey, "Seven More Myths of Formal Methods," *IEEE Software*, Vol. 12, No. 4, July 1995, pp. 34–41.

[4] J.M. Boyle, "Abstract Programming and Program Transformation: An Approach to Reusing Programs," in T.J. Biggerstaff and A.J. Perlis, eds., *Software Reusability: Concepts and Models*, ACM Press, New York, N.Y., 1989.

[5] J.C. Cherniavsky "Software Failures Attract Congressional Attention," *Computer Research Rev.*, Vol. 2, No. 1, Jan. 1990, pp. 4–5.

[6] D. Craigen, S. Gerhart, and T. Ralston, "An International Survey of Industrial Applications of Formal Methods, Mar. 1993. NISTGCR 93/626, U.S. Department of Commerce.

[7] A. Diller, *Z: An Introduction to Formal Methods*, John Wiley, Chichester, UK, 2nd ed., 1994.

[8] D. Garlan and N. Delisle, "Formal Specifications as Reusable Frameworks," in *VDM '90,* LNCS 428, pp. 150–163. Springer-Verlag, 1990.

[9] A. Hall, "Seven Myths of Formal Methods, *IEEE* Software, Vol. 7, No. 5, Sept. 1990, pp. 11–19.

[10] M.G. Hinchey and J.P. Bowen, eds., *Applications of Formal Methods*, Prentice-Hall International, Englewood Cliffs, N.J., 1995.

[11] House of Representatives, "Bugs in the Program—Problems in Federal Government Computer Software Development and Regulation," Technical Report 052-070-06604-1, Subcommittee and Oversight of the House of Representatives Committee on Science, Space, and Technology, Superintendent of Documents; Government Printing Office, Washington, D.C., 20402, 1989.

[12] C.B. Jones, *Systematic Software Development using VDM*, Prentice-Hall International, Englewood Cliffs, N.J., 1990.

[13] B. Koen. "Definition of the Engineering Methods," *American Society for Engineering Education*, 1985.

[14] D.L. Parnas, "Using Mathematical Descriptions in the Inspection of Safety-Critical Software," in M.G. Hinchey and J.P. Bowen, eds., *Applications of Formal Methods*, Prentice-Hall International, Englewood Cliffs, N.J., 1995.

[15] National Academy Press, "Computer Science and Technology Board Report: Scaling Up: A Research Agenda for Software Engineering," *Comm. ACM,* Vol. 33, No. 3, Mar. 1990, pp. 281–293. Excerpted.

[16] H. Saiedian, "Mathematics of Computing," *Computer Science Education*, Vol. 3, No. 3, 1992, pp. 203–221.

[17] H. Saiedian, "An Invitation to Formal Methods," *Computer*, Vol. 29, No. 4, Mar. 1996, pp. 16–30. (This articles includes introduction to and commentaries by 15 researchers and practitioners to a virtual roundtable on formal methods.).

[18] H. Saiedian and M. Hinchey, "Challenges in the Successful Transfer of Formal Methods Technology into Industrial Applications," *Information and Software Technology*, Vol. 38, No. 5, May 1996, pp. 313–321.

[19] D. Weber-Wulff, "Selling Formal Methods to Industry," in *Formal Methods Europe '93*, LNCS 670, pp. 671–679. Springer-Verlag, 1993.

[20] J. Woodcock and M. Loomes, *Software Engineering Mathematics*, Addison-Wesley, Reading, Mass., 1989.

A Classification of CASE Technology

Alfonso Fuggetta, Politecnico di Milano and CEFRIEL

T he design, implementation, delivery, and maintenance of software are complex and expensive activities that need improvement and better control. Among the technologies proposed to achieve these goals is CASE (computer-aided software engineering): computerized applications supporting and partially automating software-production activities.[1] Hundreds of CASE products are commercially available, offering a wide spectrum of functionalities.

The evolution and proliferation of such tools has forced CASE researchers to address a new challenging topic: How can they develop more integrated and easier to use CASE tools? In response, they have conceived and introduced new products that extend traditional operating-system functionalities to provide more advanced services, such as sophisticated process-control mechanisms and enhanced database-management functionalities.

Another growing research area is the development of technologies to support formal definition and automation of the software process, the total set of activities, rules, methodologies, organizational structures, and tools used during software production. Developers generally agree it is not possible to identify an optimal, universal, and general-purpose process. Rather, each organization must design and evolve the process according to its own needs, market, and customers. To better manage and support software processes, researchers and practitioners need new means to describe and assess them. Moreover, the descriptions must be usable by a computerized tool to guide, control, and, whenever possible, automate software-process activities. This research has produced its first results, and several industrial products have appeared on the market.

The availability of a large number of products is contributing to the improvement and wide diffusion of software-engineering practice. However, this product proliferation is creating critical problems.

It is more difficult to assess the real capabilities and features of many products on the market, and to understand how they are related to each other functionally and technologically. The terminology is often confusing or misleading. For example, terms such as tool, workbench, toolset, and environment are given very different meanings and interpretations. It is difficult, therefore, to develop a clear and systematic classification of the available technology for effective assessment and acquisition.

The variety of CASE products available today is daunting. This survey provides a classification to help in assessing products ranging from tools and environments to enabling technology.

Reprinted from *Computer*, Vol. 26, No. 12, Dec. 1993, pp. 25–38.

Critical issues in classification schemes

The basic choices and purpose of the classification scheme for CASE technology I propose in this article can be criticized in many ways. First, the acronym CASE is associated with many different definitions often less general than the one I use here.

Sodhi, for example, proposes the following definition: "Computer-Aided Software Engineering (CASE) encompasses a collection of automated tools and methods that assist software engineering in the phases of the software development life cycle."[1] This definition takes into account only the production-process technology.

Next, Pressman defines CASE as follows: "The workshop for software engineering is called an integrated project support environment, and the toolset that fills the workshop is CASE."[2] The author also includes what he calls framework tools: products supporting infrastructure development. This definition extends the scope of CASE.

And Forte and McCulley define CASE this way: "We take CASE literally, that is, CASE is software engineering enhanced by automated tools (i.e. computer-aided). . . To us, it's all part of a coordinated approach to the design and production of systems and products containing software."[3]

Finally, Sommerville proposes a CASE definition similar to the one I present in this article: "Computer-aided software engineering is the term for software tool support for the software engineering process."[4] These examples show that the term CASE is assuming a wider meaning and becoming associated with the computer-aided support offered to the entire software process.

A second criticism is that the goal of this type of classification and its approaches are shallow. It is not easy to agree on the levels of abstraction of the reference framework used to classify CASE products, or on the products' assignments to the identified classes. Moreover, it is difficult to find the right focus to technically profile the different classes of products.

Nonetheless, the need for a conceptual framework and a classification of available technology is increasing. Practitioners and researchers need to assess and compare existing technology. Customers (software-production organizations) need to have a clear overview of the available technology and its potential benefits. Educators and consultants need a solid conceptual basis for their presentations of the state of the art in the field.

Pressman makes a significant observation on this issue:[2] "A number of risks are inherent whenever we attempt to categorize CASE tools. . . Confusion (or antagonism) can be created by placing a specific tool within one category when others might believe it belongs in another category. Some readers may feel that an entire category has been omitted — thereby eliminating an entire set of tools for inclusions in the overall CASE environment. In addition, simple categorization tends to be flat. . . But even with these risks, it is necessary to create a taxonomy of CASE tools — to better understand the breadth of CASE and to better appreciate where such tools can be applied in the software engineering process."

Pressman's words point to a particularly important problem that deserves some additional comments. An ideal classification should define an equivalence relation on the considered domain. Then it becomes possible to partition the domain in equivalent classes and assign each element in the domain to just one class. An entity's class precisely and unambiguously characterizes it for easy comparison and assessment.

Often, however, it is not possible to find such an equivalence relation, and an entity might span different classes. This risk is particularly real with CASE products. Their functionalities and characteristics are not standardized, so it may be quite difficult to assign a given product to a unique class. Nevertheless, an effective classification should aim at limiting these situations to retain its overall soundness and usefulness.

References

1. J. Sodhi, *Software Eng.: Methods, Management, and CASE Tools*, McGraw-Hill, Blue Ridge Summit, Pa., 1991.

2. R.S. Pressman, *Software Eng. — A Practitioner's Approach*, McGraw-Hill, New York, 1992.

3. *CASE Outlook: Guide to Products and Services*, G. Forte and K. McCulley, eds., CASE Consulting Group, Lake Oswego, Ore., 1991.

4. I. Sommerville, *Software Eng.*, Addison-Wesley, Reading, Mass., 1992.

In this article, I propose a classification with more precise definitions for these terms. To avoid any misunderstanding, I use the term "product" to identify any object in the classification.

Even the development of a precise classification can introduce additional conceptual and practical problems that make such efforts useless or even dangerous. The criteria must clarify the rationale, purposes, and limitations of the proposed approach. The level of abstraction must strike a balance between analysis and synthesis, and avoid the introduction of useless details or vague concepts.

My classification of products supporting the software process is based on a general framework derived from the work of Conradi et al.[2] Figure 1 shows the framework. The software process is decomposed in two subprocesses: a *production process* and a *metaprocess*.

The production process includes all activities, rules, methodologies, organizational structures, and tools used to conceive, design, develop, deliver, and maintain a software product. A production process must be defined, assessed, and evolved through a systematic and continuing metaprocess.

The purpose of the metaprocess is the acquisition and exploitation of new products supporting software-production activities and, more generally, the improvement and innovation of the procedures, rules, and technologies used to deliver the organization's artifacts. In the last decade, efforts aimed at understanding the metaprocess include those of the Software Engineering Institute, whose well-known Capability Maturity Model[3] defines five levels of process maturity and provides guidelines to progressively improve it.

The production process can be supported and partially automated by the *production-process technology* — aids to software developers to specify, build, and maintain a software product. In an organization, the specific technology and related procedures and guidelines used to support the production process are called *production-process support*.

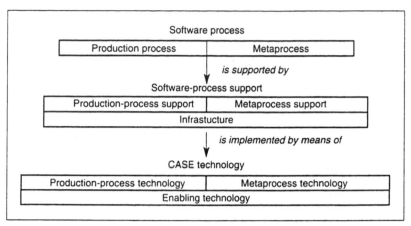

Figure 1. The general framework.

The metaprocess can be automated and supported as well with a *metaprocess technology* used to create the *metaprocess support* — the specific aids used in an organization's metaprocess to automate and guide metaprocess activities.

Related work

One of the first and most important classification attempts was that of Dart et al.,[1] who presented a taxonomy of the trends that have produced state-of-the-art software-development environments. They defined a software-development environment as "an environment that augments or automates *all* the activities comprising the software development cycle." The aim of their classification was to understand the evolution of the principles on which environments have been built.

The taxonomy identified four basic categories:

• *Language-centered environments* built around one language (for example, Interlisp, Smalltalk, or Rational). They are highly interactive, but offer limited support for programming in the large.

• *Structure-centered environments* incorporating the idea of environment generation (for example, Mentor, Cornell Program Synthesizer, and Gandalf). These environments let users directly manipulate the grammar of a programming language to produce structure-oriented tools, such as syntax-directed editors.

• *Toolkit environments* consisting of small tools intended primarily to support the coding phase (for example, Unix PWB and VMS VAX Set). They do not offer any control of the way the tools are applied.

• *Method-based environments* centered around specific methodologies for software development, such as structured analysis and design techniques or object-oriented design (for example, Excelerator, TAGS, and Software Through Pictures).

This pioneering article has several merits, but its scope is limited. It does not offer any finer grained classification of existing products, nor does it take into account the metaprocess and enabling technologies. Moreover, it tends to consider at the same level of abstraction entities that are quite different (for example, complete environments like Interlisp and Smalltalk, and more specialized products like Excelerator).

Forte and McCulley's more recent classification[2] introduces a *tool taxonomy* on two levels. (The term "tool" identifies any product considered in the Forte and McCulley classification.) At the first level, the taxonomy proposes the following classification domains to characterize a tool: application areas targeted by the tool, tasks supported in the development cycle, methods and notations, hardware platforms, operating systems, databases and transaction processing subsystems supported by the tool, network and communication protocols, and programming languages supported by the tool.

At the second level, the authors specify attributes for each domain. Figure A shows the description of the development-tasks domain. This scheme partitions the total set of CASE tools in two main classes: vertical and horizontal tools.

Vertical tools are used in a specific life-cycle phase or activity (for example, testing), while horizontal tools are used throughout the entire software process. The merit of this classification lies in the richness of the domains to characterize tools. Moreover, it is implemented in a tool called Tool Finder, which lets users retrieve product descriptions from an electronic archive.

Unfortunately, the classification does not take into account the conceptual architecture of the software process (as I discuss in the main text). It is not easy to classify tools according to the breadth of support offered to the production process. For instance, Forte and McCulley classify a compiler under the construction task, along with other more complex and sophisticated products (workbenches supporting coding, debugging, and incremental linking). They classify tool integration and process modeling in different horizontal tasks, but provide no hints for understanding their mutual dependencies or their relationships with other classes of products. Moreover, the division between vertical and horizontal tasks becomes unclear if we consider unconventional life cycles not based on the waterfall model.

Production-process and metaprocess supports are based on a common *infrastructure* that provides services and functionalities for their operation in an integrated and homogeneous environment. The infrastructure can be implemented using operating-system services and more advanced and recent products for, say, process control and database management. The products supporting infrastructure implementation are globally identified under the term *enabling technology*. The infrastructure, production-process support, and metaprocess support constitute the *software-process support*.

The classification I propose in this article considers all products in the production-process technology, metaprocess technology, and enabling technology. Globally, these products represent CASE technology.

Refining the reference framework

To refine the framework presented in the previous section, I further classify CASE products used in the production process according to the breadth of support they offer. A production process may be viewed as a set of elementary *tasks* to be accomplished to produce a software application. Examples of tasks are compiling, editing, and generating test cases from requirements specifications.

Tasks are grouped to form *activities*, sets of tasks supporting coarse-grained parts of the software-production process. For example, coding is an activity that includes editing, compiling, debugging, and so on. The activity concept is not to be confused with the phases of a waterfall life cycle. Activities are not necessarily carried out in strict sequence: They can be composed to form any type of life cycle.

According to these definitions, I classify CASE products in the production-process technology in three categories:

(1) *Tools* support only specific tasks in the software process.
(2) *Workbenches* support only one or a few activities.
(3) *Environments* support (a large part of) the software process.

Workbenches and environments are generally built as collections of tools. Tools can therefore be either standalone products or components of workbenches and environments. For exam-

---

Pressman's classification[3] is based on the identification of these different functions supported by CASE products: business systems planning, project management, support (documentation, database, configuration management, and so on), analysis and design, programming, integration and testing, prototyping, maintenance, and framework (support for environment development). Even in this case, however, little help is given for understanding the architecture of the software-process support. Moreover, Pressman does not take metaprocess technology into account.

In another important classification, Sommerville[4] defines CASE tools as the basic building blocks used to create a "software engineering environment." He classifies CASE tools according to the functions they offer and the process activities they support. CASE tools are integrated by an environment infrastructure. Integration can be achieved along four different dimensions: data integration (sharing of information), user-interface integration (common interface paradigms and mechanisms), control integration (mechanisms to control the invocation and execution of tools and applications), and process integration (integration in a defined process model). Environments are collections of tools classified in three different categories:

• *Programming environments* support programming activities, but provide limited support for software analysis and design.
• *CASE workbenches* provide support for analysis and design, but little support for coding and testing.
• *Software-engineering environments* comprise tools for all activities in the software process.

Sommerville proposes a reference framework with two levels of tool aggregations: *stand-alone tools* and *environments*.

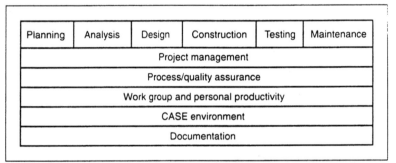

Planning	Analysis	Design	Construction	Testing	Maintenance
Project management					
Process/quality assurance					
Work group and personal productivity					
CASE environment					
Documentation					

Figure A. Development tasks in Forte and McCulley's classification.[2]

Moreover, he relates important concepts such as process integration and environment infrastructure. The classification I present in this article inherits several of these concepts and further refines the idea of a layered classification scheme.

A different type of effort is represented by the *Reference Model for Frameworks of Software Engineering Environments*, jointly developed by the European Computer Manufacturers Association (ECMA) and the National Institute of Standards and Technology.[5,6] This reference model "is a conceptual and functional basis for describing and comparing existing SEEs or SEE components."[6] (SEE stands for software-engineering environment.) Thus, it is not a classification of CASE technology, but it is important because it defines the framework for constructing, operating, and evolving a software-engineering environment. The framework is a set of interrelated services for object management, process management, user interfaces, communication, tools, policy enforcement, framework administration, and configuration.

A software-engineering environment in the ECMA model is similar to the software-process support presented in the main text. The ECMA model's goals and scope, however, are quite different: It is oriented more to the definition of the ideal func-

ple, most computer manufacturers sell tools such as compilers as stand-alone products.[1] They may also integrate compilers with other tools to support both coding and debugging. (In this section, I use "integrate" in its informal and intuitive sense.) In general, these products also include a debugger, an editor, and an incremental linker. Compilers are also very often marketed as standard components of environments (for example, the C compiler in the Unix PWB environment). Some kinds of tools are seldom available as stand-alone products. For example, graphical editors for dataflow or SADT (structured analysis and design technique) diagrams are usually embedded in products also offering other components to support analysis and design.

The distinction among tools, work-benches, and environments further extends Sommerville's classification,[4] which includes only two levels of granularity: tools and environments. Fernström, Närfelt, and Ohlsson[5] advocate a different approach based on four levels of granularity: service, tool, toolset, and environment. In their classification, the term "toolset" is equivalent to workbench, while "service" identifies an operation embedded in a tool.

Production-process support may be built by adopting and integrating one or more tools, workbenches, and environments. In general, it is composed of an environment, which acts as the "backbone." It can be further extended by introducing additional tools and workbenches to fully cover the production process. (All products mentioned in this article are examples. No evaluation is associated with their citation. Readers should refer to specialized publications[1] for a complete presentation of existing products.)

Tools

A CASE tool is a software component supporting a specific task in the software-production process. Table 1 classifies such tools.

Editing tools. Editing tools (editors) can be classified in two subclasses: *textual editors* and *graphical editors*. The first subclass includes traditional text editors and word processors used to produce textual documents such as programs, textual specifications, and documentation. Editors in the second subclass are used to produce documents

---

tionalities to be offered by the infrastructure, so it does not discuss in much detail the characteristics of CASE technology. Also, it does not present a detailed classification of tools (in the ECMA terminology) and does not evaluate the different philosophies adopted by existing environments.

ECMA concepts can be easily recognized in the classification I propose in this article. My infrastructure takes into account all the ECMA services, except for process-management services, which I consider as a separate entity in the production-process and metaprocess supports.

Perry and Kaiser's more general approach[7] for analyzing software-development environments is based on a general model consisting of three components: structures, mechanisms, and policies. Structures are the objects on which mechanisms operate. Mechanisms are the basic functionalities offered by tools. Policies are the procedures, rules, and guidelines offered to and imposed on software developers by environments. An environment can be described by specifying these three components. Classes of environments can be identified by considering analogies and commonalities. For example, toolkit environments[1] can be described by the following model:

Toolkit environment =
(
    {file system/object-management system},
    {assorted construction tools},
    {laissez-faire}
)

To describe the problems of scale in software production, the authors introduce a metaphor that distinguishes four different classes of environments: individual, family, city, and state. Environments in the individual class emphasize software-construction activities and are dominated by mechanisms. Family-class environments address coordination and are dominated by structures. The city class emphasizes co-operation among software developers and is dominated by policies. Finally, environments in the state class address the commonality issue and are dominated by higher order policies.

This classification identifies the components useful in evaluating a software-development environment. Moreover, the metaphor characterizes the different problems that software-development projects must address when scaling up. The model is less useful when applied to classifying the large variety of commercial products, since it considers only environments and does not provide any categorizations for other types of products.

In conclusion, even if the classifications available so far have substantially contributed to the state of the art, they are still incomplete. Much work is needed to provide an effective and comprehensive reference framework and the related classification scheme.

References

1. S.A. Dart et al.. "Software Development Environments," *Computer*, Vol. 20, No. 11, Nov. 1987, pp. 18-28.

2. *CASE Outlook: Guide to Products and Services.* G. Forte and K. McCulley, eds., CASE Consulting Group, Lake Oswego, Ore., 1991.

3. R.S. Pressman, *Software Eng. — A Practitioner's Approach*, McGraw-Hill. New York, 1992.

4. I. Sommerville. *Software Eng.*, Addison-Wesley. Reading, Mass., 1992.

5. "Reference Model for Frameworks of Software Engineering Environments," jointly published as ECMA Tech. Report TR/55, European Computer Manufacturers Assoc., Geneva, and NIST Special Publication 500-201, Nat'l Inst. of Standards and Technology, Gaithersburg, Md., 1991.

6. M. Chen and R.J. Norman, "A Framework for Integrated CASE," *IEEE Software*, Vol. 9, No. 2, Mar. 1992, pp. 18-22.

7. D.E. Perry and G.E. Kaiser, "Models of Software Development Environments." *IEEE Trans. Software Eng.*, Vol. 17, No. 3, Mar. 1991, pp. 283-295.

using graphical symbols. Typical examples are general drawing and painting tools (such as MacDraw), tools to enter graphical specifications (for example, those based on dataflow diagrams), and tools to paint the forms and layouts constituting an application's user interface.

Examples of textual and graphical editors are Pmate, a text editor for professional programmers running on MS-DOS personal computers; MacBubbles, a Macintosh-based editing tool for Yourdon-DeMarco diagrams; and DV Draw, an editor that creates several types of graphical output.

Syntax-directed editors are an important category of textual editor. Two examples are Key-one and DEC LSE — Language Sensitive Editor.

Programming tools. These tools are used to support coding and code restructuring. The three main subclasses are *coding and debugging tools*, *code generators*, and *code restructurers*.

The first subclass includes traditional tools used to compile, run, and debug a program. Examples are the numerous traditional compilers and interpreters available on the market, interactive tester/debuggers such as Via/Smartest, and cross-compilers such as HP Cross Compilers, a family of Unix-based C cross-compilers.

The second class includes tools that generate code starting from a high-level description of the application. Typical examples are compiler generators and Cobol generators. Compiler generators (for example, yacc/lex) automatically build lexical analyzers and parsers starting from the formal description of the language syntax. Cobol generators produce Cobol starting from a high-level program description (for example, the VAX Cobol Generator).

The third subclass includes tools used to restructure existing programs. These tools can analyze, reformat, and in some cases improve existing source code by performing actions such as elimination of "gotos" and unreachable portions of code. Examples of such tools are AdaReformat and Via/Renaissance.

Verification and validation tools. This class includes tools that support program validation and verification. Validation aims at ensuring that the product's functions are what the customer really wants, while verification aims at ensuring that the product under construction meets the requirements definition. This class has many subclasses:[6]

- *Static and dynamic analyzers* analyze a computer program without executing the program (static) or by monitoring program execution (dynamic).
- *Comparators* equate two files to identify commonalities or differences. Typically, they are used to compare test results with the expected program outputs.
- *Symbolic executors* simulate program execution using symbols rather than actual values for input data and produce outputs expressed as symbolic expressions.
- *Emulators/simulators* imitate all or part of a computer system. They accept the same data, provide the same functionalities, and achieve the same results as the imitated system.
- *Correctness proof assistants* support formal techniques to prove mathematically that a program satisfies its specifications or that a specification satisfies given properties.
- *Test-case generators* take as input a computer program and a selection of test criteria, and generate test input data that meet these criteria.
- *Test-management tools* support testing by managing test results, test checklists, regression tests, test coverage metrics, and so on.

Examples of such tools are AdaXRef, a cross-reference generator; Q/Auditor, a standards enforcer; lint-Plus, a syntax checker; Instrumentation Tool, a program instrumentor; CICS Simulcast, an execution tracer; Playback, a test-result comparator; and HP Basic Branch Analyzer, a test-coverage tool. (See the detailed classification scheme in Table 1.)

Configuration-management tools. Configuration-management techniques coordinate and control the construction of a system composed of many parts.[7] Software development and management can greatly benefit from configuration

Table 1. Classes of CASE tools.

Class	Subclass
Editing	Graphical editors
	Textual editors
Programming	Coding and debugging
	• Assemblers
	• Compilers
	• Cross-assemblers
	• Cross-compilers
	• Debuggers
	• Interpreters
	• Linkage editors
	• Precompilers/preprocessors
	Code generators
	• Compiler generators
	Code restructurers
Verification and validation	Static analyzers
	• Cross-reference generators
	• Flowcharters
	• Standards enforcers
	• Syntax checkers
	Dynamic analyzers
	• Program instrumentors
	• Tracers/profilers
	Comparators
	Symbolic executors
	Emulators/simulators
	Correctness proof assistants
	Test-case generators
	Test-management tools
Configuration management	Configuration- and version-management tools
	Configuration builders
	Change-control monitors
	Librarians
Metrics and measurement	Code analyzers
	Execution monitors/timing analyzers
Project management	Cost-estimation tools
	Project-planning tools
	Conference desks
	E-mail
	Bulletin boards
	Project agendas
	Project notebooks
Miscellaneous tools	Hypertext systems
	Spreadsheets

management, which can be decomposed into the following tasks:

- *Version management.* During software development, more than one version of each software item is produced. Versions must be managed so subsequent work incorporates the correct version.
- *Item identification.* Each software item must be unambiguously identifiable. Software-process agents (all people working in the software process) must be able to retrieve specific software items to build and rebuild coherent configurations of the product under development.
- *Configuration building.* A software product is a complex collection of versioned software items. Building a product requires invocation of operations such as preprocessing, compiling, and linking on a possibly large set of software items.
- *Change control.* Changes to a software item may have an impact on other components. Moreover, if several programmers can access the same software items, control is necessary to synchronize their activity to prevent the creation of inconsistent or erroneous versions of software items.
- *Library management.* All the software items relevant in a software process must be subject to effective storage and retrieval policies.

Products that support specific configuration-management tasks — such as configuration building (for example, make, MMS, and Pmaker), version management (SCCS and CMS), and library management (Plib86) — do not offer comprehensive and integrated support to all tasks. Most configuration-management tools in this classification constitute the first generation. The second generation of configuration-management products offers much wider support by integrating into a single product most functionalities offered by the individual tools considered here.

Metrics and measurement tools. Tools that collect data on programs and program execution fall into two subclasses:

- tools to analyze the source code and compute several source-code metrics (for example, to evaluate code complexity according to Halstead's or McCabe's metrics), and
- tools to monitor the execution of programs and collect runtime statistics.

Examples of such tools are Performance Architek and HP Apollo DPAK.

Project-management tools. Several types of products support project management. A first subclass includes products used to estimate software-production costs. These tools typically implement techniques such as Cocomo (Constructive cost model) or function points, and provide user-friendly interfaces to specify project information and analyze estimation results.

A second subclass comprises tools supporting project planning — that is, project scheduling, resource assignment, and project tracking. These tools are based on well-known concepts and notations such as WBS (work breakdown structure), Gantt, and PERT (program evaluation and review technique) charts.

A third subclass includes tools to support communication and coordination among project team members. Some permit on-line and deferred interaction among people — for example, teleconferencing systems (also called conference desks), e-mail systems, and electronic bulletin boards. Other tools are project agendas used to coordinate activities and meetings.

Examples of these tools are CA-Estimacs (cost estimation), MacProject (project planning), VAX Notes (conference desk), and DateBook (distributed agenda).

Miscellaneous tools. Products difficult to classify include spreadsheets and hypertext systems.

A spreadsheet can be used as a project-management tool to perform what-if analysis or to develop models of the development process (for example, by implementing the Cocomo model). Spreadsheets can also be used for programming. Several applications have been developed using spreadsheet languages, particularly in business administration and marketing. These applications are marketed as add-ons to standard products such as Excel. For example, Computerized Classic Accounting is an integrated accounting system developed for the Macintosh version of Excel.

Hypertext systems can replace desktop publishing systems for authoring advanced documentation. They can also be used as programming tools to develop prototypes or even final applications. Many applications for the Macintosh have been developed using HyperCard — for example, Client, a personal data manager, and MindLink, an idea processor.

Integration in CASE products

The need for integration in CASE technology is increasingly acknowledged by researchers and practitioners.[1] According to Thomas and Nejmeh, integration can be analyzed in four dimensions:[2]

- *Data integration* ensures that all the information in the environment is managed as a consistent whole, regardless of how parts of it are operated on and transformed.
- *Control integration* permits the flexible combination of an environment's functions according to project preferences and the underlying processes and environment supports.
- *Presentation integration* improves user interaction with the environment by reducing users' cognitive load.

- *Process integration* ensures that tools interact effectively in support of a defined process.

We can identify several levels of integration according to the degree of technology exploitation along these four dimensions. For example, Brown and McDermid define five levels of integration, focusing on functionalities and features that support data and control integration.[3]

References

1. *IEEE Software* special issue on integrated CASE, Vol. 9, No. 2, Mar. 1992.
2. I. Thomas and B.A. Nejmeh, "Definition of Tool Integration for Environments," *IEEE Software*, Vol. 9, No. 2, Mar. 1992, pp. 29-35.
3. A.W. Brown and J.A. McDermid, "Learning from IPSE's Mistakes," *IEEE Software*, Vol. 9, No. 2, Mar. 1992, pp. 23-28.

Workbenches

Workbenches integrate in a single application several tools supporting specific software-process activities. Hence, they achieve

- a homogeneous and consistent interface (presentation integration),
- easy invocation of tools and tool chains (control integration), and
- access to a common data set, managed in a centralized way (data integration).

Some products can enforce predefined procedures and policies within the workbench (process integration).

Table 2 shows eight classes of workbenches.

Business planning and modeling workbenches. This class includes products to support the identification and description of a complex business. They are used to build high-level enterprise models to assess the general requirements and information flows, and identify priorities in the development of information systems.

The tools integrated in such products include graphical editors (to provide diagrams and structured charts), report generators, and cross-reference generators. For example, PC Prism integrates tools to create enterprise models and automatically generate documentation from the information stored in its repository.

The borderline between this class of products and analysis and design workbenches is often quite fuzzy.

Analysis and design workbenches. Products for analysis and design activities constitute an important class of workbenches. In fact, very often the term CASE is used to denote just this class of products. Since the term CASE has a wider meaning, "upper" CASE is more properly used to denote this class of tools, which are used in the early stages of the software process. Today's upper CASE workbenches automate most of the analysis and design methodologies developed in the past decades such as SA/SD (structured analysis/structured design), object-oriented analysis and design, and Jackson System Development.

An upper CASE workbench usually includes one or more editors to create and modify specifications, and other tools to analyze, simulate, and transform them. For example, Excelerator has editors to create dataflow diagrams, structure charts, and entity-relationship diagrams. It also includes an editor and a simulator to create and test mock-ups of system inputs and outputs (forms and reports), as well as a code generator to produce skeletal Cobol source code starting from structure charts. Software Through Pictures includes several graphical editors to support the creation, for example, of control-flow diagrams, process-activation tables, and state-transition diagrams. It also includes code- and documentation-generation facilities.

The functionalities these workbenches offer depend heavily on the notations on which they are centered: If the adopted notation is not formally defined, a workbench can provide only editing and document-production facilities. Using a formal notation permits a higher degree of automation.

Table 3 shows a further classification of this class of workbenches according to level of formality, supported application, and activities covered.

Level of formality. Analysis and design workbenches support notations at different levels of formality:

- *Informal.* Structured English and other informal, textual notations, whose syntax and semantics are not formally defined.
- *Semiformal.* Notations for which it is possible to build syntax checkers. Such notations still lack a precise semantics. Dataflow diagrams are a typical example.
- *Formal.* Notations whose syntax and semantics are formally defined. Finite-state machines, Petri nets, and Statecharts are examples.

Supported applications. No notation can universally support the specification of all types of applications. In each project, the software engineer must be allowed to choose the most suitable notation — or combination of notations.

For assessment and selection, notations fall in two main categories:

(1) notations for data-intensive applications, such as banking or accounting systems (for example, dataflow and entity-relationship diagrams), and

Table 2. Classes of CASE workbenches.

Class	Sample Products
Business planning and modeling	PC Prism
Analysis and design	Excelerator Statemate Software Through Pictures
User-interface development	HP Interface Architect DEC VUIT
Programming	CodeCenter
Verification and validation	Battlemap Logiscope
Maintenance and reverse engineering	Recoder Rigi Hindsight SmartSystem
Configuration management	PCMS CCC SCLM DSEE
Project management	Coordinator DEC Plan Synchronize

Table 3. A sampling of "upper" CASE workbenches.

Sample Products	Examples of Notations Supported	Level of Formality	Class of Applications Supported	Activities Covered
Excelerator	Dataflow diagrams Entity-relationship diagrams	Semiformal	General purpose	Both
Teamwork	Dataflow diagrams Ward and Mellor	Semiformal	General purpose	Both
Statemate	Statecharts	Formal	Control intensive	Both
TAGS	Input/Output Requirements Language	Formal	Control intensive	Both
ASA	Integrated System Definition Language Finite State Machine	Formal	Control intensive	Analysis
GEODE	Specification Description Language	Formal	Control intensive	Design
ER-Designer	Entity-relationship diagrams	Semiformal	Data intensive	Both
IEW	Dataflow diagrams Entity-relationship diagrams	Semiformal	General purpose	Both
STP	Dataflow diagrams Object-oriented structured design	Formal and semiformal	General purpose	Both

(2) notations for control-intensive applications, such as avionics and control systems (for example, finite-state machines, Statecharts, and Petri nets).

According to this distinction, analysis and design workbenches can be grouped in three subclasses:

- workbenches for data-intensive applications (for example, Excelerator),
- workbenches for control-intensive applications (for example, Statemate), and
- general-purpose workbenches — products that support notations for both types of applications (for example, Teamwork).

Activities covered. I call these products analysis and design workbenches because most cover both activities. However, some cover only one. Thus, I classify analysis and design workbenches as analysis only, design only, or both.

User-interface-development workbenches. This class of CASE workbenches is distinct from the others already presented. Its products do not help with specific software-process activities but rather with user-interface design and development.

Many authors have suggested that the user interface is the most critical part of some programs. Kay has even argued that in many cases the user interface *is* the program.[8] Effective support for user-interface design and development is important.

The products in this class exploit the capabilities of modern workstations and graphical environments such as Motif or Windows. They let the developer easily create and test user-interface components and integrate them with the application program.

Typically, a user-interface workbench offers

- graphical editors to paint windows, dialog boxes, icons, and other user-interface components;
- simulators to test the developed in-

terface before integrating it with the application;
- code generators to produce the code to be integrated with the application; and
- runtime libraries to support the generation of executable code.

Examples are DEC VUIT and HP Interface Architect, both developed for the Motif standard interface.

Programming workbenches. The workbenches in this class evolved from the basic programming tools and provide integrated facilities supporting programming:

- a text editor to create and modify the source code,
- a compiler and linker to create the executable code, and
- a debugger.

For effective user interaction with the different tools, programming workbenches provide an integrated and consistent interface, and manage all information created during work sessions (source-code files, intermediate files, object- and executable-code files, and so on). Often, the workbench integrates the compiler with an interpreter or an incremental linker to speed the transition from editing to testing.

Examples of programming workbenches are Turbo C++, Turbo Pascal, and CodeCenter.

Verification and validation workbenches. This class of workbenches includes products that help with module and system testing. Products in this class often integrate several tools from both the metrics and measurement class and the verification and validation class. The functionalities offered by both classes jointly analyze the quality of code and support actual verification and validation.

A typical verification and validation workbench includes

- static analyzers to evaluate complexity metrics and call and control graphs,
- cross-reference and report generators,
- a tool to instrument a program and a tracer to support dynamic analysis, and
- a test-case generator and a test-management tool to produce, store, and manage test data, test results, and checklists.

Act and Logiscope are typical products.

Maintenance and reverse-engineering workbenches. In the past, software engineers often assumed that maintenance had only to do with fixing bugs. This approach proved inadequate for evolving software according to changes in the supported business environment, changes in the available technology, and new requirements from the customer. Now maintenance must be a component of the "forward" development process.

For maintenance, software engineers use the same tools and workbenches they normally use for development. They have to modify requirement specifications, designs, and application source code. They have to repeat the testing procedure to verify that the new version of the application can be released into service. And, with appropriate configuration-management techniques, they

have to manage the artifacts of the process (documents, source code, makefiles, and so on).

Even if most maintenance is performed with the same techniques and products used during software development, some more specific tasks must be approached with ad hoc techniques and tools — in particular, techniques identified as *reverse engineering*. Müller et al. describe this discipline as "the process of extracting system abstraction and design information out of existing software systems."[9]

This goal has not been completely fulfilled. Perhaps it will be impossible to fully achieve the automatic derivation of analysis and design information from code. Such an operation requires higher level information to be synthesized from low-level descriptions (the program statements), and it appears that this can be done only by humans with knowledge of the application.

Several available maintenance and reverse-engineering workbenches provide interesting and seemingly effective features. An example is Recoder, one of the first commercial reverse-engineering workbenches. It includes a code restructurer, a flowcharter, and a cross-reference generator. It analyzes unstructured and hard-to-read Cobol programs and produces new, more readable and modifiable versions. Rigi, another reverse-engineering workbench, can build a program's call graph and suggest possible clustering techniques to achieve strong cohesion and low coupling.

Other sample workbenches in this class are Ensemble and Hindsight.

Configuration-management workbenches. The workbenches in this class integrate tools supporting version control, configuration building, and change control. For example, the HP Apollo DSEE workbench integrates a history manager to store versions of source elements, a configuration manager to define and build configurations, and a task manager and monitor manager to control the process of changing a software item. Thus, the single product integrates and substantially extends most features offered by tools such as make, SCCS, and RCS.

A few products in this class also offer more advanced functionalities to support process modeling. For example, software-process managers can tailor

PCMS according to policies and roles they specify. Policies and roles are described through the possible states of a software item and the operations applied to them to change their state.

Other examples of configuration-management workbenches are CCC and SCLM.

Project-management workbenches. There are very few products in this class. Most potential candidates address only specific project-management tasks, and it seems more appropriate to classify them as tools.

Coordinator integrates several project-management functionalities based on an extended theoretical study of how people operate in a structured and complex organization. It lets development team members create typed messages — that is, messages with a precise meaning. requiring a specific action of the addressee (for example, requests for information or submissions of a proposal for approval). Also, Coordinator keeps track of

- the activities a person has to complete,
- temporal relations among significant actions to be completed by the organization. and
- actions that must be scheduled periodically during the project lifetime.

Other examples of project-management workbenches are Synchronize and DEC Plan. Synchronize includes several tools such as a distributed agenda, memo-distribution facilities. distributed to-do lists, and a meeting scheduler. DEC Plan offers functionalities similar to Synchronize. and also addresses project-planning and task-assignment problems.

Environments

An environment is a collection of tools and workbenches that support the software process. Some of the names I use to identify the different classes in Table 4 come from existing terminology — for example, "toolkit and "language-centered environments."[10]

Toolkits. Toolkits are loosely integrated collections of products easily extended by aggregating different tools

Table 4. Classes of CASE environments.

Class	Sample Products
Toolkits	Unix Programmer's Work Bench
Language-centered	Interlisp Smalltalk Rational KEE
Integrated	IBM AD/Cycle DEC Cohesion
Fourth generation	Informix 4GL Focus
Process-centered	East Enterprise II Process Wise Process Weaver Arcadia

and workbenches. Unlike workbenches, toolkits support different activities in the software-production process, but their support is very often limited to programming, configuration management, and project management (and project-management support is generally limited to message handling). Typically, toolkits are environments extended from basic sets of operating-system tools; the Unix Programmer's Work Bench and the VMS VAX Set are two examples.

Toolkits' loose integration requires users to activate tools by explicit invocation or simple control mechanisms such as redirection and pipes in Unix. The shared files users access for data exchange are very often unstructured or in formats that need explicit conversion so different tools can access them (via import and export operations). Because the only constraint for adding a new component is the formats of the files read or created by other tools or workbenches, toolkits can be easily and incrementally extended.

Toolkits do not impose any particular constraint on the process that users follow. Users interact through a general-purpose interface (for example, the shell or the command-language interpreter) that leaves them free to decide which procedures or operations to activate.

Language-centered environments. Examples of environments centered around a specific language are Interlisp, Smalltalk, Rational, and KEE, developed respectively for Lisp, Smalltalk (the language and the environment have the same name), Ada, and Lisp again.[11]

The peculiarity of this class of products is that very often the environment itself is written in the language for which it was developed, thus letting users customize and extend the environment and reuse part of it in the applications under development. The main drawback is that integrating code in different languages may not be feasible. Smalltalk is an environment that suffers from this problem. These environments can hardly be extended to support different programming languages, and they are often concentrated on the edit-compile-debug cycle, with little or no support for large-scale software development.

Language-centered environments offer a good level of presentation and control integration: Users are presented with a consistent interface and are given several mechanisms supporting automatic tool invocation and switching among tools (for example, among the editor, compiler, and debugger). However, these environments suffer from a lack of process and data integration. They are based on structured internal representations (usually abstract trees), but these mechanisms are invisible or hard for users to access for extending or customizing the environment with other products.

Integrated environments. The environments in this class are called "integrated" because, with some limitations, they operate using standard mechanisms so users can integrate tools and workbenches. These environments achieve presentation integration by providing uniform, consistent, and coherent tool and workbench interfaces: All products in the environment are operated through a unique interface concept. They achieve data integration through the *repository* concept: They have a specialized database managing all information produced and accessed in the environment.

The database is structured according to a high-level model of the environment, so users can develop tools and workbenches that access and exchange structured information instead of pure byte streams. This greatly enhances the functionalities and level of integration

offered to the user. Control integration is achieved through powerful mechanisms to invoke tools and workbenches from within other components of the environment.

Such mechanisms can also encapsulate[12] a tool not written to make use of any of the environment framework services. They surround the tool with software that acts as a layer between the tool and the framework. Integrated environments do not explicitly tackle process integration. This distinguishes them from the process-centered environments discussed later.

The infrastructure needed to create an integrated environment is generally more sophisticated than traditional operating-system services. Later, I discuss *integrating platforms* — extensions to operating-system services that provide the tool builder with advanced features.

The DEC Cohesion and IBM AD/Cycle integrated environments provide basic tools and workbenches, and an integrating platform that lets other companies enrich the environment with additional products. For example, DEC Cohesion is based on an integrating platform offering tool encapsulation, a repository, and user-interface-management and tool-integration facilities (ACA Services, CDD Repository, and DEC Fuse). It includes several tools and workbenches to support production-process activities (DEC Set, DEC VUIT, DEC Plan, and DEC Design), and it can be extended with third-party products.

Fourth-generation environments. Fourth-generation environments were precursors to and, in a sense, are a subclass of integrated environments. They are sets of tools and workbenches supporting the development of a specific class of program: electronic data processing and business-oriented applications. At least four characteristics distinguish these applications:

(1) The application's operations are usually quite simple, while the structure of the information to be manipulated is rather complex.

(2) The user interface is critical. Typically, it is composed of many forms and layouts used to input, display, and modify the information stored in the database.

(3) The application requirements are very often not clearly defined and can be

detailed only through the development of prototypes (very often, mock-ups of the user interface).

(4) The software process to produce such applications is generally evolutionary.

Fourth-generation environments were the first integrated environments. In general, they include an editor, an interpreter and/or a compiler for a specialized language, a debugger, database access facilities, a form editor, a simulator, simple configuration-management tools, document-handling facilities, and, in some cases, a code generator to produce programs in traditional languages such as Cobol. Often, these components are integrated through a consistent interface, data are stored in a central, proprietary repository, and built-in triggers activate tools when specific events occur in the environment.

However, fourth-generation environments provide a low degree of process integration, and ad hoc nonstandard mechanisms support the other dimensions of integration. In many cases, for example, programs and other application-related information are stored in proprietary databases. This makes it difficult (or even impossible) for other manufacturers to extend the environment with new products and components. To overcome this problem, most of these environments are migrating to standard platforms for evolution into true integrated environments.

I defined these products as "fourth-generation environments" instead of the more traditional "fourth-generation languages" to emphasize that they are more than compilers or interpreters for specific languages: They are collections of tools to manage the design, development, and maintenance of large electronic data processing applications.

Table 5 presents a more detailed division of fourth-generation environments into three classes. *Production systems* are oriented to the development of banking or accounting systems with strong performance requirements. These environments replace traditional Cobol-based environments and fall into two subclasses: *language-based systems* and *Cobol generators.* The former are based on a language that is directly compiled

Table 5. Fourth-generation environments.

Class	Sample Products
Production systems	
• Language-based systems	Natural 2
	Informix
	4GL/OnLine
• Cobol generators	Pacbase
	Transform
Infocenter systems	Focus
	Ramis
End-user systems	Filemaker

or interpreted. The latter are products that start with a high-level description of the application and generate Cobol source code for new applications to integrate with existing ones. Natural 2 is a language-based system; Pacbase is a Cobol generator.

Infocenter systems support the infocenter department of an organization in extracting and manipulating the information managed by the main electronic data processing application. To ensure high performance, the main system is usually developed using a production system. Typically, infocenter systems do not provide the same level of performance, but offer more flexible facilities to produce, say, nonstandard reports for management, based on the information stored in the main database. A typical example in this class is Ramis.

End-user systems support end users in directly defining their database and access functionalities. They provide predefined functions and forms that users customize easily through interactive facilities, without writing traditional programs. Many products developed for the Macintosh and MS-DOS personal computers can be included in this class. A typical example is Filemaker Pro (running on the Macintosh).

Process-centered environments. A process-centered environment is based on a formal definition of the software process. A computerized application called a *process driver* or *process engine* uses this definition to guide development activities by automating process fragments, automatically invoking tools and workbenches, enforcing specific policies, and assisting programmers, analysts, and project managers in their

work.[13] Thus, these environments focus on process integration. This does not mean they do not address other integration dimensions. Rather, other integration issues are the starting points for process integration.

A process engineer or process modeler (that is, someone who can analyze a process and describe it formally) produces the formal definition of the production process (called the *process model*), using specialized tools with functionalities to define, analyze, and manage it. Thus a process-centered environment operates by interpreting a process model created by specialized tools. Several research prototypes and even products on the market support both the creation and the execution of a process model. These products are therefore *environment generators*, since they can create different, customized environments that follow the procedures and policies enforced by the process model.

Process-centered environments are usually composed of parts to handle two functions:

• *Process-model execution.* The process driver interprets and executes a specific process model to operate the process-centered environment and make it available to software developers.
• *Process-model production.* Process modelers use tools to create or evolve process models.

Because of their process-model-execution function, I classify such products in Table 5 as process-centered environments, concerned with production-process technology. However, their process-model-production capabilities also qualify them as metaprocess technology.

Examples of products and research prototypes are East, Enterprise II, Process Weaver, Arcadia, Process Wise, EPOS, HPSF, Merlin, Marvel, and SPADE/S Lang (Software Process Analysis Design and Enactment/SPADE Language), whose functionalities I discuss in the later section on metaprocess technology. (EPOS, a project at Norges Teckniske Hogskole (NTH) in Trondheim, Norway, is not to be confused with an existing CASE product with the same name.)

Metaprocess and enabling technologies

The metaprocess and enabling technologies are important in developing effective software-process support. Metaprocess-technology products let a process manager create, operate, and improve production-process support. Enabling technology provides the basic mechanisms to integrate the different products in both the production-process and the metaprocess technologies.

Metaprocess technology. Toward the beginning of this article, I defined the metaprocess as the set of activities, procedures, roles, and computerized aids used to create, maintain, and further improve the production process. The metaprocess is similar to the software processes. Process managers must conceive, design, verify, use, assess, and maintain a production process (the output of the metaprocess).

To achieve these goals, process managers may be able to use traditional production-process technology — in particular, analysis and design workbenches. For instance, they can create and maintain a process model using Statecharts with the support of Statemate.[14] In this way, however, it is possible to achieve only a quite limited goal: A process model created through traditional CASE products such as Statemate can be used only as a vehicle to communicate process rules and procedures, or to document and assess the existing practice. It cannot automatically generate more advanced environments and production-process supports.

Researchers have tried to develop technologies and methodologies to provide these advanced process supports. The first results were the structure-centered environment generators[10] (for example, Gandalf and the Cornell Program Synthesizer). These metaenvironments can produce a set of tools starting from a formal description of the grammar of the language to be supported. Their initial aim was to produce a syntax-directed editor, but their scope has been progressively augmented to support more production-process tasks. These products are therefore environment generators, classified as metaprocess technology.

Recent work on process-centered environments and process modeling (discussed previously) has produced many research prototypes and a few commercial products,[15,16] whose goals I summarize:

- *Process modeling.* The development of notations to describe rules, activities, organizational structures, procedures, deliverables, and CASE products that constitute (or are used in) a software process, and the development of tools to validate and simulate the resulting model.
- *Process instantiation and enactment.* The development of runtime monitors and interpreters to execute or enact a software-process model — that is, to provide guidance to the people, tools, and workbenches involved in the process — and, whenever possible, to automate software-process activities. The resulting support to the production process is called a process-centered environment.
- *Process evolution.* Development of tools to support process-model evolution during the process lifetime.

The results of this research are encouraging, but several problems such as the process-model evolution have not yet been effectively solved. Nevertheless, some commercial products are available and, most important, the industrial community is becoming increasingly aware of the relevance of metaprocess technology.

Enabling technologies. Developing the complex products described in the previous sections requires services more sophisticated than the basic file-system-management and process-control mechanisms traditionally provided by operating systems. CASE products need functionalities such as advanced database-management systems to create and manage the repository, and sophisticated user-interface-management systems to design and develop graphical, easy-to-learn user interfaces for tools and workbenches.

To tackle these problems systematically and effectively, several industries and computer manufacturers are developing a new class of products that provide standard extensions to traditional operating systems (especially Unix). Built on top of the operating system, these products provide the tool developer with runtime libraries implementing several advanced features. Typical examples of this class are the already-mentioned DEC Cohesion Platform, HP SoftBench, and Atherton Software Backplane. Another example is PCTE (Portable Common Tool Environment), which is actually a standard interface definition, not a product. Currently, several existing or forthcoming products comply with this standard: the initial implementation by Emeraude, the Oracle-based version by Verilog, and implementations by DEC and IBM.

A key feature of these *integrating platforms* is their support for the creation of logically integrated but physically distributed systems. The development of personal computers, workstations, and local area network technology has made distributed implementations particularly suitable for advanced software-development environments. Hence, platform designers conceive and implement all the services for a distributed architecture. Moreover, the same services are very often available on different operating systems (for example, Unix, OSF/1, NT, and MS-DOS) to make the creation of heterogeneous architectures possible.

Standardization is a key aspect for such products. CASE developers can embed most of the functionalities offered by a platform in an application by adopting ad hoc components and products already available on the market. However, to develop distributed, highly integrated, and heterogeneous systems, they must identify standard mechanisms that ensure the required degree of product interoperability. (Interoperability is "the ability of two or more systems or components to exchange information and to use the information that has been exchanged."[6])

Besides the repository- and user-interface-management mechanisms, integrating platforms offer (or soon will offer) other key functionalities:

- *Advanced process-control mechanisms.* These let CASE developers encapsulate tools and workbenches, and invoke and control them through standard methods and event-generation mechanisms. Examples are the HP Encapsulator and the ACA Services offered by the DEC Cohesion Platform.
- *Support for the creation of multimedia products.* These features extend the functionalities offered by

traditional user-interface workbenches and let designers create advanced multimedia tools such as video documentation facilities and visual e-mail systems. A product offering these functionalities is the Multimedia Development Kit for Microsoft Windows.

- *Support for the creation of cooperating CASE tools and workbenches.* Typical examples of such applications are on-line agendas and concurrent/distributed editing tools. For example, DEC Fuse, Sun ToolTalk, and HP BMS give the tool developer a message-handling facility to support the integration and cooperation of CASE products.

The total value of the CASE technology market has grown from an estimated $2 billion in 1990 to $5 billion in 1993. Despite the recession Western countries have experienced in recent years, the CASE tool growth rate for the next couple of years is expected to be between 20 and 30 percent.[1]

Such high rates are justified because the total cost for human resources in software production amounts to about $250 billion per year. Therefore, even a modest increase in productivity would significantly reduce costs.[1] For this reason, CASE technology will play a key role in the information technology market, and many new products will appear.

The availability of such a large number of products and the complexity of the technologies used in software-development organizations make a reference framework for market evaluation and technology transfer essential. Moreover, it is important to facilitate comparison and exchange of experiences with other information-technology areas, such as VLSI design, factory automation, and office automation, where there have been similar efforts.

I have proposed concepts to bring in focus the state of the art of CASE technology. Attempts to classify and organize according to complex concepts may lead to extreme simplifications or, conversely, useless details. Moreover, the rapid changes in this area will quickly make some observations obsolete. As a result, this work will need to be updated incrementally as the technology develops. My aim in this article is to provide a reference framework and an initial classification of existing technology as a solid starting point for such a continuous updating. ∎

Acknowledgments

I thank Carlo Ghezzi and the anonymous referees for their stimulating and helpful comments.

References

1. *CASE Outlook: Guide to Products and Services*, G. Forte and K. McCulley, eds., CASE Consulting Group, Lake Oswego, Ore., 1991.

2. R. Conradi et al., "Towards a Reference Framework of Process Concepts," *Proc. Second European Workshop Software Process Technology*, Springer-Verlag, Berlin, 1992.

3. M.C. Paulk et al., "Capability Maturity Model for Software," Tech. Report CMU/SEI-91-TR-24, Software Eng. Inst., Carnegie Mellon Univ., Pittsburgh, 1991.

4. I. Sommerville, *Software Eng.*, Addison-Wesley, Reading, Mass., 1992.

5. C. Fernström, K.-H. Närfelt, and L. Ohlsson, "Software Factory Principles, Architectures, and Experiments," *IEEE Software*, Vol. 9, No. 2, Mar. 1992, pp. 36-44.

6. "Standard Glossary of Software Engineering Terminology," in *Software Eng. Standards*, IEEE, Spring 1991, pp. 7-38.

7. D. Whitgift, *Methods and Tools for Software Configuration Management*, John Wiley, New York, 1991.

8. A. Kay, invited address at the 11th Int'l Conf. Software Eng., 1989.

9. H.A. Müller et al., "A Reverse Engineering Environment Based on Spatial and Visual Software Interconnection Models," *Proc. Fifth ACM SIGSoft Symp. Software Development Environments*, ACM Press, New York, 1992, pp. 88-98.

10. S.A. Dart et al., "Software Development Environments," *Computer*, Vol. 20, No. 11, Nov. 1987, pp. 18-28.

11. *Integrated Programming Environments*, D.R. Barstow, H.E. Shrobe, and E. Sandewall, eds., McGraw-Hill, New York, 1984.

12. "Reference Model for Frameworks of Software Engineering Environments," jointly published as ECMA Tech. Report TR/55, European Computer Manufacturers Assoc., Geneva, and NIST Special Publication 500-201, Nat'l Inst. of Standards and Technology, Gaithersburg, Md., 1991.

13. M.M. Lehman, "Process Models, Process Programs, Programming Support," *Proc. Ninth Int'l Conf. Software Eng.*, IEEE CS Press, Los Alamitos, Calif., Order No. 767, 1987. pp. 14-16.

14. M.I. Kellner, "Software Process Modeling: Value and Experience," *SEI Tech. Rev.*, Software Eng. Inst., Carnegie Mellon Univ., Pittsburgh, 1989, pp. 23-54.

15. C. Liu and R. Conradi, "Process Modeling Paradigms: An Evaluation," *Proc. First European Workshop on Software Process Modeling*, Italian Nat'l Assoc. for Computer Science, Milan, Italy, 1991, pp. 39-52.

16. P. Armenise et al., "A Survey and Assessment of Software Process Representation Formalisms," to be published in *Int'l J. Software Eng. and Knowledge Eng.*

Alfonso Fuggetta is an associate professor of computer science at Politecnico di Milano and a senior researcher at CEFRIEL, the Italian acronym for the Center for Research and Education in Information Technology, established in 1988 by a consortium of universities, public administrations, and information-technology industries. His research interests are software-process modeling and management, CASE products, and executable specifications.

Fuggetta is chairman of the steering committee of the European Software Engineering Conference (ESEC) and a member of the steering committee of the European Workshop on Software Process Technology. He is a member of the board of directors of AICA, the Italian National Society for Computer Science, and of the Technical Committee on Software Quality Certification of Istituto Marchio Qualità. Fuggetta is also a member of IEEE and ACM.

Readers can contact Fuggetta at Dipartimento di Elettronica e Informazione, Politecnico di Milano, P.za Leonardo da Vinci, 32, 20133 Milano, Italy, e-mail fuggetta@IPMEL2.elet.polimi.it.

Traceability

James D. Palmer

*Professor Emeritus, George Mason University
and Software Consultant
860 Cashew Way
Fremont, CA 94536*

Abstract

Traceability gives essential assistance in understanding the relationships that exist within and across software requirements, design, and implementation and is critical to the development process by providing a means of ascertaining how and why system development products satisfy stakeholder requirements, especially for large complex systems. Traceability provides a path to the validation and verification of stakeholder requirements to assure these needs are met by the delivered system, as well as information on testing procedures, performance measures, non-functional characteristics, and behavioral aspects for the delivered system. Both syntactic and semantic information are needed to successfully implement tracing. It is not enough to know the form; it is also necessary to know the substance of the entities to be traced.

However, traceability is often misunderstood, frequently misapplied, and seldom performed correctly. There are many challenges to achieving traceability, particularly the absence of automated techniques to assist in the identification of linkages from requirements to design, or test, or operation needed to trace entities within and across the system development process. One of the particular challenges to providing traceability to and from system level requirements is that it becomes necessary to utilize both the constructs of language semantics as well as syntax.

Traceability is introduced, and its place in a development process, coupled with the values and pitfalls are covered. The essentials of traceability are examined together with how to implement tracing within a development life cycle for large complex systems. Working definitions and related terms are provided to assure common understanding of the terminology and application of tracing in system and software development. A review of contemporary approaches to implement tracing with an overview of several of the Computer Supported Software (or System) Engineering (CASE) tools that purport to support tracing are given and future trends are examined.

Introduction

Successful system development depends on the ability to satisfy stakeholder needs and requirements and to reflect these in the delivered system. Requirements, design, and implementation that are complete, correct, consistent, and error free, play a major role in ensuring that the delivered system meets stakeholder needs. Critical keys to this are understanding and tracing the relationships that exist amongst system requirements, design, code, test, and implementation. Large-scale complex systems are initiated by stakeholder determination that a need exists that is not met by existing systems. From this beginning, system level requirements are developed to broadly outline the desired capabilities, which, in turn, are investigated to ascertain feasibility and practicality and examine trade-offs. Once the feasibility and practicality of the desired system have been determined to be necessary and sufficient to launch a new system (or significant modification of an existing or legacy system), design is completed and systems are constructed, tested, and fielded. It is essential to maintain traceability from the system requirements to operation and maintenance to assure that the delivered system meets the stated organizational needs of the stakeholder.

System Life Cycle for Traceability Management

Generally, a system or process development life cycle is followed to produce the desired system. There are many life cycle models [1], and one of the simplest is the system development or waterfall life cycle model depicted in Figure 1. It also serves as the basis for most life cycle models in use today, such as the spiral model, the evolutionary model, and the prototyping model. Within any system development life cycle, requirements must be traced both forward and backward to assure that the correct system is being designed and produced, and that the correct design and production approaches are used.

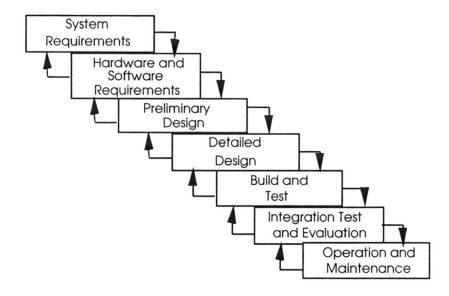

Figure 1. Typical system and software development life cycle

In the life cycle model of Figure 1, system requirements, usually prepared in natural language, are provided by the stakeholder to the developer. These system requirements, if they exist at all, may be poorly written and only vaguely define stakeholder desires for the new system. This may impact the ability to construct a system that will satisfy the stakeholder. From these system requirements, hardware and software requirements and specifications are prepared. Requirement and specification development are followed by preliminary design; detailed design; construction of the system including hardware and software; system integration, testing and evaluation; and finally installation including operation and maintenance.

These life cycle activities require documentation of needs and outcomes. Each must trace forward to the subsequent activity and backward to the preceding one. Clearly, traceability, both forward and backward, is essential to verify that the requirements of one phase translate to outcomes of that phase which become the requirements for the next phase, and so on through the development activity. Traceability is equally essential to validate that system requirements are satisfied during operation.

Need for Traceability

Traceability is essential to verification and validation and is needed to better understand the processes used to develop the system and the products that result. It is needed for quick access to information, information abstraction, and to provide visualization into the techniques used for system development. Traceability is needed for change control, develop-ment process control, and risk control. Tracing pro-vides insights to non-behavioral components such as quality, consistency, completeness, impact analysis, system evolution, and process improvement. It is equally important to have the capability to trace a requirement or design or code module to its origin, as well as test. Stakeholders recognize the value of prop-erly tracing within and across the entities of a system through risk management insights, appropriate inte-gration tests, and the delivery of a project that meets the needs statements of the requirements. [2]

Traceability supports assessment of under- or over designs; investigation of high-level behavior impact on detailed specifications, as well as non-functional re-quirements such as performance and quality factors. Moreover, traceability supports conflict detection by making it feasible to examine linkages within and across selected entities and by providing visibility into the entire system. Through tracing, there is the assur-ance that decisions made later in the system develop-ment life cycle are consistent with earlier decisions. Test cases check that coverage for code and integra-tion testing and for requirements validation is pro-vided. Traceability provides the basis for the devel-opment of an audit trail for the entire project by establishing the links within and across system entities, functions, behavior, and performance, for example.

While there is widespread acceptance of the neces-sity to trace, there is considerable controversy as to the ultimate need, purpose, and cost of tracing from re-quirements to delivered product. The controversy arises primarily because of the lack of automated approaches to implement the process and the con-comitant time and effort that must be applied with any of the presently available support tools. Developers simply do not see the benefits that may accrue to the final product when traceability is fully implemented compared to the time and effort required.

Problems and Issues Concerning Traceability

Difficulties related to tracing generally revolve around the necessity to manually add trace elements to requirements documents and subsequent work products from software development. Since these products have little or no direct consequence to the development team, assignment of trace elements generally has a low priority. The benefits of traceability are not seen until much later in the development life cycle, usually during validation testing and system installation and operation, and then primarily by integration testers and stakeholders rather than developers. Additionally, traceability is often misunderstood, frequently misapplied, and seldom performed correctly.

Issues and concerns emanate from the complexity of a project itself that must be confronted when implementing traceability. Each discipline, such as avionics, communications, navigation, security, or safety, may have languages, methods, and tools peculiar to the discipline. This results in a lack of ability to trace across disciplines, which, in turn, may lead to errors in traceability matrices used to provide linkages within and across disciplines. Some of the issues that need to be addressed by the stakeholder and developer at the time of system development include how to apportion projects by discipline, the type and nature of information that should be traced across different disciplines, and the types of tools that can be used to provide consistent and correct traceability across disciplines. Establishing threads across disciplines is also difficult due to language, method, and tool peculiarities.

Currently, there is no single modeling method or language sufficiently rich to represent all aspects of a large complex system and still be understandable to those involved. In tracing information across different disciplines and toolsets, and to provide threads across these, essential system properties and the classification schemes used are needed. Such properties and schemas do not usually exist. Thus, for verification and validation, traceability must always focus on a common denominator; the approved system requirements. Finally, internal consistency of the baseline documentation may not be adequate to support tracing. This latter is usually a significant problem in the modification of legacy systems.

Definition of Terms

There are many terms that describe, delineate, or relate to traceability. Some of these correlate to the "how and why" for traceability, while others connect to the outcomes or "what" of traceability. In general, the basic meaning of the terms is first that provided by Webster's New Collegiate Dictionary [3], while the last meaning is given in the context of systems and software engineering, as an example of usage.

Allocation: The act of distributing; allotment or apportionment; as to assign or apportion functions to specific modules.

Audit: A formal checking of records, to determine that what was stated was accomplished; to examine and verify; as to confirm a stated capability is met in the software product.

Behavior: The way in which a system acts, especially in response to a stimulus; stimulus-response mechanisms; as activity or change in reliability across sub-systems.

Bottom-up: A design philosophy or policy that dictates the form and partitioning of the system from the basic functions that the system is to perform and moving up to the top level requirements; as a design policy that provides basic modules followed by top-level constructs.

Classification: A group of entities ranked together as possessing common characteristics or quality; the act of grouping or segregating into classes which have systematic relationships; a systematic grouping of entities based upon some definite scheme; as to classify requirements according to organizational or performance characteristics.

Flowdown: To move or circulate from upper to lower levels; as to trace a requirement from a top level to designs to code to test.

Function: The characteristic action or the normal or special action of a system; one aspect of a system is so related to another that there is a correspondence from one to the other when an action is taken; as an algorithm to provide the equations of motion.

Hierarchy: A series of objects or items divided or classified in ranks or orders; as in a type of structure in which each element or block has a level number (1= highest), and each element is associated with one or more elements at the next higher level and lower levels; as a single high level requirement decomposes to lower level requirements and to design and code.

Impact Analysis: Separation into constituent parts to examine or distinguish contact of one on another, a communicating force; as to focus on software changes and the traceable consequences; relating software requirements to design components.

Policy: Management or procedure based primarily on material interest; as a settled course or level to be followed for system security.

Requirement: A requisite condition; a required quality; to demand; to claim as by right or authority; to exact; as to demand system performance by the stakeholder.

Thread: To connect; as to pass a thread through; string together; as to link behaviors of a system together.

Top-down: A design philosophy or policy that dictates the form and partitioning of the system from the top-level requirements perspective to the lower level design components; as in a design policy for all activities from high-level requirements to design and code.

Top-level requirement: A requisite condition leveled by the stakeholder; as a system level requirement for security.

Traceability: The course or path followed; to follow or track down; to follow or study out in detail or step by step, especially by going backward over evidence (as to trace requirements from design); to discover or uncover by investigation; as to trace to the source; as to follow requirements from the top level to design and code and back; or as to identify and document the allocation/flowdown path (downward) and derivation path (upward) of requirements into the hierarchy. The Department of Defense (DoD) defines traceability in the Standard for Defense System Software Development DoD-Std-2167A to be a demonstration of completeness, necessity, and consistency. Specifically, DoD- Std -21267A defines traceability as: "(1) the document in question contains or implements all applicable stipulations of the predecessor document, (2) a given term, acronym, or abbreviation means the same thing in all documents, (3) a given item or concept is referred to by the same name or description in the documents, (4) all material in the successor document has

its basis in the predecessor document, that is, no untraceable material has been introduced, and (5) the two documents do not contradict one another."

Traceability Management: To control and direct; guide; administer; give direction to accomplish an end; as to control and direct tracing from top level through to design and code.

Tree: A diagrammatic representation that indicates branching from an original stem; as software components derived from a higher level entity to more discrete lower level entities.

State of the Practice of Traceability

Traceability management applies to the entire development life cycle from project initiation through operation and maintenance as shown in Figure 2. It is presently feasible to manage tracing using a combination of manual and automated assistance, thus providing some assurance that the development of a system meets the needs as provided by the stakeholder. An essential element of successful traceability management, provided by currently available CASE tools, is the ability to provide links from requirements forward to designs, code, test, and implementation, and backward from any of these activities to requirements once these links have been manually entered into the CASE tool.

Techniques currently in use to establish and maintain traceability from requirements through designs, code, test, and operation begin with manual identification of linkages. These linkages may be subsequently supported by document managers, a database, or CASE tools specifically designed for requirements traceability management.

Contemporary Traceability Practices

Traceability has traditionally been accomplished by manually assigning and linking unique identifiers; that is, a sentence or paragraph (or other partition) requirement is assigned a particular alpha-numeric reference. This information is subsequently managed in a word processor or database, often through use of a CASE tool. Even with the use of a CASE tool, the initial identification of trace entities and linkages must be accomplished manually. By establishing a unique identification system and following this scheme throughout the life of the project, it is possible to trace these specific entities both forward and backward from

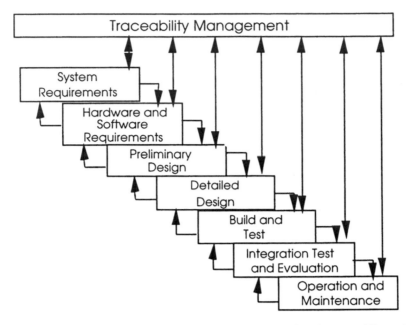

Figure 2. Traceability management across the system development life cycle

requirements to product. This unique identity may be linked within and across documents using manually derived traceability tables to assure full traceability over all aspects of the project.

A typical output of tracing is a traceability matrix that links high-level requirements to each and every other requirement or specification of the system. A typical traceability table for a large complex system is shown in Table 1. In this table, individual requirements in the Systems Requirements Document (SRD) have been manually linked to more detailed system requirements in the Systems Specification which in turn have been manually linked to particular specifications in the System Segments.

Other matrices or tables may provide more details such as cryptic messages, partial text, critical values, or the entire text. The system represented in the traceability table is configured as in Figure 3. The SRD represents stakeholder input, the SS represents the initial interpretation of these high level requirements by developers, and the segment specifi-

cations provide more detailed information to design. The Interface Control Document (ICD) provides linkages for all messages that occur within and across segments.

In most system development programs, there is the added expectation of continuous change in the system as requirements are added, modified, and deleted. Thus, the management of an ever-changing requirements base becomes a very important traceability function, as tracing provides a review of how the system requirements flowdown to lower levels and how lower level requirements are derived from higher levels. These traces may or may not contain information as to why the system is to be partitioned in a particular manner. As new requirements are added or existing ones are updated, deleted, or modified, the management process continues to provide traceability and impact analysis to assure that each of the changes is properly included in the system development process. This provides the major verification and validation procedure to assure stakeholder needs are met.

Table 1. Traceability matrix for multi-segment system

SRD	SS	Segment 1	Segment 2	Segment 3	ICD
3.1.2.1	3.3.4.5 3.3.4.6	3.2.2.5.6 3.2.2.5.7 3.4.5.6.2	3.5.3.2		3.1.4.6.7 3.1.4.6.8 3.1.4.6.9
3.4.3.1	3.6.7.2 3.8.4.3	3.5.2.5.1	3.7.4.3.1 3.7.4.3.2	3.6.4.5.2	3.3.2.4.5 3.3.2.4.7

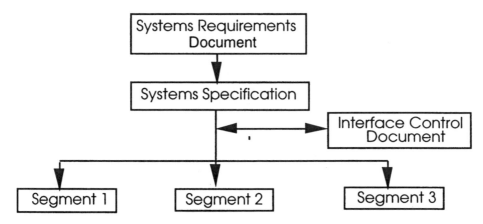

Figure 3. Typical requirements classification schema for a large complex system

Traceability is especially critical for the operation and maintenance phase. This is when significant stakeholder changes may be made and change impacts and impact analyses must be performed. Such changes are difficult to trace; however, without tracing it is nearly impossible to ascertain the extent of the full impact of additions, deletions, or modifications to the system.

An Ideal Process for Traceability

To understand what must be traced, we need a defined process for developing system architectural views, classification schemes, as well as processes for specifying and verifying the products to be constructed. This is generally provided by the stakeholder in consort with the developer. The development of these views is necessary to partition the project for design and construction.

An ideal traceability process consists of the steps of identification, architecture selection, classification, allocation, and flowdown as depicted in Figure 4. The process begins with the identification of requirements at the system level, specification of system architecture, and selection of classification schema. Following this, allocations are made in accordance with the selected schema. Following allocation, the requirements flow down to design, code, and test. This top-down approach has proven most effective in the management of traceability for large scale complex projects.

However, this approach is basically a manual activity that requires significant investment of time and effort on the part of skilled personnel. The outcomes represent a system hierarchy along the lines of the classification structure used for the architectural allocations. It is also necessary to provide threads through the various behavioral and non-behavioral aspects of the project to complete the traceability process. These thread paths are manually assigned using approaches

such as entity-relation-attribute diagrams. For example, tests are threaded back to requirements through code and design.

Once the system hierarchy, the architecture, and classification schema have been defined, identified system requirements are assigned to the top-level block of the hierarchy. At this time, they are added to the traceability database for storage, retrieval, and reuse. After appropriate analyses, these requirements are decomposed and flow down into more detailed requirements for each of the lower level blocks to which the requirement was allocated, as was shown in the example of Figure 3. The higher level requirements are sometimes referred to as parents and the lower level ones as children. Change notification should be rigorously traced to determine the impact of such activities on changes in cost, schedule, and feasibility of system design and implementation, on tests that must be conducted, and on support software and hardware.

Actual Practice for Implementing Traceability

In actual practice, tracing is a labor intensive and aggravating task. Domain experts follow a process to decompose the system that is similar to that depicted in Figure 3. Once appropriate systems architectures are identified, a classification schema or schemas for purposes of allocation of requirements to system specific architectures is prepared and requirements are assigned to specific units. As examples of the types of classification schemes used, one may be centered on functional aspects of the project; such as navigation, communications, or threat assessment; another may concentrate on performance and security; while yet another may be focused on stakeholder organization. It is not feasible to enumerate, a priori- , all the ways in which the project may need to be partitioned and

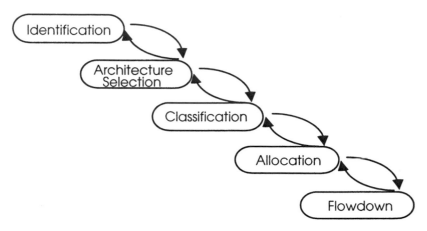

Figure 4. The ideal traceability process

viewed; thus, traceability becomes a continuous process as perspectives change and as requirements change. To validate these various views, there is only one common basis from which to form trace linkages, the system requirements.

The next step, after receipt of the requirements documents and delineation of the system architecture, is to determine the nature of the tracing to be accomplished. Several options are feasible; these include working with statements that contain "shall," "will," "should," "would," or similar verbs; or with entire paragraphs; or the total set of statements provided by the stakeholder. The strongest selection is "shall" statements, which may be the only contractually acceptable designation for a requirement. This is followed by the development of classification schemes according to function, data object, behavior, organization, or other approaches. Once the option(s) has been selected, the requirements are parsed according to the option and assigned a unique identity. For example, if "shall" has been selected as the option, sentences with "shall" as a verb are collected and are identified sequentially, while also retaining the original identification system provided by the stakeholder. This new identification system is maintained throughout the life of the project.

Syntactic and semantic information are both necessary to perform tracing. Language semantics are needed to assure the trace is related to the meaning or context of the requirement or set of requirements, while syntax is necessary to trace to a specific word or phrase, without regard to meaning or context. Integration of both constructs is required to provide for full traceability from natural language statements to the other steps as shown in Figure 2. Manual verification of outcomes is required to assure compliance with the intent and purpose of the tracing activity.

Next comes allocation according to the classification scheme. This likewise is a manual task, even with

automated assistance from one of the available CASE tools, as most of these tools require the operator to physically establish the links from one entity to another for traceability. All linkages must be designated and maintained and traceability matrices are generated from these outcomes. If a CASE tool has been used that supports generation of traceability matrices, these are created automatically; otherwise, these matrices must be manually prepared. These steps are depicted graphically in Figure 5. These results are usually stored in a traceability database. The traceability linkages are subsequently designated and maintained across the entire development project from design to code to test to operation and maintenance.

Return on Investment for Traceability

It is not feasible to measure the return on investment (ROI) for traceability. Although most of the costs associated with implementation can be documented, the benefits are quite difficult to ascertain unless comparative case studies are conducted. Costs of implementation include the investment of time and effort of domain experts to provide system architectural perspectives and classification schema, the initial cost of acquiring CASE tools to manage requirements traceability, and the expended costs of training and maintenance in the use of such tools. Due to the manual approaches required to establish architectural perspectives, classification schema, allocation, linkage, and system maintenance, fixing costs, while manageable, is a difficult task. These costs may be either estimated or accounted for with some degree of accuracy. This may be done for an ongoing project or by estimating the time, effort, capitalization costs, and expended costs involved.

The benefits are largely intangible and are related to the avoided costs associated with rework and possible failure of the product to satisfy stakeholders. To

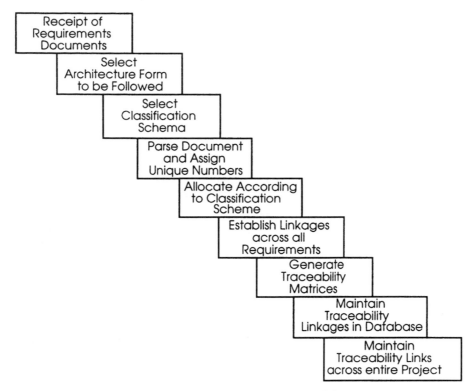

Figure 5. Steps to accomplish traceability

estimate the benefits, it would be necessary to prepare various scenarios, simulate the outcomes due to failure of various aspects of the development process, and estimate the value of avoiding these failures. Risk factors must also be taken into consideration in calculation of the potential benefits, including the potential that the project will not meet stakeholder needs. Assessing benefits without comparative analyses is generally not possible. Generating this information is considered to be unfeasible due to the costs of running such experiments and the need to develop realistic scenarios that may or may not ever be replicated in actual practice.

Current Traceability Tools

Typical of the currently available automated (or semi-automated) assistance approaches to traceability are those that provide for traceability through a variety of syntactic language components: hypertext linking, unique identifiers, syntactical similarity coefficients, or combinations of these. In hypertext linking, the "hotword" or word/phrase to be linked to other requirements is manually identified and entered into the hypertext tool. Links are automatically made and maintained by the tool to provide forward and reverse traceability for the word selection. In the unique identifier approach, an identifier is assigned that remains with the individual requirement throughout the life of

the project. To assure traceability, this unique identifier provides a "fan-out" capability within a hierarchical structure such that one system level ("A" level) requirement may be the parent to many "B" level requirements which, in turn, may be the parents for great numbers of "C" level requirements, as depicted in Table 1. Use of syntactic similarity coefficients ascertains whether or not a pre-defined set of words of a given requirement are found in another requirement. When the degree of similarity is above a pre-defined threshold, the two requirements in question are said to trace.

There are problems with each of these approaches. They do not consider the semantics or context in which the tracing is to occur. Hypertext linking finds the search text without regard to the placement in the text and without regard to the way in which the words are used. Use of a unique identifier provides access only to those requirements so identified with no perspective as to meaning or context. Syntactic similarity coefficient traceability is like hypertext linking in that it is indiscriminate as to the meaning and context of the requirement to be traced.

Commercially available requirements tools utilize straightforward traceability links that must be manually developed to relate requirements to other requirements and to design, code, and implementation. Current methods for implementing traceability with these commercial tools generally involve the manual provision of links within and across documents and then automated management of these documents. Traceability links are used to establish the one-to-one, one-to many, many-to-one, or many-to-many relationships that may exist, as may be seen from Table 1. As noted previously, linkages are not automatically established by tools during the development process, but must be manually generated. From this point, automated assistance is provided by the tool to manage traceability.

At present, there are no standards available to support tools for traceability, which has led to the development and use of a large number of commercial tools, each with differing methods, as well as proprietary tools developed by certain industries because it is considered to be a competitive advantage for most large complex projects. A number of commercially available tools have been developed to support traceability and a number of general CASE tools provide support to traceability management, especially from requirements forward to design, code, test, and operation. One of the common activities for all tools is manual development of architectural perspectives and classification schemas. Another common feature is the need to manually establish the initial linkages within and across all traceable entities. Once the initial linkages have been established, these tools effectively and efficiently manage a traceability database or word processor document.

Common Tool Characteristics

There are some common tool characteristics that are deemed to be minimal to provide support for traceability. The tool must be well understood by and be responsive to users and match the characteristics of the development environment used by the developers. Tools must also accept and utilize the data that is provided in the form provided. In addition, the tool must be flexible, capable of operation in an automated assistance mode to support various activities and services; such as active and passive data checking; batch as well as on-line processing; addition, deletion, and modification of a requirement; customization to specific domain applications; dynamic database structure for change management; and a tailorable user interface. Traceability tools will never be fully automated, as human decision making is essential to the establishment of classification schema and system architecture designation. Human interaction and decision making is both desirable and necessary to maximize the interaction of the stakeholder/developer in the development of the project.

Commercial CASE Tools for Traceability

Some commercially available tools have been developed for traceability link information expressed by a single discipline within a single phase, while others have been developed specifically to link requirements to other activities within the development life cycle. Cadre TeamWork for Real-Time Structured Analysis (CADRE) is a tool that operates on a single discipline within a single phase. Tools that link information from multiple disciplines and phases include: Requirements Traceability Manager (RTM) (Marconi Corporation) [4], SLATE (TD Technologies) [5], and DOORS (Zycad Corporation) [6]. These tools use an entity-relation-attribute-like schema to capture information on a system database, either relational or object-oriented, enable formation of queries about traceable entities, and for report generation. RTM uses a relational database structure to capture information and provide management, while DOORS provides an object-oriented database for management of information. SLATE follows a multi-user, client-server, object-oriented approach that provides dynamic representation of the system as it evolves.

Another method used by commercial tool vendors is the hypertext approach. In this approach, keywords or phrases are identified as being indicative of traces. These are linked through hypertext throughout the document or set of documents that comprise the requirements. An example of a tool that uses this approach is Document Director [7].

Some general-purpose analysis tools are also used for tracing. Some of the more robust tool sets include: Requirements Driven Design (RDD-100 by Ascent Logic) [8], which is used to document system conceptual models and Foresight [9], which is utilized to maintain a data dictionary and document system simulation.

Other tools and techniques that support requirements traceability include Software Requirements Methodology (SREM); Problem Statement Language/Problem Statement Analyzer (PSL/PSA); N2 charts; Requirement Networks (R-Nets); and ARTS (a database management system for requirements). Not all of the CASE tools support requirements traceability; however; most do support some form of requirements management.

Future Trends and Conclusions

The future in traceability support lies in the development of the capability to deal directly with requirements in natural language, the ability to provide automated assistance to allocation of requirements to various architectural and classification systems, and the ability to manage these. From this automated assistance, it becomes feasible to provide for and manage a traceable baseline for the entire system.

The following issues are being addressed in ongoing research programs:

- automated allocation of entities to architectures and classifications
- traceability that is independent of methods used to develop architectures and classifications
- tracing product attributes from requirements to the lowest levels

Several research programs are working on the problems associated with natural language; the two addressing traceability are from George Mason University and Trident Systems. The Center for Software Systems Engineering at George Mason University has developed and applied an automated assistance approach to the problems of allocation of entities to architectures and classification called the Automated Integrated Requirements Engineering System (AIRES) [10]. Trident Systems intends to develop a CASE tool called RECAP (Requirements Capture) which is intended to manage natural language requirements [11].

AIRES provides an assessment framework and techniques for integrated application of both semantic and syntactic rules for effective, efficient, and comprehensive identification of traceable and non-traceable requirements in large complex multiple-segment systems. The framework provides for the categorization of requirements in classification structures through the application of a diverse combination of rules and procedures, each of which applies unique combinations of both semantic and syntactic classification rules and tables for the categorization of requirements. These serve as the basic building blocks of the assessment framework and may be applied either singly or in combinations. AIRES supports automated development of linkages that may be transferred electronically to commercially available traceability tools such as RTM for management of a requirements database and report generation. AIRES is presently available in prototype form and has been utilized in support of several large complex system development for traceability support [12].

RECAP, presently a conceptual design, is intended to provide a set of interfaces that permit the operator to manipulate natural language requirements. RECAP proposes to combine the information management and extraction capabilities of information retrieval system approaches with knowledge-base rules. It also intends to provide sequential and string search access to any portion of the document set. Quick access to information is proposed through keywords, sentence identifiers, or rule-based queries. The user will be required to provide information for resolution of ambiguity, mistakes in statements, and addition of missing items. RECAP is intended to aid the user in making these decisions. [11].

Information linked by these tracing tools is not dependent upon a model or discipline. It is possible to link entities as needed; for example, it may be desirable to link the estimated footprint, weight, and power usage of a piece of computer equipment (stored in a hardware modeling tool) to the estimated throughput and memory requirements for a piece of software (stored in a software modeling tool). To efficiently use these tracing tools, it is necessary to automatically transfer the information captured to CASE tools used downstream in the development life cycle. This is accomplished by tracing system definitions, system development processes, and interrelationships across system units.

While tracing from origination to final product is a difficult and arduous, manually intensive task at the present time, advances in technology should soon be commercially available to assist in automated allocation and classification procedures. These advances will make the traceability task much more reasonable, feasible, and supportable for large complex system developments due to the automated assistance provided for allocation and classification, the most labor intensive aspects of tracing. In each of the approaches, the CASE tool provides automated assistance to tracing, but requires human operator inputs only for decision-making activities. These tools represent a significant advance over the present state of the practice for traceability.

References

[1] Sage, Andrew P. and Palmer, James D., *Software Systems Engineering*, John Wiley and Sons, New York, N.Y., 1990.

[2] White, Stephanie, "Tracing Product and Process Information when developing Complex Systems," *CSESAW '94,* 1994, pp. 45–50, NSWCDD/MP-94/122.

[3] *Webster's New Collegiate Dictionary*, Sixth Ed., G.&C. Merriam Co., Springfield, Mass., 1951.

[4] "RTM-Requirements & Traceability Management, Practical Workbook," GEC-Marconi Limited, Oct., 1993.

[5] Nallon, John, "Implementation of NSWC Requirements Traceability Models," *CSESAW*, 1994, pp. 15–22, NSWCDD/MP-94/122.

[6] Rundley, Nancy and Miller, William D., "DOORS to the Digitized Battlefield: Managing Requirements Discovery and Traceability," *CSESAW*, 1994, pp. 23–28.

[7] "Document Director-The Requirements Tool," B.G. Jackson Associates, 17629 E. Camino Real, Suite 720, Houston, Tex., 77058, 1989.

[8] "RDD-100-Release Notes Release 3.0.2.1, Oct., 1992," Requirements Driven Design, Ascent Logic Corporation, 180 Rose Orchard Way, #200, San Jose, Calif., 95134, 1992.

[9] Vertal, Michael D., "Extending IDEF: Improving Complex Systems with Executable Modeling," *Proc. 1994 Ann. Conf. for Business Re-engineering*, IDEF Users Group, Richmond, VA, May, 1994.

[10] Palmer, James D. and Evans Richard P., "An Integrated Semantic and Syntactic Framework for Requirements Traceability: Experience with System Level Requirements for a Large Complex Multi-Segment Project," *CSESAW*, 1994, pp. 9–14, NSWCDD/MP-94/122.

[11] Hugue, Michelle, Casey, Michael, Wood, Glenn, and Edwards, Edward, "RECAP: A REquirements CAPture Tool for Large Complex Systems," *CSESAW*, 1994, pp. 39–44, NSWCDD/MP-94/122.

[12] Palmer, James D. and Evans Richard P., "Software Risk Management: Requirements-Based Risk Metrics," *Proc. IEEE 1994 Int'l Conf. SMC*, IEEE Press, Piscataway, N.J., 1994.

Chapter 5

Requirements and Quality Management

1. Introduction to Chapter

Management involves the activities and tasks undertaken by one or more persons for the purpose of planning and controlling the activities of others in order to achieve objectives that could not be achieved by the others acting alone. *Management functions* can be categorized as planning, organizing, staffing, directing, and controlling.

Project management is a system of management procedures, practices, technologies, skill, and experience that are necessary to manage an engineering project successfully. If the product of a project is software, then the act of managing the project is called *software engineering project management*.

Quality management is all of the management aspects that concern quality assurance, quality assurance planning, and quality metrics. One of the aspects of software quality assurance is verification and validation (V&V).

Verification and validation is a unified approach to identifying and resolving software problems and high-risk issues early in the software cycle.[1] Verification and validation can also be defined as a software system engineering process employing a rigorous methodology for evaluating the correctness and quality of the software product through the software life cycle.[2] However, in most contexts, V&V retains separate, independent definitions:

- *Verification and validation (V&V)*—The process of determining whether the requirements for a system or component are complete and correct, the products of each development phase fulfill the requirements or conditions imposed by the previous phase, and the final system or component complies with specified requirements[3]

- *Verification*—The process of determining whether the products of a given phase of the

software development cycle fulfill the requirements established for them at the end of the previous phase. Verification answers the question, "Are we building the system right?"[1]

- *Validation*—The determination of the correctness of the final program or software produced from a development project with respect to the user's needs and requirements. Validation answers the question, "Are we building the right system?"[1]

Some of the major tools of V&V are reviews, inspections, walkthroughs, and traceability. A *review* is a formal meeting at which a product or document is presented to the user, customer, or other interested parties for comment and approval. It can be a review of the management and technical progress of the hardware/software development project.[4] Examples of a formal review are as follows: audit, budget review, formal qualification review (FQR), preliminary design review (PDR), software specifications review (SSR), system design review (SDR), system requirements review (SRR), and others.

A *walkthrough* is a software engineering review process in which a designer or programmer leads one or more members of the development team through a segment of design or code that he or she has written, while other members ask questions and make comments about technique, style, possible errors, violation of development standards, and other problems.[4] (In recent years, there has been a tendency to call a walkthrough an *inspection*.)

An *inspection* is a semiformal evaluation technique in which software requirements, design, or code are examined in detail by a person or group other than the originator to detect faults, violations of development standards, and other problems. The review members are peers (equals) of the designer or programmer. Error data is collected during inspections for later analysis and to assist in future inspections. *The term "peer review" may be used for either a walkthrough or an inspection.*

2. Description of Articles

The first article in this chapter, by Ray Yeh and Peter Ng, is concerned with viewing software requirements from a management perspective. The purpose of the article is to bring awareness of software requirements problems and process to management. A conceptual framework of the process, attributes, and the contents of the final product is presented. Possible pitfalls along the way are pointed out, and suggestions to software managers are provided.

Verification and validation is one of the most powerful software engineering tools available to verify intermediate software products, such as software requirements specifications, design descriptions, test cases, and test procedures. The second (and last) article in Chapter 5 discusses only one aspect of the software process—software requirements. Numerous techniques are presented to verify the software requirements as well as software testing methods used to validate the software requirements.

This article is an excerpt from a National Institute of Standards and Technology Publication 500-234, *Reference Information for the Software Verification and Validation Process,* by Dolores R. Wallace, Laura M. Ippolito, Barbara B. Cuthill, April 1996. The original publication was concerned with the entire software development life cycle. The authors rewrote the publication to cover only V&V of software requirements.

References

1. Boehm, B.W., "Verifying and Validating Software Requirements and Design Specifications," *IEEE Software,* Vol. 1, No. 1, Jan. 1984, pp. 75–88.

2. IEEE Standards for Verification and Validation Plans Seminar, The Institute of Electrical and Electronic Engineers, Piscataway, N.J., 1987.

3. ANSI/IEEE Standard 610.12-1990, *Glossary of Software Engineering Terminology,* The Institute of Electrical and Electronic Engineers, Piscataway, N.J., 1990.

4. Adapted from *IEEE Standard Glossary of Software Engineering Terminology,* ANSI/IEEE Std 729-1983, IEEE, New York, N.Y., 1983.

Software Requirements—A Management Perspective

Raymond T. Yeh

Syscorp International
9420 Research Boulevard
Suite 200
Austin, Texas 78759

Peter A. Ng

Institute for Integrated Systems Research
Department of Computer and Information Science
New Jersey Institute of Technology
Newark, New Jersey 07102

Abstract: The purpose of this paper is to bring about an awareness of the problem of deriving software requirements at the management level. No technical details concerning specific techniques, languages, or methodologies will be discussed. In this paper, a new paradigm for software development is first introduced from the point of an abstraction-based software lifecycle model. It emphasizes requirements, specification, and design rather than coding and incorporates the activities of evaluation and validation into the development process rather than at the completion of the development in each phase of the traditional waterfall model. The presentation primarily provides a conceptual framework for the requirements derivation process, attributes that might go into a requirements document, and management of the requirements derivation process. An objectives analysis is proposed for introduction preceding the process for deriving requirements, thereby allowing for a study of the organization's objectives.

1. Introduction

The 1970s marked a period of transition in and recognition of the importance of software development. The technological advancements in hardware during the 1960s not only drove the cost of equipment down, but also made possible a new level of software sophistication and a demand for it during the 1970s. In particular, software packages were introduced and distributed to thousands of users; consequently, programmers found themselves not only using programs written by others, but also more frequently, modifying and adapting existing software to suit the requirements of their companies and of the new hardware. (Even today, program maintenance alone continues to make up a significant portion of the total software development cost.) Software in the 1970s was complex, labor-intensive, error-prone, and expensive, a phenomenon known as "software crisis" [Radice 88].

Software was complex because there was no parallel procedure that could handle the rapid growth in the size of applications. As the size of the problem increased, it became completely unmanageable by a single person.

Software was labor-intensive because software development was largely a manual process. Even when only minor changes occurred, programmers had to rework most of a program.

Software was error-prone because of inadequate development and testing methods and because of incomplete documentation. Modification of software usually resulted in altered performance by components that were supposed to be unaffected by such changes. In general, it has been found that "design errors" constituted one-third to three-fourths of the total error count [Thayer 75].

Software was expensive because there were insufficient methods for formulating feasibility analyses of a user's requirements and specifications; by the time the product was finished, it may not have been what the user wanted [Boehm 73, 81]. As a result, cost overruns were the norm rather than the exception.

Finding a solution for the problem of software development became increasingly critical. Thus, the term "software engineering" was introduced at the 1968 North American Treaty Organization (NATO) Conference in Garmisch, Germany [Radice, 88], and a set of techniques for software development was introduced to combat the software crisis. Software was considered an engineering product that required techniques for the phases of plan-

Reprinted from *System and Software Requirements Engineering*, M. Dorfman and R.H. Thayer, eds., 1990, pp. 450–461.

ning, analysis, design, implementation, testing, and maintenance. The software industry's basic software engineering goals are to improve quality and productivity while reducing costs [Radice 88]. The use of process models, methods, languages, and tools enables the developer to control the process of software development, to improve user satisfaction with software products and to provide the programmer with some guidelines for producing high-quality software.

The 1980s were a period of integration of software technology and of transition from a handicraft approach to an industry approach to software engineering. The industry has replaced many of the labor-intensive development activities with software tools. Therefore, the emphasis during the next decade will be on how to integrate the set of tools further to increase the quality of software, reduce development cost, and improve the programmer's productivity.

In Section 2, we discuss the waterfall model of the software lifecycle, which was introduced to provide a systematic approach to software development. We also present a new paradigm of software development, which concentrates on requirements, specification, and design, rather than coding. In Section 3, we examine several problems in deriving requirements. In Section 4, we discuss techniques for deriving requirements and objectives analyses that can be used to alleviate those problems and we propose adding an objective analysis to precede the requirements analysis. Next, in Section 5, we address what should be included in a requirements document and discuss examples of what might go into a software requirements specification. Finally, we provide certain recommendations to managers pertaining to the process of deriving requirements.

2: An Abstraction-Based Software Lifecycle Model

The traditional waterfall model of the software lifecycle [Royce 70 and Boehm 73] is a phased refinement approach. In general, this approach consists of planning and requirements analysis, architecture, specification, design and implementation, installation and packaging, and maintenance. Verification, validation, and testing are integrated into the appropriate phases. For many reasons, the waterfall model is impractical for large projects. In addition, this approach has been criticized for running high maintenance costs for poorly motivating systems developers to perform abstract tasks in early phases of development, and for complicating systems integration. For example, with the complexity of the problem domains for today's generation of software, some user problems do not admit to "quick" solutions and their respective natures cannot be stated clearly. In these cases, a pilot version of the project may provide solutions. Using existing compo-

nents and automatic code generators can also lessen the amount of work required of the programmer. But the waterfall model's disadvantages have encouraged researchers to look for new paradigms for software development [Yeh 83, 84] based on an abstraction-based lifecycle model.

An abstract is a description, or specification, of a system that hides certain properties. Abstraction is important because it reduces the complexity of the system. The process model of this paradigm is depicted in Figure 1. It differs from the traditional phased approach in that it concentrates on the hard problems of software, namely, the requirements, specification, and design, rather than on the coding itself. Of equal importance is that evaluation and validation (E&V) are parts of the development process, rather than the completion of the development in each phase.

Central to this approach is the expression of the software system functionality specification in a form can be precisely interpreted and yet does not oversimplify the form of system design implementation. Abstraction can achieve this expression, whereby the functionality specification expresses constraints on the multiple possible embodiments that would achieve different objectives in cost, performance, error tolerance, etc.

Three types of abstractions are essential in characterizing the functional attributes of any software system: function, data, and control. Function abstractions are used to hide certain properties of some algorithms that perform certain transformations, hence allowing a function to be modified without affecting other functions. Data abstractions are used to hide certain properties of the organization of a set of data structures, allowing the interface to be specified independent of its internal representation. Control abstractions are used to hide certain properties of the order of execution of a set of operations, reducing the complexity of a system.

Given a precise statement of functionality, a set of E&V processes can be coupled closely with the design/develop-

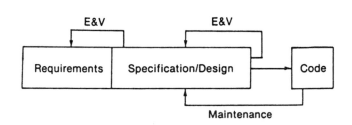

Figure 1: A process model for software evolution

426

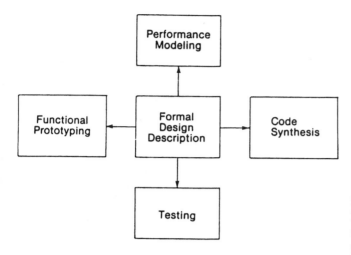

Figure 2: Interactive design steps in the new paradigm

ment process. As shown in Figure 2, rapid functional prototyping, performance modeling, and design testing are all part of this evaluation process. Rapid functional prototyping consists of the direct generation of executable code from the functional statement. This permits early users to review the proposed system's capabilities and also helps them to understand and express their needs. This early evaluation in the development can eliminate many of the causes for later system maintenance. Performance modeling at different stages of the design helps to enforce the performance issues before the system is completed, allowing for an analysis of the different design approaches. Performance evaluation is also used to provide accurate timing analyses and utilization profiles of the proposed system [Baker 89]. Design testing will help rule out poor designs early on by checking interfaces and coupling strength between modules.

The code synthesis arrow in Figure 2 also implies that in this evolutionary paradigm the code is synthesized at the highest level of specification via direct transformation or the use of previously developed components and subsystem designs. It avoids a common barrier for reusing code, namely that even if the functionality is correct, the implementation details might not fit. The reusable component is described in terms of its functionality abstraction; this strategy should make reuse possible.

This paradigm incorporates two kinds of evolution: incremental delivery and maintenance. With the functionality structure directly determining the system implementation structure, it is convenient to add functionality capabilities in increments. It is often valuable to use an implementation of a system with only limited capabilities at early stages of development in order to find specification errors. It also achieves an early pass at system integration, defective

design, and interface errors. In brief, this model calls for the design of an executable specification and design language based on abstraction.

3: Problems in Deriving Requirements

A requirement conveys an essential property that the system must satisfy. A complete set of requirements would include a complete, validated specification of the required functions, interfaces, and performances for the software product [Radice 88 and Boehm 81]. Therefore, requirements analysis focuses on studying the interface among hardware, software, and users. It is used to understand the trade-offs between conflicting constraints, to understand the available resources, and to specify the goals of the system. In this section, we discuss several factors that affect the process of requirements derivation.

3.1: Difficulties That Stem from Inherent Complexity

Todays software certainly deals with complex systems. Their complexity comes not only from the size of a system, but mainly from the interactions among its components and the constraints imposed on the system, such as real-time computing, reliability, and geographic distributions of functions and data. Many problems are associated with an inherently complex system. If the system is hard to understand and one-of-a-kind (such as many military systems), difficulties can arise in stating the problem and in deriving its requirements.

3.2: Difficulties in Dealing with Change

In many cases, customers or users do not know precisely what they want or need. As they participate in the process of deriving requirements, they become better aware of the desired system, seek to modify the requirements to fit their new understanding and, consequently, restate the problem.

3.3: Difficulties in Communication

Dealing with change can become more complicated because of difficulties in communication that may arise during the process of deriving requirements. The process requires a great deal of communication between people of diverse backgrounds, levels of expertise, interests, and goals; these people include customers, end-users, analysts, and designers, among others. To determine user requirements, the analyst needs to differentiate carefully between the needs of the end-users themselves and those of users who have some understanding of the users' problems but are not actual end-users.

3.4: Lack of Concern for the Entire Lifecycle

Most of the existing approaches for the traditional waterfall model of the software lifecycle emphasize

tional requirements (i.e., what the system is to do). It is our belief that the requirements analysis phase should begin with an objectives analysis. Also, a requirements document should contain information concerning the entire lifecycle. Cost estimates and resource allocations can be initiated from this document and a proper framework for considering design trade-offs in later phases can also be constructed, allowing vital decisions to be made based on complete information. Furthermore, many large software systems go through long lifecycles and evolve through many changes; for maintenance cost control, the ability to evolve must be considered as a major factor in the requirements phase.

4: Techniques for Understanding Requirements

In this section, we first discuss two general techniques, modeling and work breakdown structure (WBS), that can be used to alleviate the problems associated with the process of requirements derivation mentioned in Section 3. These techniques can be incorporated into any requirements methodology in varied forms. We then discuss adding an objectives analysis to precede the requirements analysis [Mittermeir 89].

4.1: Modeling

The most effective way to understand a complex system is to develop a model of that system. The model provides a basis for discussion among those concerned with the requirements derivation.

Different types of models depend on individual applications. In general, the model should include the user's environment so that the analyst who looks at the system from the user's point of view better appreciates the user's needs. This is particularly important because the desired property of an evolving system is that "a small change in the environment should affect a correspondingly small change in the system." This is possible only if both the environment and the system are modeled.

This paper presents two types of models: the conceptual model and the operational model. A conceptual model is constructed at the level at which humans formulate problems. As shown in Figure 3, it describes the interfaces between the proposed system and its environment. For complex problems, a model must be constructed so that it explicitly and formally presents the problems. It can be used by people of different backgrounds, such as users, analysts, and designers, as a basis for discussion of the problems. Therefore, a conceptual model is used to understand large, complex problems.

In many cases, a detailed operational model is required. It can be regarded as an early version of an operational prototype of the system to be developed. The operational model can be used to evaluate whether the proposed system meets the user's needs and to evaluate the feasibility of certain requirements, such as performance or time constraints in an embedded system.

4.2: Work Breakdown Structure

The technique of WBS, which systematically structures the work associated with the entire engineering process, is useful in analyzing complex systems. The purpose of a software WBS can be summarized in two goals, the "process" goal and the "product" goal. The process goal is to keep the various processes that deal with the software components under intellectual control at all times. The product goal is to organize the various software components into a product that others can comprehend.

The basic principle of any WBS is the "separation of concerns" using the mechanisms of simplification, abstraction, partition, and projection.

Simplification allows us to select the most important factors that affect our problems and to solve them. For example, in deriving his laws of motion, Newton first reduced the number of objects concerned from about 10^5 to 10 by selecting mass as the critical criterion. Second, he reduced the number of interactions from 2^{10} to 9 by considering only pair-wise interactions and only those pairs that included the sun.

Abstraction allows us to concentrate on essential properties while suppressing details that are immaterial, at least for the moment. The use of abstractions forms a natural hierarchy for elaborating details in cooperation with the intellectual control of the process.

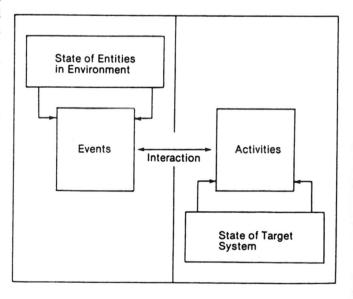

Figure 3: A conceptual model

Partition allows us to concentrate on components of a system one at a time. Partitioning the system lets us form modules; when we use abstraction to refine each partitioned component, we then have both a horizontal and vertical decomposition of the system.

Projection enables us to understand a system from different viewpoints. A projection of a system represents the entire system with respect to only a subset of its properties. The perfect physical analogy is an architectural drawing, which is a two-dimensional view of a three-dimensional building. The notion of a "view" of a database [Astrahan 76] is another example of projection.

All of these mechanisms allow us to separate particular facets of a system from the rest and thereby retain intellectual control.

4.3: Objectives Analysis

The development of software systems should not begin with the requirements analysis. At the requirements analysis phase, a number of unnecessary and possibly restricting assumptions are made because of misconceptions, managerial politics, technical ignorance, mistrust, established practices, personnel resistance, and so forth. Many managerial decisions are made to accommodate personal, rather than organizational, objectives. For the most part, task, process, and personnel assignments are given in the requirements specification without an understanding of their explicit relationships to the organization's objectives. Thus, some unnecessary constraints for the software development may arise. The addition of an objectives analysis phase preceding the requirements analysis allows us to study the organization's objectives (and similarly, the constraints against full achievement of the objectives) and their influences, interactions, and degrees of freedom [Mittermeir 89]. Therefore, an advantage of the objectives analysis is that the new system can be built so that it will accomplish the organization's objectives even when certain modifications of the system are made to account for environmental changes; certainly, modeling the proposed system can be enhanced by the results of the objectives analysis.

Generally, it is important that analysts are not misled by the problems and constraints of the current system. The solution for solving a problem may be different depending on with whom one speaks. The difficulty is that the opinion of the people involved in the daily operations is biased by the level of abstraction from which they conceive the problem, their planning horizon, their detailed acquaintance with the application, and their personal preconceptions, goals, and responsibilities. Therefore, the true picture of "the problem to be solved" can be obtained only by collecting information from all involved parties. Un-

fortunately, this is a time consuming process. But, the main advantage resulting from this process is that the system can be used effectively by the users because of their participation during the system development [Mumford 81].

4.3.1: Fundamentals of Objectives Analysis

The term "objective" refers to a fundamental, long-lasting, stable purpose of an organization or a human being. The term "goal" means a shorter-term achievement pertinent to a given objective. Thus, an objective contains goals, which in turn contain sub-goals. Goals and sub-goals pertinent to a given objective may interact in positive or negative ways. The goals pertinent to an objective and the associated interactions are called "objective structures."

Assume that an outline always exists for a potential solution to a problem within an organization. The statement that addresses the need of a system and its justification is the point of departure for the analysis effort. It serves to identify the part of the organization that will be affected by the development effort. The major activities of the objectives analysis phase are context analysis, objectives and problem analysis, and problem definition.

Context analysis: The objectives analysis phase begins with determining the preliminary scope of the development effort. This helps the analysts gain some basic understanding of the system and its immediate environment. In other methodologies, similar analysis is undertaken in an investigation phase [Miyamoto 81] or "Ist-Analyses" [Wedekind 76].

In context analysis, the analysts should learn about the basic functions to be performed by the target system, its environment, and the boundaries between the target system and its environment. They must also identify the major quantitative characteristics of the system and its environment [Putnam 78 and Basili 80], such as the number of employees, number of items produced or sold, etc. Combining modeling and context analysis can be an effective approach to understanding complex problems.

When all this information is collected, the persons who are affected by the development effort can be identified. These include the users of the new system, their managers, supervisors, and other personnel. The informants to be questioned during the following activities will be chosen from this list of personnel.

Objectives and problem analysis: A problem can be defined as the difference between an original goal set and the actual goal attained on a certain objectives dimension. For this reason, problems may be good indicators of objective dimensions. However, when solving a problem, it is important to remember those aspects of the organization's goals that have been reached well enough so as not to be mentioned in connection with problems. Since the ultimate solution must continue to accommodate these unstated goals, a simple problem analysis will not yield a complete view of the organization. The major objectives that lead the organization activities must also be considered.

After structuring the obtained objective dimensions into goal/sub-goal relationships, the analysts must determine whether complementary or adversary relationships exist between various goals and/or sub-goals (i.e., the magnitude of intergoal dependencies). The analysts must identify the objectives of adverse groups (e.g., competitors) that could hinder full goal achievement (i.e., the level of current attainment versus the desired attainment). These "negative" objectives will serve as restrictions in later analysis and during the process of selecting the best alternative solutions.

The objectives and problem analysis follows the integration of objectives structures of the different groups within the customer organization by resolving the differences through negotiation and arbitration. Finally, the objectives structure of the organization, which is relevant to the current development effort, should be formally agreed upon and accepted.

Problem definition: Problem definition investigates the definition of the system, its environment, the boundaries between the system and its environment, the problem areas that need to be addressed, and the constraints under which solutions need to be sought.

4.4: Summary

During the process of objectives analysis, the scope of the development effort and the goals of the customer's organization are identified and refined to a point where actual operations and the resources required to perform them have also been identified. As they analyze and refine the objectives, the analysts formulate ways to reach these objectives. Therefore, at the end of the objectives analysis phase, the analysts have identified the goal structure of the customer's organization and a set of alternative solutions, proposed on the basis of their own experience or a detailed study of the problems at hand. The requirements analysis can then continue, including the alternatives evaluation, system requirements analysis, medium definition, and software requirements analysis sub-phases.

5: What Should Be Included in the Requirements Document?

The conceptual model mentioned in the previous section should be a rich, complex information structure; the completeness and precison of conceptually modeling the real world can be enhanced by the process of objectives analysis. Usually there is too much information to be in-

cluded in the software requirements document (SRD). The SRD can be derived from the conceptual model by filtering and organizing, constantly aiming toward the "best engineered" specification. The SRD can be divided into two major parts: functional requirements and nonfunctional requirements. Here we discuss only examples of what might belong in a software requirements specification. For a complete set of software requirements specifications, see [ANSI/IEEE 84].

5.1: Functional Requirements

Functional requirements describe what the target system does, and these are clearly the heart of the SRD. Section 4 introduced an explicit model of the proposed system's environment as an important tool for requirements analysis, a model that led to the global model shown in Figure 3. From the viewpoint of functional requirements specification, having an explicit model of the environment creates an important advantage: since interactions between the target system and its environment can be explicitly stated, it is easy to specify the interface between system and environment in an accurate, precise, understandable, though modifiable, manner. Thus the task of the functional requirements specification is to find a formal representation for the detailed information needed to fill in Figure 3. In the following paragraphs we discuss several approaches to deriving a functional requirements specification.

5.1.1: Data Models

Data-oriented models concentrate on specifying the states of the conceptual model shown in Figure 3. The state of the target system will always be represented as a data structure, and the state of the environment can be modeled as a data structure that need never be implemented.

A data model must be interfaced with processing aspects of the system. At the very least, a set of primitive data manipulation operations should be enumerated. These operations should be defined in terms of a first-order predicate language and the operations "create," "destroy," and "modify" applied to individuals in the database.

Data-oriented models, which are the heart of requirements analysis and specification, have been very successful in the domains of data processing and business information systems.

References [Yeh 89, Roussopoulos 79, and Mittermeir 80] contain some excellent examples.

5.1.2: Dataflow Processing Models

Dataflow diagrams are the most common models of the processing activities of a system and are used in conjunction with data-oriented models. They simply name the major processing activities of the system and indicate which parts of the data model are the inputs and outputs of each activity. If iterative refinement of the dataflow diagram is supported and activities are defined (usually informally) in terms of data manipulation operations, the diagram will exhibit a level of expressive power sufficient for many data processing systems.

The dataflow approach is central to structured analysis and design technique (SADT) [Ross 77a and Ross 77b], although they also emphasize a methodology for team cooperation. The dataflow approach is supported with automated tools in the problem statement language/ problem statement analyzer (PSL/PSA) [Teichroew 77]. It can be extended with control information via Petri nets [Peterson 77] or with resource synchronization [Conner 79].

The deficiencies of the dataflow model for specifying real-time embedded systems are that the global events and activities in these kinds of systems are continuous and are not activated by the appearance of a single input or any simple combination of inputs. At a lower level, they consist of complex combinations of pieces of computation that must occur asynchronously and in parallel. Dataflow as a concept is simply not powerful enough to permit precise specification or effective decomposition of systems, such as embedded ones, in which concurrent and asynchronous operations occur at the requirements level.

5.1.3: The Process Model

The process model, which is better suited for the specification of embedded systems, emphasizes the "events" and "activities" portions of Figure 3. The central concept is the process, an autonomously computational unit that operates in parallel with and interacts asynchronously with other processes. Processes have long been used as abstractions of concurrent activity within multiprogramming systems [Horning 73], and many recent articles have shown that they can be used to model databases, monitors, functional modules, input/output devices, and presumably any other identifiable structure within a computing system (e.g., Hoare 78 and Hansen 78).

Formally, a process is a "state space," or a set of possible states, and a "successor relation" that maps predecessor states onto their possible successors. This simple concept is easily adapted into digital simulation of an object (person, machine, sensors, etc.) in the environment of a computer system.

The result of the generality of processes is that the requirements for a system can be specified by a set of asynchronously interacting processes, some of which represent objects in the environment, and some of which represent objects in the target system. Consequently, a process

model with a highly complex overall behavior is easily formed.

Using an executable model that emphasizes the active parts of the required system is the "operational" approach, which was first taken by the software requirements engineering methodology (SREM) system and its requirements specification language RSL [Bell 77, Alford 77, and Davis 77]. In RSL, processing paths from input stimuli to output responses are specified directly and can be simulated for performance purposes. Stimulus-response paths are an important aspect of operational requirements, but are incomplete, since they exclude explicit representations of system states, internal synchronization, or potentially distributed environments.

Process-oriented, applicative, interpretable specification language (PAISLey) [Zave 82 and Zave 81] is another executable language, which in comparison, is more complete than RSL in its inclusion of states, synchronization, and the system's environment. In addition, it shows that the operational approach has three significant advantages for deriving embedded system requirements. The first advantage is that the rigor of having to make a model that "runs" always proves to be a powerful influence against ambiguity and vagueness in requirements. The second advantage of operational specifications is that they provide natural structures to which performance requirements can be attached. This is especially important for embedded systems. References [Zave 79 and Zave 81] show how response time and feedback-loop requirements can be specified formally by attaching timing attributes to functions in specification. A third advantage is that operational specifications make it possible to include resource requirements when necessary. Resource requirements specify the use of a particular resource or a quantity of a resource.

5.2: Nonfunctional Requirements

Most of the literature and methodologies for requirements focus on defining functional capabilities. Nonfunctional requirements, however, have received very little attention and may be an equally important part of the SRD. Since the state of the art is quite far from a comprehensive theory or methodology for these requirements, we present an annotated outline, intended as a checklist of the various topics that should at least be considered, even if not included, in the SRD.

5.2.1: Target System Constraints

Constraints are attributes other than capabilities that restrict the kinds of solutions the designer may consider. Constraints that can be placed on the target system include, but are not limited to, performance, reliability, security, and operating and physical constraints.

431

Performance: Here, performance includes all factors that describe both the subjective and objective qualities of the target system. Performance is therefore a measurement of "success" of the target system and a constraint below which the system must not be allowed to fall.

Reliability: Reliability can be divided into two basic categories: the availability of the physical equipment and the integrity of the information [Jones 80]. For requirements, the concern is "failures" (noticeable events in which the system violates its specifications), rather than "faults" (mechanical or algorithmic defects that will generate an error) [Zelkowitz 79], since the way the system maintains its specified level of reliability is a concern of the system developers, not those who write requirements. The purpose of defining and classifying the failures is to allow constraints to be placed on the likelihood of such failures.

Security: Much of security is arguably in the realm of design, since it pertains to specific means by which the reliability of the system may be enhanced. However, in two areas security may be an appropriate requirement. The first is physical security, which may include, for example, all military standards for pressurized cable, disconnectable terminals, safes for storing classified tapes and disks, and even the criteria for destroying or reusing storage media. Operational security includes any method that must be used to cipher, modularize, limit transmission, or otherwise affect how or where sensitive information will be available. Note that the physical considerations for reuse of media are in some ways part of the operational category, since it is well known that disks, for example, even when erased or overwritten a dozen times, can be made to reveal their original information with specialized signal differentiating equipment.

Operating constraints: One operating constraint considered here is the frequency and duration of use of a proposed system. Frequency and duration of use are important not only from a staffing and maintenance point of view, but also from the standpoint of available resources. If the computer equipment is, for example, only used as part of the target system for a limited time, it might be used as a general facility at other times. Conversely, an existing facility may be able to support the needs of the target system. In designing a satellite probe, it might be very important to know that a computer module could be connected to a network and used for computational assistance when not operating in its primary capacity.

Control is an important operating constraint in many systems. An unmanned remote facility cannot be restarted by personnel if a failure occurs. Depending on whether personnel can reach the remote site, the equipment may need sophisticated automatic restart or even reconfiguration capabilities. Preventive maintenance may also be im-

possible in inaccessible locations, such as inside satellites or deep-sea probes. In addition, the location of the remote facility may affect the nature of interactions required, since distant space probes experience significant transmission delays because of speed-of-light limitations.

Physical contraints: The physical constraints requirements should include all factors relating to the physical placement of the equipment. In some applications, even camouflaging the external casing of the hardware itself might be an important physical constraint. Such constraints also include size, weight, power, temperature, humidity, and portability and ruggedness requirements.

System development, evolution, and maintenance: In many organizations, the plan for the development, evolution, and maintenance of a target system is a separate document from the requirements, since the development plan is considered to be a statement of how the requirements will be carried out. On the other hand, in many instances, large computer systems are requested and paid for by one group and developed and delivered by another. Constraints on the magnitude and cost of the development effort may very well be considered requirements by the group paying the bill. In this section, we discuss various development categories relating to the lifecycle plan.

Development strategies: The strategies for developing target systems can be divided into two gross categories: efforts directed toward the single delivery date when the completed operational system will be furnished, and efforts that plan to deliver working subsets of the requirements for evaluation in the field before embarking on a more complete version. The single full-scale effort is often itself iterative [Conn 80], but the early versions of the system are not intended for use by the customer. Prototyping may be required in time-critical situations where delivering any kind of working system will fulfill an immediate need. Similarly, in state-of-the-art projects, careful analysis of a system shell may be needed to evaluate human factors and to clarify the requirements. Most software systems are iterative; for example, operating systems are usually updated on a regular basis throughout their lives.

Scale of effort: The scale of effort is an essential factor in establishing requirements for the development strategies of a target system. In iterative efforts that envision many prototypes or versions, resources should be allocated for personnel, equipment, and overhead associated with the development of each version. When development time is included as a requirement, an evaluation can be made that assesses whether it is possible to complete the stated goals within the proposed time frame. If an extended or advanced development is foreseen for one or more iterations, this information should be incorporated into the requirements. Finally, each version should have a plan for delivery and installation. When equipment is to be installed in aircraft or naval vessels, delivery and installation may be a complex technical endeavor. When many installations are already in the field, the requirements may include special procedures for handling the logistics of updating each installation.

Quality control standards: Control over the quality of the software and hardware product is exercised to guarantee that software and hardware conform to established requirements and perform satisfactorily. Quality control is an important management technique to ensure the success of the project. In general, although the role of quality assurance in software development is vague and software quality measures are still unstandardized, it is reasonable to consider the current ideas on top-down structured, provable, and modularized software as elements of quality control. As a result, many organizations now include standardization enforcement software within their compilers and assemblers.

Milestones and review procedures: Milestones and review procedures evaluate and keep track of partly completed systems. The milestone is an identifiable stage of completion that can be used to determine whether parallel efforts are progressing on time with respect to one another. Developers themselves use review procedures to assess the progress of an effort. The contracting agency may request a feasibility study for implementing a portion of the entire system. In this case, a milestone might reflect the point at which the feasibility has been proven, thus enabling serious subsystem design efforts to begin.

Acceptance criteria: The acceptance criteria identify specific tests and evaluation factors by which the developed system can be judged. Traditionally, the acceptance criteria are the "teeth" in the contract against which disputes are settled. Since a target system can almost never be exhaustively tested, it is critical that the acceptance tests cover every significant combination of functions or activities the system is supposed to perform.

Priority and changeability: Carrying out some requirements may be very important, but other requirements may represent "goldplating." Constraints such as cost, size, training, and development time may make it necessary to delay consideration of some of the less critical requirements. A means for ranking requirements or associating some weighting factors to particular facets of a target system is very useful; these rankings could follow Parnas' modularization based on the likelihood of change [Parnas 72]. If a designer is to be expected to hide system decisions that could easily change in some modular organization, the requirements must give information about what might change. Similarly, if a general requirement can be satisfied by more than one entirely different solution, it may be

necessary to include detailed requirements for each of the solutions.

Maintenance: The maintenance category here specifically excludes the evolutionary software activities often classified under "maintenance." The requirements address the system's break down and subsequent return to working condition. For the software, the requirements might specify the staffing needed or a contractual agreement for fixing "bugs." The document might list the kinds of programs or packages that will be supplied to fix "bugs," and the kinds of software to be embedded in the system (such as error logging or path counters) that aid in discovering and tracing errors. As for hardware, it is necessary to know who will perform the preventive maintenance and repairs. The requirements may need to spell out standards for the minimal set of test points at which the repairer can probe and access the operation of the circuit.

5.2.3: Economic Context of System Development

Very few projects are undertaken without considering cost-effectiveness. Even extravagant programs give cost trade-offs serious consideration. Satisfactory economic decisions are much more likely to be made if the cost, goals, and guidelines are spelled out in the requirements documents.

Trade-offs: Requirements for cost trade-offs establish guidelines for determining whether existing equipment and software can be satisfactorily incorporated into the target system or whether a new effort is required. Very often off-the-shelf equipment is not ideal and does not entirely satisfy the requirements. However, cost/trade-off requirements can effectively overrule other requirements, if the sacrifice is not too great. Some criteria are needed to indicate just how important the ready-made requirement is and what might be given up to fulfill that requirement.

Cost of iterative system development: Many projects are developed iteratively, whether or not the customer sees the intervening stages or prototypes; to measure these iterations, almost all projects have milestones or baselines that indicate the achievement of some level of operation or functionality. Without requirements that place cost limitations on these stages, fund allocation to project phases could be unbalanced, starving, for example, later efforts due to disproportionate expenditures at the beginning of the project. In addition, if prototypes are to be delivered to the customer for interim use or evaluation, the requirements should address these costs.

Cost of each instance of the target system: The development effort may be directed at producing many similar or identical target systems. Under these circumstances, the development costs are usually amortized over the entire projected production run. Each instance of the target system will carry costs from materials and from the applicable fraction of development expenses. Any proposed evolutionary change to the target system after delivery will have to take into account the costs of updating each installation.

6: Managing the Requirements Process

In this section, we recommend ways to ensure that the requirements generation process is successful and productive.

6.1: Getting the Needed Information

One concern is how to gain access to information we may need that is hidden somewhere in the environment or in the minds of the users themselves. Another concern is how to broaden the users perspective so that enough subgoals and operational alternatives to accomplish these goals can be found. The information collected in interviews and documents analysis should be prepared so that it can be used as the starting point for refinement through the process of requirements analysis.

6.2: Getting the Users Involved

Requirements do not leap at the system analyst from their problem domain, but evolve through human interaction. Many of the problems that originate early in requirements analysis can be attributed to lack of communication between the user community and software engineers. Some common communication problems are well known: ideas may be expressed vaguely or ambiguously, goals may be contradictory or incompletely formulated, and various users may have differing views of the desired system. Realizing that these difficulties exist leads to the conclusion that good requirements analysis depends on intensive interaction with the user community at all authority levels, as well as on feedback from the software engineers on how they understand the desired system.

6.3: Getting the Baseline Requirements

Requirements will change as the users learn more about the system. Therefore, management should allocate time for changes in the requirements; otherwise, the system delivered may not be what the users desired. Once the frequency of changes settles down, however, a baseline requirement must be obtained before the first software design review. The baseline is intended to interpret mandatory provisions of the requirements specification. The baseline requirement must be "signed off" by the customer and kept firm.

6.4: Concern for Requirements Traceability and Testability

Requirements-tracing uses documentation and specification techniques to establish and maintain bidirectional

traceability in two ways from requirements through design and ultimately through coding, and from requirements to validation tests. This tracing maintains awareness of the requirements as design and development activities proceed.

The sequence of events in traceability is relatively easy to establish. Testability of requirements demands much more thought and effort. For example, if there is to be a display that queries a database, then the requirements for response time can be complex. They should include solid reasons for specifying a certain value, or proposed experiments to determine and validate the end user's real needs; the experiments should both verify what the need is and check that the final product meets the need.

6.5: Concern for the Entire Lifecycle Process

This point was stressed earlier; functional requirements are essential to, but are only part of the total requirements.

6.6: Separate the Concerns

Most of the requirements document consists of thick volumes of natural language statements; therefore, traceability and testability are difficult to perform. The document itself should be organized so that each project member can concentrate on a well-defined set of questions. This separation also makes the document easy to change, because it refines the definiton of changes. For example, hardware interfaces should be described without making any assumption about the purpose of the software, so that the hardware section can remain unchanged if the behavior of the software is changed, and vice versa.

6.7: Use Precise Notation

To avoid confusion and minimize the amount of implicit assumptions by the developer, the analyst should avoid narrative and develop a formal system of notation that presents information in a rigorous, consistent, and complete manner.

7: Conclusion

In the new paradigm for evolving software, the abstraction-based software lifecycle model is applied. This model concentrates on the hard problems of software, namely, requirements specification and design, rather than on coding. Evaluation and validation are parts of the development process, rather than the completion of the development in each phase. In this paper, we have examined the conceptual and operational models and WBS as techniques to alleviate problems encountered in the process of deriving requirements. Preceding the requirements analysis, the objectives analysis allows us to study the organization's objectives and the constraints against the full achievement of the objectives, including their influences, interactions, and degrees of freedom.

Material to be included in a software requirements document can be derived from the conceptual model by filtering and organizing, constantly aiming towards the "best-engineered" specification. Only examples of what might go into a software requirements document (functional and nonfunctional requirements) are discussed. For functional requirements, the process model is a better approach than the data-oriented model and dataflow processing model to the precise specification or effective decomposition of embedded systems. Finally, several recommendations are provided for managing the requirements derivation process.

8: References

[Alford 77] Alford, Mack, "A Requirements Engineering Methodology for Real-Time Processing Requirements," *IEEE Transactions on Software Engineering,* SE-3, Jan. 1977, pp. 60-69.

[ANSI/IEEE 84] *IEEE Guide to Software Requirements Specifications,* ANSI/IEEE Standards 830, IEEE, New York, 1984.

[Astrahan 76] Astrahan, M.M., et al., "System R: Relational Approach to Database Management," *ACM Transactions on Database Systems,* June 1976, pp. 97-137.

[Baker 89] Baker, Jerry W., Daniel Chester, and Raymond T. Yeh, "Software Design by Stepwise Evaluation and Refinement," *Modern Software Engineering: Foundations and Current Perspectives,* (eds. P.A. Ng and R.T. Yeh), Van Nostrand Reinhold, New York, Oct. 1989, pp. 239-273.

[Basili 80] Basili, V.R., *Tutorial on Models and Metrics for Software Management and Engineering,* IEEE Computer Society Press, Washington, D.C., 1980.

[Bell 77] Bell, Thomas E., Davis C. Bixler, and Margaret Dyer, "An Extenuable Approach to Computer-Aided Software Requirements Engineering," *IEEE Transactions on Software Engineering,* SE-3, Jan. 1977, pp. 48-59.

[Boehm 73] Boehm, Barry W., "Software and Its Impact: A Quantitative Assessment," *Datamation, 19,* May 1973, pp. 48-60.

[Boehm 81] Boehm, Barry W., *Software Engineering Economics,* Prentice-Hall, Old Tappan, N.J., 1981.

[Conn 80] Conn, Alex Paul, "Maintenance: A Key Element in Computer Requirements Definition," *Proc. COMSPAC,* IEEE Computer Society Press, Washington, D.C., Nov. 1980.

[Conner 79] Conner, M., "Process Synchronization by Behavior Controllers," Ph.D. thesis, Computer Sciences Department, University of Texas at Austin, 1979.

[Davis 77] Davis, Carl C. and Charles R. Vick, "The Software Development System," *IEEE Transactions on Software Engineering,* SE-3, Jan. 1977, pp. 69-84.

[Hansen 78] Hansen, Per Brinch, "Distributed Processes: A Concurrent Programming Concept," *Communications of the ACM, 21,* Nov. 1978, pp. 934-941.

[Hoare 78] Hoare, C.A.R., "Communicating Sequential Processes," *Communications of the ACM, 21,* Aug. 1978, pp. 666-667.

[Horning 73] Horning, J.J. and B. Randell, "Process Structuring," *Computing Survey, 5,* Jan. 1973, pp. 5-29.

[Jones 80] Jones, A.K. and P. Schwarz, "Experience Using Multiprocessor Systems—A Status Report," *Computing Survey, 12,* June 1980, pp. 121-165.

[Mittermeir 80] Mittermeir, Roland, "Requirements Analysis: Top Down or Bottom Up," *TRDA 80/02/02,* Institut fur Digitale Anlagen, Technische Universitat Wein, Vienna, Austria, 1980.

[Mittermeir 89] Mittermeir, Roland, Nicholas Roussopolous, Raymond T. Yeh, and Peter A. Ng, "An Integrated Approach to Requirements Analysis," *Modern Software Engineering: Foundations and Current Perspectives,* (eds. P.A. Ng and R.T. Yeh), Van Nostrand Reinhold, New York, Oct. 1989, pp. 119-164.

[Miyamoto 81] Miyamoto, I. and R.T. Yeh, "A Software Requirements and Definition Methodology for Business Data Processing," *Proc. 1981 Nat'l Computer Conference, AFIPS Conf. Proc. 50,* AFIPS Press, Reston, VA, 1981, pp. 571-581.

[Mumford 81] Mumford, E., "Participative Systems Design: Structure and Method," *Systems, Objectives, Selections 1,* 1981, pp. 5-19.

[Parnas 72] Parnas, D.L., "On the Criteria to Be Used in Decomposing Systems into Modules," *Communications of the ACM, 15,* Dec. 1972, pp. 1053-1059.

[Peterson 77] Peterson, James L., "Petri Nets," *Computing Surveys 9,* Sept. 1977, pp. 227-252.

[Putnam 78] Putnam, L.M., "A General Empirical Solution to the Macro Software Sizing and Estimating Problem." *IEEE Transactions on Software Engineering,* SE-4, July 1978, pp. 345-361.

[Radice 88] Radice, R.A. and R.W. Phillips, *Software Engineering: An Industrial Approach, Vol. I,* Prentice-Hall, N.J., 1988.

[Ross 77a] Ross, Douglas, "Structured Analysis (SA): A Language for Communicating Ideas," *IEEE Transactions on Software Engineering,* SE-3, Jan. 1977, pp. 15-34.

[Ross 77b] Ross, Douglas and Kenneth E. Schoman, Jr., "Structured Analysis for Requirements Definition," *IEEE Transactions on Software Engineering*, SE-3, Jan. 1977, pp. 6-15.

[Roussopoulos 79] Roussopoulos, Nicholas, "CSDL: A Conceptual Scheme Definition Language for the Design of Database Applications," *IEEE Transactions on Software Engineering*, SE-5, Sept. 1979, pp. 481-496.

[Royce 70] Royce., W.W., "Managing the Development of Large Software Systems: Concepts and Techniques," *Proc. WESCON*, IEEE, New York, Aug. 1970.

[Teichroew 77] Teichroew, B. and B.A. Hershey, III, "PSL/PSA: A Computer-Aided Technique for Structured Documentation and Analysis of Information Systems," *IEEE Transactions on Software Engineering*, SE-3, Jan. 1977, pp. 41-48.

[Thayer 75] Thayer, T.A., "Understanding Software through Analysis of Empirical Data," *TRW Software Series*, TRW-SS-75-04, May 1975.

[Wedekind 76] Wedekind, E., "Systemanalyse," Carl Hanser Verlag, Munich, F.R. Germany, 1976.

[Yeh 79] Yeh, Raymond T., "Systematic Derivation of Software Requirements through Structured Analysis," *Computer Science SDBEG-15*, University of Texas at Austin, Sept. 1979.

[Yeh 82] Yeh, Raymond T., "Requirements Analysis—A Management Perspective," *Proc. IEEE Sixth Int'l Computer Software and Applications Conference*, IEEE Computer Society Press, Washington, D.C., 1982, pp. 410-416.

[Yeh 83] Yeh, Raymond T., "Software Engineering," *IEEE Spectrum*, Nov. 1983, pp. 91-94.

[Yeh 89] Yeh, Raymond T., "An Alternative Paradigm for Software Evolution," *Modern Software Engineering: Foundations and Current Perspectives*, (eds. P.A. Ng. and R.T. Yeh), Van Nostrand Reinhold, New York, Oct. 1989, pp. 7-22.

[Yeh 84] Yeh, Raymond T., P. Zave, A.P. Conn, and G.E. Cole, "Software Requirements Analysis—New Directions and Perspectives," *Handbook of Software Engineering* (eds. C. Vick and C.V. Ramamoorthy), Prentice-Hall, Old Tappan, N.J., 1982, pp. 519-543.

[Zave 79] Zave, P., "Formal Specification of Complete and Consistent Performance Requirements," *Proc. Texas Conference on Computing Systems*, IEEE Computer Society Press, Washington, D.C., Nov. 1979, pp. 4B18-4B25.

[Zave 82] Zave, P., "An Operational Approach to Requirements Specification for Embedded Systems," *IEEE Transactions on Software Engineering*, SE-8, May 1982, pp. 250-269.

[Zave 81] Zave, P. and Raymond T. Yeh, "Executable Requirements for Embedded Systems," *Proc. Fifth Int'l. Conference on Software Engineering*, IEEE Computer Society Press, Washington, D.C., 1981, pp. 295-304.

[Zelkowitz 79] Zelkowitz, M.V., A.C. Shaw, and J.D. Gannon, *Principles of Software Engineering and Design*, Prentice-Hall, Old Tappan, N.J., 1979, p. 8.

Verifying and Validating Software Requirements Specifications[1]

Dolores R. Wallace
Laura M. Ippolito
Computer Systems Laboratory
National Institute of Standards and Technology
Gaithersburg, Maryland

1. Software Verification and Validation

Software verification and validation (V&V) is an aid in determining that the software requirements are implemented correctly and completely and are traceable to system requirements. (Software V&V does not verify the correctness of the system requirements, only that the software requirements can be traced to the system requirements.) The major objective of the software V&V process is to comprehensively analyze and test the software during development to determine that the software performs its intended functions correctly, to ensure that it performs no unintended functions, and to provide information about its quality and reliability [NIST165]. Software V&V evaluates how well the software is meeting its technical requirements and its safety, security, and reliability objectives relative to the system. It also ensures that software requirements are not in conflict with any standards or requirements applicable to other system components. Software V&V tasks analyze, review, demonstrate, or test all software development outputs.

Software verification examines the products of each development activity (or increment of the activity) to determine if the software development outputs meet the requirements established at the beginning of the activity. The scope of each software development activity is defined by software program management. A software design may consist of many small increments for each iteration of the total system. Hence, V&V tasks can be performed on small outputs. Validation that the software is a correct implementation of the system requirements for which the software is responsible is conducted concurrently with, and at the end of, *all* software development activities.

The software V&V process produces a software verification and validation plan (SVVP), individual plans and reports for tasks, summary reports, anomaly reports, and a final software verification and validation report (SVVR). Software V&V planning is conducted against system requirements at the highest level of planning, and then on the software requirements, which should be traceable to the system requirements. Many software V&V tasks, such as planning for software system test, are actually performed in early development activities. The software system test plan is developed concurrently with the software requirements activity. The plan is updated with additions or changes in details as the project progresses. While different management and technical staff may be responsible for different types of test, staff who perform verification of the software requirements may be staff who prepare preliminary plans for software system tests. The development of the test plans and designs may lead to discovery of software requirements errors because of the analysis needed to plan tests.

One issue that often arises in planning a project and its software V&V effort is how to ensure the objectivity of the staff performing software V&V tasks. Independent V&V (IV&V) for software grew out of this concern. Software IV&V is the performance of software V&V tasks by a team that is separate from the software development group. Independent verification and validation is described in Section 1.1.

This guideline is intended for use with any software development methodology. The software V&V process comprises the software V&V management activity and software V&V technical activities. Each activity consists of several tasks, shown in Table 1. These tasks are defined in [FIPS132] and expanded in [WALLACE94]. Software V&V management is

---

[1] Derived from Wallace, Dolores R., Laura M. Ippolito, and Barbara B. Cuthill, "Reference Information for the Software Verification and Validation Process," NIST Special Publications 500-234, National Institute of Standards and Technology, Gaithersburg, Md., Apr. 1996.

Table 1. Major Software Verification and Validation Activities

ACTIVITY	TASKS
Software V&V Management	–Planning –Monitoring –Evaluating results, impact of change –Reporting
Software Requirements V&V	–Review of concept documentation (if not performed prior to software requirements development) –Traceability Analysis –Software Requirements Evaluation –Interface Analysis –Initial Planning for Software System Test –Reporting
Software Design V&V	–Traceability Analysis –Software Design Evaluation –Interface Analysis –Initial Planning for Unit Test –Initial Planning for Software Integration Test –Reporting
Code V&V	–Traceability Analysis –Code Evaluation –Interface Analysis –Completion of Unit Test Preparation –Reporting
Unit Test	–Unit Test Execution –Reporting
Software Integration Test	–Completion of Software Integration Test Preparation –Execution of Software Integration Tests –Reporting
Software System Test [2]	–Completion of Software System Test Preparation –Execution of Software System Tests –Reporting
Software Installation Test	–Installation Configuration Audit –Reporting
Software Operation and Maintenance V&V	–Impact-of-Change Analysis –Repeat Management V&V –Repeat Technical V&V Activities

described in Section 1.2. It ensures that task selection is appropriate for achieving the software V&V objectives, ensures the performance and quality of the V&V effort, selects appropriate metrics and techniques applied to the V&V results, and conveys results of the V&V "tasks" to appropriate places. The software V&V technical activities each have several tasks. Each task is accomplished by applying one or more techniques. A specific technique, such as control flow analysis, focuses on finding a specific type of problem, for example, a logic error. An aggregate of techniques is usually necessary to achieve the objectives of a task.

[2] This document treats acceptance test as a function of the acquirer of the software system, while acknowledging that the acquirer may sometimes work with V&V staff from the software requirements V&V through software installation test to develop acceptance test. Tasks for acceptance test parallel those for software system test. Differences may exist in the specific objectives, which may influence test requirements.

Section 1.3 discusses the tasks for each activity (Section 2 describes techniques and the problem areas related to those techniques).

This article is derived from the National Institute of Standards and Technology (NIST) Special Publication 500-234. The NIST report covers all aspects of verification and validation and should be read by all serious software engineers. This extract deals only with:

- Software requirements verification
- Software system testing (software requirements validation)

1.1. Independent Verification and Validation

Some software V&V activities may be performed by two different groups. The use of a different organization (other than the software development group) for software V&V is called independent verification and validation (IV&V). The following is summarized from the chapter on IV&V in [MARCINIAK].

Technical independence requires that members of the IV&V team (organization or group) may not be personnel involved in the development of the software. This team must have some knowledge about the system design or have related experience and engineering background enabling them to understand the system. The IV&V team must not be influenced by the development team when the IV&V team is learning about the system requirements, proposed solutions for building the system, and problems encountered.

Technical independence is crucial in the team's ability to detect the subtle software requirements, software design, and coding errors that escape detection by development testing and software quality assurance reviews.

The technical IV&V team may need to share tools from the computer support environment (for example, compilers, assemblers, utilities) but should execute qualification tests on these tools to ensure that the common tools themselves do not mask errors in the software being analyzed and tested. The IV&V team uses or develops its own set of test and analysis tools separate from the developer's tools whenever possible.

Managerial independence means the responsibility for IV&V belongs to an organization outside the contractor and program organizations that develop the software. While assurance objectives may be decided by regulations and project requirements, the IV&V team independently decides which areas of the software/system to analyze and test and which techniques to use to conduct the IV&V, and determines the schedule of tasks (within the framework of the system

schedules) and the technical issues on which to act. The IV&V team provides its findings in a timely fashion simultaneously to both the development team and systems management, which act on the reported discrepancy and findings.

Financial independence means that control of the IV&V budget is retained in an organization outside the contractor and program organization that develop the software. This independence protects against diversion of funds or adverse financial pressures or influences that may cause delay or stopping of IV&V analysis and test tasks and timely reporting of results.

The extent to which each of these parameters is vested in the IV&V team's responsibilities defines the degree of independence achieved. On the basis of the definitions of IV&V and how much IV&V a specific project requires, some software V&V activities may be conducted by both the developer and another organization. For example, unit test by one organization may focus on demonstrating that specific objectives (for example, safety objectives relative to the system), which may differ from the objectives of the developer (for example, logic structure, test coverage), have been met [IEEEP1059].

1.2. Software Verification and Validation Management

The process of software V&V needs to be managed and performed comprehensively over the entire software development process. Management tasks, spanning all of the software development activities, are to:

- Plan and maintain the software V&V process
- Coordinate and interpret performance and quality of the software V&V effort
- Report discrepancies promptly to the user or development group
- Identify early problem trends and focus software V&V tasks on them
- Provide a technical evaluation of the software performance and quality attributes at each major software program review (so a determination can be made as to whether the software product has satisfied its set of software requirements well enough to proceed to the next activity)
- Assess the full impact of proposed software changes

An SVVP contains the information necessary to manage and perform software V&V. Major steps in developing an SVVP are to:

- Define (or confirm, if already provided) the quality and performance objectives (for example, verify conformance to specifications, verify compliance with safety and computer security objectives relative to the system, assess efficiency and quality of software, and assess performance across the full operating environment)
- Characterize the types of problems anticipated in the system and define how they would be manifested in the software
- Select the software V&V analysis and testing techniques to effectively detect the system and software problems
- Select the metrics and techniques applied to V&V results to measure and predict the quality of the software

The SVVP may include details for acquiring tools and for training personnel. The SVVP is revised as knowledge accumulates about the characteristics of the system, the software, and the problem areas in the software and in software V&V activities.

The software V&V process could be tailored to specific applications; however, the risk of the software failing and the subsequent consequences must be considered when selecting software V&V activities.

One software V&V management task is to monitor the software V&V technical progress and quality of results. During each software V&V activity, planned software V&V tasks are reviewed and new ones are added to focus on the critical performance/quality functions of the software and its system. The monitoring task includes formal reviews of software V&V discrepancy reports and technical evaluations to provide a check of their correctness and accuracy. Internal monitoring of the quality and accuracy of software V&V results is essential because the development group must make the necessary software changes as indicated by the software V&V results. If the software V&V results are erroneous, or of poor quality, the development group wastes its time and resources in attempting the changes, and more importantly, loses confidence in the effectiveness and helpfulness of the software V&V results. Software V&V studies [RADATZ] have shown that responding to discrepancy reports and software V&V evaluation reports consumes the largest portion of a development group's interface time with the software V&V group.

Boehm and Papaccio [BOEHM] report that the Pareto effect (that is, 20 percent of the problems cause 80 percent of the rework costs) applies to software. They recommend that software V&V "focus on identifying and eliminating the specific high-risk problems

to be encountered by a software project." This does not mean that software V&V should examine only 20 percent of the software. Rather, software V&V needs to examine *all* the software. This includes:

- Identifying potential hazards or threats to the safety and security of the system
- Prioritizing the software functions by criticality
- Allocating software V&V analysis resources to those areas of the software that contain critical[3] functions and high-risk problems (that is, are more error-prone)

Identifying and focusing on critical and high-risk areas of the software can be addressed by these software V&V methods:

- Examination of early program deliveries to software V&V staff
- Use of software hazard (or threat) analysis
- Conduct of a "criticality analysis" to identify the most critical functions of the software

Various approaches in development can provide early product information to software V&V. These include: prototypes, incremental software development, and the handing over of each unit or subfunction following development unit testing. Incremental software development is an effective method of providing early product information to software V&V. The early deliveries reinforce the systematic analysis and test approach used by software V&V to examine the software in smaller pieces while progressively evaluating larger software pieces as each new piece is integrated. High-risk software areas are easier to identify by using the incremental approach because the software V&V can:

- Provide an early lead time to evaluate each engineering solution and allow time to suggest alternative solutions that can be incorporated in subsequent incremental deliveries without adversely impacting the schedule
- Isolate each new set of requirements and evaluate their impact on the system performance
- Provide early indications of system perform-

---

[3] A critical function is a function that must be performed, correctly and reliably; otherwise the system fails in a manner that may have serious consequences.

ance so that adjustments can be made to refine the desired performance

- Develop trend information about software anomalies and risk issues to allow time to adjust the development and software V&V resources and planning to accommodate evolving software risk issues

In incremental development, a software build (or early product) represents a basic program skeleton including draft documentation containing portions of the full software capabilities. Each successive build integrates additional functions into the skeleton. On the basis of discrepancy or progress reports from software V&V, software program management can make the technical and management decisions to refocus the software V&V and development team onto the program's specific problem areas of the software.

Two related analyses, criticality and hazard, can help focus the V&V effort on those parts of the program whose consequence of failure are most severe. A hazard is an (unsafe) "condition that may lead to an unintended event that causes an undesirable outcome" [WALLACE91]. For example, a driver of a car ignores warning lights at a railroad crossing and drives the car onto the tracks. The hazard is the presence of the car and train on the track at the same time. The unintended event (mishap) is the train colliding with the car. The undesirable outcome is the probable loss of life and damage to the car and train. The term "hazard" generally is used to refer to safety problems; the term "threat" generally is used to refer to security problems. In this document, the methods and issues related to hazard analysis are also applicable to security issues; the terms "threat" and "security" could be used in place of "hazard" and "safety," respectively.

Criticality analysis locates and reduces high-risk problems and is performed at the beginning of a project. It identifies those functions and units that are required to implement critical program functions or quality requirements (for example, safety, computer security). The steps of the analysis are as follows:

- Develop a block diagram or control-flow diagram of the system and its software. Each block or control-flow box represents a system or software function (unit)

- Trace each critical function or quality requirement through the block or control flow diagram

- Classify all traced software functions (units) as critical to either the proper execution of critical software functions or the quality requirements

- Focus additional analysis on these traced software functions (units)

- Repeat criticality analysis for each activity to observe whether the implementation details shift the criticality emphasis to other or additional functions (units)

System hazard analysis is used to identify potential events and circumstances that might lead to problems of varying degrees of severity, from critical failures resulting in loss of life or national security problems, to less serious malfunctions in the system. Software hazard (or threat) analysis focuses on the role of software relative to the hazards, or threats. Specific techniques that can be used for hazard analysis are included in Section 2 with the V&V techniques; these include event tree analysis; software fault tree analysis; Petri-nets; and software failure mode, effects, and criticality analysis.

When the results of identification of high-risk areas from early deliveries, criticality analysis, and hazard (or threat) analysis are used together, the software V&V approach can focus on the most critical areas of the early software products. Software V&V results, obtained early enough in the software development process, can have a significant impact on the quality and performance of the system under development.

1.3. Software Verification and Validation Activities

Software V&V should begin when the project begins. Usually the first software V&V tasks are conducted during the software requirements V&V activity. One V&V task is to examine the early project documentation, often called the concept documents or concept of operations (ConOps) document, to verify that the system to be built is not only feasible but will use the rules, conventions, algorithms, and practices appropriate to the application domain of the system. *Software requirements V&V* is performed to ensure that the specified software requirements are correct, complete, consistent, accurate, readable, and testable, and will satisfy the system requirements. Poorly specified software requirements (for example, incorrect, incomplete, ambiguous, or not testable) contribute to software cost overruns and problems with reliability. Even when software fully meets its requirements on delivery, there may be problems in the maintenance activity because general requirements (for example, maintainability, quality, and reusability) were not accounted for during the original development. Identifying software requirements is difficult because the complexity of the problems being solved causes uncertainty in developing the intended system performance requirements. The occurrence of changes in requirements (for example, to incorporate new technologies, new missions, new knowledge, new interfacing systems, new people coming on the scene) throughout the software development process adds significantly more chance for error. Software requirements V&V is intended to prevent these problems from occurring.

Design errors can be introduced by misrepresentation of the functional requirements and by implementation constraints relating to timing, data structures, memory space, and accuracy. *Software design V&V* provides assurance that software requirements are not misrepresented or incompletely implemented, that extraneous software requirements are not designed into the solution by oversight, that software requirements are not left out of the software design, and that other constraints are managed correctly.

Clerical and syntactical errors have been greatly reduced through use of structured programming, reuse of code, adoption of programming standards and style guides, availability of more robust computer languages, better compiler diagnostics and automated support, and, finally, more knowledgeable programmers. Nevertheless, problems still occur in translating design into code and *code V&V* continues to be an important software V&V activity.

Test management is an important part of the software V&V activity, in which all testing needed for the software system is considered and planned. Software V&V test planning begins with software requirements and spans almost the full range of activities. Test planning tasks encompass different types of testing—unit test, software integration test, and software system test. The planning activities result in documentation for each test type consisting of test plan, test design, test case, and test procedure documents.

Unit test verifies the design and implementation of software units. *Software integration test* verifies functional requirements as the software units are integrated together. Special attention is focused on software, hardware, and operator interfaces. *Software system test* validates the entire software program against system requirements and software performance objectives. Software system tests validate that the software executes correctly within its stated operating environment. The software's ability to deal with anomalies and stress conditions is emphasized. *Software V&V tests are not intended to duplicate or replace the user and development group's test responsibilities*, but instead test behavior not normally checked by the user or development group.

Software installation test validates that the software operates correctly with the operational hardware system and with other software, as specified in the interface specifications. It verifies that the installation procedures are correct and adequate, that the software is the same as the executable code delivered for installation, and that all supporting software products are the proper versions. Software installation test verifies that the software has been accurately tailored for site-dependent parameters and that the configuration of the delivered product is correct.

In *software operation and maintenance V&V*, when a software change is made, all software V&V activities are considered and possibly repeated to ensure that nothing is overlooked. Software V&V activities include examining the impact of the change throughout the system to understand what software V&V activities are needed. Software V&V activities are added or deleted to address the type of software change made. In many cases, an examination of the proposed software change shows that software V&V needs to repeat its activities on only a small portion of the software. Also, some software V&V activities, such as verifying the original concepts, require little or no effort to verify a small change. Small changes can have subtle but significant side-effects in a software program; for this reason, change analysis (a software operation and maintenance V&V task) is significant in preventing unintended functions and problems from making their way into new versions of the system.

1.3.1. Software Requirements Verification and Validation. The software requirements verification activity checks that the allocation of system requirements to software is appropriate and correct, and determines how well the software requirements have been specified (for example, correct, complete, nonambiguous, testable). Software requirements verification should be structured to ensure that the software objectives have been met. Verification of the software requirements should include an examination of documentation produced earlier in system development (for example, initial feasibility studies, concepts on which the system has been designed) if this examination has not already been performed. If the assumptions, algorithms, and physical rules imposed on the software requirements previously have not been verified to be appropriate for this project, then software V&V should perform those checks. Inputs to the software requirements V&V activity may be documents written in natural or formal mathematical languages and may include graphics and charts. When formal mathematical languages are used, other forms of representations may be provided to different users of the specifications. Software requirements verification must ensure fidelity among the forms of representation [NIST223].

Concurrently with software requirements V&V,

software system test planning is initiated. Software V&V examines all the proposed testing for the system to ensure that comprehensive testing and appropriate resources are planned. Each type of testing (unit, software integration, software system) is discussed more fully in this report. When the system requirements and the software requirements have been specified and reuse of software is identified, reuse issues must be checked to ensure the software is suitable for the application domain and the operating environment.

The activities of software requirements verification are as follows:

- Conduct a concept documentation evaluation:
  - ▸ Evaluate the defined concept to determine whether it satisfies user needs and project objectives in terms of system performance requirements, feasibility (for example, compatibility of hardware capabilities), completeness, accuracy
  - ▸ Identify major constraints of interfacing systems and constraints/limitations of the proposed approach and assess the allocation of system functions to hardware and software, where appropriate
  - ▸ Assess the criticality of each software item defined in the concept

- Begin test planning[4]

- Conduct a software traceability analysis:
  - ▸ Trace software requirements to system requirements (and vice versa)
  - ▸ Check the relationships for accuracy, completeness, consistency, and correctness
  - ▸ Check that allocation is appropriate and complete

- Conduct a software requirements evaluation:
  - ▸ Evaluate the software requirements for accuracy, completeness, consistency, correctness, testability, and understandability
    - — Measure completeness by verifying existence and correctness of defining properties: initiator of action, action, object of action, conditions, constraints, source, destination, mechanism, and reason
    - — Verify correctness and appropriateness of software requirements and assertions (executable statements that may

be required in the software as fault tolerance protections for the system safety and computer security objectives; for example, checking algorithms, states, and integrity of system and the responses to unfavorable results of the assertions). Verify that the operation of the assertions will not adversely impact system performance
  - — Verify correctness and appropriateness of fault tolerance requirements. Verify that the operation of the assertions will not adversely impact system performance
  - ▸ Assess how well the software requirements accomplish the system and software objectives
  - ▸ Identify critical areas of software by assessing criticality of software requirements
  - ▸ Evaluate software requirements for compliance to software requirements standards and software engineering practices

- Conduct a software interface analysis—evaluate software requirements with hardware, user, operator, and software interface requirements for accuracy, completeness, consistency, correctness, and understandability

- Evaluate the reused software (if applicable) to verify conformance to its performance goals, to identify constraints of interfacing systems, to determine allocation of functions to hard-ware and software, and to assess criticality of each software item

- Conduct software interface analysis to evaluate reused software (if applicable) in terms of new requirements for accuracy, completeness, consistency, correctness, and understandability, relative to the operating environment of both the reused and the new software and to the application domain. When commercial-off-the-shelf (COTS) software is considered for use in a new system, this task is especially significant for ensuring that the COTS software will match the system interfaces in the operating environment

- Compare the new software system objectives to the content of the reused documentation and the reused code to ensure the:
  - ▸ Availability of all necessary files
  - ▸ Adequacy of the user manual (compared to the requirements for the user manual in

---

[4] V&V tasks related to testing are discussed in Section 1.3.2.

443

software development) and compatibility of the software, hardware, and system environment (for example, was the old system designed for a 16-bit machine and will now be on a 32-bit machine?)

- If the reused software is COTS, consider whether any functions of the software are to be blocked out from usage, if the consequences of any functions are unknown, and the operational history of the COTS software relative to failure

1.3.2. Software System Test. *Software system test*, in the context of software V&V, involves the conduct of tests to execute the completely integrated system. *Software system test is the validation that the software meets its requirements.* Validation of the complete system may involve many tests involving all system components. The software system tests exercise those system functions that invoke software to determine whether the software behaves as intended relative to complete system performance. These tests must be conducted in such a manner as to stress the system on the basis of software responses to system inputs (for example, from sensors, operators, databases). Tests and data collected from the tests are designed to provide an operational profile of the system that supports a statistical analysis of the system reliability [MUSA87, MUSA89, BUTLER]. This section of the article addresses only the tests that validate that the software implements the system requirements; other tests for other components and perspectives are necessary for complete system validation.

Acceptance testing, which involves the user/customer, is outside the scope of this article.

While software system tests are conducted after the system has been built, it is imperative that planning for these tests be conducted concurrently with the software requirements activity because:

- Analyzing the software requirements for test requirements may result in finding software requirements errors and/or discovery of untestable requirements
- Establishing test facilities (for example, model of operational environment) and computer-aided software engineering (CASE) tools (for example, test case generators, test database) may require as much time as development of the system

For reused software, software system test is performed to assure that the software is correct, consistent with prior documentation, complete for use and/or modification, and accurate. At the system level, reused software should be considered part of the system. Tests are in accordance with test procedures. Results are documented and traced as required by the software system test plan.

The activities of software requirements validation (software system test) are as follows:

- Establish the objectives of the software system test, the strategies to be employed, the coverage requirements, reporting and analysis, and close-out of anomalies
- Generate, monitor, and update a software system test plan to accomplish objectives
- Trace system and software requirements to documented test software design, cases, procedures, and execution results
- Develop test cases and procedures for unit test and continue tracing as required by software system test plans
- Test the operation of the software as an entity (sometimes a simulated environment may be used); confirm that anomalies during test are software anomalies, not problems detected for other reasons; ensure any changes to software (software requirements, software design, code, or test cases) have been made; and conduct retesting as necessary
- Document test activities and results.
- Evaluate existing test cases and reports (if available) for suitability for intended use
- Prepare test cases and test procedures if any modifications have been made to the reused software
- Follow the criteria for software system test within the boundaries of the known and documented software design

2. Software Verification and Validation Techniques

The conduct of software V&V tasks to fulfill the requirements of the V&V activities generally involves techniques selected from three major classes: static, dynamic, and formal analysis. *Static* analysis techniques are those that directly analyze the form and structure of a product without executing the product [FIPS101]. Reviews, inspections, audits, and dataflow analysis are examples of static analysis techniques. Static analysis techniques are traditionally applied to software requirements, software design, and source code. They may also be applied to test documentation, especially test cases, to verify their traceability to the software requirements, their adequacy to fulfill test requirements, and their accuracy.

Dynamic analysis techniques involve execution, or simulation, of a development activity product to detect errors by analyzing the response of a product to sets of input data [FIPS101]. For these techniques, the output values, or ranges of values, must be known. Testing is the most frequent dynamic analysis technique. Prototyping, especially during the software requirements V&V activity, can be considered a dynamic analysis technique; in this case the exact output is not always known but enough knowledge exists to determine if the system response to the input stimuli meets system requirements.

Formal analysis is the use of rigorous mathematical techniques to analyze the algorithms of a solution [FIPS101]. Sometimes the software requirements may be written in a formal specification language (for example, VDM, Z) which can be verified using a formal analysis technique like proof-of-correctness. The term *formal* often is used to mean a formalized process, that is, a process that is planned, managed, documented, and is repeatable. In this sense, all software V&V techniques are formal, but do not necessarily meet the definition of the mathematical techniques involving special notations and languages.

Table 2 lists the software V&V techniques addressed in this article and indicates under which V&V activities these techniques can be applied. This article does not necessarily address all software V&V techniques.

Table 2. Software Verification and Validation Techniques

TECHNIQUE	REQUIREMENTS VERIFICATION	SYSTEM TEST (REQUIREMENTS VALIDATION)
Algorithm analysis	✔	
Back-to-back testing		✔
Boundary value analysis		✔
Consistency analysis	✔	
Control flow analysis	✔	
Coverage analysis		✔
Database analysis	✔	
Dataflow analysis	✔	
Decision (truth) tables	✔	
Error seeding		✔
Event tree analysis	✔	
Finite state machines	✔	
Functional testing		✔
Inspections	✔	
Interface analysis	✔	✔
Interface testing		✔
Mutation analysis		✔
Performance testing		✔
Prototyping	✔	✔
Regression analysis and testing	✔	✔
Requirements parsing	✔	
Reviews	✔	✔
Simulation	✔	
SFMECA [5]	✔	
Software fault tree analysis	✔	
Stress testing		✔
Test certification		✔
Walkthroughs	✔	✔

[5] Software failures mode, effects and critical analysis

2.1. Strategies for Choosing Techniques

Some software V&V techniques used during software requirements V&V tasks are control flow analysis, dataflow analysis, algorithm analysis, and simulation. Control and dataflow analyses are most applicable for real-time and data-driven systems. These flow analyses transform logic and data requirements text into graphic flows, which are easier to analyze than the text. PERT, state transition, and transaction diagrams are examples of control flow diagrams. Algorithm analysis involves rederivation of equations or evaluation of the suitability of specific numerical techniques. Simulation is used to evaluate the interactions of large, complex systems with many hardware, user, and other interfacing software units.

Some software V&V techniques used during software design V&V tasks include algorithm analysis, database analysis, sizing and timing analysis, and simulation. Algorithm analysis examines the correctness of the equations or numerical techniques as in the software requirements activity, but also examines truncation and round-off effects, numerical precision of word storage and variables (for example, single-versus extended-precision arithmetic), and data typing influences. Database analysis is particularly useful for programs that store program logic in data parameters. A logic analysis of these data values is required to determine the effect these parameters have on program control. Sizing and timing analysis is useful for real-time programs having response time requirements and constrained memory execution space requirements.

Some software V&V techniques used during code V&V tasks are control flow analysis, database analysis, regression analysis, and sizing and timing analysis. For large code developments, control flow diagrams showing the hierarchy of main routines and their subfunctions are useful in understanding the flow of program control. Database analysis is performed on programs with significant data storage to ensure common data and variable regions are used consistently between all call routines. Data integrity is enforced and no data or variable can be accidentally overwritten by overflowing data tables. Data typing and use are consistent throughout all program elements. Regression analysis is used to re-evaluate software requirements and software design issues whenever any significant code change is made. This technique ensures project awareness of the original system requirements. Sizing and timing analysis is done during incremental code development and compared against predicted values. Significant deviation between actual and predicted values is a possible indication of problems or of the need for additional examination.

Another area of concern to software V&V is the ability of compilers to generate object code that is functionally equivalent to the source code, that is, reliance on the correctness of the language compiler to make data-dependent decisions about abstract programmer-coded information. For critical applications, this problem is solved by validating the compiler or by validating that the object code produced by the compiler is functionally equivalent to the source.

Code reading is another technique that may be used for source code verification. An expert reads through another programmer's code to detect errors. In an experiment conducted at the National Aeronautics and Space Administration Goddard Space Flight Center, code reading was found to be more effective than either functional testing or structural testing [BASILI]. The reason was attributed to the expertise of the readers who, as they read the code, were simulating its execution and were able to detect many kinds of errors.

Other techniques commonly used are walkthroughs, inspections, and reviews. These tasks occur in interactive meetings attended by a team that usually includes at least one member from the development group. Other members may belong to the development group or to other groups involved in software development. The duration of these meetings is usually no more than a few hours, in which code is examined on a line-by-line basis. In these interactive sessions, it may be difficult to examine the code thoroughly for control logic, dataflow, database errors, sizing, timing, and other features that may require considerable manual or automated effort. Advance preparation for these activities may be necessary and includes code analysis techniques. The results of these techniques provide appropriate engineering information for discussion at meetings where code is evaluated. Regardless of who conducts or participates in walkthroughs and inspections, software V&V analyses may be used to support these meetings.

A comprehensive test management approach to testing recognizes the differences in strategies and in objectives for unit, software integration, and software system test. *Unit test* verifies the design and implementation of software units. *Software integration test* verifies functional requirements as the software units are integrated. Special attention is focused on software, hardware, and operator interfaces. *Software system test* validates the entire software program against system requirements and software performance objectives. Software system tests validate that the software executes correctly within its stated operating environment. The software's ability to deal properly with anomalies and stress conditions is emphasized. These tests are not intended to duplicate or replace the user and development group's test responsibilities, but

446

instead supplement the development testing to test behavior not normally tested by the user or development group.

Effective testing requires a comprehensive understanding of the system. Such understanding develops from systematically analyzing the software's concept, requirements, design, and code. By knowing internal software details, software V&V testing is effective at probing for errors and weaknesses that reveal hidden faults. This is considered structural, or white-box, testing. It often finds errors for which some functional, or black-box, test cases can produce the correct output despite internal errors.

Functional test cases execute part or all of the system to validate that the user requirement is satisfied; these test cases cannot always detect internal errors that will occur under special circumstances. Another software V&V test technique is to develop test cases that violate software requirements. This approach is effective at uncovering basic design assumption errors and unusual operational use errors. The process of planning functional test cases requires a thorough examination of the functional requirements. An analyst who carefully develops those test cases is likely to detect errors and omissions in the software requirements. In this sense test planning can be effective in detecting errors and can contribute to uncovering some errors before test execution.

The planning process for testing must take into account the specific objectives of the software V&V for the software and the impact of different test strategies in satisfying these objectives. Frequently, the most effective strategy may be to combine two or more strategies. More information and references on software testing may be found in [MARCINIAK].

Criticality analysis may be used to identify software V&V techniques to address high-risk concerns. The selection of V&V techniques for use in each critical area of the program is a method of tailoring the intensity of the software V&V against the type of risk present in each area of the software. For example, software V&V would apply algorithm analysis to critical numerical software functions, and techniques such as sizing and timing analysis, data and control flow analysis, and interface analysis to real-time executive functions.

2.2. Descriptions of Techniques

The following are summary descriptions of techniques taken from [EWICS3], [MARCINIAK], [NBS93], [NIST209], [NIST5589], [VOAS91,92,95], and [WALLACE94] and the issues sections (in italics at the end of each description) include the types of errors the technique may find, the tasks the technique sup-

ports, and other related techniques (to or from which supporting information is provided).

Algorithm analysis examines the logic and accuracy of the software requirements by translating algorithms into some language or structured format. The analysis involves rederiving equations or evaluating the suitability of specific numerical techniques. It checks that algorithms are correct, appropriate, stable, and meet all accuracy, timing, and sizing requirements. Algorithm analysis examines the correctness of the equations and numerical techniques, truncation and rounding effects, numerical precision of word storage and variables (single vs. extended-precision arithmetic), and data typing influences. *Issues: accuracy; algorithm efficiency; correctness; consistency in computation; error propagation; numerical roundoff; numerical stability; space utilization evaluation; system performance prediction; timing*

Back-to-back testing detects test failures by comparing the output of two or more programs implemented to the same specification. The same input data are applied to two or more program versions and their outputs are compared to detect anomalies. Any test data selection strategy can be used for this type of testing, although random testing is well suited to this approach. Also known as comparison testing. *Issues: anomalies or discrepancies between versions*

Boundary value analysis detects and removes errors occurring at parameter limits or boundaries. The input domain of the program is divided into a number of input classes. The tests should cover the boundaries and extremes of the classes. The tests check that the boundaries of the input domain of the specification coincide with those in the program. The value zero, whether used directly or indirectly, should be used with special attention (for example, division by zero, null matrix, zero table entry). Usually, boundary values of the input produce boundary values for the output. Test cases should also be designed to force the output to its extreme values. If possible, a test case that causes output to exceed the specification boundary values should be specified. If output is a sequence of data, special attention should be given to the first and last elements and to lists containing zero, one, and two elements. *Issues: algorithm analysis; array size; inconsistencies between limits; specification error*

Consistency analysis compares the requirements

of any existing (used) software with the new software requirements to ensure consistency. *Issues: consistency*

Control flow analysis transforms text describing software requirements into graphic flows where they can be examined for correctness. It checks that the proposed control flow is free of problems (for example, unreachable or incorrect software design). Control flow analysis is used to show the hierarchy of main routines and their subfunctions and checks that the proposed control flow is free of problems (for example, unreachable or incorrect code elements). It detects poor and potentially incorrect program structures. *Issues: assertion testing/violations; bottlenecks; boundary test cases; branch and path identification; branch testing; cell structure of units; correctness; software design evaluation; error propagation; expected vs. actual results; file sequence error; formal specification evaluation; global information flow and consistency; hierarchical interrelationship of units; inaccessible code; software integration tests; interunit structure; loop invariants; path testing; processing efficiency; retest after change; system performance prediction; test case preparation; unit tests*

Coverage analysis measures how much of the structure of a unit or system has been exercised by a given set of tests. System-level coverage measures how many of the unit parts of the system have been called by a test set. Code coverage measures the percentage of statements, branches, or lines of code (LOC) exercised by a test set. *Issues: unit tests; software integration tests; software system tests*

Database analysis ensures that the database structure and access methods are compatible with the logical design. It is performed on programs with significant data storage to ensure that common data and variable regions are used consistently between all calling routines, that data integrity is enforced and that no data or variable can be accidentally overwritten by overflowing data tables, and that data typing and use are consistent throughout the program. *Issues: access protection; data characteristics and types; software design evaluation; file sequence error; global information flow; processing efficiency; space utilization evaluation; unit tests*

Dataflow analysis is important for designing the high-level (process) architecture of applications. It can check for variables that are read before they are written, written more than once without being read, and written but never read. *Issues: assertion testing/violations; bottlenecks; boundary test cases; branch and path identification; branch testing; cell structure of units; data characteristics; environment interaction; error propagation; evaluation of program paths; expected vs. actual results; file sequence error; global information flow and consistency; hierarchical interrelationship of units; interunit structure; loop invariants; processing efficiency; retest after changes; software design evaluation; software integration tests; system performance prediction; test case preparation; uninitialized variables; unused variables; variable references*

Decision (truth) tables provide a clear and coherent analysis of complex logical combinations and relationships. This method uses two-dimensional tables to concisely describe logical relationships between Boolean program variables. *Issues: logic errors*

Error seeding determines whether a set of test cases is adequate by inserting ("seeding") known error types into the program and executing it with the test cases. If only some of the seeded errors are found, the test case set is not adequate. The ratio of found seeded errors to the total number of seeded errors is an estimation of the ratio of found real errors to total number of errors, or

$$\frac{NumberSeededErrorsFound}{TotalNumberSeededErrors} = \frac{NumberRealErrorsFound}{TotalNumberRealErrors}$$

One can solve for the total number of real errors, since the values of the other three are known. Then, one can estimate the number of errors remaining by subtracting the number of real errors found from the total number of real errors. The remaining test effort can then be estimated. If all the seeded errors are found, this indicates that either the test case set is adequate, or that the seeded errors were too easy to find. *Issues: test case adequacy*

Event tree analysis uses a bottom-up approach to model the effects of an event that may have serious repercussions. The initiating event is the root of the event tree. Two lines are drawn from the root, depicting the positive and negative consequences of the event. This is done for each subsequent consequence until all consequences are considered. *Issues: hazard analysis; safety; threat analysis; timing*

448

Finite state machines (FSMs) check for incomplete and inconsistent software requirements by modeling the software in terms of its states, inputs, and actions. A system in state S1 receiving an input I, then carrying out action A and moving to state S2, is an example. FSMs can check that there is an action and new state for every input in every state, and that only one state change is defined for each state and input pair. *Issues: incomplete software requirements specification; inconsistent software requirements; modeling*

Functional testing executes part or all of the system to validate that the user requirement is satisfied. *Issues: boundary test cases; branch and path identification; branch testing; file sequence error; path testing; program execution characteristics; retest after change; statement coverage testing; system performance prediction; software system tests; test case preparation; test thoroughness; unit test; uninitialized variables; unused variables; variable references; variable snapshots/tracing*

Inspections are evaluation techniques whereby the software requirements, software design, or code is examined by a person or group other than the author to detect faults, violations of development standards, and other problems. An inspection begins with the distribution of the item to be inspected (for example, a specification). Each participant is required to analyze the item on his or her own. During the inspection, which is a monitored meeting of all the participants, the item is jointly analyzed to find as many errors as possible. All errors found are recorded, but no attempt is made to correct the errors at that time. However, at some point in the future, it must be verified that the errors found have actually been corrected. *Issues: accuracy; checklists (software requirements, software design, code); effective forerunners to testing; formal specification evaluation; go-no-go decisions; information flow consistency; logic errors; loop invariants; manual simulation; retest after change; space utilization evaluation; technical reviews; status reviews; syntax errors; uninitialized variables; unused variables*

Interface analysis is a static analysis technique. It is used to demonstrate that the interfaces of subprograms do not contain any errors that lead to failures in a particular application of the software. Interface analysis is especially important if interfaces do not contain assertions that detect incorrect parameter values. It is also important

after new configurations of pre-existing subprograms have been generated. The types of interfaces that are analyzed include external, internal, hardware/hardware, software/software, software/hardware, and software/database. *Issues: actual and formal parameters mismatch; inconsistencies between subroutine usage list and called subroutine; inconsistency of attributes of global variables; inconsistency between COTS parameter usage relative to other system parameters; incorrect assumptions about static and dynamic storage of values; incorrect functions used or incorrect subroutine called; input-output description errors*

Interface testing is a dynamic analysis technique. It is similar to interface analysis, except test cases are built with data that test all interfaces. Interface testing may include the following: testing all interface variables at their extreme positions, testing interface variables individually at their extreme values with other interface variables at normal values, testing all values of the domain of each interface variable with other interface variables at normal values, and testing all values of all variables in combination (may be feasible only for small interfaces). *Issues: actual and formal parameters mismatch; inconsistencies between subroutine usage list and called subroutine; inconsistency of attributes of global variables; inconsistency between COTS parameter usage relative to other system parameters; inconsistent interface parameters; incorrect assumptions about static and dynamic storage of values; incorrect functions used or incorrect subroutine called; input-output description errors*

Mutation analysis determines the thoroughness with which a program has been tested, and in the process detects errors. This procedure involves producing a large set of versions or "mutations" of the original program, each derived by altering a single element of the program (for example, changing an operator, variable, or constant). Each mutant is then tested with a given collection of test data sets. Since each mutant is essentially different from the original, the testing should demonstrate that each is in fact different. If each of the outputs produced by the mutants differs from the output produced by the original program and from each other, then the program is considered adequately tested and correct. *Issues: boundary test cases; branch and path identification; branch testing; retest after change; test case preparation*

Performance testing measures how well the software system executes according to its required response times, CPU usage, and other quantified features in operation. These measurements may be simple to make (for example, measuring process time relative to volumes of input data) or more complicated (for example, instrumenting the code to measure time per function execution). *Issues: memory allocation; synchronization; timing*

Prototyping helps to examine the probable results of implementing software requirements. Examination of a prototype may help to identify incomplete or incorrect software requirements and may also reveal if any software requirements will not result in desired system behavior. It can be used as an aid in examining the software design architecture in general or a specific set of functions. For large complicated systems prototyping can prevent inappropriate software designs from resulting in costly, wasted implementations. *Issues: behavior; omitted functions (from software requirements); incomplete software requirements specification; user interface*

Regression analysis and testing is used to re-evaluate software requirements and software design issues whenever any significant code change is made. It involves retesting to verify that the modified software still meets its specified requirements. This analysis ensures awareness of the original system requirements. It is performed when any changes to the product are made during installation to verify that the basic software requirements and software design assumptions affecting other areas of the program have not been violated. *Issues: software integration tests; retest after change; software system tests; unit tests*

Requirements parsing involves examination to ensure that each software requirement is defined unambiguously by a complete set of attributes (for example, initiator of an action, source of the action, the action, the object of the action, constraints). *Issues: accuracy; assertion testing/violations; checklists; completeness; consistency; environment interaction; feasibility; formal specification evaluation; hierarchical interrelationship of units; information flow consistency; software integration tests; interunit structure; path testing; proof of correctness; software requirements evaluation; software requirements indexing; software requirements to design correlation; retest after change; stan-*

dards check; statement coverage testing; software system tests; unit tests

Reviews are meetings at which the software requirements, software design, code, or other products are presented to the user, sponsor, or other interested parties for comment and approval, often as a prerequisite for concluding a given activity of the software development process. Reviews check the adequacy of the software requirements and software design according to a set of criteria and procedures. *Issues: effective forerunners to testing; logic errors; syntax errors*

Simulation is used to evaluate the interactions of large, complex systems with many hardware, user, and other interfacing software units. Simulation uses an executable model to examine the behavior of the software. Simulation is used to test operator procedures and to isolate installation problems. *Issues: assertion testing/violations; behavior; boundary test cases; branch and path identification; branch testing; environment interaction; execution monitoring, sampling, support; feasibility; file sequence error; interunit structure; path testing; program execution characteristics; retest after change; statement coverage testing; system performance prediction; software system tests; uninitialized variables; unused variables; variable references; variable snapshot/tracing*

Software failure mode effects and criticality analysis reveals weak or missing software requirements by using inductive reasoning to determine the effect on the system of a unit (includes software instructions) failing in a particular failure mode. A matrix is developed for each unit depicting the effect on the system of each unit's failure in each failure mode. Items in the matrix may include the failure mode and causes, effect on system, criticality, change/action required, and prevention and control safeguards. The criticality factor, that is, the seriousness of the effect of the failure, can be used in determining where to apply other analyses and testing resources. *Issues: hazard analysis; safety; incomplete software requirements specification; threat analysis*

Software fault tree analysis identifies and analyzes software safety requirements. It is used to determine possible causes of known hazards. Its purpose is to demonstrate that the software will not cause a system to reach an unsafe state, and to discover what environmental conditions would allow the system to reach an unsafe state.

450

The analyst assumes that an already identified hazard has occurred and then works backward to discover the possible causes of the hazard. This is done by creating a fault tree, whose root is the hazard. The system fault tree is expanded until it contains at its lowest level basic events that cannot be further analyzed. *Issues: hazard analysis; safety; threat analysis*

Stress testing tests the response of the system to extreme conditions to identify vulnerable points within the software, and to show that the system can withstand normal workloads. *Issues: design errors; planning for defaults when system overstressed*

Structural testing examines the logic of the units and may be used to support software requirements for test coverage, that is, how much of the program has been executed. *Issues: bottlenecks; error propagation; evaluation of program paths; parameter checking; program execution characteristics; retest after change*

Symbolic execution shows the agreement between the source code and the software requirements specification. This is an evaluation technique in which program execution is simulated using symbols rather than actual values for input data, and program output is expressed as logical or mathematical expressions involving these symbols. *Issues: assertion testing/violations; program execution characteristics; proof of correctness; retest after change*

Test certification ensures that reported test results are the actual finding of the tests. Test-related tools, media, and documentation are certified to ensure maintainability and repeatability of tests. This technique is also used to show that the delivered software product is identical to the software product that was subjected to V&V. It is used, particularly in critical software systems, to verify that the required tests have been executed and that the delivered software product is identical to the product subjected to software V&V. *Issues: incorrect product version shipped; incorrect test results; reports on test cases that were omitted*

Walkthroughs are similar to inspections, but less formal. A walkthrough is an evaluation technique in which a designer or programmer leads one or more other members of the development team through a segment of software design or code, while the other members ask questions and make comments about technique, style, and identify possible errors, violations of development standards, and other problems. *Issues: checklists; error propagation; effective forerunners to testing; formal specification evaluation; go-no-go decisions; logic errors; manual simulation; parameter checking; retest after change; small, but difficult or error-prone, sections of design or code; status reviews; syntax errors; software system tests; technical reviews*

3. Conclusions

Verification and validation is one of the most powerful software engineering tools available to verify intermediate software products, for example, software requirements specifications, design descriptions, test cases, and test procedures. This article discusses only one aspect of the software lifecycle process—software requirements. Numerous techniques are presented to verify the software requirements as well as software testing methods to validate the software requirements.

References

[BASILI] Basili, V.R. and R.W. Selby, "Comparing the Effectiveness of Software Testing Strategies," *IEEE Trans. Software Eng.*, Vol. 13, No. 12, Dec. 1987.

[BOEHM] Boehm, B.W. and P.N. Papaccio, "Understanding and Controlling Software Costs," *IEEE Trans. Software Eng.*, Vol. 14, No. 10, Oct. 1988, pp. 1462–1477.

[BUTLER] Butler, R. and G. Finelli, "The Infeasibility of Experimental Quantified Life-Critical Software Reliability," *Proc. SIGSOFT '91: Software for Critical Systems*, ACM Press, New York, N.Y., 1991.

[EWICS3] Bishop, P.G., ed., *Dependability of Critical Computer Systems 3—Techniques Directory*, The European Workshop on Industrial Computer Systems Technical Committee 7 (EWICS TC7), Elsevier Science Publishers, Amsterdam, 1990.

[FIPS132] FIPS PUB 132, "Guideline for Software Verification and Validation Plans," U.S. Department of Commerce/National Bureau of Standards (U.S.), Nov. 19, 1987.

[FIPS101] FIPS PUB 101, "Guideline for Lifecycle Validation, Verification, and Testing of Computer Software," U.S. Department of Commerce/National Bureau of Standards (U.S.), June 6, 1983.

[IEEEP1059] IEEE Std P1059-1994, "(DRAFT 7.1) IEEE Guide for Software Verification and Validation Plans," Institute of Electrical and Electronics Engineers, New York, May 24, 1993.

[MARCINIAK] Marciniak, J.J., ed., *Encyclopedia of Software Engineering,* John Wiley & Sons, New York, 1994.

[MUSA87] Musa, J.D., A. Iannino, and K. Okumoto, *Software Reliability: Measurement, Prediction, Application,* McGraw-Hill, New York, N.Y., 1987.

[MUSA89] Musa, J.D. and A.F. Ackerman, "Quantifying Software Validation: When to Stop Testing?" *IEEE Software,* Vol. 6, No. 3, May 1989 pp. 19–27.

[NBS93] NBS Special Publication 500-93, "Software Validation, Verification, and Testing Technique and Tool Reference Guide," U.S. Department of Commerce/National Bureau of Standards (U.S.), Sept. 1982.

[NIST165] NIST Special Publication 500-165, "Software Verification and Validation: Its Role in Computer Assurance and Its Relationship with Software Project Management Standards," U.S. Department of Commerce/National Institute of Standards and Technology, Sept. 1989.

[NIST209] NIST Special Publication 500-209, "Software Error Analysis," U.S. Department of Commerce/National Institute of Standards and Technology, Apr. 1993.

[NIST223] NIST Special Publication 500-223, "A Framework for the Development and Assurance of High Integrity Software," U.S. Department of Commerce/National Institute of Standards and Technology, Dec. 1994.

[NIST5589] NISTIR 5589, "A Study on Hazard Analysis in High Integrity Software Standards and Guidelines," U.S. Department of Commerce/National Institute of Standards and Technology, Jan. 1995.

[RADATZ] Radatz, J.W., Analysis of IV&V Data, RADC-TR-81-145, Logicon, Inc., Rome Air Development Center, Griffiss AFB, N.Y., June 1981.

[VOAS91] Voas, J., L. Morell, and K Miller, "Predicting Where Faults Can Hide from Testing," *IEEE Software,* Vol. 8, No. 2, Mar. 1991, pp. 41–48.

[VOAS92] Voas, J., "PIE: A Dynamic Failure-Based Technique," *IEEE Trans. Software Eng.,* Vol. 18, No. 8, Aug. 1992, pp. 717–727.

[VOAS95] Voas, J. and K. Miller, "Software Testability: The New Verification," *IEEE Software,* Vol. 2, No. 3, May 1995, pp. 17–28.

[WALLACE91] Wallace, D.R., D.R. Kuhn, and J.C. Cherniavsky, "Report on a Workshop on the Assurance of High Integrity Software," *Proc. 6th Ann. Conf. Computer Assurance* (COMPASS '91), IEEE Press, Piscataway, N.J., 1991.

[WALLACE94] Wallace, D.R., "Verification and Validation," in *Encyclopedia of Software Engineering,* Vol. 2, John Wiley & Sons, New York, N.Y., 1994.

Chapter 6

Software System Engineering Process Models

1. Introduction to Chapter

There are a number of different approaches or paradigms that can be used by system/software developers to develop their system effectively and efficiently. Baseline management is the primary development paradigm in use in the United States today.

The baseline management paradigm is a management strategy that is used to control the software development.

The baseline management approach integrates a series of life-cycle phases, reviews, and baseline documents into a software development management system (See Figure 1 for an illustration of a software development life-cycle model that is used with the baseline management paradigm.)

Specifically, baseline management:

- Is a software development process that is based on the waterfall model.[1] (The reader should be aware that the term "waterfall" or "conventional" is often used to refer to what we have called "baseline management." The authors of this tutorial feel that the distinction between the two methods is important and the terminologies should remain separate)

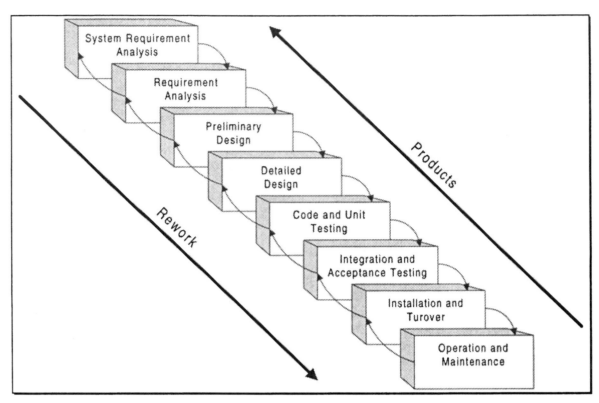

Figure 1. Illustration of a software development life cycle.

- Partitions the project into manageable phases, often called *requirements, design, implementation,* and *test,* or some variation of those names

- Establishes milestones, documents, and reviews at the end of each phase. If the review is successfully passed, the phase's products are accepted and the next phase begins

- Establishes a baseline at periodic intervals

- Uses configuration management to control the baselines. Accepted products are placed under configuration management

Alternatively, system and software requirements may be developed through prototyping and the reuse of software products (requirements and design descriptions, code, test procedures, and so on).

This chapter has three articles concerned with software engineering development strategies. The first article is an overview by Davis, Bersoff, and Comer on numerous strategies that are available to the software system engineer. The next two articles isolate each strategy discussed: iteration, risk analysis, reusable software concepts, and prototyping as a tool.

2. Description of Articles

The first article, by Al Davis, Ed Bersoff, and Ed Comer, discusses a strategy for comparing alternative software development life-cycle models. This article defines a model of a typical system development that is behind in cost and schedule and never catches up with the user's requirements. The article also defines such life-cycle metrics as *shortfall, lateness, adaptability, longevity,* and *inappropriateness.* The article then continues to discuss more approaches to software development that can reduce problems in lateness, budget, and document requirements. These strategies are as follows: rapid throw-away prototypes, incremental prototypes, evolutionary prototypes, reusable software, and automated software synthesis. Each of these different software development prototypes is individually discussed and its advantages over the conventional models are shown.

This article provides a number of paradigms that help the project manager compare and contrast all of the software development life-cycle models in terms of their ability to satisfy the user's needs and reduce software costs. These five "new models" were compared to the conventional models with respect to their ability to produce software that meets the user's needs.

The second article is a new classic by Barry Boehm entitled "A Spiral Model of Software Development and Enhancement." An earlier version of this article was presented in early 1985 by Boehm at a workshop on software requirements. The article describes a revolutionary view of the software development life cycle. The spiral model is a general software development model and treats the waterfall chart and other popular software development paradigms as special cases. The primary benefit of the spiral model is to integrate risk analysis and prototyping.

The last article in this chapter, by Hassan Gomaa, discusses rapid prototyping as a strategy for software development. The author reports that one of the main problems in developing computer applications is in specifying the user's requirements. Although prototyping is often considered too expensive, correcting ambiguities and misunderstandings at the specification stage is significantly cheaper than correcting errors in a system after it has gone into production. This article describes how to prototype and specify requirements of a computer system to manage and control a semiconductor processing facility. The cost of developing a running prototype was less than 10 percent of total software development cost. Two approaches to prototyping are described: throwaway (sometime called rapid) and evolutionary prototyping. A brief example of each type is given, and the conditions under which each type might be used are presented.

Reference

1. Royce, W.W., "Managing the Development of Large Software Systems," *Proc. IEEE WESCON*, 1970, pp. 1–9. Reprinted in *Tutorial: Software Engineering Project Management,* Thayer, R.H., ed., IEEE Computer Society Press, Los Alamitos, Calif., 1988.

A Strategy for Comparing Alternative Software Development Life Cycle Models

ALAN M. DAVIS, senior member, ieee, EDWARD H. BERSOFF, senior member, ieee, AND EDWARD R. COMER, member, ieee

Abstract—The classic waterfall model of software engineering is used throughout the production software development community. The escalating costs associated with software development and the unsatisfactory reliability, performance, and functionality of the resulting software have motivated software engineers to develop new alternate models of software development including prototyping, software synthesis, and reusable software. It is difficult to compare and contrast these new models of software development because their disciples often use different terminology, and the models often have little in common except their beginnings (marked by a recognition that a problem exists) and ends (marked by the existence of a software solution). This paper provides a framework which can serve 1) as a basis for analyzing the similarities and differences among alternate life cycle models; 2) as a tool for software engineering researchers to help describe the probable impacts of a new life cycle model; and 3) as a means to help software practitioners decide on an appropriate life cycle model to utilize on a particular project or in a particular application area.

Index Terms—Reusable software, software development life cycles, software prototyping, software synthesis, waterfall model.

Introduction

THE classic waterfall model (see Fig. 1) was defined as early as 1970 by Royce [1] and later refined by Boehm [2] in 1976 to help cope with the growing complexity of the software projects being tackled. The use of such a model

• encourages one to specify what the system is supposed to do (i.e., to define the requirements) before building the system (i.e., designing);

• encourages one to plan how components are going to interact (i.e., designing) before building the components (i.e., coding);

• enables project managers to track progress more accurately and to uncover possible slippages early;

• demands that the development process generate a series of documents which can later be utilized to test and maintain the system;

• reduces development and maintenance costs due to all of the above reasons; and

• enables the organization that will develop the system to be more structured and manageable.

Manuscript received May 12, 1986; revised November 18, 1986. This work was supported by the Software Productivity Consortium.

A. M. Davis and E. H. Bersoff are with BTG, Inc., Vienna, VA 22180.

E. R. Comer is with Software Productivity Solutions, Inc., Melbourne, FL 32936.

IEEE Log Number 8823075.

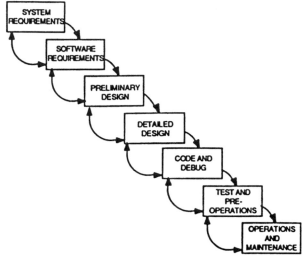

Fig. 1. The waterfall model of software development.

Most "standard" methodologies for commercial corporations, government contractors,[1] and governmental entities[1] follow some basic variation of the waterfall model, although there are a variety of different names for each of the stages. Thus, the requirements stages are often called user needs analysis, system analysis, or specifications; the preliminary design stage is often called high-level design, top-level design, software architectural definition, or specifications; the detailed design stage is often called program design, module design, lower-level design, algorithmic design, or just plain design, etc. For the most part, however, all these methodologies are equivalent.

During the past five to ten years, alternative, radically different methodologies have appeared, including rapid throwaway prototypes, incremental development, evolutionary prototypes, reusable software, and automated software synthesis.

The developers of these techniques had a variety of motivations, but primarily they were looking for ways of rescuing the software industry from what appears to be a dilemma: software is almost always more expensive and

[1]These include, for example, those methodologies derived from DoD-STD-2167, MIL-STD-490, or MIL-STD-1679A.

delivered later than expected, and to make matters worse, it is often unreliable and fails to meet the ultimate users' needs. Project managers often bypass stages or take short-cuts in order to solve the problem, but these unplanned and extemporaneous alterations of the life cycle just make the software even more expensive, later, and more unreliable.

The *rapid throwaway prototyping* approach (made popular by Gomaa [3]) addresses the issue of ensuring that the software product being proposed really meets the users' needs. The approach is to construct a "quick and dirty" partial implementation of the system prior to (or during) the requirements stage. The potential users utilize this prototype for a period of time and supply feedback to the developers concerning its strengths and weaknesses. This feedback is then used to modify the software requirements specification to reflect the real user needs. At this point, the developers can proceed with the actual system design and implementation with confidence that they are building the "right" system (except in those cases where the user needs evolve). An extension of this approach uses a series of throwaway prototypes [4], culminating in full-scale development.

Incremental development [5] is the process of constructing a partial implementation of a total system and slowly adding increased functionality or performance. This approach reduces the costs incurred before an initial capability is achieved. It also produces an operational system more quickly, and it thus reduces the possibility that the user needs will change during the development process.

In *evolutionary prototyping* (established briefly at the end of [6]), the developers construct a partial implementation of the system which meets known requirements. The prototype is then used by its intended users in order to understand the full requirements better. Whereas incremental development implies that we understand most of our requirements up front and simply choose to implement it in subsets of increasing capability, evolutionary prototyping implies that we do not know up front all of our requirements, but need to experiment with an operational system in order to learn them. Note that in the case of throwaway prototypes we are likely to implement only those aspects of the system that are poorly understood, but that in the case of evolutionary prototypes we are more likely to start with those system aspects that are best understood and thus build upon our strengths. For complex applications, it is not reasonable at this time to expect this application of prototypes to be particularly "rapid" because reliability, adaptability, maintainability, and performance (RAMP) are major forces behind making such system developments expensive and time-consuming. Since the technology is not yet available to *retrofit* RAMP requirements, they would have to be implemented up front, thus forcing software development costs high and schedules to their limit. Evolutionary prototypes will become more practical in the future as techniques for retrofitting RAMP requirements are developed.

Whereas prototyping attempts to reduce development costs through partial implementations, *reusable software* [7] is the discipline of attempting to reduce development costs by incorporating previously proven designs and code in new software products. The software industry is guilty of continuously reinventing the wheel. This is primarily because few tools are available to help reuse software designs or code from previous projects. Clearly, what is needed are techniques to create reusable components, techniques and tools to store and retrieve reusable components, and component specification techniques to help catalog and locate relevant components. The net effect of reusing components would be shorter development schedules (by using wheels rather than reinventing them) and more reliable software (by using components that have been previously "shaken down").

Automated software synthesis is a term used to describe the transformation of requirements or high-level design specifications into operational code. The transformation process may be directed by algorithmic [8] or knowledge-based [9] techniques. As Parnas [10] points out, each generation of software engineering researchers applies the term "software synthesis" to one language "higher" than the one currently used for programming. Thus, when machine language was used, software synthesis referred to the "automatic" translation of assembly language into machine code (now called assembly). Later, it referred to the translation of a high-level language into machine code (now called compilation). Now, it refers to the translation of very-high-level languages (VHLL's) into machine code. Since lines of code produced by person–month are relatively independent of the implementation language, it becomes clear that the higher the programming language used becomes, the more true productivity (as measured by the amount of functionality implemented per person–month) increases.

The purpose of this paper is to describe a paradigm[2] which can be used to compare and contrast each of the above alternative life cycle models with the more conventional waterfall model (and with each other) in the face of constantly evolving user needs.

The Paradigm

For every application beyond the trivial, user needs are constantly evolving. Thus, the system being constructed is always aiming at a moving target. This is a primary reason for delayed schedules (caused by trying to make the software meet a new requirement it was not designed to meet) and software that fails to meet customer expectations (because the developers "froze" the requirements and failed to acknowledge the inevitable changes).

Fig. 2 shows graphically how users' needs evolve over time. It is recognized that the function shown is neither linear nor continuous in reality. Please note that 1) the scale on the *x*-axis is not shown (the units can be either

---

[2]The term "paradigm" is used in this paper to mean "metamodel," i.e., a model to describe software life cycle models.

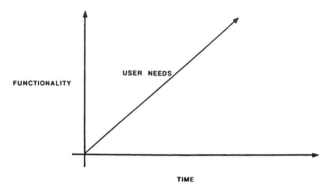

Fig. 2. Constantly evolving user needs.

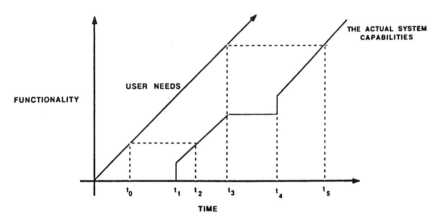

Fig. 3. Software products fall short of meeting all current user needs.

months or years), but could be assumed to be nonuniform, containing areas of compression and decompression, and 2) the units of the scale on the y-axis are not shown, but are assumed to be some measure of the amount of functionality (such as DeMarco's "Bangs for the Buck" [11]). However, none of the observations made in this paper is dependent on either the uniformity of the axes or the linearity or continuity of the curve shown in Fig. 2.

Fig. 3 shows what happens during a conventional software development. At time t_0, a need for a software system is recognized and a development effort commences with relatively incomplete knowledge of the real user needs at time t_0. At time t_1, the development effort has produced an operational product, but not only does it not satisfy the current t_1 needs, it does not even satisfy the old t_0 needs because of a poor understanding of those needs in the first place. The product now undergoes a series of enhancements (between times t_1 and t_3), which eventually enable it to satisfy the original requirements (at t_2) and then some. At some later point in time t_3, the cost of enhancement is so great that the decision is made to build a new system (once again based on poorly understood requirements), development of the product is completed at time t_4, and the cycle repeats itself.

A number of useful metrics can now be defined based on the paradigm defined above. These metrics can later be used to compare and contrast sets of alternative life

cycle approaches. These metrics are portrayed graphically in Fig. 4 and are described below.

1) A *shortfall* is a measure of how far the operational system, at any time t, is from meeting the actual requirements at time t. This is the attribute that most people are referring to when they ask "Does this system meet my needs?"

2) *Lateness* is a measure of the time that elapses between the appearance of a new requirement and its satisfaction. Of course, recognizing that new requirements are not necessarily implemented in the order in which they appear, lateness actually measures the time delay associated with achievement of a level of functionality.

3) The *adaptability* is the rate at which the software solution can adapt to new requirements, as measured by the slope of the solution curve.

4) The *longevity* is the time a system solution is adaptable to change and remains viable, i.e., the time from system creation through the time it is replaced.

5) *Inappropriateness* is the shaded area between the user needs and the solution curves in Fig. 5 and thus captures the behavior of shortfall over time. The ultimately "appropriate" model would exhibit a zero area, meaning that new requirements are instantly satisfied.

Each of the alternative life cycle models defined earlier is now analyzed with respect to the paradigm described above.

458

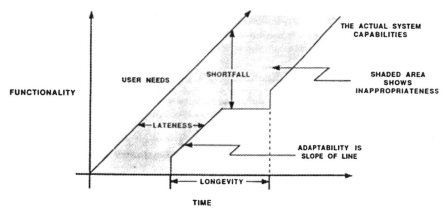

Fig. 4. Software productivity metrics.

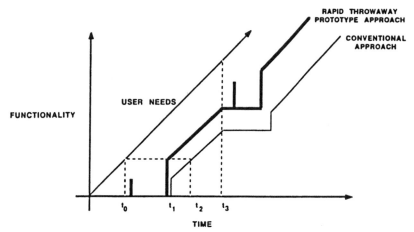

Fig. 5. Rapid prototyping versus conventional.

Rapid Throwaway Prototypes

The use of a rapid throwaway prototype early in the development life cycle increases the likelihood that customers and developers will have a better understanding of the real user needs that existed at time t_0. Thus, its use does not radically affect the life cycle model per se, but does increase the impact of the resulting system. This is shown in Fig. 5, where the vertical line (i.e., the increase in functionality provided by the system upon deployment) at time t_1 is longer than in the conventional approach. Fig. 5 also shows the rapid prototype itself as a short vertical line providing limited and experimental capability soon after time t_0. There is no reason to believe that the length of time during which the product can be efficiently enhanced without replacement is any different than with the conventional approach. Therefore, this period of time for the rapid prototype-based development (i.e., $t_3 - t_1$) is shown in Fig. 5 the same as for the conventionally developed product.

Incremental Development

When using incremental development, software is deliberately built to satisfy fewer requirements initially, but is constructed in such a way as to facilitate the incorpo-

ration of new requirements and thus achieve higher adaptability. This approach has two effects: 1) the initial development time is reduced because of the reduced level of functionality, and 2) the software can be enhanced more easily and for a longer period of time. Fig. 6 shows how this approach compares to the conventional approach. Note that the initial development time is less than for the conventional approach, that the initial functionality (A) is less than for the conventional approach (B), and that the increased adaptability is indicated by a higher slope of the curve A–C than for the conventional approach (line B–D). The stair step aspect of the graph indicates a series of well-defined, planned, discrete builds of the system.

Evolutionary Prototypes

This approach is an extension of the incremental development. Here, the number and frequency of operational prototypes increases. The emphasis is on evolving toward a solution in a more continuous fashion, instead of by a discrete number of system builds.

With such an approach, an initial prototype emerges rapidly, presumably demonstrating functionality where the requirements are well understood (in contrast to the throwaway prototypes, where one usually implements the

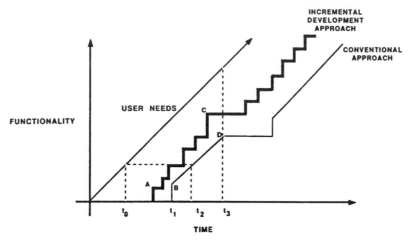

Fig. 6. Incremental development versus conventional.

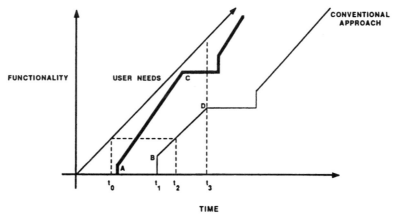

Fig. 7. Evolutionary prototyping versus conventional.

poorly understood aspects first) and providing an overall framework for the software. Each successive prototype explores a new area of user need, while refining the previous functions. As a result, the solution evolves closer and closer to the user needs (see Fig. 7). In time, it too will have to be redone or undergo major restructuring in order to continue to evolve.

As with the incremental development approach, the slope (line A–C) is steeper than in the conventional approach (line B–D) because the evolvable prototype was designed to be far more adaptable. Also, the line A–C in Fig. 7 is not stepped like line A–C in Fig. 6 because of the replacement of well-defined and well-planned system "builds" with a continuous influx of new, and perhaps experimental, functionality.

Reusable Software

Reuse of existing software components has the potential to decrease the initial development time for software significantly. Fig. 8 shows how this approach compares to conventional development. No parameters are changed, except for the development times.

Automated Software Synthesis

In the ultimate application of this approach, as an engineer recognizes the requirements, these are specified in some type of VHLL and the system is automatically synthesized. This approach has two dramatic effects: 1) the development time is greatly reduced, and 2) the development costs are reduced so much that adapting "old" systems is rarely more meritorious than resynthesizing the entire system. Thus, the longevity of any version is low, and the result is a stair-step graph, as shown in Fig. 9, where the horizontal segments represent the time the system is utilized and the time needed to upgrade the requirements. The vertical segments represent the additional functionality offered by each new generation.

Summary

Note that all five approaches reduce the area between the user need graph and actual system functionality graph when compared to conventional development. That is, all five approaches decrease shortfall, lateness, and inappropriateness to varying degrees. It is for this very reason that these alternative life cycle approaches were developed by their inventors.

460

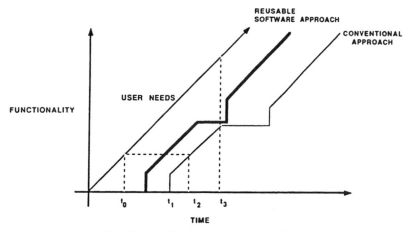

Fig. 8. Reusable software versus conventional.

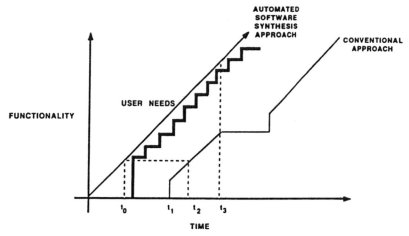

Fig. 9. Automated software synthesis versus conventional.

Other Models

The paradigm discussed in this paper makes it apparent that alternative life cycle models improve product development. It also provides insight into how we might modify the conventional life cycle model to improve our situation. For example, it is apparent by looking at all the models described above that the evolution of requirements is fundamentally ignored during development. In actuality, as important new requirements become apparent, they are reviewed by a configuration control board and either discarded (or perhaps deferred for a later release) or approved [12]. Such an approval may result in relatively expensive modifications to all existing documentation and code under development. If techniques could be developed which would make the intermediate results of the software life cycle (e.g., software requirements specifications, high-level design specifications, detailed design specifications, and code) highly adaptable, then the software development process itself could result in systems that more closely met *current* requirements. If such a scheme were possible, the result would be as shown in Fig. 10. Note that although the development time remains unchanged, the system that appears at time t_1 not only meets all the requirements of time t_0, but most of the additional t_1 requirements as well.

PRODUCTIVITY ANALYSIS

Suppose that at a particular point in time a project manager needed to meet a set of new requirements. He/she could select one of a number of choices:

1) modify the existing program,

2) build a new system from scratch using conventional software development practices, or

3) build a new system from scratch using any of the new alternative approaches.

Currently, many project managers make this selection based on fuzzy perceptions and past experiences. On the other hand, some project managers might analyze the project's aspects which affect the choice. For example, aspects of the application that might affect the selection include

• requirements volatility (i.e., the likelihood that the requirements will change);

• the "shape" of requirements volatility (e.g., discrete leaps, based on brand new threats; or gradual changes, as with a need to do things faster);

461

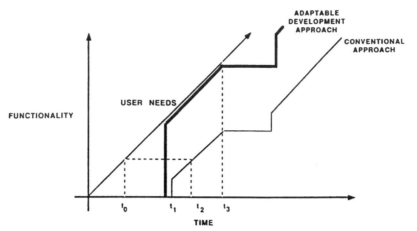

Fig. 10. Adaptable development versus conventional.

• the longevity of the application; and

• the availability of resources to develop or effect changes (i.e., it may be easier to get resources up front than to devote significant resources for enhancements).

Wise project managers must make the appropriate life cycle model selection based not only on maximum functionality in minimum elapsed time at minimum cost, but also on the above four factors. The remainder of this section describes how the paradigm can be used as a potential tool for project managers who wish to consider all the factors in making their life cycle model selections.

Comparisons of life cycle model alternatives based solely on functionality and time can be made using the graphs shown earlier in this paper (i.e., Figs. 5–10). To add cost considerations, a third dimension can be added, as shown in Fig. 11. While the cost over time is certainly projected and tracked today, the cost per unit of functionality is not. Quantifying this three-dimensional model for various development approaches would have three significant outcomes.

1) Comparisons of different life cycle model alternatives could consider not only the functionality needs of the application, but also the funding and funding profile constraints. For example, at a particular point in time, a project manager may need to make a choice between a conventional life cycle and an evolutionary prototype life cycle. He/she could plot the projected costs on a graph like that in Fig. 11 for the two approaches. The resulting plots, shown in Figs. 12 and 13, respectively, graphically show that (for this particular project) the evolutionary prototype approach costs less up front and costs more over the product's life time, but more closely meets user needs than the conventional approach.

2) Future upgrades could be weighed in importance according to the cost impact of the additional functionality.

3) Productivity would be redefined as the functionality provided (i.e., the "bang" per DeMarco [11]) per hour of labor.

Productivity today is usually measured in terms of the characteristics of the solution (e.g., lines of code per hour). This is valid only where the selected characteristic

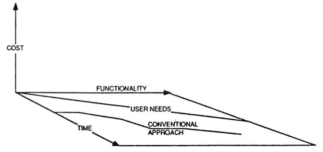

Fig. 11. The cost dimension.

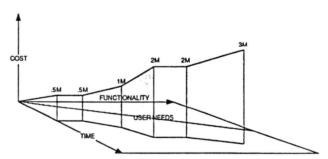

Fig. 12. Possible cost analysis for conventional development.

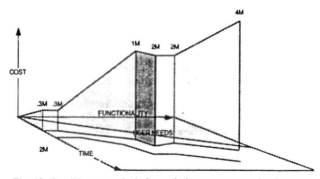

Fig. 13. Possible cost analysis for evolutionary prototype development.

of the solution, for example, lines of code, is a valid reflection of the size and complexity of the problem, which is generally true for manually developed software. This measure of productivity is, however, inappropriate for development models where lines of code are not a valid reflection of the problem space. This is one of the primary reasons that comparison of the various development models is so difficult today.

FUTURE RESEARCH

While the paradigm presented in this paper is useful for visualizing conceptual differences between development models, additional research is needed to allow precise tradeoffs to occur. Future research must tackle

* quantifying and measuring the functionality axis (i.e., the bang);
* developing the correct productivity metric in terms of effort per bang;
* understanding and measuring real user needs (in many cases, the gap between the user need and the operational system is an unquantified feeling of dissatisfaction on the user's part); and
* measuring the actual behavior (in terms of functionality, time, and cost) of the solution curves for the various models (i.e., generating techniques to arrive at accurate versions of Figs. 12 and 13 for any particular project).

Based on the paradigm presented in this paper, it follows that the "ultimate" model is one that is predictive of the user needs (i.e., the functionality is available before the user needs it) and exhibits the lowest possible cost. If the user need line could be projected with some degree of accuracy (which requires a mature application domain), then methods could be developed to provide functionality at or ahead of the need.

SUMMARY

A paradigm has been given which helps one compare and contrast alternative software development life cycle models in terms of their abilities to satisfy user needs and reduce life cycle costs. Five "new" models were compared to the conventional model with respect to their abilities to produce software which meets user needs.

ACKNOWLEDGEMENT

The authors would like to thank E. Koenke for participating in early discussions on the subject of this paper.

REFERENCES

[1] W. W. Royce, "Managing the development of large software systems: Concepts and techniques," in *Proc. WESCON*, Aug. 1970.
[2] B. W. Boehm, "Software engineering," *IEEE Trans. Comput.*, vol. C-25, pp. 1226-1241, Dec. 1976.
[3] H. Gomaa and D. Scott, "Prototyping as a tool in the specification of user requirements," in *Proc. 5th IEEE Int. Conf. Software Eng.*, Mar. 1981, pp. 333-342.
[4] B. W. Boehm, "A spiral model of software development and enhancement," *ACM SIGSOFT Software Eng. Notes*, vol. 11, no. 4, pp. 14-24, Aug. 1986; reprinted in *Computer*, vol. 21, no. 5, pp. 61-72, May 1988.
[5] E. Hirsch, "Evolutionary acquisition of command and control systems," *Program Manager*, pp. 18-22, Nov.-Dec. 1985.
[6] D. McCracken and M. Jackson, "Life cycle concept considered harmful," *ACM SIGSOFT Software Eng. Notes*, vol. 7, no. 2, pp. 29-32, Apr. 1982.
[7] T. C. Jones, "Reusability in programming: A survey of the state of the art," *IEEE Trans. Software Eng.*, vol. SE-10, pp. 488-494, Sept. 1984.
[8] H. Partsch and R. Steinbrüggen, "Program transformation systems," *ACM Comput. Surveys*, vol. 15, no. 3, pp. 199-236, Sept. 1983.
[9] D. R. Barstow, *Knowledge-Based Program Construction*. New York: North Holland, 1979.
[10] D. L. Parnas, "Can automatic programming solve the SDI software problem?," in "Software aspects of strategic defense systems," *Amer. Sci.*, vol. 73, pp. 432-440, Sept.-Oct. 1985.
[11] T. DeMarco, *Controlling Software Projects*. New York: Yourdon, 1982.
[12] E. Bersoff, "Elements of software configuration management," *IEEE Trans. Software Eng.*, vol. SE-10, pp. 79-87, Jan. 1984.

A Spiral Model of Software Development and Enhancement

Barry W. Boehm
TRW Defense Systems Group

1. Introduction

1.1 Overview

The spiral model of software development and enhancement presented here provides a new framework for guiding the software process. Its major distinguishing feature is that it creates a *risk-driven* approach to the software process, rather than a primarily document- driven or code-driven process. It incorporates many of the strengths of other models, while resolving many of their difficulties.

This section presents a short motivational and historical background of software process models and the issues they address. Section 2 summarizes the process steps involved in the spiral model. Section 3 illustrates the application of the spiral model to a software project, using the TRW Software Productivity Project as an example. Section 4 summarizes the primary advantages and implications involved in using the spiral model, and the primary difficulties in using it at its current incomplete level of elaboration. Section 5 presents the resulting conclusions.

1.2 Background

The primary function of a software process model is to determine the *order of the stages* involved in software development and evolution, and to establish the *transition criteria* for progressing from one stage to the next. Thus, a process model addresses the following software project questions:

(1) What shall we do next?

(2) How long shall we continue to do it?

Thus, a process model differs from a software *method* (often called a *methodology*) in that the latter's primary focus is on *how to navigate through each phase* (determining data, control, or "uses" hierarchies; partitioning functions, allocating requirements) and how to represent phase products (structure charts; stimulus-response threads; state transition diagrams).

Why are software process models important? Primarily because they provide guidance on the order in which a project should carry out its major tasks: phases, increments, proto- types, validation tasks, etc.. Many software projects have come to grief because they pursued their various development and evolution phases in the wrong order. The next section illustrates this via a short historical review of software process models.

1.3 Evolution of Process Models

The "Code and Fix" Model

The basic model used in the earliest days of software development contained two steps:

(1) Write some code;

(2) Fix the problems in the code.

The primary difficulties with this model were:

a. After a number of fixes, the code became so poorly structured that subsequent fixes were very expensive. This highlighted the need for a design phase previous to coding.

b. Frequently, even well-designed software was such a poor match to users' needs that it was either rejected outright or expensively redeveloped. This highlighted the need for a requirements phase previous to design.

c. Code was expensive to fix because of poor preparation for testing and modification. This highlighted the need for explicit recognition of these phases, and for test and evolution planning and preparation tasks in the early phases.

The Stagewise Model and the Waterfall Model

Even by 1956, experience on large software systems such as SAGE had led to the recognition of these problems, and to the development of a stagewise model [Benington, 1956][1] to address them. This model stipulated that software be developed in successive stages (operational plan, operational specifications, coding specifications, coding, parameter testing, assembly testing, shakedown, system evaluation).

The original treatment of the *waterfall model* given in [Royce, 1970][2] provided two primary enhancements to the stagewise model:

- Recognition of the feedback loops between stages, and a guideline to confine the feedback loops to successive stages, in order to minimize the expensive rework involved in feedback across many stages.

- An initial incorporation of prototyping in the software life-cycle, via a "build it twice" step running in parallel with requirements analysis and design.

The waterfall approach was largely consistent with the *top-down structured programming model* formulated in [Dijkstra, 1970][3] and [Mills, 1971].[4] However, some attempts to apply these versions of the waterfall model ran into the following kinds of difficulties:

- The "build it twice" step was unnecessary in applications where design issues were well-understood (e.g., developing a straightforward payroll system), and subject to such unproductive phenomena as the "second system syndrome" [Brooks, 1975][5], in which the second system is overloaded with baroque embellishments.

- The pure top-down approach needed to be tempered with a "look ahead" step to cover such issues as high-risk, low-level elements and reusable or common software modules.

These considerations resulted in the *risk-management variant* of the waterfall model discussed in [Boehm, 1975][6] and elaborated in [Boehm, 1976].[7] In this variant, each step was expanded to include a validation and verification activity to cover high-risk elements, reuse considerations, and prototyping. Further refinements of the waterfall model covered such practices as incremental development [Distaso, 1980][8], developing program families and organizing software to accommodate change via information hiding [Parnas, 1979][9] and distinguishing pre-specification and post-specification activities via the "two-leg" model [Lehman, 1984].[10]

The successive stages used in the waterfall model helped eliminate many of the difficulties previously encountered on software projects. The waterfall model has become the basis of most software acquisition standards in government and industry. But even with the extensive revisions and refinements of the waterfall model, its basic scheme has encountered significant difficulties, and these have led to the formulation of alternative process models.

The Evolutionary Development Model

A primary source of difficulty with the waterfall model has been its emphasis on fully-elaborated documents as completion criteria for early requirements and design phases. For some classes of software, such as compilers or secure operating systems, this is the most effective way to proceed. But it does not work well for many classes of software, particularly interactive end-user applications. Document-driven standards have pushed many projects to write elaborate specifications of poorly-understood user interfaces and decision-support functions, followed by the design and development of large quantities of unusable code. Further, in areas supported by fourth-generation languages (spread sheet or small business applications), it is clearly unnecessary to write elaborate specifications for one's application before implementing it.

These concerns have led to the formulation of the *evolutionary development* model [McCracken-Jackson, 1982],[11] whose stages consist of expanding increments of an operational software product, with the directions of evolution being determined by operational experience.

The evolutionary development model is ideally matched to a fourth generation language application, and well matched to situations in which users say, "I can't tell you what I want, but I'll know it when I see it." It gives users a rapid initial operational capability, and provides a realistic operational basis for determining subsequent product improvements.

But evolutionary development has its difficulties also. It is generally difficult to distinguish from the old "code and fix" model, whose spaghetti code and lack of planning were the initial motivation for the waterfall model. It is also based on the often-unrealistic assumption that the user's operational system will be flexible enough to accommodate unplanned evolution paths. This assumption is unjustified in three primary situations:

- Situations in which several independently-evolved applications must subsequently be closely integrated;

- "Information-sclerosis" situations in which temporary work-arounds for software deficiencies increasingly solidify into unchangeable constraints on evolution. A typical example is the following comment: "It's nice that you could change those equipment codes to make them more intelligible for us, but the Codes Committee just met and established the current codes as company standards."

- Bridging situations, in which the new software is incrementally replacing a large existing system. If the existing system is poorly modularized, it is difficult to provide a good sequence of "bridges" between the old software and the expanding increments of new software.

The Transform Model

The "spaghetti code" difficulties of the evolutionary development and code-and-fix models can also become a difficulty in various classes of waterfall-model applications, in which code is optimized for performance and becomes increasingly difficult to modify. The transform model [Balzer-Cheatham-Green, 1983][12] has been proposed as a solution to this difficulty.

The transform model assumes the existence of a capability to automatically transform a formal specification of a software product into a program satisfying the specification. The steps then prescribed by the transform model are:

- A formal specification of the best initial understanding of the desired product;

- Automatic transformation of the specification into code;

- An iterative loop if necessary to improve the performance of the resulting code by giving optimization guidance to the transformation system;

- Exercise of the resulting product; and

- An outer iterative loop to adjust the specification based on the resulting operational experience, and to rederive, re-optimize, and exercise the adjusted software product.

The transform model thus avoids the difficulty of having to modify code which has become poorly structured through repeated re-optimizations, since the modifications are made to the specification. It also avoids the extra time and expense involved in the intermediate design, code, and test activities.

But the transform model has various difficulties as well. Automatic transformation capabilities are only available for small products in a few limited areas: spread sheets, small fourth generation language applications, and limited computer-science domains. The transform model also shares some of the difficulties of the evolutionary development model, such as the assumption that users' operational systems will always be flexible enough to support unplanned evolution paths. And it would face a formidable knowledge-base-maintenance problem in dealing with the rapidly increasing and evolving supply of reusable software components and commercial software products.

2. The Spiral Model

The spiral model of the software process has been evolving at TRW for several years, based on experience with various refinements of the waterfall model as applied to large government software projects. The spiral model includes most previous models as special cases, and further provides guidance as to which combination of previous models best fits a given software situation. Its most complete application to date has been to the development of the TRW Software Productivity System; this application will be described in Section 3.

The spiral model is illustrated in Figure 1. The radial dimension in Figure 1 represents the cumulative cost incurred in accomplishing the steps to date; the angular dimension represents the progress made in completing each cycle of the spiral. (The model holds that each cycle involves a progression through the same sequence of steps, for each

portion of the product and for each of its levels of elaboration, from an overall concept of operation document down to the coding of each individual program). Note that some artistic license has been taken with the increasing cumulative cost dimension in order to enhance legibility of the steps in Figure 1.

2.1 A Typical Cycle of the Spiral

Each cycle of the spiral begins with the identification of:

- The objectives of the portion of the product being elaborated (performance, functionality, ability to accommodate change, etc).

- The alternative means of implementing this portion of the product (design A, design B, reuse, buy, etc).

- The constraints imposed on the application of the alternatives (cost, schedule, interface, etc.).

The next step is to evaluate the alternatives with respect to the objectives and constraints. Frequently, this process will identify areas of uncertainty which are significant sources of project risk. If so, the next step should involve the formulation of a cost-effective strategy for resolving the sources of risk. This may involve prototyping, simulation, administering user questionnaires, analytic modeling, or combinations of these and other risk-resolution techniques.

Once the risks are evaluated, the next step is determined by the relative risks remaining. If performance or user-interface risks strongly dominate program development or internal interface-control risks, the next step may be an evolutionary development step: a minimal effort to specify the overall nature of the product, a plan for the next level of prototyping, and the development of a more detailed prototype to continue to resolve the major risk issues. If this prototype is operationally useful, and robust enough to serve as a low-risk base for future product evolution, then the subsequent risk-driven steps would be the evolving series of evolutionary prototypes going toward the right in Figure 1.

On the other hand, if previous prototyping efforts have already resolved all of the performance or user-interface risks, and program development or interface-control risks dominate, the next step follows the basic waterfall approach (concept of operation, software requirements, preliminary design, etc. in Figure 1), modified as appropriate to incorporate incremental development. Each level of software specification in Figure 1 is then followed by a validation step and the preparation of plans for the succeeding cycle.

The spiral model also accommodates any appropriate mixture of a specification-oriented, prototype-oriented, simulation-oriented, automatic transformation-oriented, or other approach to software development, where the appropriate mixed strategy is chosen by considering the relative mag-

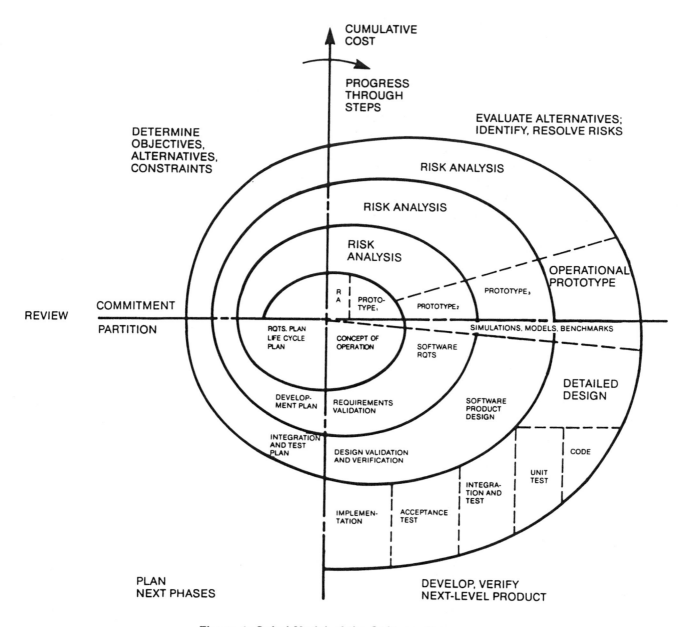

Figure 1: Spiral Model of the Software Process

nitude of the program risks, and the relative effectiveness of the various techniques in resolving the risks. (In a similar way, risk-management considerations determine the amount of time and effort which should be devoted to such other project activities as planning, configuration management, quality assurance, formal verification, or testing).

An important feature of the spiral model is that each cycle is completed by a review involving the primary people or organizations concerned with the product. This review covers all of the products developed during the previous cycle, including the plans for the next cycle and the resources required to carry them out. The major objective of the review is to ensure that all concerned parties are mutually committed to the approach to be taken for the next phase.

The plans for succeeding phases may also include a partition of the product into increments for successive development, or components to be developed by individual organizations or persons. Thus, the review and commitment step may range from an individual walkthrough of the design of a single programmer's component, to a major requirements review involving developer, customer, user, and maintenance organizations.

2.2 Initiating and Terminating the Spiral"

Four fundamental questions arise in considering this presentation of the spiral model:

(1) How does the spiral ever get started?

467

(2) How do you get off the spiral when it is appropriate to terminate a project early?

(3) Why does the spiral end so abruptly?

(4) What happens to software enhancement (or "maintenance")?

The answer to these questions involves an observation that the spiral model applies equally well to development or enhancement efforts, each of which are initiated by a hypothesis that a particular operational mission (or set of missions) could be improved by a software effort. The spiral process then involves a test of this hypothesis: at any time, if the hypothesis fails the test, the spiral is terminated. Otherwise, it terminates in the installation of the new or modified software, and the hypothesis is tested by observing the effect on the operational mission. Initiation, termination, and iteration of the tasks and products of previous cycles are thus implicitly defined in the spiral model, but not included in Figure 1 in order to simplify its presentation.

Similar spiral-type models have been defined in other fields. [Kolb, 1973][13] defines a four-stage development cycle whose stages are called divergence, assimilation, convergence, and execution. An example of its application to commercial product research and development is given in [Carlsson-Keane-Martin, 1976].[14] The book *Getting to Yes* [Fisher-Ury, 1981][15] defines a four-stage cycle for developing negotiation options; its stages are called problem, analysis, approaches, and action ideas.

3. Using The Spiral Model: The TRW Software Productivity System

The various rounds and activities involved in the spiral model are best understood via an example. This section will show how the spiral model was used in the definition and development of the TRW Software Productivity System (SPS), an integrated software engineering environment described in [Boehm et al., 1984].[16] The initial mission opportunity coincided with a corporate initiative to improve productivity in all appropriate corporate operations, and an initial hypothesis that software engineering was a potentially attractive area to investigate. This initially led to a small, extra "Round 0" circuit of the spiral to determine whether it was feasible to significantly increase software productivity at a reasonable corporate cost. (Very large or complex software projects will frequently precede the "concept of operation" round of the spiral with one or more smaller rounds to establish feasibility and to reduce the range of alternative solutions quickly and inexpensively).

Tables 1, 2, and 3 summarize the application of the spiral model to the first three rounds of defining the SPS. The major features of each round are discussed below, followed by some examples from later rounds such as preliminary and detailed design.

3.1. Round 0: Feasibility Study

This study involved five part-time participants over roughly a 2-3 month time span in 1980. As indicated in Table 1, the objectives and constraints for this round are expressed at a very high level, and in more qualitative terms: "significantly increase," "at reasonable cost," etc.

Round 0 considered a wide number of alternative approaches to significantly improve software productivity at a reasonable cost. Some of these primarily in the "technology" area could lead to the development of a software product, but these were also a number of alternatives in the management, personnel, and facilities areas which could have led to a conclusion not to embark on a software development activity.

The primary risk areas needing resolution were the possibility of situations in which the company would invest a good deal into improving software productivity and find that:

- The resulting productivity gains would not be significant; or that

- Any potentially high-leverage improvements would be incompatible with some aspects of the "TRW culture"

The risk-resolution activities undertaken in Round 0 were primarily surveys and analyses, including structured interviews of software developers and managers; an initial analysis of productivity leverage factors identified by the COCOMO software cost model (see [Boehm, 1981][16], Chapter 33); and an analysis of previous projects at TRW exhibiting high levels of productivity.

The risk analysis results indicated that it was highly likely that significant productivity gains could be achieved at a reasonable cost by pursuing an integrated set of initiatives in the four major areas. However, some candidate solutions, such as a software support environment based on a single, corporate, maxicomputer-based time-sharing system, were found to be in conflict with TRW constraints requiring support of different levels of security-classified projects. Thus, even at a very high level of generality of objectives and constraints, Round 0 was able to answer basic feasibility questions and eliminate significant classes of candidate solutions.

The plan for Round 1 involved a level of commitment on the order of 12 man-months as compared to the 2 man-months invested in Round 0 (During these rounds, all participants were part-time). Round 1 here corresponded fairly well with the initial round of the spiral model shown in Figure 1, in that its intent was to produce a concept of operation and a basic life-cycle plan for implementing whatever preferred alternative emerged.

Table 1: Spiral Model Usage: TRW Software Productivity System, Round 0

Objectives	• Significantly Increase Software Productivity
Constraints	• At Reasonable Cost • Within Context of TRW Culture — Government Contracts, High Tech., People Oriented, Security
Alternatives	• Management : Project Organization, Policies, Planning and Control • Personnel : Staffing, Incentives, Training • Technology : Tools, Workstations, Methods, Reuse • Facilities : Offices, Communications
Risks	• May be no High-Leverage Improvements • Improvements May Violate Constraints
Risk Resolution	• Internal Surveys • Analyze Cost Model • Analyze Exceptional Projects • Literature Search
Risk Resolution Results	• Some Alternatives Infeasible — Single Time Sharing System : Security • Mix of Alternatives Can Produce Significant Gains — Factor of 2 in 5 years • Need Further Study to Determine Best Mix
Plan for Next Phase	• 6-Person Task Force for 6 Months • More Extensive Surveys & Analysis — Internal, External, Economic • Develop Concept of Operation, Economic Rationale
Commitment	• Fund Next Phase

Table 2: Spiral Model Usage: TRW Software Productivity System, Round 1

Objectives	• Double Software Productivity in 5 Years
Constraints	• $10,000 per Person Investment • Within Context of TRW Culture — Government Contracts, High Tech., People Oriented, Security • Preference for TRW Products
Alternatives	• Office : Private/Modular/... • Communication : LAN/Star/Concentrators/... • Terminals : Private/Shared; Smart/Dumb • Tools : SREM/PSL-PSA/...;PDL/SADT/... • CPU : IBM/DEC/CDC/...
Risks	• May Miss High-Leverage Options • TRW LAN Price/Performance • Workstation Cost
Risk Resolution	• Extensive External Surveys, Visits • TRW LAN Benchmarking • Workstation Price/Performance
Risk Resolution Results	• Ops. Concept : Private Offices, TRW LAN, Personal Terminals, VAX • Begin with Primarily Dumb Terminals; Experiment with Smart Workstations • Defer OS, Tools Selection
Plan for Next Phase	• Partition Effort into SDE, Facilities, Management • Develop First-Cut Prototype SDE — Design-to-Cost : 15 Person Team for 1 Year • Plan for External Usage
Commitment	• Develop Prototype SDE • Commit an Upcoming Project to Use SDE • Commit the SDE to Support the Project • Form Representative Steering Group

3.2. Round 1: Concept of Operations

Table 2 provides a summary of Round 1 of the spiral along the same lines given in Table 1 for Round 0. Rather than simply elaborate on the entries in Table 2, the discussion below focuses on comparing and contrasting the features of Rounds 0 and 1:

* As mentioned above, the level of investment was greater (12 man-months vs. 2).

* The objectives and constraints were more specific ("double software productivity in 5 years at a cost of $10K/person" vs. "significantly increase productivity at a reasonable cost").

* Additional constraints surfaced, such as the preference for TRW products (particularly, a TRW-developed local area network (LAN) system).

* The alternatives were more detailed ("SREM, PSL/PSA or SADT, as requirements tools etc." vs. "tools"; "private or shared terminals, smart or dumb terminals" vs. "workstations").

* The risk areas identified were more specific ("TRW LAN price-performance within a $10K/person investment constraint" vs. "improvements may violate reasonable-cost constraint").

* The risk-resolution activities were more extensive (including the benchmarking and analysis of a prototype TRW LAN being developed for another project).

* The result was a fairly specific Operational Concept Document, involving private offices tailored to software work patterns, and personal terminals connected to VAX superminis via the TRW LAN. Some choices were specifically deferred to the next round, such as the choice of operating system and specific tools.

* The life-cycle plan and the plan for the next phase involved a a partitioning into separate activities to address management improvements, facilities development, and development of the first increment of a software development environment. (SDE).

* The commitment step involved more than just an agreement with the plan. It added a commitment for an upcoming 100-person software project to be the initial testbed user of the system, and for the environment development to focus on the needs of the testbed project. It also added the formation of a representative steering group to ensure that the separate activities were well-coordinated, and that the environment would not be overly optimized around the testbed project.

Although the plan recommended the development of a prototype environment, it also recommended that the project also employ requirements specifications and design specifications

in a risk-driven way. Thus, the development of the environment followed the succeeding rounds of the spiral model.

3.3. Round 2: Top-Level Requirements Specification

Table 3 shows the corresponding steps involved during Round 2 in defining the SPS during early 1981. Since a number of these Round 2 decisions and their rationale are covered in [Boehm et al., 1984],[16] we will not elaborate on them there. Instead, we will summarize two of the highlights dealing with risk management and the use of the spiral model.

* The initial risk-identification activities during Round 2 showed that several system requirements hinged on the decision between a host-target system or a fully portable tool set, and the decision between VMS and Unix as the host operating system. These requirements included the functions required to provide a user-friendly front-end, the operating system to be used by the workstations, and the functions required to support a host-target operation. In order to keep these requirements in synchronization with the other requirements, a special mini-spiral was initiated to address and resolve these issues. The resulting review resulted in a commitment to a host-target operation using Unix on the host system, at a point early enough to work the OS-dependent requirements in a timely fashion.

* Addressing the risks of mismatches to the user-project's needs and priorities resulted in substantial participation of the user-project personnel in the requirements definition activity. This led to several significant redirections of the requirements, particularly toward supporting the early phases of the software life-cycle into which the user project was embarking, such as an adaptation of the Software Requirements Engineering Methodology (SREM) Tools for requirements specification and analysis.

It is also interesting to note that the form of Tables 1, 2, and 3 was originally developed for presentation purposes, but subsequently became a standard "Spiral Model Template" used on later projects. These templates are useful not only for organizing project activities, but also as a residual design-rationale record. Design rationale information is of paramount importance in assessing the potential reusability of software components on future projects.

3.4. Succeeding Rounds of the Spiral"

Within the confines of this paper, it is not possible to discuss each round of the spiral in detail. But it will be useful to illustrate some examples of how the spiral model is used to handle situations arising in the preliminary design and

Table 3: Spiral Model Usage: TRW Software Productivity System, Round 2

Objectives	• User-Friendly System • Integrated Software, Office-Automated Tools • Support All Project Personnel • Support All Life-Cycle Phases
Constraints	• Customer-Deliverable SDE — Portability • Stable, Reliable Services
Alternatives	• OS : VMS/AT&T Unix/Berkeley Unix/ISC • Host-Target/Fully Portable Toolset • Workstations : Zenith/LSI-11/...
Risks	• Mismatch to User-Project Needs, Priorities • User-Unfriendly System — 12-Language Syndrome, Experts-Only • Unix Performance, Support • Workstation/Mainframe compatibility
Risk Resolution	• User-Project Surveys, Requirements Participation • Survey of Unix-Using Organizations • Workstation Study
Risk Resolution Results	• Top-Level Requirements Specification • Host-Target with Unix Host • Unix-Based Workstations • Build User-Friendly Front End for Unix • Initial Focus on Tools to Support Early Phases

Plan for Next Phase	• Overall Development Plan
	  — for Tools : SREM, RTT, PDL, OA Tools
	  — for Front End, Support Tools
	  — for LAN, Equipment, Facilities

Commitment	• Proceed with Plans

detailed design of components of the SPS: the preliminary design specification for the Requirements Traceability Tool (RTT), and a detailed design go-back on the Unit Development Folder (UDF) tool.

The RTT Preliminary Design Specification

The Requirements Traceability Tool (RTT) establishes the traceability between itemized software requirements specifications, design elements, code elements, and test cases. It also supports various associated query, analysis, and report generation capabilities. The preliminary design specification for the RTT (and most of the other SPS tools) looked different from the usual preliminary design specification, which tends to show a uniform level of elaboration of all components of the design. Instead, the level of detail of the RTT specification was risk-driven:

- In areas involving a high risk if the design was wrong, the design was carried down to the detailed design level, usually with the aid of rapid prototyping. These areas included working out the implications of various "undo" options, and the effects of various control keys used to escape from various levels of the program.

- In areas involving a moderate risk if the design was wrong, the design was carried down to a preliminary-design level. These areas included the basic command options for the tool, and the schemata for the requirements traceability data base. Here again, the ease of rapid prototyping with Unix shell scripts supported a good deal of user-interface prototyping.

- In areas involving a low risk if the design was wrong, very little design elaboration was done. These areas included details of all of the help message options and all of the report-generation options, once the nature of these options had been established in some example instances.

A Detailed Design Go-Back: The UDF Tool

The Unit Development Folder (UDF) tool collects into an electronic "folder" all of the artifacts involved in the development of a single-programmer software unit (typically 500-1000 instructions): unit requirements, design, code, test cases, test results, and documentation. It also includes a management template for tracking the programmer's scheduled and actual completion of each artifact.

During the detailed design of the Unit Development Folder (UDF) tool, an alternative was considered to reuse portions of the Requirements Traceability Tool (RTT) to provide pointers to the requirements and preliminary design specifications of the unit being developed. This turned out to be an extremely attractive alternative, not only in avoiding duplicate software development, but also in surfacing several

issues involving many-to-many mappings between requirements, design, and code which had not been considered in designing the UDF tool. These led to a rethinking of the UDF tool requirements and preliminary design, which avoided a great deal of code rework that would have been necessary if the detailed design of the UDF tool had proceeded in a purely deductive, top-down fashion from the original UDF requirements specification. The resulting go-back led to a significantly different and more capable UDF tool, incorporating the RTT in its "users-hierarchy."

Spiral Model Features Illustrated by the Two Examples

From these two examples, we can see that the spiral approach:

- Fosters the development of specifications that are not necessarily uniform, exhaustive, or formal, in that they defer detailed elaboration of low risk software elements, and avoid unnecessary breakage in their design, until the high-risk elements of the design are stabilized.

- Incorporates prototyping as a risk-reduction option at any stage of development. In fact, prototyping and reuse risk analyses were often used in the process of going from detailed design into code.

- Accommodates go-backs to earlier stages of the spiral as more attractive alternatives are identified or as new risk issues need resolution.

3.5. Results of Using the Spiral Model

The resulting Software Productivity System developed and supported using the spiral model successfully avoided the risks identified, and achieved most of its objectives. The system has grown to include over 300 tools and over 1,300,000 instructions; 93% of the instructions were reused from previous project-developed, TRW-developed, or external software packages. All of the projects using the system have increased their productivity at least 50%; most have indeed doubled their productivity (as compared with cost estimation model predictions of their productivity using traditional methods).

However, one risk area was underestimated—the risk that projects with non-Unix target systems would not accept a Unix-based host system. Some projects accepted the host-target approach, but a good many did not for various reasons (customer constraints, zero-cost target machines). As a result, the system was less widely used on TRW projects than expected. This and other lessons learned have been incorporated into the spiral model approach to developing TRW's next-generation software development environment.

4. Spiral Model Advantages, Difficulties, and Implications

4.1. Spiral Model Advantages

The primary advantage of the spiral model is that its range of options allows it to accommodate the best features of existing software process models, while its risk-driven approach helps it to avoid most of their difficulties. In appropriate situations, the spiral model becomes equivalent to one of the existing process models. In other situations, it provides guidance on the best mix of existing approaches to be applied to a given project. The application of the spiral model to the TRW Software Productivity System discussed in Section 3 provides a good example of a risk-driven mix of specifying, prototyping, and evolutionary development.

The primary conditions under which the spiral model becomes equivalent to other main process models are summarized below.

- If a project has a low risk in such areas as getting the wrong user interface or not meeting stringent performance requirements; and it has a high risk if it loses budget and schedule predictability and control; then these risk considerations drive the spiral model into an equivalence to the waterfall model.

- If a software product's requirements are very stable (implying a low risk of expensive design and code breakage due to requirements changes during development); and if the presence of errors in the software product constitutes a high risk to the mission it serves; then these risk considerations drive the spiral model to resemble the two-leg model of precise specification and formal deductive program development.

- If a project has a low risk in such areas as losing budget and schedule predictability and control, encountering large-system integration problems, or coping with information sclerosis; and it has a high risk in such areas as getting the wrong user interface or user decision support requirements; then these risk considerations drive the spiral model into an equivalence to the evolutionary development model.

- If automated software generation capabilities are available, then the spiral model accommodates them either as options for rapid prototyping or for application of the transform model, depending on the risk considerations involved.

- If the high-risk elements of a project involve a mix of the risk items above, then the spiral approach will reflect an appropriate mix of the process models above. In doing so, its risk-avoidance features will generally avoid the difficulties of the other models.

In addition, the spiral model has a number of further advantages which are summarized below.

- *It accommodates strategies for developing program families, and for the reuse of existing software.* The steps involving the identification and evaluation of alternatives accommodate these options.

- *It accommodates preparation for life-cycle evolution, growth, and changes of the software product.* The major sources of product change are included in the product's objectives, and information-hiding approaches are included in the architectural design alternatives.

- *It provides a mechanism for incorporating software quality objectives into software product development.* This mechanism derives from the emphasis on identifying all types of objectives and constraints during each round of the spiral. The GOALS approach and software engineering goal structure in [Boehm, 1981; Chapter 3][17] provide a process and checklist for incorporating quality objectives.

- *It focuses on eliminating errors and unattractive alternatives early.* The risk-analysis, validation, and commitment steps cover these considerations.

- *It accommodates iterations, go-backs, and early termination of non-viable software projects.* The first two of these aspects were illustrated in the TRW-SPS example. The example also illustrated the overall objective of the spiral approach to start small, keep the spiral as tight as possible, and thus achieve the project's objectives with a minimum resource expenditure.

- *For each of the sources of project activity and resource expenditure, it answers the key question, "how much is enough?"* How much should a project do of requirements analysis, planning, configuration management, quality assurance, testing, formal verification, etc? Using the risk-driven approach, we can see that the answer is not the same for all projects, and that the appropriate level of effort is determined by the level of risk incurred by not doing enough.

- *It can support, and be supported by, advanced software development environments.* The process steps and their associated internal and external products can be treated as data base objects to be handled by an advanced object manager. Also, process and risk-management guidance for software developers can be incorporated into an evolving Knowledge Based Software Assistant or activity coordinator.

- *It does not involve separate approaches for software development and software enhancement (or "maintenance").* This aspect helps avoid the "second class citizen" status frequently associated with software maintenance. It also helps avoid many of the problems that currently ensue when high-risk enhancement efforts are approached in the same way as routine maintenance efforts.

- *It provides a viable framework for integrated hardware-software system development.* The focus on risk-management and on eliminating unattractive alternatives early and inexpensively is equally applicable to hardware and software.

- *On the other hand, it avoids forcing software development procedures into hardware development paradigms.* A good example of this is the review called "Critical Design Review," or CDR, which occurs after the detailed design is completed. For a hardware development risk profile, this review is indeed critical: as seen in Figure 2, it is the final review before the project begins to commit the bulk of its resources into producing hardware. From this standpoint, it is indeed critical to invest in an exhaustive, across-the-board review of the detailed design specifications before proceeding. For a software project, however, the risk profile is significantly different. Typically, in order to reduce the crucial factor of software development time, a software

project will work out detailed unit interfaces by the Preliminary Design Review (PDR), and then begin to commit the bulk of its resources to large numbers of people doing detailed design and code in parallel (see Figure 2). To interrupt this process with a single, large, across-the-board CDR is not only time-consuming and expensive, but also ineffective, as the inter-unit interface specifications were necessarily verified thoroughly at the PDR. Thus, the critical review for a software project is the PDR; the "detailed design review" function is performed much more cost-effectively by a program of individual design inspections or walkthroughs, followed as appropriate by an overall review of the major issues identified in the walkthroughs.

4.2. Spiral Model Difficulties

Although the full spiral model can be successfully applied in many situations, it still has some difficulties or challenges to address before it can be called a mature, universally applicable model. The three primary spiral model challenges are summarized below.

(1) *The spiral model currently works well on internal software developments like the TRW-SPS, but it needs fur-*

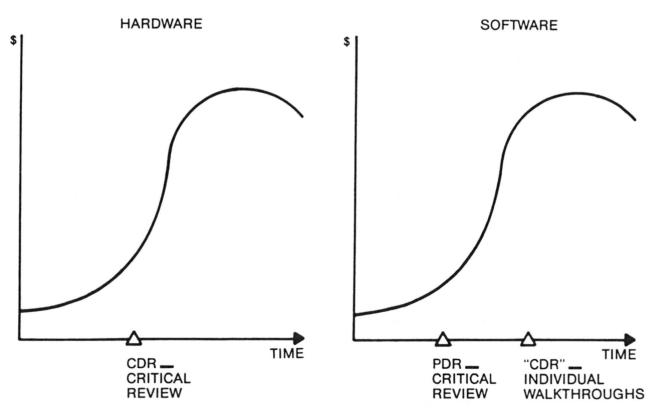

HARDWARE

SOFTWARE

CDR — CRITICAL REVIEW

PDR — CRITICAL REVIEW

"CDR" — INDIVIDUAL WALKTHROUGHS

Figure 2: Risk-Oriented Management Refocuses Software Reviews onto Key Software Issues

ther work to match it to the world of contract software acquisition.

Internal software developments have a great deal of flexibility and freedom to accommodate stage-by-stage commitments, to defer commitments to specific options, to establish mini-spirals to resolve critical-path items, to adjust levels of effort, or to accommodate such practices as prototyping, evolutionary development, or design to cost. The world of contract software acquisition has a harder time achieving these degrees of flexibility and freedom without losing accountability and control.

Recently, a good deal of progress has been made in establishing more flexible contract mechanisms, such as the use of competitive front-end contracts for concept definition or prototype fly-offs; the use of level-of effort and award-fee contracts for evolutionary development; and the use of design-to-cost contracts. Although these have been generally successful, the procedures for using them still need to be worked out to the point that acquisition managers feel fully comfortable in using them.

(2) *The spiral model places a great deal of reliance on the ability of software developers to identify and manage sources of project risk.*

A good example is the spiral model's risk-driven specification, which carries high-risk elements down to a great deal of detail, and leaves low-risk elements to be elaborated in later stages, by which time there is less risk of breakage.

However, a team of inexperienced or low-balling developers may also produce a specification with a different pattern of variation in levels of detail: a great elaboration of detail for the well-understood, low-risk elements; and little elaboration of the poorly-understood, high-risk elements. Unless there is an insightful review of such a specification by experienced developer or acquisition personnel, this type of project will proceed to give an illusion of progress during a period in which it is actually heading for disaster.

Another concern is that a risk-driven specification will also be people-dependent. For example, a design may be produced by an expert, but may be implemented by non-experts. In this case, even though the expert does not need a great deal of detailed documentation, it is necessary for him to produce enough additional documentation to ensure that the non-experts will not go astray. Reviewers of the specification must be sensitive to these concerns as well.

With a conventional, document-driven approach, the requirement to carry all aspects of the specification to a uniform level of detail eliminates some potential problems, and creates a situation in which some aspects of reviews can be adequately carried out by inexperienced reviewers. But it also creates a large drain on the time of the scarce experts, who must dig for the critical issues within a large mass of non-critical detail. And further, if the high-risk elements have been glossed over by impressive-sounding references to poorly-understood capabilities (e.g., a new synchronization concept or a commercial DBMS), then there is an even greater risk of the conventional approach giving an illusion of progress in situations which are actually heading for disaster.

(3) *In general, the spiral model process steps need further elaboration to ensure that all of the participants in a software development are operating in a consistent context.*

Some examples are the need for more detailed definitions of the nature of spiral model specifications and milestones, the nature and objectives of spiral model reviews, and the nature of spiral model status indicators and cost-vs-progress tracking procedures. Another need is for guidelines and checklists to be used in identifying the most likely sources of project risk, and the most effective risk-resolution techniques for each source of risk.

It is currently feasible for highly experienced people to successfully use the spiral approach without these elaborations. But for large scale use in situations where people bring widely differing experience bases to the project, added levels of elaboration—such as have been accumulated over the years for document-driven approaches—are important in ensuring consistent interpretation and usage of the spiral approach across the project.

Efforts to apply and refine the spiral model have largely focussed on creating a discipline of software risk management, including techniques for risk identification, risk analysis, risk prioritization, risk management planning, and risk element tracking. An example of the results of this activity is the prioritized top-ten list of software risk items given in Figure 3. Another example is the risk management plan discussed in the next section. Other recent applications and extensions of the spiral model are presented in [Belz, 1986][18] and [Iivari, 1987].[19]

4.3. Spiral Model Implications: The Risk Management Plan

Even if an organization is not fully ready to adopt the entire spiral approach, there is one characteristic spiral model technique which can easily be adapted to any life-cycle model,

Figure 3: A Prioritized Top Ten List of Software Risk Items

Risk Item	Risk Management Techniques
1. Personnel shortfalls	— Staffing with top talent, job matching; teambuilding; morale building, cross-training; pre-scheduling key people.
2. Unrealistic schedules and budgets	— Detailed, multi-source cost and schedule estimation; design to cost; incremental development; software reuse; requirements scrubbing.
3. Developing the wrong software functions	— Organization analysis; mission analysis; ops-concept formulation; user surveys; prototyping; early users' manuals.
4. Developing the wrong user interface	— Task analysis; prototyping; scenarios.
5. Gold plating	— Requirements scrubbing; prototyping; cost-benefit analysis; design to cost.
6. Continuing stream of requirement changes	— High change threshold, information hiding; incremental development (defer changes to later increments).
7. Shortfalls in externally-furnished components	— Benchmarking; inspections; reference checking; compatibility analysis.
8. Shortfalls in externally-performed tasks	— Reference checking; pre-award audits; award-fee contracts; competitive design or prototyping; teambuilding.
9. Real-time performance shortfalls	— Simulation; benchmarking; modeling; prototyping; instrumentation; tuning.
10. Straining computer science capabilities	— Technical analysis; cost-benefit analysis; prototyping; reference checking.

and which can provide many of the benefits of the spiral approach. This is the *Risk Management Plan* summarized in Table 4. The Risk Management Plan basically ensures that each project make an early identification of its top risk items (the number 10 is not an absolute requirement), develop a plan for resolving the risk items, identify and plan to resolve new risk items as they surface, and highlight the project's progress vs. plans in monthly reviews.

The Risk Management Plan has been used successfully at TRW and other organizations, and has ensured an appropriate focus on early prototyping, simulation, benchmarking, key-person staffing measures, and other early risk-resolution techniques which have helped avoid many potential project "show-stoppers." The recent U.S. Department of Defense standard on software management, DoD-STD-2167, requires

that developers produce and use risk management plans, as does its counterpart Air Force regulation, AFR 800-14.

Table 4. Software Risk Management Plan

(1) Identify the project's top 10 risk items

(2) Present a plan for resolving each risk item

(3) Update list of top risk items, plan, and results monthly

(4) Highlight risk-item status in monthly project reviews

(5) Initiate appropriate corrective actions

5. Conclusions

(1) The risk-driven nature of the spiral model is more adaptable to the full range of software project situations than are the primarily document-driven approaches such as the waterfall model or the primarily code-driven approaches such as evolutionary development. It is particularly applicable to very large, complex, ambitious software systems.

(2) The spiral model has been quite successful in its largest application to date: the development and enhancement of the TRW SPS. Overall, the spiral approach was highly effective in achieving a high level of software support environment capability in a very short time, and in providing the flexibility necessary to accommodate a high dynamic range of technical alternatives and user objectives.

(3) The spiral model is not yet as fully elaborated as are more established models such as the waterfall model. Thus, although the spiral model can be successfully applied by software-experienced personnel, it needs further elaboration in such areas as contracting, specifications, milestones, reviews, status monitoring, and risk-area identification in order to be fully usable in all situations.

(4) Partial implementations of the spiral model such as the Risk Management Plan are compatible with most current process models, and are highly useful in helping projects to overcome their major sources of project risk.

Acknowledgments

I would like to thank Frank Belz, Lolo Penedo, George Spadaro, Bob Williams, Bob Balzer, Gillian Frewin, Peter Hamer, Manny Lehman, Lee Osterweil, Dave Parnas, Bill Riddle, Steve Squires, and Dick Thayer for their stimulating and insightful comments and discussions of earlier versions of this paper, and Nancy Donato for producing its several versions.

References

(1) H.D. Benington, "Production of Large Computer Programs," *Proc. ONR Symposium on Advanced Programming Methods for Digital Computers*, June 1956, pp. 15-27. Also available in *Annals of the History of Computing*, Oct. 1983, pp.350-361, and *Proceedings, ICSE 9*, IEEE-CS, 1987.

(2) W.W. Royce, "Managing the Development of Large Software Systems: Concepts and Techniques," *Proceedings, WESCON*, August 1970. Also available in *Proceedings, ICSE 9*, IEEE-CS, 1987.

(3) E.W. Dijkstra, "Notes on Structured Programming," Technische Hogeschool Eindhoven, Report No. EWD-248, April 1970. Also in O.J. Dahl, E.W. Dijkstra, and C.A.R. Hoare, *Structured Programming*, Academic Press, 1972.

(4) H.D. Mills, "Top-Down Programming in Large Systems," in *Debugging Techniques in Large Systems*, R. Ruskin (ed), Prentice-Hall, 1971, pp. 41-55.

(5) F.P. Brooks, *The Mythical Man-Month*, Addison-Wesley, 1975.

(6) B.W. Boehm, "Software Design and Structuring" in *Practical Strategies for Developing Large Software Systems*, E. Horowitz (ed), Addison-Wesley, 1975, pp. 103-128.

(7) B.W. Boehm, "Software Engineering," *IEEE Trans. Computers*, December 1976, pp. 1226-1241.

(8) J.R. Distaso, "Software Management—A Survey of the Practice in 1980." *IEEE Proceedings, Sept. 1980, pp. 1103-1119.*

(9) *D.L. Parnas, "Designing Software for Ease of Extension and Contraction," IEEE Trans. S/W Engr., March 1979, pp. 128-137.*

(10) M.M. Lehman, "A Further Model of Coherent Programming Processes," *Proceedings, Software Process Workshop*, IEEE, Feb. 1984, pp.27-33.

(11) D.D. McCracken and M.A. Jackson, "Life Cycle Concept Considered Harmful," *Software Engineering Notes*, ACM, April 1982, pp. 29-32.

(12) R. Balzer, T.E. Cheatham, and C. Green, "Software Technology in the 1990's: Using a New Paradigm," *Computer*, Nov. 1983, pp. 39-45.

(13) D.A. Kolb, "On Management and the Learning Process," *MIT Sloan School Working Paper 652-73*, Cambridge, MA, 1973.

(14) B. Carlsson, P. Keane, and J.B. Martin, "R&D Organizations as Learning Systems," *Sloan Management Review*, Spring 1976, pp. 1-15.

(15) R. Fisher and W. Ury, *Getting to Yes*, Houghton Mifflin, 1981; Penguin Books, 1983.

(16) B.W. Boehm, M.H. Penedo, E.D. Stuckle, R.D. Williams, and A.B. Pyster, "A Software Development Environment for Improving Productivity," *Computer*, June 1984, pp. 30-44.

(17) B.W. Boehm, *Software Engineering Economics*, Prentice-Hall, 1981.

(18) F.C. Belz, "Applying the Spiral Model: Observations on Developing System Software in Ada," *Proceedings, 1986 Annual Conference on Ada Technology*, Atlanta, GA, 1986, pp. 57-66.

(19) J. Iivari, "A Hierarchical Spiral Model for the Software Process," *ACM Software Engineering Notes*, Jan. 1987, pp. 35-37.

The Impact of Prototyping on Software System Engineering

Hassan Gomaa
George Mason University
School of Information Technology and Engineering
Fairfax, VA 22030

Abstract: Traditionally, large-scale software systems have been developed by using the software lifecycle, a phased approach for developing software. However, there are several problems with this approach, particularly for systems whose requirements are not clearly understood. This paper describes how software prototyping may be used to overcome these problems in the development of large-scale software systems and describes two different types of software prototypes: throwaway prototypes and evolutionary prototypes.

1: Introduction

In the last 20 years, the cost of developing software has grown steadily, while the cost of developing and/or purchasing hardware has rapidly decreased (Figure 1). Furthermore, software now typically costs 80 percent of a total project, whereas only 20 years ago the hardware was far more expensive.

Twenty years ago the problems of developing software were not clearly understood. In the late 1960s, it was realized that a software crisis existed. The term software engineering was coined to refer to the management and technical methods, procedures, and tools required to effectively develop a large-scale software system. With the application of software engineering concepts, many large-scale software systems have been developed by using the software

lifecycle. This lifecycle, shown in Figure 2, is a phased approach to developing software and is often referred to as the waterfall model. Although certainly a major improvement over the unstructured approach used on early software projects, there remain a number of problems with the "traditional" or conventional software lifecycle:

1. It is somewhat unrealistic because it fails to effectively show iteration between phases, an important factor in any software project.

2. A working system only becomes available late in the lifecycle, typically during system testing. Thus a major problem may go undetected until the system is almost operational, at which time it is usually too late to take effective action.

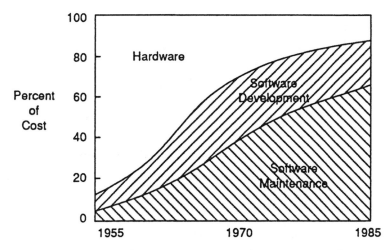

Figure 1: Hardware/software cost trends

Reprinted from *System and Software Requirements Engineering,* M. Dorfman and R.H. Thayer, eds., 1990, pp. 543–552.

3. Software requirements, a key factor in any software development, are not properly tested until a working system is available to demonstrate to the end users.

This paper describes how software prototyping may be used to overcome these problems in the development of large-scale software systems. In particular, it describes two different types of software prototypes: throwaway (also referred to as rapid) prototypes and evolutionary prototypes. The characteristics of these prototypes, tools to assist in their development, and the impact of these prototypes on the software lifecycle are described.

2: Rapid Prototyping of User Requirements

2.1: Problems in Defining User Requirements

The requirements analysis and specification phase of the software lifecycle involves analyzing the user's requirements and then specifying a system to satisfy them.

The procedure usually followed in specifying a new computer system is to write a requirements specification and submit it for the approval of the users. The main problem with this approach is that users find it extremely difficult to visualize how the system will actually function in their own environment just by reading a paper specification. This is particularly the case if the system is to be used by a wide spectrum of users, many of whom have different (sometimes conflicting) requirements and most of whom have no previous computer experience. These users often find a written specification dull to read and difficult to understand. Hence, they are uncertain whether or not the proposed system meets their requirements. It is also very difficult to determine whether a requirements specification is complete, correct, consistent, and unambiguous.

Furthermore, these problems are compounded because experience has shown that errors in requirements specification are usually the last to be detected and the most costly to correct [4]. Many data processing departments spend as much time on the maintenance of existing computer systems as on the development of new ones, and many so-called "maintenance" projects are established to correct errors in the original requirements specification.

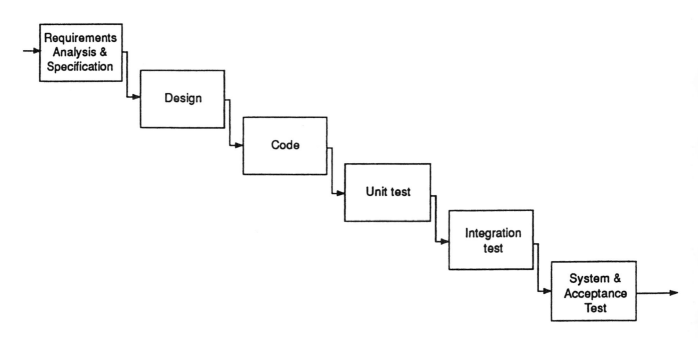

Figure 2: Software lifecycle

Figure 3 shows the types of errors that can be introduced into a software system, and when they are likely to be detected. Figure 3 shows that requirements analysis and specification errors are frequently not detected until system and acceptance test. Worse still, several errors remain undetected until the system is operational. Figure 4 shows that the longer an error goes undetected, the costlier it is to correct. Thus the most expensive errors to correct are often errors in requirements analysis and specification.

In recognition of these problems, various methods and tools have been developed to assist the requirements specification process. These tools fall into two main categories, system specification languages [5, 6] and graphical tools [7, 8], or some combination of the two. These tools tend to be of greater value to the developer than to the user. Thus, even with the assistance of these tools, the user is likely to find it difficult to visualize how the system will function in his environment.

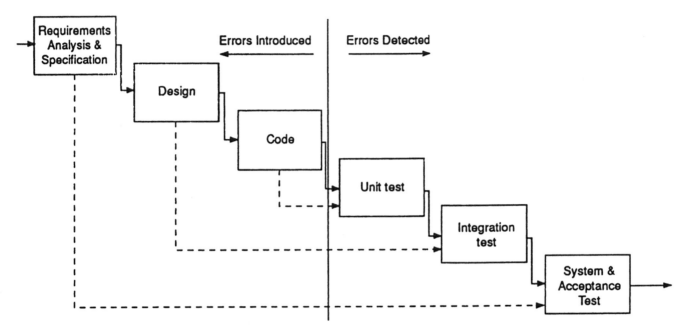

Figure 3: Error detection by phase of lifecycle

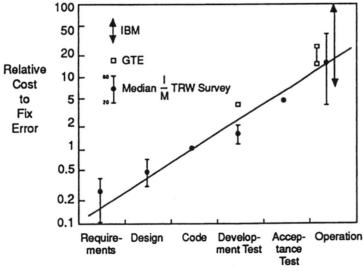

Figure 4: The cost of error correction

2.2: Plan to Throw One Away

In his classical text, "A Mythical Man Month" [9], Brooks advises us to "plan to throw one away; you will, anyhow." He points out that if this advice is not taken, the first version of a production system will in effect turn out to be a prototype. It will be replaced sooner or later by a second system, which corrects the errors in the first.

The best way to avoid these problems and to ensure that the first production system will indeed satisfy the user's requirements is to give the user "hands-on" use of the system. Prototyping is an effective way of providing this "hands-on" experience.

3: Rapid Prototyping

3.1: Nature of a Rapid Prototype

The big advantage that prototyping can bring to the requirements specification process is the capability of bridging the communications gap that exists between the system developer and the user because of their different backgrounds. With a prototype, the user can exercise the system just as though it were already operating in his own environment and thereby can provide vital feedback to the developer on the suitability of the specification.

For a prototype to be an effective tool in assisting the requirements specification process, it must satisfy the following conditions:

1. The prototype must be an actual working system with

which one can experiment and from which lessons can be learned to revise the requirements specification.

2. It must be comparatively cheap to develop the prototype (e.g., around 10 percent of the total estimated software development cost). If not, it will be difficult to justify.

3. The prototype must be developed relatively quickly so that it may be evaluated early in the software lifecycle. Because the cost of making changes to a system increases significantly as the development proceeds [4], it is necessary to obtain the user feedback well before the requirements specification is finalized.

4: Rapid Prototyping Approach

4.1: Introduction

The conventional software lifecycle is impacted by the introduction of a prototyping exercise and may be revised accordingly. The phases of the revised lifecycle are as follows:

1. Preliminary analysis and specification of user requirements

2. Design and implementation of a prototype

3. Exercising of a prototype

4. Iterative refinement of a prototype

5. Refinement of the requirements specification

6. Design and implementation of a production system

Figure 5 shows diagrammatically the impact of throwaway prototyping on the software lifecycle.

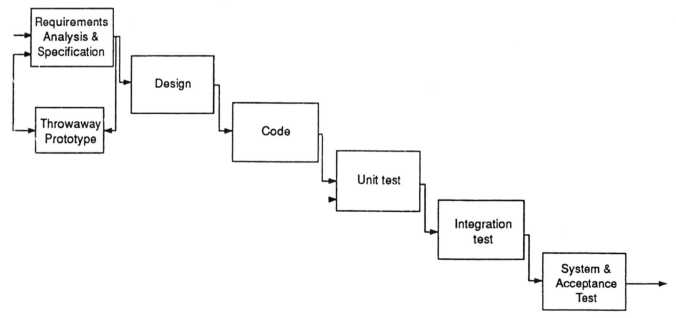

Figure 5: Impact of throwaway prototyping on lifecycle

4.2: Preliminary Analysis and Specification of User Requirements

During this phase, a first attempt is made to analyze the user's needs and to specify a system to satisfy his requirements. This preliminary specification forms the basis from which design and implementation of the prototype may proceed.

It is advantageous to have this preliminary specification to guide the development of the prototype. At this stage, the developer believes he has a reasonable understanding of the user's problem and has completed his first serious attempt at proposing a system to satisfy the user's requirements.

4.3: Design and Implementation of Prototype

The emphasis in developing the prototype is on rapid implementation and low development cost. There are a number of factors that can help achieve these objectives:

1. *Emphasis on user interface:* As the objective of the prototype is to maximize user feedback, the prototype should emphasize the user interface at the expense of lower-level software that is not visible to the user.

2. *Small development team:* Typically, a prototype should be undertaken by a small development team to minimize potential communication problems. The developers should interface closely with the specifiers. Indeed the developers may actually be the specifiers.

3. *Prototype development language:* The developers should use a programming language that helps in the rapid development of the prototype. Emphasis is on reducing development time and is not on the performance of the finished product. An interpretive language is therefore an advantage, because it can lead to rapid detection of programming errors. A language with powerful data manipulation features is also an advantage. One language that satisfies both these criteria is APL.

4. *Tools to help rapid development:* There are a number of tools that can be provided on the host system to help the rapid development of prototypes. In fact, the availability of such tools is an important criterion for the selection of the host system.

A number of languages and tools can help in the development of rapid prototypes; an interpretive language such as APL can be very helpful. The use of reusable code from previous projects is worth considering. However, until recently, effective software reuse has usually been difficult to achieve. One of the most promising class of rapid prototyping tools to emerge in the last few years is that of fourth-generation languages and application generators [15]. These tools are particularly applicable to the application domain of interactive information systems that have a large database component.

Fourth-generation languages and application generators refer to a software development environment that typically includes a database management system (often relational), a non-procedural language used for querying the database, report generation, data manipulation, screen definition, and a graphics capability. Some of these tools are sufficiently user friendly that end users can do their own prototyping.

A good fourth-generation language/application generator provides tools to allow the prototype developer to easily and rapidly:

1. Define the logical data model of the system, that is the overall structure of the database.

2. Define interactive screens that would be used to prompt the end user for data, hence allowing the end user to easily enter data into the database.

3. Provide the capability of defining the range or set of valid values for user-entered data. This capability is then used to validate the data entered by users. If a data item is incorrect, an error message is output and the user is reprompted.

4. Create reports by using the report generation capability to allow users to view data in the database.

5. Use the graphical capability to create bar charts, histograms, pie charts, scatter plots, etc.

6. Provide a query language capability so that end users can interrogate the database.

Fourth-generation languages and application generators have been effectively used to prototype interactive database oriented information systems. They have also been used to develop small to medium size applications. However for large-scale systems, it is more likely that the production system would be developed by using the conventional software lifecycle after the requirements had been prototyped by using the fourth-generation language/application generator.

4.4: Exercising of Prototype

Once the prototype has been developed, it is ready to be exercised by the users. Frequently, a system has many different users with differing requirements. Each user may exercise the prototype from his own viewpoint and may evaluate how well it performs the tasks he requires. Furthermore, use of the prototype may actually influence the user's perception of what he really wants.

The following items should be noted in this phase:

1. Time must be allocated in the software development schedule for users to exercise the prototype and to provide their feedback to the developers.

2. User management commitment must be obtained for time to be made available for users to exercise the pro-

totype. Typically, more users are involved in using the prototype than in assisting with specifying requirements.

3. It is necessary to plan a training course for users to get acquainted with the prototype. Documentation, preferably on line, should be provided for users. This documentation does not need to be as comprehensive as for a production system.

4. Vehicles, such as the provision of an online comment or mailbox mechanism and/or the use of evaluation forms, should be provided to assist in obtaining user feedback.

4.5: Iterative Refinement of Prototype

Based on user feedback, changes are made to the prototype. Depending on user comments, these changes may be minor, such as altering report formats, or they may be major, such as requiring structural modifications to the prototype.

The changes to the prototype should ideally be made quickly and the prototype should then be exercised again by the users. The iterative refinement and experimentation with the prototype continues until it reaches a stage where the benefits of further enhancements to the prototype are outweighed by the time and cost required for these modifications. At this stage, which has to be carefully monitored and evaluated by the user and the developer, further refinement of the prototype stops.

4.6: Refinement of Requirements Specification

A detailed evaluation is now made of the lessons learned through using the prototype. Some of the changes requested by users will have been implemented in the prototype and others may not have been. All user feedback is analyzed and based on this, the requirements specification is revised and forms the basis from which the design and implementation of the production system proceeds.

4.7: Design and Implementation of Production System

The design, coding, and testing of the production system proceeds by following the standard software lifecycle. Developing the prototype will probably provide insights on how the production system should be designed.

In the production system, we place emphasis on the use of software engineering methods and tools such as structured design, structured programming, systematic testing, comprehensive documentation, and walkthroughs. Thus, the primary emphasis should be to provide a maintainable system.

5: Case Study: Process Management and Information System

5.1: Introduction

An illustration of the benefits to be gained by using prototypes to assist in requirements specification is now given. A prototype was used to help specify the requirements of a computer system to manage and control an integrated circuit fabrication facility. The cost of developing and running the prototype was less than 10 percent of the total software development cost.

The system, which was prototyped, is called a process management and information system, (PROMIS) for an integrated circuit fabrication facility [10]. PROMIS was a joint development of I.P. Sharp Associates and the General Electric Company.

This section summarizes the experience gained from developing the prototype. A more detailed description of the prototype is given in [11, 12].

5.2: Overview of the Prototype

PROMIS was planned to be a highly interactive system. The user community is very varied and consists of semiconductor equipment operators, semiconductor process engineers, maintenance engineers, supervisors, and managers. The large majority of users have never used computers before. One major requirements of PROMIS was, therefore, that it should be a "user-friendly" system.

The prototype was designed to concentrate on the user interface. Most user interactions with the system were explicitly prototyped. Users interacted with the prototype through a menu that is implemented as a three-level command tree. Once a function at the lowest level of the tree has been selected, the user is presented with simple English language requests for any required data by that function. Each user input is thoroughly validated and, if an error is detected, meaningful error and information messages are issued.

Development of the prototype started after a preliminary specification of the user's requirements was completed. The prototype was developed in APL by three people over a three month period. The total manpower spent on the prototype was seven man months, which represents about six percent of the total software development effort of 10 man years. In addition, approximately $12,500 was spent in timesharing costs.

5.3: Experience with the Prototype

Users were given a two hour course and a practical demonstration on how to use the prototype. They were then given four weeks to experiment with the prototype.

Two methods were used to obtain the user's feedback: an evaluation form that they were asked to complete and an online mechanism for entering (and reading) user comments. This allowed a user to enter his comments online, while using the prototype, and to review the comments of other users.

The main points revealed by developing and using the prototype were as follows:

1. Misunderstandings between the software developers and users were revealed through use of the prototype. These were clarified.

2. Ambiguities and inconsistencies in the requirements specification were identified, as the prototype was being developed and were subsequently corrected.

3. Omissions in the requirements specification were discovered when users asked for features they considered essential, but that were not available in the prototype.

4. Software errors were discovered in the prototype that were caused by incorrect or missing requirements.

5. Some functions, although implemented, did not provide the user with the information he wanted. These were modified to provide additional or different information.

6. Users were able to give valuable feedback about which features of the system were difficult or confusing to use. Users found certain command names confusing. Certain terminology was also found confusing.

7. In some cases, the user was not sure how he wanted certain functions implemented. Developing the prototype helped him come to a decision on these.

As user feedback was received, some relatively minor modifications, primarily in the areas of report formats and user prompts, were made to the prototype. This enabled users to experience the results of their comments quickly. After five iterations, further development ceased because the primary benefits had been obtained from using the prototype.

A detailed analysis was then made of the user comments. Based on this, the requirements specification was significantly revised. The changes made to the specification were of relatively low cost and would have been considerably more expensive to implement had they been performed later in the software lifecycle.

5.4: Reasons for Low Cost of Prototype

The main reasons why the development cost of the prototype was kept to less than 10 percent of the total software development cost are as follows:

1. *Emphasis of the prototype:* The prototype emphasized the user interface to the system. The objective was to get the most benefit (i.e., user feedback) from the prototype. Consequently, not all aspects of the system were prototyped. In particular, frequently executed user functions were emphasized, not the exception conditions. Data validation, error handling, and logging were not as comprehensive in the prototype as they are in the production system. Certain subsystems, such as system recovery and facility monitoring, were not prototyped at all, because they have little or no interaction with the user and it was felt that their requirements were generally clearly understood. The prototype was a single user system whereas the production system is a multi-user system. Intertask communication and synchronization issues were therefore avoided. Performance considerations were also ignored in the prototype.

2. *Size of the prototype:* The prototype was developed by three people whereas the production system is being developed by a team of 12 people. A much more flexible and less formal development approach was therefore used for the prototype than that required for the production system.

3. *APL language:* APL is an interpretive language with many powerful features for manipulating multidimensional arrays. Consequently, APL programs are often much shorter than programs written in other languages. Because APL is interpretive, APL programmers tend to find it relatively fast to test their programs.

4. *APL system:* The APL system used, SHARP APL [13], has a number of features that assist in program development. It has a file system that is easy to use and a powerful report formatting utility, which facilitates writing and changing of sample reports, a valuable capability in any prototyping exercise. Furthermore, backup and recovery procedures are built into the system.

5.5: Experience with the Production System

The design, coding, and testing of the production system proceeded from the revised requirements specification. The production system was developed on a DEC VAX 11/780 in (structured) Fortran 77, whereas the prototype had been developed on an Amdahl system in APL.

Developing the prototype provided valuable insight to the developers on how the system should be designed, in particular how the system should be structured, how files and data should be structured, which algorithms to use and which not to use.

A more formal software engineering approach was used to develop the production system than was used in the prototype. This included top-down design, information hiding, structured programming, systematic testing, and comprehensive user and system documentation. A software quality assurance program was implemented to ensure the high quality of the software. Emphasis was placed on software usability, reliability, and maintainability.

No significant specification problems were experienced during the subsequent software development and the project was successfully completed on time. User reaction has been very favorable to the system; the most frequent comment has been how easy the system is to use. The major reason for the user friendliness of the system is the experience gained from the prototype.

6: Evolutionary Prototyping by Incremental Development

A different approach to prototyping, one in which the prototype evolves into the final system, is now described. A software development approach that encourages evolutionary prototyping is that of incremental development.

The objective of the evolutionary prototyping approach is to have a subset of the system working early which is then gradually built on. It is advantageous if the first incremental version of the system tests a complete path through the system from external input to external output.

The advantages of the evolutionary prototyping approach are:

1. It provides a good psychological boost to the team and to the management.

2. The incremental versions of the system can be used as prototypes to test certain parts of the system, such as the user interface, or to test certain key algorithms for performance, correctness, or accuracy. With this approach, the prototypes actually evolve into the final system.

3. It can be used to obtain early feedback from users.

4. Some performance measurements can be taken to determine the system response to executing a given transaction.

7: Software Lifecycle for Evolutionary Prototyping

The phases of the software lifecycle for the evolutionary prototyping approach are (see also Figure 6):

1. *Requirement analysis and specification:* This phase involves analyzing the user's requirements and specifying a system to satisfy these requirements.

2. *Architectural design:* During this phase, the system is structured into modules and module interfaces are defined.

3. *Incremental module construction:* This phase involves the complete detailed design of each module to be included in the system increment. It also includes coding and unit testing of the portion of each module to be included in the system increment.

4. *Incremental system integration:* Modules to be included in the system increment are gradually integrated and tested to form subsystems.

5. *Evolutionary construction/integration:* The previous two phases of module construction and system integration are repeated for each system increment. In some cases, the architectural design may need to be updated. The requirements specification may also need to be modified if errors are detected or to accommodate new or changed user requirements.

6. *System testing:* The whole system or major subsystems are tested to determine conformance with the functional specification. To achieve greater objectivi-

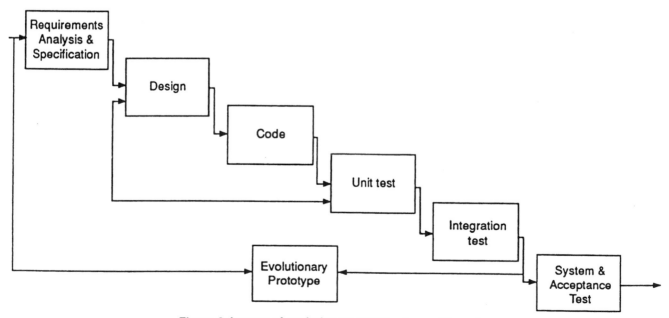

Figure 6: Impact of evolutionary prototyping on lifecycle

ty, it is preferable if system testing is performed by an independent test team.

7. *Acceptance testing:* This is performed by the user.

After the architectural design is complete, the detailed design of each module is carried out. Coding for a given module only commences after the detailed design for that module is complete. However, rather than coding the whole module prior to unit testing, the code may be developed and tested in stages.

As long as the interfaces between modules are fully defined during architectural design, module development may proceed independently. Thus it is not necessary to complete the detailed design of all modules before coding starts. This means that an incremental version of the system may be running before all module designs are completed and some may not even have been started. Thus, for example, the development of error handling modules could be delayed until after an incremental version of the system is operational.

8: Event Sequence Diagrams

A typical software system usually has to deal with a large number of external events. An external event is any external input to the system such as a sensor input or user command. The event sequence diagram is a useful development tool for both design and incremental development. The diagram shows for a group of transforms on a data flow diagram [7, 8], the sequence of actions that are expected to take place when an external event occurs.

The event sequence diagram is based on the data flow diagram. It only shows those transforms in the data flow diagram that are involved in processing the action, typically a subset of all the transforms. It should be noted that whereas a data flow diagram shows data flows and is not concerned with sequencing, the event sequence diagram is at a lower level of detail and is concerned with sequencing actions. Thus it shows the inter-dependence of events. In the event sequence diagram, the actions are numbered sequentially in the order in which they are triggered and the diagram may indeed be labelled with the specific action being performed.

The users of the diagram are to:

1. Provide a better understanding of the dynamic interactions in the system. In this way they may be used as a design tool in the system decomposition process.

   Furthermore by studying the cause-effect relationships, the designer can check whether any necessary steps have been omitted in the design.

2. A tool for deciding on how to stage the incremental software development. Thus to process one external event, features may be required from several transforms. By identifying the group of events to be sup-

ported in a given system increment, the functions that need to be provided by the transforms may be determined.

Initially a relatively small subset of events is selected such that the key elements of the system are exercised. The transforms and hence functions within modules required to support this subset are identified. Thus by classifying groups of external events to be supported, the incremental versions of the system are identified.

3. A vehicle for designing test cases during integration testing. It helps in deciding what inputs should be selected and what output data should be recorded.

9: Example of Evolutionary Prototyping

The evolutionary prototyping approach was used in the development of an industrial robot controller [14]. Event sequence diagrams were used to help identify the system increments.

The objective of the first system increment was to demonstrate that the user could initiate execution of a robot program consisting entirely of motion commands, which would result in motion of the robot arm. Subsequent increments gradually provided greater functionality including more advanced motion commands, sensor/actuator commands, additional robot language and interpreter features, and a more comprehensive user interface.

Using the evolutionary prototyping approach on the industrial controller project resulted in an early version of the system being available. This had a big morale boosting effect on both the team and management. It also had the benefits of validating the system design and of spreading the system integration workload over time.

10: Comparsion of Prototyping Approaches

The first prototyping approach is the throwaway prototype used for prototyping user requirements. Developing a throwaway prototype to assist in specifying user requirements does not eliminate or reduce the need for a comprehensive analysis and specification of user requirements. In fact, prototyping is not likely to reduce the length of the requirements process; it is more likely to increase it. However, it does result in a requirements specification that is more likely to be complete and correct. Hence, further development may proceed with greater confidence, having reduced the chances of unexpected problems arising during development because of omissions, inconsistencies, or errors in the requirements specification. Consequently, it increases the probability of a timely delivery of the product. With the rapid prototyping approach, little emphasis is placed on software quality because the tool is experimental.

The second kind of prototype is the evolutionary prototype that results from using the incremental development approach and is actually an early version of the production system. Since the prototype gradually evolves into the production system, software quality is considered to be of major importance with this prototyping approach. Thus prototype development needs to follow the software lifecycle with requirements specification, system design, and detailed design phases preceding the coding and testing of the prototype. Because the throwaway prototype can be developed much less formally than the evolutionary prototype, it can be developed much more rapidly.

The rapid prototype is considered a throwaway prototype because little emphasis is likely to have been placed on software quality. Maintainability is a much more important consideration in a production system than in a rapid prototype. This type of prototype is of most use when the user requirements are not clearly understood. It significantly reduces the risk of delivering an unappropriate production system to the user.

From a project viewpoint, development of the requirements specification by using a throwaway prototype should be viewed as a project in its own right. Once the prototyping effort has been completed and the revised requirements specification is available, the subsequent software development effort should be treated as a separate project. At this stage, it should be possible to obtain a significantly better estimate of the remaining software development effort required.

On the other hand, with the evolutionary prototype, software quality has to be an important consideration from the start. The incremental development approach may be used effectively on larger projects that can benefit substantially from being staged. In particular, this helps the system integration task by spreading the load over time. It can also be used to verify designs and performance targets at an earlier stage than usual.

11: Conclusions

This paper has described how software prototyping can be used to assist in the development of large-scale software systems. Two different approaches to prototyping have been described, throwaway prototyping and evolutionary prototyping. Examples of their use have also been given.

Rapid throwaway prototypes can be used to help understand user requirements, a major problem in many software projects. Evolutionary prototypes provide an incremental development approach, so that the system may be gradually developed and tested, allowing errors to be revealed and corrected earlier than in the conventional software lifecycle.

12: Acknowledgments

The author is indebted to J.R. DeBolt, R.F. Johnston, and D.B.H. Scott for their major contributions to the requirements specification of PROMIS and the development

of both the prototype and the production PROMIS system. The author is also indebted to his colleagues on the industrial controller development project who effectively demonstrated the benefits of the incremental development approach.

12: References

[1] W.P. Dodd, "Prototype Programs," *Computer*, Feb. 1980.

[2] *Proceedings ACM Conference on Rapid Prototyping. ACM Software Engineering Notes*, ACM, Inc., N.Y., Feb. 1983.

[3] B. McNurlin, "Developing Systems by Prototyping," *EDP Analyzer*, Vol. 19, No. 9, 1981.

[4] B. Boehm, "Software Engineering," *IEEE Transactions on Computers*, Dec. 1976.

[5] D. Teichrow and E. Hershey, "PSL/PSA: A Computer Aided Technique for Structured Documentation and Analysis of Information Processing Systems," *IEEE Transactions on Software Engineering*, Jan. 1977.

[6] T. Bell, D. Bixler, and M. Dyer, "An Extendable Approach to Computer Aided Software Requirements Engineering," *IEEE Transactions on Software Engineering*, Jan. 1977.

[7] T. DeMaro, *Structured Analysis and System Specification*, Yourdon Press, N.Y., 1978.

[8] C. Gane and T. Sarson, *Structured Systems Analysis: Tools and Techniques*, Prentice Hall, Englewood Cliffs, N.J., 1979.

[9] F. Brooks, *The Mythical Man-Month*, Addison-Wesley, Reading, Mass., 1975.

[10] J.R. DeBolt, H. Gomaa, and D.B.H. Scott, "PROMIS—A Process Management and Information System for Integrated Circuit Fabrication," *Proc. IEEE Computer Software and Applications Conf.*, IEEE Computer Society Press, Washington, D.C., Nov. 1981.

[11] H. Gomaa and D.B.H. Scott, "An APL Prototype of a Management and Control System for a Semiconductor Fabrication Facility," *Proceedings of the 1980 APL Users Meeting*, Oct. 1980.

[12] H. Gomaa and D.B.H. Scott, "Prototyping as a Tool in the Specification of User Requirements," *Proc. 5th International Conference on Software Engineering*, IEEE Computer Society Press, Washington, D.C., March 1981.

[13] P. Berry, "Sharp APL Reference Manual," I.P. Sharp Associates, 1979.

[14] H. Gomaa, "A Software Design Method for Real-Time Systems," *Communications of ACM*, Sept. 1984.

[15] J. Martin, *Fourth Generation Languages*, Vol. 1, Prentice Hall, Englewood Cliffs, N.J., 1985.

Software Requirements Engineering Glossary

Richard H. Thayer
Mildred C. Thayer
Software Management Consultants
Carmichael, CA 95608

Scope

This glossary defines the terms used in the field of system and software requirements engineering and supporting disciplines. These definitions have their roots in several management and technical domains: general (mainstream) management, project management, and system and hardware engineering. In addition, there are new definitions and old terms with new meanings. The relationships between these domains and software engineering and software engineering project management can be seen in Figure 1.

The definitions from any domain in Figure 1 usually can be applied to any domain located lower on the hierarchy. For example, a system engineering definition can apply to both system engineering and software engineering, and a project management definition can also apply to software engineering project management. But because of new technologies and meanings a software engineering definition will not necessarily apply to general engineering.

Definitions for hardware and software engineering and system and software system engineering are so similar that the terms *hardware/software* and *system/software* are frequently used to mean applicability in both domains.

The domain of the definition should be understood or identified in the first sentence of the definition. When the definition was taken from another source and the domain of definition was not obvious, the domain was added.

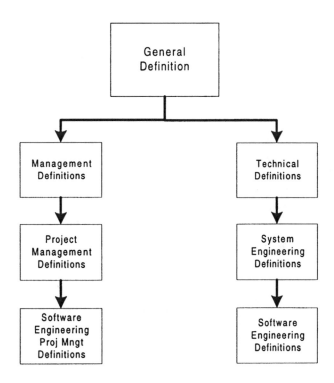

Figure 1. Hierarchical domains of software engineering and software engineering project management definitions.

Glossary Structure

Entries in the glossary are arranged alphabetically. An entry may consist of a single word, such as *requirements;* a phrase, such as *requirements engineering;* or an acronym such as *SQA.* Phrases are given in their natural order *(requirements engineering)* rather than reversed *(engineering, requirements).*

Blanks are taken into account in alphabetizing. They precede all other characters. For example, *ad hoc* precedes *Ada.* Hyphens and slashes follow blanks. Alternative spellings are shown as separate glossary entries with cross-references to the preferred spelling

No distinction is made between acronyms and abbreviations. Where appropriate, a term that has a common acronym or abbreviation contains the acronym or abbreviation in parentheses following the term. The abbreviation or acronym might also be a separate entry. The definition is placed with the term or abbreviation, depending on which one has the most usage; and the other will be cross-referenced. For example, *CASE,* an acronym for *computer-aided software engineering,* has its definition after *CASE.* In contrast, *SQA,* an acronym for *software quality assurance,* will have its definition after *software quality assurance (SQA).*

If a term has more than one definition, the definitions are listed with numerical prefixes. This ordering does not imply preference. Where necessary, examples and notes have been added to clarify the definitions.

The following cross-references are used to show a term's relationship to other terms in the glossary:

- *See* refers to a preferred term or to a term whose definition serves to define the term that has been looked up
- *See also* refers to a related term
- *Sometimes synonymous with* refers to a term that may or may not be synonymous with the defined term, that is, it is a nonstandard usage
- *Synonymous with* refers to a term that is always or nearly always synonymous with the defined term
- *Contrast with* refers to a term with an opposite or substantially different meaning

In a few cases, nonstandard cross-references are used to clarify a particular definition.

Sources

In those cases in which a definition is taken or paraphrased from another source or paper, the source is designated in brackets following the definition, for example [Smith 1988]. The use of a source reference does not imply an exact quote, but is an acknowledgment of the source of the definition. A list of all sources used in this glossary is at the end of the glossary.

Acknowledgment

The authors would like to acknowledge the hard work done by all the members of the IEEE Computer Dictionary Standards Working Group, who have worked diligently without compensation to further the discipline of software engineering.

Glossary

A

abstraction—In object-oriented development, an abstraction is a simplified description of a system that emphasizes some of the system's details or properties while suppressing others. A good abstraction is one that emphasizes details that are significant to the reader or user and suppresses details that are, for the moment, immaterial or diversionary. [Booch 1994]

acceptance criteria—In system/software engineering, the criteria a prospective user will use to determine that the proposed system will meet the software requirements.

acceptance testing—In a system/software engineering (testing): 1. A test to determine whether a hardware/software system satisfies its acceptance criteria. 2. To enable the customer to determine whether to accept the system. *See also qualification testing, system testing.*

acquisition management—The management and control of the system/software acquisition process through the use of the system acquisition lifecycle.

actor—In software engineering, an outside entity that interacts directly with a system. Actors include both humans and other quasi-autonomous things, such as machines, computer tasks, and other systems. More precisely, an actor is a role played by such an activity. [Rumbaugh 1994]

ad hoc development method—A software development methodology that is, in essence, no methodology. However, it is very popular.

adaptability—1. In software requirements analysis, a rate at which the software solution can adapt to a new requirement. [Davis et al. 1988]

490

2. In software engineering, a software quality metric that can be used to assess the ease with which software allows differing system constraints and user needs to be satisfied. [ANSI/IEEE Standard 729-1983]

adaptive maintenance—In software engineering (maintenance): 1. Consists of any effort that is initiated as a result of changes in the environment in which a software system must operate. [NBS Special Publication 500-106 1983] 2. The alteration of a program to bring it into line with changes in its operating environment. The operating environment includes the hardware on which the software runs, so adaptive maintenance includes porting the software to a new machine. [Foster et al. 1989] *Contrast with corrective maintenance; perfective maintenance.*

algorithm—A finite set of well-defined rules that provides for the solution to a problem in a finite number of steps.

allocated requirement—In system/software system engineering, requirements that have been partitioned and allocated (assigned) to a particular hardware/software subsystem for implementation. The allocated requirements form the allocated baseline.

allocation—In system/software system engineering, the assignment or budgeting of top-level functional or nonfunctional requirements among the lower level partitioned functions for accomplishment. In this manner, the elements of a system that perform all or part of specific requirements are identified.

ambiguity—A problem in developing software requirements specifications in which requirements statements can be interpreted in several different ways. The receiver must clarify these statements on the basis of the surrounding context. [Rich et al. 1987]

analysis—The process of studying a system by partitioning the system into parts (functions or objects) and determining how the parts relate to each other to understand the whole. [IEEE-STD 1362 (draft)]

annotated requirement—In system/software system engineering, annotation added to the requirements to clarify which requirements are essential and which would be nice to have; which are stable and which might be considered volatile; or which requirements are mandatory, desirable, or optional.

application model—A model of a particular application.

architectural design—In system/software system engineering: 1. The process of defining a collection of hardware and software components and their interfaces to establish a framework for the development of a system/software system. 2. The result of the architectural design process. [ANSI/IEEE Standard 729-1983] *Synonymous with internal specification, preliminary design, system design, top-level design.*

audit—1. A management review of a hardware/software project for the purpose of assessing compliance with requirements, specifications, baselines, standards, procedures, instructions, codes, and contractual and licensing requirements. 2. In system/software system engineering, an activity to determine through investigation the adequacy of, and adherence to, established procedures, instructions, specifications, codes, and standards or other applicable contractual and licensing requirements, as well as the effectiveness of implementation. [ANSI N45.2.10-1973] *See also code audit, functional configuration audit, independent audit. physical configuration audit.*

automated technique (detailed)—In software system engineering (verification and validation techniques), methods of verifying and validating a software system, which involve detailed automated models and prototypes that describe the system in detail. Detailed automated models involve large-event simulation, which can be effective in analyzing issues of accuracy, dynamic consistency, real-time performance, and lifecycle costs. The use of a prototype to demonstrate some key portion of the software will often surface numbers of ambiguities, inconsistencies, blind spots, and misunderstandings. [Boehm, *V&V Software Requirements* 1984]

availability—1. In software engineering, a software quality metric that can be used to measure the probability that software will be able to perform its designated system function when required for use. 2. The ratio of computer system uptime to total operating time. 3. The ability of a software system to perform its designated function when needed. 4. A software requirement for system operation that involves system reliability, ratio of system uptime to system operating time, and so forth.

B

baseline—1. A hardware/software work product that has been formally reviewed and accepted, which then serves as the basis for further development; it can be changed only through formal change control procedures. Each baseline must specify items that form the baseline (for example, software requirements, design documentation, and deliverable source code), the review and approval mechanisms, the acceptance criteria associated with the baseline, and the customer and project organization who participated in establishing the baseline. *See configuration management.*

baseline document—System/software documents that establish one of the configuration identifications of a hardware/software configuration item. The system specifications, requirements specifications, and design specifications are examples of baseline identification documents. *See also allocated baseline, configuration management (CM), functional baseline, product baseline.*

baseline management—A system/software project management concept that employs lifecycle phases, lifecycle phase documents, lifecycle phase reviews, and baselines to manage the project. *See also baseline, baseline document, lifecycle development model, milestone, milestone review, waterfall model.*

black-box testing—A system/software test methodology that is derived from external specifications and requirements of the system. Methods for black-box testing include random testing, testing at boundary values, and a possible error list. It verifies the end results at the system level, but does not check on how the system is implemented. Nor does it assume that all statements in the program are executed. *Contrast with white-box testing. See also functional testing.*

bottom-up development—In system/software system engineering, pertaining to a system/software system engineering development approach that starts with the lowest level system/software components of a hierarchy and proceeds through progressively higher levels to the top-level component. *See also bottom-up testing. Contrast with top-down development.*

bottom-up testing—In software system engineering (testing), the process of checking out hierarchically organized programs, progressively, from bottom to top, by using software drivers to simulate top-level components. *Contrast with top-down testing.*

bug—In software development, a euphemism for error. The first "bug" originated at Harvard University in the late 1940s. During the hunt for an error on one of the first digital computers, a moth (or bug) was found in the logic circuitry. Since then, all software errors have been called "bugs."

build—In software system engineering, an operational version of a software product incorporating a specified subset of the capabilities that the final product will include. *Sometimes synonymous with version.*

C

CASE—Acronym for computer-aided software engineering.

CASE tool—An automated software engineering development tool that can assist software engineering in analyzing, designing, coding, testing, and documenting a software system and managing a software project. John Manley, University of Pittsburgh, was apparently the first person to use the acronym CASE for computer-aided software engineering. [Manley 1984]

CCB—Acronym for configuration control board.

CDR—Acronym for critical design review.

change—In configuration management (CM), a formally recognized revision to a specified and documented program requirement. This may include a change in specification or engineering. *See also configuration control, configuration management (CM), engineering change.*

change control—In configuration management (CM), the process by which a change is proposed, evaluated, approved or rejected, scheduled, and tracked [ANSI/IEEE Standard 729-1983]. *See also configuration control, configuration management (CM).*

change status report—In configuration management (CM), details the status of all proposed changes to a hardware/software configuration item for which the developer is responsible and for which existing documentation is listed in the configuration index. The purpose of the report is to provide the customer and the developer with a summary of the current status of all proposed and approved engineering change proposals (ECPs). *See also configuration management (CM).*

changeability—In software engineering, a software quality metric that can be used to measure the ability of the software to accept change. [Boehm, *Spiral Model* 1988]

checklist—In software system engineering (verification and validation techniques), involves specialized lists of necessary activities based on previous successful software development. A checklist can be used effectively with any of the manual verification and validation methods. Checklists are excellent for catching omissions such as missing items, functions, and product. These are valuable aids in addressing some of the lifecycle feasibility considerations, such as human engineering, maintainability, reliability, availability, affordability, security, privacy, and lifecycle efficiency. [Boehm, *V&V Software Requirements 1984*] *See also verification and validation technique.*

class—In object-oriented development, a set of objects that share a common structure and behavior.

CM—Acronym for configuration management.

code—In data processing: 1. To represent data or a computer program in a symbolic form that can be accepted by a computer. 2. To write a routine. 3. Loosely, one or more computer programs or part of a computer program. [ANSI/IEEE Standard 729-1983] 4. *Synonymous with software.*

code and unit testing—In software engineering, the activity of coding the modules (units) and testing them. Unit testing is normally done by the programmers who coded them.

commercial off-the-shelf (COTS) software—*See software package.*

compatibility—In software engineering, a quality metric that can be used to measure the ability of two or more systems to exchange information. [ANSI/IEEE Standard 729-1983] *See also interoperability.*

complete—A software requirements specification is complete when the following are assured: (1) Everything that the software is supposed to do is included in the software requirements specification. (2) The system responds to all classes of input data (note: it is important to specify the responses to both valid and invalid input). (3) All pages are numbered; all figures and tables are numbered, named, and referenced; all terms and units of measure are provided; and all reference materials are present. (4) No sections are marked "to be determined" (TBD).

complexity—In software engineering, a quality metric that can be used to measure the degree of complication of a system or system component, determined by such factors as the number and intricacy

of interfaces, the number and intricacy of conditional branches, the degree of nesting, the types of data structures, and other system characteristics. [ANSI/IEEE Standard 729-1983]

computer code—*See software.*

computer program—*See software.*

computer science—The study of computers, their underlying principles, and use. It comprises such topics as compilers and operating systems; computer networks and interfaces; computer system architecture; hardware design and testing; information structures; programming languages; programming; software engineering; systems analysis and design; theories of information systems and computation; and applications from such disciplines as social sciences, economics, political sciences, engineering, business, and education.

computer software configuration item (CSCI)—[U.S. Department of Defense (DoD) usage]. *See configuration item (CI).*

computer system—1. A system composed of a computer(s), peripheral equipment, such as disks, printers, and terminals, and the software necessary to make them operate together. 2. A functional unit, consisting of one or more computers and associated software, that uses common storage for all or part of a program and also for all or part of the data necessary for the execution of the program; executes user-written or user-designated programs; performs user-designated data manipulation, including arithmetic operations and logic operations; and can execute programs that modify themselves during their execution. A computer system may be a standalone unit or may consist of several interconnected units, or it may be embedded in a larger non-data-processing system. [ANSI/IEEE Standard 729-1983] *Synonymous with embedded computer system.*

computer-aided software engineering (CASE)—The use of computers to assist in the design, development, and coding of software.

concept of operations (ConOps) document—A user-oriented document that describes the system characteristics from an end user's viewpoint. The document is used to coordinate overall quantitative and nonquantitative system goals for the user, buyer, developer, and other interfacing organizations (such as training, facilities, staffing, and maintenance elements). It describes the user organizations and mission from an integrated system point of view. [IEEE-STD 1362 (draft)]

concurrent engineering—A system engineering approach to integrate the design of a product and its development, manufacturing, coding, and other support processes starting in the study period and continuing throughout the development project, considering all elements of the product life cycle from conception through disposal. [Forsberg and Mooz 1996]

configuration accounting—In configuration management (CM), the act of reporting and documenting changes made to a baseline configuration to establish a hardware/software configuration status. *See also configuration management (CM), configuration status accounting.*

configuration auditing—In configuration management (CM), the process of verifying that all required hardware/software configuration items have been produced, that the current version agrees with specified requirements, that the technical documentation completely and accurately describes the configuration items, and that all change requests have been resolved. [ANSI/IEEE Standard 729-1983] *See also configuration management (CM).*

configuration control—In configuration management: 1. The process of evaluating, approving or disapproving, and coordinating changes to hardware/software configuration items after formal establishment of their configuration identification. 2. The systematic evaluation, coordination, approval or disapproval, and implementation of all approved changes in the configuration of a hardware/software configuration item after formal establishment of its configuration identification. [DoD Standard 480B 1988] *Sometime erroneously used synonymously for configuration management (CM). See also configuration management (CM).*

configuration control board (CCB)—In configuration management (CM), the authority responsible for evaluating and approving or disapproving proposed engineering changes to the hardware/software configuration, and ensuring implementation of the approved changes. [ANSI/IEEE Standard 729-1983] *See also configuration management (CM).*

configuration identification—In configuration management: 1. The process of designating the hardware/software configuration items (CIs) in a system and recording their characteristics. 2. The approved documentation that defines a hardware/software CI. 3. The current approved or conditionally approved technical documentation for a hardware/software CI as set forth in specifications, drawings, and associated lists, and documents referenced therein. [DoD Standard 480B 1988] *See also configuration management (CM).*

configuration item (CI)—In configuration management, an aggregation of hardware/software, or any of its discrete portions, that satisfies an end-use function and is designated by the customer for configuration management (CM). CIs may vary widely in complexity, size, and type, from an aircraft, electronic system, or ship system to a test meter, circuit board, or teddy bear. During development and initial production, CIs are only those specification items that are referenced directly in a contract (or equivalent in-house agreement). During the operation and maintenance period, any repairable item designated for separate procurement is a CI. [DoD Directive 5010.19] *See also configuration management.*

configuration management (CM)—In system/software system engineering, the discipline of identifying the configuration of a hardware/software system at discrete points in time with the purpose of systematically controlling changes to the configuration and maintaining the integrity and traceability of the configuration throughout the system lifecycle. *See also change control, change status report, configuration accounting, configuration auditing, configuration control, configuration control board (CCB), configuration identification, configuration item (CI), configuration status accounting, software configuration item (SCI).*

configuration status accounting—In configuration management (CM), the recording and reporting of the information that is needed to manage a hardware/software configuration effectively, including a listing of the approved configuration identification, the status of proposed changes to configuration, and the implementation status of approved changes. [DoD Directive 5010.19] *See also configuration management.*

CONOPS or **ConOps**—Acronym for concept of operations document.

consistency—1. In software engineering, a quality metric that can be used to measure those characteristics of software that provide for uniform design and implementation techniques and notation. 2. In software engineering (requirements specifications), a specification is consistent to the extent that its provisions do not conflict with each other, other specifications, or objectives.

context diagram—In software engineering (structured analysis methodology), a top-level diagram of a leveled set of dataflow diagrams. A dataflow diagram that portrays all the net inputs and outputs of a system, but shows no decomposition. [DeMarco 1979] *See also leveling.*

contractor—An individual, partnership, company, corporation, or association having a contract with the procuring activity to deliver manufactured products, services, or data. Manufactured products can be hardware/software configuration items.

control specification—In software engineering (realtime structured analysis methodology), a control transform description; statement of the process governing the control of data transforms. *Synonymous with state transition diagram (STD).*

control transform—In software engineering (realtime structured analysis methodology), an element of a transformation scheme that represents control of the system. Control transforms handle event flows. A control transform has the capability of generating special event flows to data transform processes within the same dataflow diagram to trigger or stop their execution. It can also generate normal event signals to be read by processes inside or outside the systems. *Contrast with data transform.*

controlling—All the management activities that ensure that actual work goes according to plan. It measures performance against goals and plans, reveals when and where deviation exists, and, by putting in motion actions to correct deviations, helps ensure the accomplishment of plans.

conventional lifecycle model—*Synonymous with waterfall model.*

correct—A software requirement is correct only if every requirement stated therein represents something that is required for a system to be built and there is no error that will affect design.

corrective maintenance—In software maintenance, refers to changes necessitated by actual errors (induced or residual "bugs") in a system. [NBS Special Pub 500-106 1983] The correction of actual errors, both simple bugs and errors, induced by misinterpretation of the requirements. *See also software maintenance.*

correctness—In software system engineering: 1. A metric that can be used to measure the extent to which software conforms to its specifications and standards. [RADC TR-85-37 1985] 2. The extent to which software is free from design and coding defects, in other words fault free. 3. The extent to which software meets its specified requirements and user objectives.

cost tradeoff—In system engineering and management, that approach to problem solving that compares and evaluates alternatives (technical) solutions, especially where advantages and costs cannot be accurately measured in numbers, by considering costs of alternatives in comparison with benefits derived.

critical (detailed) design review (CDR)—In system/software system engineering, a milestone review conducted for each hardware/software configuration item (CI) when the detail design is essentially complete. The purpose of this review will be to: (1) determine that the detail design of the CI under review satisfies the functional and performance requirements of the CI requirement specifications; (2) establish the detail design compatibility among the CI and other items of equipment, facilities, software, and personnel; (3) assess CI risk area (on technical, cost, and schedule basis); and (4) review the detailed design description (specifications). [Military Standard 1521B-1985]. *See also milestone review, review.*

customer—1. In system/software system engineering, an individual or organization who specifies the requirements for and formally accepts delivery of a new or modified hardware/software product and its documentation. The customer may be internal or external to the parent organization of the project and does not necessarily imply a financial transaction between customer and developer. 2. The person or persons who pay for the project and usually (but not necessarily) decide the requirements; the customer may or may not be the user. [ANSI/IEEE Standard 830-1984]

D

data—1. A representation of facts, concepts, or instructions in a formalized manner suitable for communication, interpretation, or processing by human or automatic means. 2. The means for communication of concepts, plans, descriptions, requirements, and instructions relating to technical projects, materials, systems, and services. These may include specifications, standards, engineering drawings, associated lists, manuals, and reports, including scientific and technical reports; they may be in the form of documents, displays, sound records, punched cards, and digital or analog data. 3. In software requirements analysis, data can be categorized as inputs and outputs, stored data, or transitory data (temporary results).

data dictionary—1. A collection of the names of all data items used in a software system, together with relevant properties of those items; for example, length of data item and representation. 2. In software engineering (structured analysis methodology), a central repository with descriptions of dataflows, data elements, files, databases, and processes referred to in a close-up dataflow diagram set. 3. In software engineering (structured analysis methodology), a technique for showing data definitions and relationships between data elements and dataflows. *See also dataflow diagram (DFD).*

data transform—In software engineering (realtime structured analysis), a part of a dataflow diagram that accepts only data as input and produces data and event flows as output. [Ward and Mellor 1986] *Contrast with control transform.*

database—1. A comprehensive collection of libraries of data normally stored in a computer or on magnetic media. 2. In software engineering (structured analysis), a data store that is accessed in more than one way and that can be modified in format without affecting the programs that accessed it.

dataflow diagram (DFD)—1. In software engineering (structured analysis methodology), a graphic representation (model) of a software system, showing data sources, data sinks, storage, and processes performed on data as nodes, and logical flow of data as links between the nodes. It can also be used to represent hardware/software systems. *See also data dictionary, leveling, process.* 2. A Structured System Analysis and Design Methodology (SSADM) tool used to show how data move in an information system and how processes act on data.

data-structure design—A software system engineering design methodology used for business applications and other systems with well-understood data structures. It produces a program structure by designing input/output data structures and relies on decomposition based on the higher level nature of these data structures. *See also Jackson System Design (JSD) method, Warnier method.*

debugging—1. In software development, the process of correcting syntactic and logical errors detected during coding. With the primary goal of obtaining an executing piece of code, debugging shares with testing certain techniques and strategies but differs in its usual ad hoc application and local scope. [FIPS Publication 101 1983] 2. In software engineering (testing), the process of locating, analyzing, and correcting suspected faults. *Synonymous with unit testing. See also testing.*

decomposition—The separation of an entity or system into its constituent parts, which are often simpler or more understandable. *See also hierarchical decomposition.*

deliverable document—In software system engineering, a document that is deliverable to a customer. Examples are user manual, operator manual, and programmer's maintenance manual. *See also documentation.*

derivation—1. In a hierarchical structure, the next lower level that is associated with a given element. The lower element is said to be derived from the higher element. 2. In system engineering, the changing or translation of a requirement through analysis into a form that is suitable for low-level analysis or design.

derived requirement—In system/software system engineering (requirements), a lower level requirements that is determined to be necessary for a top-level requirement to be met. When a requirement changes form, it becomes a derived requirement. In general, a derived requirement is more specific and is directed toward some subelement. This usually occurs through the process of analysis, which translates user requirements into parameters that a designer can relate to, such as power and weight.

design—*See architectural design, data-structure design, detailed design, external design, functional design, internal specification, preliminary design, software design, top-level design.*

design constraint (requirement)—In software system engineering, any requirement that impacts or constrains the design of a software system or software system component. Examples of design constraints are physical requirements, performance requirements, software development standards, and software quality assurance (QA) standards. [ANSI/IEEE Standard 729-1983] *See also software requirements specification (SRS).*

design review—In system/software system engineering: 1. A review that will be conducted on a periodic basis to assess the degree of completion of technical efforts related to major milestones before proceeding with further technical effort associated with a particular element of the system. The schedule and plan for the conduct of design reviews should be included in the developer's program plan and master schedule. 2. A milestone review at which the preliminary or detailed design of a system is presented to the user, customer, or other interested parties for comment and approval. 3. The formal review of an existing or proposed design for the purpose of: (1) detection and correction of design deficiencies that could affect fitness for use and environmental aspects of the product, process, or service or (2) identification of potential improvements of performance, safety, and economic aspects. [ANSI/ASQC A3-1978] [ANSI/IEEE Standard 729-1983] *See also milestone review, review.*

design specification—In system/software system engineering, a specification that documents the design of a system/software system or system/software component, for example, a system/software configuration item. Typical contents include system or component algorithms, control logic, data structures, data set-use information, input/output formats, and interface descriptions. [ANSI/IEEE Standard 729-1983] *See also design, internal specification, requirements specification.*

desirable requirement—In software system engineering (requirements specifications), a degree of necessity implying that these are requirements that would enhance the software products but are not mandatory. [ANSI/IEEE Standard 830-1984] *Contrast with essential requirement, optional requirement. See also requirement, software requirement.*

detailed design—1. In software engineering, the process of refining and expanding the softwarepreliminary design to contain more detailed descriptions of the processing logic, data structures, and data definitions, to the extent that the design is sufficiently complete to be implemented. 2. The result of the detailed design process. [ANSI/IEEE Standard 729-1983] *Synonymous with design.*

developer—In industry, the person or persons who produce a product for a customer. The customer and the developer may be members of the same organization. A developer is sometimes called a *supplier*. [ANSI/IEEE Standard 830-1984]

development baseline—In system/software system engineering, the informal baseline created when intermediate software products (such as subsystem requirement specifications, detailed design documents, user manual, and test procedures) are completed and placed under local configuration management. *See also configuration management, program librarian.*

developmental configuration—In a software engineering project, the current configuration of the system under development. The development configuration is less formal than a baseline configuration. *See also configuration management.*

document—1. A data medium and the data recorded on it. The data generally have permanence and can be read by human or machine. The term *document* is often used to describe human-readable items only, for example, technical documents, design documents, and management documents. 2. To create a document. [ANSI/IEEE Standard 729-1983] *See also deliverable document, documentation, milestone document.*

documentation—1. A collection of documents on a given subject. 2. The process of generating a document. 3. Any written or pictorial information describing, defining, specifying, reporting, or certifying activities, requirements, procedures, or results. [ANSI N45.2.10-1973] [ANSI/IEEE Standard 729-1983] 4. In software engineering, commonly used to mean user document, software maintenance manual, operator manual. *See also deliverable document, document, software documentation, software maintenance documentation, user documentation.*

document-driven model—A software development model that emphasizes elaborate documents as completion criteria for early requirement and design phases. It is asserted that document-driven standards require many projects to write elaborate specifications of poorly understood user interfaces and decision support functions. The waterfall model is sometimes called a *document-driven model*. [Boehm, *Spiral Model* 1988]

domain classes—Classes from a problem domain that are meaningful outside of any application. [Rumbaugh 1994]

driver—In software engineering (testing): 1. Code that sets up an environment and calls a module for testing. [FIPS Publication 101 1983] 2. A dummy program module used to provide top-level test data in the development and testing of a low-level module. *Contrast with stub.*

E

ease of use—In software development, the degree of user convenience in performing desired functions with the software product, as well as avoidance of overconstrained expected program behavior. *See also usability, user friendly.*

efficiency—In software engineering, a metric that can

be used to measure: 1. The relative extent to which a resource is used (that is, storage, space, processing time, communication time). [RADC TR-85-37 1985] 2. The extent to which software performs its intended functions with a minimum consumption of computing resources. [ANSI/IEEE Standard 729-1983]

embedded computer system—A computer system integral to a larger system whose primary purpose is not computational, for example, a computer system in a weapon, aircraft, automobile, communication network, intelligent point-of-sales system, automatic teller machine, and talking spelling checker for children. *See also computer system.*

embedded software—Software for an embedded computer system. *See also embedded computer system.*

encapsulation—In object-oriented development, encapsulation is the process of separating the elements of an abstraction that constitute its structure and behavior from its implementation. [Booch 1994]

engineering—The science concerned with putting scientific knowledge to practical uses. *See also software requirements engineering, software engineering, system engineering, system requirements engineering.*

engineering change—In system/software system engineering, an alteration in the configuration of a hardware/software configuration item or items, delivered, to be delivered, or under development, after formal establishment of its configuration identification.

entity—In an entity-relationship model, the principal object about which information is to be collected, usually denoting a person, place, thing, or event of informational interest. [Chen 1990] *See also entity-relationship diagram.*

entity type—In an entity-relationship model, a classification of an entity. [Chen 1990] *See also entity, entity-relationship diagram.*

entity-relationship diagram (ERD or E-R diagram)—1. A diagram that depicts a set of data elements and the logical relationship among them. 2. A tool of the structured specifications methodology that emphasizes the interfacing of objects to each other. *See also structured analysis (SA).*

E-R—Acronym for entity-relationship.

ERD—Acronym for entity-relationship diagram.

essential requirement—In software engineering (requirement specifications), a degree of necessity implying that these are mandatory requirements. The software product will not be accepted without them. *Contrast with desirable requirement, optional requirement. See also requirement, software requirement.*

event—In system/software engineering, an occurrence of an item when the value of the condition changes from true to false or vice versa. An event, therefore, specifies an instance of time, whereas a condition specifies intervals of time. [Heninger 1980]

event list—In software engineering (realtime structured analysis methodology), a list of the external events that cause the system to transform data or change state.

event table—In software engineering (requirements analysis), a table that shows when demand functions should be performed and when periodic functions should be started or stopped. Each row on an event table corresponds to a group or mode. [Heninger 1980]

evolutionary development model—A software development process whose stages consist of expanding increments of an operational software product. The directions of evolution are determined by operational experience. The evolutionary development model gives users a rapid initial operational capability and provides a realistic operational basis for determining subsequent product improvement. [Boehm, *Spiral Model* 1988] *Sometimes synonymous with evolutionary prototype.*

evolutionary prototyping—In software development strategies, the developers construct a partial implementation of the system that meets known requirements. This prototype is then used by its intended user to help understand the full requirements. Incremental development, on the other hand, implies that one understands most requirements up front, but the system is implemented in subsets of increasing capability. Evolutionary prototyping implies a need to experiment with an operational system or to learn the requirements. Note that in the case of throwaway prototypes, only those aspects that are poorly understood may be implemented, but in the case of evolutionary prototypes, those systems aspects that are best understood are more likely to be implemented. *Contrast with incremental development, rapid prototyping.*

expandability—In software engineering, a quality

metric that can be used to measure the relative effort to increase the software capability or performance by enhancing current functions or by adding new functions or data. [RADC TR-85-37 1985]

explicit requirement—In system/software system engineering, requirements that have been explicitly "spelled out." *Contrast with implicit requirement.*

exploratory prototyping—A software requirements analysis strategy involving the user interface with major system functions used to identify and define user requirements. [STARTS Guide 1987]

external design—Synonymous with requirements specifications, system/software specifications, system/software requirements specification. [Davis, *Comparison of Techniques* 1988]

external interface—In system/software system engineering, links (usually in the form of data) between the system and its environment.

external interface requirement—A specification that identifies the functional and physical exterior interfaces to the system.

external interface requirement—A system/software requirement that specifies a hardware, software, or database element with which a system/software system or system/software component must interface, or that sets forth constraints on formats, timing, or other factors caused by such an interface.

external specification—*Synonymous with requirements specification. Contrast with internal specification.*

F

feasibility—In software engineering (requirement specifications), a specification is feasible to the extent that the lifecycle benefits of a system specified will exceed lifecycle costs and that the system will satisfy the system requirements. It also implies validating that the specified system can be sufficiently maintainable, reliable, and human-engineered to keep a positive lifecycle balance. [Boehm, *V&V Software Requirements* 1984]

feasibility study—In software engineering, a study to determine the benefits and costs, in terms of time, money, and manpower, of a proposed use of a computer to accomplish a given purpose, usually with a recommendation or proposed alternatives.

final operating capability (FOC)—In acquisition management, the final capability of the system after completion of the development.

finite state machine (FSM)—A hypothetical machine that can only be in one of a given number of states at a specific time. In response to an input, the machine generates an output and changes state. Both the output and new state are purely functions of the current state and the input. An FSM is used to represent the control process in realtime structured analysis. [Davis, *Comparison of Techniques* 1988]

flexibility—In software engineering, a quality metric that can be used to measure the ease of effort for changing the software mission, function, or data to satisfy other requirements. [RADC TR-85-37 1985]

flowdown—A system engineering concept for the systematic decomposition of system requirements into allocated and derived requirements, appropriately assigned to low-level functional components. The flowdown generates a low-level requirements structure from the (system-supplied) top level. (The functional flow block diagram (FFBD) or dataflow diagram (DFD) can be used as a tool for this activity.)

FOC—Acronym for final operating capability.

formal analysis—In software engineering, formal analysis uses rigorous mathematical techniques to analyze the algorithms of a solution. The algorithms may be analyzed for numerical properties, efficiency, and correctness. [FIPS Publication 101 1983]

formal design method—In software engineering: 1. A written design specification. 2. Design methods based on mathematical formalism, for example the Vienna Development Method (VDM) and the formal specification language Z developed at the Oxford University Computing Laboratory.

formal language—1. A language whose rules are explicitly established before its use. *Synonymous with artificial language.* 2. In software development, a computer language that is used to represent a software requirement that can either be proven "correct" through proof-of-correctness methods or can be translated directly into an operational application program that implements the requirements. *See also language.*

formal mathematical analysis—A software engineering requirements methodology that uses rigorous mathematical techniques to analyze a problem and to build or produce a specification of the intended behavior of a system.

formal proof-of-correctness—In software development, the act of reviewing, inspecting, testing, checking, auditing, or otherwise establishing and documenting whether or not items, processes, services, or documents conform to specified requirements.

formal qualification review (FQR)—In system engineering, the test, inspection, or analytical process by which hardware/software products at the end-item level are verified to have met specific procuring activities or contractual performance requirements. This review does not apply to requirements verified at functional configuration audit (FCA). [U.S. Department of Defense (DoD) usage][Military Standard 1521B-1985]

formal qualification testing—In system/software system engineering, the final qualification testing on the entire contract item. The customer or a designated representative witnesses the formal qualification test, which is a basis for acceptance. [U.S. Department of Defense (DoD) usage] *See also qualification testing.*

formal review—*See review. Contrast with informal review, walkthrough, inspection.*

formal specification—In software engineering: 1. A specification written and approved in accordance with established standards. 2. A document that primarily uses mathematics to specify system requirements.

formal testing—In system/software system engineering, the process of conducting testing activities and reporting results in accordance with an approved test plan.

FQR—Acronym for formal qualification review.

FQT—Acronym for formal qualification testing.

front-end lifecycle activity—In software engineering (software development lifecycle), the software requirement and (sometimes) preliminary design phase.

function—1. In management, a major activity or group of activities that are continuous. For example, the principal functions of management are planning, organizing, staffing, directing, and controlling. 2. In project management, an activity or set of activities that span the entire duration of a software project. Examples of project functions include configuration management, quality assurance (QA), and project cost accounting. 3. In functional analysis, the system or subsystem under study. The function is the activity or behavior of the system, that is, what it does. 4. In software, a subprogram that is invoked during the evaluation of an expression in which its name appears and that returns a value to the point of invocation.

functional analysis—In system/software engineering: 1. The process of studying a system by partitioning the system into functional parts and determining how the parts relate to each other to understand the whole. *Contrast with object-oriented method.* 2. The process of studying user needs to arrive at a definition of software requirements. *Synonymous with software analysis, software requirements analysis.*

functional baseline—In system/software system engineering, the initial hardware/software configuration identification established at the end of the conceptual phase. This baseline is established by an approved system specification.

functional configuration audit (FCA)—In system/software system engineering, the formal examination of functional characteristics from test data for a hardware/software configuration item, prior to acceptance, to verify that the item has achieved the performance specified in its functional or allocated requirements. [U.S. Department of Defense (DoD) usage][Military Standard 1521B-1985] *See also formal qualification review (FQR).*

functional decomposition—In software engineering, a method of designing a system by breaking it down into its components in such a way that the components correspond directly to system functions and subfunctions. [ANSI/IEEE Standard 729-1983]

functional design—In software engineering, the specification of the working relationships among the parts of a software system. *See also preliminary design.*

functional requirement—A system/software requirement that specifies a function that a system/software system or system/software component must be capable of performing. These are software requirements that define the behavior of the system, that is, the fundamental process or transformation that software and hardware components of the system perform on inputs to produce outputs. *See also functional requirements specification.*

functional requirements specification—In system/software system engineering, a specification that sets forth the functional requirements for a system/software system or system/software component. *Sometimes synonymous with functional requirement. See also functional requirement.*

functional testing—In software system engineering (testing), the testing of the external observed functions of the system. Test cases demonstrate the external observed functions of the system. Test cases demonstrate that software functions are operational, that input is properly accepted and output is correctly produced, and that the integrity of external information is maintained. *Synonymous with blackbox testing. Contrast with structural testing.*

functionality—In software engineering (requirements analysis), the relative utility of the various computational, user interface, output, and file manager functions provided by the product.

G

Gane and Sarson technique—*Synonymous with structured analysis (SA), Structured Systems Analysis (SSA).*

H

hardware—The mechanical, magnetic, and electron design, structure, and devices of a computer. *See also computer hardware.*

hardware configuration item (HCI)—In system engineering, a hardware entity that has been established as a configuration item. The hardware configuration item exists where functional allocations have been made that clearly delineate the separation between equipment functions and software functions and the hardware has been established as a configuration item. *Contrast with software configuration item (SCI). See also configuration management (CM).*

heuristic—A procedure that often leads to an expected result, but makes no guarantee to do so. Sometime called a "rule of thumb." [DeMarco 1979]

hierarchical decomposition—In software system engineering, a method of designing a system by partitioning it into smaller and smaller pieces through a series of top-down refinements beginning with the top-most component. *See also functional decomposition, modular decomposition, stepwise refinement.*

hierarchy—1. A type of structure in which each element or block has a level, and each element is associated with one or more elements at the next higher and lower levels. [Flynn and Dorfman 1990] 2. A structure whose components are ranked into levels of subordination according to a specific set of rules. [ANSI/IEEE Standard 729-1983]

human computer interface—In software systems, the shared boundary between the human operator of the system (man) and the software system (machine). Examples of man–machine interfaces that support and enhance human capabilities are user dialogs, graphics, stream formats, and interactive devices.

I

ICD—Acronym for interface control document.

IEEE Guide to Software Requirements Specifications—A software engineering standard developed by the IEEE Computer Society, Software Engineering Standards Subcommittee in 1984, Alan M. Davis, Chair of the working group.

implementation—In software engineering: 1. Converting design to code. 2. Installing and testing the final software product. 3. In data process management, the process of installing a computer system.

implicit requirement—In software engineering, a requirement that is implied. Implicit requirements require the designer to "know" what the customer wants as well as how to design it. [ANSI/IEEE Standard 830-1984] *Contrast with explicit requirement.*

incompleteness—In software engineering (requirements), specifications in which many of the aspects of the requirements are left out. The reader must fill in these gaps by using his or her own knowledge or by asking questions. [Rich et al. 1987]

incremental development—A software development strategy that involves the process of constructing a partial implementation of a total system by slowly adding increased functionality or performance. The initial system is developed through all the system lifecycle stages, from analysis to implementation. This approach reduces the cost incurred before an initial capability is achieved. It also produces an operational system more quickly and thus reduces the possibility that the user's needs will change during the development process.

incremental testing—In system/software engineering, testing a system or program by parts or sections.

independent audit—An independent review of a software project by an outside agency or team that is separate from the organization responsible for the project for the purpose of assessing compliance with software requirements, specifications, baselines, standards, procedures, instructions, codes, and contractual and licensing requirements. *See also audit, review.*

independent verification and validation (IV&V)— In software system engineering, verification and validation of a software product by an organization that is both technically and managerially separate from the organization responsible for developing the product. The degree of independence must be a function of the importance of the software. [ANSI/IEEE Standard 729-1983] *See also validation, verification and validation, verification.*

informal review—In software engineering, a review of an existing or proposed software product and document, typically by the originators' peers, for the purpose of detecting and correcting product and documentation errors. *Contrast with formal review. See also walkthrough, inspection.*

inheritance—In object-oriented development, a relationship among classes, wherein one class shares the structure or behavior defined in another class. [Booch 1994]

inspection—In software engineering: 1. A semiformal to formal evaluation technique in which software requirements, design, or code are examined in detail by a person or group other than the originator to detect faults, violations of development standards, and other problems. The review members are peers (equals) of the designer or programmer. Traditional error data is collected during inspections for later analysis and to assist in future inspections. Sometimes called a *walkthrough* or *peer review*. *See also inspection moderator, walkthrough.* 2. A phase of quality control that by means of examination, observation, or measurement determines the conformance of materials, supplies, components, parts, systems, processes, or structures to predetermined quality requirements. [ANSI N45.2.10-1973]

inspection moderator—In software engineering (inspection), the individual who is trained in the inspection process and who is assigned to monitor the inspection. The moderator ensures that the participants are properly prepared and that the inspection is efficiently and thoroughly conducted. The moderator schedules the inspection, distributes the material being inspected, facilitates the inspection process, and ensures that the errors in the material are recorded and corrected. The moderator is responsible for recording inspection data, making sure that the actions resulting from the inspection are completed, and for conducting reinspections where appropriate. The moderator should not be the producer of the inspected item or the producer's supervisor.

integration testing—1. In system engineering, an orderly progression of testing in which software elements or hardware elements or both are combined and tested until the entire system has been integrated. 2. In software system engineering, activity that interconnects sets of previous tested modules to ensure that the sets behave as well as their independently tested module components did. *See also system testing.*

interface—In system engineering: 1. A shared boundary. An interface might be a hardware component to link two devices or it might be a portion of storage or registers accessed by two or more computer programs. 2. To interact or communicate with another system component or organizational entity.

interface analysis—In system engineering, an approach to identifying and representing functional and physical interfaces between the system and external entities or constraints or between components within the system.

interface control document (ICD)—1. In system/software system engineering, a document that describes the relationship between two components in the system hierarchy. The relationships are usually defined as requirements. 2. In system engineering, that documentation used to define all interface requirements between hardware/software development contractors. 3. A bilateral technical and administrative agreement between affected agencies and contractors. *See also documentation.*

interface requirement—*See external interface requirement.*

interface specification—*See interface control document.*

internal interface—In system/software system engineering, links between the various subunits of the system.

internal specification—*Synonymous with design specification. Contrast with external specification.*

interoperability—In software engineering, a quality metric that can be used to measure: 1. The relative effort to couple the software of one system to the software of another system. [RADC TR-85-37 1985] 2. The ability of two or more systems to exchange information and to mutually use the information that has been exchanged. [ANSI/IEEE Standard 729-1983] *See also compatibility.*

iteration—1. In software engineering, the repeating of a prior step or process as more information become available. In other words, process "*n*" can be iterated with process "*n* – 1" in which each process "*n* – 1" is reaccomplished in part or whole based on information that was determined during process "*n*." 2. In programming, the process of repeatedly executing a given sequence of programming language statements until a given condition is met or while a given condition is true. [ANSI/IEEE Standard 729-1983]

IV&V—Acronym for independent verification and validation

J

Jackson Structured Design method (JSD)—A structured software analysis methodology for the analysis and design of both data processing and realtime systems developed by Michael Jackson Systems Limited. [STARTS Tool Guide 1987]

K

There are no entries under this letter.

L

language—A systematic means of communicating ideas by the use of conventionalized signs, sounds, gestures, or marks as well as rules for the formation of admissible expressions. [ANSI/IEEE Standard 729-1983] *See also natural language, schema language, specification language.*

large-scale software development process— *Synonymous with software engineering.*

leveling—In software engineering (structured analysis methodology), leveling is the decomposition of dataflow diagrams into increasingly detailed diagrams. *See also dataflow diagram (DFD), partitioning.*

life cycle—Alternative spelling of lifecycle.

lifecycle—All the steps or phases an item passes through during its useful life. *See also software development lifecycle.*

life-cycle—Alternative spelling of lifecycle.

lifecycle development model—A model or representation of a software development lifecycle. *See software development lifecycle.*

lifecycle model—A model or representation of a software lifecycle. *See software lifecycle.*

lifecycle phase—A phase of a lifecycle model.

low-level design—*See detailed design.*

M

maintainability—In software engineering, a quality metric that can be used to measure the ease of effort for locating and fixing a software failure within a specified time period. [RADC TR-85-37 1985]

maintenance—*See software maintenance.*

maintenance manual—A software engineering project deliverable document used by the maintenance personnel of the system (in contrast to the users) to enable them to maintain the system. Maintenance means adaptive maintenance, corrective maintenance, and perfective maintenance. *Contrast with operator manual, user manual.*

maintenance project—A software development project described as maintenance to correct errors in the original requirements specification.

management—All activities and tasks undertaken by one or more persons to plan and control the activities of others to achieve an objective or complete an activity that could not be achieved by the others acting independently.

management review—In system/software system engineering, a formal meeting at which the monetary expenditures and schedule are presented to the user, customer, or other interested parties for comment and approval. The monetary expenditures are compared with the budget, and differences between the budget estimates and actual project expenditures are explained. The completion dates are compared with the master schedule, and differences between the scheduled completion dates and actual completion dates are explained.

mandatory requirement—In software engineering (requirements specifications), a degree of necessity that implies that the software will not be acceptable unless these requirements were provided in an agreed-upon manner. [ANSI/IEEE Standard 830-1984]

man–machine interface (MMI)—*See human computer interface (HCI).*

manual cross-referencing—In software engineering (verification and validation techniques), cross-referencing involves constructing cross-reference tables and various diagrams—for example, state transition, dataflow, and flow and data structure diagrams—to clarify interaction among specified entities. These entities include functions, database, and interfacing hardware, software, or personnel. [Boehm, *V&V Software Requirements* 1984] *See also verification and validation technique.*

manual model—In software engineering (verification and validation techniques), mathematical descriptions of the system that can be used to represent and analyze certain aspects of the system being specified. Manual models are good for analyzing some lifecycle feasibility issues, particularly accuracy, realtime performance, and lifecycle cause. They are also useful for risk analysis. [Boehm, *V&V Software Requirements* 1984] *See also verification and validation technique.*

manual technique (detailed)—In software engineering (verification and validation techniques), detailed manual techniques involve detailed scenarios and mathematical proofs, which are effective for clarifying human engineering aids and for verifying finite mathematics programs. [Boehm, *V&V Software Requirements* 1984] *See also verification and validation technique.*

manual technique (simple)—In software engineering (verification and validation techniques), those techniques that do not involve automation but are easily applied and implemented, such as reading, cross-referencing, interviews, checklists, and models. [Boehm, *V&V Software Requirements* 1984] *See also verification and validation technique.*

mathematical notation—In software engineering (requirements specification), notations based on predicate calculus. These express the functionality of a module in terms of pre- and postconditions. Provided that the precondition is true when the module is entered, requirements are that (1) the module terminate and (2) the postcondition be true on exit. These conditions are expressed in terms of predicate calculus. [NCC STARTS Guide 1987]

mathematical proof—In software engineering (verification and validation techniques), mathematical transformation rules can be applied to a set of statements, expressed in a precise mathematical specification language, to provide desired properties of the set of statements. These properties include internal consistencies, preservation of "invariant" relationships, and equivalence of two alternative sets of statements (such as requirements and desired specifications). Automated aids to formal specifications and verifications such as Special/HDM, Gypsy, Affirm, and Ina Jo are now available. [Boehm, *V&V Software Requirements* 1984] *See also verification and validation technique.*

measurable—In software engineering (requirements specification), a specification is measurable when some finite process exists to verify that the product meets the requirements.

methodology—In engineering, a general approach to solving an engineering problem.

metric—The theory or a system of measurements. *See also software quality metric.*

milestone—In project management, a scheduled event that is used to measure progress. Examples of major milestones include the issuance of a specification, completion of system integration, product delivery, and customer or managerial signoff. Minor milestones (sometimes called "inch pebbles") might include baselining a software module or completing a chapter of the user manual. A manager or an individual project member is identified and held accountable for achieving the milestone on time and within budget.

milestone document—A project management document that describes and documents some part of a software development lifecycle. The completion of the document signals the completion of the milestone. For example, the completion of the software requirements specification (SRS) signals the completion of the software requirements analysis phase. *See also milestone, milestone review.*

milestone review—In software engineering: 1. A project management review that is conducted at the completion of each of the hardware/software development lifecycle phases (a milestone)—requirements phase, preliminary design, detailed design phase, implementation phase, test phase, and sometimes installation and checkout phase. For example, a preliminary design review (PDR) is held at the completion of the preliminary design phase. 2. A formal review of the management and technical progress of a hardware/software development project. *See also physical configuration audit (PCA), preliminary design review (PDR), software specification review (SSR), system design review (SDR), system requirements review (SRR), test readiness review (TRR). See also review.*

mini-spec—*Synonymous with process spec, PSPEC.*

model—A representation of an artifact or activity intended to explain the behavior of some aspects of it. The model is less complex or complete than the activity or artifact modeled. A model is considered to be an abstraction of reality.

moderator—In software engineering (inspection), the

participant at a software inspection who focuses the team on defining the defect. *See also inspection.*

modifiable—In software engineering (requirements specification), a specification is modifiable if the structure and style are such that any necessary changes to the requirement can be made easily, completely, and consistently.

modular—A software system that is modular in design. *See also modular decomposition, modularity, module.*

modular decomposition—A method of designing a software system by breaking it down into modules. [ANSI/IEEE Standard 729-1983] *See also hierarchical decomposition.*

modularity—In software engineering, a quality metric that can be used to measure: 1. Those characteristics of the software that provide a structure of highly cohesive modules with optimum coupling. [RADC TR-85-37 1985] 2. The extent to which software is composed of discrete components such that a change to one component has minimal impact on other components. [ANSI/IEEE Standard 729-1983]

module—In software engineering (design): 1. A program unit that is discrete and identifiable with respect to compiling, combining with other units, and loading; for example, the input to, or output from, an assembler, compiler, linkage editor, or executive routine. 2. A logically separable part of a program. [ANSI/IEEE Standard 729-1983] *Sometimes synonymous with unit.*

N

N² chart—A system/software system engineering tool and methodology for the tabulation, definition, analysis, and description of functional interactions and interfaces. The N² chart is a fixed-format structure that graphically displays the total bidirectional interrelationships between individual functions and components in a given system or structure. The chart gets its name from the fact that for N functions there are N² intersections or squares on the diagram, each of which may contain a function or function interface. [Lano 1977]

natural language—A language spoken by people, as opposed to a formal language or a language used by computers. *Contrast with formal language.*

nonambiguous—A software requirements specification is nonambiguous only if each requirement stated therein has only one interpretation.

nonfunctional requirement—In software system engineering, a software requirement that describes not what the software will do, but how the software will do it, for example, software performance requirements, software external interface requirements, software design constraints, and software quality attributes. Nonfunctional requirements are sometimes difficult to test; therefore, they are usually evaluated subjectively. *Contrast with functional requirement.*

notation—In software engineering, a physical, graphical, or textual means of describing a software requirement design or code. [British usage]

O

object—In object-oriented development, an entity that you can do something to. An object has state, behavior, and identity. A group of objects with common structure and behavior is a class. An instance of a class is an object. [Booch 1994]

object-oriented analysis—In software engineering (requirements), the application of an object-oriented method to software requirements analysis. *Contrast with functional analysis, functional requirement, structured analysis (SA). See also object-oriented design, object-oriented method.*

object-oriented design—In software engineering (design), the application of an object-oriented method to software design. *Contrast with structured design. See also object-oriented analysis, object-oriented method.*

object-oriented development model—In software engineering, a model of a software development process with the following elements: abstraction, encapsulation, modularity, hierarchy, typing, concurrence, persistence, reusability, and extensibility. [Northrup 1996]

object-oriented method—A software engineering methodology in which the system is viewed as a collection of objects, attributes of objects, operations on the objects, and with messages passed from object to object. *Contrast with functional analysis, functional requirement, structured analysis (SA), structured design. See also object-oriented analysis, object-oriented design.*

operability—In software engineering, a quality metric that can be used to measure those operational characteristics of the software that provide useful inputs and outputs that can be assimilated. [RADC TR-85-37 1985]

operator manual—A software engineering project deliverable document used by the operators of the system (in contrast to the users) to enable them to support the users and the system. On many systems, particularly modern desktop computers, the operator and the user are the same individual; therefore the operator and user manuals are combined. *Contrast with maintenance manual, user manual.*

optional requirement—In software engineering (requirements specifications), a degree of necessity that implies a class of function that may or may not be worthwhile or necessary. The optional requirement gives its developer the opportunity to propose something that exceeds the software requirements specifications. *Contrast with desirable requirement, essential requirement. See also requirement, software requirement.*

P

partitioning—1. The separation of the whole into its parts. 2. In software engineering, the separation or decomposing of a top-level requirement or design into successively low-level detailed requirements or design. 3. In software engineering, the separation (decomposition) of a system into its logical or physical parts. *Synonymous with decomposition.* 4. A software system engineering concept, used when it is difficult or impossible to describe a problem or a solution in any way except in terms of its parts. For example, to understand the problem of defending a nation against ballistic missiles, the parts of the system might be target detection, communication, intelligence gathering and resolution, defense weapon launch, and defense weapon guidance. [Davis 1990]

path testing—In software engineering (unit testing), a test method satisfying the coverage criteria that each logical path through the program be tested at least once. Often paths through the program are grouped into a finite set of classes; one path from each class is then tested. [FIPS Publication 101 1983]

PCA—Acronym for physical configuration audit.

PDR—Acronym for preliminary design review.

peer review—In software engineering, *synonymous with walkthrough, inspection.*

perfective maintenance—In software engineering (maintenance): 1. Includes all changes, insertions, deletions, modifications, extensions, and enhancements that are made to a system to meet the evolving or expanding needs of the user. [NBS Special Publication 500-106 1983] 2. Software maintenance that incorporates new task that was not previously in the requirements. [Robson 1991] *Contrast with adaptive maintenance, corrective maintenance. See also software maintenance, preventive maintenance.*

performance requirement—A system/software system requirement specifying a performance characteristic that a system/software system or system/software component must possess; for example, speed, accuracy, and frequency.

performance requirements specification—A specification that sets forth the performance requirements for a system/software or system/software component. [ANSI/IEEE Standard 729-1983] *See also functional requirements specification, software requirements specification (SRS).*

Petri net—1. An abstract, formal model of information flow, showing static and dynamic properties of a system. A Petri net is usually represented as a graph having two types of nodes (called *places* and *transitions*) connected by arcs, and markings (called *tokens*) indicating dynamic properties. [ANSI/IEEE Standard 729-1983] 2. A network of related functions in a business operation, in which people are portrayed as nodes, and documents as connections between nodes. [DeMarco 1979] 3. An abstract structured machine with a well-defined behavior that was introduced in 1962 by Petri and later described by Peterson. This machine is used to specify process symmetry during the design phase of time critical applications. 4. A software engineering methodology used to analyze and represent realtime applications.

phase—1. The stage of development in a product or activity. 2. In software system engineering, one of the stages of the lifecycle model.

phase-dependent tool—A software tool that is applicable across one phase (or several phases but less than all phases) of the software development lifecycle, for example, a software cost-estimation tool, a structured analysis and design tool, and a test case generator.

physical configuration audit (PCA)—The formal examination of the configuration of a hardware/software configuration item against its technical documentation to establish the product or operational baseline. [U.S. Department of Defense (DoD) usage][Military Standard 1521B-1985]

PM—Abbreviation for project management, project manager.

point design—In system engineering, the selection of one design that satisfies the requirements without examining other potentially more effective designs.

polymorphism—A concept in type theory, to which a name may denote objects of many different classes that are related by some common superclass. Any object denoted by this name is able to respond to a common set of operations in a different way. [Booch 1994]

portability—In software system engineering, a quality metric that can be used to measure the relative effort to transport the software for use in another environment or to convert software for use in another operating environment, hardware configuration, or software system environment. [RADC TR-85-37 1985]

precision—A measure of the ability to distinguish between nearly equal values; for example, four-place numerals are less precise than six-place numerals; nevertheless, a properly computed four-place numeral may be more accurate than an improperly computed six-place numeral. [ANSI/IEEE Standard 729-1983]

predicate calculus—In mathematics, a symbolic logic that uses symbols for qualifiers, arguments, and predicates of propositions; as well as for unanalyzed propositions and logical connectives. A predicate may assume either of two permitted values: zero or not zero.

preliminary design—1. In system/software system engineering, the process of analyzing design alternatives and defining the hardware/software system architecture. 2. In software engineering, preliminary design typically includes definition and structuring of computer program components and data, definition of the interfaces, and preparation of timing and sizing estimates. 3. In system/software system engineering, the result of the preliminary design process. [ANSI/IEEE Standard 729-1983] *Synonymous with architectural design, internal specification, top-level design.*

preliminary design description (specification)—A specification that sets forth the preliminary design of the software system. *See also preliminary design.*

preliminary design review (PDR)—In system/software system engineering, a milestone review conducted for each hardware/software configuration item (CI) before the detail design process to: (1) evaluate the progress and technical adequacy of the selected top-level design approach, (2) determine its compatibility with the functional and performance requirements of the CI requirements specification, and (3) establish the existence and compatibility of the physical and functional interfaces between the CI and other items of equipment or facilities. [Military Standard 1521B-1985]. *See also milestone review, review.*

problem analysis—In system/software engineering, an activity during which one tries to understand fully what the problem is without defining how it will be solved. [Davis 1990] *Synonymous with requirements analysis.*

problem definition—*Synonymous with requirements analysis.*

problem domain—An area of real-world experience, such as mechanical engineering, stock trading, or the transfer of money between banks. [Rumbaugh 1994]

process—1. A unique, finite course of events defined by its purpose or by its effect, achieved under given conditions. 2. In data processing, to perform operations on data in a computer. [ANSI/IEEE Standard 830-1984] 3. In software engineering (structured analysis methodology), a description of the process or transform. Used with dataflow diagrams. *See also dataflow diagram. Synonymous with minispec.* 4. A transportation or transformation of substances, energy, or information in space or time. 5. In a formal language specification, a process is a set trace.

process free—A software requirements specification is process free when the specification does not contain management or unnecessary design information.

process group—In software engineering, a group of engineers, computer specialists, and other scientists who are concerned with the process used by the development organization for software development. Its typical functions include defining and documenting the process, establishing and defining metrics, gathering data, assisting projects in analyzing data, and advising management on areas requiring further attention. The process group typically conducts quarterly management reviews on process status and may provide review leaders. [Humphrey 1989]

process model—A representation of a system/software development process activity intended to explain the behavior of some aspects of it. The process model is less complex or complete than the activity or artifact modeled. *See also software life-cycle model.*

process specification—*Synonymous with design specification.*

process standard—A standard that defines the procedures or operations used in making or achieving a product. *See also standard, product standard.*

process work breakdown structure (WBS)—A work breakdown structure (WBS) for a process, for example, a process WBS for a software project could include at the first level: requirement analysis, design, code, and software testing. *See also product work breakdown structure, work breakdown structure (WBS).*

product assurance—1. In system/software engineering, the ability to meet reliability and quality levels as required by the contract or requirement specifications. 2. Sometimes (incorrectly) synonymous with quality assurance (QA).

product baseline—The hardware/software configuration identification established at the end of the full-scale development phase. This baseline is established by an approved "as built" configuration item product specification.

product development baseline—In system/software system engineering, the informal baseline created when the detailed design specifications are completed and placed under development control. *See also development baseline.*

product standard—A standard that defines what constitutes completeness and acceptability of items that are produced as a result of a process. *See also process standard.*

product work breakdown structure (WBS)—A work breakdown structure (WBS) for a product, for example, a product WBS for a software project could include at the first level: application programs, utility programs, and operating systems. *See also process work breakdown structure, work breakdown structure (WBS).*

program librarian—In software engineering, an individual who administers the program support library (PSL). The person responsible for establishing, controlling, and maintaining a software development library. An individual who acts as an administrator, secretary, and librarian for many teams and who maintains and controls all elements of the software configuration, for example, documentation, source listings, and data catalogs, and indexes "reusable" software models. The librarian also assists the team in research, evaluation, and document preparation.

program management directive (PMD)—In acquisition management, the official management directive that provides direction to the implementing and participating organizations. It is used during the entire acquisition cycle to standardize requirements and request studies, as well as to initiate, approve, change, transition, modify, or terminate programs. [U.S. Department of Defense (DoD) usage]

program support library (PSL)—In software engineering, a centralized and readily available depository with authorized versions of each component of a software system. It contains the necessary development control of each software configuration item. The program support library (PSL) should support three main activities: code development, software management, and configuration control. A PSL has four main components: internal libraries in machine-readable form, external libraries in hardcopy form, computer procedures, and office procedures. [Bersoff 1984] *See also configuration management.*

programming—The coding and unit testing of computer code.

programming-in-the-large—A euphemism for software engineering.

programming-in-the-small—A euphemism for coding.

project—A temporary activity characterized by having a start date, specific objectives and constraints, established responsibilities, a budget and schedule, and a completion date. (If the objective of the project is to develop a software system, then it is sometimes called a *software development* or *software engineering project.*)

project database—In system/software engineering, a repository in which all information associated with a system or project is stored. A project database should be used to store everything from requirements to source code and from user documentation to executable programs and program units, replicated as required to support multiple versions of each. [Wasserman and Pircher 1987]

project lifecycle—*See software development lifecycle, software lifecycle.*

project management—A system of procedures, practices, technologies, and know-how that provides the planning, organizing, staffing, directing, and controlling necessary to successfully manage an engineering project. Know-how in this case means the skill, background, and wisdom to apply knowledge effectively in practice. *See also software engineering project management.*

project management plan—A project management document describing the approach that will be taken for a project. The plan typically describes the work to be done, the resources required, the methods to be used, the configuration management and quality assurance (QA) procedures to be followed, the schedules to be met, and the project organization.

project manager—1. A manager who has responsibility for planning, organizing, staffing, directing, and controlling a project. 2. In software engineering, a manager who has responsibility for planning, organizing, staffing, directing, and controlling a software engineering project. *See also project management.*

project notebook—In software engineering, a central repository of written material such as memos, plans, and technical reports pertaining to a software project. *Loosely synonymous with project file, software development notebook, unit development folder (UDF).*

proof of correctness—In software engineering (formal methods): 1. A formal mathematical demonstration that a program's semantics are consistent with some specification of that program. [Oxford Dictionary of Computing 1990] 2. A formal technique of mathematical logic that infers that a relation between program variables (assumed true at program entry) implies that another relation between program variables holds at program exit. 3. A program proof that results from applying this technique.

prototype—1. In engineering, a prototype is a full-scale model and the functional form of a new system or subsystem. (A prototype does not have to be the complete system—only the part of interest.) A prototype is sometimes referred to as a *model*. 2. In software engineering, a software prototype would be a computer program that implements some part of the system requirements. This prototype can be used to assist in defining requirements or, in this case, to assist in evaluating alternatives. Examples include determining how to obtain the required accuracy in realtime performance issues, as well as user interface suitability. The process of building the prototype will also expose and eliminate a number of the ambiguities, inconsistencies, blind spots, and misunderstandings incorporated in the specifications.

Q

QA—Acronym for quality assurance.

qualification test—In system/software system engineering, a demonstration of the system/software product.

qualification testing—In system/software system engineering, this is formal testing, usually conducted by the developer for the customer, to demonstrate that the software meets its specified requirements. *See also acceptance testing, system testing.* [ANSI/IEEE Standard 729-1983]

quality—1. In software engineering, the degree of conformance of a product to its stated requirements, that is, fitness for purpose. [Rook 1986] 2. In engineering, the totality of features and characteristics of a product, or service, that affects its ability to satisfy given needs. *See also software quality.*

quality assurance (QA)—1. In software engineering, the checking of the correctness of the procedures being followed, that is, whether the development staff are following the intended procedures. [Rook 1986] 2. In project management, disciplines used by project management to monitor, control, and gain visibility into the development process. Quality assurance includes configuration management (CM), validation and verification, and test and evaluation. [Bersoff 1984] *See also software quality assurance (SQA).*

quality attribute—*See quality metric.*

quality attribute (requirement)—A requirement that specifies the degree of an attribute that affects the quality that the system/software must possess; for example, reliability and maintainability. *See also software quality attribute (requirement).*

quality metric—In software engineering, a metric that verifies complexity, correctness, coupling of modules, degree of dependency of modules, maintainability, modifiability, performance, reliability, reusability, testability, understandability, and verifiability. *See also metric, software quality metric.*

quantitative metric—In software engineering, a metric that can be used to summarize important information to make distinctions, identify outlying software characteristics, or detect trends. [Keller et al. 1990]

R

rapid prototyping—1. A software engineering development strategy that addresses the issue of ensuring that the software product being proposed meets a user's needs. The approach is to construct a "quick and dirty" partial solution to the system before (or during) the requirement stage. The potential users then use this prototype for a period of time and supply feedback to the developer concerning strengths and weaknesses. This feedback is now used to help develop the software requirements specification to reflect the user's real needs and the prototype is discarded. [Davis et al. 1988] 2. In system/software engineering, a technique enabling designers to produce an executable model of the system requirement so as to evaluate them with consistency and completeness. [ESPRIT July 1987] *See also prototype.*

rapid throwaway prototyping—*See rapid prototyping.*

readability—In software engineering (requirements specifications), the ability to read and understand the document. Readability is not associated with correctness or completeness. [Gehani 1982]

reading—In software engineering (verification and validation techniques), reading involves someone other than the originator reading the specification to identify potential problems. Because reading subjects the specification to another point of view, it pinpoints blind spots or misconceptions that the developer may have. [Boehm, *V&V Software Requirements* 1984] *See also verification and validation technique.*

realtime—In system/software engineering: 1. Pertaining to the processing of data provided by an external process according to time requirements imposed by the outside process. This term is also used to describe systems operating in conversational mode or processes that can be influenced by human intervention while in progress. 2. Pertaining to the time during which a physical process transpires; for example, the performance of a computation during the actual time that the related physical process occurs, so that results of the computation can be used in guiding the physical process. [ANSI/IEEE Standard 729-1983]

realtime structured analysis (RTSA)—A software engineering methodology that employs a modified version of structured analysis to accommodate realtime control. The constructs of realtime structured analysis include control transforms, control specifications (usually state-transition diagrams), entity-relationship diagrams, event lists, plus the usual constructs of structured analysis.

regression testing—In software engineering (maintenance and testing), the rerunning of test cases that a program has previously executed correctly in order to detect errors created during software correction or modification activities. [FIPS Publication 101 1983]

relationship diagram—*See entity-relationship diagram (ERD or E-R diagram).*

reliability—In software engineering, a quality metric that can be used to measure the extent to which the software will perform without any failure within a specified time period. [RADC TR-85-37 1985]

requirement—In system/software engineering: 1. A capability needed by a user to solve a problem or achieve an objective. 2. A capability that must be met or possessed by a system or system component to satisfy a contract, standard, specification, or other formally imposed document. 3. The set of all requirements that form the basis for subsequent development of the software or software component. 4. Short description sometimes used in place of the term *software requirements specification. See also software requirement, system requirement. See also requirements specification, software requirements specification, system requirements specification.*

requirements analysis—In system/software engineering: 1. The process of studying user needs to arrive at a definition of system or software requirements. 2. The verification of system or software requirements. [ANSI/IEEE Standard 729-1983] 3. The systematic process of reasoning about a problem and its constituent parts to understand what is needed or what must be done. Analysis also involves communication with all persons involved with both the requirements and the requirements specifications. [Rzepka and Ohno 1985] *See also software requirements analysis.*

requirements engineering—In system engineering, the science and discipline concerned with analyzing and documenting requirements. It comprises needs analysis, requirements analysis, and requirements specifications. *See also requirement.*

requirements engineering environment—In system/software engineering, provides the requirements engineer with appropriate mechanisms to facilitate the analysis, documentation, and checking activities. [Rzepka and Ohno 1985]

requirements flowdown—In system/software system engineering, the systematic decomposition of system requirements into allocated and derived requirements, appropriately assigned to low-level functional components.

requirements management—In system/software system engineering, the process of controlling the identification, allocation, and flowdown of requirements from the system level to the module or part level, including interfaces, verification, modifications, and status monitoring. [Flynn and Dorfman 1990]

requirements specification—In system/software engineering, a document that states the functions that software must perform, the required level of performance (speed, accuracy, etc.), the nature of the required interfaces between the software product and its environment, the type and severity of constraints on design, and the quality of the final product. *Synonymous with external specification. See also software requirements specification, system requirements specification.*

requirements traceability—*See traceability.*

requirements verification—*See verification.*

resource—In engineering and management, the people, money, equipment, facilities, transportation, and so forth that are needed or can be used to satisfactorily complete an activity or build a product. Resources can be expendable (money and materials) or nonexpendable (people and machines).

reusability—In software engineering: 1. A bottom-up approach of designing systems from existing modules and then connecting them together to form bigger modules, thereby eliminating the need to design modules from scratch. [Ramamoorthy et al. 1984] 2. A metric used to measure the relative effort to convert software components for use in another application.

reusable code—In software engineering, code that can be reused in another application. To be valuable, the reused code must have been tested and used successfully in an application.

reusable software—In software engineering, software that can be reused in another application. To be valuable, the reused software must have been tested and used successfully in an application.

reuse—In software development, the act of using a software product (requirement specification, design description, code, etc.) in a different project.

reverse engineering—A software engineering approach that derives the design or requirements of a system from its code. The design can be represented by a program design language (PDL) or a formal language. By creating a logical view from a physical system, reverse engineering assists in maintaining and enhancing existing systems. [Sayani 1990]

review—1. In system/software system engineering, a formal meeting at which a product or document is presented to the user, customer, or other interested parties for comment and approval. It can be a review of the management and technical progress of the hardware/software development project. 2. In hardware/software engineering, the formal review of an existing or proposed design for the purpose of detection and remedy of design deficiencies that could affect fitness for use and environmental aspects of the product, process, or service, and for identification of potential improvements of performance, safety, or economic aspects. [ANSI/IEEE Standard 729-1983] 3. In the spiral software development model, the review covers all products developed during the previous cycle, including the plans for the next cycle and the resources required to carry them out. The major objective of the review is to ensure that all concerned parties are mutually committed to the approach to be taken for the next phase. [Boehm, *Spiral Model 1988*] *See also audit, critical (detailed) design review (CDR), formal qualification review (FQR), functional configuration audit (FCA), independent audit, informal review, milestone review, physical configuration audit (PCA), preliminary design review (PDR), software specification review (SSR), system design review (SDR), system requirements review (SRR). See also inspection, walkthrough.*

risk—1. In system/software system engineering, a potential occurrence that would be detrimental to the project. Risk is measured as the combined effect of the likelihood of the occurrence and a measured or assessed consequence given that occurrence. 2. In software engineering (require-ments specifications), if the lifecycle cost effectiveness of a specified system is extremely sensitive to some system aspect and that aspect is not well known or understood, there is a high risk involved in the system. If such high-risk issues are not identified and resolved in advance, then there is a strong likelihood of disaster if this risk occurrence is realized. [Boehm, *V&V Software Requirements* 1984]

risk analysis—In system/software system engineering, the methodical process of identifying areas of potential risk, the associated probability of occurrence, and the seriousness of the consequences of the occurrence.

risk management—In system/software system engineering, the integration of risk identification, risk assessment, and risk reduction to optimize the probability of success.

risk management plan—In system/software system engineering project management, a plan that would describe the programmatic aspects of risk identification, risk assessment, risk reduction, and risk management to be performed. The risk management plan should relate the developer's approach for handling risk—avoidance, prevention (control), assumption (retention), transfer, knowledge, and research. A typical risk management plan would: (1) identify the project's top risk items, (2) present a plan for removing each risk item, (3) update monthly lists of top risk items, plans, and results, (4) highlight the risk-item status at monthly project reviews, and (5) initiate appropriate corrective actions. [Boehm, *Risk Management* 1989]

risk reduction—In system/software system engineering, an approach for reducing risk through avoidance, prevention (control), transfer, knowledge, and research.

RTSA—Acronym for realtime structured analysis. *See realtime structured analysis (RTSA).*

S

SA—Acronym for structured analysis. *See structured analysis (SA).*

scenario—1. A description of a series of events that could be expected to occur simultaneously or sequentially. 2. An account or synopsis of a projected course of events or actions.

schema—1. In data processing, a set of relationships among data elements in a complex file structure. 2. In software engineering, a diagrammatic presentation of a database. [British usage] 3. In software development (formal methods), a way of decomposing a specification into small elements. [Spivey 1989]

schema language—In the formal language Z, the language that provides the presentation framework for the mathematical portion of a Z specification. [Norris 1986]

SCM—Acronym for software configuration management.

SDR—Acronym for system design review.

security—1. In software engineering (quality metrics), this is fault tolerance against deliberate intrusive faults from internal or external sources. [IEE/BCS Safety-Related Systems 1989] 2. In software engineering, the establishment and application of safeguards to protect data, software, and computer hardware from accidental or malicious modification, destruction, or disclosure.

SEI—Acronym for Software Engineering Institute.

sensitivity analysis—In system/software system engineering, a sensitivity analysis must be performed on all trade studies to determine the value of results to the decision makers. Where the total weighted scores of several alternatives are proximate, a small change in the estimated performance of any alternative against any criteria may change the decision. In these instances, it may be useful to indicate a range of estimated performance values having a known confidence level that can be transformed to the weighted scores. [DoD, *Engineering Management Guide* 1986]

SEPM—Acronym for software engineering project management. [Thayer, Pyster, and Wood 1981]

simulation—In system/software system engineering: 1. Physical or mathematical representation of a system to expedite the evaluation of selected system parameters. Simulation is used to explore the effects that alternative system characteristics will have on system performance, without actually producing and testing each alternative system. 2. Use of an executable model to represent the behavior of an object. During testing, the computational hardware, the external environment, and even code segments may be simulated. [FIPS Publication 101 1983] 3. An imitation so that, for example, one program acts like another program.

smoking—In system/software system engineering (requirements engineering), a strategy in which the user requests many system features, but wants only one of them.

software—In computer science, data processing, and software engineering, a sequence of instructions suitable for processing by a computer. Processing may include the use of an assembler, a compiler, an interpreter, or a translator to prepare the program for execution, as well as to execute it. [ANSI/IEEE Standard 729-1983] *Synonymous with code, computer code, computer program. Contrast with hardware.*

software analysis—*See analysis.*

software configuration item (SCI)—In software system engineering, a software entity that has been established as a configuration item. The software configuration item exists where functional allocations have been made that clearly delineate the separation between equipment functions and software functions and the software has been established as a configuration item. *Contrast with hardware configuration item (HCI). See also configuration management (CM).*

software configuration management (SCM)—*See configuration management.*

software configuration status accounting—*See configuration status accounting.*

software crisis—The term used since the 1960s to describe the recurring system development problem in which software problems cause the system to be late, over cost, and not responsive to the users' or customers' requirements including functionality, performance, usability, and maintainability.

software design—In software engineering, the process of defining the software architecture (structure), components, modules, interfaces, test approach, and data for a software system to satisfy specified requirements. [ANSI/IEEE Standard 729-1983]

software design constraint (requirement)—*See design constraint (requirement).*

software development file (SDF)—In software engineering, a repository for a collection of material pertinent to the development or support of software. Contents typically include (either directly or by reference) design considerations and constraints, design, documentation and data, schedule and status information, test requirements, test cases, test procedures, and test results. *Sometimes synonymous with unit development folder (UDF).*

software development library—In software engineering, a software library containing computer-readable and human-readable information relevant to a software development effort. [ANSI/IEEE Standard 729-1983]

software development lifecycle—A software development model/strategy that begins with the decision to develop a software product and ends when the product is delivered. It depicts the relationships among the major milestones, baselines, reviews, and project deliverables that span the life of the project. A project lifecycle model must include project-initiation and project-termination activities. The software development lifecycle typically includes a requirements phase; design phase; implementation (coding) phase; test phase; and, sometimes, installation and checkout phases..

software development methodology—In software engineering: 1. An integrated set of software engineering methods, policies, procedures, rules, standards, techniques, tools, languages, and other methodologies for analyzing, designing, implementing, and testing software. 2. A set of rules for selecting the correct methodology, process, or tools.

software development notebook—In software engineering, a collection of materials pertinent to the development of a given software module or subsystem. Contents typically include the requirements, design, technical reports, code listings, test plans, test results, problem reports, schedules, and notes for the module or subsystem. [ANSI/IEEE Standard 729-1983] *See also project notebook, unit development folder (UDF).*

software development plan—*See software project management plan.* [U.S. Department of Defense (DoD) usage]

software development project—*See software engineering project.*

software development project—The same skills and techniques that are used for the design of a significant software system should be applied to the design of the project process and organization. The output of each phase of the whole software development project consists entirely of documentation, or of documentation and code. Documents are the sole means by which the successive stages of the design process are recorded, and against which each phase is validated. [McDermid 1991]

software documentation—In software engineering: 1. The collection of technical data or information that is used to develop, support, and use a software system. This includes proposals, management plans and documents, requirement specifications, design specifications, computer listings, test documentation, standards, user manuals, operator manuals, and maintenance manuals that describe or specify the design or details, explain the capabilities, or provide operating instructions to obtain desired results from the system. 2. A term used informally to define the documents accompanying a software system that are necessary to use, operate, and maintain the system. *See also documentation.*

software engineering—1. The practical application of computer science, management, and other sciences to the analysis, design, construction, and maintenance of software and its associated documentation. 2. An engineering science that applies the concept of analysis, design, coding, testing, documentation, and management to the successful completion of large, custom-built computer programs. 3. The systematic application of methods, tools, and techniques to achieve a stated requirement or objective for an effective and efficient software system. 4. The application of scientific principles to: (1) the early transformation of a problem into a working software solution and (2) subsequent maintenance of that software until the end of its useful life. [Davis, *Comparison of Techniques* 1988]

software engineering assessment—A Software Engineering Institute (SEI) evaluation of the software engineering capabilities of software developers in order to measure their abilities to develop software in accordance with modern software engineering methods. *See also Software Engineering Institute (SEI).*

Software Engineering Institute (SEI)—A U.S. federally funded software engineering laboratory operated by Carnegie Mellon University (Pittsburgh, PA), under contract to the DoD.

software engineering project—In software engineering, the set of all activities, functions, and tasks, both technical and managerial, required to satisfy the terms and conditions of the project agreement. A software engineering project is a temporary activity characterized by having a start date, specific objectives and constraints, established responsibilities, a budget and schedule, and a completion date. The project consumes resources and has the goal of producing a product or set of products that satisfies the project requirements, as specified in the project agreement. A software engineering project may be self-contained or may be part of a larger project. In some cases, the project may span only a portion of the software product lifecycle. In other cases, the project may span many years and consist of numerous subprojects, each in itself being a well-defined and self-contained software engineering project. [ANSI/IEEE Standard 1058.1-1987] *Synonymous with software project, software development project.*

software engineering project management (SEPM)—A system of procedures, practices, technologies, and know-how that provides the planning, organizing, staffing, directing, and controlling necessary to successfully manage a software engineer-

ing project. Know-how in this case means the skill, background, and wisdom to apply knowledge effectively in practice. *See also project management.*

software external interface requirement—*See external interface requirements.*

software functional requirement—*See functional requirement.*

software lifecycle—In software engineering: 1. A model of the phases of a software system that starts when a software product is conceived and ends when the product is no longer available for use. It depicts the relationships among the major milestones, baselines, reviews, and project deliverables that span the life of the system. The software lifecycle typically includes a requirements phase, design phase, implementation (coding) phase, installation and checkout phase, operation and maintenance phase, and, sometimes, retirement phase. *See also software development lifecycle.* 2. A strategy for developing a system that includes the development of requirements, product design, and detailed design that involves the development of verification and validation, approval or disapproval, and baselining of each of these specifications. [Boehm, *V&V Software Requirements* 1984]

software lifecycle model—A representation of a software lifecycle. Examples are the "waterfall model" or "incremental development model." *See software lifecycle.*

software maintenance—In software engineering: 1. The performance of activities required to keep a software system operational and responsive after it is accepted and placed into production. [NBS Special Publication 500-106 1983] 2. Modification of a software product after delivery to correct faults, to improve performance or other attributes, or to adapt the product to a changed environment. [ANSI/IEEE Standard 729-1983] *See also adaptive maintenance, corrective maintenance, perfective maintenance.*

software package—A commercial "preprogrammed" software system used for particular applications. Examples are: payroll packages, accounting packages, or a statistical packages. The software system is purchased rather than developed. *Synonymous with commercial off-the-shelf (COTS) software. See also reusable software.*

software performance requirement—*See performance requirement.*

software project—*See software engineering project.*

software project management plan (SPMP)—In software engineering project management, the controlling document for managing a software project. A software project management plan defines the technical and managerial functions, activities, and tasks necessary to satisfy the requirements of a software project, as defined in the project agreement. *Synonymous with software development plan.*

software prototyping—*See evolutionary prototyping, prototyping, rapid prototyping.*

software quality—In software engineering: 1. The totality of features and characteristics of a software product that bears on its ability to satisfy given needs, for example, to conform to specifications. 2. The degree to which software possesses a desired combination of attributes. 3. The degree to which a customer or user perceives that software meets his or her composite expectations. 4. The composite characteristics of software that determine the degree to which the software in use will meet the expectations of the customer. [ANSI/IEEE Standard 729-1983] 5. Attributes of software that affect its perceived value, for example, correctness, reliability, maintainability, and portability.

software quality assurance (SQA)—In software system engineering, a planned and systematic pattern of all actions necessary to provide adequate confidence that the software and the delivered documentation conform to established technical requirements. [ANSI/IEEE Standard 729-1983]

software quality attribute (requirement)—In software engineering: 1. A condition or set of conditions defined in terms of software quality metrics that must be satisfied to meet a software need. 2. A requirement that specifies the degree of an attribute that affects quality that the software system must possess,]for example, correctness, reliability, maintainability, and portability. *See also software quality metric, software requirements specification (SRS).*

software quality metric—In software engineering, a quantitative measure of the degree to which software possesses a given attribute that affects quality. An attribute of software that affects its perceived value for example, correctness, reliability, maintainability, and portability. *See also software quality attribute (requirement).*

software reliability—*See reliability.*

software requirement—In software engineering: 1. A software capability needed by a user to solve a problem to achieve an objective. 2. A software capability that must be met or possessed by a system or system component to satisfy a contract, standard, specification, or other formally imposed document. 3. The set of all software requirements that forms the basis for subsequent development of the software or software component. [ANSI/IEEE Standard 729-1983] 4. Short description sometimes used in place of the term *software requirements specification. See also software requirements analysis, software requirements specification (SRS).*

software requirement viewpoint—In software engineering (requirements), the organizing and structuring of the software requirements specifications around the different views of a software requirement. These views are described by different actors (or participants, agents) and can be based on different environments and perspectives. The collection of system requirements information from multiple perspectives. [Kotonya and Sommerville 1996]

software requirements analysis—In software engineering, the process of studying user needs to arrive at a definition of software requirements. *Sometimes synonymous with analysis, software analysis, software requirements engineering. See also software requirements specification (SRS).*

software requirements elicitation—The process through which the customers (buyers and/or users) and the developer (contractor) of a software system discover, review, articulate, and understand the users' needs and the constraints on the software and the development activity.

software requirements engineering—In software system engineering, the science and discipline concerned with analyzing and documenting software requirements. It involves transforming system requirements into a description of software requirements, performance parameters, and a system configuration through the use of an iterative process of definition, analysis, tradeoff studies, and prototyping. *Sometimes synonymous with software requirements analysis. See also requirement, requirements engineering.*

software requirements management—Planning and controlling the requirements elicitation, specification, analysis, and verification activities

software requirements review (SRR)—*Synonymous with software specification review (SSR).*

software requirements specification (SRS)—1. In software system engineering, a document that clearly and precisely describes each of the essential requirements (functions, performance, design constraints, and quality attributes) of the software and the external interfaces. Each requirement is defined in such a way that its achievement can be objectively verified by a prescribed method, for example, inspection, demonstration, analysis, or test. [ANSI/IEEE Standard 830-1984] 2. Data item description of a software requirements specification. [U.S. Department of Defense (DoD) usage][DoD Standard 2167A 1988] See also detailed design description (specification), preliminary design description (specification), software design constraint (requirement), software external interface requirement, software functional requirement, software performance requirement, software quality attribute (requirement), software requirements analysis, version description document (VDD).

software requirements verification—Ensuring that the software requirements specification is in compliance with the system requirements, conforms to document standards of the requirements phase, and is an adequate basis for the architectural (preliminary) design phase

software specification review (SSR)—In software system engineering, a milestone review conducted to finalize software configuration item (SCI) requirements so that the software developer can initiate preliminary software design. The SSR is conducted when SCI requirements have been sufficiently defined to evaluate the developer's responsiveness to and interpretation of the system/segment level technical requirements. A successful SSR is predicated on the developer's determination that the software requirements specification and interface specifications form a satisfactory basis for proceeding into the preliminary design phase. [Military Standard 1521B-1985] *See also milestone review, review.*

software system—In system engineering, a collection of related software that allows the accomplishment of some system engineering requirement.

software system engineering—1. A technical and management process. The technical process is the analytical effort necessary to transform an operational need into a software design of the proper size and configuration, and its documentation in requirements specifications. The management process involves assessing the risk and cost, integrating the engineering specialties and design groups, maintaining configuration control, and continuously auditing the effort to ensure that cost, schedule, and technical performance objectives are satisfied to

meet the original operational need. [adapted from Sailor 1990] Software system engineering has the same relationship to software engineering as system engineering has to hardware engineering (all types). 2. A special case of system engineering.

software testing—*See testing. See also black-box testing, white-box testing.*

software unit—In a software system, the lowest element of a software hierarchy that contains one or more of the following characteristics: (1) a unit comprising one or more logical functional entities, (2) an element specified in the design of a computer software component (CSC) that is separately testable [DoD Standard 2167A 1988], (3) the lowest level to which software requirements can be traced, and (4) the design and coding of any unit that can be accomplished by a single individual within the assigned schedule. *Sometimes synonymous with module.*

software utility—In data processing, a software system or tool to support other software systems or tools.

software-intensive system—A system that contains a significant amount of software in relationship to hardware and manual procedures. [Dorfman 1990] *See also system.*

specification—In engineering: 1. A document that prescribes, in a complete, precise, verifiable manner, the requirements, design, behavior, or other characteristics of a hardware/software system or hardware/software system component. 2. The process of developing a specification. 3. A concise statement of a set of requirements to be satisfied by a product, material, or process. The specification indicates, whenever appropriate, the procedure used to determine whether the requirements given are satisfied. [ANSI N45.2.10-1973] [ANSI/IEEE Standard 729-1983] *See also software requirements specification (SRS), system requirements specification. See also formal specification, interface specification, requirements specification, software requirements specification.*

specification language—A software requirements language with one or more of the following properties: (1) Simplifies the process of delivering system specifications and information from informal user requirements. A specification language should assume an appropriate model for software structure that simplifies the development with specifications from informal requirements; (2) permits the specification to be analyzed for internal consistency, precision, and completeness; (3) facilitates the validation that specifications really meet the user's requirements. [Ramamoorthy et al. 1984].

specification tree—In system/software system engineering, a set of specifications arranged in a tree-like order. *See also traceability.*

specification-driven approach—*Synonymous with waterfall model.*

spiral model—1. A software development strategy developed by Barry W. Boehm that creates a risk-driven approach to the software process in contrast to a document-driven or code-driven process. The spiral model holds that each cycle involves a progression through the same sequence of steps, for each portion of the product, and for each of its levels of elaboration, from an overall concept of operations document down to the coding of each individual programs. [Boehm, *Spiral Model* 1988] 2. A software development process model that represents combinations of the conventional (baseline management), prototyping, and incremental models to be used for various portions of a development. It shifts the management emphasis from development of products to risk analysis and avoidance and explicitly calls for evaluation concerning whether a project should be terminated. [Dorfman 1990] *See also process model, waterfall model.*

SQA—Acronym for software quality assurance. *See software quality assurance (SQA).*

SRR—Acronym for software requirements review, system requirements review. *See software specifications review (SSR), system requirements review (SRR).*

SRS—Acronym for software requirements specification, system requirements specification.

SSADM (Structured System Analysis and Design Methodology)—A United Kingdom (U.K.) government software development method used on software development projects developed by Learmonth and Burchett Management Systems (LBMS). Three main classes of diagrams used in SSADM: logical data structures, which represent the relationship between data elements within the system; dataflow diagrams, which show how data move around an information system; and that processes act on; and the entity life history, which gives a third view of data, showing all events affecting the entity during the life of the system. An entity life history, for example, includes those who created it, those who modified it in some way, and those who deleted it. [Williams 1987]

SSR—Acronym for software specification review.

SSS—Acronym for system/segment specification.

stable requirement—In software engineering (requirements specifications), a requirement may be considered stable if the needs it addresses will not change in the expected life of the software. [ANSI/IEEE Standard 830-1984] *Contrast with volatile requirement.*

standard—1. A standard is an approved, documented, and available set of criteria used to determine the adequacy of an action or object. 2. A document that sets forth the standards and procedures to be followed on a given project or by a given organization. 3. A software engineering standard is a set of: (1) procedures that define the processes for and (2) descriptions that define the quantity and quality of a product from a software engineering project. *See also process standard, product standard.*

state chart—A software requirements analysis methodology that is an extension to the finite state machine. The extension provides a notation and set of conventions to facilitate the hierarchical decomposition of finite state machines and a mechanism for communicating between concurrent finite state machines. [Davis, *Comparison of Techniques* 1988]

state transition diagram (STD)—In software engineering (realtime structured analysis methodology), a representation of how the external events cause the system to change from performing one set of transforms to another.

statement of work (SOW)—In system/software projects, a description of all the work required to complete a project. The statement of work (SOW) is normally part of a contract and is written by the customer or procuring agency. It may or may not include a procurement specification.

state-of-the-art—In engineering, the current (latest) technology, but not necessarily in use. *Contrast with state-of-the-practice.*

state-of-the-practice—In engineering, the current (latest) technology in use. *Contrast with state-of-the-art.*

static analysis—In software engineering (verification and validation techniques), direct analysis of the form and structure of a product without executing the product. It may be applied to the requirements, design, or code. [FIPS Publication 101 1983]

stepwise refinement—A system/software development methodology in which data definitions and processing steps are defined broadly at first and then with increasing detail. [ANSI/IEEE

Standard 729-1983] *See also hierarchical decomposition, modular decomposition, top-down development.*

structural testing—In software engineering (testing), the testing at the module level of the internal structure of the system. It may execute all the statements or branches in the program to check on how the system is implemented. Some methods of structural testing are: statement coverage, branch coverage, and path coverage. [Ramamoorthy et al. 1984] *Synonymous for white-box testing. Contrast with functional testing.*

structural testing—In software engineering (testing), the testing of the internal structure of the system. Logical paths through the software are tested by providing test cases that exercise specific sets of conditions or loops. *Synonymous with white-box testing. Contrast with functional testing.*

structure chart—In software engineering (structured methodology), a treelike representation of a program structure. It is used to represent the organization (usually hierarchical) of program components (modules), the hierarchy of control, and the flow of data and control. A structure chart is used in structured design. *See also structured design.*

structured—In software engineering, a term that means that the artifact or methodology is logical in nature and is documented and implemented in a consistent manner throughout all levels of the system. [Nelsen 1990]

structured analysis (SA)—In software engineering (methodology), a state-of-the-art software analysis technique that uses dataflow diagrams (DFDs), data dictionaries, and process descriptions to analyze and represent a software requirement. The technique supports both nonrealtime and realtime systems. *See also dataflow diagram (DFD), data dictionary, leveling, process.*

structured design—1. In software engineering, a design technique that involves hierarchical partitioning of a modular structure in a top-down fashion, with emphasis on reduced coupling and strong cohesion. [DeMarco 1979] 2. A disciplined approach to software design that adheres to a specified set of rules based on principles such as top-down design, stepwise refinement, and dataflow analysis. [ANSI/IEEE Standard 729-1983]

structured programming—1. A computer program (software) consisting of a basic set of control structures, each having one entry point and one exit point. The set of control structures typically in-

cludes sequences of two or more instructions, conditional selection of one of two or more instructions (or sequences of instructions), and repetition of an instruction or a sequence of instructions. [ANSI/IEEE Standard 729-1983] *See also structure chart, structured programming.* 2. In the mid-1970s, *synonymous with software engineering.*

structured specification—In system/software engineering, a requirements analysis methodology and representation method that consists of the following tools: dataflow diagram (DFD), data dictionary, and tools that specify processes (structured English, state transition diagram, decision trees, and decision tables).

Structured Systems Analysis (SSA)—A structured system analysis methodology that was developed by C.P. Gane and T. Sarson and documented in their book, *Structured System Analysis: Tools and Techniques.* [Gane and Sarson 1979] It is a spinoff of the earlier structured analysis work of Ross and is closely related to the design work of Constantine and Yourdon. SSA is a pure top-down technique in which the analyst starts with a single process showing all system inputs and outputs then repeatedly decomposes the process to show greater and greater detail. The Gane and Sarson textbook by the same name is well illustrated and easy to read. [Gane and Sarson 1979]

stub—In software development (testing), a low-level, dummy program module used to receive and respond to test data produced during the development and testing of a high-level module. 2. In software development, a program statement substituting for the body of a program unit and indicating that the unit is or will be defined elsewhere. [ANSI/IEEE Standard 729-1983] *Contrast with driver.*

subsystem—In engineering, a group of assemblies or components or both combined to perform a single function. [ANSI/IEEE Standard 729-1983]

survivability—In software engineering (metrics), a quality metric used to measure how well the software will perform and support critical functions without failures, within a specified time period, when a portion of the system is inoperable. [RADC TR-85-37 1985]

SwSE or SWSE—Acronym for software system engineering.

system—1. A collection of hardware, software, people, facilities, and procedures organized to accomplish a common objective. 2. A set of components that interact according to a design. A component of a system can also be another system (called a *subsystem*). Such components (subsystems) may be: controlling or controlled system; hardware, software, human interaction; input and output subsystems. [IEE/BCS Safety-Related Systems 1989] 3. A bounded physical entity that achieves within its domain a defined objective through interaction of its parts. [Def Stan 00-56/1 1991]

system analysis—*See analysis. See also system requirements engineering.*

system analysis group—In system engineering, a designated group of individuals responsible for all simulations and fundamentals analysis done at the systems level. [Sailor 1990]

system architecture—In system engineering, the structure and relationship among the components of a system. The system architecture may also include the system's interface with its operational environment. [ANSI/IEEE Standard 729-1983]

system design review (SDR)—In system/software system engineering, a system milestone review conducted when the definition effort has proceeded to the point where system requirements and the design approach are defined. Alternative design approaches and corresponding test requirements have been considered and the developer has defined and selected the required equipment, logistic support, personnel, procedural data, and facilities. This normally is late in the definition phase. This review is conducted in sufficient detail to ensure a technical understanding between the system developer and the customer. The system segments are identified in the system design specification, and the hardware/software configuration items are identified in the requirements specifications. *See also milestone review, review.*

system documentation—In system engineering, technical data or information, including specifications, standards, engineering drawings, associated lists, manuals, computer listings, and printouts that describe or specify the design or details, explain the capabilities, or provide operating instructions to obtain desired results from the system. *See also documentation.*

system engineer—An engineer who practices system engineering. *See also system engineering.*

system engineering—The application of scientific and engineering efforts to: (1) transform an operational need into a description of system perform-

ance parameters and a system configuration through the use of an iterative process of definition, synthesis, analysis, design, test, and evaluation; (2) integrate related technical parameters and ensure compatibility of all related, functional, and program interfaces in a manner that optimizes the total system definition and design; (3) integrate reliability, maintainability, safety, survivability, human factors, and other such factors into the total engineering effort to meet cost, schedule, and technical performance objectives. [Military Standard 499A 1974]

system engineering organization—In a system engineering project, a selected group of engineers responsible for conducting certain aspects of system engineering. Not all system engineering activities are done in the system engineering organization; and not all engineers in a system engineering organization are system engineers. [Sailor 1990]

system engineering process—In engineering, the multidisciplinary activity that begins with function analysis and arrives at a total system design through a process that considers and evaluates a spectrum of user requirements and economic and technical variables that are relevant to candidate approaches. [Searle 1981]

system engineering project—The set of all activities, functions, and tasks, both technical and managerial, required to satisfy the terms and conditions of the project agreement. A system engineering project is a temporary activity that is characterized by having a start date, specific objectives and constraints, established responsibilities, a budget and schedule, and a completion date. A system engineering project consumes resources and has the goal of producing a product or set of products that satisfies the project requirements, as specified in the project agreement. In some cases, a system engineering project may span many years and consist of numerous subprojects, each being a well-defined and self-contained system engineering project. *See also software engineering project.*

system integration—In system/software system engineering, the action to ensure that the various segments and elements of the total system can operate together and interface with the external environment as required and expected.

system requirement—In system engineering: 1. A system capability needed to solve a problem or achieve an objective. 2. A system capability that must be met (or possessed) by a system or component to satisfy a contract, standard, specification, or other formal document. 3. The set of all system requirements that forms the basis for subsequent development of the system or system component. [ANSI/IEEE Standard 729-1983] *See also system requirements specification (SRS), software requirement.*

system requirements engineering—The science and discipline concerned with analyzing and documenting system requirements. It involves transforming an operational need into a system description, with system performance parameters and a system configuration, through the use of an iterative process of definition, analysis, tradeoff studies, and prototyping. *See also requirement.*

system requirements review (SRR)—In system engineering, a system milestone review that ascertains the adequacy of the system developer's efforts in defining system requirements. It will be conducted when a significant portion of the system functional and performance requirements has been established, normally in the definition phase (or equivalent effort). *See also milestone review, review.*

system requirements specification (SRS)—In system engineering, a specification that sets forth the requirements for a system or system segment. Typically included are functional requirements, performance requirements, interface requirements, design requirements, and development standards.

system testing—1. In system engineering, the process of testing integrated hardware and software systems to verify that they meet specified requirements. [ANSI/IEEE Standard 729-1983] *See also acceptance testing, qualification testing.* 2. In software system engineering, the activity of checking that the complete software system is fully integrated with its hardware environment according to the requirements specification.

T

task—1. In SEPM, the smallest unit of management accountability for work assignment usually assigned to one or a few individual project members. A task specification includes the specific objectives of the task, staffing requirements, the expected duration of the task, the resources to be used, and any special considerations. Similar tasks are usually grouped together to form functions and activities. [ANSI/IEEE Standard 1058.1-1987] *See also function.*

TBD—Acronym for "to be determined" or "to be done."

TBR—Acronym for "to be resolved."

TBS—Acronym for "to be supplied."

technical review—In software system engineering, a formal team evaluation of software requirements specification. This review identifies any discrepancies from system specifications and standards. It also provides recommendations after the examination of alternatives. This examination may require more than one meeting, and typically has a larger audience than walkthroughs or inspections. In this midprocess examination approach, the technical review meets the need for widespread requirements exposure to assure correctness, completeness, and feasibility. [Hollocker 1990] *See also review.*

technology—A collective term for a practices, tools, techniques, and/or methods.

technology transfer—The awareness, convincing, selling, motivating, collaboration, and special effort required to encourage industry, companies, organizations, and projects to make good use of new technology products. *See also technology transfer gap.*

technology transfer gap—The time interval (measured in years) between the development of a new product, tool, or technique and its use by the consumers of that product, tool, or technique. *See also technology transfer.*

termination—In a software process model, the ending of the software development lifecycle.

test bed—In software engineering (testing): 1. A test environment containing the hardware, instrumentation, tools, simulators, and other support software necessary for testing a system or system component. 2. The repertoire of test cases necessary for testing a system or system component. [ANSI/IEEE Standard 830-1984] *See also testing.*

test case—In software engineering (testing), a specific set of test data and associated procedures developed for a particular objective, such as to exercise a particular program path or to verify compliance with a specific requirement. [ANSI/IEEE Standard 729-1983] *See also testing.*

test case specification—In software engineering (testing), a document specifying inputs, predicted results, and a set of execution conditions for a test item. [ANSI/IEEE Standard 829-1983] *See also testing.*

test coverage—In software engineering (testing): 1. The selection of test cases so that all statements are executed at least once. 2. In software engineering (metrics), the ratio of executed code to potential code during the test process. Metrics to measure test coverage include the percentage of the total statements executed (statement coverage), the percentage of the total branches taken (decision or branch coverage), and the percentage of the total conditions in all decisions in the system covered (path or condition coverage). Test coverage is typically embodied in standards describing metrics, test procedures, and test reports. [Ramamoorthy et al. 1984] *See also software testing, testing.*

test data—In software engineering (testing), data developed to test a system or system component. [ANSI/IEEE Standard 729-1983] *See also test, test case, testing.*

test design specification—In software engineering (testing), a document specifying the details of the test approach for a software feature or combination of software features and identifying the associated tests. [ANSI/IEEE Standard 829-1983] *See also testing.*

test document—*See test case specification, test design specification, test plan, test procedure specification.*

test plan—In software engineering (testing), a document describing the scope, approach, resources, and schedule of intended testing activities. The test plan identifies test items, the features to be tested, the testing tasks, who will do each task, and any risks requiring contingency planning. [ANSI/IEEE Standard 829-1983] *See also testing.*

test procedure specification—In software system engineering (testing), a document specifying a sequence of actions for the execution of a test. [ANSI/IEEE Standard 829-1983] *See also test, testing.*

test readiness review (TRR)—In software system engineering, a milestone review to determine that the software test procedures are complete and to ensure that the software developer is prepared for formal software performance testing. The results of informal testing also are reviewed. [Military Standard 1521B-1985]. *See also milestone review, review, testing.*

testability—1. In software engineering, a software quality metric that can be used to measure those characteristics that provide for testing. 2. In soft-

ware engineering (requirements specifications), the extent to which one can identify an economically feasible technique for determining whether the developed software will satisfy this specification. To be testable, specifications must be specific, unambiguous, and quantitative wherever possible. [Boehm, *V&V Software Requirements* 1984]

testing—In software system engineering: 1. A verification method that applies a controlled set of conditions and stimuli for the purpose of finding errors. This is the most desirable method of verifying the functional and performance requirements. Test results are documented proof that the requirements were met and can be repeated. The resulting data can be reviewed by all concerned for confirmation of capabilities. 2. The process of analyzing a system/software item to detect the differences between existing and required conditions and to evaluate the features of the system/software item. [ANSI/IEEE Standard 729-1983] 3. The process of exercising or evaluating a system or system component by manual or automated means to verify that it satisfies specified requirements or to identify differences between expected and actual results. *Compare with debugging.*

to be determined (TBD)—In system/software system engineering, a term (normally written "TBD") that is placed in the system/software requirements specifications where decisions have been postponed for a later time. Each TBD entry should be annotated with the following: (1) the reason for the TBD, (2) who is responsible for removing the TBD, (3) the expected date of removal of the TBD, and (4) under what conditions the TBD can be removed. [Boehm, *V&V Software Requirements* 1984]

to be supplied (TBS)—In system/software engineering (requirements), a term that means that the system item identified in the requirements specification will be supplied to the developer.

top-down analysis—A system/software engineering methodology that means requirements are allocated and decomposed from the top, or system level, down through subsystems, hardware components, and software programs in an orderly fashion. [Nelsen 1990]

top-down development—In system/software engineering, pertaining to an approach that starts with the highest-level system/software component of a hierarchy and proceeds through progressively lower levels; for example, top-down analysis, top-down design, top-down programming, and top-down testing. *Sometimes called stepwise refinement.*

top-down testing—In software engineering (testing), the process of checking out hierarchically organized programs, progressively, from top to bottom, using simulations of low-level components (called *stubs*). [ANSI/IEEE Standard 729-1983] *Contrast with bottom-up testing.*

top-level dataflow diagram—In software engineering (structured analysis methodology), the highest level of dataflow diagrams.

top-level design—*Synonymous with architectural design, preliminary design.*

traceability—1. In software engineering, a quality metric that can be used to measure those characteristics of software that provide a thread of origin from the implementation to the requirements, with respect to the specific development envelope and operational environment. [RADC TR-85-37 1985] 2. In software engineering (requirement specifications), identification and documentation of the derivation path (upward) and allocation/flowdown path (downward) of requirements in the hierarchy.

traceable—A software requirements specification is traceable if the origin of each of the requirements is clear and if it facilitates the referencing of each requirement in future development or enhancement documents.

tracing—In software engineering: 1. To track the implementation of each software requirement into tested code. 2. A procedure for providing an auditable track from the requirements, through design, to the completed and tested product, and back.

trade study—In system/software system engineering, consists of comparing two or more candidate designs with respect to all the characteristics that are important to the intended applications. Characteristics to be considered include not only the identified performance, but also factors of cost, availability, and development times. The factors include affordability, maintainability, growth potential, safety, impact on interfaces, support to the system, and flexibility with respect to low-level design solutions. [Searle 1981]

tree—In a software engineering (methodology), a hierarchy in which it is expected that an element at a given level has only one derivation, that is, flows from one element at a given level to the next higher level. Occasional multiple derivations are permitted. A tree is a graphical representation of such a hierarchy. [Flynn and Dorfman 1990]

TRR—Acronym for test readiness review.

U

UDF—Acronym for unit development folder.

unambiguous—A software requirement specification is unambiguous if the requirement stated has only one semantic interpretation.

unit—*See software unit. See also module.*

unit development folder (UDF)—In software engineering project management, a central depository for recording the progress that has been made toward a "unit's" objectives. A UDF is used by project management for monitoring software work accomplished. A unit can be a single project member or project team. Initial development credited to Frank Ingrassia. *Sometimes synonymous with software development file.*

unit testing—In software engineering (testing), the process of ensuring that the unit executes as intended. This usually involves testing all statements and branch possibilities. *Sometimes synonymous with debugging.*

untestable requirement—In system/software engineering, requirements that cannot be tested. For example, some realtime, critical defense systems cannot be tested because actual inputs are not available. Other requirement attributes that sometimes cannot be tested properly are constraints and nonfunctional requirements, such as flexibility and evolvability. [Rama-moorthy et al. 1984]

usability—1. In software engineering, a metric that can be used to measure the relative effort for using software (training and operation), for example, familiarization, input preparation, execution, and output interpretation. [RADC TR-85-37 1985] 2. A metric used with computer-aided software engineering (CASE) tools that can be used to measure the ease with which the tool can be learned and used. Usability includes a consistent-use interface and should hide the underlying system software from those users who do not wish to see it. [Wasserman and Pircher 1987]

use case—In software engineering (requirements), a method of describing the possible sequences of interactions among the system and one or more actors in response to some initial stimulus by one of the actors. It is a set of possible scenarios, each starting with some initial event from an actor to the system and following the ensuing transaction to its logical conclusion. [Rumbaugh 1994]

use-center analysis—In software engineering

(requirements), the process of capturing requirements from the user's point of view. *See concept of operations document.*

user—1. One who uses the services of a computer system. [IEEE *Computer Applications Technology Glossary* 1986] 2. The person or persons who operate or interact directly with the computer system. The user and the customer are often the same individuals or entities. *Sometimes synonymous with customer.*

user documentation—*See user manual.*

user friendly—1. In software development, the capability for a consistent user interface, default parameter settings, the use of icons and windows, self-explanatory commands, and online help messages. A user-friendly system should hide the underlying system software from those users who do not wish to see it. 2. Pertaining to a computer system, device, program, or document designed with ease of use as a primary design objective. [IEEE *Computer Applications Technology Glossary* 1986] 3. A software system that has been designed for use by inexperienced people and includes one or more helpful features to assist the user.

user interface—In software engineering (human computer interface), the partition between software, input and output devices, screens, procedures, and dialogue between people and the software system. *See also interface.*

user interface requirement—In software engineering, the specified requirements for the user interface. *See also user interface.*

user manual—In software engineering projects, a manual used to provide a computer system user or customer personnel with the necessary instructions concerning usage of a software system and instructions on how it is to be operated. The manual content and format are specifically designed to meet the needs of the intended user. *Contrast with maintenance manual, operator manual.*

V

V&V—Acronym for verification and validation *See verification and validation (V&V).*

validation—In software engineering, determination of the correctness of the final program or software produced from a development project with respect to the user's needs and requirements. Validation

answers the question, "Am I building the right product?" [Boehm, *V&V Software Requirements* 1984]

validation method—In software engineering, a method of validating systems/software requirements using tests, demonstrations, analysis, similarity, and examinations. [Nelsen 1990] *See also testing.*

VDM (Vienna Definition Method)—A software requirements methodology. VDM is a formal method for software development based on work carried out at IBM's laboratory in Vienna, Austria. It is a formal specification language that uses set theory and logic to create abstract specifications that can be proved correct. Data and associated operations are presented in a mathematical language. VDM is useful for specifying functional behavior and derives a correct design from the specification. VDM cannot express nonfunctional requirements. [STARTS Guide 1987]

Vee chart—In system engineering, a type of system process model characterized by its "V" shape. The left leg represents the decomposition and definition of the project. The right leg of the Vee represents the integration and verification of the system starting at the lowest level and building to the completed solution. [Forsberg and Mooz 1996]

vendor—A company or firm that manufactures and sells goods. A software vendor (sometimes called a *software house*) develops and sells software and software packages. A tool vendor is a company or agent who distributes and sells a tool.

verifiability—1. In software engineering (metrics), a metric used to measure the relative effort to verify specified software operation and performance. [RADC TR-85-37 1985] 2. In software requirements analysis, a software requirements specification is verifiable only if every requirement stated therein is verifiable. A requirement is verifiable only if there exists some finite cost-effective process by which a person or machine can check that the actual, as-built software product meets the requirement.

verification—In software engineering: 1. The process of determining whether the products of a given phase of the software development cycle fulfill the requirements established during the previous phase. Verification answers the question, "Am I building the product right?" *See also validation.* 2. The act of reviewing, inspecting, testing, checking, auditing, comparing, or otherwise establishing and documenting whether items, processes, services, or documents conform to specified requirements. 3. Formal proof of program correctness. *See also formal (verifiable) requirements language.* 4. In system/software system engineering, a generalized term that can mean: test (using precision instrumentation), demonstration (a functional test), analysis (or simulation), or examination (or documentation). [Sailor 1990]

verification and validation (V&V)—In software engineering, a software quality assurance (SQA) procedure that includes both verification and validation. The basic objectives in verification and validation of software requirements and design specifications are to identify and resolve software problems and high-risk issues early in the software cycle. [Boehm, *V&V Software Requirements* 1984] *See also independent verification and validation, validation, verification.*

verification and validation technique—In software systems engineering, a methodology for performing software requirements and design verification and validation. *See also automated technique (detailed), checklist, manual cross-referencing, manual model, manual technique (detailed), manual technique (simple), mathematical proof, prototype, reading.* [Boehm, *V&V Software Requirement* 1984]

version—In a software system, an operational software product that differs from other like products in terms of capability, environmental requirements, and configuration. *Sometimes synonymous with build. See also configuration management.*

version description document (VDD)—In system/software system engineering, a specification that sets forth the exact version of a hardware/software configuration item and its interim changes. It is used to identify the current version and, accordingly, accompanies each version of a hardware/software configuration item and each release of an interim version change to a configuration item. [U.S. Department of Defense (DoD) usage][DoD Standard 2167A 1988]

visibility—In software engineering, a quality metric that can be used to measure those characteristics of software that can be used to provide visibility and insight to decision makers. [Keller et al. 1990]

volatile requirement—In software engineering (requirements specifications), a requirement may be considered volatile when it is thought that the requirements will change (sometimes rapidly) during the expected life of the software. [ANSI/IEEE Standard 830-1984] *Contrast with stable requirement.*

W

walkthrough—In software engineering, a software inspection process, conducted by the peers of the software developer, to evaluate a software element. Although usually associated with code examination, this process is also applicable to the software requirements and software design. The major objectives of the walkthrough are to find defects (such as omissions, unwanted additions, and contradictions) in a specification and other products and to consider alternative functionality, performance objectives, or representations. [Hollocker 1990] *See also inspection.*

Warnier method—A software engineering methodology based on the data structure developed by Jean Warnier in the early 1970s. Similar to Jackson's JSD method, it assumes that the data structure is the key to a successful software design effort. The logical construction of programs approach employs four different design representation schemes: data organization diagrams, logical sequence diagrams, instruction lists, and pseudocode.

waterfall—*See waterfall model.*

waterfall chart—*See waterfall model.*

waterfall model—A software development lifecycle strategy first developed by Winston W. Royce [1970], that partitions the project into manageable phases—requirements, design, implementation, and test—and establishes milestones, documents, and reviews at the end of each phase. In the model, the successful completion of one lifecycle phase in the waterfall chart corresponds to the achievement of the counterpart goal in the sequence of software engineering goals for the software process. The waterfall model recognizes the iteration between phases.

WBS—Acronym for work breakdown structure.

white-box testing—In software engineering (testing), a software test methodology at the module level in which test cases are derived from the internal structure of the program. It may execute all the statements or branches in the program to check on how the system is implemented. Some methods of white-box testing are statement coverage, branch coverage, and path coverage. [Ramamoorthy et al. 1984] *Contrast with black-*

box testing, functional testing. See also structural testing.

work breakdown structure (WBS)—In project management, a method of representing in a hierarchical manner the parts of a product or process. A WBS can be used to represent a process (requirement analysis, design, code, or software test) or a product (application programs, utility programs, or operating systems). *See also process work breakdown structure, product work breakdown structure.*

X

There are no entries under this letter.

Y

Yourdon technique—*Synonymous with structured analysis (SA) and structured design.*

Z—A formal software requirements language (pronounced "ZED") that evolved from research work carried out by the Programming Research Group at the Oxford University Computing Laboratory. Z uses a mathematical-notation-based conventional set theory and predicate calculus with some minor extensions. Note: Z cannot easily model concurrency, nor is it integrated with other software engineering techniques. [Norris 1986]

References

[ANSI N45.2.10-1973] ANSI N45.2.10-1973, *Quality Assurance Terms and Definitions*, American National Standards Institute, NY, 1973.

[ANSI/ASQC A3-1978] ANSI/ASQC A3-1978, *Quality Systems Terminology,* American National Standards Institute, NY, 1978.

[ANSI/IEEE Standard 729-1983] ANSI/IEEE Standard 729-1983, *IEEE Standard Glossary of Software Engineering Terminology,* The Institute of Electrical and Electronics Engineers, New York, N.Y., approved by American National Standards Institute Aug. 9, 1983.

[ANSI/IEEE Standard 829-1983] ANSI/IEEE Standard 829-1983, *IEEE Standard for Software Test Documents,* The Institute of Electrical and Electronics Engineers, New York, NY, approved by American National Standards Institute Aug. 19, 1983.

[ANSI/IEEE Standard 830-1984] ANSI/IEEE Standard 830-1984, *IEEE Guide for Software Requirements Specifications*, The Institute of Electrical and Electronics Engineers, New York, N.Y., approved by American National Standards Institute July 20, 1984.

[ANSI/IEEE Standard 1058.1-1987] ANSI/IEEE Standard 1058.1-1987, *IEEE Standard for Software Project Management Plans,* The Institute of Electrical and Electronics Engineers, New York, N.Y., approved by American National Standards Institute Oct. 6, 1988.

[Bersoff 1984] Bersoff, E.H., "Elements of Software Configuration Management," *IEEE Trans. Software Engineering,* Vol. SE-10, No. 1, Jan. 1984, pp. 79–87. Reprinted in Thayer, R.H., and M. Dorfman, eds., *System and Software Requirements Engineering,* IEEE Computer Society Press, Los Alamitos, Calif., 1990.

[Boehm, *Risk Management* 1989] Boehm, B.W., *Software Risk Management*, IEEE Computer Society Press, Los Alamitos, Calif., 1989.

[Boehm, *Spiral Model* 1988] Boehm, B.W., "A Spiral Model of Software Development and Enhancement," in Thayer, R.H., ed., *Tutorial: Software Engineering Project Management,* IEEE Computer Society Press, Los Alamitos, Calif., 1988. Also published in *Computer*, Vol. 21, No. 5, Apr. 1988, pp. 61–72.

[Boehm, *V&V Software Requirements* 1984] Boehm, B.W., "Verifying and Validating Software Requirements and Design Specifications," *IEEE Software*, Vol. 1, No. 1, Jan. 1984, pp. 75–88. Reprinted in Thayer, R.H., and M. Dorfman, eds., *System and Software Requirements Engineering,* IEEE Computer Society Press, Los Alamitos, CA, 1990.

[Booch 1994] Booch, Grady, *Object-Oriented Analysis and Design*, Benjamin/Cummings, Redwood City, Calif., 1994.

[British usage] Either the term is unique to the United Kingdom or the definition is different from that used in the United States.

[Chen 1990] Chen, P.P., "Entity-Relationship Approach to Data Modeling," in Thayer, R.H., and M. Dorfman, eds., *System and Software Requirements Engineering,* IEEE Computer Society Press, Los Alamitos, Calif., 1990.

[Davis 1990] Davis, A.M., "The Analysis and Specification of System and Software Requirements," in Thayer, R.H., and M. Dorfman, eds., *System and Software Requirements Engineering,* IEEE Computer Society Press, Los Alamitos, Calif., 1990.

[Davis et al. 1988] Davis, A.M., E.H. Bersoff, and E.R. Comer, "A Strategy for Comparing Alternate Software Development Life Cycle Models," *IEEE Trans. Software Eng.,* Vol. SE-14, No. 10, Oct. 1988, pp. 1453–1461. Reprinted in Thayer, R.H., and M. Dorfman, eds., *System and Software Requirements Engineering,* IEEE Computer Society Press, Los Alamitos, Calif., 1990.

[Davis, *Comparison of Techniques* 1988] Davis, A.M., "A Comparison of Techniques for the Specification of External System Behavior," *Comm. ACM,* Vol. 31, No. 9, Sept. 1988, pp. 1098–1115. Reprinted in Thayer, R.H., and M. Dorfman, eds., *System and Software Requirements Engineering,* IEEE Computer Society Press, Los Alamitos, Calif., 1990.

[DEF Stan 00-56/1 1991] MoD, *Hazard Analysis and Safety Classification of the Computer and Programmable Electronic System Elements of Defence Equipment,* Def Stan 00-56/Issue 1, Ministry of Defence, United Kingdom, Apr. 5, 1991.

[DeMarco 1979] DeMarco, T., *Structured Analysis and System Specification,* Prentice-Hall, Englewood Cliffs, N.J., 1979.

[DoD Directive 5010.19] DoD Directive 5010.19, *Configuration Management,* U.S. Department of Defense, Oct. 28, 1987.

[DoD Standard 480B 1988] DoD Standard 480B, *Configuration Control—Engineering Changes, Deviation and Waivers,* U.S. Department of Defense, July 15, 1988.

[DoD Standard 2167A 1988] DoD Standard 2167A, *Defense System Software Development,* U.S. Department of Defense, Feb. 29, 1988.

[DoD, *Engineering Management Guide* 1986] Technical Management Department, Defense Systems Management College (DSMC), *System Engineering Management Guide,* 2nd ed., DSMC, Fort Belvoir, V.A., 1986.

[Dorfman 1990] Dorfman, M., "System and Software Requirements Engineering," in Thayer, R.H., and M. Dorfman, eds., *System and Software Requirements Engineering,* IEEE Computer Society Press, Los Alamitos, Calif., 1990.

[ESPRIT July 1987] Draft ESPRIT *Workprogramme,* Commission of the European Communities, Brussels, July 22, 1987.

[FIPS Publication 101 1983] FIPS Publication 101, *Guideline for Lifecycle Validation, Verification, and Testing of Computer Software,* Federal Information Processing Standards Publication 101, Institute for Computer Science and Technology, National Bureau of Standards, Gaithersburg, M.D., 1983.

[Flynn and Dorfman 1990] Flynn, R.F., and M. Dorfman, "The Automated Requirements Traceability System (ARTS): An Experience of 8 Years," in Thayer, R.H., and M. Dorfman, eds., *System and Software Requirements Engineering,* IEEE Computer Society Press, Los Alamitos, Calif., 1990.

[Forsberg and Mooz 1996] Forsberg, K., and H. Mooz, "System Engineering Overvi7ew," in *Software Requirements Engineering,* Thayer, R.H., and M. Dorfman, eds., IEEE Computer Society Press, Los Alamitos, Calif., 1997.

[Foster et al. 1989] Foster, J.R., A.E.P. Jolly, and M.T. Norris, "An Overview of Software Maintenance," *British Telecom Technology Journal,* Vol. 7, No. 4, October 1989, pp. 37-46.

[Gane and Sarson 1979] Gane, C.P., and Sarson, T., *Structured Systems Analysis: Tools and Techniques,* Prentice-Hall, Englewood Cliffs, NJ, 1979.

[Gehani 1982] Gehani, N., "Specifications: Formal and Informal—A Case Study," *Software Practices and Experiences,* Vol. 12, 1982, pp. 433–444.

[Heninger 1980] Heninger, K.L., "Specifying Software Requirements for Complex Systems: New Techniques and Their Application," *IEEE Trans. Software Eng.,* Vol. SE-6, No. 1, Jan. 1980, pp. 2–13. Reprinted in Thayer, R.H., and M. Dorfman, eds., *System and Software Requirements Engineering,* IEEE Computer Society Press, Los Alamitos, Calif., 1990.

[Hollocker 1990] Hollocker, C.P., "Requirement Specification Examinations," in Thayer, R.H., and M. Dorfman, eds., *System and Software Requirements Engineering,* IEEE Computer Society Press, Los Alamitos, Calif., 1990.

[Humphrey 1989] Humphrey, W.S., *Managing the Software Process,* Addison-Wesley, Reading, Mass., 1989.

[IEE/BCS Safety-Related Systems 1989] IEE/BCS, *Software in Safety-Related Systems,* The Institution of Electrical Engineering and The British Computer Society, Oct. 1989.

[IEEE-STD 1362 (draft)] IEEE P1362, *IEEE Guide for Concept of Operations Document,* Draft 2.5, The Institute of Electrical and Electronics Engineers, NY, Feb. 26, 1996.

[Keller et al. 1990] Keller, S.E., L.G. Kahn, and R.B. Panara, "Specifying Software Quality Requirements with Metrics," in Thayer, R.H., and M. Dorfman, eds., *System and Software Requirements Engineering*, IEEE Computer Society Press, Los Alamitos, Calif., 1990.

[Kotonya and Sommerville 1996] G. Kotonya, G., and Sommerville, I., "Requirements Engineering with Viewpoints," *Software Engineering J.*, Vol. 11, No. 1, Jan. 1996, pp. 5-18.

[Lano 1977] Lano, R.J., "The N² Chart," TRW-SS-77-04, TRW Defense and Space Systems Group, Redondo Beach, CA, 1977. Republished as *A Technique for Software and Systems Design*, Vol. 3, North-Holland Publishing Co, New York, N.Y., 1979. Extract published in R.H. Thayer and M. Dorfman (eds.), *System and Software Requirements Engineering*, IEEE Computer Society Press, Los Alamitos, Calif., 1990.

[Manley 1984] Manley, J.H., "Computed Aided Software Engineering (CASE): Foundation for Software Factories," *Proc. IEEE COMPCON '84 Fall Computer Conference on the Small Computer (R)* IEEE Computer Society Press, Los Alamitos, Calif., 1984, pp. 84–91.

[McDermid 1991] McDermid, John A., *Software Engineering Reference Book*, Butterworth Heinemann, Jordon Hill, Oxford, England, 1991.

[Military Standard 499A-1974] Military Standard 499A, *Engineering Management (USAF)*, U.S. Department of Defense, May 1, 1974.

[Military Standard 1521B-1985] Military Standard 1521B (USAF), *Technical Reviews and Audits for Systems, Equipment, and Computer Programs*, U.S. Department of Defense, 1985.

[NBS Special Pub 500-106 1983] Martin, R.J., and W.M. Osborne, *Guidance on Software Maintenance*, NBS Special Publication 500-106, Institute for Computer Science and Technology, National Bureau of Standards, Gaithersburg, MD, 1983.

[NCC STARTS GUIDE 1987] The National Computer Centre, *The Starts Guide*, 2nd Ed., Vol. I, Chapter 5, The National Computer Centre, Manchester, England, 1987.

[Nelsen 1990] Nelsen, E.D., "System Engineering and Requirement Allocation," in Thayer, R.H., and M. Dorfman, eds., *System and Software Requirements Engineering*, IEEE Computer Society Press, Los Alamitos, Calif., 1990.

[Norris 1986] Norris, M., "Z (A Formal Specification Method): A Debrief Report," The National Computing Centre, Manchester, England, 1986. Reprinted in *System and Software Requirements Engineering*, Thayer, R.H., and M. Dorfman, eds., IEEE Computer Society Press, Los Alamitos, Calif., 1990. *See also STARTS Debrief Reports for reports on other software tools and methods.*

[Northrup 1996] Northrop, Linda M., "Object-Oriented Development," in *Software Engineering*, Dorfman, M., and R.H. Thayer, eds., IEEE Computer Society Press, Los Alamitos, Calif., 1996.

[Oxford Dictionary of Computing 1990] *Oxford Dictionary of Computing*, 3rd Ed., Oxford University Press, Oxford, England, 1990.

[RADC TR-85-37 1985] Bowen, T.P., G.B. Wigle, and J.T. Tsai, *Specification of Software Quality Attributes*, Vol. 1, *Final Technical Report;* Vol. 2, *Software Quality Specifications Guidebook;* Vol. 3, *Software Quality Evaluation Guidebook;* RADC TR-85-37, prepared by Boeing Aerospace Company for Rome Air Development Center, Griffiss AFB, N.Y., Feb. 1985.

[Ramamoorthy et al. 1984] Ramamoorthy, C.V., A. Prakash, W. Tsai, and Y. Usuda, "Software Engineering: Problems and Perspectives," *Computer*, Vol. 17, No. 10, Oct. 1984, pp. 191–209. Corrected copy reprinted in Thayer, R.H., ed., *Tutorial: Software Engineering Project Management*, IEEE Computer Society Press, Los Alamitos, Calif., 1988.

[Rich et al. 1987] Rich, C., R.C. Waters, and H.B. Reubenstein, "Toward a Requirements Apprentice," *Proc. 4th Int'l Workshop Software Specifications and Design*, IEEE Computer Society Press, Los Alamitos, Calif., 1987, pp. 79–86. Reprinted in Thayer, R.H., and M. Dorfman, eds., *System and Software Requirements Engineering*, IEEE Computer Society Press, Los Alamitos, Calif., 1990.

[Robson 1991] Robson, D.J., K.H. Bennett, B.J. Cornellius, and M. Munro, "Approaches to Program Comprehension," *J. Systems and Software*, Vol. 14, No. 2, Feb. 1991, pp. 79–84.

[Rook 1986] Rook, P., "Controlling Software Projects," *Software Engineering J.*, Jan. 1986, pages 7–16. In R.H. Thayer (ed.), *Software Engineering Project Management*, IEEE Computer Society Press, Los Alamitos, Calif., 1988.

[Rumbaugh 1994] Rumbaugh, J., "Getting Started: Using Use Cases to Capture Requirements," *J. Object Oriented Programming*, Sept. 1994, pp. 8–12, 23. Reprinted in *Software Requirements Engi-*

neering, Thayer, R.H., and M. Dorfman, eds., IEEE Computer Society Press, Los Alamitos, Calif., 1997.

[Rzepka and Ohno 1985] Rzepka, W., and Y. Ohno, "Requirements Engineering Environments: Software Tools for Modeling User Needs," Guest Editors' Introduction, *Computer,* Vol. 18, No. 4, Apr. 1985, pp. 9–12.

[Sailor 1990] Sailor, J.D., "System Engineering Overview," in *System and Software Requirements Engineering,* Thayer, R.H., and M. Dorfman, eds., IEEE Computer Society Press, Los Alamitos, Calif., 1990.

[Sayani 1990] Sayani, H.H., "PSL/PSA at the Age of Fifteen," in *System and Software Requirements Engineering,* Thayer, R.H., and M. Dorfman, eds., IEEE Computer Society Press, Los Alamitos, Calif., 1990.

[Scharer 1981] Scharer, L., "Pinpointing Requirements," *Datamation,* April 1981, pp. 139–151. Reprinted in Thayer, R.H., and M. Dorfman, eds., *System and Software Requirements Engineering,* IEEE Computer Society Press, Los Alamitos, Calif., 1990.

[Searle 1981] Searle, L.V., *An Air Force Guide to System Specification,* ESD TR-81-128, Electronic Systems Division, Hanscom AFB, Mass., 1981.

[Spivey 1989] Spivey, J.M., "An Introduction to Z and Formal Specifications," *Software Engineering J.,* Vol. 4, No. 1, Jan. 1989, pp. 40–50.

[STARTS Guide 1987] National Computing Centre, The *STARTS Guide,* 2nd Ed., The National Computing Centre, Manchester, England, 1987.

[Thayer, Pyster, and Wood 1981] Thayer, R.H., A.B. Pyster, and R C. Wood, "Major Issues in Software Engineering Project Management," *IEEE Trans. Software Eng.,* Vol. SE-7, No. 4, July 1981, pp. 333–342.

[U.S. Department of Defense (DoD) usage] The term is primarily used by the U.S. Department of Defense and the aerospace industry.

[Ward and Mellor 1986] Ward, P.T., and S.J. Mellor, *Structured Development for Real-Time Systems:* Vol. 1, *Introduction & Tools;* Vol. 2, *Essential Modeling Techniques;* Vol. 3, *Implementation Modeling Techniques*; Yourdon Press, New York, N.Y., 1986. (Note: The principal [first] author for Vol. 3 is S.J. Mellor.)

[Wasserman and Pircher 1987] Wasserman, A.I., and P.A. Pircher, "A Graphic, Extensible Integrated Environment for Software Development," *Proc. 2nd ACM SIGSOFT/SIGPLAN Software Engineering Symp., Practical Software Development Environment* ACM Press, New York, N.Y., 1986. Published in *ACM SIGPLAN Notices,* Vol. 22, No. 1, Jan. 1987, pp. 131–142. Reprinted in Thayer, R.H., and M. Dorfman, eds., *System and Software Requirements Engineering,* IEEE Computer Society Press, Los Alamitos, Calif., 1990.

[Williams 1987] Williams, J., "SSADM—System Building Made Simple," *Systems International,* Nov. 1987, pp. 91–92. Reprinted in Thayer, R.H., and M. Dorfman, eds., *System and Software Requirements Engineering*, IEEE Computer Society Press, Los Alamitos, Calif., 1990.

Biography of Richard H. Thayer

Richard H. Thayer, PhD, is a Professor of Computer Science at California State University, Sacramento, California, United States of America. He travels widely where he consults and lectures on software requirements analysis, software engineering, project management, software engineering standards, and software quality assurance. He is a Visiting Researcher at the University of Strathclyde, Glasgow, Scotland. As an expert in software project management and requirements engineering, he is a consultant to many companies and government agencies.

Prior to this, he served over 20 years in the U.S. Air Force as a senior officer in a variety of positions associated with engineering, computer programming, research, teaching, and management in computer science and data processing. His numerous positions include six years as a supervisor and technical leader of scientific programming groups, four years directing the U.S. Air Force R&D program in computer science, and six years of managing large data processing organizations.

Thayer is a Senior Member of the IEEE Computer Society and the IEEE Software Engineering Standards Subcommittee. He is Chairperson for the Working Group for a Standard for a Concept of Operations (ConOps) document and past chairperson for the Working Group for a Standard for a Software Project Management Plans. He is a Distinguished Visitor for the IEEE Computer Society.

He is also an Associate Fellow of the American Institute of Aeronautics and Astronautics (AIAA) where he served on the AIAA Technical Committee on Computer Systems, and he is a member of the Association for Computing Machinery (ACM). He is also a registered professional engineer.

He has a BSEE and an MS degree from the University of Illinois at Urbana (1962) and a PhD from the University of California at Santa Barbara (1979) all in Electrical Engineering.

He has edited and/or co-edited numerous tutorials for the IEEE Computer Society Press: *Software Engineering Project Management* (1988), *System and Software Requirements Engineering* (1990), and *Software Engineering—A European Prospective* (1992). He is the author of over 40 technical papers and reports on software project management, software engineering, and software engineering standards and is an invited speaker at many national and international software engineering conferences and workshops.

Biography of Merlin Dorfman

Merlin Dorfman, PhD, is a Technical Consultant in the Space Systems Product Center, Lockheed Martin Missiles and Space Company, Sunnyvale, Calif. He specializes in systems engineering for software-intensive systems (requirements analysis, top-level architecture, and performance evaluation), in software process improvement, and in algorithm development for data processing systems. He has performed concept exploration, system implementation, and operations and maintenance of data systems and has worked on proposal teams and company-funded technology projects as well as on development contracts. He was in charge of the development of the Automated Requirements Traceability System (ARTS). He was the first chairman of Space Systems Division's Software Engineering Process Group. He represented the Lockheed Corporation on the Embedded Computer Software Committee of the Aerospace Industries Association, and was Vice-Chairman of the Committee.

Dorfman wrote and taught a four-day course, "Software Requirements and Design Specifications," for Learning Tree International of Los Angeles, Calif. He co-teaches a two-week course in Software Project Management for the Center for Systems Management of Cupertino, Calif. He has been a guest lecturer on software systems engineering at the Defense Systems Management College. He is a Fellow of the American Institute of Aeronautics and Astronautics (AIAA), a member of its System Engineering Technical Committee, past chairman of the Software Systems Technical Committee, and past Chairman of the AIAA San Francisco Section, and is currently Assistant Director of Region 6 (West Coast). He is an affiliate member of the Institute of Electrical and Electronics Engineers (IEEE) Computer Society.

He has a BS and MS from the Massachusetts Institute of Technology and a PhD from Stanford University, all in Aeronautics and Astronautics. He is a registered Professional Engineer in the states of California and Colorado and is a member of the Tau Beta Pi and Sigma Gamma Tau honorary societies.

He is co-editor of two IEEE Tutorial volumes, *System and Software Requirements Engineering* and *Standards, Guidelines, and Examples for System and Software Requirements Engineering*, and co-editor of a volume, *Aerospace Software Engineering*, in the AIAA "Progress in Aeronautics and Astronautics" Series.

9 780818 677380